CONTENTS AT A GLANCE

TABLE OF CONTENTS

INTRODUCTION

THE ARRAY OF BOOKS AVAILABLE TO HELP YOU LEARN AND USE LOTUS 1-2-3 Release 2.3 can be intimidating. How do you know which is the right one for you? Though many of these books may look the same, there are important differences. The first step is to determine what you need to know and how you want to learn it. This introduction will explain just that, and give you a quick tour of what's inside *PC Magazine Guide to 1-2-3 Release 2.3*.

Who This Book Is For

If you fit into one of these categories, you'll find that this book is just what you need:

- You're new to Lotus 1-2-3 and to spreadsheets

- You know how to use another spreadsheet program and also need to learn Lotus 1-2-3

- You've used an earlier version of Lotus 1-2-3, and want to learn about the new features of Release 2.3

- You're a veteran 1-2-3 user, but need a comprehensive book to use as a reference for access to less frequently used features

If you've never used Lotus 1-2-3, you'll appreciate this book's easy-to-use format. Throughout you'll find step-by-step instructions and exercises in which you'll create and print spreadsheets, graphs and charts, and database reports. These instructions are accompanied by screen illustrations that you compare to the screen on your computer to check on your progress. It's like having an expert at your side as you learn.

Experienced spreadsheet and 1-2-3 users will find many expert hints and tips in this book that are not available anywhere else. *PC Magazine Guide to 1-2-3 Release 2.3* will quickly bring you up to date on all the new features of Release 2.3, and will serve as a valuable reference to the features in 1-2-3 that you use less frequently, but need information about quickly.

A Quick Tour of the Chapters

Chapter 1 introduces you to Lotus 1-2-3 Release 2.3. You'll begin with the basics—starting the program and using the 1-2-3 keyboard—and move on to overviews of how to enter data and use the menu system using some hands-on exercises to create a worksheet. A summary of the new features in Release 2.3 is also in this chapter.

In Chapter 2 you'll learn about some fundamental commands that will enable you to manage your files, correct and modify data, determine how you want to display numbers, work with columns and rows, and enter values and labels. You'll also get an introduction to formulas, where the real power of a spreadsheet lies.

Chapter 3 explains how to use commands that perform mathematical tasks using dates and times. You'll work through a hands-on exercise to learn how to enter dates in a spreadsheet to enable 1-2-3 to carry out a math function.

Moving beyond basic spreadsheet design, Chapter 4 shows you how to work with groups of cells, or ranges. You'll learn how to work more quickly and accurately by assigning names to ranges, then using those names in formulas. Helpful tips are also given for managing range names, searching for information within a range or an entire worksheet, and converting a formula to an actual value.

Chapter 5 is an in-depth exploration of functions—built-in formulas that allow you to perform sophisticated calculations. You'll learn how to apply formulas in typical spreadsheet operations, and how to avoid the common pitfalls in formula writing. This chapter includes a review of 1-2-3's most important functions.

Chapter 6 brings spreadsheet viewing and printing features together. Basic printing commands are covered, and you'll produce a printed report of spreadsheet data.

You'll learn how to handle files efficiently and how to share information between files in Chapter 7. Here you'll find some DOS fundamentals, tips on saving and retrieving files and navigating lists of files, and time-saving hints on copying, combining, and linking information in 1-2-3 files. 1-2-3's add-in programs are also covered here, including the file management program Viewer, the customization features of Wysiwyg, and Auditor, which enables you to analyze the logical structure of your worksheet by examining the formulas they contain.

Chapter 8 examines two aspects of working with 1-2-3: sorting information and working with 1-2-3's database features. Fast and accurate sorting not only helps you keep your spreadsheet data organized, but is also a valuable aid in working with databases. In this chapter you'll see the versatility of 1-2-3 as you learn how to create new databases, and how to work with spreadsheets as databases.

Graphs and charts are discussed in Chapter 9. Lotus 1-2-3's many graph types are explained and illustrated. You'll also learn the ins and outs of printing graphs, and how to use 1-2-3's add-in program PrintGraph.

Chapter 10 shows you how to improve the appearance of your spreadsheets and presentations with Wysiwyg, a program with sophisticated presentation features such as fonts, shading, and drawing tools. Here you'll learn how to customize and dress up spreadsheets to meet your presentation needs. This chapter also features a complete guide to the Wysiwyg commands.

The commands for working with text are covered in Chapter 11. The text editor capabilities of 1-2-3 are discussed, as well as how to transfer 1-2-3 files to a word-processing program (and bring word-processing files into 1-2-3) and how to use text in formulas.

Chapter 12 explores some of the commands and functions you can use to perform statistical analysis. You will learn how to calculate and graph linear regressions, how to perform frequency distributions, and how to create data tables to perform "what-if" calculations on your data.

Chapters 13 and 14 discuss 1-2-3's powerful macro features. Chapter 13 is your introduction to macros, a fixed set of instructions activated by a simple keystroke that you would otherwise have to laboriously enter in one keystroke at a time. You'll see how easy it is to save time and work by using simple, easy-to-create macros. Chapter 14 explores the more complex aspects of creating macros. Here you'll learn to use macros that prompt for user input in programs that you create. This chapter is also your guide to 1-2-3's built-in functions that are primarily used in macros and advanced spreadsheets.

PC Magazine Guide to 1-2-3 Release 2.3 is rounded out with three appendices that give you instructions for installing 1-2-3, hints for using 1-2-3 on a network, and a collection helpful tables and tips.

How to Use This Book

Here are a few things you should know before you begin:

- Material that you are to type in at the keyboard appears in boldface type, as in "Type **941.34** and press Enter."

- Longer excerpts of text that you are to type in, material that needs to be emphasized, and information that you should see on your screen as a result of carrying out a command or procedure appears on its own line in a different typeface, as in this example:

Type **S** or choose Spreadsheet to display these options:

```
1 Import   2 Create   3 Link Edit   4 Link   5 Link Options
```

Now you're ready to begin learning Lotus 1-2-3 Release 2.3. Whether you're new to 1-2-3 or an experienced user, start with Chapter 1—you'll find useful information there about 1-2-3 basics, and about new features in Release 2.3. Experienced users can move on to other chapters of interest; new users should read the chapters in order to take advantage of the building-block design of this book. Whatever your level, you'll find that *PC Magazine Guide to 1-2-3 Release 2.3* is the perfect companion to unlock the many powerful features of 1-2-3.

C H A P T E R

Getting Started

THIS CHAPTER DESCRIBES 1-2-3 RELEASE 2.3, HOW IT COMPARES WITH other software, how to load it into your computer, and how to start using it for a variety of tasks. As you read, you will learn the basics about 1-2-3 Release 2.3 and will become better equipped to understand the many features covered in the rest of this book.

What Is 1-2-3 Release 2.3?

1-2-3 Release 2.3 is a spreadsheet program with integrated database and graphics capabilities. The terms spreadsheet, database, and graphics refer to ways of organizing and analyzing information. A *spreadsheet* arranges information in columns and rows like a columnar accountant's pad. A *database management* program helps organize and manipulate collections of information such as customer lists and inventory records, or any set of data that you could store on a set of index cards. A *graphics* program presents information graphically, as in pie charts, line charts, and bar graphs.

An Electronic Spreadsheet

The *1* in 1-2-3 refers to an electronic spreadsheet, sometimes referred to as a *worksheet,* the computer equivalent of a columnar pad. As you can see from Figure 1.1, the column and row format of the 1-2-3 screen creates a grid, or matrix, within which numbers and words, known as *values* and *labels*, can be arranged. You can perform calculations on numbers in the spreadsheet cells. You can also enter instructions to add, subtract, or otherwise manipulate values into cells and then display the results.

An example of an instruction, or *formula,* appears at the top of Figure 1.1. Because formulas in 1-2-3 follow a consistent pattern or *syntax*—much like ordinary math—they are easy to write.

1-2-3 provides commands for altering the appearance of numbers, the location of words, and the width of the columns. There are also commands to control procedures like storing and printing data that has been entered into the spreadsheet. The commands are organized into an easy-to-use structure known as a *menu.* You can see the menu displayed along the top of the screen in Figure 1.2. You can operate the menu from the keyboard or by using a mouse. When using the keyboard, you activate the menu by pressing the slash key (/). You select a command from the menu either by typing its first letter or by moving the highlight bar onto the command using the space-bar or arrow keys and then pressing the Enter key. To activate the menu with the mouse, simply move the mouse pointer into the menu area. To select a menu item with the mouse, place the mouse pointer over the item and click the left mouse button. (Using the mouse will be covered in more detail later in the chapter.)

Figure 1.1

The 1-2-3 spreadsheet

Formula

Column heading

Row label

Value

Label

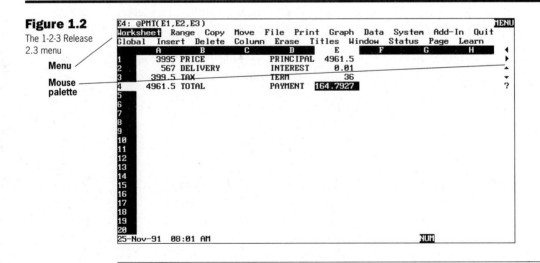

Figure 1.2

The 1-2-3 Release 2.3 menu

Menu

Mouse palette

Besides the menu, there are several differences between Figures 1.2 and 1.1. 1-2-3 Release 2.3 includes a new feature known as *Wysiwyg* ("what you see is what you get"). This feature is at work in Figure 1.1 but not in Figure 1.2. When you use Wysiwyg, you can see the column and row grid of worksheet cells. You can also see the exact size, shape, and color of font in which your work will be printed. Note that you can use a mouse with 1-2-3 Release 2.3 whether or not you are using Wysiwyg. When you have a mouse installed on your computer, a small *mouse palette* automatically appears on the right of the 1-2-3 Release 2.3 screen as shown in Figure 1.2. (Use of the mouse palette will be discussed later in the chapter.)

Wysiwyg creates dazzling screens on a large high-resolution color monitor; however, such screens do not look quite as stunning reduced to a size that will fit comfortably in a book. In addition, not everyone who uses 1-2-3 Release 2.3 will use Wysiwyg all the time, since it takes up space in memory which may be required for large worksheets or other programs. For these reasons, many of the illustrations in this book show 1-2-3 Release 2.3 without Wysiwyg loaded. Whenever Wysiwyg and related commands are being illustrated, Wysiwyg screens will be shown.

Graphics Ability

The *1* in 1-2-3 refers to the electronic spreadsheet; the *2* refers to the program's graphics capabilities. Prior to 1-2-3, if you had to draw charts based on the information in a spreadsheet, you had to use a separate program. In contrast, 1-2-3 allows you to create and print graphs without learning a second software package. Figure 1.3 shows a basic 1-2-3 graph.

Since the introduction of electronic spreadsheets, users have sought increasingly sophisticated chart-making software. As a result, there are now programs to enhance 1-2-3's graphics capabilities. In fact, the Wysiwyg program of 1-2-3 Release 2.3 provides graphing features comparable to those found in stand-alone charting programs, as you can see from the example in Figure 1.4.

The enhanced capabilities of Wysiwyg include a mixture of fonts and direct access to graphs from the spreadsheet. Indeed, Wysiwyg allows you to insert graphs directly into a spreadsheet. This means that you can use 1-2-3 to assemble documents that contain both data and charts of data.

The Wysiwyg feature not only gives you an opportunity to make full use of the graphics capability of your system, it also gives you complete control over the way the 1-2-3 Release 2.3 work area is displayed on screen. You can choose your own colors and shading for the work area; you can turn on or off the frame of row numbers and column letters; you can also display gridlines between worksheet cells, as shown in Figure 1.1.

Figure 1.3

A basic 1-2-3 graph

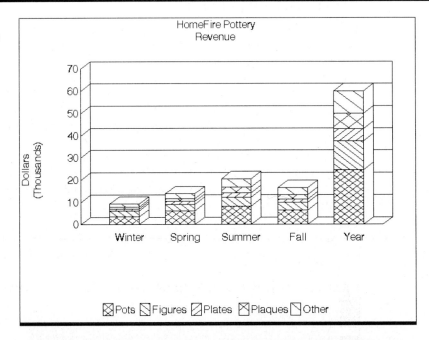

Figure 1.4

A 1-2-3 Release 2.3 graph enhanced by Wysiwyg

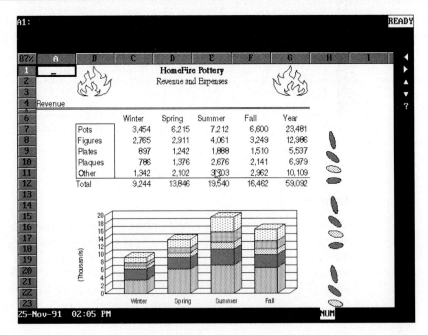

Database Management

If the *1* and the *2* of 1-2-3 represent spreadsheet and graphics, respectively, the *3* stands for database management. Many lists compiled with spreadsheet programs are more manageable if they can be sorted. What's more, much of the information stored in spreadsheets can be considered a database. Because of this, 1-2-3 includes several database management capabilities, including the ability to sort lists and to isolate those items that match specified selection criteria. These features are essential to organizing and extracting information from databases.

For example, you might sort the database in Figure 1.5 by the number of items on hand to reveal quickly which items need to be reordered. The ability to "query" a database lets you frame questions such as "which items in the inventory cost over $1000?"

Figure 1.5

A database list

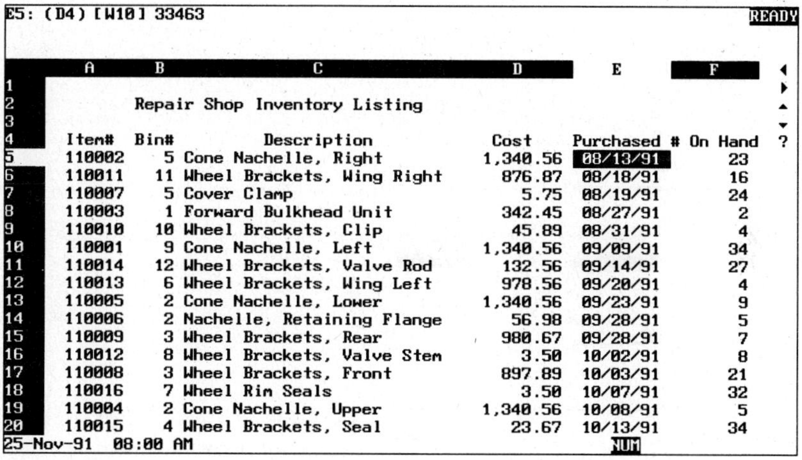

Macros

1-2-3 also provides a tool for automating spreadsheet, graphics, or database management operations that you perform regularly. You can think of this feature as 1-2-3's fourth capacity—one that helps you manage the other three more efficiently. In 1-2-3, you can type in a series of commands and then replay them at will. This feature is like the macro keys used by some word processing programs. The replay feature is especially popular among those preparing spreadsheets for other less skilled users.

1-2-3 has special commands that you can include in macros to make them more than just keystroke recordings. Using the macro command language, you can develop customized applications that can be operated with only a basic knowledge of 1-2-3. Figure 1.6 shows a sample macro menu, a method of presenting customized commands using the 1-2-3 macro command language. Notice how the design of this menu matches the regular menu seen in Figure 1.2.

Figure 1.6

A macro menu

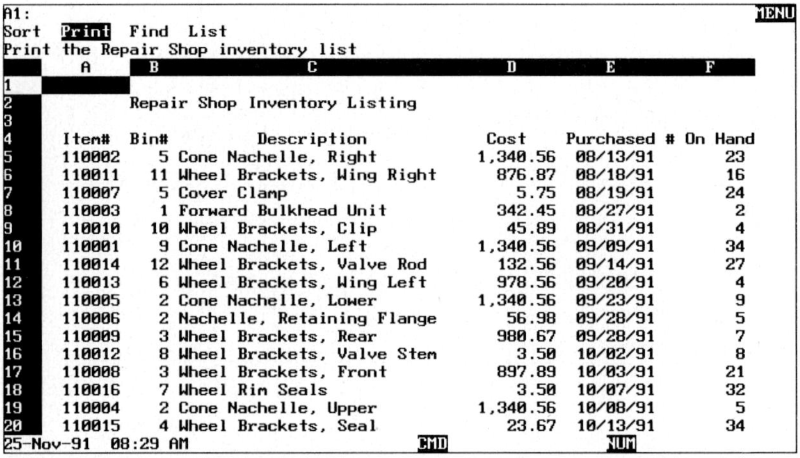

```
A1:                                                               MENU
Sort  Print  Find  List
Print the Repair Shop inventory list
        A        B            C              D        E        F
1
2              Repair Shop Inventory Listing
3
4     Item#  Bin#        Description        Cost    Purchased # On Hand
5     110002    5 Cone Nachelle, Right    1,340.56  08/13/91      23
6     110011   11 Wheel Brackets, Wing Right 876.87 08/18/91      16
7     110007    5 Cover Clamp                 5.75  08/19/91      24
8     110003    1 Forward Bulkhead Unit     342.45  08/27/91       2
9     110010   10 Wheel Brackets, Clip       45.89  08/31/91       4
10    110001    9 Cone Nachelle, Left      1,340.56 09/09/91      34
11    110014   12 Wheel Brackets, Valve Rod 132.56  09/14/91      27
12    110013    6 Wheel Brackets, Wing Left 978.56  09/20/91       4
13    110005    2 Cone Nachelle, Lower    1,340.56  09/23/91       9
14    110006    2 Nachelle, Retaining Flange 56.98  09/28/91       5
15    110009    3 Wheel Brackets, Rear      980.67  09/28/91       7
16    110012    8 Wheel Brackets, Valve Stem  3.50  10/02/91       8
17    110008    3 Wheel Brackets, Front     897.89  10/03/91      21
18    110016    7 Wheel Rin Seals             3.50  10/07/91      32
19    110004    2 Cone Nachelle, Upper     1,340.56 10/08/91       5
20    110015    4 Wheel Brackets, Seal       23.67  10/13/91      34
25-Nov-91  08:29 AM                    CMD              NUM
```

Add-Ins and Versions

Starting with Release 2.0, Lotus 1-2-3 introduced the ability to run *add-in programs*—optional programs that attach to 1-2-3 and become part of the main program for as long as necessary. This approach allows the main program to remain a reasonable size while permitting 1-2-3 to accommodate specialized needs. Lotus provides several add-in programs with Release 2.3, including the Wysiwyg feature. By supplying powerful features as add-ins, 1-2-3 enables you to work at various levels, from a basic spreadsheet on a small laptop computer, to a sophisticated graphics program on a desktop workstation.

Each revision of 1-2-3 has both expanded the program's capabilities and increased its demands on the computer hardware, requiring more memory and more disk space for acceptable performance. Since some people are still using older computer models, Lotus created several different but compatible versions of the program, each one optimized for a different range of machines. There is now a complete family of 1-2-3 products, including

- 1-2-3 Release 2.3, the most widely used version, is suitable for all types of computers running DOS.

- 1-2-3 Release 3.1 is a version for more advanced hardware running DOS.

- 1-2-3/G is a version for more advanced hardware running OS/2.

New and Improved: 1-2-3 Release 2.3

If you are already familiar with 1-2-3 or with other spreadsheets, you may want to know what is new in Release 2.3. Perhaps the most striking difference is the Wysiwyg feature, already seen at work in Figures 1.1 and 1.4, and discussed in greater depth in a moment. There are other, more subtle differences, that make Release 2.3 a more powerful yet more accessible successor to Release 2.2.

Ease of Use

The mouse has become an inexpensive and widely used device, and full support for mouse users is built into Release 2.3, whether or not you use the Wysiwyg feature. As mentioned, you can activate the main menu by simply moving the mouse pointer into the area above the worksheet frame and you can select menu items by pointing and clicking. If you are working with Wysiwyg, the right mouse button switches you from the regular 1-2-3 Release 2.3 menu to the Wysiwyg menu.

You can select a rectangular group of adjacent cells, known as a *range*, with the mouse before issuing a command that affects those cells. You can also use the mouse to select files and other items that 1-2-3 Release 2.3 presents in list form.

A new feature that will appeal to keyboard users as well as mouse users is the *dialog box*. This is a method of presenting in a summary form a large number of different settings, such as those for printing. Figure 1.7 shows the dialog box used in Release 2.3 to establish global settings for the worksheet.

Dialog boxes make a large group of settings much easier to work with. 1-2-3 Release 2.3 now has so many commands that they do not all fit comfortably into the original menu structure. The dialog box in Figure 1.7 employs all of the old keystrokes in the Worksheet Default command but makes it much easier to see what the current choices are. Dialog boxes are provided for Data Sort, Data Query, Graph, Print, as well as all Worksheet Global and Worksheet Global Default settings. (See "Using Dialog Boxes" in Chapter 2 for more information.)

There are several other features in Release 2.3 that contribute to considerably greater ease of use. These include reminders to save work when using the File Retrieve and Worksheet Erase commands plus the use of the Del key to delete the contents of the current cell. (In previous versions of 1-2-3, you needed to issue the Range Erase command to erase a cell.) The prompts for the Copy and Move commands are now much clearer (they are "Copy what?" and "To where?" as opposed to "Enter range to copy FROM" and "Enter range to copy TO"). The help system has been completely overhauled and is heavily cross-referenced. There is even an on-screen tutorial that you can launch from within 1-2-3 Release 2.3 or from DOS. A separate tutorial is supplied for the Wysiwyg feature.

Figure 1.7

A typical 1-2-3 Release 2.3 dialog box

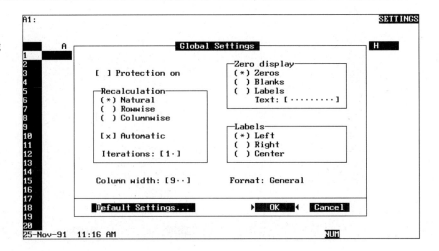

The Wysiwyg Add-In

You have already glimpsed how the Wysiwyg feature can alter the appearance of your work with 1-2-3 Release 2.3. Wysiwyg is an add-in program supplied with 1-2-3 Release 2.3. Indeed, you may elect to do all of your 1-2-3 Release 2.3 work in Wysiwyg mode. If you use Wysiwyg, you can embellish your graphs with drawings and clip art, enhance spreadsheets with a variety of fonts and type styles, and all in a "what-you-see-is-what-you-get" mode of operation.

This is only part of what Wysiwyg can do. You can use the Display command to customize the worksheet display with your choice of colors and styles. You can display the worksheet frame with sculpted buttons for row and column identifiers. You can adjust row height and column width with the mouse. You can turn off the worksheet frame or use it as a ruler, measuring your work area in inches, centimeters, or points. You can use the Display Zoom command to shrink or enlarge your worksheet to give you an overview of a large range of cells, or a closer look at details. Figure 1.8 shows the effect of "zooming in" on a worksheet. Note that the worksheet gridlines have been turned off and a variety of fonts are in use.

Figure 1.8

Using the Wysiwyg Display Zoom command

```
A4: {DUTCH12 Bold Italic} 'POLK ST.                                READY
```

	A	B	C	D	E	F	G
1	Revenue Projection, Based on Monthly Growth Factor of						1.12
2							
3		Jan–92	Feb–92	Mar–92	Apr–92	May–92	Jun–92
4	*POLK ST.*						
5	Tour	3,350	3,752	4,202	4,707	5,271	5,904
6	Flight	1,875	2,100	2,352	2,634	2,950	3,304
7	Hotel	950	1,064	1,192	1,335	1,495	1,674
8	Rental	875	980	1,098	1,229	1,377	1,542
9	Group	800	896	1,004	1,124	1,259	1,410
10	*VAN NESS*						
11	Tour	3,400	3,808	4,265	4,777	5,350	5,992
12	Flight	2,175	2,436	2,728	3,056	3,422	3,833
13	Hotel	1,350	1,512	1,693	1,897	2,124	2,379
14	Rental	975	1,092	1,223	1,370	1,534	1,718
15	Group	1,100	1,232	1,380	1,545	1,731	1,939
16	*UNION SQ*						

```
25-Nov-91  08:07 AM                                                NUM
```

To match the display virtuosity of Wysiwyg, 1-2-3 Release 2.3 includes some powerful print commands. A print-to-fit feature compresses the information that you want to print so that it fits onto a single page, or as few pages as possible, while still maintaining legibility. To cope with the versatility of the print feature in Wysiwyg and the additional layout settings now possible, you can create a print layout library that stores a variety of named settings.

If you want to be creative, the graph editing commands in Wysiwyg allow you to turn a 1-2-3 Release 2.3 worksheet into a canvas for your own graphic designs. If you want to avoid doing your own drawings, you can make use of a library of clip art that you can paste into worksheets. To match the graphic improvements in Wysiwyg, the regular Graph command in Release 2.3 has been improved. New styles of graph are possible, including area, horizontal bar, and high-low-close.

More Power

More advanced users will appreciate several improvements in areas such as macros, file management, and spreadsheet auditing. There are new macro commands to turn on and off spreadsheet borders and dialog boxes. Several new commands make it easier to create spreadsheet data entry forms and append information to a database. There are also commands for displaying graphs during macro execution, enabling you to create slide shows.

The Viewer add-in supplied with 1-2-3 Release 2.3 uses technology from another Lotus product, Magellan, to list directories and files on your disks. While browsing through spreadsheet files you can see the file contents, making it much easier to locate the correct file. You can also use the Viewer to establish links with other spreadsheets, pointing to the cell required in the link without having to retrieve the worksheet. Figure 1.9 shows the Viewer at work. In this figure, the file LB32.WK1 is highlighted at the left side of the screen and its contents are displayed on the right.

Figure 1.9

The Viewer displaying a worksheet file

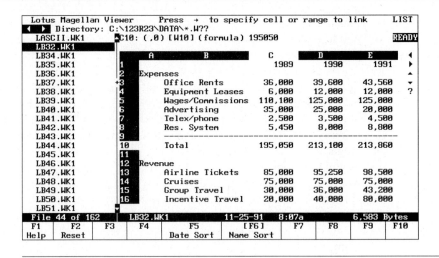

To help you design better and more accurate worksheets, 1-2-3 Release 2.3 has an add-in called Auditor. This gives you a breakdown of complex formulas and shows which cells supply information to the formula. The Auditor also helps locate circular references.

Running 1-2-3 Release 2.3

Despite this impressive array of features, 1-2-3 Release 2.3 has relatively modest minimum hardware requirements and can be used with a wide range

of popular personal computers. The following sections describe the hardware requirements of 1-2-3 Release 2.3.

Memory Requirements

Your computer's *memory* is the area where programs and data are temporarily held while they are in use. When you load a program, the program's instructions are copied from storage on disk into memory. Some programs are loaded into memory in sections; a section is loaded only when it is needed. With 1-2-3 Release 2.3, in contrast, most of the program is loaded into memory at once.

To run 1-2-3 Release 2.3, your computer needs at least 512 kilobytes of random access memory (that is, 512k of RAM). To learn how much RAM is in your computer, use the Check Disk command (CHKDSK) from the disk operating system disk, as described in Appendix A. If you plan on using the Wysiwyg add-in, you will need 640k of RAM.

RAM has become fairly inexpensive and it is definitely worth upgrading to at least 640k. For example, with 512k of RAM in your PC, 1-2-3 Release 2.3 can handle a modest spreadsheet. This capacity increases when you have 640k, depending on your operating system and other programs you might be using.

There are basically two types of memory beyond the 640k recognized by DOS: expanded memory and extended memory. *Expanded memory* is a method of making additional RAM available even on older PCs. Expanded memory cards, like the Intel Above Board, that conform to the Lotus/Intel Expanded Memory Specification can increase your PC's RAM to several megabytes. 1-2-3 Release 2.3 can use this area to store spreadsheets. As long as you install the memory board and its software correctly, 1-2-3 Release 2.3 will automatically detect and use the added space. The investment in such cards is more than returned, since enhanced memory enables you to apply the power of 1-2-3 Release 2.3 to much larger collections of information.

If you have an 80286- or 80386-based system, such as an IBM AT or a Compaq 386, you may have extended memory already built into your computer. *Extended memory* is memory beyond 640k that is counted and checked by your system when it is powered up. Your system thinks of this memory as simply an extension of the basic 640k, but DOS cannot recognize it as such. Fortunately, although 1-2-3 Release 2.3 cannot directly recognize this memory, programs like 386MAX from Qualitas and QEMM from QuarterDeck Office Systems can make this extended memory like expanded memory, allowing 1-2-3 Release 2.3 to use it. See Appendix A for more about memory expansion.

Disks and Drives

The memory in your computer is simply a huge set of electrical switches. Information is held in memory as current flowing through switches that are either on or off. When you turn off the power or leave a particular application, everything in memory is forgotten. To store information beyond the current work session, you therefore need to copy it from memory into some form of storage, typically a disk—either a floppy or a fixed disk. Floppy disks have the advantage of being removable and easily transported. Fixed or hard disks are faster and have a larger capacity.

1-2-3 Release 2.3 comes to you on several floppy disks, the number depending upon the disk size. To ensure that it can be loaded by a wide range of systems, 1-2-3 Release 2.3 is available on 5¼-inch 360k disks as well as 3½-inch 720k disks, as used by the IBM PS/2 models and laptop systems like the Toshiba T1000.

1-2-3 Release 2.3 must be installed on a hard disk. Since the price of hard-disk drives continues to drop, they are an increasingly attractive proposition for almost anyone who uses a computer. A hard-disk drive provides faster access to files on the disk, more room for larger files, and the ability to store all of the parts of a program like 1-2-3 Release 2.3 on one disk. You can also place many different programs on the hard disk and can then move between them quickly and easily. Appendix A describes hard-disk installation and organization for 1-2-3 users.

If you have a laptop or other computer that does not have a hard disk you can still run 1-2-3 Release 2.3, but you will not have immediate access to all of the features. Once you have installed 1-2-3 Release 2.3 on a hard disk, you can transfer the essential program files to a floppy disk for use on a floppy-disk system. This procedure is described in Appendix A. Note that the licensing agreement for 1-2-3 Release 2.3 does not allow you to use one copy of the program on two different computers at the same time.

Display Screens

Your computer's screen is an output device, used by the computer to display results. It is also used to monitor input. Computer monitors present images on the screen in two ways. The first display method is referred to as *character* or *text mode.* In text mode, your monitor uses a set of characters (A through Z, numbers, and symbols) to display information that is mainly text, but which can also include simple drawings and designs. 1-2-3 Release 2.3 can use this mode to display the spreadsheet, as you saw in Figure 1.6.

The other display technique is referred to as *graphics mode.* In this mode, your monitor uses a series of dots to show everything from simple letters and numbers to complex shapes and a wide variety of character sizes and styles. This is how 1-2-3 Release 2.3 displays graphs, as shown in Figure

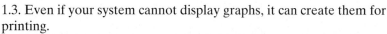

1.3. Even if your system cannot display graphs, it can create them for printing.

If you have a computer system with graphics display capability, you will be able to see the graphs drawn by 1-2-3 Release 2.3. This graphics capability is provided by a combination of a suitable display card/adapter and an appropriate monitor—for example, a VGA adapter and a VGA monitor, or a Hercules monochrome adapter and a monochrome monitor. These days most PCs can display graphs. Unless you have the original IBM PC monochrome display adapter, you will be able to see 1-2-3 Release 2.3 graphs.

If you have a Hercules, EGA, or VGA system, you can use the Wysiwyg add-in to display the 1-2-3 Release 2.3 spreadsheet in graphics mode. This enables you to see the fonts used for spreadsheet entries as well as any graphs that are pasted into the worksheet. You can see a worksheet in graphics mode in Figure 1.8. In graphics mode, you can enlarge or reduce the worksheet to provide a better view of your work.

Printing and Plotting

1-2-3 Release 2.3 can print information on paper in a number of ways. When you are working with text and numbers in the spreadsheet, you can select the Print option from the menu bar. This option enables you to send text reports to your printer and set print factors such as paper size and margins.

Since graphic images are more complex than text reports, you need a special program to print them. One method is to save the graph in a special file, exit the main 1-2-3 program, and load the PrintGraph program. There you can choose from a variety of printers and plotting devices. If you have a color output device such as the HP Colorpro plotter, you can assign colors to the various parts of the graph. If you use the Wysiwyg add-in, you can print graphs without using PrintGraph and without saving the graph in a special graph file. You simply paste the graph into a section of your worksheet.

The Wysiwyg add-in provides a sophisticated method of printing both graphs and sections of spreadsheet. It gives you greater control over print features such as fonts, shading, and lines. You can use the preview feature in Wysiwyg to see what your graphs and spreadsheets will look like before you print them.

At times you may want to print exactly what appears on the screen. Unless you are displaying a graph, you can usually print whatever is on the screen with the Print Screen (PrtSc) key. Printing graphics screens usually requires a special program such as INSET or Collage. Chapter 9 describes how to use such programs with 1-2-3.

Starting 1-2-3 Release 2.3

1-2-3 Release 2.3 is easy to start on almost any computer. You just follow two simple steps: Install the program and then issue the command that begins the program. Since many of you will already have the program installed, the first step is described in Appendix A.

There are several ways to load the 1-2-3 Release 2.3 program. The approach shown here uses the 1-2-3 Access System, which allows you to move between the main 1-2-3 Release 2.3 program and the supplemental utility programs PrintGraph, Translate, and Install. To get to the 1-2-3 Access System from the DOS prompt, first move to the directory in which 1-2-3 has been installed. Usually this directory is called 123, so you type **CD \123** and press Enter. This changes the directory to the area of the disk where the 123 program files are located. Now you can type **Lotus** and press Enter. You will see a screen like the one in Figure 1.10.

Figure 1.10

The 1-2-3 Access System

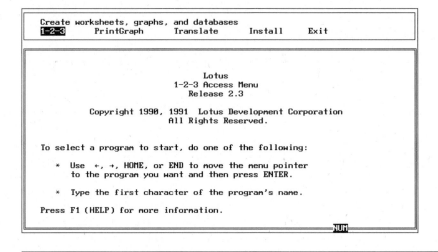

The top part of this screen is a two-line menu. As you can see, the first item, 1-2-3, is highlighted. The second line explains that you select this item to use 1-2-3. Because 1-2-3 is highlighted, it is called the *current* selection. To choose the current selection, simply press Enter. The main 1-2-3 program will be loaded and you should see a screen like the one in Figure 1.11. This is a blank 1-2-3 worksheet; you are now ready to start working with the program.

If you do not know what the DOS prompt is or how to get to it, if you have difficulty following this installation process, or if you do not see the screen shown in Figure 1.11, you should consult Appendix A.

Figure 1.11

The 1-2-3 worksheet

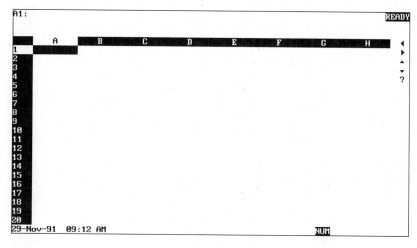

The Worksheet

When you first load 1-2-3, you'll see an empty electronic work space called a worksheet, in which to place numbers, words, and instructions (formulas and calculations). As you can see in Figure 1.11, there is a line of letters near the top of the screen and a list of numbers down the left-hand side. The letters represent a series of columns and the numbers represent a series of rows. The intersection of each column and row forms a box, called a *cell*, into which you put information.

Every cell has a name based on its location, or column and row *coordinates*, just like squares on a map. For example, the cell highlighted in the figure is called A1 because it is in column A on row 1. When you first start 1-2-3, you are in cell A1 and if you enter information it will be placed in that cell. The cell you are in is called the *current cell*.

Your Lotus worksheet is larger than what you see on the screen. The columns continue through column Z, additional columns are designated AA through AZ, then BA through BZ, and so on. After repeating the alphabet nearly ten times, you get to the last column, IV, a total of 256 columns. The rows go down to 8192. Multiplying the columns and rows together gives you the total number of cells: over two million. Obviously, your monitor can show you only a tiny portion of this huge work area. The screen acts like a window, showing you different parts of the worksheet as you move the cell pointer.

The highlighting that marks the current cell is called the *cell pointer*. You can move the cell pointer with the arrow keys and other cursor-movement keys. When you do, your exact location is recorded in the upper-left corner of the screen. 1-2-3 provides important information around the edge of the screen. The horizontal and vertical borders, the control panel, and the status area work like a dashboard. The *status area* tells you the status of the Caps Lock, Num Lock, and Scroll Lock keys. This area also displays error messages to help you when you make mistakes and tells you whether the UNDO feature is active.

In the upper-right corner of the screen, the *mode indicator* shows you a variety of messages about the current task. (When you first load 1-2-3, the mode indicator says READY, meaning that 1-2-3 is ready to accept new data or commands.) The *cell address indicator* in the upper-left corner of the screen shows you the address and contents of the current cell, as well as its display format and its width setting. For example, in Figure 1.5 cell E5 is shown to contain the following:

```
(D4) [W1Ø] 33463
```

These three items are the cell format, the cell width, and the cell contents, respectively. Note that in the worksheet itself, E5 appears to contain the date 08/31/91 rather than the number 33463. This is because Lotus stores dates internally as numbers, and 33463 is the number that corresponds to August 31, 1991 whereas 08/31/91 is that number displayed in date format. There is often a difference between the cell contents, as shown next to the cell address indicator, and what 1-2-3 actually displays and prints. This allows you to alter the appearance of numbers to suit your needs.

About Keyboards and Mice

The traditional method of issuing commands to 1-2-3 Release 2.3 is the keyboard. An alternative means of input, the mouse, is also supported. The following sections describe how to use both keyboard and mouse to issue instructions.

Keyboard Layouts

There are several different personal computer keyboard layouts in use today. As you can see in Figure 1.12, the basic differences are in the placement of the cursor-movement and function keys.

Although there are different keyboard layouts, the keys are basically the same. For example, the key marked Esc or Escape may be on the left or right side of the keyboard, but pressing Esc does the same thing in either case. Like many other programs, 1-2-3 Release 2.3 uses the Escape key to let you change your mind. After you have chosen an option from a menu, pressing the Escape key lets you "unchoose" the option. Keys used extensively by 1-2-3 Release 2.3 are shown in Table 1.1.

Figure 1.12

Popular keyboard layouts

Function keys   ESC key

Ctrl key

Scroll Lock key

Shift key   Shift key

Function keys   Num Lock key

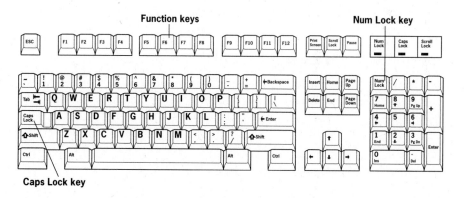

Caps Lock key

Table 1.1   Frequently Used Keys

Key	Purpose
Enter	Used to enter data into the worksheet, select highlighted menu items, and confirm range coordinates and other settings.
Escape	Cancels changes on the editing line, takes you out of menus, returns you to READY mode, and unlocks range coordinates.
Backspace	Removes characters to the left on the edit line, unlocks range coordinates, and returns beginning coordinate to current cell.
Delete	Removes current character from editing line.
Ins	Activates overstrike mode when editing.
Tab	Used in POINT and READY modes to move cell pointer one screen to the right. Used in EDIT mode to move edit cursor five characters to the right. Note that holding down Shift and pressing Tab reverses the action.
Shift	Displays "upper half" of any key, including capitals A-Z, symbols such as $, and numbers on numeric key pad. Also used with function keys.
Caps Lock	Continuously capitalizes letter (A-Z) without use of Shift key; does not affect any other keys.
Num Lock	Locks numeric keypad into numbers; locks out cursor movement with those keys.
Scroll Lock	Tells 1-2-3 to move the worksheet instead of the cell pointer when using cusor-movement keys.
Ctrl	Used with certain keys to execute commands, such as Ctrl-Break, which halts macro execution.
Alt	Used with selected characters to execute macros; also used with function keys.
Print Screen	Prints current screen but will not print graphs.
@ (at)	Precedes built-in formulas known as the @functions.
/ (slash)	In READY mode activates menu; used in formulas for division.
\ (backslash)	Used as special label prefix to repeat characters; also used in naming "instant" macros.
* (asterisk)	Used for the multiplication sign.
. (period)	Used as a decimal point and when setting ranges (used to move active corner of a range once the starting point has been set).
% (percent)	Enter after a number to divide by 100 (for example, entering 10% results in 0.1).

In 1-2-3 Release 2.3, you will use the cursor-movement keys extensively to highlight options and move around the screen. These keys include Up Arrow, Down Arrow, Left Arrow, Right Arrow, PgUp, PgDn, Home, and End. On all PC keyboards, they share keys with various numbers on the numeric keypad. On some keyboards, they are replicated in separate cursor-movement keypads. If your keyboard does not contain separate cursor-movement keypads, the arrow/number keys on the numeric keypad are set to arrows when you turn on your computer, just as the alphabet keys are set to lowercase. Use the Shift key to produce numbers instead of arrows, or lock in numbers by pressing the Num Lock key. This process is the same as using either Shift for the capital letters A through Z or locking in capital letters with the Caps Lock key. If your keyboard does contain separate cursor-movement keypads, Num Lock will probably be turned on when you turn on your computer. You can press the Num Lock key if you want to turn it off.

In addition to Caps Lock and Num Lock, there is the Scroll Lock key, which is described in Chapter 5.

Function Keys

1-2-3 Release 2.3 makes extensive use of the *function keys*—the keys labeled F1, F2, and so on. These keys are either down the left side or across the top of the keyboard. The individual function keys will be explained as they come up in the text. A keyboard template packaged with the 1-2-3 Release 2.3 manual lists the function keys, which are also shown in Table 1.2. Further assistance with function keys is available from the 1-2-3 program itself. You can press F1, the Help key, at any time during a 1-2-3 session to get on-screen assistance. If you press F1 right after you have loaded the program, you get the Help Index, shown in Figure 1.13.

You select items from this list by highlighting them and pressing Enter. For example, to get help with Entering Data you would press the Down Arrow key several times until that topic was highlighted, and then press Enter. You can use the F8 key to return to the previous help topic. If you press F3, you will get information about other keys you can use with the help system. To leave the help system and return to 1-2-3, simply press Escape.

Cursor-Movement Keys

To explore the work area, lightly press the Right Arrow key once. The highlighting will move to the next cell to the right, B1. You are now in cell B1. Lightly press the Down Arrow key once and you will be in cell B2. Notice that your current location is being monitored in the upper-left corner of the control panel, in the cell address indicator. This is very helpful, since it's difficult to eyeball your location, particularly after several hours at the screen. Make sure you press these keys lightly. Your keyboard can repeat keystrokes

Table 1.2   **Function Keys**

Key	Name	Description
F1	Help	Displays the Help screens.
F2	Edit	Places 1-2-3 in EDIT mode, displaying the contents of the current cell on the editing line.
F3	Name	Displays a list of names. Name produces a full-screen list of file names when a single-line list is displayed, produces a full-screen list of range names when a single-line list is displayed, and lists range names when used with F4 or when creating a formula.
F4	Abs	When used in POINT or EDIT mode, adds absolute cell addressing with $ sign (cycles cell through absolute, mixed, and relative addresses).
F5		Moves cell pointer directly to a particular cell or named range.
F6	Goto	Moves cell pointer between two windows. Turns off the display of setting sheets (MENU mode only).
F7	Query	Repeats most recent Data Query operation.
F8	Table	Repeats most recent Data Table operation.
F9	Calc	In READY mode, recalculates all formulas. In VALUE and EDIT modes, converts formula to its value.
F10	Graph	Draws a graph using current graph settings.

To use one of the following 1-2-3 keys, hold down the Alt or Shift key, press the function key, and then release both keys.

Key	Name	Description
Alt-F1	Compose	When used with alphanumeric keys, creates characters you cannot enter directly from the keyboard.
Alt-F2	Step	Activates STEP mode, which causes macros to execute one step at a time for the purpose of debugging.
Alt-F3	Run	Displays a menu of named ranges in the worksheet so you can select the name of a macro to run.
Alt-F4	Undo	Cancels any changes made to the worksheet since 1-2-3 was last in READY mode. Press Alt-F4 again to redo changes.
Alt-F5	Learn	Turns Learn feature on and records keystrokes in the learn range. Press Alt-F5 again to turn off the Learn feature.
Alt-F7	App1	Activates add-in program assigned to this key, if any.
Alt-F8	App2	Activates add-in program assigned to this key, if any.
Alt-F9	App3	Activates add-in program assigned to this key, if any.
Alt-F10	App4	Activates add-in program assigned to this key, or displays Add-In menu if there is no add-in program assigned to the key.

and will do so if you hold down rather than tap a key. In this book, the term *press* means tap lightly rather than hold down.

To see the keyboard repeat feature, hold down the Down Arrow key for two seconds. The cell pointer will move quickly down the screen and the numbers at the left will scroll by rapidly. You are dragging the screen with you to view a different area of the spreadsheet. Now try pressing the Home key: It takes you back to A1.

Figure 1.13
The Help Index

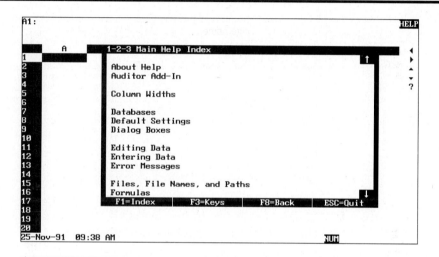

Figure 1.14 shows the full range of cursor-movement keys. The Up Arrow, Down Arrow, Left Arrow, and Right Arrow keys move you one cell in each of their respective directions. Used with the Ctrl key, the Right Arrow and Left Arrow keys move one screen at a time across the worksheet. You can achieve a similar effect with the Tab and Shift-Tab keys, respectively. The PgUp and PgDn keys move you 20 lines at a time up and down the worksheet. The Home key always places you in A1 (unless you are using worksheet titles, which are described in Chapter 5). The End key is slightly more complicated and is covered in the next chapter.

Using Your Mouse

If you have a mouse installed on your computer, 1-2-3 Release 2.3 presents a mouse pointer on the screen. This pointer is shaped like either a small rectangle or an arrow, depending upon the display mode you are using. The pointer will move as you move the mouse. There are three basic actions you perform with a mouse: pointing, clicking, and dragging.

Figure 1.14

Close-up of the
cursor-movement
keys

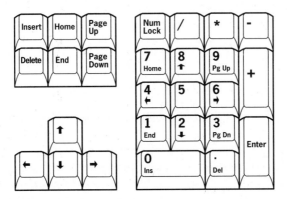

Pointing with the mouse simply means moving the pointer to an object or area on the screen. To see how pointing works, move the pointer into the area above the column letters. A menu will appear. Move the pointer onto the spreadsheet and the menu will disappear.

Clicking with the mouse involves pointing to an object on the screen and then selecting it by pressing a button on the mouse (normally the left button). Clicking means giving the button a quick tap; you do not hold down the mouse button when clicking. Try clicking to select any one of the cells on the screen: Place the mouse pointer on the cell and click the left mouse button. The cell pointer will move to the cell and make it the current cell, just as though you had used the cursor movement keys. You can also use the mouse to emulate the cursor-movement keys by means of the four arrow symbols on the right of the screen above the question mark. This area of the screen is known as the *mouse palette.* Place the mouse pointer on the down arrow symbol and click the left mouse button—the cell pointer will move down one cell. You can use this method when entering data, as described later in this chapter. You can also use the four *mouse arrows* with the End key, as described in Chapter 4.

Dragging with the mouse involves moving the mouse pointer to a location on the screen, pressing a mouse button, holding it down while moving the mouse pointer to another location, and then releasing the mouse button. You can use dragging to select a group of cells. Place the mouse pointer over cell B2 and hold down the left mouse button while moving the mouse pointer over and down to cell F10. You will see the area between B2 and F10 outlined on screen. Remember, a rectangular group of cells like this is referred to as a range; you will learn more about range commands in Chapter 2. When you select cells in this way, a message on the second line of the screen will say "Range: B2..F10." To cancel the range, simply click on a single cell or press Escape.

Many of the actions you perform in 1-2-3 Release 2.3 can be executed by one of the three basic mouse techniques—point, click, and drag. However, you will still need to use the keyboard for typing entries into the worksheet and other actions. Since operating 1-2-3 Release 2.3 with a mouse is fairly intuitive, this text describes commands and actions for keyboard users first, and includes tips for mouse users when appropriate.

Mouse users can click on the question mark in the mouse palette to get help, instead of pressing F1. Note that the Install program, described in Appendix A, allows you to switch the functions of the left and right mouse buttons. Although this is a considerate gesture to left-handed users, the left-handed author of this text has found it quite easy, and far less complicated, to work with the normal assignment of mouse keys, which are described as left and right throughout this text. Users of three-button mice will find that 1-2-3 Release 2.3 uses the first two buttons, counting from the left, and ignores the third.

Entering Data

1-2-3 categorizes all information into one of two types of data: values or labels. In general, *values* are numbers and calculations and *labels* are words or text. 1-2-3 looks at the first character of each new entry in the worksheet to determine whether that data should be treated as a value or a label. The following sections describe how to enter data into the worksheet and make changes to your entries.

Entering Values

To learn how to enter values into 1-2-3, try the following exercise. Press Home to make sure that the cell pointer is in cell A1, and note the flashing cursor in the cell. Now type **789** from the row of numbers at the top of the keyboard. Do not press Enter or any other key; just observe that the cursor has moved from the worksheet cell to the second line of the screen. Also note that the number 789 has not yet been placed into the worksheet; instead, it is on the second line of the control panel, as shown in Figure 1.15. This line acts as an editing area for your cell entries. The cursor should be flashing after the number 9, indicating that this is where the next characters you type will appear.

At this point, you can either continue to type or use the Backspace key to erase what you have typed. Each time you press Backspace, it erases one character to the left of the cursor. If you want to completely erase what you have typed, you can press Escape. (If you pressed the Enter key prematurely or otherwise caused the number to leave the second line of the screen, just type **789** again and observe what happens *before* you press Enter.)

Figure 1.15

Entering a value

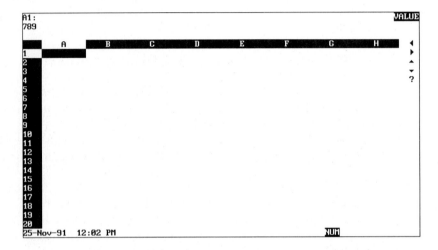

When you started typing 789, the mode indicator in the upper-right corner of the screen changed from READY to VALUE. This tells you that 1-2-3 is reading what you have typed as a value. If you had started your entry with a letter instead of a number, 1-2-3 would have assumed that you were creating a label rather than a value. When an entry begins with a number, or any of these characters

$$+ \quad - \quad \# \quad \$ \quad @ \quad (\quad .$$

1-2-3 assumes a value is being entered (for this reason, these characters are referred to as *value indicators*).

You can now place the number 789 into the worksheet. To do so, press Enter and notice that the number disappears from the editing line and is placed into the worksheet in the cell you are highlighting. The cell address indicator in the upper-left corner of the control panel now lists the contents of the cell. This might seem like a duplication of effort since the cell pointer's location is clearly visible on the screen. However, what's in the cell address indicator is sometimes different from what's displayed in the worksheet. The cell address indicator shows the exact contents of the cell as 1-2-3 reads it.

When you press Enter, notice that the mode indicator returns to READY. Note also that the numbers you have entered are placed on the

right-hand side of the cell. 1-2-3 normally aligns numbers even with the right
edge of the column, which is referred to as *right alignment.*

Entering Labels

Now that you are back in READY mode, you can move to another cell.
Press the Right Arrow key once to move to cell B1, where you will enter a
label. Before you type, locate the Caps Lock key on your keyboard. Press
Caps Lock once and notice that the status area reflects this change with the
message "CAPS."

    Next you will enter the word PRICE; you are going to use 1-2-3 to deter-
mine the cost of a swimming pool. When you type the letter "P," notice that
the mode indicator changes from READY to LABEL. Also note that the
word is being typed on the editing line so you can change it with the Backspace key if you make an error. Type **PRICE**, press Enter, and observe the
cell address indicator.

    1-2-3 precedes the word you typed with an apostrophe (') to remind you
that this is a label. Although you're unlikely to confuse this particular label
with a number, later you will encounter values that look like labels.

    The apostrophe also signifies that this label is left aligned. Labels can be
either left aligned, right aligned, or centered in the column. Right-aligned
labels are preceded by a quotation mark ("). Centered labels begin with a
caret (^), which is the shifted 6 on the keyboard. 1-2-3 will assume one of
these three label prefixes, which is called the *default label prefix.* As you can
see, the default in this case is an apostrophe, indicating left alignment.

    To enter a label aligned differently from the default, just type the
desired prefix before the label text. (If you want the actual label to begin
with one of the prefixes, you must use two of them. In other words, entering ""**DELUXE**" will produce the right-aligned label "DELUXE.") Later
you will learn how to change the prefix for a group of labels or how to
change the default itself.

Entering Data with the Arrow Keys

You will now enter another label, DELIVERY, directly below PRICE. How-
ever, you will use a slightly different method to enter this label into the cell.
First press the Down Arrow to move to cell B2 and then type **DELIVERY**.
The label will appear on the editing line, as did 789 and PRICE. Pressing the
Down Arrow key again will both enter the label and move you down to the
next row (much as if you had pressed Enter and then pressed Down Arrow).
The cursor-movement keys will enter what you are typing and move you in a
particular direction with one keystroke, a very useful feature if you want to
enter a series of labels or numbers. At the same time, this means that you

cannot use the cursor-movement keys to move through data on the editing line when you are entering information into a cell. Practice this method of entering by typing **TAX** and pressing the Down Arrow key, and then entering **TOTAL** and pressing the Down Arrow key. The results should look like Figure 1.16.

Figure 1.16

Labels entered in a column

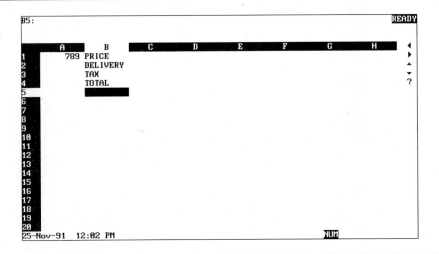

Editing Cells

Even the most careful spreadsheet user will occasionally need to correct mistakes and change entries. In this example, you will change the figure of 789, which is rather low for a swimming pool. Press Home to move the cell pointer to A1 and the number 789. To change a cell entry completely, just type a new entry. Type **2000** and press Enter. The new number completely replaces the old one. (Do *not* use commas when entering numbers in 1-2-3; they will be inserted later.)

Suppose you want to modify rather than completely replace the contents of the cell. For example, you might want to change 2000 to 2095 to reflect a price increase. When you don't need to change a cell completely, you can use the Edit key, F2. In this case, you press F2 while your cell pointer is in A1. When you do so, the contents of the cell are returned to the editing line, as shown in Figure 1.17. Press Backspace twice to back over the last two zeros and type **95**. Now press Enter to return the modified entry to the cell.

Figure 1.17

Editing the
contents of a cell

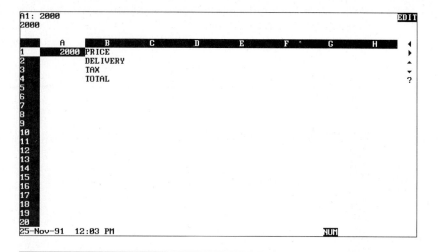

Entering and Editing with a Mouse

There are several ways to use a mouse when you enter and edit worksheet
data. You can select the cell into which you want to make an entry by clicking
on it. If you start typing an entry, you can click the right mouse button to cancel the entry. (The right mouse button often works like the Escape key, cancelling the current command.) If you use the mouse arrows on the mouse palette,
you can simulate the use of cursor-movement keys to place entries into cells.
For example, typing **789** and then clicking on the down arrow in the mouse palette will enter 789 in the current cell and move the cell pointer to the next cell
down the column.

If you are typing a label, you can also enter it by clicking the left mouse
button while pointing to the top three lines of the screen. If you are editing a
value entry, you can enter it with the same technique. However, if you are
typing a new value entry you cannot use this method of entry, but you can
still use the mouse arrows.

Instructions and Formulas

You now want to enter the delivery costs in your worksheet. First press
Down Arrow once. You will be in cell A2. Now type the number **567** and
enter it into the cell by pressing the Down Arrow key. You are now in cell
A3 and ready to do some math with 1-2-3.

In cell A3, you want a figure for the sales tax that must be paid on the
price of the pool (not including the delivery charge). Assume that the tax
rate is 10% or 0.1. The figure you want in cell A3 is 2095 x 0.1. You want

1-2-3 to calculate this for you, so you will type an instruction into cell A3 that tells 1-2-3 to multiply the number in cell A1 by 0.1 and place the answer in cell A3.

Note that you are not simply telling 1-2-3 to multiply the number 8095 by 0.1. Instead, you want to establish a relationship between the two cells A1 and A3 so that A3 will continue to give you 0.1 times the contents of A1 even if the number in A1 changes.

The instruction for performing this calculation will be entered as **.1*A1** (1-2-3 uses the asterisk as a multiplication sign). Although the instruction contains a letter as well as numbers, 1-2-3 considers the decimal point to be a *value indicator,* reading what follows it as a value. Type **.1*A1** and press Enter. You will immediately see thc tax calculated, as shown in Figure 1.18.

Figure 1.18

The tax calculation

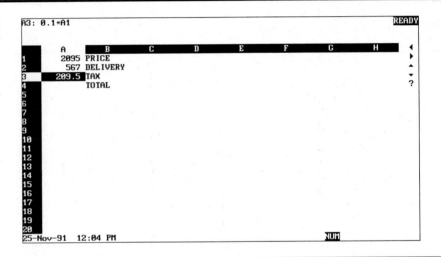

The cell address indicator on the second line of the screen should look like this:

```
A3:  0.1*A1
```

What's important to 1-2-3 is not the actual value displayed in cell A3, but the relationship between the two cells A1 and A3. This relationship will remain the same, whatever number is in cell A1.

Suppose that the price goes up. Press Home to get to the value 2095 in cell A1. Type **2995**, the new price, and press Enter. 1-2-3 will update cell A3 automatically. Now move your cell pointer down to cell A3 and look at the cell address indicator. The cell contents have not changed; you'll still see the formula you entered before.

Now you want to calculate a total cost for the pool, including price, delivery, and tax. You need to add together the data in several cells. To do this, you will first place the cell pointer in the cell that is to contain the answer—in this case, cell A4. Then you will type an instruction that tells 1-2-3 that this cell will contain the sum of cells A1, A2, and A3.

You might think that you could type **A1+A2+A3**, and this is almost correct. However, instructions involving only cell references need special treatment because 1-2-3 will read the letter *A* as the first character of a label. To ensure that 1-2-3 knows you are typing a value, first type a plus sign, then type the cell reference (as in **+A1+A2+A3)**, and finally press Enter. Make sure that your cell pointer is in A4 and then type the formula and press Enter. The results can be seen in Figure 1.19.

Figure 1.19
The completed
formula

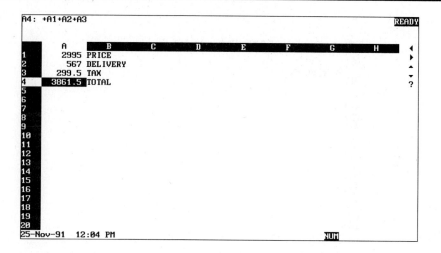

The Ability to UNDO

As you work with 1.2.3, you will notice the word UNDO in the status area. This message indicates that the UNDO feature is active. This feature allows you to reverse the last action you performed. For example, press Home to return to A1, type a new price of **2750**, and then press Enter. Now press the Undo key, which is Alt-F4 (hold down Alt and press the F4 key). The previous entry will return as your entry of 2750 is undone.

Now move the cell pointer down to A4. Press Alt-F4 again. Note that UNDO does not reverse cell pointer movement, but it does undo the last change you made to a cell, even if that cell is no longer highlighted. Press

Alt-F4 once more; 2995 is displayed in A1. In other words, UNDO will undo itself, and you can use UNDO to switch between two values and instantly compare the effect they have on the rest of the worksheet.

If you do not see the UNDO message when you are in READY mode, this feature has been turned off in your copy of 1-2-3. This may have been done to save memory since UNDO uses about 145k of RAM. Chapter 2 explains how to turn UNDO on and off.

Using the Menu System

The manipulation of facts and figures in cells is only part of the power of 1-2-3. There is a whole collection of 1-2-3 commands in a series of menus and submenus that you access by pressing the Menu key. The Menu key is the forward slash (/) that is usually on the same key as the question mark.

Menu Navigation

When you press /, the main 1-2-3 menu appears at the top of the screen. The first line of the menu lists currently available options, with the first option, Worksheet, already highlighted, as shown in Figure 1.20. The second line of the menu either describes what the current option does or indicates what options will become available if the currently highlighted item is selected. For example, if you select Worksheet, the items Global, Insert, Delete, and so on will move up to the first line of the menu. Note that the word MENU appears in the mode indicator when the menu system is in use.

You can press the Right Arrow key once to highlight Range, and continue across the bar to highlight each of the items in turn. You can also press Left Arrow to move the highlighting the other way. Press End to highlight the last item and Home to highlight the first. In addition, you can use the spacebar to move through the menu items. The spacebar cycles to the right through each item and then begins again at the beginning of the menu, just like the Right Arrow key.

Now move the highlighting onto the item called Move. The second line of the menu will display an explanation of the item. Highlight File and on the second line you will see Save, Retrieve, Combine, and so on. When a menu item leads to further menu selections, these appear on the second line. When a menu item does not lead to a further menu but actually carries out a command, the second line contains an explanation of the command. This allows you to browse through the menu system and always know what comes next, even if you are not familiar with all of the commands.

Figure 1.20

The 1-2-3 menu system

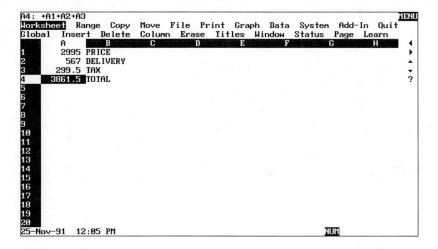

Exploring the Menu Levels

To explore how the menu works, move the highlighting to File and press Enter. The Retrieve, Save, and Combine options are now moved up to the first line of the menu. The first item, Retrieve, is highlighted and explained on the second menu line. Now highlight Admin (press End or Left Arrow) and press Enter to select it. Next select Table. At this point, you are several layers down into the menu system. A simple way to move back up the menu system to the top, or main, menu is to press the Escape key. This takes you back one level at a time. If you keep pressing the Escape key, the menu will eventually disappear altogether and you will be back in READY mode. Try this now.

There are two ways to select items from the menu. You can highlight the item and press Enter—also known as the point-and-shoot interface method. Alternately, you can type the first character of the item you want. For example, press / to display the menu and then press F followed by A followed by T. You will have reached the same level as last time, but with fewer keystrokes.

Selecting menu items by pressing their first letter is convenient if you are familiar with the menu selections and the keyboard. The point-and-shoot method is better if you are not a good typist and want to see where you are heading before you get there. For the rest of the book, you should use the menu item selection method that you prefer. In the interests of accuracy, the text will sometimes tell you which letters to press to select a specific command. In some cases, you will be asked to highlight a specific menu item in order to see what comes next, but in most cases the text will leave the selection method up to you.

There is another way to leave the menu system. Escape takes you out one step at a time; Ctrl-Break immediately returns you to READY mode. Try this now (hold down the Ctrl key and then press the Break key, which is sometimes on the Scroll Lock key).

Using Menus with a Mouse

You can activate the menu with your mouse. Simply move the mouse pointer into the area above the column letters. The menu automatically appears, as seen in Figure 1.20. You can press the right mouse button to make the menu disappear. To select an item from the menu, point at it and click the left mouse button. You should select items from the top line of the menu, not the second line. Once you have selected an item, you can use the right mouse button to reject it (in this situation the right mouse button acts like the Escape key).

You can use the mouse arrows to move the highlighting through a list of menu items. As you've seen, in some menus, such as those involving file lists, there is a special mouse palette on the top line of the screen to help you move through the file list quickly.

When you move your mouse pointer into the menu area, you may see a menu that begins with Worksheet Format instead of Worksheet Range. This is the Wysiwyg menu, which appears when you have the Wysiwyg add-in loaded. In this case, you can press the right mouse button to switch between the two menus. When Wysiwyg is loaded, the mouse pointer activates the last menu you used. If you last used the Wysiwyg menu, it appears when you move the mouse pointer into the menu area. Switch to the regular menu and it will appear the next time you call up the menu with your mouse.

Saving and Ending

Having completed this swimming-pool cost calculation, you may decide to take a break. So far, all of your work is in the computer's memory and that memory is only as good as the power to your computer. If you suffer an electrical failure or accidentally pull the plug, the memory's contents are lost. To produce a permanent record of your work, you must transfer a copy of the memory's contents to permanent storage on the disk. This is known as *saving* and has to be done on a regular basis, particularly before you leave your PC unattended. You also need to save your work to disk before leaving 1-2-3 if you want to be able to retrieve it in future work sessions.

To save your work, press / to bring up the menu and then press F for File. Now press S for Save; you should see a prompt like the one on the second line of Figure 1.21.

Figure 1.21

The File Save prompt

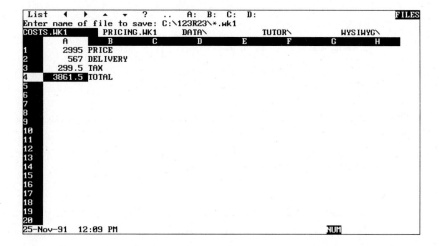

```
List   ◄   ►   ▲   ▼   ?   ..   A:  B:  C:  D:                    FILES
Enter name of file to save: C:\123R23\*.wk1
COSTS.WK1        PRICING.WK1      DATA\           TUTOR\         WYSIWYG\
       A         B         C         D         E         F         G         H
1      2995 PRICE
2       567 DELIVERY
3     299.5 TAX
4    3861.5 TOTAL
5
6
7
8
9
10
11
12
13
14
15
16
17
18
19
20
25-Nov-91  12:09 PM                                          NUM
```

Any files that have already been created with 1-2-3 will appear in an alphabetical list on the third line of the screen. The first time you use the program, it will suggest storing on the same drive and directory from which you started the program, typically C:\123. The list will include any files stored in this area of the disk, followed by any subdirectories of the main 1-2-3 directory (subdirectory names are followed by a backslash, as in DATA\ and WYSIWYG\).

Now type a name for the file in which you want 1-2-3 to store this worksheet. The name can consist of up to eight letters or numbers, like SWIMPL01, but cannot include spaces. However, you can use the underline character, as in S_POOL01. Although you can use some punctuation in file names, not all punctuation characters are allowed and it is thus best to avoid punctuation.

Note that the file names in the list actually have two parts. The first part, up to eight characters, is followed by a period and three more characters. The second part of the file name—the part after the period—is called the *extension*. It is often used like a surname, to show the family or group to which the file belongs. 1-2-3 worksheet files are all automatically assigned the extension .WK1; you do not need to type it in. For more details on file naming, see Chapter 6. For this example, simply type **POOL** and press Enter. The file will be stored as POOL.WK1.

If you want to avoid storing data files among program files, you will need a data directory for your 1-2-3 worksheets, for example C:\123\DATA. If you have created such a directory, you can tell 1-2-3 to store your files there using the File Directory command or the Worksheet Global Default Directory command. For more on these commands, see Chapter 7, which also describes how to use your mouse to navigate file lists, using the special mouse palette.

Now that you have saved your work, you can either turn off your system or return to DOS. However, you may want to continue with the example in the next section before you quit. To leave 1-2-3 and return to DOS, perhaps to use different software, press / to activate the menu and select Quit. 1-2-3 asks you to confirm that you want to quit, presenting a No/Yes choice, with No as the default. If you highlighted Quit on the main menu and then pressed Enter too hard, 1-2-3 would select Quit followed by No, and return you to READY mode. You can only complete the Quit command by pressing Y or highlighting Yes and pressing Enter.

If you confirm the Quit command but have not saved your latest changes, 1-2-3 will beep and require you to confirm the command again with a second No/Yes menu. You can select No to return to READY mode and then use the File Save command to save your work. Alternately, you can quit without saving by choosing Yes.

If you used the 1-2-3 Access System to load 1-2-3, completing the Quit command returns you to the Access menu, from which you choose Exit to return to DOS. If you did not use the 1-2-3 Access System to load 1-2-3, the Quit command returns you directly to DOS.

If you do not want to stop working with 1-2-3 but want to begin a fresh file after saving the last one, you can clear the worksheet area by pressing / and selecting Worksheet followed by Erase. Again, 1-2-3 will prompt for confirmation of this choice in case you have not saved changes to the current worksheet.

Suppose you leave 1-2-3 and want to return to the POOL file later. Reload 1-2-3, press /, and then select File followed by Retrieve. Type **POOL** and then press Enter to retrieve a copy of the file from disk. The next chapter includes more information on file saving and retrieving.

More Math: Using Functions

The swimming-pool cost calculation didn't really stretch 1-2-3's mathematical capabilities. Taken together, the entries you have made so far constitute a spreadsheet *model*—a numerical picture of a set of related values. This particular model shows the total cost of an item given a specific delivery charge and rate of tax. If you change the price or delivery value, the spreadsheet displays, or models, the result. You may want to expand this model to explore

1-2-3's ability to work with numbers. Suppose you are considering taking out a loan to finance the cost of the swimming pool. You would want to know your monthly payments, which 1-2-3 can model for you.

A loan payment calculation involves three pieces of information. You will type labels for these three items into column D, starting in D1. Move the cell pointer to D1 now. Then enter the labels **PRINCIPAL**, **INTEREST**, **TERM**, and **PAYMENT** in cells D1, D2, D3, and D4, using the Down Arrow key to move from one cell to the next. Then move back to cell E1 where you will enter the principal amount. Your screen should look like Figure 1.22.

Figure 1.22
Worksheet ready for principal

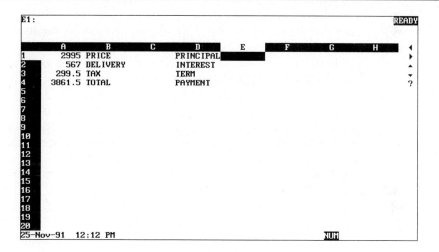

The amount you want to finance, or the principal, is the total from cell A4. Instead of typing the number again, simply type **+A4** and press Enter. This establishes a relationship between E1 and A4 so that whatever number appears in cell A4 also appears in cell E1.

Now move the cell pointer to E2. Here you want to enter the rate of interest, which should be expressed as a rate per period of the loan. Suppose you are going to make monthly payments. You need to enter the amount of interest you will pay in one month. Assume that the bank is charging 12% per year (sometimes referred to as 12% annual percentage rate)—that is, 1% per month. You type **.01** in cell E2 and press the Down Arrow key. In cell E3, type the term, the number of months for the loan, say **36**, and press Down Arrow.

In E4, you will enter a formula for the payment. You do not need to know the exact formula. 1-2-3 has a special built-in function for calculating a loan payment given the principal, interest, and term. In fact, 1-2-3 includes dozens of built-in functions for most common calculations. These are often referred to as @functions ("at" functions) because they are always preceded by the @ sign (a shifted 2 on most keyboards). However, for simplicity this book will omit the @ sign from the word "function."

The function you need in this case is called @PMT. Type **@PMT** in cell E4 but do not press Enter yet. The @PMT function needs to know the amounts for the principal, interest, and term of the loan—amounts referred to as *arguments*. You enclose the arguments for the @PMT function within parentheses and separate them with commas. Instead of typing the actual amounts for the principal, interest, and term, you use the coordinates of the cells in which these amounts have been entered. To complete the formula type **(E1,E2,E3)** and then press Enter to place it into the cell. The entire formula is thus:

```
@PMT(E1,E2,E3)
```

This produces the monthly payment, as seen in Figure 1.23.

Figure 1.23

The completed @PMT formula

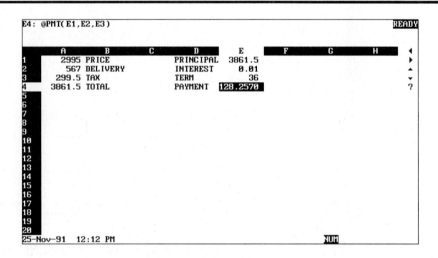

To see how flexible a spreadsheet is, you can now try changing the assumptions that produce the answer in E4. For example, if you were considering a more expensive model, you could type the new price in A1 and immediately see the new payment in E4. Press Home and enter **3995** in A1. To lower the monthly payment, enter a longer term, such as 48 months, into E2. Now press the Undo key, Alt-F4, to change the entry back to 36.

You can save the new version of this worksheet. Press / and select File followed by Save. Type **POOLPMT** and press Enter. The new file is saved as POOLPMT.WK1. To clear the worksheet for further practice, press / and choose Worksheet followed by Erase and then Yes. Alternatively, you can select Quit to leave 1-2-3 and reload the program later for more practice.

Spreadsheet Practice

So far, you have learned how to enter labels, numbers, and formulas. To practice your data entry skills, try entering the values and labels shown in Figure 1.24. This model is a four-year record of passenger volume figures for a small airline. Four main destinations are served by Magic Carpet Airlines (MCA), and the figures are listed by destination.

Figure 1.24

Passenger volume figures

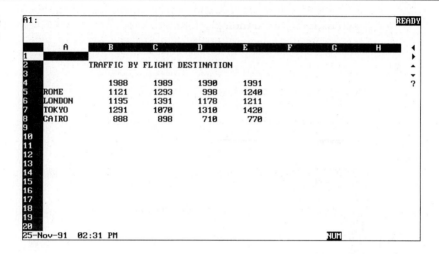

```
A1:                                                              READY
          A        B        C        D        E     F     G     H    ◄
1                                                                     ►
2                  TRAFFIC BY FLIGHT DESTINATION                      ▲
3                                                                     ▼
4                 1988     1989     1990     1991                     ?
5    ROME         1121     1293      998     1240
6    LONDON       1195     1391     1178     1211
7    TOKYO        1291     1070     1310     1420
8    CAIRO         888      898      710      770
9
10
11
12
13
14
15
16
17
18
19
20
25-Nov-91   02:31 PM                                  NUM
```

In a new worksheet, move the cell pointer to B4, ready to type the first year of the model. Later in this book, you will learn several different ways of handling dates and calendar information, including sophisticated date arithmetic. In this situation, you can just type the number **1988** and press Right Arrow to enter it and move to C4 for the next year.

Instead of simply typing **1989**, you will create the year by adding one to the previous year. This is the formula 1+B4 (which does not need a preceding plus sign because 1 is a value indicator). Type **1+B4** and press Right Arrow. Now type **1+C4** and again press Right Arrow to move to cell E4. Finally, type **1+D4** and this time press Enter. Returning to B4, you can change that cell to 1989 and see the other years change automatically. Press Undo (Alt-F4) to change B4 back to 1988.

Now go to column A, on line 5, and enter the city names. Again, use the Down Arrow key to move from one cell to the next. Follow the city names with the numbers shown in the figure. These numbers will be used later in several examples, and you can practice using the keyboard as you enter them. When you are done entering all of the data, move the cell pointer to B2 to enter the main title. A quick way to do this is to press the Goto key,

F5. When you press F5, you will see the prompt "Enter address to go to." Type **B2** and press Enter. This shortcut is particularly useful when you are moving around in large worksheets. In cell B2, type **TRAFFIC BY FLIGHT DESTINATION** and press Enter.

To finish the model, you will enter formulas in cells B9 through E9 to total the number of passengers for each of the years. In B9 you could enter **+B5+B6+B7+B8** to get the total. However, you can also use a function to add the cells, in this case the @SUM function. The argument for this function is the group of cells to be summed, in this case B5 through B8. This group of cells form what 1-2-3 calls a range, a rectangular group of adjacent cells.

You can describe a range by giving the first and last cells of the group, separated by two periods, as in B5..B8. In other words, you can sum these cells by entering **@SUM(B5..B8)**. However, you do not actually have to type two periods. In B9, type the formula **@SUM(B5.B8)** and then press Enter. As you can see from Figure 1.25, 1-2-3 records this as @SUM(B5..B8), giving you one period for free. The use of functions and ranges will be discussed in more detail in the next chapter.

Figure 1.25

The @SUM formula

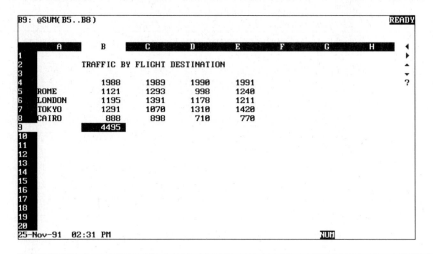

To complete the model, you need to create similar formulas in C9, D9, and E9. There is a quick way to do this: Copy the formula from B9. The theory and practice of copying formulas will be dealt with in the next chapter, but for now you can just follow these steps to copy the formula in B9 and complete the model:

1. With the cell pointer on the @SUM formula in B9, press / to bring up the menu. Select Copy.

2. Press Enter to accept B9..B9 as the range you are going to copy. You will then be asked "To Where?"

3. Type a period and then press Right Arrow three times so that the To Where? range is B9..E9. Press Enter. The results will appear, as shown in Figure 1.26.

Figure 1.26
The results of the
Copy command

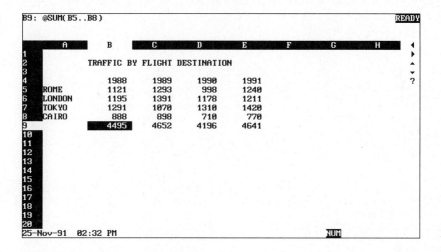

The formula from B9 is now copied across all of the years. This is one way that 1-2-3 simplifies building mathematical models. To save this worksheet, use the File Save command and the file name PASSVOL. You will then be able to recall the file for use in Chapter 2.

Summary

In this chapter, you explored the basic concepts of the electronic spreadsheet as implemented by 1-2-3 Release 2.3. You learned how data is entered, altered, and calculated. You saw how the menu system works and how files are stored on disk for later use. Chapter 2 covers the finer points of data entry as well as the range commands that allow you to alter the appearance of data and build extensive models out of a few basic ingredients.

Spreadsheet Commands

CHAPTER 1 INTRODUCED THE 1-2-3 SPREADSHEET AND GAVE A FEW examples of how it can be used. During the exercises at the end of the chapter, you learned how the 1-2-3 screen acts like a dashboard, providing you with valuable information as you navigate around the huge worksheet. You also entered some data and stored your work in a disk file for later retrieval. In this chapter, you will review the main elements of 1-2-3 in greater depth and explore examples of how they are applied.

File Management in a Spreadsheet Session

When you load 1-2-3, you are presented with an empty and unnamed grid of more than two million cells. You can enter new information into these cells and then store them in a file. If you have already stored a worksheet file on disk, you can retrieve it into the worksheet.

Bringing Back Stored Files

You use the File Retrieve command to work on a worksheet that you have already stored on disk. When you use this command to read a worksheet file from disk, you are replacing all two million cells of the worksheet area with the contents of the file. This means that you erase from memory anything that had been entered into the worksheet prior to the File Retrieve command. For this reason, you should make sure that you have saved to disk any work in progress before performing the retrieval operation. 1-2-3 will *not* prompt you before overwriting the current worksheet with the retrieved worksheet. If changes to the current worksheet have not been saved when you issue the File Retrieve command, 1-2-3 warns you and asks you to confirm the command. Select No to cancel the command or Yes to continue.

Using the File List

If you start 1-2-3 and decide to retrieve a worksheet stored on disk, you press / to activate the menu and select File (either press F or press Right Arrow four times to highlight File and then press Enter). When you select Retrieve from the File menu, you see a list of previously saved worksheet files from which to select, as shown in Figure 2.1.

This alphabetical list grows as you add more files. The maximum number of files you can see at one time is five. Any more files must be scrolled into view with the cursor-movement keys or the spacebar. You use Right Arrow or spacebar to move one name to the right, and Left Arrow to move one name to the left. Press End for the very last file, and Home for the very first. You can use Tab or Ctrl-Right Arrow to highlight the last name out of those currently displayed, and Shift-Tab or Ctrl-Left Arrow to highlight the first name out of those currently displayed.

Figure 2.1

The file list

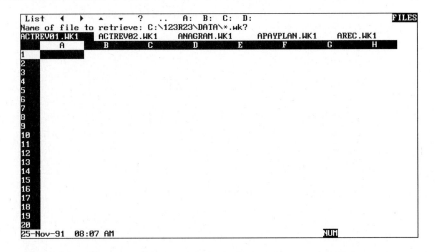

You can also view the available files by pressing F3, the Name key. This produces an extended full screen list that can show up to 105 files at once, arranged in five columns, as shown in Figure 2.2. You can use the cursor-movement keys to select the desired file.

If you are using a mouse, the File Retrieve command places a special mouse palette on the top line of your screen, as shown in Figures 2.1 and 2.2. You can use the mouse arrows on this palette to move through the file list. You can also click on List instead of pressing F3 to view the full-screen file list. To select a file from either the single-line list or the full-screen list, simply click on the file name. If you need help, you can click on the question mark (?). To abort the File Retrieve command, click the right mouse button. You will also see drive letters in the special mouse palette (A:, B:, and so on). These enable you to list files on other disks. Use of the drive letters is covered in Chapter 7.

As mentioned, you can toggle between the single-line list and the full-screen list by pressing F3, or clicking on List in the special mouse palette. Entries in the list that end with a backslash (\) represent subdirectories of the current directory. If you select a subdirectory, 1-2-3 will list files in that area of the disk. You can also list files in the directory above the current directory, that is, the *parent directory*. For example, if the current directory is C:\123\DATA, C:\123 is the parent directory. To view the parent directory, press Backspace, or click on the pair of dots (..) in the special mouse palette.

Figure 2.2

The extended file list

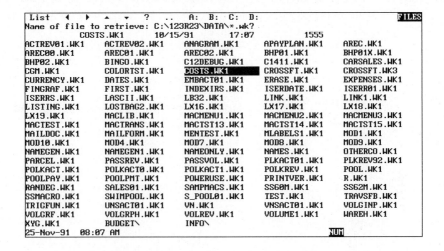

Besides displaying more files, the full-screen file list provides more information about individual files. The file you highlight is detailed on the second line of the screen. For example, in Figure 2.2, the second line includes the following information:

```
COSTS.WK1      10/15/91       17:07        1555
```

This tells you that COSTS.WK1 was last stored onto disk on 10/15/91 at 17:07 (seven minutes past five in the afternoon) and that the file is 1,555 bytes in size. (For more on file sizes, see Chapter 6.) When you have many files, this detailed information can help you locate the correct one. Note that you can only use the Name key when a file list is already on screen—that is, after issuing the File Retrieve or File Save command. It does not work in READY mode.

To complete the File Retrieve command, highlight the name of the file you want and press Enter. Alternatively, you can type in the file name and press Enter (you don't need to type the file name extension). When you complete the File Retrieve command, a copy of the file is read from the disk into the computer's memory. In Figure 2.3, you can see the passenger volume worksheet from Chapter 1 (the one that you saved as PASSVOL.WK1).

Notice that the cell pointer is still where you left it when you stored the file to disk. This feature allows you to return to the point where you left off. If you leave the cell pointer on the edge of your worksheet and then retrieve the file later, you may be confused about the cell pointer location. For this reason, some people prefer to press Home before saving work so that the worksheet looks familiar when it is retrieved.

Figure 2.3

The retrieved file

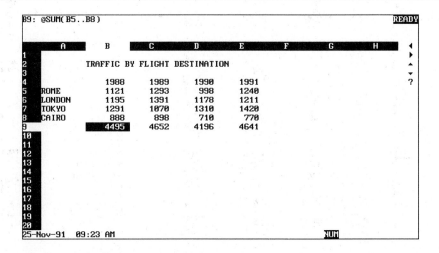

```
B9:  @SUM(B5..B8)                                                    READY

         A         B          C          D          E       F       G       H    ◀
1                                                                                 ▶
2               TRAFFIC BY FLIGHT DESTINATION                                     ▲
3                                                                                 ▼
4               1988       1989       1990       1991                             ?
5    ROME       1121       1293        998       1240
6    LONDON     1195       1391       1178       1211
7    TOKYO      1291       1070       1310       1420
8    CAIRO       888        898        710        770
9               4495       4652       4196       4641
10
11
12
13
14
15
16
17
18
19
20
25-Nov-91   09:23 AM                                               NUM
```

Resaving Old Files

Once you begin to change a worksheet, you should remember to resave the file on a regular basis. Remember, the copy of the worksheet that is in memory disappears if your PC is turned off or restarted. Try to save every 15 minutes and whenever you leave your computer unattended.

When you save a worksheet, you can either overwrite the old version of the worksheet with the new version, or put the new version in a new file and give it a different name. To save a worksheet, press / and then select File followed by Save (/FS). As you can see from the prompt in Figure 2.4, 1-2-3 automatically assumes that you want to use the same file name.

At this point, you can accept the name by pressing Enter. 1-2-3 will always check whether a file of the same name exists on disk. If it does, you will see a prompt like the one in Figure 2.5. Your choices are Cancel, Replace, and Backup.

Generally, you will choose Replace to replace the older version until the worksheet design is complete. Then you may want to save different sets of numbers in different files, in which case you choose Cancel and repeat the File Save command, this time entering a new file name.

To save the current file quickly, using the same name but without overwriting the previous version, you can select the File Save Backup option. This option assigns the file extension .BAK to the previous version of the spreadsheet and saves the current version with the extension .WKS. If you save PASSVOL.WK1 using the Backup option, the original PASSVOL.WK1 file will be renamed PASSVOL.BAK and the new version of the spreadsheet will be saved as PASSVOL.WK1. If you repeat the same command later, 1-2-3 will replace the existing PASSVOL.BAK file with a new version.

Figure 2.4
The file save prompt

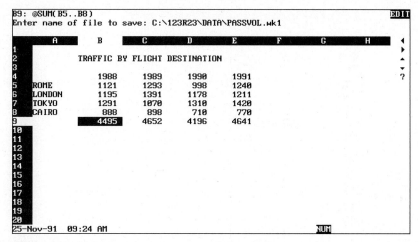

Figure 2.5
Cancel, Replace,
and Backup options

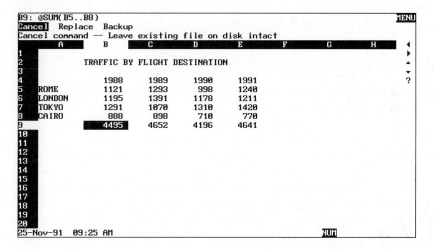

To change the default file name at the file save prompt, just type the desired name. This will automatically replace the existing name. Alternatively, you can edit the default file name by pressing spacebar and Backspace, and then using other editing keys to change the name. Table 2.1 lists the keys for editing the file save prompt. When the name is typed correctly, you can press Enter to confirm the save operation.

Table 2.1   **Keys for Editing the File Save Prompt**

When the file has not yet been saved:

Esc	Places the prompt in EDIT mode, removing the *.WK1 file specification. Pressed a second time, removes the rest of the prompt so that you can enter your own prompt. (If you enter a directory name followed by \, 1-2-3 will add *.WK1 to list files in that directory.)
Backspace	Lists files in the next directory above the current directory. If the current directory is the root, places the prompt in EDIT mode, and eventually erases the drive letter.

When the file has previously been saved:

Esc	Removes the existing name and lists worksheets in the current directory. Pressed a second time, places the prompt in EDIT mode, removing the *.WK1 file specification. Pressed a third time, removes the rest of the prompt so that you can enter your own.
Backspace	Active only in EDIT mode.
Spacebar	Activates EDIT mode.

When the prompt is in EDIT mode:

Home	Moves edit cursor to first character of prompt.
End	Moves edit cursor to last character of prompt.
Ins	Activates overstrike mode.
Ctrl-Right Arrow	Moves edit cursor 5 characters to the right.
Ctrl-Left Arrow	Moves edit cursor 5 characters to the left.

Erasing a Worksheet

When you have saved a spreadsheet and want to build a new one, use the Worksheet Erase command to clear the entire worksheet window. Press / and then select Worksheet followed by Erase. You are asked to confirm that you want to erase the worksheet, whether or not it has been changed since you last saved it. If you choose Yes to confirm the command and your current work has not been saved, 1-2-3 asks for a second confirmation. This is because the Worksheet Erase command erases all two million cells from memory.

Note that in this and other confirmation prompts, the No option is highlighted initially. This helps prevent you from accidentally selecting Yes. Also note that the Worksheet Erase command does not affect files that are stored on disk: It only erases the contents of memory. To delete files from disk, you will use the File Erase command described in Chapter 6.

More About Data Entry

In Chapter 1, you learned about the two types of data in a spreadsheet: values and labels. You also discovered two methods of entering data into the spreadsheet. You can type your entry and press Enter, which inserts the data into the cell and leaves that cell highlighted. Alternately, you can type your entry and press a cursor-movement key, which enters the data and moves you in the direction of the key you pressed. In both cases, you place the cell pointer on the cell into which you want to receive the data before you begin typing.

Inevitably you will make a few mistakes in data entry as you construct your worksheets. The following sections present several methods of correcting mistakes and modifying data.

Changes Before Entering

At times you will need to change or cancel an entry as you type it. For example, suppose you start typing some new data and realize that your cell pointer is in the wrong cell, possibly one that already contains data. When you type data, it first appears on the editing line, just below the cell address indicator in the upper-left corner of the screen. Pressing Enter or an arrow key at this point will place this data into the wrong cell. If there is already data in the cell, the new data will replace the old, and you will have to reenter the old data. If the cell is empty, you will simply have to remove the incorrect entry.

Fortunately, 1-2-3 lets you change your mind before you enter what is on the editing line. If you press the Escape key or click the right mouse button, whatever you typed is removed from the editing line, and you are back in READY mode. Now you can move the cell pointer to the correct location.

If you start typing new data in the right place but make an error or a spelling mistake, use the Backspace key to erase the error, and then resume typing. Remember, you should *not* press the Left Arrow key to go back and correct mistakes while typing a new entry. Doing so will enter the data into the cell.

Undoing Data Entry

Entering data into a cell is an action that can be reversed with the Undo feature. If you have pressed Enter to place the data in the cell but have not used a menu command or made another entry, pressing the Undo key returns the cell pointer to the last entry and reverses it. If you placed the entry in a blank cell, Undo makes the cell blank again. If you overwrote a previous entry, the previous entry will be restored.

The Undo key only works if the Undo feature is active, in which case the message "UNDO" is displayed in the status line while 1-2-3 is in READY mode. To turn on the Undo feature, you select Undo from the Worksheet Global Default Other menu and then select Enable. You can also select Disable to turn the feature off. You may want to turn Undo off to make more memory available to worksheets and add-ins. Unfortunately, you cannot turn Undo on if you already have a worksheet loaded. You must save your work and clear the work area before enabling Undo. To record the Undo status so that it stays the same in the next session, use the Update command on the Worksheet Global Default menu.

If you have entered data into a formerly empty cell, you can also undo that operation by leaving the cell pointer on the new entry and pressing the Delete key. This erases the contents of the current cell. You can undo the delete operation and thus switch between two different entries.

Cell Editing

You can change the contents of a cell in several ways. The method you use will depend upon the type of change you need to make. The following paragraphs explain the different ways of editing, using Figure 2.3 as an example.

As explained in Chapter 1, the simplest editing method involves typing the new data over the old. This will completely replace the old data. For example, if you place the cell pointer on the word LONDON, type **PARIS**, and press Enter, the entire word LONDON will disappear, not just the first five letters. This is often the fastest way to correct data entry errors. However, it is occasionally easier to edit the existing entry.

The Edit Key

For example, if you want to change LONDON to LONDON - HEATHROW, you can avoid retyping the entire entry by using function key F2, the Edit key. As you saw in Chapter 1, when you place the cell pointer on a cell and press F2, the contents of the cell are returned to the editing line. The mode indicator also changes from READY to EDIT. The cell address indicator at the top of the screen describes what cell you are editing; next to it you see what was in the cell before the editing began. With the cell contents back on the editing line, you can now edit the cell contents and place the revised entry in the worksheet by pressing Enter.

When you are in EDIT mode, several keys behave differently. Pressing Home moves the cursor to the left side of the entry. Pressing End returns the cursor to the right side. You can also move through the entry with the Left

Arrow and Right Arrow keys. Thus, if you mistakenly enter LUNDON - EATHROW, you can press F2 to edit the cell, press the Left Arrow key until your cursor is under the erroneous U, and press the Delete key to remove it, changing LUNDON - EATHROW to LNDON - EATHROW. You then type **O** to insert it into the text to the left of the cursor. The input line should now contain LONDON - EATHROW. Next, you use the Right Arrow key to position the cursor under the E, where you type **H** to complete the editing. As soon as you're done you can press Enter, regardless of where your cursor is within the data, and the revised information will be placed back into the cell.

While you are editing a cell in EDIT mode, you are in what is called INSERT mode, where what you type is inserted into the text instead of replacing what is there. However, you can get into OVERSTRIKE mode by pressing the Ins key. When you press Ins during editing, the message "OVR" appears in the status area at the bottom of the screen. Once you are in OVERSTRIKE mode, the characters you type replace existing characters, rather than simply pushing them to the right. 1-2-3 automatically reverts to INSERT mode when you leave EDIT mode. Table 2.2 lists the keys you can use to make changes to the current cell while in EDIT mode.

Editing with the Mouse

Once you have pressed F2 to edit the contents of a cell, you can use the mouse in several ways. You can use the left and right mouse arrows to move the edit cursor through the contents of the editing line. You can use the up and down mouse arrows to enter the edited data and move the cell pointer to the next cell up or down the current column. You can also click the left mouse button anywhere in the top three lines of the screen to enter the edited data and return to READY mode. If you decide to abandon your edits, you can click the right mouse button, the equivalent of pressing Esc.

Deleting Cell Entries

At times, you will want to erase the entire contents of a cell. The correct way to clear out a cell is with the Delete key. Simply put the cell pointer in the cell you want to erase and press Del. You may already have found another method of erasing a cell: If you place the cell pointer on the cell you want to delete, press spacebar, and then press Enter, the cell appears to have emptied. However, if you look next to the cell address indicator, you see that the apostrophe, which begins a left-aligned label, still remains. You have replaced what was in the cell with a blank label.

It's not good to get into the habit of deleting cells in this way, since the cell is not really emptied. Blank cells can affect some calculations that include them. In addition, they are hard to find since you can see nothing in a blank cell unless the cell pointer is on it and you observe the characters to the right of the cell address indicator. Remember to use the Delete key to delete a single cell. You can always reverse the effect of Delete by pressing Undo (Alt-F4).

Table 2.2   **Keys Used in EDIT Mode**

Key	Action
Left Arrow	Moves edit cursor one character to the left
Right Arrow	Moves edit cursor one character to the right
Home	Moves edit cursor to the first character
End	Moves edit cursor to the right of last character
Tab	Moves edit cursor five characters to the right
Ctrl-Right Arrow	Moves edit cursor five characters to the right
Shift-Tab	Moves edit cursor five characters to the left
Ctrl-Left Arrow	Moves edit cursor five characters to the left
Del	Deletes character at edit cursor
Ins	Toggles between insert and overstrike modes
Backspace	Deletes character to the left of edit cursor
Esc	Cancels editing, returns to READY mode
Enter	Enters contents of cell and returns to READY mode with cell pointer in same cell
Down Arrow	Enters contents of cell and returns to READY mode, moving cell pointer down one cell
Up Arrow	Enters contents of cell and returns to READY mode, moving cell pointer up one cell
PgDn	Enters contents of cell and returns to READY mode, moving cell pointer down one page
PgUp	Enters contents of cell and returns to READY mode, moving cell pointer up one page
Ctrl-[	Erases all characters in entry but remains in EDIT mode
Alt-F1	The Compose key, allows you to create special characters
F2	The Edit key, switches back to VALUE or LABEL mode
F3	The Name key, lists range names if pressed after a math sign
F4	The Abs key, adds dollar signs to make cell reference absolute if edit cursor is on a cell reference
F9	The Calc key, converts a formula to its current value

Replacing Formulas with Their Results

When you enter a formula into a 1-2-3 cell, what you see on the worksheet is the current value of that formula. However, 1-2-3 records the formula itself, rather than its result. This allows the formula to remain dynamic—that is, to change value when cells or functions referenced in the formula change. Sometimes you will want to "freeze" the results of a formula and convert the formula to the value it created. One way to do this is to edit the cell.

When you press F2 to edit a cell that contains a formula, the formula is placed on the editing line. Pressing F9 (the Calc key) converts the formula to its result. You then press Enter to place the value in the worksheet and replace the formula. For example, suppose you are assembling the passenger volume figures shown in Figure 2.3 and are missing the number of passengers for Rome in the last year of the table (cell E5). If you are in a hurry, you might decide to estimate the number by using a formula that multiplies the numbers for the previous year by a factor, as in 1.1*D5. However, entering this formula into cell E5 makes E5 permanently dependent on D5. To convert the formula into a number, just highlight E5, press F9, and then press Enter to replace the formula with its current result. In Chapter 5, you will learn how to convert whole ranges of formula cells into their values, using the Range Values command.

Data Entry Errors

If you enter data that 1-2-3 cannot read, pressing Enter to place the data in a cell will result in a beep. For example, since 1-2-3 does not accept numbers that contain commas or include text, entering **4 CITY TOTAL** in cell A9 will produce a beep and change the mode indicator to EDIT when you press Enter. 1-2-3 has automatically placed you in EDIT mode so that you can correct your error. In fact, 1-2-3 is trying to point out your error by placing the cursor at your first mistake, in this case the space after 4.

You need either to change the entry so that it does not begin with a number or type a label prefix before the number. Then you can place the corrected data into the cell by pressing Enter. You can also press the Escape key twice after a data entry error to cancel the erroneous entry completely.

Worksheet Defaults

Each time you start 1-2-3 or issue the Worksheet Erase command, some basic settings, known as *defaults*, are reinstated. A default is what the program assumes unless you tell it differently. For example, when you start 1-2-3, the columns in which you enter data are nine characters wide. In other words, the default column width is nine characters. But you can also change the column width in a particular worksheet to anything from one to 240 characters.

In a new worksheet, the columns can accommodate nine characters, labels are normally aligned on the left, and a general format is used to display numbers. (Changing the worksheet to other formats is described in detail in the section "Formatting Numbers.") When you start working on a spreadsheet design, you can change the default settings for that sheet by using the Worksheet Global command. For example, you can establish the right label prefix as the default prefix for all new labels in a worksheet. You can have all numeric entries appear in a Currency format, that is, preceded by a dollar sign and including a fixed number of decimal places. You can make all of the columns ten characters wide using the Worksheet Global Column-Width command. (The commands for controlling columns are discussed in more detail later in the section "Commanding Columns.")

Having established the desired default settings for a worksheet, you can always vary sections of the worksheet from the default. For example, you can change one or more columns to a width other than the default, as described under "Commanding Columns." You can format one or more cells with a different format from the default. In addition, you can give any number of labels a different prefix from the default, as described under "Labels."

Note that changes to the worksheet defaults apply only to the current worksheet. You cannot establish a default label prefix other than left or a column width other than nine for all new worksheets. There are some program defaults, such as the international formatting of values and dates, that you can change permanently, so that they become the new defaults. Chapter 5 explains how to make these changes.

Using Dialog Boxes

When you select the Worksheet Global command, you will see a screen like the one in Figure 2.6, most of which is taken up by a box called Global Settings. Boxes such as this one are known as dialog boxes. Several commands in 1-2-3 use a dialog box as well as a regular menu. This section explains how to use dialog boxes in 1-2-3. The instructions here apply to all commands that use dialog boxes.

The Role of Dialog Boxes

Dialog boxes both show you the status of current settings, and allow you to change those settings. Dialog boxes are like a form that you fill in, with fields that you need to complete and lists that you can check. The items in the dialog box are grouped together in logical order. You can use dialog boxes both with the keyboard and with a mouse.

Figure 2.6
The Global Settings
dialog box

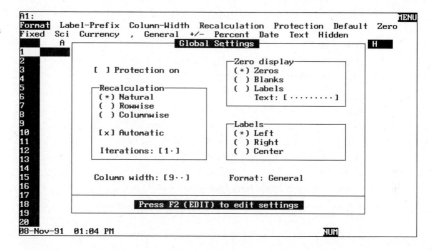

There are two ways of changing the settings in a dialog box. You can use the menu displayed above the box. When you choose an item from the menu, you are prompted to supply a response. For example, when you select Format you are asked to choose from a list of formats that appears as a single line on the screen. The choice you make then appears in the dialog box. Earlier versions of 1-2-3 had no dialog boxes, so you couldn't see values supplied for the settings.

You can also change dialog box settings by editing them directly in the dialog box. To do this, press the Edit key (F2) or click the left mouse button with the mouse pointer anywhere in the settings box. Your screen should now resemble Figure 2.7. The menu disappears from the top of the screen and the mode indicator changes to SETTINGS.

Editing a Dialog Box

To edit settings in a dialog box, choose the item you want to change, make the change, and then confirm the new settings. There are several ways of choosing items and confirming the settings, which will be discussed after you learn about these objects within a dialog box:

- Command buttons
- Option buttons
- Check boxes
- Text boxes
- Pop-up dialog boxes
- Three-dot buttons
- List boxes

Figure 2.7
Editing dialog box
settings

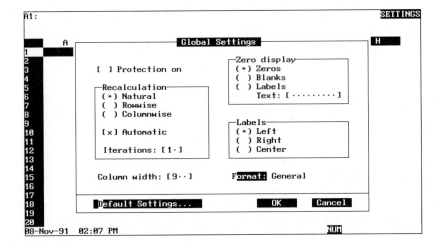

Command Buttons

When you edit a dialog box, the OK and Cancel buttons appear at the bottom of the box; these are called command buttons. When you first press Edit (F2), the OK field is selected, as indicated by the arrow on either side. If you press Enter or the spacebar while OK is selected, or click on OK, the command button is activated. 1-2-3 assumes that you have finished editing the Global Settings and returns you to the Worksheet Global menu, with your settings in effect. You can achieve the same result by pressing Shift-Enter at any time while in SETTINGS mode.

The Cancel command button cancels the editing of settings and returns you to the menu, wiping out any of the changes you made to the settings. You use the Cancel button by pressing the spacebar or Enter key while Cancel is selected, or by clicking on the button with your mouse. Pressing the Escape key or clicking the right mouse button while editing the dialog box has the same effect.

OK and Cancel appear in all dialog boxes, and additional command buttons are also displayed when appropriate. Three-dot buttons, which lead to further dialog boxes, are described in a moment.

Option Buttons

In Figure 2.7 the group marked Labels contains three option buttons. The current selection, the Left option, is marked by an asterisk. Only one option in the list can be selected, but at least one option must be selected (this type of arrangement is sometimes referred to as radio buttons, after the push-button station selectors on old car radios). If you select Right, Left is automatically deselected.

Check Boxes

A check box is used for settings that can either be on or off. For example, the Automatic setting in the Recalculation group in Figure 2.7 can either be on or off. The default setting is on, marked by the x within the square brackets. Note that square brackets and x's distinguish check boxes from option buttons, which use parentheses and asterisks.

Text Boxes

A text box is a field in the dialog box that contains a typed entry, such as the Column width setting in Figure 2.7. When you select this field, you must type your preference. Text boxes are enclosed in square brackets and preceded by the field name and a colon.

Pop-up Dialog Boxes

Some dialog box options lead to further choices that are displayed in a pop-up dialog box. For example, when you select Format from the Global Settings dialog box, the Format dialog box appears, as shown in Figure 2.8. This dialog box within a dialog box is complete with its own OK and Cancel command buttons. After you make your choice and activate the OK button, you are returned to the previous dialog box, where your selection will be displayed.

Figure 2.8

The Format pop-up dialog box

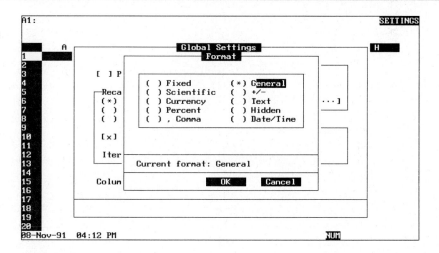

Three-Dot Buttons

Sometimes it is helpful for a dialog box to refer you to a further set of options. For example, when you are working on global settings for the current worksheet, you may want to alter the global program defaults. In Figure 2.7, the Global Settings dialog box refers you to the Default Settings box with a special command button, called a three-dot button. The ellipsis indicates that activating this button brings up another dialog box, in this case the Default Settings box shown in Figure 2.9.

Figure 2.9

The Default
Settings dialog box

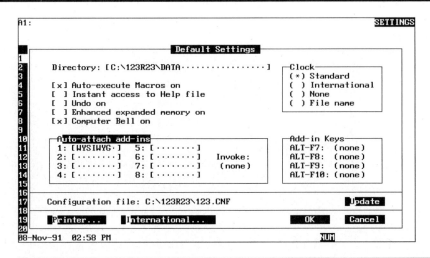

As you can see from the figure, this dialog box includes the setting for the default data directory, the place where 1-2-3 will look for your data files, as well as a list of automatically attached add-on programs. Note that there are two further three-dot buttons at the bottom of this menu, plus another command button called Update, which is used to save your new settings as defaults for future work sessions.

List Boxes

A list box is used within a dialog box when you have to choose from a list that varies, such as a list of range names or file names, as described in Chapter 4. For example, when you are using the Default Settings dialog box in Figure 2.9 you can tell 1-2-3 the name of add-in programs to use all the time, known as auto-attach add-ins. A typical example would be the Wysiwyg program mentioned in Chapter 1 and already included in the settings in Figure 2.9.

The entry of WYSIWYG in field 1 of Figure 2.9 is the name of the actual Wysiwyg program file. The field is a text field, one that you can type in. However, when you select a vacant auto-attach add-in field, such as field 2, you can press F3 to see a list of available program files, as shown in Figure 2.10. Note that you can scroll through the list by clicking on the up or down arrows so that the desired item is brought into view. Keyboard users can use the cursor-movement keys to scroll through the list. To select an item from the list, highlight it and then press Enter or click on OK. In fact, if the name you want appears in the list, you can just click on it to select it.

Figure 2.10

Using a list box

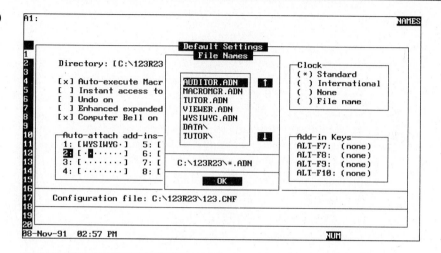

Navigating the Dialog Box

When you press F2 or click in a dialog box to edit it, you need to be able to choose the setting that you want to alter. Mouse users can simply click on the item they want. For example, to alter the format, click on Format to bring up the Format dialog box shown in Figure 2.8, click on the format you want, then click on OK. If the format uses a variable decimal place setting, a small box appears for you to enter the desired number of decimal places. To select a number other than the default, type the number and then click on OK. You are returned to the Global Settings dialog box with your selection reflected in the Format field.

To alter an option button or check box setting with a mouse, just click on the item. The appropriate asterisk or cross will appear or disappear to mark the change.

Keyboard users will need to use keystrokes to change the active field on the dialog box. When you first press F2, the OK command button is active. If you press Home, the first setting, the one in the upper-left corner of the dialog box, will be activated. In Figure 2.7 this is the Protection on setting. When a setting is active it is highlighted or marked by arrows. You move to the next setting by pressing Tab. Repeatedly pressing Tab will activate each setting in turn. You move in the opposite direction by pressing Shift-Tab.

Pressing Tab or Shift-Tab takes you from setting to setting, but does not highlight each possible choice in turn. Thus the Labels setting counts as one, and Tab will not move the highlight through the three choices for this setting. To move from choice to choice, you use the Up, Down, Left, and Right arrow keys. Also notice that settings are grouped together. For example, there are three settings within the Recalculation box. You can move among the settings in a group of settings with the arrow keys.

To use the keyboard to alter settings, press Enter or the spacebar when the choice you want is highlighted. For example, to alter the Labels setting, move the highlighting to Labels, press Enter, and use the cursor-movement keys to highlight the desired choice, and then press Enter or the spacebar to select it. Many items have key letters that you can use instead of using the highlight-and-enter method. For example, once you have activated the Labels setting by highlighting it and pressing Enter, you can type L to select Left, R to select Right, or C to select Center.

If the setting you activate uses a pop-up dialog box, you can make your choice from there. If the setting you activate requires a text entry, type it and then press Enter. If the setting is a check box, simply press Enter or the spacebar to toggle it on or off. For settings that require ranges, like those in the Data Sort dialog box, you can press F4 to switch to the worksheet and point out the range. Alternatively, you can press F3 to list named ranges, which are described in Chapter 4.

To confirm the changes you have made in a dialog box, you can press Shift-Enter. You can also activate the OK button and press the spacebar or Enter. To cancel changes, press Esc or activate Cancel and press the spacebar or Enter. Alternatively, you can press Ctrl-Break to cancel the entire operation, leave the menu system, and return to READY mode. If you select a menu item that displays a dialog box that you do not want to use or even see, you can press F3 to turn it off.

Most examples in this book simply say which command to use and let you decide how to issue the command. The text will read "issue the Worksheet Global Format command" rather than "press / and then type W followed by G." This approach allows you to relate to the program in the way that fits your style of working, level of program knowledge, and type of hardware. Dialog boxes, in particular, can be operated in a number of ways. You will probably need to work with the program for a while before deciding which technique is best for you.

Formatting Numbers

Recall that 1-2-3 does not permit commas in numbers when you enter them. Features such as commas, leading dollar signs, parentheses for negative numbers, and the number of decimal places shown are all functions of *numeric formats,* which you can control using the format commands. For example, the difference between the way numbers are shown in Figure 2.3 and Figure 2.11 is a result of a change in their format, affected with the Worksheet Global Format command.

Figure 2.11

Formatted numbers

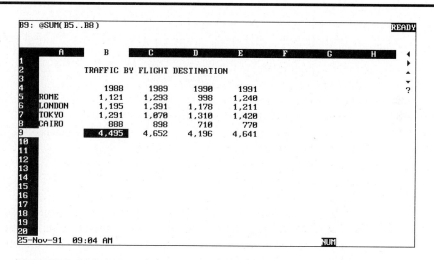

Being able to change the way a number is displayed saves you a great deal of effort. When you start a fresh worksheet, 1-2-3 uses the General format, which displays no commas in the thousands and no decimal places unless they are entered or calculated by a formula. In the General format, entries or calculation results with many decimal places are shown with as many decimal places as will fit in the cell. When you enter or calculate a number with decimal places, the General format displays the decimal places until the complete number is shown or until the cell is filled, whichever comes first. For example, given the following values, the General format will show 502.5 in cell D4, 3.333333 in cell D5, and 0.333333 in cell D6:

```
B4: 1005      C4: 2      D4: +B4/C4 =      502.5
B5:   10      C5: 3      D5: +B5/C5 = 3.333333
B6:    1      C6: 3      D6: +B6/C6 = 0.333333
```

Even when you enter numeric constants (as compared to formulas), the General format can present problems because it only displays digits that affect the number's value. For example, if you enter 100.00, 1-2-3 displays 100, and 99.50 shows up as 99.5. The only way to get the decimal points to line up within a column is to assign a different format.

The Default Format

You can change the default 1-2-3 format for part or all of the worksheet. Suppose that you want commas in the passenger volume numbers, as shown in Figure 2.11. You can achieve this effect by choosing Comma as your default format.

To change the overall or global format, press /, select Worksheet, and then select Global. 1-2-3 displays a screen indicating all the current default settings. This screen will be discussed in Chapter 8. For now, just note that the cell display format is currently G for General. Select Format to display a menu with the following format choices:

```
Fixed Sci Currency , General +/- Percent Date Text Hidden
```

Some of the formats require that you indicate the number of decimal places. For example, when you choose the Comma format (represented by the , in the menu) the following prompt appears:

```
Enter number of decimal places (0..15): 2
```

As you can see, the options are from 0 to 15, with 2 displayed as the suggested default setting. While formats such as Fixed, Comma, and Currency suggest using two decimal places, you can always type your own choice before pressing Enter to confirm the format selection. Figure 2.12 shows what happens to the worksheet in Figure 2.3 when the Worksheet Global format is set to Comma with 0 decimal places. The various formats are listed in Table 2.3.

Figure 2.12

The Comma format applied with Worksheet Global format

```
B4: 1988                                                            READY

          A        B        C        D        E        F        G        H     ◄
 1                                                                              ►
 2               TRAFFIC BY FLIGHT DESTINATION                                  ▲
 3                                                                              ▼
 4               1,988    1,989    1,990    1,991                               ?
 5     ROME      1,121    1,293      998    1,240
 6     LONDON    1,195    1,391    1,178    1,211
 7     TOKYO     1,291    1,070    1,310    1,420
 8     CAIRO       888      898      710      770
 9               4,495    4,652    4,196    4,641
10
11
12
13
14
15
16
17
18
19
20
25-Nov-91   09:03 AM                                        NUM
```

Table 2.3   **The 1-2-3 Format Options**

Format Name	Format Identifier	Description/Example
Fixed	(F2)	No commas in thousands, negatives in parentheses, user-defined decimal places: 2000.99 (2000.99)
Scientific	(S2)	Exponential notation, negatives in parentheses, user-defined decimal places: 2.00E+03 (2.00E+03)
Currency	(C2)	Commas in thousands, negatives in parentheses, user-defined decimal places, $ sign prefix: $2,000.99
, (Comma)	(,2)	Commas in thousands, negatives in parentheses, user-defined decimal places: 2,000.99
General	(G)	As many decimal places as entered or will fit, exponential notation for large numbers
+/-	(+)	Positive numbers as plus signs (+), negatives as minus signs (-) for simple bar charts
Percent	(P2)	Contents divided by 100, % sign as suffix
Date	(D1)	Various options described in Chapter 3, including formats for time values (D1 is the first date format)
Text	(T)	Formulas displayed rather than their values in cells
Hidden	(H)	Cell contents hidden from view; contents shown next to the cell address indicator only when the cell is highlighted

Note that you can alter the details of some formats with the Worksheet Global Default Other International setting. For example, you can change the punctuation used for decimal points and thousands separators as described in Chapter 7.

As Figure 2.12 illustrates, changing the Worksheet Global format affects the appearance of all values in the worksheet, including the years in row 4. However, the underlying values have not changed, as you can see from Figure 2.12 where the cell pointer is highlighting B4. Obviously, since you don't want commas in the years, 1-2-3 needs to be told that the range of cells from B4 through E4 must be formatted differently.

Range Formats

You can format sections of the worksheet with the Range Format command. Formats assigned by the Range Format command are not affected by changes to the Worksheet Global format. You normally begin a Range command by placing the cell pointer on the cell you want to change or in the upper-left corner of the group of cells to be changed. In Figure 2.12, this cell is B4. Having selected the correct cell, press / and choose Range to display the following choices:

```
Format Label Erase Name Justify Prot Unprot Input Value
Trans Search
```

Since the Format option is listed first, you can press Enter to select it. This reveals a set of options almost identical to those offered by the Worksheet Global Format command:

```
Fixed Sci Currency , General +/- Percent Date Text Hidden
Reset
```

However, this menu has an option to Reset the format. You use this option when you want a cell formerly formatted with Range Format to appear in the spreadsheet's global format, in effect undoing the previous Range Format command.

To remove commas from the years, you can use the Fixed or General format. If you choose the Fixed format, you must tell 1-2-3 that there are to be zero decimal places for these years. When you press Enter to confirm the format, you will also have to tell 1-2-3 to which cells this format applies.

1-2-3 assumes that when you enter the Format command you want to format at least the cell where the cell pointer is located. In this case, this is referred to as range B4..B4, which means the cell B4. The fact that 1-2-3 displays two cell references (B4..B4) rather than one (B4 by itself) indicates that the range is already *anchored*. This means that when you press any of the cursor-movement keys, the cell pointer will expand rather than simply move from one cell to the next. To extend the current range, press Right Arrow three times, pointing out the cells to be included, as shown in Figure 2.13. The cell in which you anchor the beginning point of the range is usually the top cell in a column of cells or the left cell in a row. If the range includes cells from more than one column or row, you can begin pointing in the upper-left corner of the range, although any corner will do. The section "Working with Ranges" in this chapter explains ranges in greater detail.

When the highlighting covers the cells and the range prompt shows B4..E4, as in Figure 2.13, you press Enter to complete the command. As you can see from Figure 2.14, all the cells within the range are changed.

Figure 2.13

Highlighting the
cells to be
formatted

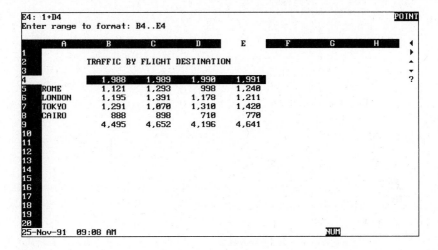

Figure 2.14

A range format
applied

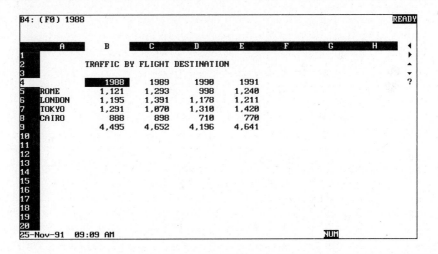

Note that after the format is applied, 1-2-3 displays the characters (F0) next to the cell address indicator, telling you that cell B4 has a Fixed format of zero decimal places assigned to it. (The full list of format identifiers is given in Table 2.3.)

A cell's formatting and format identifier remain in place even if you change or erase the cell's contents. For example, if you erased any of the cells from B4 to E4 at this point and then entered a new number, that number would be displayed in Fixed format with zero decimal places. In addition, when you copy a cell, its assigned format (or lack thereof) is copied along with its data, so that all the copies are formatted just like the original. This means that copying an unformatted cell to a formatted one, in effect, removes the cell's formatting.

Note that when you issued the Range Format command, the range was automatically anchored at the current cell. Sometimes you will want to point out a range that does not start from the current cell. If the cell pointer was in A1 when you issued the last command, for example, the range would have been anchored at cell A1. In this case, you would need to press Esc to "unanchor" the range. (You could tell that the range was no longer anchored because only one reference to A1 would appear on the input line.) Then you would move the cell pointer to one corner of the desired range (B4 or E4) and type a period to reanchor the range. You could then use the arrow keys to highlight the range and press Enter.

Of Mice and Ranges

If you are using a mouse with 1-2-3, you can select ranges with it. Whenever a 1-2-3 command prompts you to point out a range, place the mouse pointer over the upper-left cell in the range and then hold down the left mouse button as you drag the mouse pointer to the lower-right corner of the range. This expands the highlighting to cover the range; the corresponding coordinates are reflected in the range prompt. When you release the mouse button, the range remains selected until you complete the command by pressing Enter or by clicking the left mouse button while the pointer is anywhere outside of the selected range. You can cancel the range by clicking the right mouse button.

You can also select a range with the mouse while you are in READY mode, before issuing a command to affect the range. Place the mouse pointer over the upper-left cell in the range, hold down the left mouse button, and drag the mouse pointer to the lower-right corner of the range. The highlighting expands to cover the range and the coordinates are reflected in a special range prompt on the second line of the screen. Release the mouse button and the range stays selected.

You can now choose any command that requires range coordinates from the menu and 1-2-3 automatically uses the coordinates of the preselected range. The preselected range remains selected after the command has been executed, allowing you to carry out a series of commands on the same range without having to select it repeatedly.

To clear a preselected range, click the right mouse button or press Esc to leave the cell pointer in the upper-left cell of the range you have just cancelled. You can also select a different range, or use the mouse or cursor-movement keys to move the cell pointer.

There is another way to use the mouse when working with ranges. If you have not preselected a range, you can use the arrows in the mouse palette to alter the coordinates of the range. For example, suppose the cell pointer is in B4 in Figure 2.13. You have selected the Range Format Fixed command and typed 0 for the number of decimal places. You then use the mouse equivalent of pressing Enter, clicking in the top three lines of the screen, to confirm the decimal place setting. 1-2-3 prompts for the range to be formatted. Click on the right mouse arrow three times to expand the range to B4..E4. Now click in the top three lines to confirm the range and complete the command.

Finally, you can use the mouse to accept values in commands like Range Format. For example, when you are prompted to enter a number for the decimal place setting, you can click with the mouse in the top three lines of the screen to accept either the default value or a value you have entered.

Preselecting Ranges with F4

Keyboard users can also select ranges before issuing range related commands. To select a range from the keyboard, use the F4 key while in READY mode. This key is knows as Abs, short for Absolute. It has completely different functions when you press it in POINT or EDIT mode, as described in Chapter 5.

Suppose you want to select B4..E4 before issuing the Range Format command. Check that the mode indicator says READY and then press F4. A special range prompt appears on the second line of the screen and the current cell is anchored as the first cell in the range, as in B4..B4. The mode indicator changes from READY to POINT. Now use the cursor-movement keys to extend the range; for example, press Right Arrow to expand the range to B4..E4. When you are satisfied with the range, press Enter to return to READY mode. The range remains selected on the screen so that when you use the menu to issue a range command, the selected range is used automatically. The range remains selected when the command is completed.

To cancel a selected range, press Esc or any cursor-movement key while in READY mode. If you press F4 to define a range and want a cell other than the current cell to be the starting point, you can press Esc to unlock the range coordinates. Move the cell pointer to the cell you want as a starting point and type a period to anchor the range.

When you have learned to use range names, you can select named ranges by pressing F4, typing the name of the range, and pressing Enter. You can also press F4, press F3 to list range names, and select a name from the list. In most cases, examples in this book describe range related commands in terms of selecting the range after issuing the command; however, you are free to preselect with F4 if you want to. In fact, preselection is more efficient when you want to apply several range commands to the same range.

Format Considerations

When a format change establishes the number of decimal places that can be displayed, 1-2-3 rounds the number for display purposes only. 1-2-3 remembers the number to 15 decimal places, even if the format indicates that zero decimal places are to be displayed. Chapter 4 discusses the @ROUND command, which causes 1-2-3 to round numbers permanently.

The normal width of 1-2-3 columns is nine characters. Because 1-2-3 needs to prevent the numbers in adjacent cells from appearing to run together, there is always a single character space to the right of a value entry. This means that a nine-character column can only accept eight digits. Figure 2.15 shows what happens when you apply a default format that produces numbers longer than will fit into the nine-character columns.

Figure 2.15
The asterisk effect

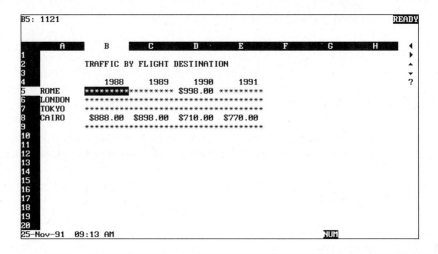

The Worksheet Global Format Currency command with two decimal places turns the number 1121 in cell B5 into $1,121.00. However, the cell shows ********* to let you know you need to widen the column or change the format. Figure 2.16 shows what happens when you widen the columns: The numbers reappear. The commands for widening columns are discussed in the section "Commanding Columns."

Note that you didn't alter the cells that were formatted with the Range Format command by changing the global format. If you wanted the cells B4 through E4 to assume the global format, you would have to use the Range Format Reset command and point out the range B4..E4.

Figure 2.16

After widening the columns

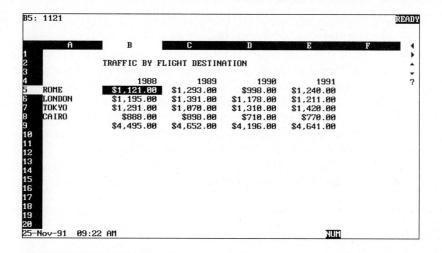

```
B5: 1121                                                            READY

          A           B           C           D           E           F     ◄
1                                                                            ►
2                 TRAFFIC BY FLIGHT DESTINATION                              ▲
3                                                                            ▼
4                     1988        1989        1990        1991               ?
5        ROME     $1,121.00   $1,293.00     $998.00   $1,240.00
6        LONDON   $1,195.00   $1,391.00   $1,178.00   $1,211.00
7        TOKYO    $1,291.00   $1,070.00   $1,310.00   $1,420.00
8        CAIRO      $888.00     $898.00     $710.00     $770.00
9                 $4,495.00   $4,652.00   $4,196.00   $4,641.00
10
11
12
13
14
15
16
17
18
19
20
25-Nov-91   09:22 AM                                          NUM
```

In this example, the Currency format is not appropriate. To change the global format back to the General format that 1-2-3 uses by default, select Worksheet Global Format General. All cells that are not range formatted will revert to the General format.

If you set the correct global format, you spend less time changing the appearance of separate ranges of cells. You also save space both in memory and on disk because you are not storing formatting codes in individual cells. When you need to distinguish a group of cells from the whole, use the Range Format command.

Entering Values

As you know, 1-2-3 distinguishes between values and labels by the first character of a new cell entry. Anything that begins with one of the following value indicators is treated as a value:

```
0 through 9 . + - ( @ # $
```

If you do not begin an entry with one of these characters, 1-2-3 will treat it as a label. Occasionally, you will need to enter items that look like numbers but are not, such as zip codes or phone numbers. This problem is dealt with in a moment under the section "Wrong Numbers."

Cell References

Whenever you enter instructions or formulas involving both numbers and cells, such as 1.1*A1, you can type the number first. This lets 1-2-3 know that what follows is a value. When formulas consist of cell references only, such as A3+A4, you must precede the entry with a value indicator. In the last chapter, you learned that this value indicator can be a plus sign, as in +A3+A4. The plus sign does not alter the value of the cell reference it precedes. You can also use a parenthesis to begin a value entry, as in (A3+A4). Parentheses are excellent value indicators when you need to control the order of calculation, as in (A2+A3)*(B2+B3). However, for every opening parenthesis there must be a closing parenthesis, so you may want to use the single + for simple formulas. (The gray + on the numeric keypad does not require that you use the Shift key.)

Large Numbers

You will occasionally need to enter a large number into a 1-2-3 worksheet. Given the General display format and the default column width of nine characters (eight digits), entering the number **123456789** displays 1.2E+08 in the worksheet. The cell address indicator lets you know that the number 123456789 is still stored by 1-2-3. What you are seeing is the scientific notation 1.2 x 10 to the power of 8. Widening the column to ten characters will restore the number to its normal appearance.

If you work with numbers in the millions and billions, you can set Exponential as the default format, using the Worksheet Global Format command, and see all of your numbers in scientific notation. The Fixed, Currency, and Comma formats all show asterisks instead of converting numbers that are too large into a scientific notation.

Wrong Numbers

Sometimes you need to work with numbers that are not values. For example, suppose you enter the phone number **555-1212** and press Enter. You get -657 in the cell because 1-2-3 thinks the 5 means that a value is coming and reads the entry as 555 minus 1212. To overcome this problem, you must precede the first character with one of the label indicators described later in the "Labels" section. For example, you can use the apostrophe to indicate a label aligned on the left of the cell. Thus '555-1212 will enter the phone number as a left-justified label. You can also precede a number with a space to make it a label.

Another common wrong number is a street address. For example, if you type **123 Main Street** without first typing a label indicator, 1-2-3 will reject your entry because it expects a value since you began with the number 1.

When you press Enter, 1-2-3 will beep and automatically switch you to EDIT mode so that you can clarify the error. This often occurs when you type a formula or a number incorrectly—for example, if you omit a closing parenthesis, enter a space in a formula, or type a comma in a number. When you are placed in EDIT mode, 1-2-3 positions the cursor where it thinks the problem lies, usually the first character that caused the confusion.

For example, if you type **1:00 AM** 1-2-3 will position the cursor under the colon. In this case, you can simply press Home to place the cursor at the beginning of the entry and add an apostrophe, telling 1-2-3 to treat the entry as a label. (Note that 1-2-3 can deal with time values, but not as ordinary numbers. See Chapter 11 for more on time and date values.) Remember that in EDIT mode you use Enter to put the data into the cell. If you want to retype the entire entry, press the Escape key to leave EDIT mode and return to READY mode.

Number Series

1-2-3 provides several methods for entering a series of numbers, such as 101, 102, 103, and so on. Such series are sometimes needed to number consecutive columns and rows, as in the numbering of inventory items and their locations shown in the example in Figure 2.17.

Figure 2.17
A series of numbers

B4: 101 READY

	A	B	C	D	E	F	G	H
1	Location & Quantity							
2								
3				Warehouse Number				
4		101	102	103	104	105	106	
5	Item:							
6	35650	61	46	44	110	0	93	
7	35651	55	104	0	0	109	0	
8	35652	48	122	0	120	0	0	
9	35653	80	26	109	71	114	0	
10	35654	115	0	49	0	0	48	
11	35655	83	0	123	56	121	80	
12	35656	91	0	112	46	0	121	
13	35657	35	60	96	0	89	80	
14	35658	0	32	0	32	103	27	
15	35659	0	57	0	120	41	0	
16	35660	111	33	122	0	53	81	
17	35661	32	114	80	0	0	81	
18	35662	103	97	101	27	0	0	
19	35663	106	59	72	82	106	118	
20	35664	116	77	58	75	0	36	

25-Nov-91 09:34 AM NUM

1-2-3 has a command called Range Fill that lets you automatically fill a group of cells with consecutive numbers. (Range Fill is covered in detail in Chapter 3.) You can also generate consecutive numbers using formulas. However, as you saw in the exercise at the end of Chapter 1, you can create these numbers with a simple formula. Look at the years on row 4 of Figure 2.16. They appear as

```
1988      1989      1990      1991
```

If 1988 is in cell B4, then cell C4 can be 1+B4, cell D4 can be 1+C4, and cell E4 can be 1+D4. When you enter the years this way, you can simply change 1988 and all the other years will adjust accordingly. For example, changing the contents of B4 to 1989 produces the following results:

```
1989      1990      1991      1992
```

In the section "The Copy Command," you will learn how to copy a formula from one cell to another to create a series of related values very quickly.

Formulas

Formulas are where much of the power of a spreadsheet lies. Whether you are adding cells or calculating the internal rate of return on an investment, being able to establish a relationship between cells gives you tremendous number-crunching ability. The following sections discuss various methods of entering formulas. (1-2-3's built-in formulas, sometimes referred to as "@functions," are discussed in greater depth in Chapter 5.)

Entering Formulas

So far you have seen formulas typed into the cell that is to contain the answer. For example, you know that the total of the three items in Figure 2.18 is going to be +A1+A2+A3, and you can enter this formula in A4.

However, if you are not a good typist, you might want to try the pointing method of entering formulas. Practice this in a fresh worksheet after saving your current worksheet and then using the Worksheet Erase command. You begin this method with the plus sign or a value, if there is one in the formula. Then, when 1-2-3 is in VALUE mode, you use the arrow keys to highlight the first number you want in the formula. For example, you can achieve the results in Figure 2.19 by typing the plus sign and then pressing the Up Arrow key three times. As you can see, 1-2-3 displays the address of the cell occupied by the cell pointer. Also note that the mode indicator has changed from VALUE to POINT.

Now you can type the next math sign, in this case another plus. The cell pointer moves back down to the cell in which the formula is being built, as shown in Figure 2.20. The basic procedure is: math sign, point, math sign, point. Note that 1-2-3 treats commas and parentheses, as well as numeric operators like plus and minus, as math signs.

Figure 2.18

Adding numbers

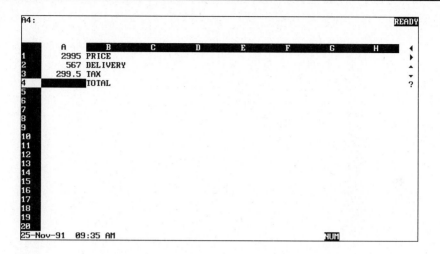

Figure 2.19

Building formulas
by pointing

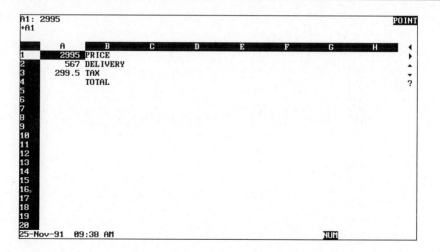

The next step is to point to the next cell that needs to go into the formula, in this case A2. When you highlight A2 with the cell pointer, it too is added to the editing line at the top of the screen, as shown in Figure 2.21.

After typing another plus sign, you repeat the process for the third cell. The formula on the editing line now reads +A1+A2+A3, and pressing Enter places it in the cell.

Figure 2.20
The second plus sign

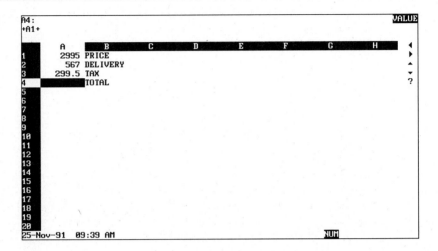

Figure 2.21
Another cell added

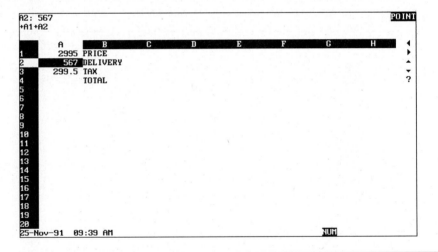

You can use a mouse when pointing out cells in formulas. However, you cannot simply type a plus sign and then click on the cell you want to include in the formula. Instead, you must point out the cell you want by using the mouse arrows in the mouse palette. Alternately, you can point out cells by clicking with the mouse, but only after you have moved the cell pointer at least one cell with either the cursor-movement keys or the arrows on the mouse palette. This prevents you from accidentally adding the wrong cells to formulas through careless clicking.

Note that when you are constructing formulas with the pointing method, you need to be careful about clicking the mouse in the top three lines of the screen. This enters the formula you have constructed so far, and if done prematurely may result in an incomplete formula.

This method is useful when you have values scattered throughout the spreadsheet and you cannot remember a particular number's exact address. You can also use the pointing method effectively when building formulas that involve ranges.

Functions and Ranges

As discussed in Chapter 1, there is another way to add the three items in cells A1 through A3. Instead of the formula +A1+A2+A3, you can consider these cells as part of a group, or range, and then apply the @SUM function to the contents of the range. You describe ranges by giving the first and last cells, separated by one or two periods. The completed formula would thus be @SUM(A1.A3).

Instead of typing, you can enter the same formula using the pointing method. Place the cell pointer in the cell that is to contain the formula and type **@SUM** and a left parenthesis. Then move the cell pointer to the first cell in the range of cells to be summed, A1 in this case. 1-2-3 will display the cell coordinate on the editing line, which shows

    @SUM(A1

While you are pointing to this first cell, type a period to anchor the range at this cell. The editing line will change to read

    @SUM(A1..A1

Now when you use the arrow keys to move the cell pointer, the first cell of the range will remain A1 and the cell pointer will stretch to encompass a range of cells. For example, if you press Down Arrow once, the result will be

    @SUM(A1..A2

When a range has been anchored, moving the cell pointer alters the second cell in the range reference. This allows you to expand the range using the cursor-movement keys. This method of pointing out a range is sometimes referred to as *painting* the range. If you anchored the beginning of the range in the wrong cell, you can press the Escape key to unlock that cell and move to another.

When you have highlighted all of the cells to be summed, in this case A1..A3, you can type the closing parenthesis. The completed formula is placed in the worksheet when you press Enter. The completed formula is

```
@SUM(A1..A3)
```

You can use a mouse to point out a range used in a formula. For example, after you have typed **@SUM(** you can use your mouse to define the range. However, before you point out the range you must move the cell pointer. For example, to create the formula @SUM(A1..A3) in A4, you first type **@SUM(** and then press the Up Arrow key or click on the up mouse button. Now you can use the mouse to define the range A1..A3. Place the cell pointer over A1, holding down the left button and dragging to A3 before releasing. Then type **)** to finish the formula and press Enter.

Labels

Although spreadsheets are number-crunching tools, labels are also extremely important because they tell you what the numbers mean. In fact, you should never enter numbers and formulas without first including labels to indicate what the numbers represent. 1-2-3 creates a label whenever a new cell entry begins with one of the following label indicators:

```
A through Z ' " ^ { [ ! \ > ; ~ ? } ] _ | ) * = & %
```

A space at the beginning of an entry also tells 1-2-3 that you are typing a label. If you have the Wysiwyg add-in loaded, the colon (:) brings up the Wysiwyg menu; otherwise, it is a label indicator. The less-than sign (<) activates the regular 1-2-3 menu on most keyboards.

Lining Up Labels

Normally, 1-2-3 aligns labels on the left and precedes them with an apostrophe to remind you that they are labels. To center a label in the column, you simply start the label with the caret sign (^). To right align a label, precede it with the double quotation mark (").

You can add label prefix characters to labels in several ways. To vary individual labels from the default label prefix setting, simply type the desired prefix before the label text. You can also tell 1-2-3 to right align, left align, or center all new labels in a worksheet by default. In this case, 1-2-3 automatically adds the appropriate label prefix character whenever you enter a new label. To do this, you press / to activate the menu, pick Worksheet followed by Global and then Label-Prefix, and select the alignment you prefer. This label alignment command only affects the current worksheet, not the current

1-2-3 session. It also does not affect any labels entered in the current worksheet before you issued the command.

To vary a group of cells from the default alignment, you use the Range Label command. Press / to activate the menu, pick Range, and select Label. You will see the three choices Left, Right, and Center. When you make your selection, you will be prompted to specify the range of cells you want to affect. Select the cells and press Enter to confirm the change. Alternatively, you can preselect the range with your mouse, and then issue the Range Label command.

Long Labels

1-2-3 labels can contain as many as 240 characters. You are unlikely to need labels that are this long, but you should know how 1-2-3 treats labels that are wider than one column. In Chapter 11, you learn that 1-2-3 can wrap long labels into a rectangular area on the spreadsheet to let you compose text for letters, memos, and notations on spreadsheet models.

In Figure 2.22, the title for the table of numbers is wider than one column. The title was entered in cell B2. When you enter a label like this, 1-2-3 gives no indication that it will exceed the nine-character width of the cell. When you press Enter to put this label into the cell, it exceeds the cell width but is still legible and will print when you print this worksheet.

Figure 2.22
The long label in B2

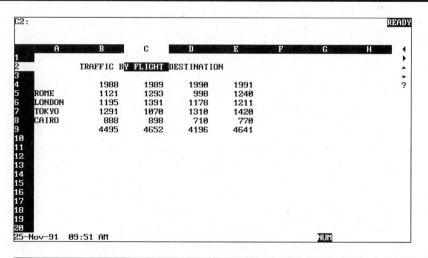

Long labels simply borrow space from adjacent cells to display their contents. If you place the cell pointer in C2 and look next to the cell address indicator, you'll notice that there is nothing in this cell. As you can see from

Figure 2.22, cell C2 is empty. The contents of cell B2 simply flow over into that display area. Unfortunately, this display method presents a problem when you want to enter a long label to the left of an occupied cell.

Consider the labels in column A of the example: city names that all fit neatly into a column with the default width of nine characters. If you change the label ROME to SAN FRANCISCO, the cell to the right of A5 is occupied and 1-2-3 cannot display the full label, as shown in Figure 2.23. Nevertheless, the missing letters are not lost, as you can see from the cell contents displayed next to the cell address indicator.

Figure 2.23

A label that is wider than its column

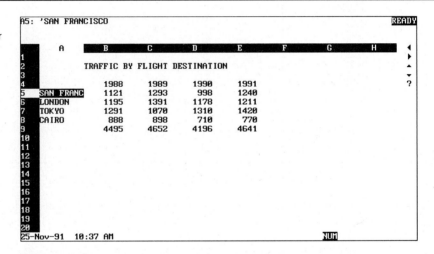

To solve this problem, you need to either abbreviate the label (for example, change it to SAN FRAN) or widen the column. Most likely you will want to widen the column using the column commands. However, you may choose to shorten the label, particularly if you are trying to keep the worksheet small or if you want the entries in a column to be more consistent in width.

Underlines and Repeating Labels

Cell entries in 1-2-3 cannot be underlined unless you use the Wysiwyg add-in. However, if you want to create the impression of a line beneath a label or across a spreadsheet, you can enter a line into a separate row. Figure 2.24 shows equal signs used for a dividing line. (See Chapter 10 for details on how to use Wysiwyg to underline numbers and labels within a cell and to draw lines above, below, and around cells.)

Figure 2.24

Adding a line of characters

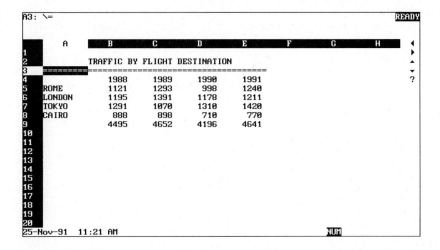

```
A3: \=                                                              READY

             A        B        C        D        E     F     G     H   ◄
                                                                       ►
1                                                                      ▲
2           TRAFFIC BY FLIGHT DESTINATION                             ?
3   =================================================
4                1988     1989     1990     1991
5   ROME         1121     1293      998     1240
6   LONDON       1195     1391     1178     1211
7   TOKYO        1291     1070     1310     1420
8   CAIRO         888      898      710      770
9               4495     4652     4196     4641
10
11
12
13
14
15
16
17
18
19
20
25-Nov-91   11:21 AM                                    NUM
```

To create the line in Figure 2.24, you need to fill each cell with a single character, the equal sign. Instead of typing as many characters as it takes to fill the column, you can use the backslash (\), which is the *cell fill* character. The \ is followed by the character you want to repeat. Thus, entering \= in A3 produced

=========

Alternatively, entering * would fill the cell with asterisks, while \+= would produce

+=+=+=+=+

This technique is much quicker than entering a series of symbols manually. In addition, when columns are altered in width, the cell fill method adjusts the number of characters in the cell accordingly. You will get a chance to create a line out of equal signs using the \ character in the section "The Copy Command."

Commanding Columns

There are several commands that you can apply to the columns from which the worksheet is built. You can add new columns, delete columns, and hide columns. You can also change the width of one or more columns.

Current Column Width

Suppose that you need to change ROME to LOS ANGELES in cell A4 of the example. Enter the new label now and note how it overflows the cell. You decide to widen the column so that the new label will fit. The column your cell pointer is occupying is referred to as the *current column*. To widen the current column, press / to activate the menu and then select Worksheet, Column, and Set-Width. As you can see from Figure 2.25, you are prompted for a width setting and reminded that the column can be from 1 to 240 characters wide. The default width of 9 is shown as the current setting.

Figure 2.25

Setting the width of column A

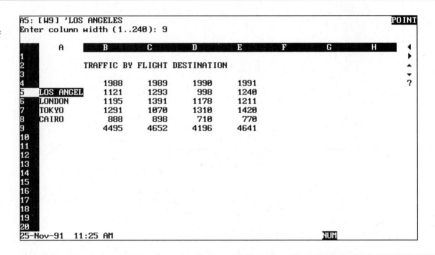

At this point, you can either type the number of characters for the width, or press the Right Arrow or Left Arrow key to widen or narrow the column on the screen. The width number changes as you do this. If you use the arrow keys, you can adjust the width visually until it is suitable. When the column is an appropriate width, in this case 11 or 12, press Enter to confirm it and to return to READY mode. The result can be seen in Figure 2.26.

The column width changes for the full length of the column. You cannot mix cells of varying widths within a column. When you have set the width of the current column manually, 1-2-3 displays a width reminder next to the cell address indicator when you highlight any cell in the column. As you can see from Figure 2.26, the notation in this case is [W12]. This notation is helpful if you change numerous columns in a worksheet.

If you are running 1-2-3 with the Wysiwyg add-in attached, you can use your mouse to alter the width of a column. To do this, move the mouse pointer to the column heading, over the line to the right of the column you want to adjust. For example, to adjust column A, place the cell pointer on the line between A and B. Then press the left mouse button, which changes the mouse pointer to two arrows on either side of a vertical line that indicates the new edge of the column, as shown in Figure 2.27.

Figure 2.26

Column A expanded

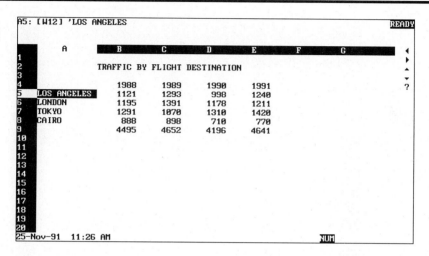

You can move the arrow and associated line to the left or right to narrow or widen the column. When you release the mouse button, the column width is set wherever you placed the border indicator line. If you use this technique when the worksheet grid is not displayed, a second border line appears on the left of the column you are adjusting to help you keep track of the column. This second line is barely visible when you are adjusting column A, since it tends to blend with the worksheet frame. Note that you can use the mouse to change the width of a column other than the current column. The technique does not move the cell pointer.

The Global Width

You can also change all the column widths in a worksheet at once. To redefine the global width, press / and select Worksheet, Global, and then Column-Width. Select the new width either by typing the desired number of characters or by pressing the Left Arrow or Right Arrow key. Press Enter to confirm the setting.

Changing the default column width does not change the width of columns that have been set manually. If column A is set to 12, it will remain at 12 when you change the global width. This feature is useful since it preserves the effort you have put into setting certain columns correctly. However, at times you may want a column to revert to the global setting. To do this, place your cell pointer in the column you want to reset. Press / to activate the menu and select Worksheet, Column, and then Reset-Width. The column will now take its width measurement from the default setting.

Figure 2.27
Changing column width in Wysiwyg mode

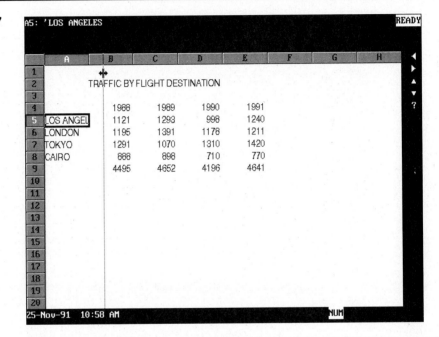

The Column-Range Command

If you want to set the width of several adjacent columns, you can use the Column-Range command on the Worksheet Column menu. When you choose Column-Range, you can select Set-Width to establish widths that differ from the global setting, or Reset-Width to return widths to the global setting.

When you choose either Set-Width or Reset-Width, you are prompted for a range. 1-2-3 needs to know the columns to which you want the command applied, so you point out a range of cells that encompasses those columns. For example, to alter the width of columns B through E you could enter the range B1..E1, B4..E4, or even B1..E4. The row reference does not affect the command, which is simply a shortcut for adjusting several columns at once.

Lastly, 1-2-3 will prompt you for a width. As with the other column width commands, you can either type in a number or use the Left Arrow and Right Arrow keys to adjust the width manually.

Inserting and Deleting Columns

At times you may discover that you need an extra column. To create a new column, just press /, select Worksheet, and then select Insert from the Worksheet menu. You will be asked if you want to insert a Row or Column. Choose Column and you will be asked to indicate the number of columns to insert. Columns are added to the left of the current column. Press Enter to insert one column. Press the Right Arrow key once for each additional column you want to add, and then press Enter.

The new columns are added down all 8192 rows of the worksheet, so consider whether any unseen data will be affected at the time of the insert. While inserting a column, you can press End plus Down Arrow, End plus Up Arrow, or any of the other cursor-movement keys to view lower and upper areas of the worksheet before you press Enter to confirm the insertion.

You can delete columns in much the same way. Select Delete from the Worksheet menu and then choose Column. Next highlight the columns you want to delete. Since deleting removes all the data in those columns, you should use this operation with extreme care. Check areas above and below the current screen for valuable data that you might delete with the column. The integrity of formulas in the worksheet is normally preserved whenever you insert columns; however, deleting columns can have an adverse effect on formulas. Assuming the Undo feature is on, you can press Alt-F4 to undo any damage.

1-2-3 also has a command for hiding columns from view to improve the appearance of your worksheet, to prepare for printing summary reports, or to conceal confidential data. This command is covered in Chapter 6.

Working with Rows

You can use the Worksheet Insert and Delete commands to manipulate spreadsheet rows. At times you may enter data only to discover that you need an extra row. Just select Insert from the Worksheet menu and then choose Row. You will be prompted for the number of rows to be inserted. New rows are added above the current row. Press Enter to insert one row. Press the Down Arrow key once for each additional row you want to add, and then press Enter. New rows are added across all 256 columns of the worksheet, so consider whether any unseen data will be affected at the time of the insert. You can press End plus Left Arrow and End plus Right Arrow while inserting a row to view other areas of the worksheet before you press Enter to confirm the insertion.

You can delete a row in much the same way. Pick Delete from the Worksheet menu, and then select Row. Next, highlight the rows you want to remove. The Delete Row command removes all the data in those rows, across all 256 columns, so you should use it with care. Check the areas to the left and right of the current screen for valuable data that you might unintentionally delete with the rows.

Suppose you want to insert a row between the totals and the rest of the numbers in the example in Figure 2.26. You can use the Worksheet Insert command to do this. First, place your cell pointer somewhere in row 9. Then issue the Worksheet Insert Row command. You will get the prompt "Enter row insert range." At this point you can use the cursor-movement keys to view the rest of the worksheet, checking that the new row will not cause a problem. However, in this case there are no off-screen cell entries. To insert just one row, simply press Enter. The new row will be added above the cell pointer, as shown in Figure 2.28.

Figure 2.28

A new row entered

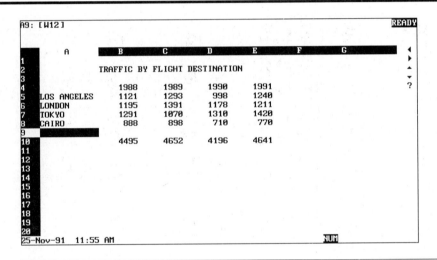

Note that the sum formulas, which moved from row 9 to row 10, still give the same answers. When a 1-2-3 command relocates formulas, 1-2-3 makes sure that they remain correct. If you have Undo enabled, you can press the Undo key (Alt-F4) to revert to the screen shown in Figure 2.26. If you do not have Undo enabled, you can use the Worksheet Delete Row command to remove the blank row you just inserted. Now you can explore another way to make space in a spreadsheet.

Working with Ranges

As you have seen, the Insert and Delete commands on the Worksheet menu work with rows and columns. There are other commands, such as Copy and Move, that you can apply to a range of cells. Since these are among 1-2-3's most powerful commands, you should know exactly what constitutes a range. A *range* is any rectangular group of cells on the spreadsheet. You can refer to a range of cells by any two diagonal coordinates. The diagram in Figure 2.29 shows what is and is not a range.

Figure 2.29
Diagram of
acceptable ranges

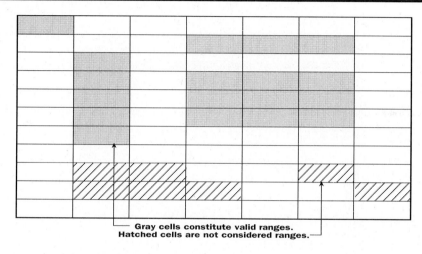

Gray cells constitute valid ranges.
Hatched cells are not considered ranges.

Moving Cells

Occasionally, you will need to move a group of cells from one location to another. If you need a few extra columns or rows in a spreadsheet, you may be able to use the Worksheet Insert command to accomplish the desired changes. At other times you can use the Worksheet Delete command to remove extra space. However, these commands do not work well in a crowded spreadsheet, and sometimes you will need to move a group of cells.

To use the Move command, you must highlight the cells to be moved and then indicate their destination. Note that any cell entries within the selected destination will be overwritten by the cells you are moving. The Move command preserves the integrity of the formulas within the range. For example, in the worksheet in Figure 2.26, you can move the sum formulas from B9..E9 to B10..E10 to make way for a new row of labels. To do this, place the cell pointer in B9, press /, and then select Move. You are prompted for the range of cells you are moving, as shown in Figure 2.30.

As with other range related commands, 1-2-3 assumes you want to include at least the current cell, and presents it as the default response (in this case B9..B9). The appearance of two cell addresses on the input line indicates that the range is anchored. In other words, if you point to other cells,

B9 will remain the beginning point of the range. In fact, you want to extend this range to include the other sum formulas. A quick way of doing this is to press End followed by Right Arrow to move the highlighting across to the last of the cells in the row, E9, as shown in Figure 2.31. The prompt will now show B9..E9.

Figure 2.30

The "Move what?" prompt

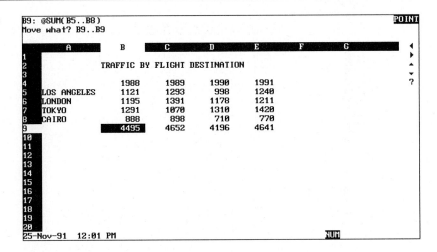

```
B9: @SUM(B5..B8)                                                    POINT
Move what? B9..B9
          A         B        C        D        E        F        G       ◄
1                                                                         ►
2               TRAFFIC BY FLIGHT DESTINATION                            ▲
3                                                                         ▼
4               1988     1989     1990     1991                          ?
5  LOS ANGELES  1121     1293      998     1240
6  LONDON       1195     1391     1178     1211
7  TOKYO        1291     1070     1310     1420
8  CAIRO         888      898      710      770
9               4495     4652     4196     4641
10
11
12
13
14
15
16
17
18
19
20
25-Nov-91  12:01 PM                                         NUM
```

At this point you can press Enter to confirm the range. 1-2-3 will ask "To where?", the destination range of the cells being moved. This will be B10..E10. However, because the range will maintain its size and shape during the move, you do not need to enter the full range. Instead, you can just enter the cell in the upper-left corner of the range, in this case B10. Note that when 1-2-3 asks "To Where?" it does not provide an anchored cell reference. In this case you get just a plain, unanchored B9. Press Down Arrow once and the cell reference will change to B10. You don't need to anchor the destination cell reference; just press Enter. 1-2-3 will relocate B9..E9 to B10..E10. In fact, the results will be exactly the same as those in Figure 2.28 (except that the cell pointer will be in B9).

Note that the formula that was in B9, @SUM(B5..B8), is now in B10. In most situations, Move does not affect the way your formulas work; however, as a precaution, save your worksheet before a large move so that you can retrieve the unchanged version if the move does not work out as planned. Unless you have turned off the Undo feature, you can also use the Alt-F4 (Undo) key to reverse the Move command. Large moves may take some time for the computer to complete; the mode indicator will read WAIT until the operation is completed.

Figure 2.31
The full "Move
what?" range

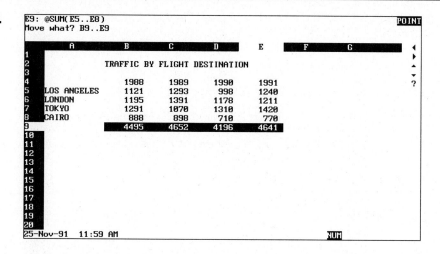

The Copy Command

Computers are very useful for copying information. When building a work-sheet, you will use the Copy command to replicate ranges of cells any time you want to use the same labels, numbers, or formulas more than once.

A Simple Copy

Now you will enter some labels into the empty cells in row 9 of the sample worksheet. You can do this very quickly using the Copy command. Place the cell pointer in A9 and enter \=. This will fill the cell with the equal sign char-acter. Instead of typing this same entry in B9 through E9, you can copy it there from A9. Leaving the cell pointer on A9, press / and select Copy. You will be asked "Copy what?", as shown in Figure 2.32. At this prompt, you enter the cells you want to copy data from.

In this case, the answer is A9..A9, the range that 1-2-3 suggested auto-matically because you began the command with A9 as the current cell. Press Enter to accept A9. You will be asked where you want the data copied to, as shown in Figure 2.33. Note that A9 is the unanchored default response to this prompt.

An accurate response to this prompt would be B9..E9, which you can type if you want. (Remember, you only need to type **B9.E9** since 1-2-3 will generate the second period.) In fact, you can always type range coordinates instead of pointing them out, whether you are using range related commands or functions. However, many users find pointing out ranges more intuitive and more accurate.

Figure 2.32

The Copy prompt

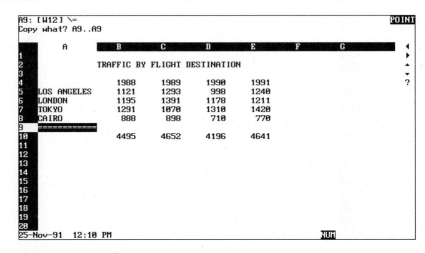

Figure 2.33

The "To Where?" prompt

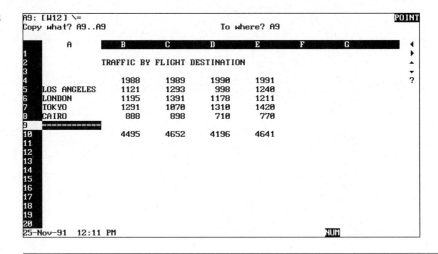

With the pointing method, there are actually two ways to copy the contents from A9..A9 to B9..E9. You can move the cell pointer to B9, type a period to anchor B9 as the first cell of the destination range, press Right Arrow three times to make the range B9..E9, and then press Enter. Alternatively, you can leave cell A9 as the first cell in the destination range. Simply type a period and press the Right Arrow key four times. This will make the destination range A9..E9, as shown in Figure 2.34.

Figure 2.34
Pointing out the
destination range

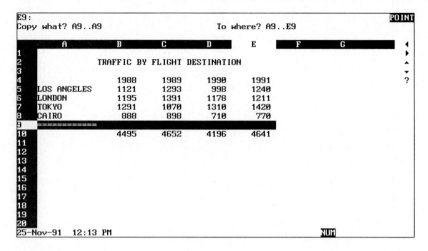

```
E9:                                                                  POINT
Copy what? A9..A9                    To where? A9..E9
         A           B        C        D        E      F        G      ◄
1                                                                      ►
2                 TRAFFIC BY FLIGHT DESTINATION                       ▲
3                                                                     ▼
4                 1988     1989     1990     1991                     ?
5  LOS ANGELES    1121     1293      998     1240
6  LONDON         1195     1391     1178     1211
7  TOKYO          1291     1070     1310     1420
8  CAIRO           888      898      710      770
9  ==========
10                4495     4652     4196     4641
11
12
13
14
15
16
17
18
19
20
25-Nov-91   12:13 PM                                           NUM
```

It does not matter that A9 will be copied over itself. However, anchoring the range in the cell you are copying saves a step in the copy process. When you press Enter, 1-2-3 will complete the copy and the results will appear as shown in Figure 2.35.

Figure 2.35
The completed
Copy

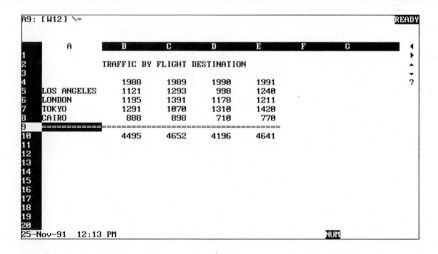

```
A9: [W12] \=                                                        READY
         A           B        C        D        E      F        G      ◄
1                                                                      ►
2                 TRAFFIC BY FLIGHT DESTINATION                       ▲
3                                                                     ▼
4                 1988     1989     1990     1991                     ?
5  LOS ANGELES    1121     1293      998     1240
6  LONDON         1195     1391     1178     1211
7  TOKYO          1291     1070     1310     1420
8  CAIRO           888      898      710      770
9  =====================================================
10                4495     4652     4196     4641
11
12
13
14
15
16
17
18
19
20
25-Nov-91   12:13 PM                                           NUM
```

Copying with a Mouse

You can use your mouse with the Copy command. Click on the cells you want to copy and then select Copy from the menu. Click on the "Copy what?" prompt to confirm the current cell as the source range (you can also click on the source range itself to confirm it). After confirming the source range, you can select the destination range by pointing to the first cell and holding down the left mouse button as you drag the mouse pointer to the last cell in the range. When you release the mouse button, the range will remain selected and the "To where?" prompt will show the range coordinates. To confirm the range you have selected, click on the "To where?" prompt or within the selected range. To cancel the range, press the right mouse button.

You can use the mouse to select a multicell source range before issuing the Copy command. If you select a multicell range and then issue the Copy command, 1-2-3 assumes the source range is correct and moves straight to the destination range prompt.

Copying a Formula

The Copy command is useful for duplicating formulas as well as labels. Consider the formulas you used to produce a series of years by adding 1 to the previous year. They can be summarized as follows:

```
B4: 1985    C4: 1+B4    D4: 1+C4    E4: 1+D4
```

When you create the formula 1+B4 in cell C4, you are telling 1-2-3 "add 1 to the cell on the left." The formulas 1+C4 and 1+D4 also mean "add 1 to the cell on the left." Instead of entering each of these formulas separately, you can enter the first one in C4 and then copy the formula from C4 to D4 and E4. You can do this because ordinary cell references in 1-2-3 are *relative*. When copying relative cell references, 1-2-3 replicates the formulas function *relative* to the position of the formula cell itself, rather than copying specific cell references. In other words, it adjusts each copy of the formula to "fit" its new location.

To copy the formula, place the cell pointer in the cell to be copied (C4), press /, and select Copy. You will be prompted for the source range. Since 1-2-3 assumes you want to include the current cell, the prompt shows C4..C4. Just press Enter to accept that cell as the range to be copied. The destination prompt will appear, asking for the cells you are going to copy into, in this case C4..E4. You can indicate this range either by typing **C4.E4** or by pressing the period to anchor the beginning point of the range at C4 and then pressing Right Arrow to include the other cells through to E4. (You could use D4.E4 as the destination, but it is faster to use C4..E4 as the range, copying C4 over itself.) Having indicated the destination cells for the copy, you press Enter. 1-2-3 copies the formula as instructed and modifies each new formula to fit its location. Being able to address cells in a relative manner makes this kind of copying very useful. In Chapter 6 you will learn how to make cell references absolute so that they don't change when copied to a new location.

Larger Copies

The Copy command works for much larger groups of cells and labels. For example, suppose you want to expand the sample worksheet to include revenue figures, as shown in Figure 2.36. First you make a copy of the entire model so far. Then you modify the copy to reflect revenues instead of volume. Begin by placing the cell pointer in A2. Press / and use the arrow keys to extend the source range to A2..E10, as shown in Figure 2.37.

Figure 2.36
The completed volume/revenue model

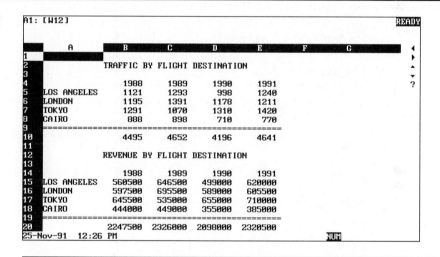

Press Enter to confirm this source range and then move the cell pointer down to A12, the upper-left cell of the destination range. Now press Enter. The copy is completed, and 1-2-3 assumed that the cells below and to the right of A12 were free to receive the copied data. If these cells had not been empty, 1-2-3 would have overwritten their contents. In other words, you must exercise some care when carrying out large copy operations. You can see the results of this copy operation in Figure 2.38.

Now move the cell pointer to B12 to change the word TRAFFIC in the title to REVENUE. A quick way to get there is to press F5, the Goto key, and then type **B12** and press Enter. When you get to B12, press F2, the Edit key. This places the contents of B12 on the editing line. Press Home and then Right Arrow. This will move the cursor under the T in TRAFFIC. Press Insert and type **REVENUE**. This will replace TRAFFIC with REVENUE. Finally, press Enter to return the edited title to the cell.

Figure 2.37
Copying the entire model

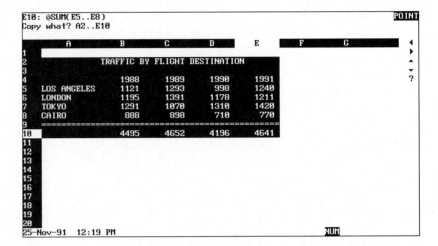

Figure 2.38
Results of large copy operation

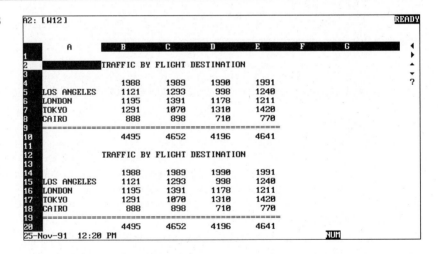

To perform the revenue calculations, move the cell pointer to B15. Assume that the average fare for all years and destinations is $500. You will create the revenue numbers by multiplying all of the traffic numbers by 500. In B15, enter **500*B5**. To 1-2-3 this means make B15 equal to 500 times the cell ten rows above. You can now copy this formula across the model. With the cell pointer still in B15, press / and select Copy. Press Enter to accept B15 as the source range. Press a period to anchor B15 as

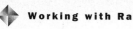

the upper-left corner of the destination range. Press Down Arrow three times to take the range down to B18. Now press End followed by Right Arrow to take the range to the end of the model, as shown in Figure 2.39.

Figure 2.39

The destination range

```
E18: 770                                                                 POINT
Copy what? B15..B15                       To where? B15..E18
┌──────────────────────────────────────────────────────────────────────┐
│      A        B        C        D        E      F        G          ◄  │
│1                                                                    ►  │
│2           TRAFFIC BY FLIGHT DESTINATION                            ▲  │
│3                                                                    ▼  │
│4            1988     1989     1990     1991                         ?  │
│5  LOS ANGELES  1121   1293      998     1240                           │
│6  LONDON      1195     1391     1178    1211                           │
│7  TOKYO       1291     1070     1310    1420                           │
│8  CAIRO        888      898      710     770                           │
│9  ================================================                    │
│10           4495     4652     4196     4641                            │
│11                                                                      │
│12          REVENUE BY FLIGHT DESTINATION                               │
│13                                                                      │
│14           1988     1989     1990     1991                            │
│15 LOS ANGELES 560500  1293      998     1240                           │
│16 LONDON      1195     1391     1178    1211                           │
│17 TOKYO       1291     1070     1310    1420                           │
│18 CAIRO        888      898      710     770                           │
│19 ================================================                    │
│20          563874    4652     4196     4641                            │
│25-Nov-91   12:25 PM                                          NUM       │
└──────────────────────────────────────────────────────────────────────┘
```

When you press Enter, the copy is completed and the formula from B15 is placed into all the cells through to E18, replacing the previous contents. 1-2-3 has translated the cell references in the original formula so that each formula means 500 times the cell ten rows above. The results were shown in Figure 2.36.

To preserve the extensive changes in this model you should save it using the File Save command. Type the name **VOLREV** at the File Save prompt and then press Enter. This will create a new file, separate from the original model.

Tips on Copying

You will use the Copy command extensively when building spreadsheet models. As you do, the rhythm of the command keys will become second nature. To copy one cell to many cells, the pattern is

1. Highlight the cell you wish to copy.

2. Press / and select Copy to pick the command.

3. Press Enter to accept the current cell as the one to be copied.

4. Point to one corner of the destination range.

5. Anchor the range by typing a period.

6. Point to the diagonally opposite corner of the destination range.

7. Press Enter to complete the command.

To copy from many cells to one destination, move the cell pointer to one corner of the range you want to copy. Then use the sequence copy, point, Enter, point, Enter. When copying a range of several cells to multiple locations, use the sequence copy, point, Enter, point, anchor, point, Enter. An example of this and other types of copying can be found in Chapter 6.

Always remember that the Copy command does not check for existing data in the destination cells. You can lose data by inadvertently copying over it. Proceed carefully the first few times you use Copy and always save the worksheet as a precaution before large copy operations. In Chapter 7, you will learn how to perform a reverse copy, and how to make multiple copies of a group of cells.

Range Erase

Now that you know how to move cell entries and copy them, it is important to learn how to get rid of them. You do this with the Range Erase command, which removes the contents of one or more cells (it does not affect the format or width setting of cells). After choosing the Erase command from the Range menu, you simply highlight the range to be modified (using the techniques described earlier for moving and copying cells), and then press Enter. The contents of all selected cells will be erased. Remember that the Undo key combination (Alt-F4) will reverse the Range Erase command if you delete the wrong cells, but only if you use Undo right away. Also remember that the Delete key will perform a Range Erase on the current cell.

Summary

In this chapter, you have reviewed the basic elements of spreadsheet modeling: labels, values, formulas, columns, rows, and ranges. You have seen how 1-2-3 can copy information to make your work easier. The ability to copy formulas will enable you to build large models quickly. In the next chapter, you will learn about a special type of 1-2-3 cell entry: dates.

3

Working with
Dates and Times

Date Data

About Time

I N THE FIRST TWO CHAPTERS, YOU SAW HOW 1-2-3 DISTINGUISHES BETWEEN values and labels. One category of data that presents special problems for software is dates, which appear to combine text and numbers. In this chapter, you will learn how to enter dates in 1-2-3 and perform math with date and time information.

Date Data

Consider the date April 1, 1991. If you enter this date as 4/1/91 you get a decimal number, the result of dividing 4 by 1 and then by 91. If you enter 1-Apr-91 you will get an error, since the entry begins with a number but contains nonnumeric characters. If you precede the 1 with an apostrophe or enter April 1, 1991, you get a label. While this is fine if you are entering the date purely as descriptive text, it is not adequate if you want to perform date calculations.

Date arithmetic is a common need. For example, suppose you want to find out how many days past due your accounts receivable are running. In order to treat dates mathematically, 1-2-3 stores them as numbers known as *date serial numbers*. 1-2-3 starts with a base date of January 1, 1900 and treats each day as a unit of 1. In other words, the date serial number of January 2, 1900 is 2, while January 31, 1900 is 31, and so on. Day 500 was May 14, 1901. Day 30,000 was February 18, 1982. Date serial numbers and the functions you can use to manipulate them are covered in detail in Chapter 11, but the following material will help you get started.

Using date serial numbers, you can compare any two dates and calculate the difference between them. For example, to determine the number of days that elapsed between April 4, 1990 and June 15, 1990, you can simply subtract 33039 (the date serial value for 4/4/90) from 32967 (the date serial value for 6/15/90) to get 72 days.

The @DATE Function

Rather than making you calculate date serial numbers yourself, 1-2-3 provides a function called @DATE that lets you generate them automatically. To enter a date with the @DATE function, you supply three arguments: the year, the month, and the day. You enclose these arguments within parentheses and separate them by commas; thus you enter April 1, 1991 as

```
@DATE(91,4,1)
```

For dates past December 31, 1999 you use a year argument that is greater than 100. For example, you would enter the first day of the year 2001 as

```
@DATE(101,1,1)
```

You would enter December 31, 2099 as

```
@DATE(199,12,31)
```

This is the highest date available with the @DATE function. Its serial number is 73050. Thus the arguments of the @DATE function, the function's *syntax,* can be described as

```
@DATE(YY,MM,DD)
```

where YY is a numeric value between 0 and 199, MM is a numeric value between 1 and 12, and DD is a numeric value between 1 and 31. Any invalid dates—for example, @DATE(87,2,29)—return the value ERR. For example, @DATE (87,2,29) returns ERR because there was no February 29th in 1987.

When you enter a date using the @DATE function, 1-2-3 displays the result as a date serial number. For example, @DATE (91,4,1) returns the value 33329. To make this date serial number look like a date, you must apply a Date numeric format using the Range Format command. That is, entering a date in 1-2-3 is a two-step process. First you enter a date serial value using the @DATE function, and then you display it as a date using Range Format.

A Date Example

You can test 1-2-3's date math by posing a simple question: How many days have you been alive? Begin with a fresh worksheet (issue the Worksheet Erase command if necessary) and follow these steps:

1. In A1, enter your date of birth using the @DATE function. For example, if your date of birth were October 3, 1957 you would type

```
@DATE(57,10,3)
```

2. Now press Down Arrow to enter the date and move down to the next cell. Note that when you enter the @DATE function, 1-2-3 shows the date serial number in the worksheet—for example, the preceding date has the serial number 21096.

3. In A2, type today's date in the same format. For example, if today is August 12, 1991, type

```
@DATE(91,8,12)
```

4. Press Down Arrow to enter the date and move down to the next cell. Again note that @DATE produces a date serial number, in this case 33462.

5. In A3, type the formula **+A2–A1** and press Enter. The result is the length of time, measured in days, that you have been alive—that is, the number of days from your date of birth to today.

6. To check this date math, press Down Arrow to move to cell A4 and enter the formula **+A3/365**. This will calculate approximately how many years you have been alive, as shown in Figure 3.1. If you get an incorrect answer, check how you have entered the dates in A1 and A2.

Figure 3.1

A date math example

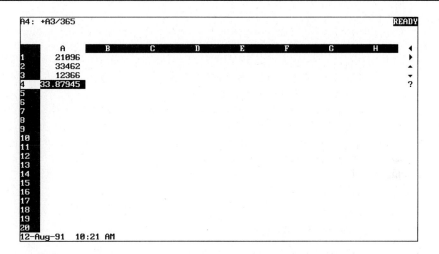

Notice that the formula +A3/365 only gives an approximate answer because some years have 366 rather than 365 days. Also note that the dates you have entered appear to be numbers rather than dates. You can make the entries in cells A1 and A2 look like dates by using a date format.

Date Formatting

To apply a date format to cells A1 and A2, press Home to highlight A1, press /, select Range, and then select Format. Now select Date. There are five date formats, which are described in Table 3.1. (The Time option will be explained in the section "About Time.") Select the first format and 1-2-3 will prompt you for the range of cells to be formatted. Press Down Arrow once and then press Enter to select the range A1..A2.

Table 3.1   **Date Formats**

Format	Example	Description
1 (DD-MMM-YY)	03-Oct-57	Full date display
2 (DD-MMM)	03-Oct	Day and month shown, no year
3 (MMM-YY)	Oct-57	Month and year shown, no day
4 (Long Intn'l)	10/03/57	Full date with slash separator
5 (Short Intn'l)	10/03	Month and day with slash separator

The immediate result of applying date format 1 will be asterisks in A1..A2. This is because the first date format creates a date too wide for the default column width of nine characters. 1-2-3 is attempting to display 03-Oct-57, which is nine characters. Since the date is a value and 1-2-3 will display only eight digits of a value in a nine-character column, this series of asterisks tells you to change the format or column width.

To remove the asterisks and reveal the date in date format 1, widen the column by one character. Press / and select Worksheet followed by Column and Set-Width. Press Right Arrow once and then press Enter to achieve the result shown in Figure 3.2. Note that the cell address indicator provides the cell address, and next to that you see the format identifier, the width setting, and the cell contents, respectively:

```
A1: (D1) [W10] @DATE(57,10,3)
```

If much of your work includes dates and you plan to use the first date format, you can change the default column width to ten using the Worksheet Global Column-Width command. However, since few worksheets contain nothing but dates, you probably won't want to use a date format as a global format.

The @TODAY Function

When you calculated how many days you have been alive, you entered today's date with the @DATE function. You can also enter the current date using the @TODAY function, which reads the current date from the date setting in DOS. As long as you have the date set correctly in DOS, the @TODAY function will return the correct date. However, since this date is displayed as a serial number, you may want to format the cell to make it look more like a date.

Figure 3.2

Date format 1

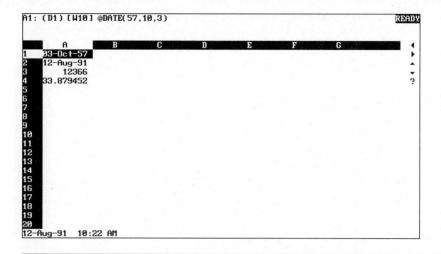

```
A1: (D1) [W10] @DATE(57,10,3)                                    READY

         A         B       C       D       E       F       G       ◄
1   03-Oct-57                                                       ►
2   12-Aug-91                                                       ▲
3       12366                                                       ▼
4   33.879452                                                       ?
5
6
7
8
9
10
11
12
13
14
15
16
17
18
19
20
12-Aug-91   10:22 AM
```

Whenever you retrieve a worksheet containing the @TODAY function, 1-2-3 reads the date from DOS so that the worksheet date is current. Sometimes you may want to use the current date when making a worksheet entry, but *fix* that date so that it does not change in the future. For example, when creating invoices you usually use the current date and want this date to remain unchanged the next time you retrieve the file. To enter a fixed date with @TODAY, simply type **@TODAY** and then press F9, the Calc key. This replaces the function with its current result, a date serial number. You can then press Enter to place the value into the worksheet. For more about other date-related functions, see the Date/Time function section in Chapter 5.

More About Date Formats

The five different date formats give you various options when working with dates. While the first format shows a full date, the second, third, and fifth formats show abbreviated dates. The second format (DD-MMM) is useful when you don't need the year—for example, when you enter daily sales transactions, as shown in Figure 3.3.

The third format (MMM-YY) is useful when you want to use month names for column or row headings—for instance, when working on a month-by-month budget breakdown. Suppose that you want January through June of 1992 as column headings in row 3, starting in column B. You would enter

```
@DATE(92,1,1)
```

in B3, and then format with date format 3. The result would be Jan-92. To get Feb-92 in C3, you enter **+B3+31** and then format with date format 3. You can then copy this formula from C3 to D3 through G3 to achieve the results shown in Figure 3.4.

Figure 3.3

The DD-MMM format

```
A4: (D2) [W7] @DATE(91,1,3)                                    READY

      A        B                C                 D     E       F        ◀
1  Repair Shop Transactions: 1991                                        ▶
2                                                                        ▲
3    Date    Item#          Description          Price  Qty    Total     ▼
4  03-Jan    1002 Wheel Brackets, Wing Right   1,096.09   1  1,096.09    ?
5  04-Jan    1023 Wheel Brackets, Wing Left    1,223.20   2  2,446.40
6  04-Jan    1008 Forward Bulkhead Unit          428.06   1    428.06
7  04-Jan    1082 Wheel Rim Seals                  4.38   3     13.14
8  04-Jan    1003 Cover Clamp                      7.19   1      7.19
9  05-Jan    1015 Wheel Brackets, Clip           57.36   1     57.36
10 05-Jan    1030 Cone Nachelle, Lower         1,675.70   4  6,702.80
11 05-Jan    1016 Cone Nachelle, Left          1,675.70   1  1,675.70
12 06-Jan    1008 Forward Bulkhead Unit          428.06   1    428.06
13 07-Jan    1041 Wheel Brackets, Rear         1,225.84   2  2,451.68
14 08-Jan    1022 Wheel Brackets, Valve Rod      165.70   1    165.70
15 09-Jan    1060 Wheel Brackets, Front        1,122.36   3  3,367.08
16 10-Jan    1084 Wheel Brackets, Seal            29.59   1     29.59
17 11-Jan    1000 Cone Nachelle, Right         1,675.70   2  3,351.40
18 12-Jan    1049 Wheel Brackets, Valve Stem       4.38   1      4.38
19 13-Jan    1040 Nachelle, Retaining Flange      71.23   2    142.46
20 14-Jan    1082 Wheel Rim Seals                  4.38   1      4.38
12-Aug-91   10:25 AM
```

Figure 3.4

Month headings using MMM-YY format

```
C3: (D3) +B3+31                                               READY

        A        B       C       D       E       F       G       H     ◀
1   Office Budget: 1992                                                 ▶
2                                                                       ▲
3               Jan-92  Feb-92  Mar-92  Apr-92  May-92  Jun-92          ▼
4   Rent                                                                ?
5   Heat
6   Light
7   Phones
8   Equipment
9   Supplies
10
11
12
13
14
15
16
17
18
19
20
12-Aug-91   10:26 AM
```

Although adding 31 days to the previous month does not always produce the first of the month, this problem does not affect the appearance of dates in the MMM-YY format. Because some months have fewer than 31 days,

this technique yields a sequence in which dates fall progressively later in the month. This is not a problem initially because you are only displaying the month and year. However, in the fifth year the sequence will jump from a date near the end of one month to a date early in the month two months later—from late March to early May or, if the first year in the sequence is a leap year, from late May to early July. Note that in the years 2000 and after, this format will actually be MMM-YYYY—January 1, 2000 will appear as Jan-2000, and so on.

The fourth date format, long international, usually takes the form MM/DD/YY, while the short international format is usually MM/DD. However, you can vary these formats using the International settings, as described in Chapter 6. The long international format is useful when you want a full date that will fit into the default column width of nine characters.

About Time

When you select Date from the Range Format menu, you are presented with the five date formats plus the Time option. When you select Time, 1-2-3 lists four different formats for displaying values as times, as shown in Table 3.2. Figure 3.5 also shows an example of how you can use times in a worksheet.

Table 3.2 **Time Formats**

Format	Example	Identifier
1 (HH:MM:SS AM/PM)	07:15:00 PM	D6
2 (HH:MM AM/PM)	07:15 PM	D7
3 (Long Intn'l)	19:15:00	D8
4 (Short Intn'l)	19:15	D9

The @TIME Function

To enable 1-2-3 to treat the time of day as a value rather than a label, you enter times with the @TIME function. This function takes three arguments: hours, minutes, and seconds. You enter the hours in 24-hour format, as a number from 0 to 24. (At 1 p.m. the hour is 13, and so on.) You enter the minutes and seconds as numbers from 0 to 60. Thus you enter 6:30 a.m. as

```
@TIME(6,30,0)
```

Figure 3.5

Using times in a spreadsheet

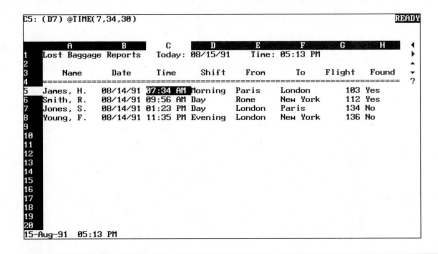

If you entered this data into an unformatted cell, you would get the result .270833 because 1-2-3 treats the time of day as a fraction of 1 day. That is, exactly 6:00 a.m. is .25, noon is .5, and so forth.

Much like @DATE entries, @TIME entries only look like times when displayed with time formats. Since you select time formats by first choosing Time from the Format Date menu, the time formats are identified as D6 through D9 (as noted in Table 3.2). Thus time format 1 is known as D6, time format 2 is D7, and so on. The control panel in Figure 3.5 shows that cell C5 has been formatted with time format 2, or D7.

Time Math

Entering times with the @TIME function allows you to perform time arithmetic. For example, suppose you are a lawyer and you bill your clients at $75 per hour. You start a project for a client at 8:34 a.m., finish at 1:22 p.m., and you want to calculate the bill. In essence, you want to subtract your starting time from the time you finished and multiply the result by your rate. To do this, you could set up a simple worksheet like the one in Figure 3.6. Note that the times in C2 and C3 are formatted to appear as times rather than as fractions of a day.

The correct calculation of the number of hours worked is not as straightforward as it might appear. The formula in cell E2, +C3-C2, returns 0.2, which is not the correct number of hours. In fact, 0.2 is the amount of time worked expressed as a decimal fraction of one day. You could only use this number for billing purposes if the rate in cell E3 were a daily rate rather than an hourly one. However, since the rate *is* hourly, you must convert this decimal fraction of a day into hours by multiplying it by 24. The correct answer is returned by the amended formula shown in Figure 3.7—that is, 24*(+C3-C2).

Figure 3.6
A time math example

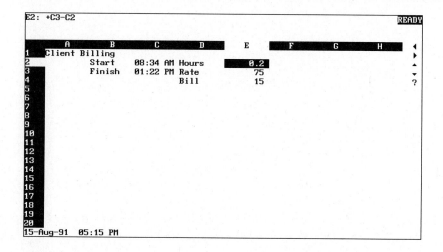

Figure 3.7
Corrected time math example

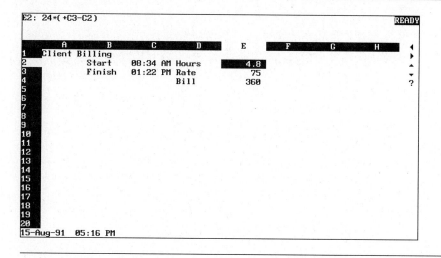

As you can see, when working with time values you must pay careful attention to the way that 1-2-3 quantifies time. To convert decimal time into hours, multiply by a factor of 24. To convert hours to decimal time (for purposes of billing at a daily rate, for example) you divide by 24. In other words,

```
0.2*24 = 4.8
```

and

```
4.8/24 = 0.2
```

Remember that you can find the decimal equivalent of any given time simply by entering it with @TIME in an unformatted cell.

Because 1-2-3 treats time of day as a fraction of a single day, you can combine times with dates to calculate the passage of time over periods longer than one day. For example, Figure 3.8 shows one way of calculating the number of hours a patient spent in the hospital. The patient was admitted on August 1 and discharged the next day. The date and time of discharge are added to produce a single number:

```
C8+C9 = 33452.556944
```

From this number, the single number representing the time and date of admission is subtracted

```
C5+C6 = 33451.356944
```

so that

```
33452.556944 - 33451.356944 = 1.2 days
```

This value is then multiplied by 24 to give the result in hours. The complete formula (shown next to the cell address indicator in Figure 3.8) is

```
((C8+C9)-(C5+C6))*24
```

The use of parentheses in formulas is explained in Chapter 6. Note that the number of decimal places can be considerable, particularly since many of the digits are recurring. Bear in mind that 1-2-3 is performing math to 15 decimal places even though it can only show a part of the decimal fraction in a nine-character column.

The @NOW Function

Earlier you learned how to use the @TODAY function to read the date from DOS. When you need time-of-day information as well, you can use the @NOW function, which returns the current date and time, read from DOS. Entering the @NOW function when the time is 3:43 p.m. and the date is August 16, 1991 yields the answer 33466.65 in a nine-character cell. (The full answer is 33466.655046.) This answer will change as the time changes and the worksheet is updated. Several actions cause 1-2-3 to update the @NOW function:

- Entering new data in the worksheet

- Editing existing data in the worksheet

- Pressing the Calc key (F9)

Figure 3.8
Time math
including days

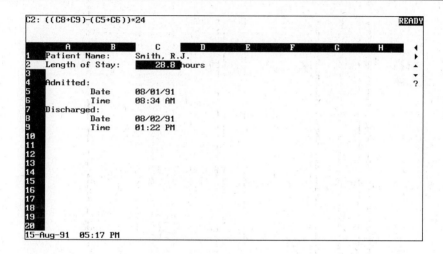

```
C2: ((C8+C9)-(C5+C6))*24                                    READY

        A       B       C       D       E       F       G       H    ◄
1    Patient Name:   Smith, R.J.                                     ►
2    Length of Stay:     28.8 hours                                  ▲
3                                                                    ▼
4    Admitted:                                                       ?
5            Date    08/01/91
6            Time    08:34 AM
7    Discharged:
8            Date    08/02/91
9            Time    01:22 PM
10
11
12
13
14
15
16
17
18
19
20
15-Aug-91   05:17 PM
```

You may want to use @NOW to read the date and time and then fix the resulting value so that it does not change—for example, when logging in a patient using the worksheet in Figure 3.8. Simply type **@NOW**, press F9 (Calc), and press Enter to create a fixed date/time reading.

If you format the @NOW entry with a time format, the result will appear as a time. If you use a date format (D1 through D5), the @NOW entry will appear as a date. If you want just the current time without the date, you can enter **@NOW-@TODAY**. Note that 1-2-3 will automatically convert your entry into @NOW-@INT(@NOW), which gives the same result. The @INT (integer) function is covered in Chapter 5.

Summary

Date and time information can be very important in a wide range of projects. By mastering the 1-2-3 commands that relate to dates and times you will widen the range of tasks you can undertake. As you become more adept at working with formulas, you can try the date- and time-related examples given in Chapter 5.

4

Range-Related Commands

I N THIS CHAPTER, YOU WILL LEARN MORE ABOUT WORKING WITH RANGES and cell entries. You will learn to move the cell pointer from one end of a range to the other and from one range to the next with the End key. You will learn how to fill a range with a series of numbers, how to attach names to ranges, and how to use the powerful Search/Replace feature.

All About the End Key

When you are building a worksheet or moving around a finished model, the End key can be very helpful. In READY mode the End key alone does nothing. But if you follow it with an arrow key or Home, the End key moves the cell pointer for you. The action of End and the arrow keys is described in Table 4.1 and diagrammed in Figure 4.1.

Table 4.1   **The End Key**

End Up Arrow	If the current cell contains an entry, the cell pointer moves up to the next nonblank cell beneath an empty one. If the current cell is blank, it moves up to the next nonblank cell encountered.
End Down Arrow	If the current cell contains an entry, the cell pointer moves down to the next nonblank cell above an empty one. If the current cell is blank, it moves down to the next nonblank cell encountered.
End Right Arrow	If the current cell contains an entry, the cell pointer moves right to the next nonblank cell followed by an empty one. If the current cell is blank, it moves to the next nonblank cell to the right.
End Left Arrow	If the current cell contains an entry, the cell pointer moves left to the next nonblank cell preceded by an empty one. If the current cell is blank, it moves to the next nonblank cell to the left.
End Home	Moves to the "last" cell, the lower-right corner of the active part of the spreadsheet.

As you can see, the End key alters the normal action of the arrow keys, taking the cell pointer to the last *active* cell in the direction in which you point. This is the last occupied cell in a row or column of contiguously occupied cells or the last blank cell if all of the cells in the direction you point are blank. You are taken to the next occupied cell if you are on a blank cell and use End followed by an arrow key pointing in the direction of additional data.

To get to the bottom of a column of numbers, you can press End followed by Down Arrow, as long as there are no gaps in the numbers. To get to the cell below the last number in the column—when summing a column, for instance—you would press Down Arrow one more time. If you press End and then Down Arrow with the cell pointer in an empty column, you will suddenly be on row 8,192. Similarly, if you press End and then Right Arrow with the cell pointer in an empty row, you will wind up in column IV. The Home key is useful for recovering from such mistakes.

Figure 4.1

Diagram of the End and arrow keys

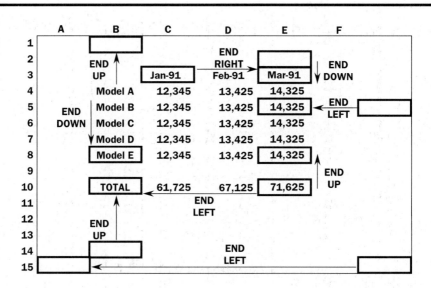

You might find it easier to think of the End key as moving from one range of occupied cells to the next. If you are within a range of occupied cells, End followed by an arrow key takes you to the end of that range, moving in the direction of the arrow. If you are at the end of a range of occupied cells or in a blank cell, End plus an arrow key takes you to the beginning of the next range of occupied cells if there is one; otherwise, it takes you to the edge of the worksheet.

Note that when you press End in READY or POINT mode, you turn on the message "End" at the lower-right corner of the screen. This message reminds you that the End feature has been activated. It stays on screen until you either press End again or press an arrow key or Home. This is true even if you use the menu system or issue function key commands after turning on End.

Moving to the Last Cell

You can also use the End key with the Home key. The sequence End Home moves the cell pointer to what 1-2-3 calls "the last cell"—this is the cell farthest from A1 that has been used. The area from A1 to the last cell is sometimes referred to as the *active work area*. In many worksheets, the last cell will coincide with the lower-right corner of your model. However, in some cases, End Home may take you to an apparently blank area. For example, if the entry farthest down in the worksheet is in cell A100 and the entry farthest to the right is in Z1, End Home will take the cell pointer to Z100, even if there is nothing in this cell and most of the model occupies A1..N50. The significance of the last cell is that each cell between A1 and the last cell takes up space in memory, even if it is not being used. As a rule of thumb, you should keep entries as close to A1 as possible if you want to make the most efficient use of memory. For more on using End Home when working on large models, see the section "Tidying Up" in Chapter 6.

Using Your Mouse with the End Key

You can also use your mouse with the End key. After pressing End you can click one of the four mouse arrows on the mouse palette to move the cell pointer in the direction of the particular arrow you click. This technique is particularly useful when pointing out ranges. Unfortunately, there is no mouse equivalent of the End key.

Data Fill

1-2-3 provides several commands for handling information arranged in tables—from sorting lists that you have entered in a worksheet to creating lists of results from spreadsheet formulas. These commands are grouped under Data on the main 1-2-3 menu. The Data Fill command can be very useful when you are building spreadsheets, since it automatically creates a sequence of values.

Simple Fills

To see the Fill command in action, issue the Worksheet Erase command so that you can begin with an empty worksheet. Suppose that you want to enter the series of years 1990 through 1996 for column headings on row 3, beginning in column B. Move the cell pointer to B3 and press / to bring up the menu. Select Data and then Fill. 1-2-3 will ask you to enter a range of cells to fill, as shown in Figure 4.2. Note that the range is not anchored at this point, as indicated by the appearance of only one cell address on the input line.

Type a period to anchor the range at B3 and then press Right Arrow several times to increase the fill range. The range needs to be large enough to accommodate the seven numbers from 1990 to 1996, so extend it from B3 through H3 and then press Enter. At this point, 1-2-3 requests the Start value. The default is 0 but you can type 1990 over this. When you press Enter to confirm the Start value, 1-2-3 asks for the Step, the amount by which you want to increment each value in the series. Since the default is 1, the value you need for the year series, press Enter to confirm this default. Now you are asked for the Stop value, which is 8191 by default. You want 1-2-3 to stop at 1996, but since the defined fill range won't allow the series to exceed 1996, you can simply press Enter to accept 8191. 1-2-3 fills the cells B3..H3 with a series of values starting at 1990, incremented by 1, and stopping at 1996, as shown in Figure 4.3.

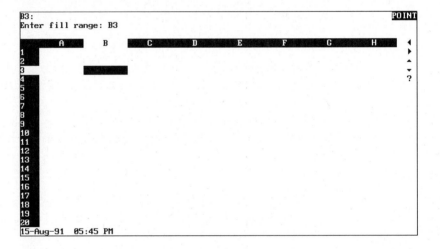

Figure 4.2

The fill range prompt

You can also control Data Fill by defining a fill range larger than you actually need for the planned series, and then giving the exact Stop value. With this method, you don't have to determine how much space the data will occupy. Note that the default Stop value of 8191 comes from numbering all 8192 rows in the spreadsheet, starting with the number zero. In addition, the range setting for Data Fill is *sticky*—that is, the second time you issue the command in the same worksheet, 1-2-3 remembers the range you used the first time. This feature allows you to refill the same range with different values quickly, but you also have to *unstick* the range if you want to fill a different group of cells. You can do this with either the Escape or Backspace key.

Suppose that in the worksheet shown in Figure 4.3 you also want a series of numbers in column A, starting at A4, that represent the 12 months of the year. Move the cell pointer to A4 and press / to bring up the menu. Select Data and then Fill. Note that 1-2-3 remembers the previous range and displays it as a default.

Figure 4.3
Completed series
of years

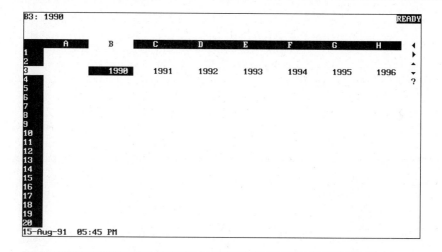

To reject the remembered range, press Backspace. This unlocks the range coordinates and moves the beginning point of the range to the cell that was current when you issued the Data Fill command. Pressing Escape would unlock the range, but would not change the start of the range, which would remain at B3 rather than returning to A4 automatically. This technique works with all remembered ranges in 1-2-3.

After you have typed a period to anchor the new fill range at cell A4, you can press PgDn once to select A4..A24 as the fill range. This range includes more than enough room for the series you need, and it saves you the trouble of identifying the correct cell for the last number in the series.

When you press Enter to confirm this fill range, notice that 1-2-3 also remembers the Start value from the last Data Fill command. In this case you want the series to start at 1, so type **1** to replace the previous entry and press Enter. The Step value of 1 is still acceptable, so press Enter to accept it. You should change the Stop value to 12; otherwise 1-2-3 will fill the entire range from A4 to A24, instead of stopping at 12. When you press Enter, the series is created, as shown in Figure 4.4.

Fill Tips

You can preselect the Data Fill range with your mouse. When you issue the Data Fill command, you will go straight to the Start prompt. Note that a series created by the Data Fill command is not dynamic: If you alter the value in the first cell in the series, the other numbers in the series do not change. However, since the fill range is remembered, you can easily repeat the Data Fill command with different Start, Step, and Stop values. Bear in mind that the Step value can be a negative, resulting in a declining rather than ascending series. If you use a negative Step value, make sure that the Stop value is less than the Start value. You can also use a fractional Step value; for example, you could use .5 to increment the numbers by one half. You can even use a formula for the Step, as in $^3/_{16}$ to increment by three sixteenths or 0.1875.

Figure 4.4

Completed series of months

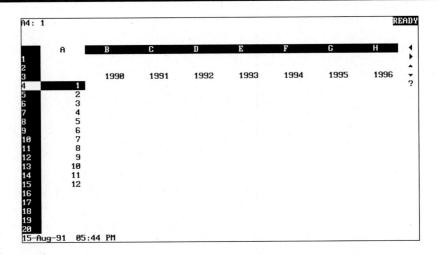

You can use the Data Fill command to create a series of dates if you enter the Start value using @DATE. For example, to create the series of months (previously shown in Figure 3.4 in Chapter 3), you would enter

```
@DATE(92,1,1)
```

as the Start value, use 31 as the Step, and format the cells with the third date format (MMM-YY). The Stop value would need to be much greater than the default of 8192 since January 1, 1992 is day number 33604. You can easily enter a very large Stop value, such as 999999, by holding down the 9 key.

You can use a formula or single cell reference as the Start value as long as the formula or cell reference amounts to a value. If A1 contained the number 5, you could enter A1 as the Start value and 1-2-3 would start the fill with 5. You could enter A1/5 as the Start value to have the series start with one fifth of the value in A1. If you refer to a cell that contains a label, no series is created. If you provide a cell reference or formula as a Start value, 1-2-3 does not remember the reference or formula itself, only its value.

Finally, you can use Data Fill for series that include both columns and rows. Suppose that in Figure 4.4 you want to model a steady increase in passenger volume, beginning with 400 passengers in January of 1990 (cell B4) and increasing by five passengers every month until December, 1996 (cell H15). With the cell pointer in B4, press /, select Data Fill, and then press Backspace. Type a period to anchor B4 as the start of the range, extend the range from B4 to H15, and then press Enter. Now enter 400 as the Start value, 5 as the Step value, and 99999 as the Stop value. The results can be seen in Figure 4.5, which also includes a label in A1. Since this worksheet will be used as an example in the next section, save it using the file name CAIROVOL.

Figure 4.5

A large range fill

```
B4: 400                                                                  READY

          A         B         C        D        E        F        G        H      ◄
1  Projected Volume: Cairo                                                        ►
2                                                                                 ▲
3                   1990      1991     1992     1993     1994     1995     1996    ▼
4          1        400       460      520      580      640      700      760    ?
5          2        405       465      525      585      645      705      765
6          3        410       470      530      590      650      710      770
7          4        415       475      535      595      655      715      775
8          5        420       480      540      600      660      720      780
9          6        425       485      545      605      665      725      785
10         7        430       490      550      610      670      730      790
11         8        435       495      555      615      675      735      795
12         9        440       500      560      620      680      740      800
13        10        445       505      565      625      685      745      805
14        11        450       510      570      630      690      750      810
15        12        455       515      575      635      695      755      815
16
17
18
19
20
15-Aug-91   05:53 PM
```

Pointers for Pointing

You can use the period key (.) to help you view and change a range's current corners while issuing any 1-2-3 command. This technique is particularly useful for checking the coordinates of a "sticky" range, which you may have defined in an earlier work session. Normally, when a range is highlighted and 1-2-3 is in POINT mode, the lower-right corner of the range is active. This is indicated by the flashing cursor and the fact that any cursor-movement key you press affects the lower-right corner of the range setting. When you press the period key, 1-2-3 activates other corners, moving clockwise around the four corners of the range. Thus, the first press activates the lower-left corner, the next activates the upper-left corner, and a third press activates the upper-right corner. A fourth press of the period key reactivates the lower-right corner.

You will find this technique useful for viewing cells in all four corners of a large range. When a range is too large to be seen in one screen, you can check the accuracy of the range coordinates without either altering the range or using the period key.

You can also use the period key feature to extend the range but leave the lower-right corner where it is. By activating a different corner, you alter the way in which 1-2-3 extends the range when you press the cursor-movement keys. For example, if the top corner is active, the Up Arrow key adds rows to the top of the range and the Down Arrow key removes them. The Left Arrow key adds columns to the left edge of the range while the Right Arrow key narrows the range by removing columns from the left edge.

Range Names

As you start building more complex spreadsheets, you will want to start using names for cells or groups of cells. Such names are known as *range names*. The following sections explain how to use range names to improve the accuracy of your work and make your worksheets more professional. 1-2-3 provides extensive facilities for naming ranges. There are also commands that help you keep track of range names to better manage their use.

Why Name Ranges?

If you do a lot of work with the same range of cells, you can save time by attaching a name to that range. For example, you may want to perform several calculations on the projected figures for passenger volume in Figure 4.5. If you give the name TOTVOL (for total volume) to the cells in the range B4..H15, you can enter the formula @SUM(TOTVOL) to get an immediate total for all the numbers in those cells. Figure 4.6 shows this formula at work.

Once you've assigned the name TOTVOL, you can use it whenever you need to refer to the range B4..H15. For example, you can use the formula @AVG(TOTVOL) to get the average monthly volume for the seven-year period. (The @AVG function returns the average value of cells in a range.) You are also less likely to make errors when writing formulas that use range names. If you typed B5..H13 by mistake, 1-2-3 wouldn't know you had missed rows of numbers. If you typed TOTVAL by mistake, however, 1-2-3 would recognize the error. Furthermore, you needn't type TOTVOL in formulas or remember its exact spelling, since you can select range names from a list when writing formulas.

Figure 4.6

Using a range
name in a formula

```
H19:  @SUM(TOTVOL)                                                    READY

        A        B        C        D        E        F        G       H    ◄
1    Projected Volume: Cairo                                                ►
2                                                                           ▲
3             1990     1991     1992     1993     1994     1995     1996    ▼
4        1     400      460      520      580      640      700      760    ?
5        2     405      465      525      585      645      705      765
6        3     410      470      530      590      650      710      770
7        4     415      475      535      595      655      715      775
8        5     420      480      540      600      660      720      780
9        6     425      485      545      605      665      725      785
10       7     430      490      550      610      670      730      790
11       8     435      495      555      615      675      735      795
12       9     440      500      560      620      680      740      800
13      10     445      505      565      625      685      745      805
14      11     450      510      570      630      690      750      810
15      12     455      515      575      635      695      755      815
16
17
18
19                                                             Total    51030
20
15-Aug-91   05:53 PM
```

Creating Range Names

To name a range of cells, such as the volume figures in Figure 4.5, first place
the cell pointer on the upper-left cell of the group to be named (in this case
B4). Now activate the menu, select Range, and then select Name. You'll see
a menu containing these five options:

```
Create Delete Labels Reset Table
```

Select Create to assign a new name. 1-2-3 prompts you to enter the
name. If you have already created some range names, they will be listed
below the "Enter name" prompt. To create TOTVOL, simply type the name
at the prompt and press Enter. (1-2-3 converts all range names to uppercase
when it records them, so you can type names in either upper- or lowercase.)

After typing the range name and pressing Enter, you are prompted for
the range of cells to be included, as with other Range commands. Notice that
the range is already anchored at the current cell, in this case B4. Press End
followed by Down Arrow to extend the highlighting to the last row of numbers. Pressing End followed by Right Arrow will extend the highlighting to
the last column and make the range B4..H15. Press Enter to complete the
operation. The range name is now recorded.

Using Range Names

Once you have created a name, you can begin to refer to it in formulas. For
example, move the cell pointer to H19 and type **@SUM(** to prepare for summing the numbers in B4..H15. Now press the Name key (F3). 1-2-3 will

display a list of existing range names immediately below the input line. Mouse users should note the special mouse palette that can be used to navigate the list.

In this case, only the name TOTVOL is displayed. When more than one range name exists, the names are presented in alphabetical order, just like file names. You navigate this list much as you navigate the File Retrieve list. (Pressing Name again, or clicking on List, displays a full screen list, with the cell coordinates of the highlighted range name shown at the top of the screen.)

To copy a range name from the list into a formula, highlight the range name and press Enter or click on it with your mouse. When there is only one range name, it is highlighted automatically. Press Enter to select the name and then type the closing parenthesis to complete the formula:

```
@SUM(TOTVOL)
```

Press Enter to insert this formula into cell H19. The result will be similar to Figure 4.6, where the right-aligned label Total has been added in cell G19.

If you assign a range name to cells that are already referred to in formulas, the range name will appear in place of the cell reference in the control panel when you highlight the formula cell. For example, if you had used the formula @SUM(B4..H15) before attaching a range name to those cells, and then assigned the name TOTVOL to B4..H15, the formula would change to @SUM(TOTVOL) automatically. Whenever you use F2 to edit a formula that contains a range name, 1-2-3 displays range coordinates in place of the range name so that you can change the coordinates individually. As soon as you press Enter, those coordinates are converted back to range names.

You can use range names in place of cell coordinates in many commands. For example, if you want to copy the cells in TOTVOL to another location, you can select Copy from the menu and then type TOTVOL as the range to copy from. (You cannot use the Name key in this instance.)

In addition, you can use range names when moving around a worksheet. For example, press Home to move the cell pointer to A1, press the Goto key (F5), and then press Name (F3). Select TOTVOL from the list that appears and note that the cell pointer moves to B4. When you move the cell pointer to a named range that consists of more than one cell, the cell pointer is placed in the upper-left cell of the range.

Managing Range Names

Suppose that you decide to create more range names in the sample worksheet, one for each year of the table, beginning with 1990. With the cell pointer in B4, select Range Name Create. You will see the name TOTVOL that has already been created. Type **CAIRO90** and press Enter. Then press End followed by Down Arrow to include the range B4 through B15, and

press Enter to confirm the range. Repeat this process for the remaining years, naming C4..C15 as CAIRO91, D4..D15 as CAIRO92, and so on.

Each time you use the Range Name Create command, the existing range names are listed alphabetically. Remember that you can press Name while the single-line list is displayed to display a full-screen list, as shown in Figure 4.7. Note that the cell coordinates of the highlighted range name are given on the second line of the display.

Figure 4.7

The full-screen range name list

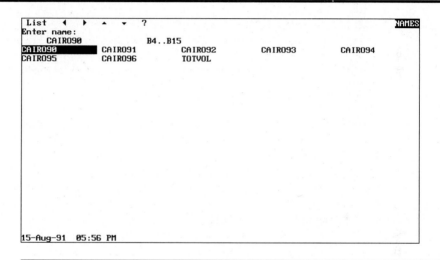

If you want to delete a range name, use the Range Name Delete command. (This removes the name from the cells, but does not affect the contents of the named cells.) The Labels command on the Range Name menu allows you to assign names to cells using labels in the spreadsheet (a process discussed in detail in Chapter 13). The Range Name Reset command deletes all range names at once. (1-2-3 does not require that you confirm this action, so be very careful not to select it by mistake.)

The Range Name Table command places a list of the range names, together with their cell coordinates, in a designated area of the spreadsheet. This feature is useful when you need to keep track of a large number of range names. Normally, you place the table in an area of the worksheet set aside for housekeeping tasks, as shown in Figure 4.8.

You can move the cell pointer out of the way of the main model, as shown here, by pressing Home, Tab, Down Arrow, and then Right Arrow to place the cell pointer in J2. Then you issue the Range Name Table command. 1-2-3 assumes that it's okay to use the current cell for the table, plus the cell immediately to the right and as many rows as it takes to list all of the names (which is why you should use an empty area of the worksheet for this command).

Figure 4.8

A range name table

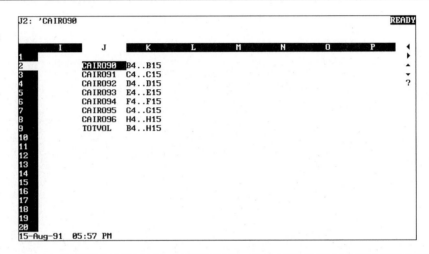

The result of the Range Name Table command is merely a series of labels, but it provides a useful check on the accuracy of your work. (If you had accidentally used the range BC3..C15 for CAIRO91, the error would be immediately apparent from the table.) Remember, this table is not dynamic— that is, if you create a new range name or alter the coordinates of an existing name, the table will not reflect the change until you update it by repeating the Range Name Table command. If you repeat the command using the same cell as the starting point, 1-2-3 will completely update the table, removing names that have been deleted and adding those that are new. Unfortunately, 1-2-3 does not remember the location of the last range name table, so you must reselect it manually. Note that if you have created long range names, they may be difficult to read in regular nine-character columns.

The names you use for ranges must follow certain rules. They can contain as many as 14 characters. You can use the letters A through Z, the numbers 0 through 9, and punctuation characters. Range names should bear some meaningful relationship to the contents of the cells, but should not be too long, which would defeat their purpose. To avoid confusion and critical errors, range names should not be the same as values, which is why the example used CAIRO90 instead of 1990. Similarly, range names should not be the same as any valid cell reference. For example, do not use C90 as a range name because there is a cell called C90 on row 90 in column C. Using C_90 or 90C would be better. You can use any number of range names and the ranges can overlap.

You will learn more about range names when working with macros in Chapters 12 and 13. At this point, you may want to save the sample worksheet for use in the next section.

Search and Replace

When you start to create larger worksheets, you will appreciate the worksheet editing command Range Search. This command enables you to find specific information within a range of cells or an entire worksheet. You can search the contents of either formulas or labels (but not numeric constants). In addition, the Range Search command can replace the target data with something else, either in all or in selected cases.

Preparing to Search

Imagine that somewhere in a large worksheet like the one in Figure 4.9, you have entered a formula that multiplies the value in another cell by 6%. You think that you might have entered 6% as .6 instead of .06, and want to check that the formula is correct. Even if you cannot recall where the error is, the Range Search command can locate it for you.

Figure 4.9

A test case for
Range Search

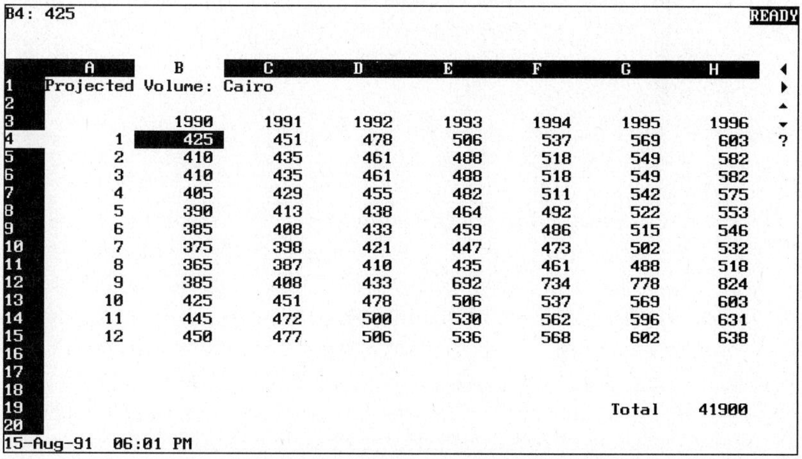

B4:	425							READY

	A	B	C	D	E	F	G	H	
1	Projected Volume: Cairo								
2									
3		1990	1991	1992	1993	1994	1995	1996	
4	1	425	451	478	506	537	569	603	?
5	2	410	435	461	488	518	549	582	
6	3	410	435	461	488	518	549	582	
7	4	405	429	455	482	511	542	575	
8	5	390	413	438	464	492	522	553	
9	6	385	408	433	459	486	515	546	
10	7	375	398	421	447	473	502	532	
11	8	365	387	410	435	461	488	518	
12	9	385	408	433	692	734	778	824	
13	10	425	451	478	506	537	569	603	
14	11	445	472	500	530	562	596	631	
15	12	450	477	506	536	568	602	638	
16									
17									
18									
19							Total	41900	
20									

15-Aug-91   06:01 PM

To test this command, you can use a variation of the worksheet used for the range name examples. To prepare the worksheet, first enter the set of values seen in B4..B15 of Figure 4.9. These values represent seasonally adjusted expectations for monthly volume. The values in the remaining columns are all formulas, creating projected figures through multiplication by a growth factor. For example, the formula in C4 is +B4*1.06, increasing B4 by a factor of 6%. Entering this formula will produce the result 450.5. Now, with the cell pointer still on C4, press / and select Copy. Press Enter to accept C4 as the source range. Type a period to anchor the destination range at C4. Now press End followed by Right Arrow, and then End followed by Down Arrow to select C4..H15 as the destination range. Press Enter to complete the copy. The results will appear as shown in Figure 4.10.

Figure 4.10

The initial results

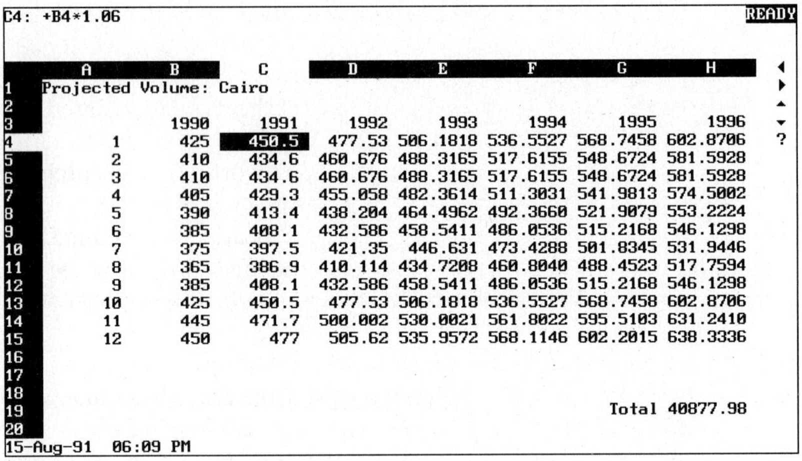

```
C4: +B4*1.06                                                           READY

         A         B         C       D        E        F        G        H      ◄
1  Projected Volume: Cairo                                                       ►
2                                                                                ▲
3                1990      1991     1992     1993     1994     1995     1996      ▼
4          1      425     450.5   477.53  506.1818 536.5527 568.7458 602.8706    ?
5          2      410     434.6  460.676  488.3165 517.6155 548.6724 581.5928
6          3      410     434.6  460.676  488.3165 517.6155 548.6724 581.5928
7          4      405     429.3  455.058  482.3614 511.3031 541.9813 574.5002
8          5      390     413.4  438.204  464.4962 492.3660 521.9079 553.2224
9          6      385     408.1  432.586  458.5411 486.0536 515.2168 546.1298
10         7      375     397.5   421.35   446.631 473.4288 501.8345 531.9446
11         8      365     386.9  410.114  434.7208 460.8040 488.4523 517.7594
12         9      385     408.1  432.586  458.5411 486.0536 515.2168 546.1298
13        10      425     450.5   477.53  506.1818 536.5527 568.7458 602.8706
14        11      445     471.7  500.002  530.0021 561.8022 595.5103 631.2410
15        12      450       477   505.62  535.9572 568.1146 602.2015 638.3336
16
17
18
19                                                      Total 40877.98
20
15-Aug-91   06:09 PM
```

To tidy up these calculations, you will format them using the Range Format command and the range name TOTVOL you assigned to B4..H15. Press / and select Range Format Fixed. Type **0** for decimal places and press Enter to confirm it. At the "Enter range to format:" prompt, press the Name key (F3) to display a list of named ranges. Press Name again to see the full-screen list. Now press End to highlight TOTVOL, the last name in the list. Press Enter to select this as the range to be formatted and the Fixed format will be assigned to cells B4..H15.

Note that the cell totaling these figures has also been assigned the same format. If you do not do this, the total will display several decimal places while summing numbers that appear to be rounded. This type of visual inconsistency should be avoided whenever possible.

To set up the target cell for the search command, move the cell pointer to E12 by pressing the Goto key, F5, typing **E12**, and pressing Enter. To change this cell, press the Edit key (F2) and then press Backspace twice. Now type **6** and press Enter. The formula in E12 should now read +D12*1.6, which is incorrect. Next you will use the Range Search command to locate the one cell that contains .6 instead of .06.

Using Range Search

When you select Search from the Range menu, you are prompted for the range of cells in which to conduct the search. Like the Data Fill range, the search range is "sticky": 1-2-3 remembers the range you specify and offers it as the default range for the next search operation.

If you have no idea where the target information is located, you will probably want to select the entire worksheet as the search range. To do this, press Home to reach A1, type a period to anchor the cell pointer there, and then press End followed by Home to move to the intersection of the last occupied row and column in the worksheet. If you created the range name table in columns J and K, End Home should take you to K19, making the search range A1..K19. However, don't worry if your search range is slightly different. You don't have to search the entire worksheet if you have some idea where the target cell or cells are located. For example, you could select a named range to be searched by pressing Name when the "range to search" prompt appears. In this example, you could search the range named TOTVOL, or B4..H15.

When you have entered the search range, you'll see the prompt "Enter string to search for:". Here you enter the characters that make up the target information—that is, what you are searching for. Note that 1-2-3 often uses the term *string* to refer to a series of characters that can be numbers or letters. In this case, you are looking for .6, so just type **.6**. When you are searching for labels, 1-2-3 is not case sensitive. In other words, if you are looking for Bush you can enter **Bush**, **BUSH**, or **bush** as the search string. If you are looking for a cell reference, such as AB3, you can enter **ab3**, **AB3**, or even **Ab3**. After typing the target information for the search, press Enter.

At this point, 1-2-3 offers you a choice between Formulas, Labels, or Both. If you select Formulas, 1-2-3 will look for the search string in the formulas entered into cells. Bear in mind that 1-2-3 only searches the contents of formulas: It does not examine their results. For example, if you specify a search string of 4, then 1-2-3 will not stop on a cell containing 2*2. You want the Formulas option in this example, since the .6 is part of a formula. You use the Labels option when searching for entries that are labels. The Both option, which searches both labels and formulas, is useful when you are looking for a string that could be in both, such as a word that is used as a title and a range name. For example, in a spreadsheet reporting profits from the Cairo office you might have used Cairo as a title and CAIRO as a range name in a formula.

After you've told 1-2-3 the range to be searched, the string to look for, and what kind of data to examine, you must choose either Find or Replace. The Find option locates entries that match the search string, which is what you need in this example. By contrast, the Replace option allows you to substitute a new string of characters for those that are being found. For example, if you had used .06 in many formulas and needed to change it to .07, you would use the Replace option.

When you select Find, 1-2-3 locates the first cell within the search range that contains the target string, and actually highlights the string, as shown in Figure 4.11. At this point, you can either select Next to have 1-2-3 find further instances of the string, or Quit to end the search. If you select Next and 1-2-3 finds another instance of the target string, it is highlighted and the Next and Quit options return. If there are no more instances of the target string, 1-2-3 beeps and displays the message "No more matching strings" in the status line at the bottom of the screen. At the same time, the mode indicator flashes ERROR. Press the Escape key and 1-2-3 will return to READY mode with the cell pointer in the last cell located by the Range Search command.

Figure 4.11

The Find command in operation

```
E12: (F0) +D12*1.6                                                    MENU
Next  Quit
Find next matching string
     A         B         C         D         E       F         G         H     ◄
1      Projected Volume: Cairo                                                 ►
2                                                                              ▲
3                1990      1991      1992      1993    1994      1995      1996 ▼
4          1      425       451       478       506     537       569       603 ?
5          2      410       435       461       488     518       549       582
6          3      410       435       461       488     518       549       582
7          4      405       429       455       482     511       542       575
8          5      390       413       438       464     492       522       553
9          6      385       408       433       459     486       515       546
10         7      375       398       421       447     473       502       532
11         8      365       387       410       435     461       488       518
12         9      385       408       433       692     734       778       824
13        10      425       451       478       506     537       569       603
14        11      445       472       500       530     562       596       631
15        12      450       477       506       536     568       602       638
16
17
18
19                                                              Total     41900
20
15-Aug-91  06:14 PM
```

If you select Quit, you will also be returned to READY mode with the cell pointer in the last cell located by the Range Search command. In this example, 1-2-3 leaves the cell pointer in E12 and you can change the .6 to .06.

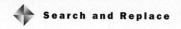

Using Search and Replace

In a search and replace operation, 1-2-3 searches for every instance of one sequence of characters and replaces it with another. For example, if you used the word "New York" many times in a worksheet and realized that in some cases it should be "Newark," you might think you would have to change each cell manually. Instead, you can highlight the area of the worksheet containing the words to be changed and have 1-2-3 do a search and replace within that range to make the changes for you. You can have the Range Search command stop at each instance of the target string and ask if you want to replace it. Alternately, you can have the command instantly change all occurrences to the replacement string.

You can use search and replace with numbers as well as labels. For example, suppose that in the model in Figure 4.11 you decide growth from 1995 to 1996 will be 7% instead of 6%. Rather than entering a new formula in H4 and copying it down the column, you can use the Range Search command and select the Replace option. You will search for .06 and replace it with .07. Furthermore, if you have named H4..H15 as CAIRO96, you can use the range name to speed up the operation.

First, select Search from the Range menu. 1-2-3 prompts you for the range of cells in which to conduct the search, offering the range used in the previous search as a default. To change the range to CAIRO96, simply press Name twice, highlight CAIRO96 in the full-screen list of range names, and press Enter. (If you have not named H4..H15, select it as the search range by pressing Backspace to reject the existing search range, moving the cell pointer to H4, typing a period, and pressing End, Down Arrow, and then Enter.)

When you have entered the search range, you'll see the prompt "Enter string to search for:" with the last search string as a default. Press Backspace once and then type **06** for the string and press Enter. Now select Formulas. After you've indicated the range to be searched, the string to look for, and what kind of entries to look in, choose Replace.

Enter the requested Replacement string with an eye to results. Using ambiguous search and replace strings can produce incorrect results. For example, searching for 6 and replacing with 7 would adversely affect formulas that refer to cells on row 6—for one, +G6*1.06 would be changed to +G7*1.07. You want to change .06 to .07, so make sure to enter .07 as the replacement string. With labels, 1-2-3 is not case sensitive in the Search but is literal in the replacement process and does not adjust the capitalization of the replacement string. Thus, searching for BUSH and replacing it with TREE will replace Bush (as well as bush and Bush) with TREE rather than tree or Tree. (If you have used search and replace in WordPerfect, you will be familiar with a case-sensitive replacement function.)

As soon as you enter your replacement string, 1-2-3 displays the first cell that contains the search string, as shown in Figure 4.12. If there are no instances of the search string within the defined range, 1-2-3 beeps and displays ERROR in the mode indicator. In this case, press Esc to return to READY mode and try the command again, checking your search range, search string, and type of search (Formulas, Labels, or Both). In this example, the first cell found is H4.

Figure 4.12

The search/replace prompt

```
H4: (F0) +G4*1.06                                                          MENU
Replace  All  Next  Quit
Replace string and proceed to next matching string in range
      A          B         C         D         E         F         G         H      ◀
1  Projected Volume: Cairo                                                          ▶
2                                                                                   ▲
3                 1990      1991      1992      1993      1994      1995      1996   ▼
4            1     425       451       478       506       537       569       603   ?
5            2     410       435       461       488       518       549       582
6            3     410       435       461       488       518       549       582
7            4     405       429       455       482       511       542       575
8            5     390       413       438       464       492       522       553
9            6     385       408       433       459       486       515       546
10           7     375       398       421       447       473       502       532
11           8     365       387       410       435       461       488       518
12           9     385       408       433       459       486       515       546
13          10     425       451       478       506       537       569       603
14          11     445       472       500       530       562       596       631
15          12     450       477       506       536       568       602       638
16
17
18
19                                                                    Total    40878
20
15-Aug-91  06:17 PM
```

The contents of the cell located by the search are displayed on the first line of the screen. The second line displays your options. When you select Replace, 1-2-3 replaces this instance of the search string and searches for the next instance. Select Replace now and note that the cell pointer moves to the next cell within the search range that contains .06. However, H4 shows 0, a slightly disconcerting result. This is because 1-2-3 does not recalculate formulas altered by a search and replace operation until you return to READY mode.

When 1-2-3 pauses at cell H5 (the next cell that contains .06), select All to replace all remaining instances of the search string within the defined range. Normally, you should only use this option when you are familiar with search and replace operations and are sure of the result, since you are performing what amounts to a global replace with the All command. When the All command is completed, you are returned to READY mode, the altered formulas are calculated, and the cell pointer is in the last cell that was altered, as shown in Figure 4.13. Save your spreadsheet at this point because you will use it in future examples.

Pick Next during a search and replace to move on to the next instance without changing anything. Next enables you to review the cells that contain the search string without affecting them. To return to READY mode without changing the current instance of the search string, select Quit. If you keep selecting Replace and Next, 1-2-3 will eventually say "No more matching strings." You can press Enter or Esc to return to READY mode. The cell pointer will be in the last cell located by the search command.

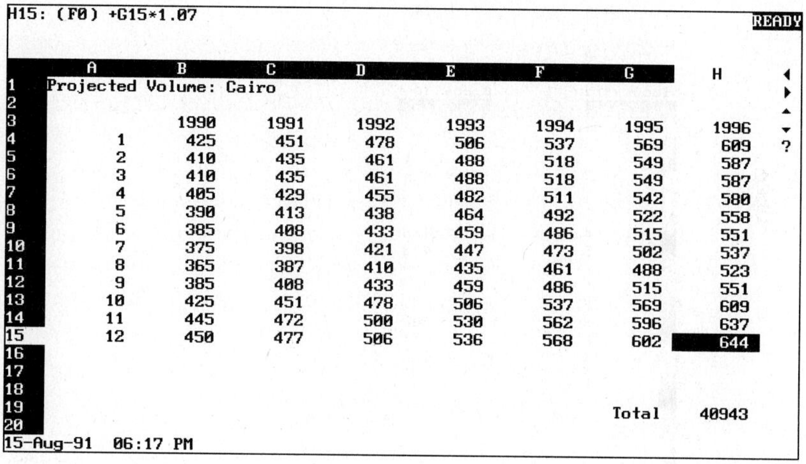

	A	B	C	D	E	F	G	H
1	Projected Volume: Cairo							
2								
3		1990	1991	1992	1993	1994	1995	1996
4	1	425	451	478	506	537	569	609
5	2	410	435	461	488	518	549	587
6	3	410	435	461	488	518	549	587
7	4	405	429	455	482	511	542	580
8	5	390	413	438	464	492	522	558
9	6	385	408	433	459	486	515	551
10	7	375	398	421	447	473	502	537
11	8	365	387	410	435	461	488	523
12	9	385	408	433	459	486	515	551
13	10	425	451	478	506	537	569	609
14	11	445	472	500	530	562	596	637
15	12	450	477	506	536	568	602	644
16								
17								
18								
19							Total	40943
20								

Figure 4.13 Results of search/replace

After a search and replace, 1-2-3 will remember the settings that you entered so that you can easily repeat the command. To perform a search and replace with different settings, just type them over the remembered ones. Note that 1-2-3 can undo a search and replace, so you can use Undo to switch between "before" and "after" states and compare their effects.

Using Range Value

At times you may want to convert formulas into permanent values. You can easily convert a single cell from a formula to a value by pressing Calc (F9) while editing the cell. When you press Enter, the resulting value is placed in the cell, replacing the formula. However, when you need to convert a lot of formulas to values or you want to preserve the formulas, the Range Value command is a useful alternative to the Edit/Calc sequence (F2, F9). For example, you might create a budget using formulas that multiply the current year's expenses by 1.1. Once the budget is approved, however, you will want to freeze that set of numbers using Range Value so that they no longer respond to changes in this year's figures.

The Range Value command works just like the Copy command, except that it converts all formulas to values. Suppose that you want to copy the numbers projected in Figure 4.13. Place the cell pointer on B4 and press / to bring up the menu. Select Range and then Value. 1-2-3 asks you for a range to convert and a destination for the converted data. Press End and then Down Arrow followed by End and Right Arrow to select B4..H15. When you press Enter, 1-2-3 requests the range to copy TO. Press PgDn to move the cell pointer to B24, and then press Enter. You will be returned to READY mode.

Now press PgDn to see the values created by Range Value. Move the cell pointer to C24 and note that the formula +B4*1.06 is now the value 450.5, as shown next to the cell address indicator. On the worksheet itself, this value is rounded to 451 because of the worksheet's global format. At this point, press Undo (Alt-F4) to reverse the Range Value command.

Changing formulas to their resulting values saves memory, allowing you to create larger worksheets within the same amount of random access memory (RAM). When you are working with large worksheets, you can economize on RAM by identifying calculated values that you know will not change, and converting the formulas to values. You do this by using the same source and destination ranges with the Range Value command. However, this overwrites the formulas so that they are permanently lost unless you use Undo.

Transposing a Range

In some situations, you may want to rearrange information so that columns are rows and rows are columns. For example, you can rearrange the information in Figure 4.12 to look like that in Figure 4.14. (Note that not all of the transposed range is visible in the figure: Some of the data is off screen to the right.) You can switch columns and rows with the Range Trans (transpose) command, which uses a source range and a destination range, just like Copy and Range Value. While copying cells, Range Trans also converts any formulas to values.

You can replicate Figure 4.14 by placing the cell pointer on A3, the upper-left cell of the row and column area to be transposed. Then issue the Range Trans command and select A3..H15 as the source range. Select cell A23 as the destination range. Like Range Value, Range Trans can be undone with the Undo key (Alt-F4). You needn't save the sample worksheet after the Range Value and Range Trans examples.

Figure 4.14

Transposed range

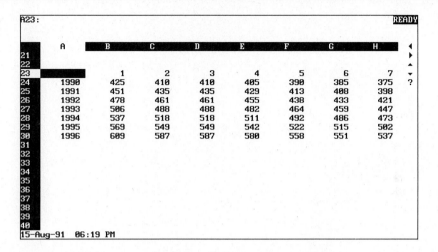

Summary

By skillful manipulation of ranges, you can accomplish otherwise time-consuming tasks with a minimum of keystrokes. Naming ranges can make your worksheets easier to use, both for yourself and for others, while you can use search and replace operations to perform large-scale editing with ease. In the next chapter, you will learn more about creating formulas in 1-2-3, and will review many of the built-in formulas, or functions, that 1-2-3 provides.

Functions in Depth

PREVIOUS CHAPTERS MENTIONED THAT 1-2-3 PROVIDES YOU WITH THE basic building blocks of complex formulas in the form of functions. These built-in formulas allow you to perform sophisticated calculations. This chapter explains how formulas are applied in typical spreadsheet operations, and reviews most of 1-2-3's functions. You have already learned how to create simple formulas with 1-2-3. Now you will learn how to build more complex ones, and how to avoid some of the common pitfalls in formula writing.

More About Formulas

In the context of 1-2-3, the term *formula* simply means an instruction written in a form that 1-2-3 understands. The way you give instructions to 1-2-3 can be as straightforward as "add cell A1 and cell A2." Even complex instructions follow a consistent format, or *syntax*.

Formula Syntax

Simple 1-2-3 formulas combine values, such as numbers or cells containing numbers, with operators, such as the division sign or a plus sign. The values in a 1-2-3 formula can be cells containing values, as in the formula B16*B17 in cell B18 of Figure 5.1. These cells can be described by range names as well as coordinates. For example, if you assign the names WIDTH and LENGTH to cells B16 and B17, respectively, the formula in cell B18 can be entered as **WIDTH*LENGTH** and 1-2-3 will display WIDTH*LENGTH in the control panel whenever that cell is highlighted.

Values in formulas can also be constants. A *constant* is a number, date, or piece of text that you enter directly and which does not change, such as the 1 in 1+B3. Constants are often used in formulas for projections. For instance, in the last chapter a constant of 1.06 was used to calculate one year's figures based on those in the previous year. A constant is also used in the formula for finding the circumference of a circle. The formula $2\pi R$ involves three constants: the number 2, the value of π (3.141...), and the radius (R).

You can also use functions in formulas—either by themselves or as part of longer formulas. For example, the formula

```
@SUM(EXPENSES)*1.06
```

would multiply the sum of the values in the block named EXPENSES by 1.06.

Note that 1-2-3 capitalizes cell references, range names, and function names entered in formulas, regardless of whether you enter them as upper- or lowercase letters.

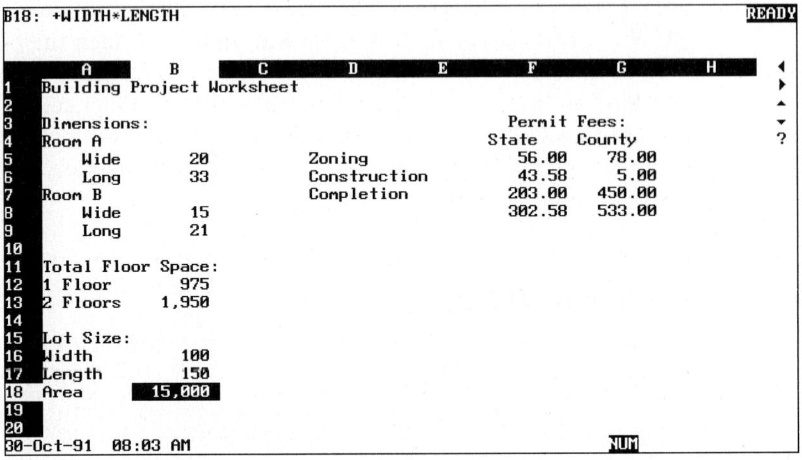

Figure 5.1

Sample formulas

```
B18: +WIDTH*LENGTH                                                    READY

         A          B          C          D       E       F        G         H      ◀
1   Building Project Worksheet                                                       ▶
2                                                                                    ▲
3   Dimensions:                                          Permit Fees:                ▼
4   Room A                                               State    County             ?
5       Wide       20          Zoning                    56.00     78.00
6       Long       33          Construction              43.58      5.00
7   Room B                     Completion               203.00    450.00
8       Wide       15                                   302.58    533.00
9       Long       21
10
11  Total Floor Space:
12  1 Floor              975
13  2 Floors           1,950
14
15  Lot Size:
16  Width                100
17  Length               150
18  Area              15,000
19
20
30-Oct-91   08:03 AM                                             NUM
```

Operators and Priorities

You can use many different operators in 1-2-3 formulas, including the standard arithmetic operators add (+), subtract (−), multiply (*), and divide (/). Another operator, the exponent (^), produces powers of a number (as in 4^3=64). In Chapter 8, you will learn how to set out conditions using logical operators such as the greater-than sign (>). All of the operators recognized by 1-2-3 are listed in Table 5.1.

Table 5.1 also shows the order of operations in a formula. If all the operators are the same or have the same precedence, as in

```
2 * 3 * 4 = 24
```

the calculation is performed from left to right. If there are operators of mixed precedence, higher precedence operators are calculated first. For example:

```
4 + 3 * 2 = 10
```

This formula adds 4 to the product of 3 and 2, even though the plus comes before the asterisk in the formula entry.

You can also affect the order of calculation by using parentheses, as in

```
2 * (4 + 3) = 14
```

When you nest calculations within several parentheses, the innermost calculations are performed first. For example, in Figure 5.1, cell A13 contains the formula ((B5*B6)+(B8*B9))*2. This formula calculates the total floor area of a two-story house with two rooms (called A and B on the spreadsheet) on each floor. The arrangement of parentheses in this formula means that both the B5*B6 and B8*B9 calculations will occur first, then the two products will be added, and finally that sum will be multiplied by the constant value 2 that stands outside the parentheses. Actually, the two inner sets of parentheses are not necessary because, as you saw in Table 5.1, the multiplication will occur before the addition. However, you can use extra parentheses in formulas to make them easier to read.

Table 5.1   **Operators in Order of Precedence**

Operator	Precedence	Definition	Example
^	1	Exponentiation (to the power of)	B2^2 (square B2)
- +	2	Negative and positive values	+B2, -C2
* /	3	Multiplication and division	B2*C2, C2/B2
+ -	4	Addition and subtraction	B2+C2, B2-C2
= <>	5	Equal-to and not-equal-to	B2=12, B2<>12
< >	5	Less-than and greater-than	B2<12, B2>12
> =	5	Greater-than-or-equal-to	B2 > = 12
< =	5	Less-than-or-equal-to	B2 < = 12
#NOT#`	6	Not condition 1	#NOT#B2<12
#AND#	7	Both condition 1 and condition 2	B2>12#AND#B2<100
#OR#	7	Either condition 1 or condition 2	B2=12#OR#B2=C2
&	7	String concatenation	+"Joe"&" "&"Doe"

* 1-2-3 performs operations with lower precedence numbers first and performs operations with equal precedence from left to right. To override the order of precedence, enclose an operation in parentheses.

Common Formula Errors

Remember, if you make a mistake in a formula, such as a typo or an invalid cell reference, 1-2-3 will not accept the formula when you press Enter. Instead, it will beep and change to EDIT mode so you can correct your error. 1-2-3 attempts to put the cursor near the error, so look there first. You may have neglected to close a pair of parentheses or quotations, or omitted the @ sign before a function name. Or, you might have inadvertently included a space while typing the formula.

In addition, you may succeed in entering a formula only to see the message "CIRC" at the bottom of the screen. This message signals a circular reference in a formula, meaning that the formula refers to itself. For example, you cannot ask 1-2-3 to multiply the current cell by 1.1 and to put the answer in the current cell. If you do, the initial result may appear acceptable, but each time the worksheet is recalculated, the result will be further exaggerated. You can usually solve this kind of problem by retyping the formula. If you see the "CIRC" message and cannot determine which cell is producing it, use the Worksheet Status command. As you can see from Figure 5.2, the menu provided by the Worksheet Status command shows the location of the circular reference. You can then press any key to leave the menu and edit the cell in question.

Figure 5.2

The Worksheet
Status display

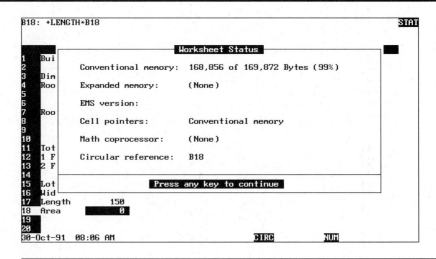

Referring to an unnamed range is another common error. When this happens, you must stop typing the formula to name the range, which is especially annoying when the formula is complex and lengthy. To save your typing on a rejected formula, you can press Home when 1-2-3 places you in EDIT mode. Then type an apostrophe. This will allow you to enter the formula as a label and then review it. When you have corrected the formula and are ready to reenter it as a value, simply press Home and then Del to remove the apostrophe before pressing Enter.

Another problem than can occur with formulas is the ERR result. ERR appears in a worksheet cell when 1-2-3 cannot understand what you want it to do. For example, suppose you sum the range B4..B7 with a formula like this:

```
@SUM(B4..B7)
```

Then suppose you delete row 7. This confuses 1-2-3 and the formula turns into @SUM(ERR) while the cell containing the formula just displays ERR. This error has a domino effect: Any cell that depends on a result that is ERR will also result in ERR. To solve this problem, you need to correct the source of the error and then work through the formulas that depend upon it to make sure they are correct. A common cause of ERR is dividing a value by zero. This can occur when a value required in a formula is missing. For example, the formula +B5/C5 will result in ERR if C5 contains 0, because the user does not yet know what C5 should be. For techniques to avoid this problem, see Chapter 14 and the discussion of @ISERR.

Calculating Formulas

1-2-3 normally recalculates all formulas in a worksheet whenever you make a new entry or edit an existing entry. Formulas are calculated from least dependent to most dependent, thus ensuring that formulas that use the results of other formulas have updated results with which to work. This calculation method is called *automatic natural recalculation*. However, to control when recalculation takes place and the order in which formulas are calculated, you can alter the way that 1-2-3 normally handles recalculation.

Worksheet Global Recalculation

You alter the way that 1-2-3 recalculates a worksheet with the Worksheet Global Recalculation command. When you select Recalculation from the Worksheet Global menu, you have the choice of Natural, Columnwise, Rowwise, Automatic, Manual, and Iteration. The current choices are displayed in the Global Settings box under Method, Order, and Iterations. The Method options are Automatic and Manual; the default is Automatic. The Order options are Natural, Columnwise, and Rowwise; the default is Normal. The Iteration options are 1 to 50; the default is 1. The settings you choose are attached to the current worksheet when it is saved. They do not affect worksheets you retrieve later from disk or new worksheets. When you issue the Worksheet Erase command, the Recalculation settings revert to the defaults.

Manual Recalculation

While a worksheet is recalculating, 1-2-3 cannot respond quite as quickly to commands and cell pointer movements. When you are working on a large worksheet, this delay can become annoying. To alleviate this problem, 1-2-3 allows you to switch from Automatic to Manual recalculation by using the Worksheet Global Recalculation command.

Choosing Manual will stop 1-2-3 from doing any recalculation until you issue the Calc command (the F9 key). If you change recalculation to Manual and alter the worksheet, you will see the message "CALC" at the bottom of the screen. This reminds you that the worksheet is not up to date. You can then press F9 to recalculate the entire worksheet at once. Manual recalculation tells 1-2-3 to recalculate only in the following situations:

■ When a formula is entered or edited, the result of that formula alone is calculated.

■ When you press F9 (the Calc key), all formulas are calculated.

■ When you turn Automatic recalculation back on and prompt a recalculation by entering new data or editing a cell, all formulas are calculated.

Iterations and Order

In some rare situations, the order of calculation used by 1-2-3 will not produce accurate results. For example, older spreadsheet programs could only calculate one row or column at a time. This meant that users would design models so that when recalculation occurred moving down the worksheet row-by-row, or across it column-by-column, the results would come out right. If you are using a design that depends upon such recalculation, you should select either Columnwise or Rowwise from the Worksheet Global menu. Sometimes such designs had formulas in upper rows that depended upon answers in lower rows, thus requiring a second calculation of the spreadsheet for all of the results to be accurate. To accommodate this requirement, 1-2-3 allows you to alter the number of passes it makes through the worksheet during recalculation, known as the *number of iterations,* from the default of 1 to any number up to 50. You should only change the Iteration setting if you know that your worksheet design requires multiple iterations for accurate results.

Calculating Big and Little Numbers

There is a limit to 1-2-3's mathematical capabilities. In particular, you may experience problems with very large numbers or small rounding errors in calculations. Using scientific notation, 1-2-3 can work with very large numbers—for example, $1.23*10^21$ (this represents 1,230,000,000,000,000,000,000). However, when a value or formula result reaches $1*10^100$, 1-2-3 can no longer display the number and returns asterisks, regardless of the width of the column.

Normally, arithmetic is done with numbers that can be described as base 10, such as 1, 10, 100, and so on. For your computer to perform arithmetic, base 10 numbers must be converted to binary, or base 2 numbers. 1-2-3 does this for you, but the programming techniques it uses will sometimes produce extremely small, and occasionally significant, rounding errors. For example, a formula result that appears as 12.3 may in fact be stored in computer memory as 12.30000000000000000001.

For this reason, it is possible to enter a formula that compares two supposedly equal numbers and have 1-2-3 tell you that they are not equal. Suppose you have a table of numbers in B2..D5, a series of column totals in B6..D6, and a series of row totals in E2..E5. The sum of B6..D6 should equal the sum of E2..E5. You could enter the following formula to check that the two sums are in fact equal:

```
@SUM(B6..D6)=@SUM(E2..E5)
```

The result will be 1 if the two numbers are equal, 0 if the numbers are not equal.

However, there is a chance that 1-2-3 will return 0 when in fact it should return 1. After checking your formulas, you decide that the values being compared are, in fact, equal. The problem disappears if you use the @ROUND function, which limits the number of decimal places used by 1-2-3 (@ROUND is described later in this chapter). This formula will definitely give the correct answer:

```
@ROUND(@SUM(B6..D6),2)=@ROUND(@SUM(E2..E5),2)
```

This anomaly in 1-2-3 is not really cause for concern once you know it exists. The point is that you should never base important decisions on formulas that you have not tested, particularly if the answers sound too good to be true.

Functions: Built-in Formulas

Functions allow you to perform calculations that would be difficult or cumbersome to perform using standard arithmetic operators. For example, you can work out a loan payment using multiplication, division, and subtraction, but @PMT is much easier to use. In this section, you will learn the rules for using functions, before going on to an in-depth review of the major functions.

Function Arguments

Some functions simply generate values by themselves. For example, @PI gives the value of pi. The date function @NOW tells you the current date and time according to your PC. However, most functions require additional information, called *arguments*. For example, the principal, interest, and term required by the @PMT function are said to be the arguments of @PMT. Some functions require just one argument. For instance, @SUM only needs to know what range of cells you want to sum. Other functions, such as @PMT, require several arguments.

There are three types of arguments required by functions:

- *Numeric arguments,* such as numbers entered into cells or supplied as constants, as in @PMT(E1,E2,36)

- *Range arguments,* such as a range of cells being summed with @SUM(B1..B3), or a named range, such as @SUM(TOTAL SALES)

- *String arguments,* such as a label or piece of text entered into a cell, entered into a function in quotes, or produced by another function

In functions that can accept more than one argument, the arguments are separated by commas, as in:

```
@SUM(B1..B3,C1..C3,E1..E3)
```

This function totals the first three rows of columns B, C, and E. Functions are often combined with operators and values in formulas, just like any other formula element. For example, this formula produces a loan payment rounded to two decimal places with the @ROUND function:

```
@ROUND(@PMT(E1,APR/12,TERM),2)
```

Function Types and Syntax

There are around 90 functions in 1-2-3 Release 2.3 and several ways of classifying them. The distinction between numeric and string functions closely follows that between values and labels. In addition, you can group functions by the type of work they apply to: financial, date, logical, and so on.

The database functions will be covered in Chapter 8. String (text) functions are covered in Chapter 11. The @TRUE, @FALSE, and @IS functions (@ISAAF, @ISAPP, and so on), as well as the special functions such as @@ and @CELL, will be covered in Chapter 14. Chapter 3 covered the basic date and time functions. At the end of this chapter, you will learn how to combine these and other date/time functions with other functions to create sophisticated formulas. However, you enter all 1-2-3 functions using a standard arrangement of parts, or *syntax,* that includes the function name and any required arguments. All function statements follow these rules:

- They begin with the @ sign.

- Next is the function name, spelled accurately and typed in upper- or lowercase or a combination.

- When required, arguments enclosed in parentheses follow the function name.

- When there are several arguments, they are separated by commas (unless you have selected a different argument separator, such as a semicolon, as described in the next chapter).

- Arguments must be in the proper order.

- There should be no spaces between the statement's components.

Aggregate Functions

Aggregate functions perform some of the most common spreadsheet calculations. In addition to @SUM, which was used in Chapters 1 and 2, this group includes functions that aggregate a range of cells, count the contents and average the range, find the largest and smallest numbers in the range, and determine the degree of variance. These functions also work with several different ranges at once or with numerous individual cells.

The @SUM Function

@SUM, one of the most frequently used functions, totals a group of values. In Figure 5.3, @SUM adds the values in a range of cells that has been named TOTVOL. It also totals the individual columns B through H.

Figure 5.3
Using @SUM

```
H19: (,0) @SUM(TOTVOL)                                              READY

        A         B        C        D        E        F        G       H    ◄
1  Projected Volume: Cairo                                                  ►
2                                                                           ▲
3               1990     1991     1992     1993     1994     1995    1996    ▼
4           1    425      451      478      506      537      569     609    ?
5           2    410      435      461      488      518      549     587
6           3    410      435      461      488      518      549     587
7           4    405      429      455      482      511      542     580
8           5    390      413      438      464      492      522     558
9           6    385      408      433      459      486      515     551
10          7    375      398      421      447      473      502     537
11          8    365      387      410      435      461      488     523
12          9    385      408      433      692      734      778     832
13         10    425      451      478      506      537      569     609
14         11    445      472      500      530      562      596     637
15         12    450      477      506      536      568      602     644
16             4,870    5,162    5,472    6,034    6,396    6,780   7,254
17
18
19                                                         Total   41,968
20
30-Oct-91   08:11 AM                                         NUM
```

You can use @SUM to total columns, rows, and ranges that include both columns and rows. @SUM just needs to know the coordinates of the range to be summed. The range needn't have values in every cell; the empty cells will be ignored.

The syntax of the @SUM function is as follows:

```
@SUM(list)
```

The argument is *list* rather than *range* because @SUM can actually be used to sum a list of values, including one or more ranges, single cells, or numeric expressions. @SUM(YEAR,A100,1000) would add the values in YEAR plus the value in cell A100 plus 1000. Whenever you sum more than one value or range of values you must separate the items in the list with commas. For example, @SUM(YEAR,MONTH) would sum two ranges, one named YEAR and one called MONTH.

There are several advantages to using @SUM rather than a cell+cell+cell formula to total the values in a range. Rows or columns inserted within a summed range are automatically included in the range. For example, consider these two approaches to adding up values:

```
B2:            100      B2:            100
B3:            200      B3:            200
B4:            300      B4:            300
B5:          =====      B5:          =====
B6: @SUM(B2..B4)        B6: +B2+B3+B4
```

In the example on the left, you can easily insert an extra row into the spreadsheet to include another value in the calculation. If you place the cell pointer on row 4 and issue the Worksheet Insert Row command to include one more row, cells B4, B5, and B6 become cells B5, B6, and B7. The formula that was in B6 but is now in B7 becomes @SUM(B2..B5). If you enter a value in B4, it will be included in the @SUM calculation.

The same is not true if you have used the cell+cell+cell method of adding. Here are the results for both of the examples after a row and a new value of 250 have been inserted at B4:

```
B2:            100      B2:            100
B3:            200      B3:            200
B4:            250      B4:            250
B5:            300      B5:            300
B6:          =====      B6:          =====
B7: @SUM(B2..B5)        B7: +B2+B3+B5
```

Inserting new rows within the summed range increases the range to include the new cells. Individually referenced cells are not automatically added to + formulas.

There is one potential pitfall when you insert rows for new items, even if you use @SUM. In the example, the integrity of the @SUM formula is preserved if you insert a row at row 3, 4, or 5. If you insert at row 2, the whole set of numbers is moved down. However, because 1-2-3 inserts new rows above the current cell, the new B2 is not included in the @SUM formula and, if you enter a value into B2, it is therefore not included in the total.

As a rule, you add a cell to a summed column if you insert a row between the first and last cell of the range. Since it is quite natural to add numbers to the bottom of a list, you might want to include the row below the last number when you create an @SUM formula, assuming that cell is blank or contains a label. For instance, you can change B7's formula in the previous example to @SUM(B2..B6), including the set of dashes in B6 in the @SUM range. You can then place the cell pointer on row 6, below the last number, insert a new row, and have that row be included in the range. When 1-2-3 calculates the @SUM function, labels in the range have a value of 0 and do not affect the answer.

The @COUNT Function

The @COUNT function counts the number of items or nonempty cells in a list of ranges and/or single cells. Most often it is used to count the number of items in a single range. This function is useful for worksheets that include lists, since it can tell you how many entries there are in a column, and thus how many items there are in a list. You simply need to tell @COUNT the location of the cells to be counted. Its syntax is as follows:

```
@COUNT(list)
```

Note that 1-2-3 includes labels when calculating @COUNT. Thus the count for a summed range that includes a line of labels might be greater than you expect. For example, the following arrangement results in an answer of 6 when summed, as opposed to an answer of 4 when counted:

```
B1:              2        B1:              2
B2:              2        B2:              2
B3:              2        B3:              2
B4:           ====        B4:           ====
B5:  @SUM(B1..B4) B5:  @COUNT(B1..B4)
```

Only if cell B4 were empty would the count be 3.

The @AVG Function

The @AVG function gives the average of values in a range of cells and has the following syntax:

```
@AVG(list)
```

In Figure 5.4, this function is used to calculate the average monthly volume.

Figure 5.4
Using @AVG

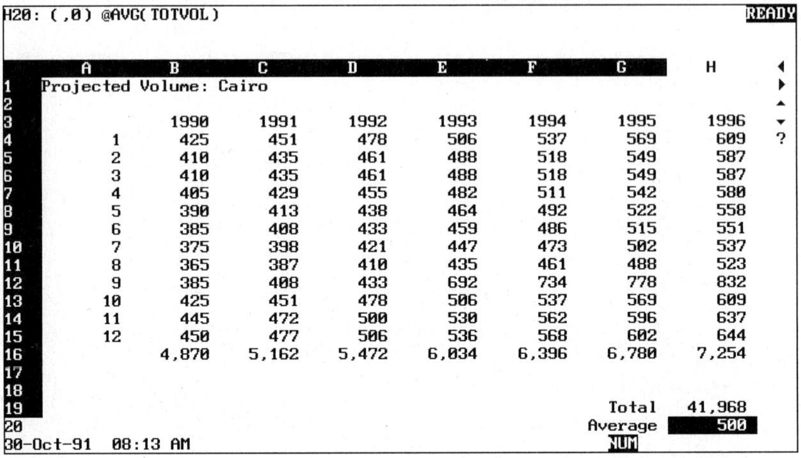

```
H20: (,0) @AVG(TOTVOL)                                              READY

        A         B         C         D         E         F         G         H      ◀
1   Projected Volume: Cairo                                                           ▶
2                                                                                     ▲
3                 1990      1991      1992      1993      1994      1995      1996     ▼
4           1      425       451       478       506       537       569       609    ?
5           2      410       435       461       488       518       549       587
6           3      410       435       461       488       518       549       587
7           4      405       429       455       482       511       542       580
8           5      390       413       438       464       492       522       558
9           6      385       408       433       459       486       515       551
10          7      375       398       421       447       473       502       537
11          8      365       387       410       435       461       488       523
12          9      385       408       433       692       734       778       832
13         10      425       451       478       506       537       569       609
14         11      445       472       500       530       562       596       637
15         12      450       477       506       536       568       602       644
16               4,870     5,162     5,472     6,034     6,396     6,780     7,254
17
18
19                                                            Total    41,968
20                                                            Average      500
30-Oct-91   08:13 AM                                          NUM
```

Like @SUM, the @AVG function works well with columns, rows, and larger ranges, particularly if you use a range name. However, label cells are used in calculating the average. Essentially, the @AVG function combines @SUM with @COUNT. You could say that @AVG=@SUM/@COUNT. Since @COUNT gives a value of 1 to a label, the arrangement seen here would produce 6 when summed, but 1.5 when averaged:

```
B1:                 2            B1:             2
B2:                 2            B2:             2
B3:                 2            B3:             2
B4:             ====            B4:         ====
B5: @SUM(B1..B4)               B5: @AVG(B1..B4)
```

Only if cell B4 were empty would @AVG correctly determine the average of the values, 2.

The @MAX Function

The @MAX function finds the largest value in a specified group of cells and/or numeric expressions, and requires the following syntax:

```
@MAX(list)
```

Like the @SUM function, @MAX works well with range names. In Figure 5.5, for example, the range name TOTVOL was used in the formula @MAX (TOTVOL), which returns the highest value among all of the volume figures.

Figure 5.5
Using @MAX

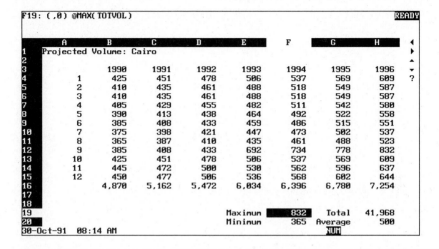

You can also use @MAX with single cells if you separate them with commas. Thus @MAX(B5,G3,K7) will tell you the largest amount in those three cells. In addition, you can use @MAX to compare a cell to a number. Thus @MAX(G5,10) returns the value in G5 if it is greater than 10; otherwise, it returns the value 10. This feature is handy when you must enter zero instead of the result of a subtraction whenever that subtraction results in a negative number. For example, in a tax-form spreadsheet, you might use a formula like (@MAX,G5,0) to enter the amount from line 5 or 0, whichever is greater.

The @MIN Function

A corollary to the @MAX function, the @MIN function returns the smallest value in a group of cells and/or numeric expressions, using the syntax:

    @MIN(list)

In Figure 5.5, @MIN was used to determine the lowest monthly volume figure.

You can use @MIN to identify the lowest value in lists such as inventories. You can also use @MIN to determine the lowest balance for a customer's credit or checking account. Like @MAX, @MIN works with several arguments, some of which can be constants. For instance, @MIN(100,G2..G15) will return 100 or the lowest value in G2..G15 if this is lower than 100.

The @STD Function

The standard deviation function (@STD) returns the standard deviation for a given group of cells and/or numeric expressions that represent a population of data. It requires the syntax:

```
@STD(list)
```

Like other aggregate functions, @STD is usually applied to a single range of cells. The standard deviation of a set of values is a measure of how much variation there is from the average of the values. The standard deviation is the square root of the variance.

The @VAR Function

The @VAR function returns a measure of variance for a list of ranges, cells and/or numeric expressions. That is, it returns the amount of variation between individual values and the mean of the population, using the syntax:

```
@VAR(list)
```

The result of the @VAR function is the square of the standard deviation of the same set of values.

Arithmetic Functions

Arithmetic functions affect the way numbers are calculated. They are often used when the outcome of a formula needs to be modified—for example, when a result should be rounded or a negative number turned into a positive number.

The @ABS Function

The @ABS function returns the *absolute value,* or positive equivalent, of a number. Its syntax is as follows:

```
@ABS(x)
```

The formula @ABS(B5) returns the absolute value of the value in B5. In other words, if B5 is either 1.5 or –1.5, @ABS(B5) equals 1.5.

The @INT Function

The @INT function drops the decimal places from a number. Its syntax is as follows:

```
@INT(x)
```

Thus, the formula @INT(B5) results in 2 when B5 contains 2.75. The value is stripped of digits that follow the decimal place, rather than rounded up to 3.

The @MOD Function

You use the modulus function (@MOD) when you need the number that remains after one number is divided by another. @MOD returns the remainder of x divided by y, as in

    @MOD(x,y)

Thus, the formula @MOD(B5,5) = 1 when B5 contains the value 36, since 36 divided by 5 yields 7 with a remainder of 1. The @MOD function is useful when you need to figure shipping factors. For example, you could use

    @MOD(CASES_ORDERED,CASES_PER_TRUCK)

to determine how many cases will be left after a large order has been loaded onto trucks. Note that you cannot use zero as the value for the y argument in an @MOD formula, since you cannot divide by zero. Doing so produces an ERR message in the formula cell.

The @RAND Function

When you need a random number in a cell, you can use the @RAND function, which produces a uniformly distributed random number greater than or equal to 0 and less than 1. @RAND takes no argument. You will normally want to combine the results of @RAND with a formula to produce a number within a certain range. You do this by enclosing the high end and low end of the range, separated by a hyphen, within a pair of parentheses, and then multiplying that by the @RAND function added to the low-end number. Thus,

    (49-1)*@RAND+1

would produce a random number from 1 to 49. If you need to get a whole number from the @RAND function, you must use @INT or @ROUND.

Although random numbers might not seem useful in a program designed to help you organize and accurately analyze information, they can come in handy when you want to fill cells with numbers to test a spreadsheet design. Several of the models in this book were created from random numbers.

Note that the result of an @RAND function changes each time the worksheet is recalculated. You can trigger recalculation of a formula containing @RAND by using the Edit key (F2). Highlight the cell containing the formula and press F2. When you press Enter to return the formula to the cell, notice that the @RAND function has picked a new number.

Because @RAND returns a new result every time the worksheet recalculates, you may have problems creating values used elsewhere in the worksheet. However, you can fix data generated by @RAND by using the Range Value command to change the formula to a value.

The @ROUND Function

The @ROUND function controls the number of decimal places associated with spreadsheet values. Its syntax is

```
@ROUND(x,n)
```

where x is a value or expression resulting in a value, or a reference to a cell containing a formula or value, and n is the desired number of decimal places. The value of n should be between –15 and +15 and should be an integer (whole number). 1-2-3 will round the n argument to an integer. The result of @ROUND(1/3,2) is thus .33.

Normally, 1-2-3 retains up to 15 decimal places in calculations that result in fractions. When you use a display format that limits the number of decimal places, fractions are not displayed in their entirety but are still active. However, when you're summing numbers that contain longer fractions than are revealed, totals can appear incorrect as the fractions accumulate. Thus, in the following example, if each of the cells B1 through B3 contained the value 3.33 displayed in Fixed format, with zero decimal places, the total would look wrong:

```
B1  3.33 displayed as 3
B2  3.33 displayed as 3
B3  3.33 displayed as 3
B4  @SUM(B1..B3)  = 10
```

To solve this problem, you need to round the numbers being totaled with @ROUND. The function rounds off x, using n as the number of digits to round to. The effect on the above example is shown here:

```
B1  @ROUND(3.33,0) = 3
B2  @ROUND(3.33,0) = 3
B3  @ROUND(3.33,0) = 3
B4  @SUM(B1..B3)   = 9
```

Of course, this does not resolve the problem that recurring fractions can cause. You can see an example of this in Figure 5.6, which makes two attempts to show an even distribution of a $10,000 grant between three colleges. The numbers on the left are created by dividing B3 by 3 and then summing the results. The numbers on the right use @ROUND(B3/3,0) to remove the decimal places. Both sets of figures are formatted to two decimal places with the Currency format. In many situations, adding @ROUND to a series of formulas simplifies the task of balancing a worksheet, but you should be aware of problems like the one in the figure.

Figure 5.6

Using @ROUND

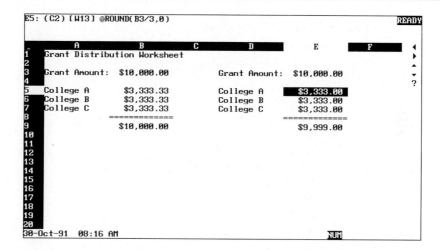

You can combine @ROUND with @RAND to produce a whole number within a specified range, as in the following formula:

```
@ROUND(((49-1)*@RAND+1),0)
```

This produces a number from 1 to 49 with no decimal places.

Using a negative number as the *n* argument rounds up values to the next highest unit of 10. For example, @ROUND(1257,–1) results in 1260 and @ROUND(1257,–2) results in 1300. This feature is useful when you want to deal in approximate values. However, you should use negative *n* arguments sparingly because the larger the negative value the further the result moves from the original figure. Thus @ROUND(1257,–3) results in 1000, and if the negative *n* argument is equal to or greater than the number of digits in the value being rounded, the result is 0. That is, @ROUND(1257,–4) = 0.

You can also use @ROUND to resolve problems that may arise from slight inaccuracies in the way that 1-2-3 handles numbers, as described earlier in this chapter under "Calculating Big and Little Numbers." If you are comparing two formula results, you might want to use @ROUND to limit the number of decimal places that can affect the outcome. For example, when working with numbers that should be dollars and whole cents, you can use @ROUND with a decimal place argument of 2. An example of this is given later in this chapter under "Crossfooting with @IF."

The @EXP Function

The @EXP (exponent) function returns the value of e (a constant approximately equal to 2.7182818285) raised to the power of x, as in

```
@EXP(x)
```

where x is equal to a numeric value less than or equal to 709. Thus, if x is 2, e has been squared. The @EXP function is the inverse of a natural logarithm, @LN. If the value of x is greater than 230.25 or less than or equal to –228, 1-2-3 can calculate and store the result, but cannot display it. (Instead, it fills the cell with asterisks.) If x is greater than 790, the @EXP function returns ERR.

The @SQRT Function

You can find the square root of a number or formula in 1-2-3 with the @SQRT function, which uses the syntax:

```
@SQRT(x)
```

For example, @SQRT(B5) returns the square root of the value in B5. Square roots of negative numbers produce the response ERR. Use the @ABS function to make the value a positive number.

One typical application of @SQRT is in the calculation of the hypotenuse, or slope, of a triangle. For example:

```
@SQRT(base*base+height*height)
```

An example of this is given later in this chapter in the section "Trigonometrical Functions."

The @LN and @LOG Functions

The @LN(x) and @LOG(x) functions return the log base e of x and the log base 10 of x, respectively. Thus @LN(100) = 4.60517 and @LOG(100) = 2. If the value of x is less than or equal to 0, these functions return the ERR message in the cell in which they were applied.

Financial Functions

1-2-3 provides extensive functions for financial calculations. Using these functions, you can calculate annuities and mortgage payments, present values, and numerous other figures that would otherwise require a lengthy formula.

Terminology

There are some basic terms and conditions common to all 1-2-3 financial functions. Table 5.2 explains the arguments used in these functions. Note that 1-2-3 stipulates that interest rates be stated as a percentage per period. For example, when figuring monthly loan payments with the @PMT function, you must state the interest argument as a percentage per month.

Table 5.2   **Arguments Used in Financial Functions**

Argument	Definition
cost	The amount paid for an asset.
future-value	An amount to be accumulated.
interest	A constant periodic interest rate. Must be stated to match the period of time assumed in the calculation, such as that implied by a term argument (for example .15/12 would state a 15.00% annual percentage rate as a monthly rate).
guess	An estimated rate of return.
life	The number of periods it will take to depreciate an asset.
payments	A single value representing a series of equal regularly timed payments.
period	The time period for which you want to find the depreciation allowance.
present-value	An amount valued today.
principal	An amount to be borrowed.
range	A group of cells containing a series of values representing cash flows at regular intervals (negative numbers representing cash outflows).
salvage	The estimated value of an asset at the end of its useful life.
term	A number of periods of time; determines the unit used in the interest argument. For example, if term is stated as 12, meaning 12 months, then interest must be stated at a monthly rate.

The @PMT Function

As you saw in Chapter 1, the @PMT function calculates the amount required to pay back a loan in equal payments based on a given principal or amount borrowed, a rate of interest, and a loan term. The syntax for @PMT is as follows:

```
@PMT(principal,interest,term)
```

Principal is the amount being borrowed. *Interest* is the interest being charged. *Term* is the life of the loan. Note that *interest* must be greater than –1 and *term* cannot be zero. The values for *principal*, *interest*, and *term* can be numeric constants, numeric fields, or formulas that result in numbers.

Figure 5.7 shows a loan calculation worksheet that demonstrates the argument requirements of the @PMT function. Since the *interest* argument needs to be supplied as a percentage per period but is normally quoted as an annual percentage rate, the loan payment formula divides the rate in E4 by the number of payments per year (E3). Likewise, the term of the loan is stated in years (E2) for convenience and then multiplied by the payments per year (E3) in the formula.

You could adjust this payment-per-year value for quarterly (4), semi-annual (2), or annual (1) payments. Also note that the payment formula uses @ROUND to give a practical amount.

Figure 5.7
Using @PMT

```
E5: (,2) [W12] @ROUND(@PMT(E1,E4/E3,E2*E3),2)                          READY

        A       B        C        D          E      F      G
1   Principal............................  12,500.00
2   Loan term in years...................      4
3   Number of payments per year..........      12
4   Annual interest rate (%A.P.R).........  12.50%
5   Payment per period....................    332.25
6   Total of payments.....................  15,948.00
7   Total interest paid...................   3,448.00
8
9   PMT  Paid in   Paid in   Cumulative  Remaining
10   #   Interest  Prinicpal  Interest   Balance
11   1    130.21    202.04     130.21    12,297.96
12   2    128.10    204.15     258.31    12,093.81
13   3    125.98    206.27     384.29    11,887.54
14   4    123.83    208.42     508.12    11,679.12
15   5    121.66    210.59     629.78    11,468.53
16   6    119.46    212.79     749.24    11,255.74
17   7    117.25    215.00     866.49    11,040.74
18   8    115.01    217.24     981.49    10,823.49
19   9    112.74    219.51   1,094.24    10,603.99
20  10    110.46    221.79   1,204.70    10,382.20
30-Oct-91   08:17 AM                                        NUM
```

A Payment Table

Often you want to see a loan payment table that shows the split between interest and principal as well as the amount of principal left unpaid. You can lay out a table of payments below the mortgage calculations, as shown in Figure 5.7. The table consists of five columns. Column A, the payment number, runs from 1 to 48 in cells A11 through A58. Column B calculates the portion of each payment that is interest, while column C shows the portion paid to reduce the principal. Column D maintains a running total of interest, and column E tracks the declining principal. Figure 5.8 exposes the first few rows of the formulas that make up this table. This is done with the Text format, which shows formulas instead of their results.

Figure 5.8
Payment table
formulas

```
B11: (T) [W14] +E1*$E$4/12                                                   READY
        A        B          C            D            E          F    ◄
1   Principal.................................     12,500.00           ▲
2   Loan term in years........................            4           ▼
3   Number of payments per year...............           12
4   Annual interest rate (%A.P.R).............       12.50%           ?
5   Payment per period........................       332.25
6   Total of payments.........................    15,948.00
7   Total interest paid.......................     3,448.00
8
9   PMT  Paid in     Paid in      Cumulative   Remaining
10   #   Interest    Prinicipal   Interest     Balance
11   1   +E1*$E$4/12 +$E$5-B11    +B11         +E1-C11
12   2   +E11*$E$4/12 +$E$5-B12   +D11+B12     +E11-C12
13   3   +E12*$E$4/12 +$E$5-B13   +D12+B13     +E12-C13
14   4   +E13*$E$4/12 +$E$5-B14   +D13+B14     +E13-C14
15   5   121.66      210.59       629.78       11,468.53
16   6   119.46      212.79       749.24       11,255.74
17   7   117.25      215.00       866.49       11,040.74
18   8   115.01      217.24       981.49       10,823.49
19   9   112.74      219.51       1,094.24     10,603.99
20  10   110.46      221.79       1,204.70     10,382.20
30-Oct-91   08:20 AM                                       NUM
```

At the bottom of the table, you can create totals for columns B and C to check the accuracy of the calculations. The total principal reduction is not exactly equal to the principal of the loan because of the need to accept payments in dollars and whole cents. As any banker knows, there are several ways of dealing with this kind of minor imbalance in a loan amortization. Figure 5.9 displays the bottom of this particular table, where the last value in column E is displayed as (0.00). The actual value is –0.00085705, but this number is too small to be of significance. The formulas used in Figure 5.7 are not the only ways to generate a loan table. However, this example is fairly typical.

Finally, note that Figures 5.7 through 5.9 calculate the remaining balance on the loan using simple interest, the method commonly used by banks for mortgages and personal loans. Some lending institutions use the so-called rule of 78 to calculate the amount left unpaid, determining interest with a system like sum-of-the-years, seen later under the @SYD function.

Investment Functions

1-2-3 offers several financial functions that help you evaluate investments. These functions—@PV, @NPV, @FV, @RATE, and @IRR—are discussed in the following sections.

The Importance of Present Value

When you evaluate a potential investment, it helps to know the investment's present value. Suppose that you are offered an investment opportunity that will pay you $1,050 after one year if you invest $1,000 now. You know that simply putting the $1,000 in a good savings account will yield $1,060, so the

Figure 5.9
The bottom of the payment table

```
B59: (,2) [W14] @SUM(B11..B58)                                        READY
      A          B          C          D            E          F       ◀
41    31       56.54      275.71     2,951.67     5,151.92            ▶
42    32       53.67      278.58     3,005.33     4,873.33            ▲
43    33       50.76      281.49     3,056.10     4,591.85            ▼
44    34       47.83      284.42     3,103.93     4,307.43            ?
45    35       44.87      287.38     3,148.80     4,020.05
46    36       41.88      290.37     3,190.67     3,729.67
47    37       38.85      293.40     3,229.52     3,436.27
48    38       35.79      296.46     3,265.32     3,139.82
49    39       32.71      299.54     3,298.02     2,840.27
50    40       29.59      302.66     3,327.61     2,537.61
51    41       26.43      305.82     3,354.04     2,231.79
52    42       23.25      309.00     3,377.29     1,922.79
53    43       20.03      312.22     3,397.32     1,610.57
54    44       16.78      315.47     3,414.10     1,295.10
55    45       13.49      318.76     3,427.59       976.34
56    46       10.17      322.08     3,437.76       654.26
57    47        6.82      325.43     3,444.57       328.82
58    48        3.43      328.82     3,448.00       (0.00)
59 Totals     3,448.00  12,500.00
60
30-Oct-91   08:24 AM                                            NUM
```

investment does not seem worthwhile. In other words, the investment promises a 5% return whereas you can get 6% elsewhere.

You can also compare the promised yield of an investment with your estimate of realistic alternative yields by discounting the total payments you would receive from the investment. *Discounting* means using a reasonable return rate (a rate you could expect on a safe alternative investment) to determine how much you would need to invest today to acquire the same amount of money in the specified time frame. If this discounted value is greater than the amount you are considering investing, the investment is a good one. Another term for the discounted value is present value.

For example, suppose you want to determine the present or discounted value of the venture offering a 12-month return of $1,050 on an initial investment of $1,000. You would take the $1,050 and divide it by the number of payments plus the rate of return on the alternative investment, in this case, 6%. The formula is thus 1050/(1+.06) and the answer, the present value of $1,050 received a year from now discounted at a rate of 6%, is $991. Since the present value of the promised return is less than the price of the investment, $1,000, the investment is not a good one. To use 1-2-3 for this kind of analysis, you use the @PV and @NPV functions, which can handle investments promising more than one annual payback amount.

The @PV Function

To calculate the present value of a simple annuity (a regular series of equal payments), use the @PV function, which has the following syntax:

```
@PV(payments,interest,term)
```

Payments, *interest*, and *term* can be numeric constants, numeric cells, or a formula that results in a number. *Interest* must be greater than –1.

For example, suppose someone has offered to make five annual payments of $30,000 in return for your investment of $110,000. You know that you can get a 12% return if you invest this money elsewhere. To determine the present value of the payments you would receive under this plan, you would create a spreadsheet like that shown on the left side of Figure 5.10. Note that the @PV function returns $108,143.29, indicating that this is the most you should consider investing in return for the five $30,000 payments.

Figure 5.10
Using @PV

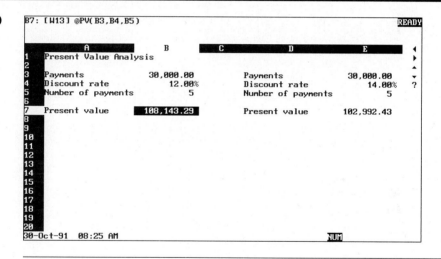

Suppose that you were offered the five payments of $30,000 in return for an initial investment of $100,000. Since the present value of the promised return is shown to be greater than the proposed investment amount, you might want to approve the investment. However, while the @PV function allows you to take into account the time value of money when comparing investment opportunities, you must still bear in mind less readily quantifiable factors such as risk. Typically, the discount rate represents a zero risk alternative such as CDs or Treasury notes. The right of Figure 5.10 illustrates that if the safe rate of return is 14% the present value falls from just over $108,000 to just less than $103,000.

The @NPV Function

Closely related to @PV is the @NPV function, which calculates the *net present value* of returns on an investment, based on a discount rate. The net present value of an investment should be greater than zero, otherwise it offers no better return than investing at the discount rate. Whereas @PV assumes equal amounts of cash flow from the investment or a single lump sum, the @NPV function handles unequal amounts returned from the investment, using the syntax

```
@NPV(interest,range)
```

where *interest* is the discount interest rate and *range* is a group of cells containing the cash outlay and flows from the investment. Typically, the first value in *range* is the amount invested and further values are returns on the investment. The stream of cash is assumed to be constant (at regular intervals) but the amounts can vary. For example, suppose you are promised three annual payments—of $30,000, $40,000, and $50,000—in return for your investment of $100,000. You would calculate the net present value of this proposition with the formula:

```
@NPV(.12,CASH)
```

The first argument is the discount interest rate of 12%. The second argument is the name of the range containing the values –100000,30000,40000,50000. In other words, the first value is the investment you make, and the second, third, and fourth values are the returns to you. The result is less than zero (–5,122.78 in fact), which suggests that this is not a good investment.

Suppose you are still interested in the investment and counter with a demand for returns of $35,000, $45,000, and $50,000. The values in CASH would be –100000,35000,45000,50000.

The result is positive, 2,422.09, suggesting that the investment is now much more profitable. Figure 5.11 contains a worksheet used to evaluate a further proposal that offers payments over four years in return for an initial investment of $110,000. The formula in B17 of Figure 5.11 is @NPV(B13,CASH).

Timing Investments

With all financial functions, including @NPV, you need to pay attention to the assumptions that 1-2-3 makes about timing. In @PV and @NPV calculations, 1-2-3 assumes payment at the end of the period. That is, the model in Figure 5.12 actually represents putting out $110,000 one year from the beginning of the project and receiving the first payment of $27,500 at the end of the second year. However, it's more likely that you will want to base calculations upon investing at the beginning of the first period and receiving the first return payment at the beginning of the second period.

To accommodate this assumption, you take the initial investment out of the @NPV argument and place it at the end of the formula, as in cell B17 of Figure 5.12. The result shows a slightly improved investment based on the new assumptions.

Figure 5.11
Using @NPV

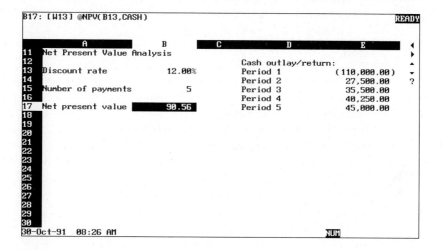

Figure 5.12
Revised @NPV
calculation

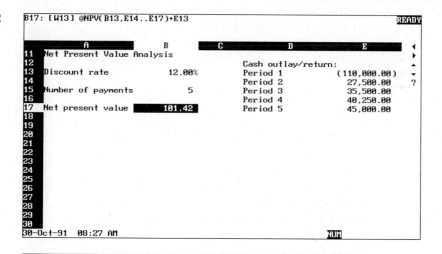

Also note that you can make a similar adjustment to the assumptions used with @PV. In Figure 5.13, the formula in B7 is as follows:

```
@PV(B3,B4,B5-1)+B3
```

This formula now reflects payments at the beginning rather than the end of the periods.

Figure 5.13
Revised @PV
calculation

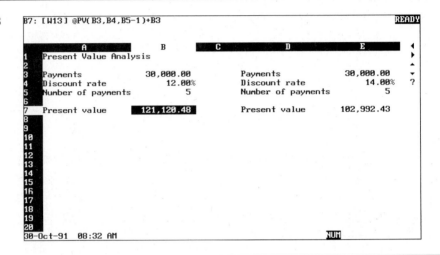

The @RATE Function

Suppose you have a sum of money to invest and an idea of the amount of money you want to accumulate. The @RATE function enables you to calculate the interest rate required to achieve your goal. Its syntax is as follows:

```
@RATE(future-value,present-value,term)
```

The @RATE function returns the rate of interest required to grow a present value into a specified target value over a stated term. For example, suppose you want to accumulate $30,000 to pay for college. You have $15,000 in a savings account, and college is six years away. The @RATE function will tell you what interest rate you need to achieve this goal:

```
@RATE(30000,15000,6) = .122462 or roughly 12.25%
```

The @IRR Function

When you want to compare your yields from different investments, you can use the @IRR function to calculate their internal rate of return. This function uses the syntax

```
@IRR(guess,range)
```

where *guess* is your estimate of what the answer will be and *range* is a reference to a range of cells containing amounts of cash flow. Typically, the first number in the range will be a negative one, indicating the initial payment or investment. The @IRR function assumes that the payments occur at the end of the period.

Generally, an investment is attractive if it shows an internal rate of return greater than the rate you can obtain elsewhere, the so-called *comparison* or *hurdle* rate. Figure 5.14 uses the @IRR function to compare three different investments. The third investment offers the best return, as it results in the highest @IRR. If you enter an @IRR formula and get an error, try altering the guess argument, using a percentage closer to the probable return.

Figure 5.14

Using @IRR

```
F12: (P2) @IRR(F4,F6..F10)                                              READY

      A    B       C       D      E       F      G    H        I
1
2         Compare different pay back schedules - internal rate of return
3
4         Estimate   12.00%      Estimate   12.00%      Estimate   12.00%   ?
5
6         Payment 1 (10,000)     Payment 1 (10,000)     Payment 1 (10,000)
7         Payment 2  2,500       Payment 2  2,500       Payment 2  5,000
8         Payment 3  2,500       Payment 3  2,500       Payment 3  3,000
9         Payment 4  2,500       Payment 4  3,000       Payment 4  2,500
10        Payment 5  3,000       Payment 5  5,000       Payment 5  2,500
11
12          IRR =    1.92%         IRR =    10.03%        IRR =    13.22%
13
14
15
16
17
18
19
20
30-Oct-91  08:39 AM                                              NUM
```

The @FV Function

The @FV function calculates future value, as shown in Figure 5.15. Here the @FV function returns the future value of an annual retirement fund investment of $10,000 per year, earning 15% per year over a 20-year term using the formula @FV(D2,D3,D4) in cell D5. The @FV function has the following syntax:

@FV(*payments,interest,term*)

Payments is a numeric value representing the amount of equal payments to be made. *Interest* is a numeric value greater than zero representing periodic interest rate. *Term* is a numeric value representing the number of periods of the investment. You can use @FV to see the effects of regular savings plans and evaluate such investments against alternative uses of funds. @FV assumes that the payments are made at the beginning of the period.

The @TERM Function

@TERM is an alternative function if you have a target figure or goal in mind for your investments. This function calculates how long it will take a series of equal, evenly spaced investments to accumulate to a target amount based on a steady rate of interest. The syntax of the @TERM function is as follows:

@TERM(*payments*,*interest*,*future-value*)

Figure 5.15

Using @FV, @TERM, and @CTERM

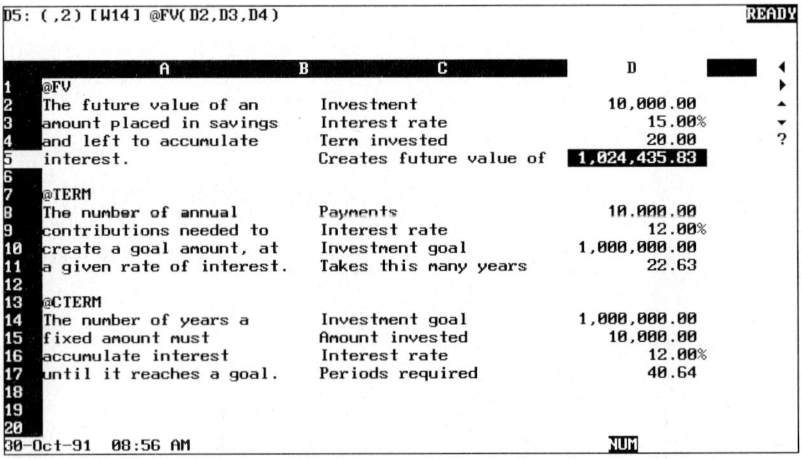

```
D5: (,2) [W14] @FV(D2,D3,D4)                                      READY

                    A              B           C            D          ◄
                                                                       ►
1   @FV                                                                ▲
2   The future value of an     Investment            10,000.00        ▼
3   amount placed in savings   Interest rate            15.00%
4   and left to accumulate     Term invested            20.00          ?
5   interest.                  Creates future value of 1,024,435.83
6
7   @TERM
8   The number of annual       Payments             10,000.00
9   contributions needed to    Interest rate           12.00%
10  create a goal amount, at   Investment goal   1,000,000.00
11  a given rate of interest.  Takes this many years   22.63
12
13  @CTERM
14  The number of years a      Investment goal   1,000,000.00
15  fixed amount must          Amount invested      10,000.00
16  accumulate interest        Interest rate           12.00%
17  until it reaches a goal.   Periods required        40.64
18
19
20
30-Oct-91  08:56 AM                                       NUM
```

In Figure 5.15, the formula

@TERM(D8,D9,D10)

in cell D11 is used to calculate the number of years it will take to accumulate $1,000,000 if you invest $10,000 per year at 12%.

The @CTERM Function

The @CTERM function calculates the time it takes for a single investment to grow to some future amount. It has the following syntax:

@CTERM(*interest*,*future-value*,*present-value*)

The *interest* is a numeric value representing the fixed interest rate per compounding period. The *future-value* argument is a numeric value representing the future value that an investment will reach at some point. The *present-value* argument is a numeric value representing the present value of the investment. In Figure 5.15, the formula

@CTERM(D16,D14,D15)

in cell D17 shows that it will take over 40 years to achieve the goal of reaching $1,000,000 from an initial investment of $10,000 earning 12% per year.

Financial Functions

Depreciation Functions

1-2-3's three different methods for calculating depreciation are shown in Figure 5.16, which displays both results and formulas. Depreciation is a method of accounting for the fact that most goods lose value over time. Calculations of income and valuations of assets often require an assessment of depreciation. In some cases, depreciation can be offset against revenue to reduce taxable income.

Figure 5.16

Depreciation functions

```
A1: [W6] 'Depreciation Methods:                                  READY

     A    B  C    D      E        F              G              
1  Depreciation Methods:                    Assumptions:
2
3  Straight Line                   Formulas      Value to depreciate
4        Year  1    2,089.00       @SLN(G4,G6,G8)        11,785.00
5        Year  2    2,089.00       @SLN(G4,G6,G8)     Salvage value
6        Year  3    2,089.00       @SLN(G4,G6,G8)          1,340.00
7        Year  4    2,089.00       @SLN(G4,G6,G8)     Estimated life
8        Year  5    2,089.00       @SLN(G4,G6,G8)              5
9  Double Declining
10       Year  1    4,714.00       @DDB(G4,G6,G8,C16)
11       Year  2    2,828.40       @DDB(G4,G6,G8,C17)
12       Year  3    1,697.04       @DDB(G4,G6,G8,C18)
13       Year  4    1,018.22       @DDB(G4,G6,G8,C19)
14       Year  5      187.34       @DDB(G4,G6,G8,C20)
15 Sum-of-the-years-digits
16       Year  1    3,481.67       @SYD(G4,G6,G8,C16)
17       Year  2    2,785.33       @SYD(G4,G6,G8,C17)
18       Year  3    2,089.00       @SYD(G4,G6,G8,C18)
19       Year  4    1,392.67       @SYD(G4,G6,G8,C19)
20       Year  5      696.33       @SYD(G4,G6,G8,C20)
30-Oct-91  08:58 AM                              NUM
```

Straight-Line Depreciation

The straight-line method results in an equal amount of depreciation per period. Its syntax is as follows:

```
@SLN(cost,salvage,life)
```

This form of depreciation is the simplest. As in all depreciation functions, *cost* is a numeric value representing the amount paid for an asset. *Salvage* is a numeric value representing the worth of an asset at the end of its useful life. *Life* is a numeric value representing the expected useful life of an asset.

Double-Declining-Balance Depreciation

The @DDB function calculates depreciation based on the double-declining method, using the following syntax:

```
@DDB(cost,salvage,life,period)
```

The @DDB function determines accelerated depreciation values for an asset, given the initial cost, end value, life expectancy, and depreciation period. *Period* is a numeric value representing the time period for which you want to determine the depreciation expense.

Sum-of-Years Depreciation

The @SYD function uses a method called the sum-of-the-years-digits to vary the rate at which depreciation is taken. This function needs to know the year for each calculation, and has the following syntax:

@SYD(*cost,salvage,life,period*)

You can use the @SYD function to compute a loan payout based on the rule of 78, which results in a larger payoff for loans than the simple interest calculation seen in Figure 5.7. Figure 5.17 shows a rule of 78 payout table, where the @SYD function is applied in cell B71. Note that this formula uses the @IF function, described next under "Logical Functions." This function ensures that the formula returns a zero if the payment number is greater than the total number of periods. Otherwise, it returns the @SYD result, rounded to two decimal places.

Figure 5.17

Loan table using @SYD

```
B71: (,2) [W12] @IF(A71>E62*E63,0,@ROUND(@SYD(E67,0,E62*E63,A71),2))    READY
```

	A	B	C	D	E	F	G
61	Principal.............................				12,500.00		
62	Loan term in years......................				4		
63	Number of payments per year..............				12		
64	Annual interest rate (%A.P.R)............				12.50%		
65	Payment per period.......................				332.25		
66	Total of payments.......................				15,948.00		
67	Total interest paid......................				3,448.00		
68							
69	PMT	Interest	Principal	Cumulative	Remaining		
70	#	paid	reduction	interest	balance		
71	1	140.73	191.52	140.73	12,308.48		
72	2	137.80	194.45	278.53	12,114.03		
73	3	134.87	197.38	413.40	11,916.65		
74	4	131.94	200.31	545.34	11,716.34		
75	5	129.01	203.24	674.35	11,513.10		
76	6	126.07	206.18	800.42	11,306.92		
77	7	123.14	209.11	923.56	11,097.81		
78	8	120.21	212.04	1,043.77	10,885.77		
79	9	117.28	214.97	1,161.05	10,670.80		
80	10	114.35	217.90	1,275.40	10,452.90		

```
30-Oct-91   09:20 AM                                                  NUM
```

Accelerated Cost Recovery

Some tax calculations use yet another method of depreciation known as the accelerated cost recovery system (ACRS). The rate of depreciation allowed by ACRS varies each year of the asset's life and depends on when the asset was placed in service. There is no ACRS function in 1-2-3, but you can use the @INDEX function to create tables of depreciation rates, based on the month the asset was placed in service and the year of the asset's life. @INDEX is a logical function and is described in the next section.

Logical Functions

1-2-3 provides a variety of functions that are useful when you need to enter logical arguments into formulas. Careful use of logical functions can greatly enhance the sophistication of your worksheets because formulas can be made to evaluate one or more conditions in a model. Formulas can choose between one or more answers and look up values within tables.

The Big If

@IF is one of 1-2-3's most powerful functions. It instructs 1-2-3 to choose between two actions based on whether a condition is true or false. For example, suppose that you are budgeting quarterly revenue and expense for a computer store, using a spreadsheet like the one shown in Figure 5.18. You have gotten good results from spending 5% of all revenue on advertising. Thus, advertising is normally revenue multiplied by .05. However, you know that money spent on advertising beyond a certain dollar amount, say, $2,500, is not effective.

To budget your advertising expenditures with a ceiling of $2,500, you can add the @IF function to the advertising expense formula, producing the formula shown in the control panel of Figure 5.18. This formula dictates that:

- If revenue times .05 is less than 2500

- Then advertising = revenue times .05

- Otherwise advertising = 2500

  The syntax for the @IF function is

  `@IF(condition,x,y)`

When the condition is true, the formula returns the result stated in the x part of the argument. Otherwise, it returns the result in the y part. True and false results can be constants, value or label cells, or other formulas. The true result and the false result can be any type of data.

Crossfooting with @IF

The @IF function is extremely versatile because it allows the spreadsheet to become intelligent—that is, to return one of two values based on a condition that you establish. You can use @IF in numerous situations in a typical worksheet. For example, you can use it to test the integrity of a spreadsheet, as in the expense report worksheet shown in Figure 5.19. Anyone who has filled out expense reports knows that the sum of the rows should equal the sum of the columns. When you lay out this kind of report in 1-2-3, the calculation is done for you. However, you should never assume that the work is always done correctly just because it is done electronically. The worksheet should be *crossfooted*, meaning that the aggregate of the row totals should be checked against the aggregate of the column totals.

Figure 5.18
Using @IF

```
B15: (,0) [W11] @IF(B9*0.05>2500,2500,B9*0.05)                          READY

        A          B          C         D          E        F          ◀
1  Computer Store                                                       ▶
2                                                                       ▲
3              Quarter 1  Quarter 2  Quarter 3  Quarter 4               ▼
4  Revenue:                                                             ?
5      Sales     24,550     28,560    34,330     38,770
6      Service    8,100      9,420    11,330     12,790
7      Training   8,910     10,360    12,460     14,070
8  ------------------------------------------------------------
9      Total     41,560     48,340    58,120     65,630
10
11 Expenses:
12     Lease      5,000      5,000     5,000      5,000
13     Salaries  18,000     18,000    18,000     18,000
14 Phones, etc.     850        850       850        850
15 Advertising    2,078      2,417     2,500      2,500
16 ------------------------------------------------------------
17     Total     25,928     26,267    26,350     26,350
18
19 Profit:
20             15,632     22,073    31,770     39,280
30-Oct-91  09:21 AM                                        NUM
```

The @IF formula in cell G17 of Figure 5.19 says that if the sum of the columns (the range called TOTD) equals the sum of the rows (the range called TOTA), the cell should contain the sum of the rows. Otherwise, it should contain an error message (produced by the @ERR function) to show that a mistake has been made. When a mistake has been detected, the ERR message appears as a label in cell G17. Note that the @ROUND function is used with the @SUM function to remove any errors arising from the way that 1-2-3 stores numbers.

Suppose that the formula in G17 returns ERR. You review the spreadsheet and discover that someone typed a number over a formula in column G, causing the sum of the columns to be incorrect. When you replace the erroneous value with the correct formula, the ERR message will disappear and the expense report will be correct.

Nesting the @IF Function
When you want to apply several conditions to a calculation, you can nest @IF statements. For example, nested @IF statements are used in Figure 5.20 to calculate commissions based on a percentage (4% to 6%) of sales. As you can see, the statement in D5 reads

```
@IF(C5<40000,0.04*C5,@IF(C5<50000,0.05*C5,C5*0.06))
```

This formula says that if the sales in C5 are less than $40,000, the commission will be 4% (0.04) of sales. If sales are greater than or equal to $40,000 but less than $50,000, the commission will be 5%. If sales are greater than or equal to $50,000, the commission will be 6%. It takes a little planning to nest @IF statements. However, if you write out the statement in English first, you can usually frame the actual formula to fit most conditional situations.

Figure 5.19
Crossfooting with @IF

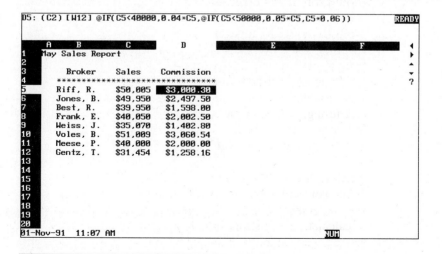

Figure 5.20
Nested @IF statements

The @IF function can return labels as well as values. For example, in the Broker Transaction Record in Figure 5.21, the word "Yes" in cell K9 is the result of an @IF formula. The record needs to show if special handling is required, based on the amount of the transaction, which is shown in H11. The formula in K9 states

```
@IF(H11>20000,"Yes","No")
```

Thus the word "Yes" is returned here because the amount in H11 is greater than 20,000.

Figure 5.21

Using @IF to return a label

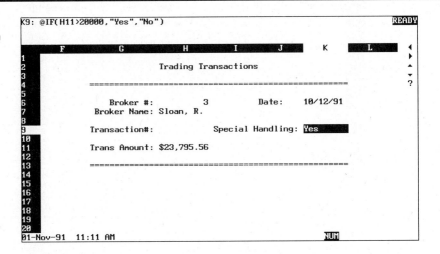

You could also enter the name of the broker with an @IF formula that looks for the broker number entered in H6 and responds with one of three names, like this:

```
@IF(H6=3,"Sloan, R.",@IF(H6=2,"Doe, J.",
@IF(H6=1,"James, E.",@ERR)))
```

This formula will result in the ERR message if the broker number is not 1, 2, or 3.

Lookup Tables

When you want to make a formula dependent on a range of conditions, there is an alternative to nesting @IF statements. You can instead have 1-2-3 refer to a table of conditions. Such *lookup tables* are vertical or horizontal lists of numbers with related values. Figure 5.22 shows a commission table that offers a simple way to determine the rate based on a broader range of sales levels.

The vertical list of sales levels in column E and related commission rates in column F show the rate applicable to any given level of sales. Any sales amount below \$35,000 earns a commission of 3.50%. Sales from \$35,000 to \$35,999 earn 3.75%, and so on. The bottom of the table shows that sales of \$50,000 and up earn 8.00%. This table of numbers, cells F23 through F39, was then named TABLE with the Range Advanced Create command. In cell D23 the formula reads

```
@VLOOKUP(C23,$TABLE,1)*C23
```

Figure 5.22

A vertical lookup table

```
D23: (C2) [W12] @VLOOKUP(C23,$TABLE,1)*C23                                READY

      A      B          C          D               E              F            ◄
21           Broker     Sales      Commission      Sales Level Commission      ►
22    ***************************************************************************▲
23           Riff, R.   $50,005    $4,000.40                    $0      3.50%   ▼
24           Jones, B.  $49,950    $3,621.38               $35,000      3.75%   ?
25           Best, R.   $39,950    $1,897.63               $36,000      4.00%
26           Frank, E.  $40,050    $2,002.50               $37,000      4.25%
27           Weiss, J.  $35,070    $1,315.13               $38,000      4.50%
28           Voles, B.  $51,009    $4,080.72               $39,000      4.75%
29           Meese, P.  $40,000    $2,000.00               $40,000      5.00%
30           Gentz, T.  $31,454    $1,100.89               $41,000      5.25%
31                                                         $42,000      5.50%
32                                                         $43,000      5.75%
33                                                         $44,000      6.00%
34                                                         $45,000      6.25%
35                                                         $46,000      6.50%
36                                                         $47,000      6.75%
37                                                         $48,000      7.00%
38                                                         $49,000      7.25%
39                                                         $50,000      8.00%
40
01-Nov-91   11:13 AM                                              NUM
```

In other words, the vertical lookup function is invoked to look up the value of cell C23 (the sales amount) in the range of cells named TABLE in column 1. The value that is found in the table, in this case the commission rate of 8.00%, is then multiplied by cell C23 to calculate the commission amount.

The syntax of the vertical lookup function is thus:

```
@VLOOKUP(x,range,column)
```

The *x* argument is the cell containing the value you are looking up in the table. The *range* should be consecutive columns of values. The *column* is the number of the column in the table that the formula should look to for its result. The column numbering is 0 for the first column, 1 for the next column to the right, and so on. In the example, the contents of C23 and column 0 of the lookup table must be values, and column 0 must contain a consecutive range of values. However, the contents of offset column 1 and any additional columns in the table can be labels.

You can also arrange lookup tables horizontally, as seen in Figure 5.23. The formula in H25 uses the @HLOOKUP function. This example supposes that each broker has a number and writes that number on sales transaction slips. A clerk then records the slips in the format seen in Figure 5.23. As the clerk enters the broker number, 1-2-3 looks up that number in the horizontal table of names.

The first row of a horizontal table is row 0, successive rows are numbered 1, 2, 3, and so on. The syntax of the @HLOOKUP function is as follows:

@HLOOKUP(*x*,*range*,*row*)

The first row of the table, row 0, must be a series of values. Successive rows can be values or labels. Row 1, which the formula references in this case, is a set of labels. The *row* argument is the number of the row from which you want the result taken.

Note that you do not have to use a range name for the lookup table reference in the formula. However, it's easier to refer to the cells of the table with a range name than it is to type something like G33..N34. This is particularly true if you want to copy the formula containing the reference to the table and thus need to make the cell references absolute, as in $G$33..$N$34. You can make a reference to a range named TABLE absolute by preceding it with a dollar sign. This was done in Figure 5.23 so that the formula could be correctly copied to cells C6 through C12. Absolute cell references are discussed in greater detail in the next chapter.

Figure 5.23

A horizontal lookup table

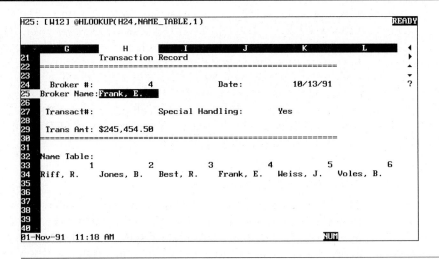

The @CHOOSE Function

Like a lookup table, the @CHOOSE function selects its responses based on a number. For example, if there were just a few brokers, you could use @CHOOSE in place of @HLOOKUP in cell H25 of Figure 5.23. If there were just four brokers, the formula in H25 could read

```
@CHOOSE(H24,"Riff, R.","Jones, B.","Best, R.","Frank, E.")
```

The number entered in cell H24 would thus determine the name placed into H25. The syntax of the @CHOOSE function is as follows:

```
@CHOOSE(offset,list)
```

If *offset* = 1, the first result in the *list* is used. If *offset* = 2, the second result is used, and so on. The value of *offset* must be a number between 1 and the total number of results in the argument. Values of *offset* outside that range will cause an error. If *offset* includes a decimal, 1-2-3 rounds off the value. *Offset* can be a numeric constant, a cell, or a formula. The results can be constants or formulas of any data type. However, all results must have the same data type.

The @ERR Function

When you want a cell to reflect an error, you can use the @ERR function, which takes no argument. The @ERR function returns the value ERR in the current cell. In addition, in most cases it creates the ERR message in any other cells that reference a cell that contains the ERR condition. The exceptions to this are the @COUNT, @ISERR, @ISNA, @ISNUMBER, @ISSTRING, @CELL, and @CELLPOINTER formulas. These formulas do not result in ERR if they reference a cell that contains ERR. The ERR value resulting from the @ERR function is the same as the ERR value produced by 1-2-3 when it encounters an error.

The @NA Function

The @NA function is like @ERR but it returns the value NA (not available) rather than the ERR message that 1-2-3 uses when you type a formula incorrectly. Note that if you calculate the @SUM, @AVG, @MIN, @MAX, @STD, or @VAR of a range that includes @NA, the result is @NA. Similarly, @NA plus, minus, times, or divided by anything equals @NA.

The @INDEX Function

The @INDEX function is a hybrid of the vertical and horizontal lookup tables. For this function, you state the column and row numbers for a value set in a table of values. @INDEX has the syntax:

@INDEX(*range,column-offset,row-offset*)

This function has a number of interesting applications, including the accelerated depreciation schedule seen in Figure 5.24. This figure is a table of the allowed rates of depreciation for real property placed in service between January 1, 1980 and March 15, 1984. The months are numbered across the top and the years of asset life listed down the side.

Figure 5.24
Using @INDEX

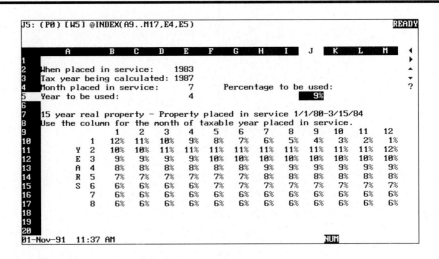

By answering the questions in the upper-left corner of the screen, you provide the index data needed for the formula used in J5:

@INDEX(A9..M17,E4,E5)

The number 7 in E4 is the column coordinate; the number 4 in E5 is the row coordinate. The cell at which they intersect, H13, contains the value 9% returned by the @INDEX formula. Note that the location of the coordinates within the indexed range corresponds to the number of columns and rows in the range, with the first row being 1, the second being 2, and so on. This is not the 0, 1, 2, 3 numbering used in the @VLOOKUP function or the A1, A2, A3 numbering of the cell coordinates.

Trigonometric Functions

If you work with geometry and trigonometry, 1-2-3 offers many helpful functions. While these functions are mainly used in engineering and scientific applications, they can be handy in many situations. You can calculate the angles, areas, and lengths of various shapes using these functions. You can even use them to generate curves in graphs.

The @PI Function

The @PI function provides the value of pi to ten decimal places. For calculations that require the value of pi, you can just type in **@PI**. The @PI function takes no argument; it simply returns the value 3.1415926536. The formula for calculating the circumference of a circle is thus:

```
2*@PI*radius
```

You can calculate the area of a circle by combining @PI and the exponent operator:

```
@PI*radius^2
```

This formula calculates pi times the square of the radius. Note that the exponent operator (^) is calculated before the multiplication (*) is performed.

Degrees and Radians

You can also use @PI to convert radians to degrees. In 1-2-3, the trigonometric functions like @SIN and @ASIN, described in a moment, work with values in radians. You can use @PI to convert degrees to radians, using these formulas:

```
1 degree = (@PI*2*radian)/360
```

or

```
@PI/180
```

You can convert angles expressed in radians to degrees using these formulas:

```
1 radian = 360/(@PI*2)
```

or

```
180/@PI
```

For example, suppose you have a plot of land in the shape of a right-angled triangle with sides of 30, 40, and 50 feet. You want to know the angle between the shortest and longest sides. One way to calculate this is to use @ASIN with the other two sides, as in

```
@ASIN(40/50)
```

The result is 0.927295, the angle expressed as a radian. To convert this value to degrees, you multiply by 180/@PI, like this:

```
@ASIN(40/50)*180/@PI
```

The result is approximately 53.13 degrees.

Sine, Cosine, Tangent

The @SIN, @COS, and @TAN functions return the trigonometric sine, cosine, and tangent of x, an angle measured in radians. You can convert an angle measured in degrees to one expressed in radians by using the @PI function. Thus @SIN(60*@PI/180) returns the sine of a 60-degree angle.

The inverse trigonometric functions—@ASIN, @ACOS, and @ATAN—save you from having to create these values from the @COS, @SIN, and @TAN functions. Each function returns an angle, measured in radians, given its sine, cosine, or tangent. For example, @ATAN2(x,y) calculates a four-quadrant arctangent from the x and y coordinates of a point.

Trigonometric Applications

You can use trigonometric functions in a wide variety of ways. The diagram in Figure 5.25 shows how various angles and lengths would be calculated using the trigonometric functions in 1-2-3 plus the @SQRT function described earlier.

Figure 5.25

Using trigonometric functions

Y = X/@TAN(@P/180*a)

Z = Y/@SIN@PI/180*b)

X = @SQRT(Z^2-Y^2)

b = 180/@PI*@ATAN(Y/X)

Z = Y/@COS(@PI/180)*a)

Calculations are based on a right-angle triangle using @COS, @SIN, @TAN, @ATAN, @PI, and @SQRT.

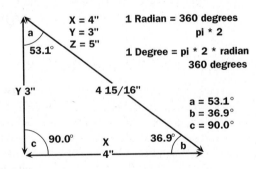

X = 4"
Y = 3"
Z = 5"

1 Radian = 360 degrees
pi * 2

1 Degree = pi * 2 * radian
360 degrees

a = 53.1°
b = 36.9°
c = 90.0°

Besides calculating angles and sides of triangles, trigonometric functions can generate a sequence of values that result in a curve when plotted. An example of this is a biorhythm chart, used to plot a person's physical, emotional, and mental energy on a time scale. In its simplest form, a biorhythm chart consists of three different cycles: 22 days for the physical level, 28 for the emotional level, and 32 for the mental level. The @SIN function is used to generate curves from these cycles, seen in Figure 5.26, which shows a simple biorhythm chart as drawn by the 1-2-3 Graph command.

Figure 5.26
A biorhythm chart

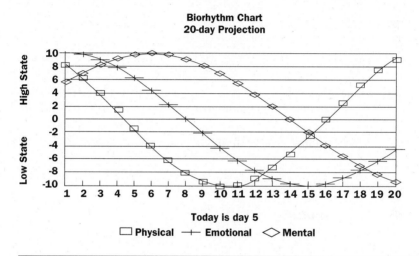

The worksheet from which this graph was generated is seen in Figure 5.27. The current date and the subject's date of birth are recorded and then extrapolated for the three different cycles. The numbers are then graphed on a scale of days. For more on the graphing of spreadsheet data, see Chapter 9.

Further Date and Time Functions

In Chapter 3, you learned how to use the basic date and time functions @DATE, @TIME, @NOW, and @TODAY. There are several other date and time related functions that can be useful when dealing with chronological data. This section reviews the use of the date part functions @DAY, @MONTH, @YEAR. The two date/time string functions @DATEVALUE and @TIMEVALUE are dealt with in Chapter 11.

Figure 5.27

A biorhythm
worksheet

```
F9: [W10] 10*@SIN(E9*@PI/11.5)                                    READY
        A        B      C     D        E        F        G        H
1                       BIORHYTHM CHARTING
2  Subject's birthday:                      Days charted:
3           10/07/53                                      20
4  The date today:                          Today is day:
5           11/25/91                                       5
6
7  Difference between:                      Cycles:
8                     Today - Birthday   Physical Emotional  Mental
9  Day number: 1      33,562    13,923        8.17    10.00    5.56
10             2      33,563    13,924        6.31     9.75    7.07
11             3      33,564    13,925        3.98     9.01    8.31
12             4      33,565    13,926        1.36     7.82    9.24
13             5      33,566    13,927      (1.36)     6.23    9.81
14             6      33,567    13,928      (3.98)     4.34   10.00
15             7      33,568    13,929      (6.31)     2.23    9.81
16             8      33,569    13,930      (8.17)     0.00    9.24
17             9      33,570    13,931      (9.42)   (2.23)    8.31
18            10      33,571    13,932      (9.98)   (4.34)    7.07
19            11      33,572    13,933      (9.79)   (6.23)    5.56
20            12      33,573    13,934      (8.88)   (7.82)    3.83
25-Nov-91  02:13 PM                                   NUM
```

Date Part Functions

When you enter a date with the @DATE function, 1-2-3 converts it to a date serial number, allowing you to perform math with dates. The statement @DATE(99,12,25) returns the value 33597, which appears as 25-Dec-91 when formatted with date format 1. There are several 1-2-3 functions designed to extract part of a date from a date value.

The @DAY function extracts the day of the month from a date value. It has the syntax

```
@DAY(date-number)
```

where *date-number* is a number under 73050.9999999. This number represents the highest date possible, December 31, 2099, and @DAY(73050) actually returns 31. The @DAY function converts the date serial number you supply as *date-number* into the number (1 through 31) associated with that day. The formula @DAY(A1) would return the answer 25, if A1 contained the number 33597 or the formula @DATE(91,12,25).

The @MONTH function returns the number (1 through 12) that corresponds to the month of the year represented by *date-number*. The @MONTH function has the syntax:

```
@MONTH(date-number)
```

Thus @MONTH(A1) returns 12, if the number in A1 is 33597 or A1 contains @DATE(91,12,25).

The @YEAR function returns the year of a date value and has the syntax:

```
@YEAR(date-number)
```

The formula @YEAR(A1) would produce the answer 91, if the value in A1 were any date serial number within 1991. You could use the formula @YEAR(A1)+1900 to get the result 1990. The @YEAR function returns 100 for dates in the year 2000, 101 for dates in the year 2001, and so on. This means that the formula @YEAR(A1)+1900 is accurate for all valid years.

You can use date part functions with cell references or in combination with other date functions. Thus, the formula

```
@MONTH(@DATE(91,12,25))
```

returns the answer 12. You can combine date functions with other functions for some useful formulas, such as this one, which results in the full name of the month corresponding to the date value in A1:

```
@CHOOSE(@MONTH(A1)-1,"January","February","March","April",
"May","June","July","August","September","October",
"November","December")
```

The @MONTH function finds out the month number from A1, which will be from 1 through 12. This number is then reduced by 1 to give a value from 0 to 11. This value is used as the first argument for the @CHOOSE function, which then looks up the corresponding case argument, from case0 to case11, which are the month names. Because the names are text, they have to be enclosed in quotes. For more on text in formulas see Chapter 11. A variation of the preceding formula can give you the name of the day of the week from a date in A1:

```
@CHOOSE(@MOD(A1,7),"Saturday","Sunday","Monday","Tuesday",
"Wednesday","Thursday","Friday")
```

You can also use @CHOOSE when you want a series of dates that are on the same day of the month, such as 3/1/91, 4/1/91, and so on. Because of the varying number of days in a month, this sort of series cannot be generated by either the Data Fill command or the simple formula of adding 30 days to the previous date. The following formula looks up the number of the month in A1, and then uses it to find the number of days in that month from a list of case arguments:

```
+A1+@CHOOSE(@MONTH(A1)-1,31,@IF(@MOD(@YEAR(A1),4)=0,29,28),
31,30,31,30,31,31,30,31,30,31)
```

The first case, corresponding to January, is 31. If the date in A1 were January 1, 1991, the above formula would add 31 days to that to get February 1. The second case uses the @IF function to return 29 if the year in A1 is a leap year; otherwise, it returns 28. The condition tested by the @IF statement is the year number modulo 4. If this is 0, meaning that the year is exactly divisible by 4, then the second case is 29. Since 91 modulo 4 is 3, the second case will be 28 if the year in A1 is 1991. The remaining cases list the days of the months for March through December.

Time Part Functions

You can use the @TIME function to enter a time value. For example, the time 11:35:00 p.m. is expressed as @TIME(23,35,00). The basic unit of time math is one day; thus 12 hours is represented by 0.5 and 1 hour by 0.04166, recurring. 1-2-3 can extract parts of the date from a date value, and it can also extract the elements of a time value. The time part functions are @HOUR(*time*), @MINUTE(*time-number*), @SECOND(*time-number*). For example, the formula @HOUR(A1) produces 10 and @MINUTE(A1) produces 30, if A1 contains either the value @TIME(10,30,00) or the number 0.4375, which is the serial number of 10:30 a.m.

You can use the time part functions in several ways. Suppose you want to indicate the shift during which a production report was made. You have entered the time in D5. The following formula will return the word "Late" if the hour is 12 or later and "Early" if the hour is before 12:

```
@IF(@HOUR(D5)>=12,"Late","Early")
```

Summary

You can make full use of functions by following these techniques:

- Always assume there is an appropriate function. The calculation you want to perform is probably one that many other spreadsheet users need to perform, so it may be provided by 1-2-3. Sometimes you may need to combine several functions in one formula to do the job. Occasionally, you will need to use an intermediate cell to produce part of the answer before completing the calculation in another cell. In Chapter 6, you will learn how to hide columns from the display and printed reports so that extra columns for calculations need not affect the worksheet appearance.

- Save particularly useful function statements. When you come up with a good formula, you can save the worksheet under a different name to keep a copy of the formula for reference. In the next chapter, you will discover how to save a portion of a spreadsheet into a separate file and combine several files into one. This will allow you to build a library of functions. You can also save useful formulas by highlighting the appropriate cell and using the PrtSc key to print all of the information on the screen, including the contents of the highlighted cell.

■ Use the Help key to look up functions. There is no need to memorize the more than 90 1-2-3 functions. You can use the Help key (F1) to display the functions and their arguments.

If you follow these guidelines and spend some time experimenting with functions, you will find that they offer tremendous power. The next chapter explains how you can apply common functions in practical situations. It also explores the links between spreadsheets and the use of absolute cell references in formulas.

6

Building, Viewing, and Printing Spreadsheets

Building a Spreadsheet

Using and Viewing
the Model

Updating the Model

Worksheet Printing

Setting Setups

Print Destinations and
Background Printing

I N PREVIOUS CHAPTERS, YOU LEARNED SEVERAL METHODS OF ENTERING information into 1-2-3. You saw how to create and copy formulas to produce extensive spreadsheets from a few simple entries. This chapter reviews the process of building spreadsheet models, introducing several tricks for doing so with maximum efficiency. It also explains commands for viewing large spreadsheets on the screen and for printing spreadsheets.

Building a Spreadsheet

This chapter provides step-by-step instructions for creating a typical spreadsheet. It explains how to organize and print the worksheet, as well as how to dress it up with format commands. You can perform these steps yourself as a practical exercise, or simply use them as a reference when building your own models. The methods presented here are effective, but they are not hard-and-fast rules. As you become more experienced with 1-2-3, you may develop other techniques that are more suited to your work.

This chapter assumes that you are working with the "traditional" 1-2-3 display, which is 80 characters wide and 25 lines long. With this display, you can view 20 lines of the worksheet at once and can also view eight columns of nine characters each. With the Wysiwyg add-in, 1-2-3 can show more columns and rows in a single screen. While this does not affect the basic operation of the program, it may mean that your views of the model look slightly different from the illustrations as the example develops. For more on using Wysiwyg to alter your view of 1-2-3, refer to Chapter 7.

Basic Design

The spreadsheet presented in this chapter is a 12-month revenue projection for a travel agency with four separate offices. Part of the model can be seen in Figure 6.1. Five revenue categories are calculated for each of the four offices:

- Tour indicates the sales of packaged holidays.

- Flight displays the ticketing of regular airline flights.

- Hotel represents the commissions from hotel bookings.

- Rental indicates the commissions from rental car bookings.

- Group shows the revenue from special group events.

The January figures are multiplied by a growth factor to produce the February figures. In each successive month, the revenue is assumed to increase by the same factor.

Figure 6.1

Sample
spreadsheet

A1:								READY
	A	B	C	D	E	F	G	H
1								
2		Jan-92	Feb-92	Mar-92	Apr-92	May-92	Jun-92	Jul-92
3	POLK ST.							
4	Tour	2,350	2,374	2,397	2,421	2,445	2,470	2,495
5	Flight	1,875	1,894	1,913	1,932	1,951	1,971	1,990
6	Hotel	950	960	969	979	989	998	1,008
7	Rental	875	884	893	902	911	920	929
8	Group	800	808	816	824	832	841	849
9	VAN NESS							
10	Tour	3,400	3,434	3,468	3,503	3,538	3,573	3,609
11	Flight	2,175	2,197	2,219	2,241	2,263	2,286	2,309
12	Hotel	1,350	1,364	1,377	1,391	1,405	1,419	1,433
13	Rental	975	985	995	1,005	1,015	1,025	1,035
14	Group	1,100	1,111	1,122	1,133	1,145	1,156	1,168
15	UNION SQ.							
16	Tour	2,875	2,904	2,933	2,962	2,992	3,022	3,052
17	Flight	4,500	4,545	4,590	4,636	4,683	4,730	4,777
18	Hotel	1,150	1,162	1,173	1,185	1,197	1,209	1,221
19	Rental	925	934	944	953	963	972	982
20	Group	950	960	969	979	989	998	1,008
05-Nov-91 10:19 AM							NUM	

Building Principles

In general, it's best to build spreadsheets by entering data in the following
order:

1. First you use *labels* to identify the contents and arrangement of the model.
   Don't worry about the exact titles for columns and rows, since you can
   change them later. Also, don't worry about the width of columns, since
   these too can be adjusted after most of the model has been built.

2. Next you enter *numbers,* which make up the basic data in a worksheet.
   As you enter the numbers, you will get a general idea of the dimensions
   of the model.

3. Then you enter the first few *formulas* and make sure they work before
   copying them. Range Format the results of formulas before copying
   them, since cell formats are copied along with cell contents.

4. When you know what kind of numbers you are using, make any necessary
   format changes. Use the Worksheet Global Format command for the
   most common format, but avoid global formats with zero decimal places
   because these obscure fractional values. Use the Range Labels command
   to align labels before copying, as the alignment will also be copied.

5. Adjust column *widths* as needed. Use a global setting for the most common width (Worksheet Global Column-Width) and adjust other columns individually (Worksheet, Column).

It's quicker to work in this order than to adjust formats and column widths before entering most of the data. You will probably need to readjust some widths and formats after the model is completed anyhow.

Whether you build the model column by column or row by row depends upon the kind of data you are working with. The sample model in this chapter will be built column by column. That is, the column of labels will be followed by the starting values and then the first column of formulas. The first formula column will then be copied to the rest of the columns. This approach follows the natural progression of the data and requires the least keystrokes.

Entering and Copying Labels

Whenever possible, you should use the Copy command to reuse labels that you have already entered into the worksheet. This strategy saves time and also helps prevent typos and inconsistent spellings. Make sure you check your data before copying it. If the labels are aligned in a special way, apply the alignment command before copying to reduce the need for later adjustments. For example, to create and copy the labels for the sample worksheet, follow these steps:

1. Type the first labels in column A as they appear in Figure 6.2. The uppercase label is the name of the office, which is followed by five categories of revenue generated by that office. All six lines are normal left-aligned labels that you can enter with the Down Arrow key.

Figure 6.2

Entering and aligning labels

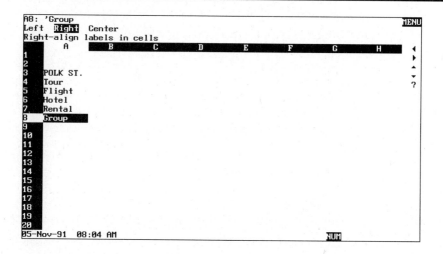

2. To differentiate between the revenue categories and the office names, you will right align the labels in cells A4 through A8. With your cell pointer in A8, activate the menu and select Range. Select Label, and then choose Right from the menu shown in Figure 6.2.

3. When prompted for the range to be modified, you can use the Up Arrow key to expand the range from A8 to A4. Note that to 1-2-3 both A4..A8 and A8..A4 are acceptable. When you press Enter to confirm A8..A4 as the range to right align, the command deletes the current label prefix and replaces it with one you specify, in this case " (double quote) for right alignment.

Working with Ranges

As described in Chapter 2, you can use the F4 key to select a range before you issue a range-related command. The technique will work to select A4..A8 for the Range Label Right command. Press F4 while in READY mode with the cell pointer in A8. The Range prompt appears on the second line of the screen. Press the Up Arrow key to include the cells through A4. Now you can issue the Range Label Right command and 1-2-3 will assume you want to alter cells A8..A4.

In many of the examples in this chapter, you can preselect cells with F4 before issuing a range-related command, including the Copy command. However, the steps given in the examples assume you will be selecting the range after you have issued the command.

If you are using a mouse, you can use it to select the range A4..A8 before you issue the Range Label Right command. To do this, click on A4 while in READY mode, press the left mouse button, and drag the mouse pointer to A8 before releasing. The cells remain highlighted when you activate the menu. When you select Range Label Right, the command assumes A4..A8 is the range you want to affect, applies the command, and returns you to READY mode. The range will remain selected. You can press the right mouse button or click on any single cell to deselect the range.

You can also use your mouse to select cells at a range prompt. For example, if you issue the Range Label Right command before you have selected, you can still use your mouse at the "Enter range of labels" prompt. Simply point to the first cell in the range, press the left mouse button, and then drag the mouse pointer to the last cell in the range before releasing the button. To confirm the range, simply click the left mouse button while the mouse pointer is still within the selected range.

You can use either technique for identifying cells during other commands discussed in this chapter. Specific directions for mouse users will only be given when a new technique or shortcut is introduced.

Multiple Copies

You can use the set of labels you have just created for each of the four offices. You can make three copies of the labels in A3..A8 and place them in A9 through A26. Then you simply change the office names from POLK ST. to VAN NESS, UNION SQ., and EMBARCADERO. In earlier chapters, you learned how to copy a single cell to many cells and how to make a single copy of many cells. When you want to make multiple copies of a range containing more than one cell, however, you include blank cells in the source range so that it matches the range required by the desired number of copies, as described here:

1. Move the cell pointer up to A3 and select Copy. 1-2-3 assumes that the source range begins at A3, where your cell pointer was located when you issued the command. This coordinate is already anchored as the start of the source range, as indicated by the double dots in A3..A3.

2. Include the other labels to be copied in the source range by pressing End followed by Down Arrow. This extends the source range to A3..A8.

3. Note that this source range is six rows long. If you indicated A9 as the destination range, you would create entries in the six cells A9 through A14. However, you want to create new entries in A9..A26, a range that is 18 rows long. To do this, you extend the source range to match the range required by the desired number of copies. In this case, you want the source range to be A3..A20, so press Down Arrow to extend the source range to A20.

    You can also use a series of questions and answers after highlighting the entries to be copied. First ask "how many cells have I highlighted?" The answer is 6. Now ask "how many copies do I want?" The answer is 3. Multiply these two answers together ($6 \times 3 = 18$). This means you need to highlight 18 cells. Now ask "how many cells have I already highlighted?" The answer is 6. Subtract this from 18 ($18 - 6 = 12$). This means that you need to highlight 12 more cells, so press the Down Arrow key 12 times. Your screen should look like the one in Figure 6.3.

4. Press Enter to confirm A3..A20 as the source range. 1-2-3 will ask for the destination range. This is simply the starting cell for the copies you are making, or A9. In response to the "To Where?" prompt, indicate A9 as the destination range and press Enter. Your screen should resemble Figure 6.4.

If you press PgDn, note that the copies continue down through A26. You have made three copies of the original labels with one command.

Figure 6.3

Highlighting the source range

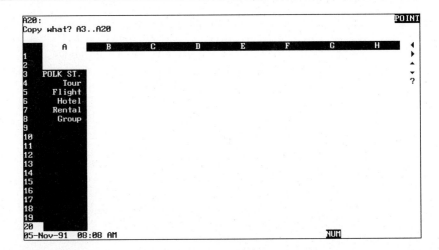

Figure 6.4

Results of the multiple copy

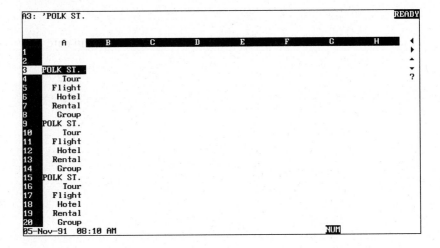

The alignment of the labels is also copied, so that the right-aligned entries remain that way. Now change the office names in A9, A15, and A21 so that they read VAN NESS, UNION SQ., and EMBARCADERO, respectively. Since the label EMBARCADERO is more than nine characters, it will extend into column B. We'll deal with this issue later. To complete the entries for the first column of the model, enter the label **TOTALS** in A28. Row 28 will contain totals for each of the columns of values in the model.

The Second Column

Now you're ready to create the data in the second column. Follow these steps:

1. Move the cell pointer to B2 to enter the month heading Jan-92 in the second column of the model. To create this heading, enter the date January, 1, 1992, using the @DATE function, as in

   `@DATE(92,1,1)`

   This results in date serial number 33604.

2. To format this number as a month heading, use Range Format Date and select format 3. Press Enter to confirm B3..B3 as the cell to be formatted. The result is Jan-92.

3. Now you need to enter the starting values for this projection, which are given in Table 6.1. (The first entry in the table, POLK ST., goes in cell A3.) You can enter the values with the Down Arrow key to minimize keystrokes. If you are experienced with a ten-key pad, you might want to enter the numbers using your keyboard's numeric keypad. On newer keyboards, this keypad is separate from the cursor-movement keys so that, after making sure Num Lock is on, you can enter a number and then press Down Arrow all with the same hand. If your keyboard has a combined cursor-movement and numeric keypad, you can alternate between arrows and numbers either by pressing Num Lock, or by holding down the Shift key when numbers are required and releasing it to switch to arrows.

4. The revenue figures in column B need to be formatted to show commas as thousands separators. Use the Range Format command to apply the Comma format with zero decimal places to the numbers in B4 through B26.

5. At the bottom of column B, you want to enter a formula that will sum the January expenses for all four offices. Move the cell pointer to B28 to create the formula, which will use the @SUM function. Type **@SUM(** to begin the formula. This places 1-2-3 in value mode and you can use the pointing method to indicate which cell block is to be summed.

6. Use the PgUp and Up Arrow keys to move the cell pointer to B4. Mouse users can then click on B4 and drag through to B26 to select the range to be summed, going to step 10 to complete the operation. If you are a keyboard user, you must anchor the start of the range at B4 by typing a period. Now you need to move the highlighting down the column. If you use the End and Down Arrow keys, the cell pointer will only go

Table 6.1   **Starting Values for the Sample Spreadsheet**

Column A	Column B
POLK ST.	
Tour	2350
Flight	1875
Hotel	950
Rental	875
Group	800
VAN NESS	
Tour	3400
Flight	2175
Hotel	1350
Rental	975
Group	1100
UNION SQ.	
Tour	2875
Flight	4500
Hotel	1150
Rental	925
Group	950
EMBARCADERO	
Tour	3140
Flight	2100
Hotel	1250
Rental	950
Group	2500

to the next gap in the rows. A faster method of moving to the bottom of a column involves moving your cell pointer to a solid column of data.

7. Press Left Arrow and your cell pointer will be in column A, which contains consecutive rows of data, as shown in Figure 6.5.

8. Now press End followed by Down Arrow. This moves the cell pointer directly to row 26, as shown in Figure 6.6. Do not press Enter yet.

Figure 6.5
Moving into column A

Figure 6.6
Highlighting to the bottom of column A

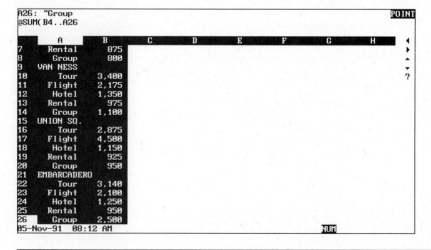

9. You have just "hitched a ride" on a range of occupied cells. At this point, press Right Arrow to move the cell pointer back into the original column. The highlighted range is now B4..B26.

10. Complete the formula by typing the closing parenthesis and pressing Enter. Use the Range Format command to apply the Comma format with zero decimal places to the result in B28.

This method of moving with the cell pointer is very useful for building a model, since you often need to move the cell pointer to the end of the model in a row or column that is not yet completely filled. Of course, you must remember to come back to the original column or row before completing the maneuver.

The Third Column

The first entry in column C is the month heading, which will go in C2.

1. Move the cell pointer to C2 and enter the formula **31+B2**. This creates a date serial number equivalent to February 2, 1992.

2. Format the result with the Range Format Date command and select date format 3. The result should now appear as Feb-92.

Most of the values in column C are formulas that multiply the revenue figures in column B by a factor that increases them. These formulas are repeated across the model to project a steady month-to-month increase in revenue. To begin with, this rate will be 1% a month.

3. Move the cell pointer to cell C4, enter the formula **1.01*B4,** and format the cell with the Comma format, zero decimal places. Formatting a cell before copying ensures that the format as well as the contents are duplicated.

4. Use the Copy command to copy this formula to the other cells in column C, making each cell in the third column 1.01 times the value in the cell to the left. The source range will be C4..C4, which 1-2-3 is already suggesting. Press Enter to confirm this range.

5. To point out the destination range for the Copy, type a period while the cell pointer is still in C4, anchoring this cell as the start of the range. Then press PgDn once and Down Arrow twice to move the highlight down to C26, as shown in Figure 6.7.

6. Press Enter to confirm C4..C26 as the destination. This will complete the Copy process; your results should resemble those shown in Figure 6.8.

Figure 6.7
The destination range

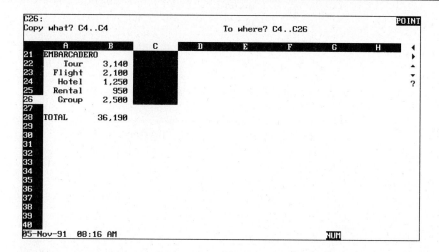

Figure 6.8
Results of the Copy command

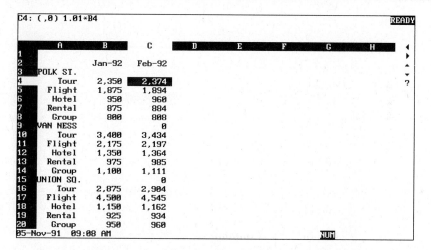

Note that including cell C4 in both the source and destination ranges copies that cell over itself, but this causes no problems. However, there is a slight problem with the Copy results, because each cell in column C from rows 4 to 26 is now 1.01 times the value of the corresponding cell in column B, including cells on rows that do not have values in column B. This means that there is a 0 in cells C9, C15, and C21. You can simply highlight each of these cells and delete its contents with the Delete key.

To complete column C, you need a sum formula in C28. You can simply copy the formula from B28 using a technique known as *reverse copy*. As a spreadsheet grows, you might find it inconvenient that the Copy command leaves the cell pointer in the upper-left cell of the range you copied from. This feature can be particularly cumbersome when you are copying across several screens' worth of worksheet. Reverse copy overcomes this problem, because it invokes the Copy command from the destination of the copy—in this case, C28.

1. Move the cell pointer to cell C28 and issue the Copy command. Initially, the suggested source range will be locked in at C28, represented as C28..C28. Press Esc to unlock this range. The display at the top of the screen now shows C28 only.

2. Move the cell pointer left to the formula in cell B28. The source range now changes to B28. Press Enter to confirm that this is the cell you want to copy.

3. Because you started the copy from C28, 1-2-3 assumes that this is where you want the formula to be copied to. You needn't lock the destination point; simply press Enter to confirm it. Figure 6.9 shows the result you should see.

Figure 6.9

Results of the reverse copy

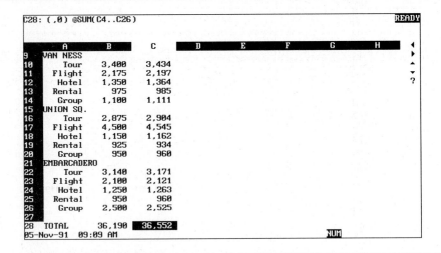

Further Columns

You can now copy the entries in column C to complete the projection for 12 months. Use the following steps to copy column C, from C2 through C28, into columns D through M.

1. Move the cell pointer to C2 and issue the Copy command. The source range, initially suggested as C2..C2, needs to be expanded downward. Press PgDn once to move the highlighting to C22. Press the Down Arrow key six times to include C28. Then press Enter to confirm C2..C28 as the source range.

2. With the cell pointer still in C2, anchor the destination range there by typing a period.

3. Now press Tab once. This will move the cell one screenful of columns to the right, extending the destination range to I2. Now press Right Arrow four times to make the destination range C2..M2. At this point, you can press Enter to complete the copy.

Note that when you issue this command, 1-2-3 copies data all the way down to row 28. In some cases, you may want to expand the destination range highlighting to view the full range of destination cells. In this case, such a precaution is not essential since you are building a new worksheet and know that nothing has been entered in D2..M28. The results of the copy command appear in Figure 6.10. Check your own results against those shown in the figure to make sure that you have not made mistakes either in entering the formula in C4 or in copying column C.

Figure 6.10

The completed Copy

```
C2: (D3) 31+B2                                                         READY

      A        B        C        D        E        F        G        H      ◄
 1                                                                          ►
 2              Jan-92   Feb-92   Mar-92   Apr-92   May-92   Jun-92   Jul-92 ▲
 3    POLK ST.                                                              ▼
 4       Tour   2,350    2,374    2,397    2,421    2,445    2,470    2,495  ?
 5     Flight   1,875    1,894    1,913    1,932    1,951    1,971    1,990
 6      Hotel     950      960      969      979      989      998    1,008
 7     Rental     875      884      893      902      911      920      929
 8      Group     800      808      816      824      832      841      849
 9    VAN NESS
10       Tour   3,400    3,434    3,468    3,503    3,538    3,573    3,609
11     Flight   2,175    2,197    2,219    2,241    2,263    2,286    2,309
12      Hotel   1,350    1,364    1,377    1,391    1,405    1,419    1,433
13     Rental     975      985      995    1,005    1,015    1,025    1,035
14      Group   1,100    1,111    1,122    1,133    1,145    1,156    1,168
15    UNION SQ.
16       Tour   2,875    2,904    2,933    2,962    2,992    3,022    3,052
17     Flight   4,500    4,545    4,590    4,636    4,683    4,730    4,777
18      Hotel   1,150    1,162    1,173    1,185    1,197    1,209    1,221
19     Rental     925      934      944      953      963      972      982
20      Group     950      960      969      979      989      998    1,008
05-Nov-91  09:17 AM                                              NUM
```

As you can see, 1-2-3 reproduces a set of formulas very quickly. Since much of your work with numbers will require repetition of the same calculations, you will probably use the Copy command frequently in your own spreadsheets.

Saving Your Work

At this point, you might want to issue the File Save command to store your work. When you issue the File Save command for a worksheet that has not yet been saved, you are provided with a list of files in the current directory. You should enter an appropriate name, such as REVENU01.

Summing the Rows

Now you are ready to perform a further calculation on the model. Column N will hold the totals for each office and revenue category over the 12-month period. The figures in this column will be a series of @SUM formulas, the first of which is entered in N4.

1. In cell N2, enter the centered label **^TOTALS**.

2. In cell N4, type **@SUM(** to begin the formula. Then press Left Arrow followed by End and Left Arrow. This will move the cell pointer to the extreme left of the model. Now press Right Arrow once so that the cell pointer is in cell B4. Type a period to anchor the beginning point of the range in this cell.

3. Now press End and then Right Arrow to include all the cells in the range B4..M4. Type the closing parenthesis to complete the formula and press Enter to place the formula in N4. The result should be 29803.88.

4. With the cell pointer still in N4, issue the Range Format command and apply the Comma format with zero decimal places.

5. To sum all the rows in the model, issue the Copy command with the cell pointer still in N4. Press Enter to accept N4..N4 as the source range.

6. Type a period to anchor N4 as the start of the destination range and press the PgDn key. Press the Down Arrow key several more times to include the last row of the model, making N4..N28 the destination range. Press Enter to confirm the copy.

7. Use the Delete key to erase the unnecessary formulas in cells N9, N15, N21, and N27.

Checking Your Work

The formula in cell N28 is actually the grand total of all the revenue, since it sums the row of column totals. To make sure that the model is working correctly, you can replace this formula with one that makes sure the sum of the rows is equal to the sum of the columns, as described in Chapter 5 under "Crossfooting with @IF."

The first step is to assign range names that will make the formula easier to write. The range B28..M28 will be called FOOT while N4..N26 will be called CROSS.

1. With the cell pointer in M28, issue the Range Name Create command.

2. Type **FOOT** and press Enter.

3. Press End and then Left Arrow followed by Right Arrow. This will select M28..B28 as the range. Press Enter.

4. With the cell pointer in N26, issue the Range Name Create command.

5. Type **CROSS** and press Enter.

6. Press PgUp once and Down Arrow three times. This will select N26..N4 as the range. Press Enter.

Having named the ranges that represent the sum of the rows (CROSS) and the sum of the columns (FOOT), you can use them in the following formula, which should be entered in cell N28:

```
@IF(@ROUND(@SUM(CROSS),0)=@ROUND(@SUM(FOOT),0),
@ROUND(@SUM(FOOT),0),"Error")
```

The result should be 458,980, the sum of the range called FOOT. However, if there is an error in the model—that is, if the sum of the range CROSS does not equal the sum of the range FOOT—you will see Error in N28. A typical cause of error is the accidental replacement of a column or row sum formula by a fixed value. Note the use of @ROUND in this formula—this is a precaution against minuscule math errors, as discussed in Chapter 5.

To prepare for the next stage of the exercise, press Home to move the cell pointer to A1 and view the top of the model. It should look like Figure 6.1. Now save the model again.

Using and Viewing the Model

The model you have created has several practical uses. You can use it to determine the expected revenue for the year based on the assumed beginning values and growth factor. You can also record actual revenue in a similar worksheet and compare this against projections. However, you should first experiment with the 1-2-3 commands for moving around a large spreadsheet and changing the way it is displayed.

Navigation

Having built the model, you might want to review your results. This involves moving around the worksheet. The following keys will be of assistance.

The Big Keys

When you want to move the cell pointer more than one row or column at a time, 1-2-3 offers several options. Pressing the Tab key moves the cell pointer one screen's worth of columns to the right. Holding down Shift and pressing Tab moves the cell pointer one screen to the left. The Ctrl-Right Arrow and Ctrl-Left Arrow key combinations duplicate the Tab and Shift-Tab keys and are sometimes referred to as "big right" and "big left." The PgDn and PgUp keys move the cell pointer one screen's worth of rows down and up. Normally this is 20 rows.

The End Keys

As you have seen, the End key can be of great help during copy operations. Now that you have built the model, you can use End and Right Arrow to move to the right side of the model. Place the cell pointer in B2 and press End followed by Right Arrow. This will move the cell pointer to N2 and scroll the right half of the model into view. Press Home to return to A1. With the cell pointer in A3, press End and then Down Arrow to move the cell pointer to A26. Press End and then Right Arrow to move the cell pointer to N26. Mouse users can press End and then click on the mouse arrows in the mouse palette.

   Note that when there are gaps between entries in a column or row, you cannot use End and an arrow key to get to the last occupied cell in that column or row. Instead, you press End followed by Home to move the cell pointer to the junction of the column and row furthest from A1 that have been used for data or contain formatting. For example, to see the grand total at the end of this model, press End and then Home. The cell pointer should be in N28 because N is the last column and 28 the last row to contain data or formatting. If your cell pointer goes to a row beyond 28 or a column beyond N, you may want to adjust your worksheet as described later in the section "Tidying Up."

The Goto Key

The arrow keys are not always the most efficient way to move to a specific location, particularly if that location is some distance from your current position. You can instead use the Goto key, F5, which was introduced in Chapter 1. Simply press F5, type in the coordinates of your destination, and press Enter. If the destination cell is already visible on the screen when you press F5, the cell pointer is moved to the destination cell and the worksheet is not rearranged on the screen. However, if the destination cell is not on screen when you issue the Goto command, 1-2-3 scrolls the worksheet, placing the destination cell in the upper-left corner of the screen. This feature can be disorienting, as you can see from Figure 6.11, which shows the effect of moving from A1 to N28 using Goto. 1-2-3 displays just N28, and there are no other occupied cells visible to give any context or meaning to N28. However, Goto is very useful when you want to locate a specific cell, perhaps for editing, and can be effective in conjunction with range names.

Figure 6.11
Moving to N28 with
Goto

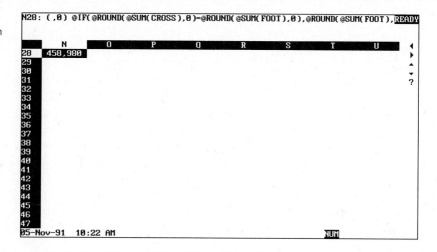

Scrolling

If you want to view an area of the worksheet rather than move to a specific cell, you can employ the Scroll Lock key. Like Caps Lock, Scroll Lock is a toggle key, and when it is active you will see the status message SCROLL in the lower-right corner of the screen. When SCROLL is active, 1-2-3 responds to the cursor-movement keys by moving the worksheet relative to the worksheet borders rather than moving the cell pointer relative to the columns and rows. For example, press Home, Goto, and enter **N28** as the destination. Press Scroll Lock so that SCROLL is visible in the lower-right corner of the screen. Now press Up Arrow several times. Notice how this moves up the border, revealing more rows of the model. Press Left Arrow several times and the left border will move to the left relative to the worksheet.

If you keep pressing Left Arrow, cell N28 will reach the right edge of the screen. At this point, continuing to press Left Arrow moves the cell pointer to M28, L28, and so on, while scrolling the border to the left. The Scroll Lock key can take some getting used to, so you may want to experiment with it. To return the cursor keys to their normal role, simply press Scroll Lock a second time. The SCROLL message will disappear.

Navigating with Range Names

In this particular model, you know that the grand total is in cell N28, and you can use several different keys to bring this cell into view. However, you probably have enough names and numbers to remember without adding worksheet cell coordinates to the list. By using a consistent set of range names with your worksheets, you can avoid having to remember either names or cell addresses when navigating a worksheet.

As discussed in Chapter 4, you can attach a name to a single cell or group of cells just for viewing purposes. After you have attached a name to a cell or group of cells, you can enter the name at the Goto prompt. Alternatively, you can use the Name key (F3) to list range names, and then simply highlight the destination on the list, pressing Enter to insert it at the GOTO prompt line and Enter again to complete the Goto command. If the range name refers to a group of cells, your cell pointer will be placed in the cell at the upper-left corner of the range. Unless that cell is already on screen when the Goto command is issued, it will be placed in the upper-left corner of your screen.

For example, to move quickly to the lower-right section of the example spreadsheet, you can name the range K16..N28 as ENDVIEW. You can then press Goto followed by Name and select ENDVIEW from the list. (If you have many range names in the worksheet, you can press Name a second time to get a full-screen list of names.) When you complete the Goto command, cell K16 will be in the upper-left corner of the screen and N28 will be clearly visible. If you are consistent in your range names—for example, if you always use ENDVIEW for the lower-right corner of your models—you will not need to remember specific names and coordinates for separate worksheets.

Note that the list of range names is alphabetical. This means that if you choose names carefully, ranges that are referenced frequently will appear at the top of the list. For example, if you move constantly between A1 and three separate areas of a worksheet, you can call the three areas 1HOME, 2HOME, and 3HOME. These three names will then appear at the beginning of the range name list, and will be easy to select.

Worksheet Titles

As you could see in Figure 6.11, and as you should know from navigating the sample worksheet, the column headings disappear if row 2 scrolls off the screen, and the row headings are lost if column A is scrolled out of view. This makes it difficult to tell which months and which revenue category you are viewing. The solution to this problem is to freeze certain rows and columns as titles that remain on screen no matter where you are in the worksheet, as shown in Figure 6.12.

Figure 6.12
Diagram of
worksheet titles

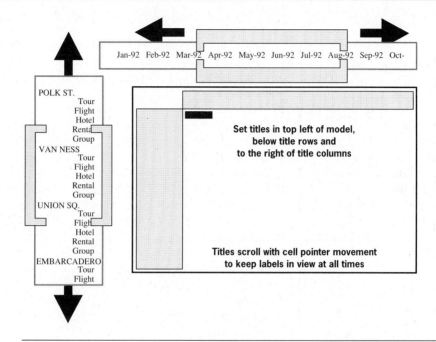

To freeze titles, you place the cell pointer in the upper-left cell of the area you want to move, in this case B3, and then issue the Worksheet Titles command. You are offered four choices:

- Horizontal freezes the area above the cell pointer.

- Vertical freezes the area to the left of the cell pointer.

- Both freezes areas above and to the left of the cell pointer.

- Clear unfreezes all titles.

In this case, you want both the months and the revenue categories to stay on the screen while you scan the model, so pick Both. When you make your Titles choice, you are returned to the spreadsheet. Try moving the cell pointer to the right past column H and note that the row headings in column A remain on screen. Similarly, the column headings in row 2 remain visible even if you move the cell pointer down past row 20. Now press End followed by Home. Cell N28 will be displayed, as shown in Figure 6.13, with the column and row headings visible on the screen. As you can see, titles make it much easier to tell what is going on when you are navigating the model.

Figure 6.13

Using worksheet titles

```
N28: (,0) @IF(@ROUND(@SUM(CROSS),0)=@ROUND(@SUM(FOOT),0),@ROUND(@SUM(FOOT), READY
            A       H       I       J       K       L       M       N
1
2                 Jul-92  Aug-92  Sep-92  Oct-92  Nov-92  Dec-92  TOTALS
11      Flight    2,309   2,332   2,355   2,379   2,403   2,427   27,584
12      Hotel     1,433   1,447   1,462   1,476   1,491   1,506   17,121
13      Rental    1,035   1,045   1,056   1,066   1,077   1,088   12,365
14      Group     1,168   1,179   1,191   1,203   1,215   1,227   13,951
15 UNION SQ.
16      Tour      3,052   3,082   3,113   3,144   3,176   3,208   36,462
17      Flight    4,777   4,825   4,873   4,922   4,971   5,021   57,071
18      Hotel     1,221   1,233   1,245   1,258   1,270   1,283   14,585
19      Rental      982     992   1,002   1,012   1,022   1,032   11,731
20      Group     1,008   1,019   1,029   1,039   1,049   1,060   12,048
21 EMBARCADE
22      Tour      3,333   3,367   3,400   3,434   3,469   3,503   39,823
23      Flight    2,229   2,251   2,274   2,297   2,320   2,343   26,633
24      Hotel     1,327   1,340   1,354   1,367   1,381   1,395   15,853
25      Rental    1,008   1,019   1,029   1,039   1,049   1,060   12,048
26      Group     2,654   2,680   2,707   2,734   2,762   2,789   31,706
27
28 TOTAL         38,416  38,801  39,189  39,580  39,976  40,376  458,980
05-Nov-91  10:29 AM                                           NUM
```

Now press Home and notice that the cell pointer moves to B3 rather than A1. This is because B3 is the cell in which you performed the title lock. If you press Left Arrow or Up Arrow, a beep will tell you that cells above and to the left of B3 are off limits.

The restriction on movement imposed by titles can be a problem when you are still adjusting your worksheet. For example, in Figure 6.13 the label EMBARCADERO is wider than cell A21. This means that the label gets truncated when you are using titles. Suppose you decide to widen column A. Unless you are working with a mouse in Wysiwyg mode, widening a single column normally requires that you place the cell pointer in the column to be widened. However, with the titles locked at B3, column A is off limits. There are two ways around this problem. You can use the Goto key (F5), which can select a cell in the titles area. For example, you can press F5, type **A21**, and then press Enter to position the cell pointer in A21. However, the effect on screen is a little confusing as you will see two of column A, as shown in Figure 6.14.

At this point, you can edit A21 or make changes to other cells in the column. You can also use the Worksheet Column Set-Width command to alter the width of column A. Do this now and change the width to 12. To remove the duplicate column, press PgDn, Tab, and then Home.

There is an alternative technique for altering the width of a title column without using the Goto key. You can issue the Worksheet Column Column-Range Set-Width command from any cell in the worksheet and alter just one column. This command prompts you for a range of columns to alter. Simply press Esc to unlock the default range coordinates and move the cell pointer to the column you want to change, in this case A. You can then press Enter and get the "Select a width for range of columns" prompt. Choose the width and press Enter. This command, like other range commands that you might use on title cells, automatically removes the duplicate column from your screen.

Figure 6.14
Moving to A21 with Goto

A21:	'EMBARCADERO							READY
	A	A	B	C	D	E	F	G
1								
2			Jan-92	Feb-92	Mar-92	Apr-92	May-92	Jun-92
21	EMBARCADE	EMBARCADERO						
22	Tour	Tour	3,140	3,171	3,203	3,235	3,267	3,300
23	Flight	Flight	2,100	2,121	2,142	2,164	2,185	2,207
24	Hotel	Hotel	1,250	1,263	1,275	1,288	1,301	1,314
25	Rental	Rental	950	960	969	979	989	998
26	Group	Group	2,500	2,525	2,550	2,576	2,602	2,628
27								
28	TOTAL	TOTAL	36,190	36,552	36,917	37,287	37,659	38,036
29								
30								
31								
32								
33								
34								
35								
36								
37								
38								
05-Nov-91 10:43 AM							NUM	

You can use the Goto key when you need to edit title cells. For example, you may want to change the year in cell B2 to 1993. Press Goto and type the address of the title cell you want to edit; then press Enter. A copy of cell B2 appears at the cell pointer. At this point, you can press F2 to edit the cell and then press Enter to place the cell contents back in the cell. (You needn't actually change B2 at this point.) After altering a title cell, you remove the duplicate display by pressing PgDn, Tab, and then Home.

The titles work very well when you have built a model and are only updating the data. However, you may need to unlock the titles when making major changes to the spreadsheet. To clear the titles, select Worksheet Titles Clear. In this example, leave the titles in place because they work well with windows.

Windows on a Worksheet

There may be times when you want to view two separate parts of a worksheet at once. 1-2-3 allows you to split the screen either horizontally or vertically into two parts, called *windows*. Using a vertical window with the sample worksheet will allow you to see the left and right ends of the model at the same time. In turn, this will allow you to see how changes to starting values in column B affect totals in column N. First position the cell pointer anywhere in column E. Vertical windows are inserted to the left of the cell pointer, meaning that the window will be placed between D and E if you issue the command with the cell pointer in E. Now issue the Worksheet command followed by Window. The options are as follows:

■ Horizontal splits the screen horizontally at the current row.

■ Vertical splits the screen vertically at the current column.

■ Sync synchronizes worksheet scrolling so that the same rows appear in both vertical windows or the same columns in both horizontal windows. This is the default method of scrolling in windows.

■ Unsync allows the worksheet to be scrolled independently in each window.

■ Clear removes windows.

In this case, you want to select Vertical, which produces the effect shown in Figure 6.15. Note that 1-2-3 returns you to READY mode so that you need to reenter the menu system if you want to use another window command. Also notice that the cell pointer has been moved to the column immediately to the left of the window.

Figure 6.15

A vertical window

```
D4: (,0) 1.01*C4                                              READY

          A        B        C        D          E        F        G     ◄
                                                                         ►
1                                          1
2               Jan-92   Feb-92   Mar-92   2    Apr-92   May-92   Jun-92  ▲
3    POLK ST.                              3                              ▼
4         Tour   2,350    2,374    2,397   4    2,421    2,445    2,470   ?
5       Flight   1,875    1,894    1,913   5    1,932    1,951    1,971
6        Hotel     950      960      969   6      979      989      998
7       Rental     875      884      893   7      902      911      920
8        Group     800      808      816   8      824      832      841
9    VAN NESS                              9
10        Tour   3,400    3,434    3,468   10   3,503    3,538    3,573
11      Flight   2,175    2,197    2,219   11   2,241    2,263    2,286
12       Hotel   1,350    1,364    1,377   12   1,391    1,405    1,419
13      Rental     975      985      995   13   1,005    1,015    1,025
14       Group   1,100    1,111    1,122   14   1,133    1,145    1,156
15   UNION SQ.                             15
16        Tour   2,875    2,904    2,933   16   2,962    2,992    3,022
17      Flight   4,500    4,545    4,590   17   4,636    4,683    4,730
18       Hotel   1,150    1,162    1,173   18   1,185    1,197    1,209
19      Rental     925      934      944   19     953      963      972
20       Group     950      960      969   20     979      989      998
05-Nov-91  04:01 PM                                           NUM
```

You move the cell pointer between split windows by pressing the Window key, F6. Each time you press F6, the cell pointer moves to the other window. For example, if you place the cell pointer in the right window, in cell E4, and then press End followed by Right Arrow, column N moves into view on the right side of the screen. Now press F6 again and the cell pointer moves back to D4 in the left window.

At the moment, the two windows are *synchronized*. In other words, pressing PgDn, for example, moves the cell pointer to D24 in the left window, as shown in Figure 6.16. It also moves the equivalent rows into view on the right side of the screen.

Figure 6.16

Synchronization
with a vertical split

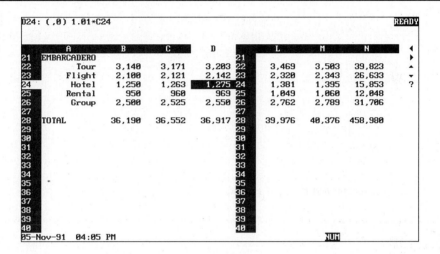

With a vertical split, synchronization means that pressing Up Arrow or Down Arrow scrolls the worksheet the same number of rows on both sides of the split. Note that the row numbers in the dividing line match those in the left border. Also note that because the titles are locked, the month headings remain visible. With horizontal window synchronization, Right Arrow or Left Arrow will move the worksheet on the top and bottom halves of the screen, and the column letters in the dividing line will match those in the top border.

The Window key is affected by the synchronization of windows. With synchronized vertical windows, when you move from the first window to the second the cell pointer moves to the column it last occupied in the second window and the row it last occupied in the first window. With horizontal synchronized windows, the cell pointer moves into the second window in the row it occupied the last time the second window was used, in the column that it was in before moving out of the first window.

Suppose that you want to alter the starting value in B4 and immediately observe the effect on the grand total in N28. To do this, you need to unsynchronize the windows by selecting Worksheet Window Unsync. With the cell pointer still in the left half of the screen, press Home. The upper-left portion of the model slides into view while the model on the other side does not move. Now enter the value **3350** in B4. The effect on N28 is visible immediately, as you can see from Figure 6.17.

Figure 6.17

Unsynchronized windows

```
B4: (,0) 3350                                                            READY

          A          B        C        D           L        M        N     ◄
                                                21                          ►
1                  Jan-92    Feb-92   Mar-92  22    3,469    3,503   39,823  ▲
2                                             23    2,320    2,343   26,633  ▼
3   POLK ST.                                  24    1,381    1,395   15,853  ?
4         Tour   3,350     3,384    3,417     25    1,049    1,060   12,048
5         Flight  1,875    1,894    1,913     26    2,762    2,789   31,706
6         Hotel    950      960      969      27
7         Rental   875      884      893      28   41,081   41,492  471,662
8         Group    800      808      816      29
9   VAN NESS                                  30
10        Tour   3,400     3,434    3,468     31
11        Flight  2,175    2,197    2,219     32
12        Hotel   1,350    1,364    1,377     33
13        Rental   975      985      995      34
14        Group   1,100    1,111    1,122     35
15  UNION SQ.                                 36
16        Tour   2,875     2,904    2,933     37
17        Flight  4,500    4,545    4,590     38
18        Hotel   1,150    1,162    1,173     39
19        Rental   925      934      944      40
20        Group    950      960      969
05-Nov-91   04:06 PM                                              NUM
```

Note that the row numbers in the window dividing line no longer match those in the left border. Also note that when windows are not synchronized, the cell pointer always moves back to the position it occupied before the Window key was pressed.

To clear windows, simply select Worksheet Window Clear. Do this now. Also clear the titles with Worksheet Titles Clear. Later in this chapter, you'll review the commands for printing worksheets. Note that neither titles nor windows affect the way that the worksheet is printed. Also note that when you are working with windows, the Worksheet Column, Worksheet Global Column-Width, and Worksheet Titles commands only affect the current window.

Hiding Columns

You can also alter the way a model is displayed on screen by hiding some of the columns. 1-2-3 lets you place selected columns in the background, as outlined in Figure 6.18. In essence, 1-2-3 allows you to pick and choose which columns to view. Hidden columns do not appear in printouts. However, the hidden data is not lost, and hidden formulas continue to be active.

Suppose that you want to hide the first six months of the sample model. First place your cell pointer on any row in column B and then select Worksheet Column Hide. You are asked to specify the column to hide. You can select one or more columns. In this example, you anchor B as the beginning column by typing a period, and then press Right Arrow to move the highlighting through to column G. When you press Enter, the columns disappear from view, as shown in Figure 6.19.

Figure 6.18

Hiding columns

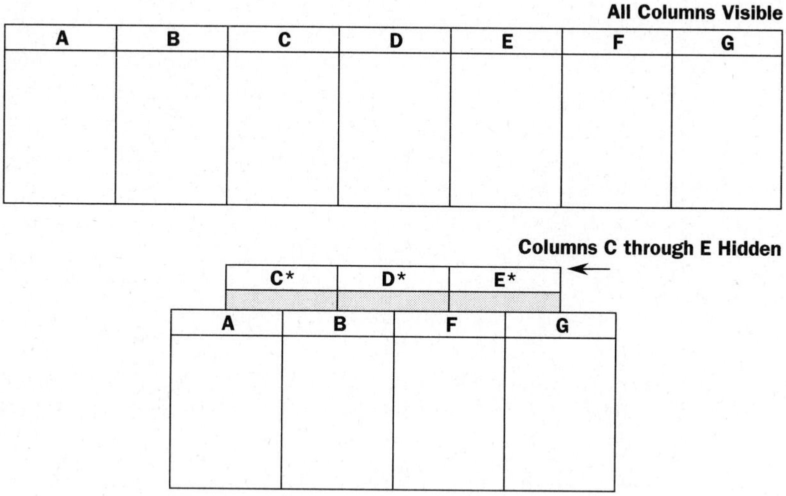

All Columns Visible

A	B	C	D	E	F	G

Columns C through E Hidden

	C*	D*	E*	←

A	B	F	G

Figure 6.19

Columns B through G hidden

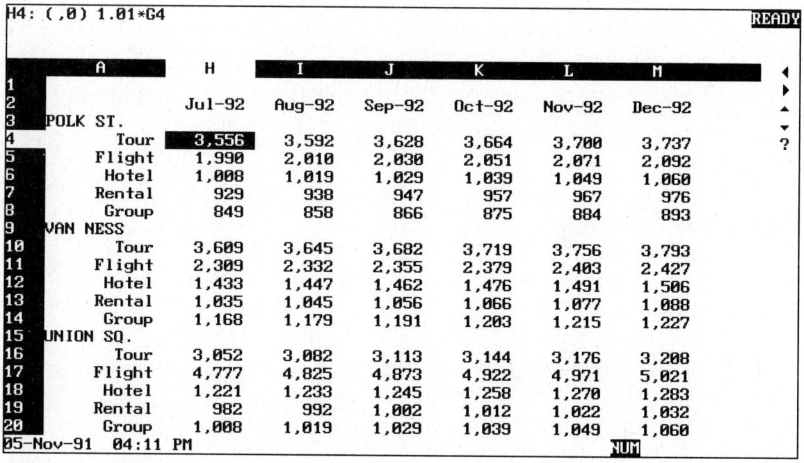

```
H4: (,0) 1.01*G4                                          READY
              A      H      I      J      K      L      M    ◄
1                                                            ►
2                 Jul-92 Aug-92 Sep-92 Oct-92 Nov-92 Dec-92  ▲
3  POLK ST.                                                  ▼
4        Tour   3,556  3,592  3,628  3,664  3,700  3,737     ?
5      Flight   1,990  2,010  2,030  2,051  2,071  2,092
6       Hotel   1,008  1,019  1,029  1,039  1,049  1,060
7      Rental     929    938    947    957    967    976
8       Group     849    858    866    875    884    893
9  VAN NESS
10       Tour   3,609  3,645  3,682  3,719  3,756  3,793
11     Flight   2,309  2,332  2,355  2,379  2,403  2,427
12      Hotel   1,433  1,447  1,462  1,476  1,491  1,506
13     Rental   1,035  1,045  1,056  1,066  1,077  1,088
14      Group   1,168  1,179  1,191  1,203  1,215  1,227
15 UNION SQ.
16       Tour   3,052  3,082  3,113  3,144  3,176  3,208
17     Flight   4,777  4,825  4,873  4,922  4,971  5,021
18      Hotel   1,221  1,233  1,245  1,258  1,270  1,283
19     Rental     982    992  1,002  1,012  1,022  1,032
20      Group   1,008  1,019  1,029  1,039  1,049  1,060
05-Nov-91  04:11 PM                                    NUM
```

To redisplay the columns, select Worksheet Column Display. Asterisks next to the column letters will indicate the columns that are currently hidden. To return columns to the display, include them in the range and press Enter. (In this case, type a period to anchor the range, press Right Arrow six times to extend the range to column B, and press Enter.) If you press Esc and do not select any columns, the marked columns remain hidden.

The column width and format remain unaffected by the hide-and-display process. When you carry out any command using the POINT mode to indicate cell references, 1-2-3 temporarily reveals hidden columns, marked by asterisks, so that they can be considered in the command. For example, if you use the Move or Copy command or build formulas with the point-and-shoot method, any hidden columns will be temporarily revealed so you can correctly complete the operation.

Adding a Title

Although 1-2-3 has a command for centering labels within a column, there is no command for centering a title over a model. If you want titles to be centered over models, you must estimate a centered location yourself, or settle for a title on the left. In this example, the title will be on the left. If you load the Wysiwyg add-in, you can center a title over a model, as described in Chapter 10. Move the cell pointer to cell A1, issue the Worksheet Insert Row command, and press Enter to insert a new row at the top of the spreadsheet. Enter the following label in A1:

```
Revenue Projection, Based on Monthly Growth Factor of:
```

In cell G1, enter the actual figure for the growth factor: 1.01. Now format the cell with the Fixed format, using two decimal places. The results will appear as shown in Figure 6.20.

Now is a good time to repeat the File Save command and replace the previous version of the file with the new one.

Updating the Model

Having built the model and explored several ways of making it easier to view, you may want to update it to reflect a revised estimate of how much revenue will rise. As you recall, the expenses in columns C through M were calculated using a growth factor of 1.01. To change this growth factor to 1.02, you could enter 1.02*B5 in C5 and then copy it to the other cells. However, that would involve several steps, which would have to be repeated every time you wanted to see the effect of a different growth factor. Fortunately, you can make the spreadsheet easier to modify by using formulas that refer to the growth factor stored in cell G1.

Figure 6.20

Adding a title

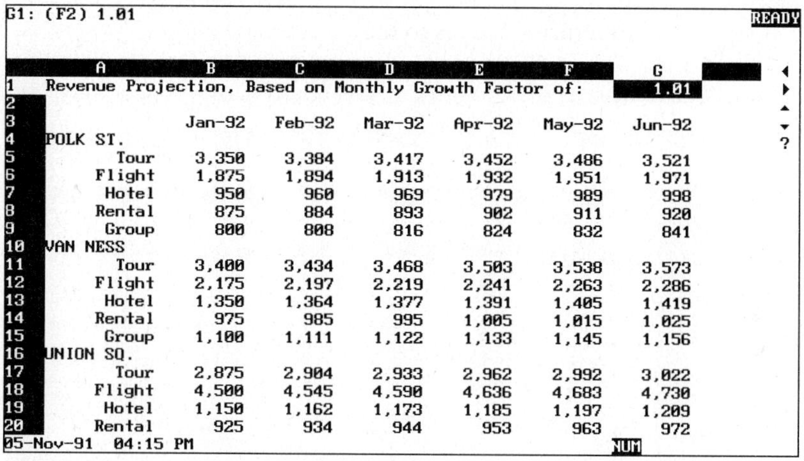

```
G1: (F2) 1.01                                                      READY
         A         B         C         D         E         F        G        ◄
1   Revenue Projection, Based on Monthly Growth Factor of:       1.01       ►
2                                                                           ▲
3             Jan-92    Feb-92    Mar-92    Apr-92    May-92    Jun-92       ▼
4   POLK ST.                                                                ?
5        Tour    3,350     3,384     3,417     3,452     3,486     3,521
6      Flight    1,875     1,894     1,913     1,932     1,951     1,971
7       Hotel      950       960       969       979       989       998
8      Rental      875       884       893       902       911       920
9       Group      800       808       816       824       832       841
10  VAN NESS
11       Tour    3,400     3,434     3,468     3,503     3,538     3,573
12     Flight    2,175     2,197     2,219     2,241     2,263     2,286
13      Hotel    1,350     1,364     1,377     1,391     1,405     1,419
14     Rental      975       985       995     1,005     1,015     1,025
15      Group    1,100     1,111     1,122     1,133     1,145     1,156
16  UNION SQ.
17       Tour    2,875     2,904     2,933     2,962     2,992     3,022
18     Flight    4,500     4,545     4,590     4,636     4,683     4,730
19      Hotel    1,150     1,162     1,173     1,185     1,197     1,209
20     Rental      925       934       944       953       963       972
05-Nov-91   04:15 PM                                              NUM
```

Problems with Relatives

Since the growth rate is stated in G1, you might be tempted simply to enter the formula G1*B5 in C5 and copy it to the other cells. This way you could just change the factor in G1 and the change would be reflected throughout the model. Although that approach is basically a good idea, it can create problems. Remember that entering a formula like 1.01*B5 in C5 means that C5 is 1.01 times the cell to the left of C5. When you copy this formula to D5, D5 becomes 1.01*C5, 1.01 times the cell to the left of D5. The formula +G1*B5 in C5 returns the product of the cell that is up four rows and over four columns, and the cell to the left. If you copy this formula from C5 to D5, you get +H1*C5, the cell that is up four rows and over five columns, times the cell to the left. Since H1 is empty, the answer will be 0. The same would apply to all other cells in the row if you copied the formula across the row, as shown in Figure 6.21.

If you copy a formula and the answer is an unexpected zero, move the cell pointer to the first offending cell and check the contents next to the cell address indicator. In the case of D5, it is +H1*C5, as predicted.

Absolute Solutions

To solve this problem, you need a way to keep the reference to cell G1 from changing as you copy the formula. You can do this by making that reference *absolute* instead of relative. What you want to say is that C5 is absolutely G1 times B5. To make a cell reference absolute, you place a dollar sign in front of the coordinates. Thus you can copy $G$1*B5 from C5 to any cell and the result will be G1 times the cell to the left of the formula.

Figure 6.21

Problems copying a formula

```
D5: (,0) +H1*C5                                                         READY

            A          B          C          D          E          F          G          ◄
1    Revenue Projection, Based on Monthly Growth Factor of:                    1.01       ►
2                                                                                          ▲
3                     Jan-92     Feb-92     Mar-92     Apr-92     May-92     Jun-92         ▼
4    POLK ST.                                                                              ?
5            Tour      3,350      3,384          0          0          0          0
6            Flight    1,875      1,894      1,913      1,932      1,951      1,971
7            Hotel       950        960        969        979        989        998
8            Rental      875        884        893        902        911        920
9            Group       800        808        816        824        032        041
10   VAN NESS
11           Tour      3,400      3,434      3,468      3,503      3,538      3,573
12           Flight    2,175      2,197      2,219      2,241      2,263      2,286
13           Hotel     1,350      1,364      1,377      1,391      1,405      1,419
14           Rental      975        985        995      1,005      1,015      1,025
15           Group     1,100      1,111      1,122      1,133      1,145      1,156
16   UNION SQ.
17           Tour      2,875      2,904      2,933      2,962      2,992      3,022
18           Flight    4,500      4,545      4,590      4,636      4,683      4,730
19           Hotel     1,150      1,162      1,173      1,185      1,197      1,209
20           Rental      925        934        944        953        963        972
05-Nov-91   05:56 PM                                                        NUM
```

There are two ways to add dollar signs to a cell reference: You can type them in yourself, or, with the cursor next to the cell reference on the editing line, you can press the Absolute key, F4, and 1-2-3 will add dollar signs for you. In fact, if you keep pressing F4, 1-2-3 will show you the four possible cell references:

- $G$1   Absolutely cell G1

- $G1   Absolutely column G, but relative row

- G$1   Relative column, but absolutely row 4

- G1   Completely relative

The Absolute key, F4, can be used either while entering or editing a formula and always affects the cell reference at or to the left of the cursor. In the sample model, either type the formula $G$1*B5 into C5 or press F2, move the cursor back to the asterisk, press F4 once, and press Enter. Then copy the formula to the range C5..M27. (You will create several extra rows of zeros that you can remove with Range Erase.) The formula will work correctly now, and you can update the rate in G1 to 1.02 and see all of the affected cells change, as shown in Figure 6.22.

The absolute reference is necessary whenever you are writing formulas that are going to be copied but need to refer to a specific cell or range of cells in their new locations. A typical example of this is a reference to a rate, growth factor, or other spreadsheet assumption that is located outside the main body of the model.

Figure 6.22

Altering the growth factor

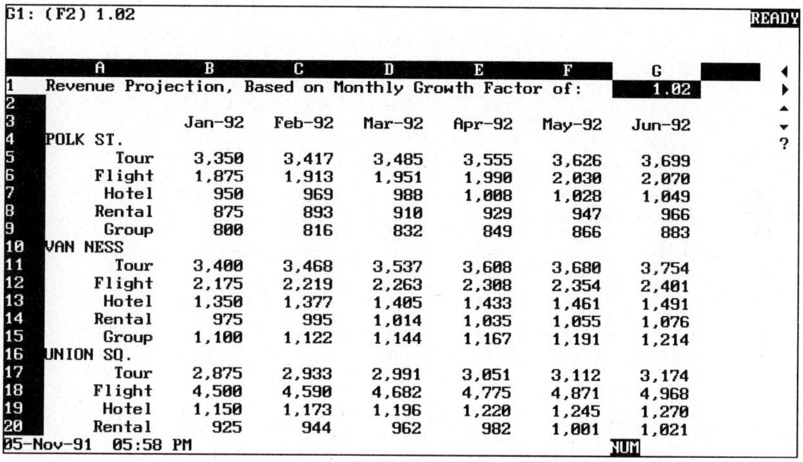

```
G1: (F2) 1.02                                                        READY

             A        B        C        D        E        F        G        ◀
1  Revenue Projection, Based on Monthly Growth Factor of:         1.02      ▶
2                                                                            ▲
3                 Jan-92   Feb-92   Mar-92   Apr-92   May-92   Jun-92         ▼
4  POLK ST.                                                                  ?
5          Tour     3,350    3,417    3,485    3,555    3,626    3,699
6        Flight     1,875    1,913    1,951    1,990    2,030    2,070
7         Hotel       950      969      988    1,008    1,028    1,049
8        Rental       875      893      910      929      947      966
9         Group       800      816      832      849      866      883
10 VAN NESS
11         Tour     3,400    3,468    3,537    3,608    3,680    3,754
12       Flight     2,175    2,219    2,263    2,308    2,354    2,401
13        Hotel     1,350    1,377    1,405    1,433    1,461    1,491
14       Rental       975      995    1,014    1,035    1,055    1,076
15        Group     1,100    1,122    1,144    1,167    1,191    1,214
16 UNION SQ.
17         Tour     2,875    2,933    2,991    3,051    3,112    3,174
18       Flight     4,500    4,590    4,682    4,775    4,871    4,968
19        Hotel     1,150    1,173    1,196    1,220    1,245    1,270
20       Rental       925      944      962      982    1,001    1,021
05-Nov-91   05:58 PM                                              NUM
```

Tidying Up

Your improved and expanded model is almost ready to print. Before you do this, you might want to tidy up the worksheet—that is, remove any unnecessary columns and rows. Earlier you saw that the End, Home sequence moves the cell pointer to the "last cell" of the worksheet, the junction of the column and row furthest from A1 that have been used. In this example, and in many of your own worksheets, this cell should coincide with the last cell of a model. If it does not, your worksheet may be taking up unnecessary space in memory because 1-2-3 remembers columns and rows that are no longer in use.

To see how this can happen, press Home, press Tab three times, and then press PgDn three times. This will move the cell pointer to Y61. Now type **9** and press Enter. This means that 1-2-3 must use space in RAM to remember all of the cells from A1 to Y61. Next use the Range Erase command to remove the contents of Y61. Press Home to move back to A1. Now press End followed by Home. The cell pointer will return to Y61, even though the cell is empty. At this point, 1-2-3 is still using space in RAM to remember all of the cells between N29 and the phantom entry in Y61, even though they are not in use.

To correct this problem, you save and then retrieve the worksheet. When you do so, 1-2-3 forgets phantom entries and corrects the "last cell" to reflect accurately the junction of the column and row in use and furthest from A1. While you are working on a model, the End, Home sequence is a handy way of checking how much of the worksheet area you have used, and it may reveal redundant entries that can be erased. Bear in mind that if you format a cell, that cell is considered to be in use even if its contents have been erased.

A quick way of cleaning up a model is to delete all columns and rows that are beyond the last cell of the model. To do this with the sample worksheet, you would place the cell pointer in the cell that is one row and one column past the end of the model, in this case O30, and then issue the Worksheet Delete Row command. To define the rows to be deleted, you would press End and then Home. This would ensure that row 30 and all rows down to the end of the worksheet were included. Then you would press Enter. The operation is repeated with the Worksheet Delete Column command. When completed, the two commands will have cleared any worksheet entries that were outside the model. Of course, before performing any delete operation you should make sure that the areas being erased do not contain any valuable data.

Worksheet Printing

Now that you know how to view and update your model, you need to learn how to produce a printed copy. 1-2-3 can produce anything from a simple, one-page printout to a carefully formatted multiple-page report with headers, footers, and other enhancements.

There are essentially two ways to print spreadsheet reports with 1-2-3: You can use the Print command on the main menu, or you can use the Wysiwyg add-in. The Print command is preferable for quick jobs when output quality is not critical. You should use the Wysiwyg option, discussed in detail in Chapter 10, for complex formatting tasks that you may not be able to accomplish with Wysiwyg. Even if you plan to use Wysiwyg for most of your printing, however, you should first familiarize yourself with the regular Print command since many of its features are similar to Wysiwyg.

The Print Command

To initiate printing, you select the Print command from the main menu. 1-2-3 will display a menu with the choices Printer, File, Encoded, and Background. If you want to send output directly to your printer, choose Printer. (The other options are covered later in this chapter.) When you choose Printer, you see the Print Settings dialog box shown in Figure 6.23.

This screen shows 1-2-3's initial default print settings. These settings make several assumptions about your printer and paper. It is assumed that the paper is $8^1/_2$-by-11-inch American letter size. It is assumed that the printer will be printing at ten characters per inch (10 pitch)—a fairly common setting on most printers. This gives a maximum number of 85 characters that could be printed on one line (10 × 8.5). With the default margin settings of 4 and 76, both measured in characters from the left edge of the page, 1-2-3 will put a maximum of 72 characters on each line (76–4=72). It is further assumed that the printer will be spacing the lines of print six to the inch, giving a page length of 66 (6 × 11).

Figure 6.23
The Print Settings
dialog box

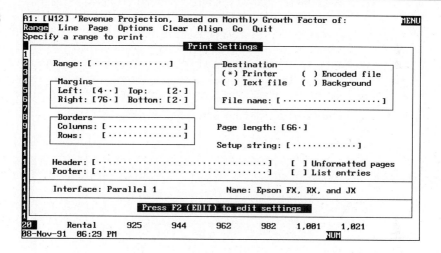

You can alter these settings for the current worksheet. The new settings will then be recorded with the worksheet when you use the File Save command. Also, you can record your own print defaults, which then take effect for all new worksheets, as described in the next section.

The Print Settings Dialog Box

Most of the screen shown in Figure 6.23 is taken up by the Print Settings dialog box. The use of dialog boxes in general was described in Chapter 2. This particular box determines the appearance of the printed output produced when you issue the Go command that tells 1-2-3 to print your worksheet.

Dialog boxes both show you the current settings and allow you to change the settings. You can change the settings with your mouse, or you can edit the settings from the keyboard by pressing the F2 key. Alternatively, you can change the settings by choosing the appropriate menu items. Changes you make with the menu system will be reflected in the dialog box. If you don't want to use the dialog box, you can press F6 to turn it off and reveal the worksheet underneath. (Pressing F6 a second time restores the dialog box.)

Towards the bottom of the Print Settings dialog box are the current settings for your printer interface and printer model. These settings cannot be changed from the Print Settings dialog box. Instead you must use the Default Printer Settings dialog box, which you access by issuing the Worksheet Global Default Printer command. If you need to change the printer model or printer interface, refer to the section on printer defaults in the next chapter.

Range-Align-Go

While 1-2-3 provides numerous options for print operations, you may get acceptable results with just three commands: Range, Align, and Go. You use Range to tell 1-2-3 which cells are to be printed; you specify the desired coordinates either by typing them in or by pointing out the cells. Align resets the line counter to zero and the page number to one, ensuring that the printer and 1-2-3 agree about where on the page the printing should begin. Go initiates the actual printing once you have specified a range and aligned the paper.

Make *sure* not to choose Go unless you have followed the four steps to proper PC printer operation: Plug in, turn on, load up, and go on-line. In other words, before you initiate printing you should have a printer connected to your PC, the printer must be powered up and loaded with paper, and the on-line light must be on. If not, you may confuse 1-2-3. A good precautionary measure is to save your worksheet before you begin printing.

The Print Range

To see how 1-2-3 handles basic printing, try printing the first six months of the sample worksheet. The basic operation is as follows:

1. If you haven't already, select Print followed by Printer. Then select Range. The initial coordinate is not locked, so you can move it freely to identify the upper-left corner of the range of cells to be printed.

2. Select A1..G29 as the print range. If you are using the keyboard, press Home and the cell pointer will move to A1. (If your titles are still frozen, you may have to use the arrow keys to move to A1.) Anchor the print range coordinates at A1 by typing a period and then press Right Arrow to move to column G. Now press PgDn and Down Arrow to include all cells through G29. Press Enter to confirm this range.

3. 1-2-3 returns you to the Print Settings menu. If your printer is hooked up, powered up, has paper in it, and is on-line, you can now select Align followed by Go.

The mode indicator will flash the word WAIT and, if you are using a dot-matrix or daisy wheel printer, you will hear the printer printing. When the mode indicator changes back to MENU, select the Page option to eject the page. (The Page option is explained more in the next section.) The results will look something like Figure 6.24 if you are using letter size paper and ten characters per inch.

```
Revenue Projection, Based on Monthly Growth Factor of:      1.02

               Jan-92  Feb-92  Mar-92  Apr-92  May-92  Jun-92
POLK ST.
         Tour  3,350   3,417   3,485   3,555   3,626   3,699
       Flight  1,875   1,913   1,951   1,990   2,030   2,070
        Hotel    950     969     988   1,008   1,028   1,049
       Rental    875     893     910     929     947     966
        Group    800     816     832     849     866     883
VAN NESS
         Tour  3,400   3,468   3,537   3,608   3,680   3,754
       Flight  2,175   2,219   2,263   2,308   2,354   2,401
        Hotel  1,350   1,377   1,405   1,433   1,461   1,491
       Rental    975     995   1,014   1,035   1,055   1,076
        Group  1,100   1,122   1,144   1,167   1,191   1,214
UNION SQ.
         Tour  2,875   2,933   2,991   3,051   3,112   3,174
       Flight  4,500   4,590   4,682   4,775   4,871   4,968
        Hotel  1,150   1,173   1,196   1,220   1,245   1,270
       Rental    925     944     962     982   1,001   1,021
        Group    950     969     988   1,008   1,028   1,049
EMBARCADERO
         Tour  3,140   3,203   3,267   3,332   3,399   3,467
       Flight  2,100   2,142   2,185   2,229   2,273   2,319
        Hotel  1,250   1,275   1,301   1,327   1,353   1,380
       Rental    950     969     988   1,008   1,028   1,049
        Group  2,500   2,550   2,601   2,653   2,706   2,760

TOTAL         37,190  37,934  38,692  39,466  40,256  41,061
```

If you want to select the print range by means of the dialog box, you can use either keystrokes or a mouse. With a mouse, click on the Range field in the dialog box to activate it. Then press F4 to switch to the worksheet in POINT mode. Now indicate the range by clicking and dragging. Click within the range you have selected in order to confirm it and return to the dialog box.

Using the keyboard, press F2 to edit the dialog box settings, and then press Home to move the highlighting to the Range field. Now press Enter to activate the Range field. At this point, you can press F4 to switch to POINT mode and select the range using the keystrokes described above. When you press Enter, the range is confirmed and you are returned to the dialog box. Of course, you can also activate the Range field by typing **R** after pressing F2.

Sometimes you don't need to print your entire spreadsheet, but you may want to print more than will fit neatly onto a regular page. For example, you may want to print the entire sample model. In this case, you need something more than simple Range-Align-Go printing. You also need to understand how 1-2-3 measures the printed page and relates the print range to it.

Adjusting the Printer

When working with 1-2-3 printouts, you may want to advance the paper in the printer. You should avoid the temptation to advance the paper by hand because this spoils the line count that 1-2-3 maintains as it sends data to the printer. To advance paper and maintain the accuracy of the line count, use the Line command on the main print menu to move the paper forward one line at a time.

Similarly, you can use the Page command to eject the current sheet of paper. This command is often used to eject the last page of a report when the report does not take up the entire page. The Page command is particularly important if you have a footer that contains a page number. If you eject the last page with the Page command, the page number will be printed, whereas it may not appear if you simply remove the paper by hand.

If you do advance the paper by hand, use the Align command to let 1-2-3 know that the current position of the paper in the printer is correct, that is, the printhead is at the top of the form. If you use background printing, described at the end of this chapter, the last page is automatically ejected for you.

Page Layout

How much you can print on a page depends on both the size of your print range and your print settings, including the size of the paper and the margins that define the printing area. The following print settings affect what will fit on the page:

- You can create headers and footers to appear at the top and bottom of every page of a report.

- You can change margins to accommodate different sizes of paper and different type sizes.

- You can define borders so as to repeat column and row labels in multiple-page reports.

- You can define a setup string to turn on or off special printer features.

- You can alter page length to match differences in page size and character height.

- You can print output with various types of print formatting.

Several of these settings appear in Figure 6.25.

Figure 6.25

Diagram of print parameters

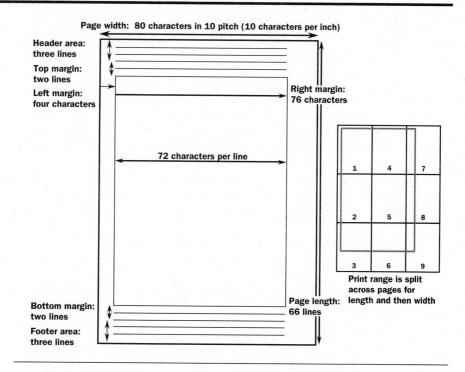

You can familiarize yourself with the way 1-2-3 relates to your printer by defining the entire sample spreadsheet as the print range, from A1..N29. Then use the Align and Go commands to print the model using the default settings. Typical results are shown in Figure 6.26.

Note that the information flows over two pages but has no page numbers and that the second page lacks row labels to explain the data. There are several different ways to solve these problems. You can increase the size of the paper, reduce the size of the type, repeat some information on successive pages, and add headers and footers.

Figure 6.26

A two-page report

```
Revenue Projection, Based on Monthly Growth Factor of:      1.02

             Jan-92  Feb-92  Mar-92  Apr-92  May-92  Jun-92

POLK ST.
         Tour   3,350   3,417   3,485   3,555   3,626   3,699
         Flight 1,875   1,913   1,951   1,990   2,030   2,070


   Jul-92  Aug-92  Sep-92  Oct-92  Nov-92  Dec-92   TOTALS

   3,773   3,848   3,925   4,004   4,084   4,165   44,931
   2,112   2,154   2,197   2,241   2,286   2,331   25,148
   1,070   1,091   1,113   1,135   1,158   1,181   12,741
     985   1,005   1,025   1,046   1,067   1,088   11,736
     901     919     937     956     975     995   10,730

   3,829   3,906   3,984   4,063   4,145   4,227   45,601
   2,449   2,498   2,548   2,599   2,651   2,704   29,171
   1,520   1,551   1,582   1,613   1,646   1,679   18,106
   1,098   1,120   1,142   1,165   1,189   1,212   13,077
   1,239   1,264   1,289   1,315   1,341   1,368   14,753

   3,238   3,302   3,369   3,436   3,505   3,575   38,560
   5,068   5,169   5,272   5,378   5,485   5,595   60,354
   1,295   1,321   1,347   1,374   1,402   1,430   15,424
   1,042   1,063   1,084   1,105   1,128   1,150   12,406
   1,070   1,091   1,113   1,135   1,158   1,181   12,741

   3,536   3,607   3,679   3,753   3,828   3,904   42,114
   2,365   2,412   2,460   2,510   2,560   2,611   28,165
   1,408   1,436   1,465   1,494   1,524   1,554   16,765
   1,070   1,091   1,113   1,135   1,158   1,181   12,741
   2,815   2,872   2,929   2,988   3,047   3,108   33,530

  41,882  42,720  43,574  44,445  45,334  46,241  498,796
```

Setting Borders

The report in Figure 6.26 would be easier to read if the revenue categories were repeated on the second page. To accomplish this, select the Options command on the Print Settings menu and choose Borders. You can select Columns to identify a column or columns of cells to be printed down the left side of each page (row headings). Select Rows to identify rows of cells to be printed across the top of each page (column headings). In this example, the Borders Columns setting should be A4..A29 and the Borders Rows setting should be B3..N3.

When you use print borders, you must redefine the print range to exclude areas included in the borders. (Otherwise, you will get some duplicated columns/rows in your printout.) Thus the print range in this case should be B4..N29. The first page of the printout that results from these settings is much the same as that in Figure 6.26. However, the second page is different, as shown in Figure 6.27.

Figure 6.27
Printing with borders

	Jan-92	Feb-92	Mar-92	Apr-92	May-92	Jun-92
POLK ST.						
Tour	3,350	3,417	3,485	3,555	3,626	3,699
Flight	1,875	1,913	1,951	1,990	2,030	2,070
Hotel	950	969	988	1,008	1,028	1,049

	Jul-92	Aug-92	Sep-92	Oct-92	Nov-92	Dec-92
POLK ST.						
Tour	3,773	3,848	3,925	4,004	4,084	4,165
Flight	2,112	2,154	2,197	2,241	2,286	2,331
Hotel	1,070	1,091	1,113	1,135	1,158	1,181
Rental	985	1,005	1,025	1,046	1,067	1,088
Group	901	919	937	956	975	995

	TOTALS
POLK ST.	
Tour	44,931
Flight	25,148
Hotel	12,741
Rental	11,736
Group	10,730
VAN NESS	
Tour	45,601
Flight	29,171
Hotel	18,106
Rental	13,077
Group	14,753
UNION SQ.	
Tour	38,560
Flight	60,354
Hotel	15,424
Rental	12,406
Group	12,741
EMBARCADERO	
Tour	42,114
Flight	28,165
Hotel	16,765
Rental	12,741
Group	33,530
TOTAL	498,796

The second page includes labels for the offices and revenue categories that are missing from Figure 6.26. However, there are two problems with the results in Figure 6.27. The title from row 1 has been excluded, and the last column of numbers has been pushed onto a third page. The answer appears to be further adjustment of the width settings.

Margins and the Width Factor

You saw in Figure 6.25 that the margins are a critical factor when adjusting print settings. If you used the Options Margins command to decrease the left margin or increase the right margin, you might be able to fit the entire report on two pages. However, you cannot increase the left and right margins by much without exceeding the limits of the page.

You could also use wider paper. However, 1-2-3 won't know that you have changed the paper unless you use the Options Margins Right command to increase the right margin. Assuming that you still use a 10 pitch type size, the 15-inch paper used in many wide-carriage printers will accept a right margin of 140. A sheet of 8 1/2-by-14-inch legal paper turned sideways can use a 132-character right margin. You must also increase margins if you reduce printer pitch. The condensed pitch of 17 characters per inch used on many printers allows a right margin of 140 on 8 1/2-inch paper and 250 on 15-inch paper.

You can place more cells on a page without changing the margins by narrowing the widths of some columns in the model. In the sample model, you could easily change columns B through M to eight characters using the Worksheet Column Column-Range command. This would save 12 characters of space (12 columns times 1 character per column)—a sufficient reduction in the width of the print range to allow the model to fit on two pages. You can see the results in Figure 6.28, which also shows a title supplied by a header, an option described in a moment.

A quick way to alter the width of a group of columns is to use the Column-Range command on the Worksheet Column menu. Choose Set-Width and then define the columns to be altered as a range, in this case B4..M4. When you enter the desired column width, all columns within the range are adjusted to that width at the same time.

Page Size and the Length Factor

Just about every popular printer can print characters at six lines per inch, making an 11-inch piece of paper 66 lines long. As you saw in Figure 6.25, 1-2-3 leaves a top and bottom margin of two lines, plus room for a header and footer. If you are working with paper longer or shorter than 11 inches, you must indicate the length measured in lines. Thus an 8 1/2-by-11-inch piece of paper printed on its side is 53 lines long. You can actually tell 1-2-3 that you have a 33-line sheet of paper and it will treat a regular sheet of paper as though it were two sheets. This feature can be useful if you print a model that is less than 18 rows long.

Figure 6.28
Report with
narrower columns

```
        Revenue Projection, Based on Monthly Growth Factor of: 1.02

          Jan-92  Feb-92   Mar-92   Apr-92   May-92    Jun-92  Jul-92
POLK ST.
      Tour  3,350   3,417    3,485    3,555    3,626     3,699   3,773
    Flight  1,875   1,913    1,951    1,990    2,030     2,070   2,112
     Hotel    950     969      988    1,008    1,028     1,049   1,070
```

```
        Revenue Projection, Based on Monthly Growth Factor of:   1.02

          Aug-92   Sep-92   Oct-92   Nov-92   Dec-92    TOTALS
POLK ST.
      Tour  3,848    3,925    4,004    4,084    4,165    44,931
    Flight  2,154    2,197    2,241    2,286    2,331    25,148
     Hotel  1,091    1,113    1,135    1,158    1,181    12,741
    Rental  1,005    1,025    1,046    1,067    1,088    11,736
     Group    919      937      956      975      995    10,730
VAN NESS
      Tour  3,906    3,984    4,063    4,145    4,227    45,601
    Flight  2,498    2,548    2,599    2,651    2,704    29,171
     Hotel  1,551    1,582    1,613    1,646    1,679    18,106
    Rental  1,120    1,142    1,165    1,189    1,212    13,077
     Group  1,264    1,289    1,315    1,341    1,368    14,753
UNION SQ.
      Tour  3,302    3,369    3,436    3,505    3,575    38,560
    Flight  5,169    5,272    5,378    5,485    5,595    60,354
     Hotel  1,321    1,347    1,374    1,402    1,430    15,424
    Rental  1,063    1,084    1,105    1,128    1,150    12,406
     Group  1,091    1,113    1,135    1,158    1,181    12,741
EMBARCADERO
      Tour  3,607    3,679    3,753    3,828    3,904    42,114
    Flight  2,412    2,460    2,510    2,560    2,611    28,165
     Hotel  1,436    1,465    1,494    1,524    1,554    16,765
    Rental  1,091    1,113    1,135    1,158    1,181    12,741
     Group  2,872    2,929    2,988    3,047    3,108    33,530

TOTAL     42,720   43,574   44,445   45,334   46,241   498,796
```

Bear in mind that 1-2-3 normally reserves three lines at the top and bottom of each page for a header and footer, features that are described in the next section. Even if you do not use a header or footer, 1-2-3 reserves space for them in addition to the two-line top and bottom margins. This means that you can reduce the top and bottom margins to zero without printing too close to the leading or trailing edge of the page. It also means that you cannot print more than 56 lines per page when the page length is 66.

Note that some printers cannot print over the entire surface of the page. For example, many laser printers cannot print close to the top and bottom edges of the page. For this reason, you may need to set a page length of 60 rather than 66. (This page length is definitely advisable with a Hewlett-Packard LaserJet.)

By now you probably noticed that 1-2-3's Print command is line oriented rather than page oriented. This is because much of the printing done with 1-2-3 is on what are sometimes called *line printers*—dot-matrix printers that feed paper past a moving printhead that prints information one line at a time. This approach is quite different from that used in *page printers* such as the LaserJet, which print an entire page at once.

One advantage of this line-oriented approach is that you can send several different ranges to the printer, one after the other, without each one having to be on a separate piece of paper. This means that you can print several small ranges one after another on the same page. To do this, you define the first range, issue the Align command followed by the Go command, and then redefine the range. You print the second range without issuing the Align command. Without the Align command, 1-2-3 assumes that it can resume printing where it left off. 1-2-3 will keep track of how many lines have been used on the current page and will feed a second page when the total page length has been exceeded.

Creating Headers and Footers

Besides setting parts of the spreadsheet as border headings, you can repeat other information on each page of a multiple-page printout. The header and footer commands provide areas into which you type the text to be printed, along with formatting instructions that tell 1-2-3 how to align the text and special codes that print such information as the correct page number. The # sign tells 1-2-3 to enter the page number in a header or footer. The @ sign prints the current date, according to your PC's clock, in the format currently used by the on-screen clock/calendar.

The straight line symbol (|) is used like a tab stop to position header and footer text across the line. If you type the header text with no | symbol, 1-2-3 left-aligns everything. If you precede text with one |, 1-2-3 centers all header and footer text. Using two || symbols right-aligns the text. In the sample worksheet, you could enter the following as a header:

```
Revenue Projection, Based on Monthly Growth Factor of: 1.12
```

This would center the title over each page of the report, as seen in Figure 6.28. For a footer you might enter

```
Prepared on @|By P. Smith||Page #
```

This will print a footer that includes the date and the page number, like this:

```
Prepared on 03-Oct-91        By P. Smith              Page 1
```

Bear in mind that if you do not issue the Align command before printing, the page numbers will not start with 1. To print the footer on the last page with the page number in place, use Page to eject the paper; do not use the printer's form feed button.

Headers and footers are limited to one line in length, and can include as many characters as are permitted on one line by the current margin settings. You can use the contents of a cell as a header or footer by entering the cell reference preceded by a backslash, as in \A1. You can also use a range name for a header or footer, as in \HEADER, which will cause the contents of the upper-left cell of the range called HEADER to be used. However, you can only use one cell reference per header or footer and you cannot combine the cell/range reference feature with others such as the alignment character (|) or the page number symbol (#).

As mentioned, 1-2-3 always reserves three lines for headers and footers: one line for the text of the header or footer, the other two to separate the header or footer from the body of the report. If you do not use a header or footer, the three lines are still reserved. If you want to cancel a header or footer, simply select the Header or Footer command, press Backspace to clear the current entry, and then press Enter to confirm a blank header or footer. You can also leave headers and footers out of a report without cancelling them. The Unformatted option on the Options Other menu tells 1-2-3 to print reports without headers, footers, or page breaks. This option will be discussed in more detail in the section "Formatting Output."

Making Page Breaks

1-2-3 automatically inserts page breaks in reports according to the page length setting. Page breaks inserted by 1-2-3 are referred to as *soft page breaks,* since they change position according to the page length and top and bottom margin settings. However, you can specify *hard page breaks* to force breaks at chosen points in your document. A hard page break consists of the | character followed by two colons (|::). You insert this special code into the worksheet in an otherwise empty row. Since the row is not printed, you can insert a fresh row in a model solely to hold the page break code. The code is stored as part of the worksheet and is not removed until you delete it.

To create a hard page break, either type the code in a blank row or select Page from the Worksheet menu. The Page command inserts a row and enters the code. Note that the page break code should be in the left-hand column of the print range, and not in any border range.

Print Defaults

When you save a worksheet, the print settings in effect at the time of the save are stored with the worksheet data. If you need to change the print settings, perhaps to print a different section of the same worksheet, you can use the Clear command on the Print Settings menu. This provides the following four options:

- All restores default values for all print settings and clears the current print range.

- Range clears the current print range.

- Borders clears any row or column ranges used for borders.

- Format returns to default values all margin, page length, and setup string settings.

Of course, you may want to edit your print settings within the dialog box rather than using the Clear command. For example, to clear the print range, simply activate the Range field in the dialog box, press Esc or the right mouse button to clear the cell coordinates, and then press Enter or select OK. (To activate the Range field without a mouse, press F2 to edit the settings, and then type **R** to select Range.) Note that you can use Esc to clear a range from a dialog box setting, but not from a menu setting. If you select Range from the menu and then press Esc, you will not clear the range; instead you end up with a single cell range.

If you will be using the same basic print settings on a regular basis, you can incorporate them into the system defaults, as described in the next chapter.

Formatting Output

Unfortunately, the term "format" is rather overused in 1-2-3 and this can lead to confusion in the print commands. You use the print command Clear Format to return all margin, page length, and setup string settings to the default values. However, the Print Options Other menu uses the term "formatted" in a slightly different context. When you select Other from the Print Options menu, 1-2-3 displays a menu with the following options:

```
As-Displayed Cell-Formulas Formatted Unformatted
```

The As-Displayed and Formatted choices constitute the default setting and together they simply mean that the contents of the print range will appear in print as they do on screen. By using the four items on this menu, you control the data format—the appearance of printed data—which can be either As-Displayed or Cell-Formulas. You also control the print format—the arrangement of information on the page—which can be either Formatted or Unformatted.

You use the Cell-Formulas option if you want a list of what is in every cell in a worksheet, including the cell format and width if it differs from the global setting. This option corresponds to choosing List entries in the Print Settings dialog box. The resulting printout lists the cells that are in the print range down the left margin of the page. This is a useful reference when you are checking a worksheet for accuracy or exchanging worksheet details with other users. In Figure 6.29, you can see the range A1..G6 of the sample worksheet printed in this way. The cell contents are printed as they appear at the top of the screen when the cell is highlighted. Another user could re-create a spreadsheet design from a listing such as this, as all formulas and format information is included.

Figure 6.29

Printout with Cell-
Formulas as the
Output setting

```
A1:  [W12] 'Revenue Projection, Based on Monthly Growth Factor of:
G1:  (F2)   [W8]  1.02
B3:  (D3)   [W8]  @DATE(92,1,1)
C3:  (D3)   [W8]  31+B3
D3:  (D3)   [W8]  31+C3
E3:  (D3)   [W8]  31+D3
F3:  (D3)   [W8]  31+E3
G3:  (D3)   [W8]  31+F3
A4:  [W12] 'POLK ST.
A5:  [W12] "Tour
B5:  (,0)   [W8]  1875
C5:  (,0)   [W8]  +$G$1*B5
D5:  (,0)   [W8]  +$G$1*C5
E5:  (,0)   [W8]  +$G$1*D5
F5:  (,0)   [W8]  +$G$1*E5
G5:  (,0)   [W8]  +$G$1*F5
A6:  [W12] "Flight
B6:  (,0)   [W8]  1875
C6:  (,0)   [W8]  +$G$1*B6
D6:  (,0)   [W8]  +$G$1*C6
E6:  (,0)   [W8]  +$G$1*D6
F6:  (,0)   [W8]  +$G$1*E6
G6:  (,0)   [W8]  +$G$1*F6
```

Normally, 1-2-3 prints as much data per page as it can while recognizing hard page break codes, inserting soft page breaks as needed, and allowing room for headers and footers. This is the type of printing you get when Formatted is selected. The Unformatted option on the Other menu tells 1-2-3 to disregard headers, footers, and page breaks. This corresponds to selecting Unformatted pages from the dialog box and is useful if you want a continuous stream of output—for example, to print mailing labels or to send data to a text file. For more on printing to a text file, see Chapter 10. To restore normal printing after selecting either Cell-Formulas or Unformatted, choose As-Displayed and Formatted, or edit out the crosses from the List entries and Unformatted pages check boxes in the Print Settings dialog box.

Setting Setups

You can change the print style, print pitch, and other aspects of many printers via codes transmitted as part of the print data sent from the program. 1-2-3 accommodates these codes as printer setup strings, which are sent ahead of the data to set the printer. For example, to most IBM and EPSON dot-matrix printers, the characters \015 mean small print (15 pitch).

You use the Setup command on the Options menu to enter a setup string. To activate small print on an Epson, you would select Setup, type **\015**, and press Enter. This code would then precede the rest of the print data the next time you issue the Go command. Note that this code turns on the small print, but does not turn it off after the print job. To turn off the feature, you either send a "small print off" setup string with the next print job, or reset the printer. (This usually involves turning it off and then back on again.) If you do not turn off a feature, you risk annoying others who use the printer. For example, if you turn on boldface with a 1-2-3 setup string and forget to switch it off, other users may get boldface when they expect regular print.

You can combine several strings in one setup string. For example, entering **\015\0270** as a setup string turns on condensed print and eight line per inch spacing for most Epson and IBM dot-matrix printers. Note that 1-2-3 does not know what the codes mean; it merely carries them to the printer. If you activate 15 characters per inch, you will presumably want to alter the right margin to make room for more characters per line. (120 should work nicely.) Likewise, if you alter the line spacing to eight lines per inch you will want to change the page length to reflect the added lines (88 lines on an 11-inch sheet).

You can also activate print features by inserting setup strings into the worksheet. To do this, you first insert a blank row above the range to which you want the print feature applied. Then you insert a special code into the first column of the blank row. This code consists of two vertical bars followed by the setup code. Thus, if you want to turn on italic printing for a section of the worksheet and \0274 is the setup string, the code would be ||\0274. (This is the code used by an Epson FX printer.) Note that this code will turn on the feature, which will stay on until another code is received. If you want just part of the report to be italicized, you can enter the code for normal print in another blank row just above where you want normal print to resume. For the Epson FX, the code would be ||\0275. Bear in mind that you can also implement printer features by printing your worksheet with the Wysiwyg add-in, described in Chapter 10. This allows you to use a variety of fonts without resorting to setup strings.

Print Destinations and Background Printing

You will have noticed the group of Destination settings in the Print Settings dialog box. These setting include a text box called File name and four option buttons called Printer, Text file, Encoded file, and Background. These four option buttons correspond to the choice you make when you first select Print from the main 1-2-3 menu. For basic printing of paper reports, the Printer option is usually satisfactory. However, you may want to direct printer output to a file instead of a printer, or you may want to have 1-2-3 print while you continue working with the program. This section describes the destination options other than Printer.

Printing to a Text File

When you select Go from the Print menu, the information that 1-2-3 sends to your printer is actually a series of electronic codes representing each letter, digit, space, and line ending. These are known as ASCII codes (American Standard Code for Information Interchange). Most computer programs can read ASCII codes.

1-2-3 can divert the information from your printer into a file on disk that is made up of ASCII codes. This type of file, sometimes referred to as a text file or DOS printer file, contains nothing but the letters, digits, and spaces that would have been printed. Because this information is represented by ASCII codes, many different programs will be able to read it. This makes text files a useful tool for exporting information from 1-2-3 to other programs.

Chapter 11 contains a detailed example of how to use this feature. You select Print and then File from the 1-2-3 menu, at which point 1-2-3 asks you to name the file. Later, when you actually "print" the spreadsheet, it will be stored on disk with the first name you specified and the extension .PRN, as opposed to the .WK1 extension used for worksheet files. Having named the file, you will see the Print Settings menu with the file name included in the Destinations box. There will be an asterisk by the option button called Text file.

Now select the print parameters you want and issue the Go command. The print range is directed to the PRN file. This file remains open until you select Quit from the Print menu, allowing you to send several different print ranges to the same file.

Printing to an Encoded File

The PRN file created by the File option just described contains nothing but letters, digits, spaces, and line endings. It includes none of the details needed by your specific printer model, such as setup strings. If you select Print and then Encoded from the 1-2-3 menu, you can create a file that stores not only the data contained in your report but also the printer codes needed to format it properly on your printer.

This encoded file will have the extension .ENC. When you select Encoded and name the file, you can choose the print settings you want and then issue the Go command. The ENC file remains open, allowing you to send several different print ranges to the same file. When you select Quit from the Print menu, the file will be closed and written to disk.

An ENC file created in this manner can later be printed at the DOS prompt, after you have left 1-2-3. Suppose that you named the file REPORT. 1-2-3 will add the extension .ENC so the full file name is REPORT.ENC. You can enter the following command to send the report to the printer:

```
COPY REPORT.ENC/B LPT1:
```

The /B option helps DOS interpret the file correctly, and LPT1: is the DOS name for your parallel printer port. If you issue the command from a directory other than the one that contains the ENC file, you also need to include the path name, as in

```
COPY C:\123\DATA\REPORT.ENC/B LPT1:
```

Bear in mind that the information in the .ENC file is specific to the printer model selected when the file was created. Sending the file to a different type of printer may result in printing errors.

Background Printing

When printing a lot of lengthy reports, you might find it annoying that you have to wait until printing is completed before continuing your work with the program. The solution to this problem is background printing, a task performed by a special print management program that you load before the main 1-2-3 program. The program is called BPRINT and the program file, BPRINT.EXE, should have been copied to your 1-2-3 program directory when you installed 1-2-3.

To use background printing, you must type **BPRINT** at the DOS prompt before you load 1-2-3. You should not use the System command, described in the next chapter, to temporarily return to DOS and load BPRINT. (Doing so can prevent you from returning to 1-2-3, which could lead to loss of data.) See Appendix A if you want to include BPRINT in a batch file that starts 1-2-3.

Assuming you have started your 1-2-3 session with BPRINT, you can select Print and then Background when you want to print a report. At this point, 1-2-3 asks you to supply a file name. This will be an ENC file of the type used by the Encoded option; however, 1-2-3 will automatically erase the file as soon as the report has been printed to prevent redundant files from filling up your disk. By default, 1-2-3 uses your data directory for the ENC files. You can use a name like SPOOL, which will be stored temporarily as SPOOL.ENC while printing takes place, after which it will be deleted.

After naming a file, you will get to the Print Settings screen where the file name will be displayed in the Destination settings group and the Background option button will be marked with an asterisk. From this point print operations proceed as normal. When you issue the Align and Go commands there is a brief pause as the ENC file is written to disk, after which the Print Settings screen reappears. Background printing does not actually start until you select Quit to leave the Print Settings menu. At this point the ENC file is sent to the printer while you carry on working. Note that 1-2-3 will automatically eject the last page of the report.

Choosing a Destination

Now that you know more about the alternative print destinations you might want to experiment with them. Bear in mind that you can always change the print destination after you have reached the Print Settings screen. Simply check the box you want. If you choose any other than Printer you will also need to fill in the File name box. If you want to see a list of existing print files, press F3 while the File name box is active. This will pop up a list box showing appropriate files.

Summary

Before going on to the next chapter, you should save the sample worksheet one last time. Print settings are not stored until you save your worksheet on disk. You may spend quite a bit of time getting just the right settings for your report, only to lose your work if you do not save the worksheet. Also, the sample worksheet will be used in the next chapter when various aspects of spreadsheet file handling and linking are explored.

In this chapter, you learned how to create and work with a typical worksheet. You saw how the Print command controls printing of worksheet data. The alternative method of printing, using Wysiwyg, is covered in Chapter 10. The next chapter explains how to adjust the default settings in 1-2-3, and describes how you can link 1-2-3 files and exchange data between them.

CHAPTER

7

Files, Links, and Defaults

THIS CHAPTER EXPLAINS HOW TO HANDLE THE FILES YOU CREATE WITH
1-2-3 and discusses a variety of techniques for sharing information
between files. It details the use of add-in programs, including the
Viewer, which is used to manage files. You will also learn how to
customize underlying aspects of the program's operation, so that it more
closely meets your personal requirements.

Files, Disks, and DOS

The File menu shown in Figure 7.1 is one of the most important menus in
1-2-3. Among other things, you use this menu to store and retrieve your
worksheet files. As you know, the data you enter into a worksheet window is
not immediately stored in a file on disk. Instead, it is temporarily retained in
the computer's random access memory (RAM). You can think of RAM as an
electronic desktop on which the work that you do, such as entering and calculating, is performed very quickly.

Figure 7.1

The File menu

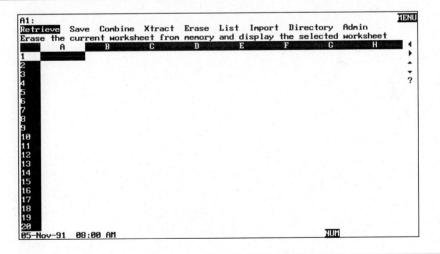

By retaining most of your worksheet in RAM, 1-2-3 can respond to commands and perform calculations very quickly. However, everything you have
entered into RAM is erased when the power to your PC is turned off or
interrupted. This is why it is critical to use the File menu on a regular basis to
transfer a copy of the worksheet from memory to disk. If you are already
familiar with how a computer stores data on disk and in memory, you may
want to skip the next section.

Operating-System Basics

When you turn it on, your computer first looks to the disk drives for information. Disks store information magnetically, as do music cassette and video tapes. On a disk, this magnetic storage medium is laid out flat. The *format*, an arrangement of concentric circles and pie-shaped wedges, divides the disk into a collection of numbered boxes or *sectors*. Information is both stored onto and retrieved from a disk by a device called the *read/write head*. Unlike the stationary read/write head in a tape recorder, the disk drive read/write head moves across the disk, locating information according to the system of sectors.

The first disk drive the computer looks to is floppy drive A. If there is no disk in the floppy-disk drive, the computer looks for a hard disk. What the computer always looks for first is the *operating system,* a collection of programs that control the flow of information between hardware and software, and manage the filing of information on disk. On an IBM PC or PC-compatible, the operating system is called the *disk operating system*, or DOS. This system can be PC-DOS, distributed by IBM; DR DOS from Digital Research; or MS-DOS, the version Microsoft licenses to many computer manufacturers.

The role of DOS is twofold. First, DOS manages the flow of information into and out of the computer, as illustrated in Figure 7.2. When you type the letter **A**, DOS makes sure that an A appears on the screen and that the character is stored and printed as an A. Although you may instruct 1-2-3 to print data, 1-2-3 actually passes that request on to DOS for execution.

Figure 7.2
DOS manages the flow of information

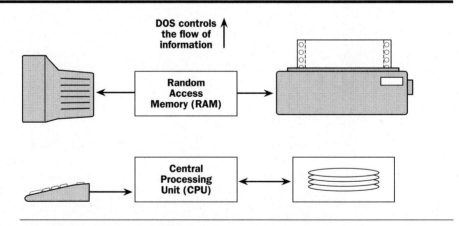

Besides being a flow manager, DOS is a file manager. The information your computer uses is stored in either program files or data files. DOS manages the arrangement of these files on the disk. Thus, it is actually DOS that executes your 1-2-3 File Save request, deciding which sectors of the disk the file will occupy and recording the sector numbers so that the file can be retrieved later.

When the computer finds DOS on either a floppy disk or the hard disk, it reads the essential files from the disk and loads them into memory. While the disk and disk drive use a combination of electronic and mechanical components, the computer's memory is purely electronic. It is a place where information can be changed much faster than on a disk. 1-2-3 takes good advantage of this speed by loading as much of the program as possible into memory.

Once the computer has loaded DOS into RAM, it can start handling your information. The date and time are usually supplied to the disk operating system at this point. You can type them in manually or they can read from a clock within the computer. DOS stores a record of the date and time whenever a file is written to disk. This information can be displayed when the file is listed, either by DOS or by a program like 1-2-3. 1-2-3 also uses the date and time for the on-screen clock/calendar display.

Disks and Directories

Just as 1-2-3 comes to you on disks, data created with the help of programs is also stored on disks. Information is stored on disks in files. As you work with your computer, you quickly create many files, and there is a practical limit to how many files you should store *en masse* on a disk. Large-capacity disks, particularly hard disks, are often divided into small, manageable sections called *directories* and *subdirectories*. This division is much like that used in the telephone directory of a large company. The main directory may list departments in its main section, rather than listing every single person in the company, and each department might have its own subdirectory listing each staff member. Directories and subdirectories are an important part of organizing your 1-2-3 work on your hard disk.

Hard Disks and Paths

A hard-disk directory system for a computer running 1-2-3 and WordPerfect might look like the one in Figure 7.3. When using a hard disk, you cannot be in two places at once. There is always one directory that is the current directory. When you issue a command, DOS normally assumes that the program and data files referred to in the command are stored in this directory. If you want DOS to find either a program file or a data file in another directory, you must specify a path for it to follow. For example, the path to the file EDITOR.DOC is C:\WP\LETTERS\. The path to the purchase-order entry worksheet in the SALES subdirectory of the 123 directory is C:\123\SALES\.

You can have more than one file with the same name on your hard disk if you keep the files in separate directories. However, it is generally safer to give each file a unique name. To accurately identify files on a hard disk, include the path to the file as part of the file name. In other words, the full name of the EDITOR.DOC file is

```
C:\WP\LETTERS\EDITOR.DOC
```

Figure 7.3
A hard-disk
directory system

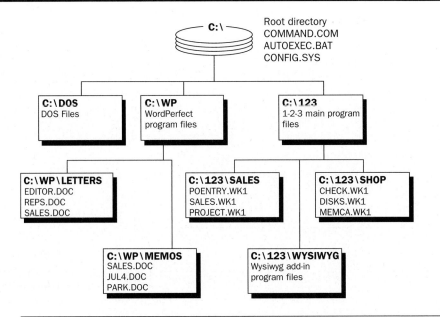

When you begin working with a disk, the best place to start is the root directory. The *root directory* of a drive is the highest level of the directory tree; it is signified by a single backslash, as in C:\. You can ensure that you are in the root directory by typing **CD** at the DOS prompt and pressing Enter. This command tells DOS to change to the root directory. You can quickly learn which directory is current by entering **CD** without the back-slash. Your system may already be set up to tell you the current directory in the DOS prompt, as described later in the section "Hard Disks and Paths."

You can also use the DOS PATH command, which creates a path setting that tells DOS the directories to look in when you issue a command to run a program. For example, suppose you enter **LOTUS** at the DOS prompt and DOS does not find a program file called LOTUS in the current directory. It will look in each of the directories listed in the path setting until it finds the LOTUS file. You can determine the current path setting on your PC by entering the word **PATH** at the DOS prompt. A typical response would be

```
C:\;C:\DOS;C:\123R23
```

If the program file you are trying to run is not in the current directory, this path tells DOS to look first in the root directory, then in the DOS directory, and finally in the 123R23 directory. To change the path setting, you simply enter the word **PATH** followed by an equal sign and the names of the directories you want to include, separated by semicolons. For instance, the following command created the previous path setting:

```
PATH=C:\;C:\DOS;C:\123R23
```

To avoid having to type a path statement every time you use your PC, you can include the PATH command in the AUTOEXEC.BAT file that is run whenever you start your PC. For more on AUTOEXEC.BAT, see Appendix A.

If your 1-2-3 program directory is included in the path setting, you can load 1-2-3 from any directory on your hard disk. For more about this feature, see the section "Where to Store Data" later in this chapter.

Programs and Prompts

After you have started, or *booted up*, your computer, it asks what programs you wish to execute by displaying the *system prompt*. The prompt can consist of several pieces of information. The first is usually the name of the drive that the computer is using (normally C for a hard drive) and the last is usually a > (greater than) sign. The DOS prompt can appear as C>, C:\>, or even Hello C:\>. For more on adjusting the prompt, see the section "Hard Disks and Paths." Following the prompt is the cursor, which points out where you are and where the next character you type will appear.

The System Command

Programs like 1-2-3 are called *applications* because they apply the power of the computer to useful tasks. To start an application program, you normally type the program name at the system prompt and then press the Enter key to send the request to the disk operating system. DOS will then look on the disk for the program and begin to load it into memory. In the case of 1-2-3, this means you type either **LOTUS** or **123** and press Enter. Entering **LOTUS** loads the 1-2-3 Access System from which you can access 1-2-3, PrintGraph, Translate, and Install. Entering **123** bypasses the access system and takes you straight into 1-2-3.

Once an application has been loaded into memory, you issue commands to the application and not to DOS. However, applications use DOS to carry out many important commands, such as File Save and File Retrieve in 1-2-3. When you load 1-2-3, part of DOS stays in memory. You can access DOS without actually unloading 1-2-3 from memory by using the System command. When you select System from the main 1-2-3 menu, you are taken to the operating system prompt, as shown in Figure 7.4.

Figure 7.4

The system prompt

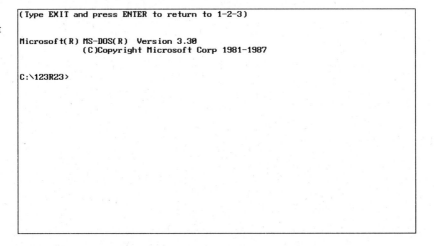

```
(Type EXIT and press ENTER to return to 1-2-3)

Microsoft(R) MS-DOS(R)  Version 3.30
          (C)Copyright Microsoft Corp 1981-1987


C:\123R23>
```

You can now issue DOS commands such as COPY. In Figure 7.5, you can see that the DOS command CHKDSK has been run. To return to 1-2-3, type **EXIT** and press Enter, as instructed at the top of the screen. (As you work with DOS, the message may disappear from the screen, so don't forget this procedure for getting back to 1-2-3.)

When you return to 1-2-3, your worksheet will be as you left it. Nevertheless, it is a good idea to save the worksheet before using the System command, since it is possible to issue commands at the DOS prompt that "lock up" your computer when you try to exit back to 1-2-3.

At the system prompt, you can use most DOS commands and even run other software, but the amount of memory available to run programs is limited, as you can see from the memory report in Figure 7.5. This is because both DOS and 1-2-3 are already loaded into memory. When you use the System command, you should be careful to run only programs that cleanly remove themselves from memory when they quit. This rules out loading any memory-resident software such as SideKick or even BRINT, the background print program described in Chapter 6, but it does allow you to use well-behaved utility software such as Norton Utilities or QDOS II.

Naming Files

You can enter commands at the DOS prompt in either upper- or lowercase, since DOS does not distinguish between the two. Similarly, when you ask

1-2-3 to store information in a file on the disk and 1-2-3 passes this request on to DOS, you can type the file name in either upper- or lowercase. However, DOS will remember the name in uppercase.

Figure 7.5

Using DOS at the system prompt

```
(Type EXIT and press ENTER to return to 1-2-3)


Microsoft(R) MS-DOS(R)  Version 3.30
              (C)Copyright Microsoft Corp 1981-1987


C:\123R23>chkdsk
Volume COMPANY PC  created Aug 25, 1991 10:32a

 32333824 bytes total disk space
   311296 bytes in 30 hidden files
   122880 bytes in 36 directories
 28811264 bytes in 1820 user files
  3088384 bytes available on disk

   655360 bytes total memory
   161728 bytes free

C:\123R23>
```

Every file stored in the same area of a disk must have a unique name. As described in Chapter 1, this name is composed of three parts: a first name, a period, and an optional extension. The first name consists of one to eight letters or numbers without spaces. You can use some punctuation marks in a file name, but it is usually easier to use numbers and letters. Valid punctuation characters for file names are

  ( ) ! @ # $ % & - _ ` { } ~ ' ^

If you use invalid characters, both 1-2-3 and DOS will respond with error messages.

The period has a special role in file names: It connects the first part of the file name with its extension. The extension is usually three characters long and follows the rules for file names. When extensions are used, they are often chosen to distinguish between types of files. For example, 1-2-3 Release 2.3 worksheets automatically have the extension .WK1. Note that Version 1A uses the extension .WKS for worksheet files, and the student edition of 1-2-3 uses .WKE. You should always allow 1-2-3 to assign the standard extension since worksheets named with other extensions will not show up in the worksheet file list.

Copying Files

At the DOS prompt you can copy files from one disk to another or from one subdirectory of a disk to another. You can also make a duplicate copy of a file and give it another name. If you want to copy a group of files, you can use special characters called *wildcards* to denote more than one file. DOS recognizes two wildcard characters. The asterisk represents any number of characters, and the question mark represents a single character.

For example, the command

```
COPY *.WK1 A:
```

tells the system to copy all files with the .WK1 extension in the current directory of the current disk to the disk in drive A. The term *file specification* is used to describe the characters *.WK1 since they specify a certain group of files. The command

```
COPY SALES.WK? A:
```

tells the system to copy to drive A all of the files with SALES as the file name and WK as the first two letters of the extension (this would include WKS and WK1 files). Because the question mark represents only one character, the file specification SALES?A.* includes SALES1A.WK1, SALES1A.DBF, and SALES2A.WK1, but not SALES3.WK1.

The COPY command is helpful when you need to make one or more copies of a worksheet for colleagues or when you want to create several versions of a file. For example, the sample worksheet in the last chapter showed revenue projections for four offices. If you want to make four separate files each tailored to a particular office, you could begin by using COPY at the DOS prompt to create four copies of the worksheet within the same directory, as in

```
COPY REVENUE.WK1 POLKREV.WK1
```

then

```
COPY REVENUE.WK1 VANSREV.WK1
```

and so on.

File Size

The size of files is measured in bytes: the amount of space it takes to store one character, number, space, or piece of punctuation. However, you cannot directly relate the size of a data file to the number of characters you type into it. For example, files may contain information about how the data is arranged. 1-2-3 stores a typical worksheet of 1,250 active cells in 38,750 bytes of disk space.

Since one byte is a very small unit of measurement, you will often see bytes measured in units of *kilobytes*, abbreviated as k. Each kilobyte is 1,024 bytes, but just use 1,000 when converting from bytes to kilobytes. Thus, a worksheet that contains 38,750 bytes can be described as 38k in size. Extremely large files occupy megabytes—one *megabyte*, or Mb, is 1,024k, over a million bytes. The capacity of your disks is usually measured in kilobytes and megabytes. The older 5¼-inch floppy disks (known as double-sided double-density disks) store 360k. The newer 5¼-inch disks (known as high-density disks) used in the IBM PC AT can store 1.2 megabytes. The hard-jacketed 3½-inch disks used in many laptop PCs and the IBM PS/2 can store 720k, or 1.4 megabytes, depending on how they are formatted. Most hard disks hold at least 10 megabytes and some exceed 250 megabytes in capacity.

Backing Up

Earlier you learned that the COPY command is useful for copying worksheet files onto a floppy disk. In fact, you should regularly copy important worksheet files from your hard disk to a floppy disk just in case something goes wrong with your hard disk. This process is known as making an archive or backup copy. However, the COPY command is not really suitable as a backup tool, particularly since it cannot copy a group of files that takes up more than one floppy disk. BACKUP, the DOS command for making backup copies, is described in your DOS manual. While BACKUP comes free with DOS, it is not the most efficient program and you might want to consider a commercial alternative such as Backit or PC-FullBack. Another alternative is a hard-disk management utility such as QDOS II, which provides menu-driven file copying.

Working with Directories

The following sections provide tips for working with hard-disk directories, including how to make and remove directories and navigate through them.

Improving the Prompt

To navigate more easily in a hard disk with one or more subdirectories, it is useful to change the uninformative default DOS prompt. This prompt (usually C>) merely displays the current drive followed by a greater-than sign. A better prompt is C:\>, which tells you the drive you are using (C) and the current directory (in this case the root directory). If you move into subdirectory 123R23 of the root directory, the prompt reads C:\123R23>, as shown in Figure 7.5. (If your hard disk is not drive C but drive D or E or another valid letter, just substitute that letter for C in the discussions that follow; substitute your program directory for 123 if you used a different directory name.)

To change the prompt to this more informative version, you can enter **PROMPT PG** at the DOS prompt. When you press Enter, you will see the drive letter and the path (represented by $P) plus the greater-than sign (represented by $G). Once you enter the PROMPT command, the new prompt remains in effect until you turn off or reset your computer. To avoid having to reenter the command each time you turn on your computer, you might want to add the prompt command to your AUTOEXEC.BAT file, as described in Appendix A.

Making Directories

To see the path prompt in action and to explore the directory commands, change your location to a subdirectory such as the one for 1-2-3. Type **CD \123** and press Enter. Your prompt will change. To change your current location back to the root directory, type **CD ** and press Enter. To make a subdirectory directly below the root directory, type

```
MD \TEMP
```

and press Enter. MD is short for "make directory," and the long version of the command is MKDIR. To make a directory called MINE that is a subdirectory of the TEMP directory, type

```
MD \TEMP\MINE
```

and press Enter.

Suppose you want to copy all the files from a disk in drive A into this new directory. There are two ways of doing this. You can move into the subdirectory by entering

```
CD \TEMP\MINE
```

and then issue the command

```
COPY A:*.*
```

In this case, DOS assumes that the destination of the files is the current directory. Alternatively, you can type the more explicit command

```
COPY A:*.* C:\TEMP\MINE
```

while in the root or any other directory.

To remove a subdirectory, you must first remove all data and program files from it. Using the command DEL *.* from within a subdirectory deletes files only in that subdirectory, not across the whole disk. You can delete files from any subdirectory, not just the current one. For example, if you were in the root directory you could enter

```
DEL \TEMP\MINE\*.WK1
```

to delete all files with the .WK1 extension in the MINE subdirectory of the TEMP subdirectory. To remove an empty subdirectory you use the RD (remove directory) command. You must completely empty a directory of both files and subdirectories before you can remove it. To delete the directories you have created, start with the lowest level first. For example, enter

```
RD \TEMP\MINE
```

followed by

```
RD \TEMP
```

This will remove the TEMP and MINE directories.

Help with Directories and DOS

If the DOS directory commands seem difficult to grasp, you may want to use a program called a hard-disk organizer. A good example of this is type of program is QDOS II from Gazelle Systems. This program draws a picture of your directory system and provides sorted lists of files. QDOS II uses menus similar to those in 1-2-3 for all of the DOS commands such as COPY and DEL. Magellan from Lotus is another excellent program designed to help you organize your hard disk. This program works particularly well with 1-2-3 files.

Since DOS commands are not the easiest to learn and apply accurately, you may sometimes make mistakes. One of the worst is to delete the wrong file. Fortunately there is a cure for this. If you realize you have unintentionally erased a file, do not continue to move or store additional files. Instead, reach for an *undelete utility,* a special program that can reverse the delete procedure used by DOS. Several software packages include such undelete programs, including Norton Utilities and Mace Utilities.

Saving and Retrieving Files

You use 1-2-3's File Save command to store an up-to-date copy of the worksheet currently in memory into a file on disk. You use the File Retrieve command to erase the current worksheet from memory and replace it with a worksheet that is already stored in a file on disk. Since both File Save and File Retrieve list existing files, you can use them to choose which directory to save into or retrieve from. This section reviews the commands for saving

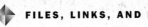

and retrieving files, including the management of file reservations used in networking, and the protection of files with passwords.

Where to Store Data

Chapter 1 mentioned that 1-2-3 generally assumes you want to save data files in the drive and directory in which you installed the program. However, when you first install 1-2-3, it makes no assumptions about where you want to store data files. The directory that a newly installed version of 1-2-3 uses for data files is the one that is current when the program is started. Since Chapter 1 recommended loading 1-2-3 from the 1-2-3 program directory, this is the directory that first appears when you use File Save. Thus, if you have stored 1-2-3 in C:\123, this will be the initial data directory.

To handle the occasional file that is not in the default directory, you need to edit the path when using the File Save or File Retrieve command, as described in the following sections. However, suppose you have 1-2-3 installed in C:\123, but you want 1-2-3 to store a series of worksheets on drive A. In this case, you can make a temporary change to the default directory by using the File Directory command. Select the Directory command from the File menu; you are prompted to "Enter current directory." The currently selected directory, in this case C:\123, is shown as the default.

Note that the cursor flashes under the first letter of this path name. When you type the path name of the new storage area, in this case **A:**, it replaces the current one. If you want to specify a particular directory you have created on A, you add a backslash (\) and the name of the directory, as in A:\WORK. When you have typed the new directory, press Enter. From now until you end the current 1-2-3 session or use the File Directory command again to select a different area, 1-2-3 will store files to and retrieve files from the new directory.

To make a more permanent change to the data directory setting, use the Worksheet Global Default Directory command and specify the directory you want 1-2-3 to use. You must then use the Worksheet Global Default Update command to record this preference in the configuration file that is read each time 1-2-3 is loaded (changing defaults is described in detail later in this chapter).

You can also leave the Worksheet Global Default Directory setting blank and allow 1-2-3 to use whatever directory is current when the program is loaded as a data directory. You can then start 1-2-3 from the directory that contains the files you need for the current session, and this will be the assumed directory when you issue the Save or Retrieve command. For example, when working on budget worksheets you might enter the following at the DOS prompt:

```
CD \123\DATA\BUDGET
```

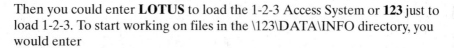

Then you could enter **LOTUS** to load the 1-2-3 Access System or **123** just to load 1-2-3. To start working on files in the \123\DATA\INFO directory, you would enter

```
CD \123\DATA\INFO
```

at the DOS prompt before starting 1-2-3. For this approach, the 1-2-3 program directory must be in the current path setting, and there must not be a directory permanently recorded in the Worksheet Global Default Directory setting. To clear this setting, simply choose Directory from the Worksheet Global Default menu, press Esc, press Enter, and then choose Update. For more on the Worksheet Global Default Directory command, see "The Default Directory" later in this chapter.

File Saving

When you are ready to save a worksheet that you have built from scratch, select File Save. 1-2-3 asks you to "Enter name of file to save:" The name you supply must be from one to eight characters in length, and must follow the file-naming conventions already described. 1-2-3 will automatically give the file a WK1 extension.

If the current worksheet has not yet been saved on disk, the "Enter name of file to save:" prompt is followed by the current data directory path and a generic file specification (*.wk1). The current directory is usually the directory that was current when 1-2-3 was loaded. However, you may have selected a permanent default directory with the Worksheet Global Default Directory command, and recorded it with the Update command. In this case, the permanent default directory is the current directory, unless you have set a temporary directory with the File Directory command.

Below the data directory path and the generic file specification is an alphabetical list showing the first five files that meet this specification. Note that the mode indicator changes to FILES while files are being listed. Also note that a special mouse palette appears on the top line of the screen.

If the worksheet you are about to save was originally retrieved from a file on disk, you are prompted with the name of that file, as shown in Figure 7.6. For example, if you retrieve the file SALES01.WK1 from the DATA subdirectory of the 123R23 directory on drive C and update the figures, you will be prompted with the name

```
C:\123R23\DATA\SALES01.WK1
```

when you go to save the file.

Note that the mode indicator says EDIT, meaning that you can alter this name if you want. Techniques for editing file names are described in a moment. If you press Esc at this point, the suggested name will be replaced with the generic file specification *.wk1 and the mode indicator will change from EDIT to FILES. This change is accompanied by a list of files in the current directory that match the file specification *.wk1, and the special mouse palette.

Figure 7.6

Saving a preexisting file

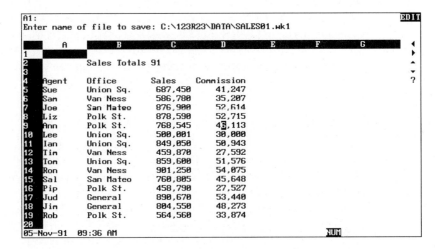

When you're saving a file, 1-2-3 lists the file names already in use. You can pick a file from this list and save the current worksheet into it, but doing so will replace the contents of that disk file with the worksheet you are about to store. To pick a name from the list, simply highlight the desired name and press Enter. Several techniques for navigating the file list will be discussed in a moment.

When you save a file that already has a name, as in Figure 7.6, 1-2-3 initially displays EDIT in the mode indicator, suggesting that you can edit the existing file name. There are two ways of doing this. You can simply start typing the new name, which will completely replace the current name but leave the directory path unchanged. Alternatively, you can change the existing name by pressing the spacebar and Backspace. This rather inconsistent key combination activates the EDIT mode for file names. You can then use the normal editing keys to alter the file name and directory path to your liking. Press Enter to store the file under the new name. 1-2-3 will automatically check that the new name is not already in use. If it is, you will be asked to confirm the File Save command.

Save Confirmation

When you have the right path and file name entered for the worksheet you are about to save, press Enter to confirm the name. Before saving the file, 1-2-3 will check whether a file of the same name already exists in the current storage area. If such a file exists, 1-2-3 responds with the choices Cancel, Replace, and Backup. Select Cancel to prevent the existing file from being overwritten. Select Replace to confirm that you want to overwrite the old file. Use this option when updating a file or saving successive unfinished versions of a model. Backup preserves the existing file by changing the extension to .BAK and then saving the new file with the name you requested and the regular extension.

Retrieving Files

You use the Retrieve command from the File menu when you want to bring back into memory a copy of a worksheet that you have stored on disk. The command assumes that you want to retrieve a worksheet from the current drive and directory. When you select File Retrieve, 1-2-3 helps you identify the file you want by displaying a one-line alphabetical list of files, similar to the one used by File Save. When you have highlighted the file you want to retrieve, press Enter and 1-2-3 reads that file into memory.

If you use File Retrieve when you already have data in the current worksheet, 1-2-3 assumes that you want to replace the current contents of the worksheet with the data you are going to read from disk. The data read from the file will replace all that was there before it, from cell A1 through cell IV8192. In other words, you can potentially lose your work when issuing the File Retrieve command. If you always use File Save before File Retrieve, you can prevent any such losses. Also, if the UNDO feature is active you can reverse a File Retrieve and switch back to the previous worksheet, *if* you use UNDO promptly. For details on when UNDO will work, refer to "The UNDO feature" later in the chapter.

Basic File Listing

The list of existing files that appears with File Save and File Retrieve initially occupies a single line. As discussed in Chapter 2, you can change the display to a full-screen list by pressing the Name key (F3) or by clicking on List in the special mouse palette at the top of the screen. Tips for using the full-screen file list are given in the next section. If you press Name or click on List a second time, the list returns to the single-line format. You can move through the single-line file list using the cursor-movement keys, as described in Table 7.1. For example, the End key moves the highlighting to the last name in the list, as shown in Figure 7.7.

Table 7.1   Keys for Navigating File Lists

Key	Action in Single-Line List
Left Arrow	One item to the left
Left Arrow (when first key)	Last item in list
Right Arrow	One item to the right
Up Arrow	Five items to the left
Down Arrow	Five items to the right
End	Last item in list
Home	First item in list
Tab and Ctrl-Right	Four items to the right
Shift-Tab and Ctrl-Left	Four items to the left
PgDn	Five items to the left
PgUp	Five items to the right
Enter	Select highlighted item
Esc	Cancel list

Key	Action in Full-Screen List
Left Arrow	One column to the left
Left Arrow (when first key)	Last item in list
Right Arrow	One column to the right
Up Arrow	One item up
Down Arrow	One item down
End	Last item in list
Home	First item in list
Tab and Ctrl-Right	Last column on right; repeat to move down one item
Shift-Tab and Ctrl-Right	Last column on left; repeat to move down one item
PgDn	Twenty items down the current column (last item in current column)
PgUp	Twenty items up the current column (first item in current column)
Enter	Select highlighted item
Esc	Cancel list

Figure 7.7
The end of the
single-line list

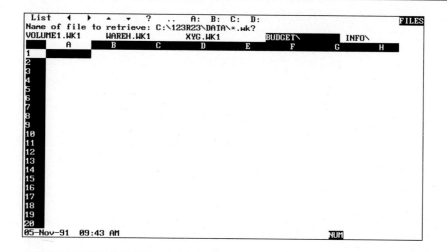

Any subdirectories of the current data directory will be listed alphabetically at the end of the file list. Subdirectories are designated by a backslash. You can see two directories in Figure 7.7: BUDGET\ and INFO\. Since the current data directory is C:\123\DATA, the full names of these two directories are C:\123\DATA\BUDGET and C:\123\DATA\INFO, respectively. If you want to list files in a subdirectory of the current directory, highlight the subdirectory name and press Enter. The file list changes, as shown in Figure 7.8, which lists the files in the BUDGET directory.

Figure 7.8
Listing files in a
subdirectory

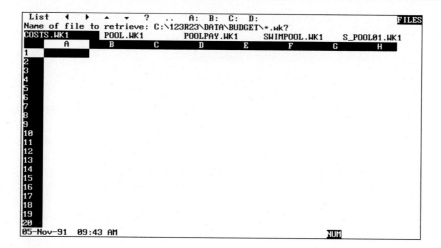

If you want to list files in a directory above the current one, press Backspace while the file list is displayed. You back up one level in the hierarchy of directories each time you press Backspace. For example, pressing Backspace in Figure 7.8 will take you from a list of files in C:\123\DATA\BUDGET to a list of files in C:\123\DATA. Pressing Backspace a second time will display files in C:\123, and pressing it a third time will list files in C:\. Each time 1-2-3 will list files according to the *.wk? specification. If you are using a mouse, you can back up the directory tree by clicking on the pair of dots in the mouse palette.

If you press Backspace while viewing files in the root directory of the current drive (with the C:*.wk? prompt), 1-2-3 beeps and changes to EDIT mode. You can then edit the path and the file specification. For example, you might want to look for files on another disk. You could enter **D:** and 1-2-3 would display all files in the root directory of drive D. 1-2-3 would automatically add the *.wk? specification so that worksheet files plus any subdirectories of D:\ were listed. Having changed the drive, you can navigate the drive either by pressing Backspace or by highlighting a subdirectory name and then pressing Enter. To switch drives with a mouse, simply click on the appropriate drive letter in the mouse palette.

At times you may want to display files other than those meeting the *.wk? specification. For example, you might want to look at files created by another Lotus program, Symphony, which gives files the extension WRK or WR1. As you have seen, pressing Backspace repeatedly eventually allows you to edit the file specification. However, it's quicker to press the Escape key when the standard file specification of *.wk? is displayed. Escape removes the *.wk? and places you in EDIT mode so that you can immediately type the desired specification, such as *.wr? to list Symphony files or even *.* to see all files. After typing the specification you want, press Enter to produce the list.

The Full-Screen File List

Sometimes it's easier to locate the file you want by viewing a full-screen display of files like the one shown in Figure 7.9. You produce this display by pressing the Name key (F3) when the single-line file list is displayed. For example, you may want to know the date and time that a file was last saved to the disk. This information, as well as the size of the worksheet, is displayed at the top of the screen next to the name of the currently highlighted file.

The full-screen list works much like the single-line list. You highlight a file and press Enter to select it. The keys for navigating this list were shown in Table 7.1.

Figure 7.9

The full-screen display

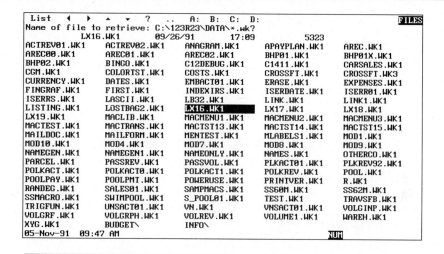

```
List  ◄   ►   ▲   ▼   ?   ..   A:  B:  C:  D:                           FILES
Name of file to retrieve: C:\123R23\DATA\*.wk?
          LX16.WK1          09/26/91        17:09              5323
ACTREV01.WK1   ACTREV02.WK1   ANAGRAM.WK1   APAYPLAN.WK1   AREC.WK1
AREC00.WK1     AREC01.WK1     AREC02.WK1    BHP01.WK1      BHP01X.WK1
BHP02.WK1      BINGO.WK1      C12DEBUG.WK1  C1411.WK1      CARSALES.WK1
CGM.WK1        COLORTST.WK1   COSTS.WK1     CROSSFT.WK1    CROSSFT.WK3
CURRENCY.WK1   DATES.WK1      EMBACT01.WK1  ERASE.WK1      EXPENSES.WK1
FINGRAF.WK1    FIRST.WK1      INDEXIRS.WK1  ISERDATE.WK1   ISERR01.WK1
ISERRS.WK1     LASCII.WK1     LB32.WK1      LINK.WK1       LINK1.WK1
LISTING.WK1    LOSTBAG2.WK1   LX16.WK1      LX17.WK1       LX18.WK1
LX19.WK1       MACLIB.WK1     MACMENU1.WK1  MACMENU2.WK1   MACMENU3.WK1
MACTEST.WK1    MACTRANS.WK1   MACTST13.WK1  MACTST14.WK1   MACTST15.WK1
MAILDOC.WK1    MAILFORM.WK1   MENTEST.WK1   MLABELS1.WK1   MOD1.WK1
MOD10.WK1      MOD4.WK1       MOD7.WK1      MOD8.WK1       MOD9.WK1
NAMEGEN.WK1    NAMEGEN1.WK1   NAMEONLY.WK1  NAMES.WK1      OTHERCO.WK1
PARCEL.WK1     PASSREV.WK1    PASSVOL.WK1   PLKACT01.WK1   PLKREV92.WK1
POLKACT.WK1    POLKACT0.WK1   POLKACT1.WK1  POLKREV.WK1    POOL.WK1
POOLPAY.WK1    POOLPMT.WK1    POWERUSE.WK1  PRINTVER.WK1   R.WK1
RANDEG.WK1     SALES01.WK1    SAMPMACS.WK1  SS60M.WK1      SS62M.WK1
SSMACRO.WK1    SWIMPOOL.WK1   S_POOL01.WK1  TEST.WK1       TRAVSFB.WK1
TRIGFUN.WK1    UNSACT01.WK1   VN.WK1        VNSACT01.WK1   VOLGINP.WK1
VOLGRF.WK1     VOLGRPH.WK1    VOLREV.WK1    VOLUME1.WK1    WAREH.WK1
XYG.WK1        BUDGET\        INFO\
05-Nov-91  09:47 AM                                            NUM
```

File Admin Tables

When managing disk files, you can use the File Admin Table command to produce file lists within the current worksheet. You can make a table showing any particular group of files, and the file size, date, and time information is listed. Admin Table provides the following five options:

- Worksheet lists files that match the *.wk? specification.

- Print lists files that match the *.prn specification.

- Graph lists files that match the *.pic specification.

- Other lists all files—that is, files that match the *.* specification.

- Linked lists files that are linked to the current file (as described in the next section).

After selecting the desired option, you must point out where in the worksheet you want the table placed. This area should be a range containing four columns and at least as many rows as there are files meeting the specification. The easiest response is to select a single cell that is to the right of or below all other worksheet entries. 1-2-3 will then use as many cells as are needed for the table.

The first four Admin Table options all present a file prompt that assumes the current data directory and is similar to the prompt for saving or retrieving files. You can edit this prompt to apply to a different directory or a different group of files. For example, *.w?? would include WRK files as well as those with the extensions WK1 and WKS. The final option, Linked, is explained in the section "Managing Links." Figure 7.10 shows the results of a File Admin Table Worksheet command. You can see that the file names and the date/time information are hard to read with the default format and column width. Figure 7.11 shows the same table improved by customized column width settings and formats.

Figure 7.10

Results of the File Admin Table Worksheet command

```
A1:  'ACTREV01.WK1                                                    READY

        A           B        C          D        E       F       G       H      ◄
1   ACTREV01.     33510  0.821018    7724                                       ►
2   ACTREV02.     33511  0.009965    7724                                       ▲
3   ANAGRAM.W     33531  0.762546    3848                                       ▼
4   APAYPLAN.     33537  0.533495    6682                                       ?
5   AREC.WK1      33544  0.557210    7302
6   AREC00.WK     33544  0.579930    3597
7   AREC01.WK     33544  0.567523    7729
8   AREC02.WK     33544  0.565451    4171
9   BHP01.WK1     33538  0.884097    7279
10  BHP01X.WK     33539  0.458553    7158
11  BHP02.WK1     33536  0.780138    7321
12  BINGO.WK1     33509  0.876481    4646
13  C12DEBUG.     33563  0.485486    4608
14  C1411.WK1     33590  0.546030    3073
15  CARSALES.     33601  0.963518    1399
16  CGM.WK1       33251  0.476527    2284
17  COLORTST.     33184  0.657928    2057
18  COSTS.WK1     33526  0.713495    1555
19  CROSSFT.W     33547  0.512835    3043
20  CROSSFT.W     33542  0.514120    2281
05-Nov-91   09:49 AM                                          NUM
```

Figure 7.11

An improved file table

```
B1:  (D4) [W11] 33510                                                 READY

        A             B           C          D        E       F       G        ◄
1   ACTREV01.WK1    09/29/91    19:42     7,724                                 ►
2   ACTREV02.WK1    09/30/91    00:14     7,724                                 ▲
3   ANAGRAM.WK1     10/20/91    18:18     3,848                                 ▼
4   APAYPLAN.WK1    10/26/91    12:48     6,682                                 ?
5   AREC.WK1        11/02/91    13:22     7,302
6   AREC00.WK1      11/02/91    13:55     3,597
7   AREC01.WK1      11/02/91    13:37     7,729
8   AREC02.WK1      11/02/91    13:34     4,171
9   BHP01.WK1       10/27/91    21:13     7,279
10  BHP01X.WK1      10/28/91    11:00     7,158
11  BHP02.WK1       10/25/91    18:43     7,321
12  BINGO.WK1       09/28/91    21:02     4,646
13  C12DEBUG.WK1    11/21/91    11:39     4,608
14  C1411.WK1       12/18/91    13:06     3,073
15  CARSALES.WK1    12/29/91    23:07     1,399
16  CGM.WK1         01/13/91    11:26     2,284
17  COLORTST.WK1    11/07/90    15:47     2,057
18  COSTS.WK1       10/15/91    17:07     1,555
19  CROSSFT.WK1     11/05/91    12:18     3,043
20  CROSSFT.WK3     10/31/91    12:20     2,281
05-Nov-91   09:51 AM                                          NUM
```

Sharing Data Between Files

1-2-3 provides several commands that allow you to share data between work-sheets. You can copy sections of one worksheet to a new file (File Xtract). You can move all or part of a worksheet on disk into another worksheet in memory (File Combine). You can also create formulas that link values in one file with those in another. 1-2-3 Release 2.2 introduced this ability to link worksheets, making data in one dependent upon data from another. Although Release 2.3 does not allow you to view more than one file at once, being able to link files opens up a new realm of spreadsheet design possibilities.

Worksheet Recycling

Sometimes you may want to copy information from one worksheet to another or create several variations of a single worksheet. Suppose that you are the general manager of the four travel agencies whose revenue was projected in the last chapter, using a worksheet like the one shown in Figure 7.12. In this model, the revenue figures in column C are created by multiplying those in column B by the growth factor in G1. Column D is column C times G1, and so on. Column N contains totals for the year and row 29 contains totals for each month.

Figure 7.12

Revenue projection worksheet

```
A1: [W12] 'Revenue Projection, Based on Monthly Growth Factor of:        READY

          A         B        C        D        E        F        G       ◄
 1   Revenue Projection, Based on Monthly Growth Factor of:        1.02   ►
 2                                                                         ▲
 3             Jan-92   Feb-92   Mar-92   Apr-92   May-92   Jun-92         ▼
 4   POLK ST.                                                             ?
 5       Tour    3,350    3,417    3,485    3,555    3,626    3,699
 6     Flight    1,875    1,913    1,951    1,990    2,030    2,070
 7      Hotel      950      969      988    1,008    1,028    1,049
 8     Rental      875      893      910      929      947      966
 9      Group      800      816      832      849      866      883
10   VAN NESS
11       Tour    3,400    3,468    3,537    3,608    3,680    3,754
12     Flight    2,175    2,219    2,263    2,308    2,354    2,401
13      Hotel    1,350    1,377    1,405    1,433    1,461    1,491
14     Rental      975      995    1,014    1,035    1,055    1,076
15      Group    1,100    1,122    1,144    1,167    1,191    1,214
16   UNION SQ.
17       Tour    2,875    2,933    2,991    3,051    3,112    3,174
18     Flight    4,500    4,590    4,682    4,775    4,871    4,968
19      Hotel    1,150    1,173    1,196    1,220    1,245    1,270
20     Rental      925      944      962      982    1,001    1,021
05-Nov-91   09:53 AM                                         NUM
```

When the manager of the Polk Street office receives a printout of the revenue projected for her office, she requests a copy of the worksheet file in order to plot actual revenue against projections. You don't want to send her the entire worksheet, since this reveals projections for all four offices. There are several ways of creating a worksheet just for the Polk Street office.

One method is to use DOS to create a copy of the original worksheet, and then retrieve the copy and edit out all of the information not pertaining to the Polk Street office. In this example, you could use Worksheet Delete Row to get rid of sections of the worksheet that you no longer need.

Alternatively, you can use 1-2-3 to make the copy. Retrieve the original file into memory, issue the File Save command, and type a new name for the file. Pressing Enter will create a copy of the original file. Again, you can now edit out all of the information not pertaining to the Polk Street office and save the file.

File Xtract

When you want to create a worksheet that is a subset of a larger worksheet, there is an alternative to copying the file and then editing the copy. You can actually copy data directly from a worksheet in memory into a new file on disk using a procedure called file extraction. This procedure involves the Xtract command on the File menu. The basic procedure for the File Xtract command is as follows:

1. Place the cell pointer in the upper-left cell of the range you want to extract. (This step is not essential but will save you a few keystrokes when you point out the range in steps.)

2. Issue the File Xtract command.

3. Choose between Formulas and Values.

4. Name the file in which you want the extracted cells stored.

5. Indicate the range of cells to be copied to the file.

If you choose Formulas, the formulas themselves are copied to the new file. If you choose values, the formulas are converted to their results during the extraction process. The difference is much like this difference between the Copy command and Range Value command.

To use File Xtract to create a new file containing just the Polk Street information, begin with the cell pointer in A1. After you issue the File Xtract command, 1-2-3 offers you the choice between Formulas and Values. Choose Formulas. Then type **POLKREV** as the name for the new file you are creating. When you press Enter, you are asked to point out the range to be extracted. In this case you would select A1..N9, as shown in Figure 7.13.

When you press Enter to confirm the extract range, 1-2-3 writes a new file to disk with the name POLKREV.WK1 and contents that match A1..N9 of the current worksheet. (If there is a file named POLKREV.WK1 in the current data directory, 1-2-3 gives you a chance to change the name, presenting the Cancel/Replace/Backup menu.) Note that the File Xtract command does not remove the extract range from the current worksheet, which remains unchanged. Xtract works like Copy rather than Move. Also note that you can preselect the range to be extracted.

Figure 7.13

The extract range

```
N9: (,0) @SUM(B9..M9)                                              POINT
Enter extract range: A1..N9

        H        I        J        K        L        M        N        O    ◄
1                                                                            ►
2                                                                            ▲
3    Jul-92   Aug-92   Sep-92   Oct-92   Nov-92   Dec-92   TOTALS            ▼
4                                                                            ?
5    3,773    3,848    3,925    4,004    4,084    4,165    44,931
6    2,112    2,154    2,197    2,241    2,286    2,331    25,148
7    1,070    1,091    1,113    1,135    1,158    1,181    12,741
8      985    1,005    1,025    1,046    1,067    1,088    11,736
9      901      919      937      956      975      995    10,730
10
11   3,829    3,906    3,984    4,063    4,145    4,227    45,601
12   2,449    2,498    2,548    2,599    2,651    2,704    29,171
13   1,520    1,551    1,582    1,613    1,646    1,679    18,106
14   1,098    1,120    1,142    1,165    1,189    1,212    13,077
15   1,239    1,264    1,289    1,315    1,341    1,368    14,753
16
17   3,238    3,302    3,369    3,436    3,505    3,575    38,560
18   5,068    5,169    5,272    5,378    5,485    5,595    60,354
19   1,295    1,321    1,347    1,374    1,402    1,430    15,424
20   1,042    1,063    1,084    1,105    1,128    1,150    12,406
05-Nov-91   09:54 AM                                            NUM
```

You can now retrieve the new file you have created to see what it looks like. After making sure that any important changes to the current worksheet have been saved, issue the File Retrieve command and select POLKREV.WK1. The results should look like those in Figure 7.14.

The upper-left cell of the extract range was placed in cell A1 of the new file, and this is where the cell pointer is located when you first retrieve the file. Note that the cell formats and column widths of the original file have been faithfully preserved. In addition, cells that were formulas, such as C3 and C5, are still formulas. To complete this file, you just need to add a row of totals in columns B through N.

The formulas shown in Figure 7.14 are still *live*, meaning that a change to the growth rate in G1 will result in a change to all of the values in columns C through N. However, you may want to give the manager of the Polk Street office a frozen set of figures. To do this, you would choose the File Xtract Values option instead of Formulas. This would convert formulas to values, so that the actual contents of C5 would be 3,417 rather than +$G$1*B5.

You will also want to use the Values option when the cells to be extracted don't contain all of the data needed by the formulas within the extract range. For example, if you were creating a worksheet for the Van Ness office you could extract cells A10 through N15. However, if you did this

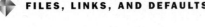

with the Formulas option, the resulting file would be somewhat garbled because many of the formulas refer to G1, which was not included in the new file. The results can be seen in Figure 7.15, where the cell pointer has been moved to C2, the first erroneous entry.

Figure 7.14

The Xtract file retrieved

```
A1: [W12] 'Revenue Projection, Based on Monthly Growth Factor of:        READY

        A          B        C        D        E        F        G          ◄
1  Revenue Projection, Based on Monthly Growth Factor of:            1.02    ►
2
3                  Jan-92   Feb-92   Mar-92   Apr-92   May-92   Jun-92       ▲
4  POLK ST.                                                                  ?
5          Tour    3,350    3,417    3,485    3,555    3,626    3,699
6          Flight  1,875    1,913    1,951    1,990    2,030    2,070
7          Hotel     950      969      988    1,008    1,028    1,049
8          Rental    875      893      910      929      947      966
9          Group     800      816      832      849      866      883
10
11
12
13
14
15
16
17
18
19
20
05-Nov-91   09:56 AM                                              NUM
```

Figure 7.15

A problem created by File Xtract Formulas

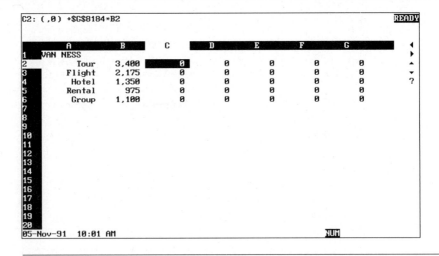

```
C2: (,0) +$G$8184*B2                                              READY

        A          B        C        D        E        F        G          ◄
1  VAN NESS                                                                  ►
2          Tour    3,400        0        0        0        0        0        ▲
3          Flight  2,175        0        0        0        0        0        ?
4          Hotel   1,350        0        0        0        0        0
5          Rental    975        0        0        0        0        0
6          Group   1,100        0        0        0        0        0
7
8
9
10
11
12
13
14
15
16
17
18
19
20
05-Nov-91   10:01 AM                                              NUM
```

Note that 1-2-3 replaced $G$1 with $G$8184 in an effort to replicate the meaning of the original formula in a file that lacks the required data. In this particular example, it wouldn't be too difficult to correct the problem created by the Formulas option (you could insert several new rows at the top of the model, add a growth rate in G1, and use Range Search/Replace to change the appropriate references to $G$1). However, with more complex models, such corrections might not be feasible. A safer option when extracting ranges that do not include all of the supporting cells is to use the Values option.

Combining Files

In some situations, it is helpful to be able to read all or part of another worksheet into the current worksheet. For example, consider the revenue worksheet in Figure 7.16. This file, called ACTREV.WK1, was created from a copy of the model in Figure 7.12. The contents of row 1 were changed and the projected values were replaced by zeros.

Figure 7.16

Actual revenue worksheet

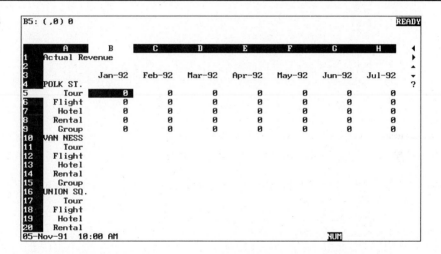

As general manager, you want to use this worksheet to consolidate the actual revenue figures reported by the four offices, filling in the worksheet with actual values reported each month. Each of the four offices sends in a report each month as a worksheet file on disk. In Figure 7.17, you can see the January figures from the Polk Street office. This worksheet was also created from a copy of the main worksheet and each of the four offices uses a similar model, the only difference being the name in A4. This file is called PLKACT01.WK1 because it contains the actual revenue for January, the first month.

To read the data from the worksheet in Figure 7.17 into the model in Figure 7.16, you use the Combine command on the File menu. The following is the basic procedure for the File Combine command.

Figure 7.17
The actual revenue
for Polk Street in
January

```
A1: [W12] 'Actual Revenue                                              READY

        A          B        C        D        E        F        G       ◀
1   Actual Revenue                                                       ▶
2                             1        3                                  ▲
3                  Jan-92   Feb-92   Mar-92   Apr-92   May-92   Jun-92    ▼
4   POLK ST.                                                             ?
5          Tour   2,876       0        0        0        0        0
6        Flight   1,983       0        0        0        0        0
7         Hotel   1,023       0        0        0        0        0
8        Rental     567       0        0        0        0        0
9         Group     432       0        0        0        0        0
10
11  TOTAL          6,881       0        0        0        0        0
12
13
14
15
16
17
18
19
20
05-Nov-91   10:02 AM                                            NUM
```

1. Place the cell pointer in the upper-left cell of the range in the current worksheet into which you want to copy information from another file.

2. Issue the File Combine command.

3. Choose between Copy, Add, or Subtract.

4. Choose between Entire-File and Named/Specified-Range.

5. Enter the range if you selected Named/Specified-Range.

6. Name the source file, the one from which you want to combine data.

When you complete the command, 1-2-3 reads cells from the source file you have specified into the current worksheet at the current cell pointer location. The choice between Copy, Add, and Subtract determines how 1-2-3 handles values in cells of the current worksheet that are being overwritten:

- Copy copies the exact contents of the source file cells over existing entries in the current worksheet.

- Add copies only values from the source file, not labels and formulas. The Add option adds these to values in the current worksheet. Labels or formulas in the area of the current worksheet covered by the incoming data are not affected.

- Subtract copies only values from the source file, not labels and formulas. The Subtract option takes these values away from values in the current worksheet. Labels or formulas in the area of the current worksheet covered by the incoming data are not affected.

Note that the Copy option copies labels and formulas as well as numeric constants. Any relative references in the copied formulas are adjusted to fit the formulas' location in the current file. The Add and Subtract options are reviewed in the next section.

Selecting either Entire-File or Named/Specified-Range determines whether all or part of the source file is read into the current worksheet. You can identify a range either by a range name or a set of coordinates. Unfortunately you cannot use the Name key to list ranges in the source file: You must know the correct name or cell coordinates before starting the File Combine command.

If you want to add data from Figure 7.17 into Figure 7.16, you begin by placing the cell pointer in B5 of the consolidated worksheet. Then you issue the File Combine command. You are asked to choose Copy, Add, or Subtract. In this case, either Copy or Add is suitable. (It makes no difference whether you simply copy the Polk Street office's figures into the January column of the current spreadsheet or add them to the zeros currently in that column.) Next you are asked to choose between the entire file and a specific range. Choose Named/Specified-Range and enter **B5..B9** as the coordinates. Although these happen to be the same cells as the range into which the data from the source file will be copied, the two ranges do not have to have the same coordinates.

Finally, you must select the file to combine from. In this case, the file name is PLKACT01.WK1. The file list provided works just like the one used in Save and Retrieve operations. If the supporting worksheet is supplied on a floppy disk, make sure you change the drive specifier from C: to A: if necessary. When you've selected the file name, the specified cells from that file are read into the current worksheet, as shown in Figure 7.18.

Figure 7.18
Results of the File Combine

```
B5: (,0) 2876                                                      READY

        A           B      C        D        E        F        G      ◄
1   Actual Revenue                                                    ►
2                                                                     ▲
3               Jan-92  Feb-92   Mar-92   Apr-92   May-92   Jun-92    ▼
4   POLK ST.                                                          ?
5          Tour   2,876      0        0        0        0        0
6        Flight   1,983      0        0        0        0        0
7         Hotel   1,023      0        0        0        0        0
8        Rental     567      0        0        0        0        0
9         Group     432      0        0        0        0        0
10  VAN NESS
11         Tour       0      0        0        0        0        0
12       Flight       0      0        0        0        0        0
13        Hotel       0      0        0        0        0        0
14       Rental       0      0        0        0        0        0
15        Group       0      0        0        0        0        0
16  UNION SQ.
17         Tour       0      0        0        0        0        0
18       Flight       0      0        0        0        0        0
19        Hotel       0      0        0        0        0        0
20       Rental       0      0        0        0        0        0
05-Nov-91  11:32 PM                                        NUM
```

Note that the formatting and column width settings are stripped from the incoming data and do not affect the current worksheet. If you specify the wrong cells or file, you can reverse the File Combine command with the UNDO feature.

To continue combining reports from the four offices, you would move the cell pointer to B11 and repeat the previous steps. If the Van Ness office used a worksheet like the one in Figure 7.19, you could simply change the name of the source file; the coordinates of the range being combined would be the same.

Figure 7.19
The Van Ness worksheet

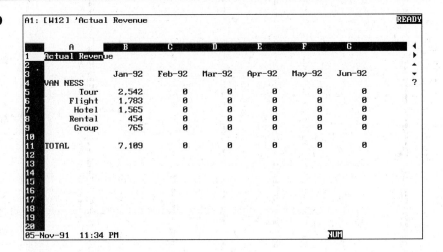

Combine Add and Subtract

The Add and Subtract options of the File Combine command only read in numeric constants from the source worksheet. This means that labels in the target worksheet are ignored, as are formulas. For example, suppose you want to consolidate actual revenue for all four offices in a worksheet like the one shown in Figure 7.20. You can see that the Polk Street figures have already been input in B5..B9.

If you issue the File Combine Add command with B5 as the current cell and specify the range B5..B9 from the Van Ness office as the range to be combined, the numbers from that file will be added to those already in B5..B9. If you used B3 as the current cell and B3..B11 as the range, the results would be exactly the same. This is because B3 and B11 are both formulas and the Add option does not alter cells containing formulas. The formula in B3 is a date entered with the @DATE function, while B11 is the sum formula @SUM(B5..B9). This would continue to add the contents of B5..B9 after the Combine Add.

Figure 7.20

Consolidation with
Combine Add

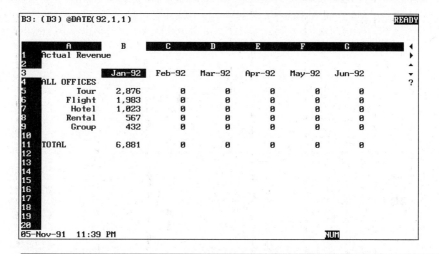

```
B3: (D3) @DATE(92,1,1)                                              READY

         A         B        C        D        E        F        G    ◄
 1 Actual Revenue                                                     ►
 2                                                                    ▲
 3              ║ Jan-92   Feb-92   Mar-92   Apr-92   May-92   Jun-92  ▼
 4 ALL OFFICES                                                        ?
 5         Tour   2,876        0        0        0        0        0
 6       Flight   1,983        0        0        0        0        0
 7        Hotel   1,023        0        0        0        0        0
 8       Rental     567        0        0        0        0        0
 9        Group     432        0        0        0        0        0
10
11 TOTAL          6,881        0        0        0        0        0
12
13
14
15
16
17
18
19
20
05-Nov-91  11:39 PM                                          NUM
```

The Subtract option has the opposite effect of Add: It subtracts the incoming numbers from those in the specified range of the current spreadsheet. This option can be useful when you want successive reductions of a figure—for example, when a debt reduction goal has to be met. As with the Add option, the main problem with Subtract is keeping track of which files have been combined. Remember that you can undo a File Combine with UNDO.

Combine and Xtract Tips

The Combine and Xtract commands are diagrammed in Figure 7.21. Combine is primarily for consolidating in one worksheet data that has been generated in a number of other files. Effective use of this command depends on consistency in file design so that there are no surprises about the contents of incoming cells. The File Xtract command is mainly used to pass pieces of information from one worksheet to another without having to copy the entire file. You can also use Xtract to divide one large worksheet into several smaller, more manageable files. These smaller files can still share data if you use the file-linking feature described in a moment.

The File Xtract command is not particularly dangerous, unless you use the Formulas option incorrectly. You should always check a file created by Xtract Formulas to make sure that the formulas in the new file make sense. The File Combine command can be very destructive, since incoming data can overwrite valuable entries in the current worksheet. Always save the current worksheet before executing a File Combine. Then make sure that the UNDO feature is active so that you can reverse the effects of a Combine operation that goes wrong. Finally, pay close attention to the location of the cell pointer before issuing the File Combine command, since you cannot move it during the command, and this location determines where the incoming data will be placed.

Figure 7.21

Diagram of File
Combine and Xtract

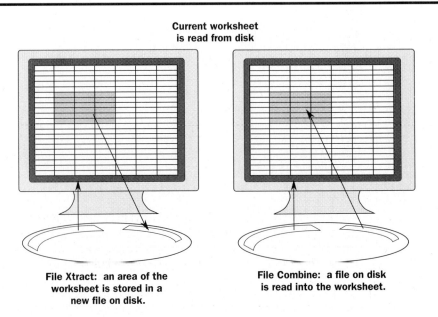

**Current worksheet
is read from disk**

**File Xtract: an area of the
worksheet is stored in a
new file on disk.**

**File Combine: a file on disk
is read into the worksheet.**

Linking Files

Lotus 1-2-3 Release 2.2 introduced *file linking,* the ability to enter in the current worksheet a cell reference that refers to a worksheet on disk. To do this, you simply precede the cell reference with a plus sign and the name of the file, enclosed in two pairs of angle brackets. In an earlier example of file combining, data from cell B5 of a file called PLKACT01.WK1 was copied into a consolidation worksheet called ACTREV.WK1. File linking offers an alternative method of achieving the same end. You simply enter the following link formula in B5 of ACTREV.WK1:

```
+<<PLKACT01>>B5
```

You can see this formula at work in Figure 7.22. Note that 1-2-3 adds the WK1 extension when you enter this formula.

Figure 7.22

A link formula at work

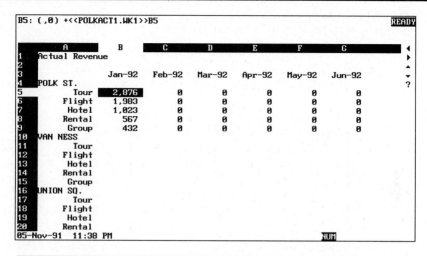

This formula means that whatever value is in cell B5 of the file PLKACT01.WK1 will be displayed in cell B5 of the current worksheet. Note that the link formula cannot contain anything other than a reference to a single cell in another worksheet. Also note that link formulas return one of three results:

- If the referenced cell contains a formula, the results of the formula are returned.

- If the referenced cell contains a value, the value is returned.

- If the referenced cell contains a label, the label is returned.

A link formula has no effect on the formatting or width of the cell in which it is entered.

A worksheet containing link formulas is referred to as a *dependent worksheet*, since it depends upon one or more worksheets for its values. A worksheet that supplies values to a dependent worksheet is called a *supporting worksheet*. A supporting worksheet can reside in the same directory as the dependent worksheet, in which case the angle brackets in the link formula only contain the name of the file. If the supporting file is in a different directory, the link formula must specify the full path. For example, if PLKACT01.WK1 were in the BUDGET subdirectory of the 123\DATA directory, the formula might look like this:

```
+<<\123\DATA\BUDGET\PLKACT01.WK1>>B5
```

Note that 1-2-3 will assume that the directory referred to is on the same disk as the current data directory. If it is not, you must include a drive letter in the formula, as in

```
+<<C:\123\DATA\BUDGET\PLKACT01.WK1>>B5
```

1-2-3 assumes that you are linking to a file with the WK1 extension and enters this in the formula for you. If this is not the case—for example, if you are linking to a Lotus Symphony file with the WRK extension—you need to type the extension when entering the formula.

You can only link files in Release 2.3 by referencing single cells in other worksheets; you cannot reference ranges in links. For example, you cannot include a range of cells from a supporting worksheet in an @SUM formula in the dependent worksheet. To use multiple values from other worksheets in the current worksheet, you must reference all of the cells you need and then use the cells of the current worksheet in the necessary formula. However, you can reference a cell that contains an @SUM formula in the supporting worksheet.

You cannot use link references within more complex formulas in the dependent worksheet. You cannot even use a constant with a link reference. Thus the following formula would not be acceptable:

```
+<<PLKACT01.WK1>>B5^1.1
```

Instead you would need to pull B5 from PLKACT01.WK1 into a separate intermediate cell in the dependent worksheet, say B40, and then use the formula +B40*1.1.

Like other formulas, link formulas can be copied. Relative cell references are adjusted accordingly. For example, in Figure 7.22, cell B5 was copied to B6, producing the formula

```
+<<PLKACT01.WK1>>B6
```

The same formula was also copied to the other months, columns C through M. The zeros in column C reflect the zeros in the supporting file. Figure 7.23 shows the completed consolidation worksheet.

The cell B11 contains a reference to B5 in the Van Ness file, VNS-ACT01.WK1. That formula was copied down to row 15 and across to column M. The entries for the Union Square and Embarcadero offices carry similar formulas that pull in values from separate worksheets. You can see the entries for the Embarcadero office in Figure 7.24. Note that the formula in cell B23 refers to drive B, which is where the EMBACT01.WK1 file is located. Note that if you link to a worksheet on a floppy disk, you must insert that disk in the disk drive *before* you load the dependent worksheet.

Figure 7.23
Consolidation with
file links

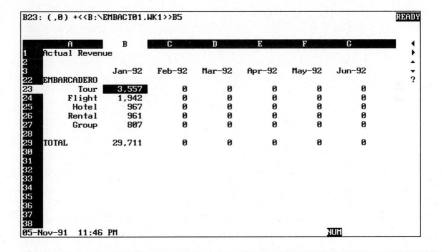

Figure 7.24
The rest of the
consolidation
worksheet

Later in this chapter, you will learn how to load the Viewer add-in program, which enables you to establish links simply by pointing at the appropriate cell in the supporting worksheet.

Managing Links

The ability to share data between files permits you to split large and cumbersome worksheets into more manageable, interrelated units. Since you can copy data from one 1-2-3 worksheet to another with File Xtract, it is easy to divide a large worksheet into more manageable parts. Knowing that 1-2-3 supports links between files allows you to approach new projects in a different way, following more closely the traditional accounting model of consolidated sheets and supporting sheets.

Links can also work across a network of connected PCs. The main requirement is that you correctly describe the networked drive in the link formula. For example, many networks set up a common file storage area on a machine called a file server. This area is often referred to as drive F by the PCs that share it. By using this network drive letter and the correct file name, you can link a worksheet on your own PC to one stored on the server.

Given the ability to link between drives and even between separate PCs, you may wonder how 1-2-3 handles changes to supporting files. In the example in Figure 7.24, someone could remove the disk from drive B and alter the values it contains. 1-2-3 always updates link references when a dependent worksheet is retrieved, then assuming that the values supplied by the links are correct. You can make sure that the values supplied by the links are correct by *refreshing* them with the File Admin command.

The File Admin command is useful for a number of file-management tasks. The File Admin menu contains the three options Reservation, Link-Refresh, and Table. The Reservation option is used when you are networking files and is discussed in the next section. The Link-Refresh option tells 1-2-3 to check that all link references are current. If necessary, values in the current worksheet are updated. If there is any chance that data in the supporting worksheet may have changed since you loaded the dependent worksheet, you should use Link-Refresh before printing or basing any decisions on results from a dependent worksheet. For example, if you are working with a dependent worksheet on a network, a co-worker may be altering the supporting worksheet at the same time. In this case, Link-Refresh will read in the current values. Similarly, if your supporting worksheet is on a floppy disk supplied by someone else, be sure to use Link-Refresh if you receive a disk with an updated version of the file after you load the dependent worksheet. If you select the Link-Refresh option and 1-2-3 cannot find a file to which you have referred, as would be the case in Figure 7.24 if the floppy disk containing EMBACT01.WK1 was removed from drive B, then the link formula in question returns ERR.

The File Admin Table command, introduced earlier in this chapter, offers a Link option that lists all files linked to the current worksheet. When you issue this command, 1-2-3 does not let you alter the file specification; it simply asks for the location of the table and then lists all files referred to in the current worksheet. This type of table is very valuable when documenting linked worksheets.

Other Management Issues

You need to manage several other aspects of 1-2-3 to maximize your productive use of the program. These include disk space, memory usage, and the way worksheet files are accessed on a network.

File Reservations

Every 1-2-3 worksheet file is assigned a *reservation*. This ensures that only one person can save changes to a file, even if several people are using it at once on a network. If you have the file reservation, you are the only one who can save changes to the file. Other users can retrieve the file while you are using it, but 1-2-3 will not let them save the file. As soon as you stop using the file, either by retrieving a different file or using the Worksheet Erase command, the reservation can pass to the next user. If you no longer need the reservation but still want to use the file, you can release the reservation by selecting the Release option under the File Admin Reservation command.

   If you have retrieved a worksheet and do not at first have the reservation (you'll see the message RO at the bottom of the screen), you can request it later by selecting the Get option under the Reservation command. This tells 1-2-3 to check whether the person who has the reservation has released it or is no longer using the file. If so, you will be given the reservation and can save your changes to the file.

Out-of-Space Problems

Large worksheets can grow with surprising rapidity. The Copy command in particular quickly generates a lot of data. This can result in space problems, both on disk and in memory. When you attempt to save a file that is too large to fit in the remaining free space on your disk, 1-2-3 responds with a "disk full" error message. You can respond to this situation in the following ways:

■ You can save to a floppy disk. If you have been saving to a floppy disk and the current disk cannot accommodate your worksheet, you can retry the save after inserting a disk with more free space. You can use the System command on the File menu to exit temporarily to DOS and format a fresh floppy disk if you need one. The System command does not affect your unsaved work.

■ You can clean up your hard disk. If you have been saving to a hard disk that has now filled up, you might consider saving to a floppy disk as a temporary measure. Then you can exit 1-2-3 and create some more space on your hard disk (basically this means copying old files to floppy disks and then deleting them from the hard disk).

■ You can convert values. Formulas take up more space than values in a worksheet. If you use the Range Value command to convert into values the numbers that are generated by formulas, the worksheet can be stored in less space.

■ You can divide the worksheet. When you attempt to save a worksheet and get a "disk full" message, you may want to consider splitting the worksheet into separate, smaller worksheets and then storing them on different disks.

Memory Space

1-2-3 displays the message "memory full" when you attempt to retrieve a file that is too large to fit in currently available memory. You get a similar message when you expand the current worksheet beyond the limits of available memory. If you want to check on the amount of memory you have available, use the Worksheet Status command and read the current memory status from the display, which will resemble Figure 7.25.

Figure 7.25
Worksheet Status
display

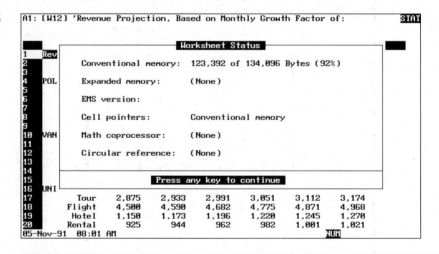

If you already have a worksheet loaded when you read the Status menu, you can see how much room there is for expansion. If you just have a blank worksheet, you can tell how large a file you can retrieve. Figure 7.25 indicates that approximately 134k of conventional memory is available for data. (This is the amount of memory not already occupied by 1-2-3, DOS, and other programs.) Of this total, 123k (92%) has not been used by the current spreadsheet. 1-2-3 needs enough free memory to read the entire file from disk plus

5% to 10% more space for manipulating the data in the worksheet. Thus, if you have 128,000 bytes available, it's unwise to retrieve anything larger than 120,000 bytes.

When you use a command that results in the "memory full" message, you should save parts of the worksheet to separate files using File Xtract. This will allow you to store the data safely so that you can redesign the worksheet, perhaps free up more memory, or add more memory to the system. You can free up memory by saving the current worksheet, exiting 1-2-3, and removing any memory-resident programs you might have loaded.

If a Copy command caused the "memory full" message, probably only part of the range was copied. However, the data you had before the Copy operation should still be intact. Likewise, if you tried to retrieve a file that was too large, only part of the file will be in your worksheet, but the entire file will still be safely stored on disk.

The item below Conventional memory in Figure 7.25 is Expanded memory, which refers to memory added to your system beyond the 640k limit of RAM normally recognized by DOS. If you have expanded memory properly installed in your computer it should be listed here. Furthermore, the item called EMS version should tell you what version of expanded memory you have. The item Cell pointers refers to how you want 1-2-3 to use your expanded memory. The options here are determined by the Expanded-Memory option on the Worksheet Global Default Other menu, described later in the section "Expanded Memory."

Password Protection

To prevent unauthorized access to a worksheet stored on disk, you can assign a password to the worksheet while you are saving it. Select File Save and then type in the file name followed by a space and the letter P. When you press Enter, 1-2-3 prompts you for a password. This password can consist of several words, numbers, and spaces—up to a total length of 15 characters. Pick a password that you can remember. No one can see the letters of the password as you type, because 1-2-3 shows only a blank rectangle for each letter, as shown in Figure 7.26.

When you have typed the password, press Enter. You will be asked to verify the word by typing it again. (Presumably, if you can type the word twice you did not make a mistake the first time you entered it.) After typing the word a second time, press Enter. The file-saving process continues as usual.

When you attempt to retrieve or open the password-protected file, you are prompted for the password. This time you just need to type the password once and then press Enter to access the file. If you type an incorrect password, 1-2-3 beeps and gives you the message "Incorrect password." 1-2-3 is sensitive to the distinction between upper- and lowercase letters in passwords. The password "Fred's File" will not be accepted if supplied as "FRED'S FILE" or even "Fred's file".

Figure 7.26

Entering a password

```
A1: [W12] 'Revenue Projection, Based on Monthly Growth Factor of:          EDIT
Enter password: ▮▮▮▮▮▮
          A         B        C        D        E        F        G           ◄
1  Revenue Projection, Based on Monthly Growth Factor of:          1.02       ►
2                                                                             ▲
3            Jan-92   Feb-92   Mar-92   Apr-92   May-92   Jun-92               ▼
4  POLK ST.                                                                   ?
5       Tour    3,350    3,417    3,485    3,555    3,626    3,699
6     Flight    1,875    1,913    1,951    1,990    2,030    2,070
7      Hotel      950      969      988    1,008    1,028    1,049
8     Rental      875      893      910      929      947      966
9      Group      800      816      832      849      866      883
10 VAN NESS
11      Tour    3,400    3,468    3,537    3,600    3,600    3,754
12    Flight    2,175    2,219    2,263    2,308    2,354    2,401
13     Hotel    1,350    1,377    1,405    1,433    1,461    1,491
14    Rental      975      995    1,014    1,035    1,055    1,076
15     Group    1,100    1,122    1,144    1,167    1,191    1,214
16 UNION SQ.
17      Tour    2,875    2,933    2,991    3,051    3,112    3,174
18    Flight    4,500    4,590    4,682    4,775    4,871    4,968
19     Hotel    1,150    1,173    1,196    1,220    1,245    1,270
20    Rental      925      944      962      982    1,001    1,021
05-Nov-91   08:06 AM                                              NUM
```

When you save a file with password protection, 1-2-3 *encrypts* the file, scrambling the data to make it unintelligible even to a sophisticated, well-trained programmer. Don't expect to be able to retrieve the data if you forget the password. Neither Lotus Corporation's staff nor anyone else can retrieve the data if you forget the password. Trying to get around the password by using the partial file retrieval command, File Combine, does not work either. You should leave a copy of the password in a secure place such as a locked desk drawer or in another password-protected 1-2-3 file. You can use a spreadsheet or word processor to list files and their passwords. You might want to code passwords on any printed listing. A further technique for remembering passwords is to use the first letters of a favorite phrase or song title. Thus the password SOTDOTB might appear hard to remember, but would be easy for an Otis Redding fan.

When you want to remove password protection from a file, you must first open the file, and then use the File Save command. 1-2-3 will remind you that the file is password protected, as in Figure 7.27. You can now press Backspace to remove the protection message. Then press Enter to complete the File Save and the file will no longer be password protected.

Since using passwords can be a nuisance, you should decide if the need for security is real. If it is, make sure you use proper passwords. The protection is of little use if you use a password such as "password," "pass," your first name, the file name, and so on. Believe it or not you can buy lists of common passwords, so the serious data thief is likely to guess most words that do not have the following features:

- At least eight characters

- A mixture of text and numbers

- Some odd characters like @, spaces, and commas

- A mixture of upper- and lowercase characters

- A lack of logic

Figure 7.27
Password reminder

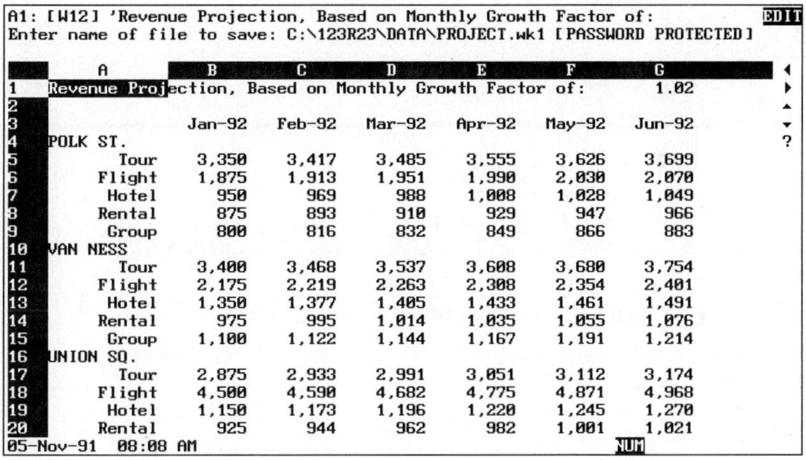

```
A1: [W12] 'Revenue Projection, Based on Monthly Growth Factor of:          EDIT
Enter name of file to save: C:\123R23\DATA\PROJECT.wk1 [PASSWORD PROTECTED]
         A          B        C        D        E        F        G        ◄
1    Revenue Projection, Based on Monthly Growth Factor of:        1.02     ►
2                                                                           ▲
3               Jan-92   Feb-92   Mar-92   Apr-92   May-92   Jun-92         ▼
4    POLK ST.                                                              ?
5         Tour   3,350    3,417    3,485    3,555    3,626    3,699
6       Flight   1,875    1,913    1,951    1,990    2,030    2,070
7        Hotel     950      969      988    1,008    1,028    1,049
8       Rental     875      893      910      929      947      966
9        Group     800      816      832      849      866      883
10   VAN NESS
11        Tour   3,400    3,468    3,537    3,608    3,680    3,754
12      Flight   2,175    2,219    2,263    2,308    2,354    2,401
13       Hotel   1,350    1,377    1,405    1,433    1,461    1,491
14      Rental     975      995    1,014    1,035    1,055    1,076
15       Group   1,100    1,122    1,144    1,167    1,191    1,214
16   UNION SQ.
17        Tour   2,875    2,933    2,991    3,051    3,112    3,174
18      Flight   4,500    4,590    4,682    4,775    4,871    4,968
19       Hotel   1,150    1,173    1,196    1,220    1,245    1,270
20      Rental     925      944      962      982    1,001    1,021
05-Nov-91  08:08 AM                                        NUM
```

To implement a lack of logical connection between the content of the file and the password protecting it, you need to be imaginative. For example, a banker might use the names of birds to protect a series of salary recommendation files. Combined with the other features, something like Gull@5476 would be difficult to guess. Since such a name would also be difficult to remember, you must make proper provisions for recording and securing passwords. A sheet of paper locked in a drawer is usually a good technique. Note that password protection of files is different from cell protection. Cell protection, described in detail in Chapter 13, prevents changes to worksheets but allows you to retrieve and view them.

The 1-2-3 Defaults

As you develop a clearer idea of the type of work you will be doing with 1-2-3, you will want to customize the program to suit your needs. You do this with the Worksheet Global Default command. When you issue this command, you get a dialog box like the one shown in Figure 7.28. Besides the obligatory Quit option, the Worksheet Global Default menu offers six items: Printer, Directory, Status, Update, Other, and Autoexec. Of these items, Update deserves to be mentioned before the rest.

Figure 7.28

The Default
Settings dialog box

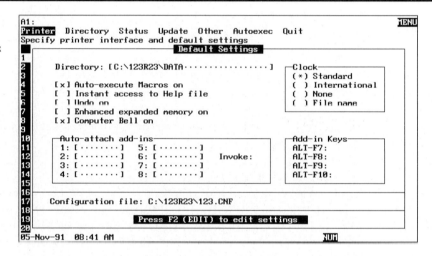

The Worksheet Global Default Update command records the current default settings in a file on disk so that 1-2-3 can read them the next time it is loaded. The file is called 123.CNF and is stored in the same directory as the 1-2-3 program files. You can see this file at the bottom of the dialog box. If you want to retain changes you have made to your default settings, be sure to use the Update command before quitting 1-2-3. Note that you can use a different set of defaults with 1-2-3 by loading a configuration file other than 123.CNF. For more information on this feature, see Appendix A.

If you edit the Default Settings dialog box, either with a mouse or the keyboard, several useful buttons will appear, as shown at the bottom of Figure 7.29. The Printer and International buttons allow you to move to special dialog boxes where you can edit the printer and international settings. The Update button allows you to record your choices without reverting to the menu.

Default Printer Settings

The first option on the Worksheet Global Default menu is Printer. When you select this option you get the Default Printer Settings dialog box shown in Figure 7.30, which covers several aspects of printing with the 1-2-3 Print command. Chapter 6 introduced the Print Settings dialog box that controls

Figure 7.29
The Default settings in SETTINGS mode

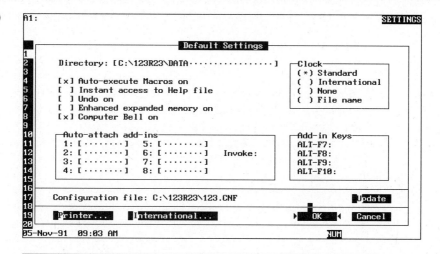

each print job from a specific worksheet. The Default Printer Settings dialog box controls the overall operation of your printer.

By adjusting the default printer settings, you can avoid repeating the same changes for each print job. For example, if you normally use a left margin of 5 instead of 4, you can change the default Left setting to 5 and, by using the Worksheet Global Default Update command, store this setting in the configuration file. The next time you create a worksheet, the left margin setting will automatically be 5 instead of 4.

If you use a mouse there are several ways to get to the Default Printer Settings dialog box. If you click on the Default Settings dialog box to edit it, a button called Printer appears, as shown in Figure 7.29. You can click on this button to get to the Default Printer Settings dialog box.

The Default Printer Settings dialog box includes the following options:

■ The Interface setting determines which of your PC's printer ports 1-2-3 uses for printed output. The basic choice is between parallel and serial.

■ The AutoLF (Automatic Line Feed) setting is a simple yes/no choice that is normally set to No because most printers do not advance the paper automatically, instead allowing the software to control this task. Some older printers automatically advance the paper one line for every end-of-line signal they get in a printout. Such printers need this setting changed to Yes. (If your reports come out double-spaced when you were expecting single-spacing, make sure this option is set to No.)

■ The Left setting sets the left margin as a number of characters. The default is 4, which leaves a margin of almost half an inch for a standard ten pitch type. You may need to change this setting if you always use a different pitch or always want a wider margin. Settings of much less than 4 can result in reports that are too close to the left edge of the printed page.

Figure 7.30

The Default Printer Settings dialog box

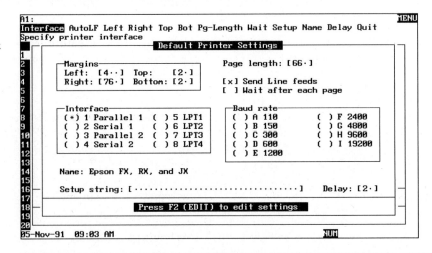

- The Right setting sets the right margin as a number of characters from the left edge of the page. The default setting of 76 leaves a margin of just less than an inch when printing in ten pitch type on 8½-by-11-inch paper. The A4 paper used all over Europe is approximately 8¼ inches wide, so the default Right setting of 76 leaves a margin of a little more than half an inch.

- The Top setting sets the top margin as a number of lines from the top of the page. The default setting is 2.

- The Bottom setting sets the bottom margin as a number of lines from the bottom of the page. The default setting is 2.

- The Pg-Length setting must be coordinated with the length of the sheets of paper on which your reports are being printed as well as the number of lines per inch your printer is using. 1-2-3 assumes that you are using 8½-by-11-inch paper and printing at six lines per inch. If you are using A4 paper, the standard paper size in Europe, the length of 11.625 inches accommodates 70 lines. You can change the lines per inch setting either through hardware switches on your printer or through an appropriate setup string. A popular alternative when printing in small type is eight lines per inch, which gives a page length of 88 lines for an 11-inch-long sheet. Note that some printers cannot print over the entire surface of a page. This requires some adjustment to the page-length setting. For example, when using an HP LaserJet with 11-inch-long sheets, you need to set the page length to 60 for multipage reports to be evenly spaced across pages.

- The Wait setting determines whether or not 1-2-3 will wait for you to insert a new sheet of paper before printing the next page. The default setting is No, since most people use continuous feed paper or a sheet feeder. If your printer requires manual feeding, change this setting to Yes.

- The role of setup strings in activating printer features such as condensed print was discussed in the last chapter. If there is a setup string that you use with every print task, you can enter it with the Setup option and it will be used all the time.

- In 1-2-3 Release 2.3, you can use the Install program to select a number of different printer models. You can then use each of these during a 1-2-3 session without having to return to the Install program. Each printer model you select with Install is given a number (1, 2, 3, and so on). The Name option allows you select the model you want as the default. If your printed reports are not coming out as expected, you might check this setting to make sure you have the correct model selected.

- The Delay setting determines how many minutes 1-2-3 waits before deciding there has been a printer error. The initial default is 2 minutes. If you are sharing a printer on a network, you might want to increase this setting to avoid what is sometimes referred to as "timing out." This is when a program like 1-2-3 keeps trying to print a document only to get a busy signal from the printer. The program eventually stops trying and decides that the printer is not working properly. The range of settings is from 0 to 30. The shortest possible setting is 1, which represents 1 minute. As the on-screen prompt states, a setting of 0 means "wait forever."

The Default Directory

The Directory option on the Default Settings menu is where you record the directory that 1-2-3 uses for data files. If you do not record a specific directory with this option, 1-2-3's File commands will assume the directory that was current when the program was loaded. If you do select the Directory option, enter a directory path, and then use the Update command, that directory will be used for the rest of the current session and for all future sessions (unless you use the File Directory command to set a temporary directory for a single session).

If you want 1-2-3 to use the directory that is current when the program is loaded, you must clear the Default Directory setting by selecting Directory from the Default menu, pressing Esc to clear the existing directory name, and then pressing Enter and choosing Update. At this point, the Directory section of the Default Settings box will be blank. Unfortunately, 1-2-3 fails to leave this setting blank. The next time you load 1-2-3, the name of the current directory will appear in the box. This makes it impossible to tell from the Default Settings screen whether or not a specific directory has been recorded as a preference. If you cleared the Directory setting and then loaded the program later, things should be clear, but this anomaly can make matters rather confusing on machines used by several different people.

The Default Status

The Default Status command appears at first to be another anomaly: It merely replaces the dialog box shown in Figure 7.28 with a summary of the settings and a message saying "Press any key to continue." However, as you can see from Figure 7.31, the status screen includes both Printer and International settings that are not visible in Figure 7.28. Note that the mode indicator changes to STAT.

Figure 7.31

The Worksheet Global Default Status screen

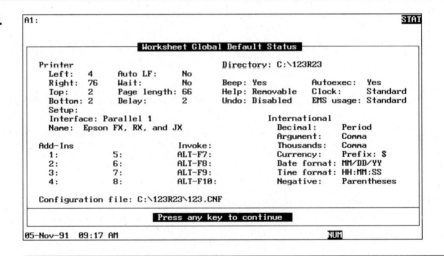

```
A1:                                                                    STAT
┌────────────────────────────────────────────────────────────────────────┐
│                    ┌ Worksheet Global Default Status ┐                   │
│   Printer                          Directory: C:\123R23                  │
│     Left:    4    Auto LF:    No                                         │
│     Right:  76    Wait:       No    Beep: Yes        Autoexec:  Yes       │
│     Top:     2    Page length: 66   Help: Removable  Clock:     Standard  │
│     Botton:  2    Delay:      2     Undo: Disabled   EMS usage: Standard  │
│     Setup:                                                                │
│     Interface: Parallel 1           International                         │
│     Name:  Epson FX, RX, and JX       Decimal:      Period               │
│                                       Argument:     Comma                 │
│   Add-Ins                  Invoke:    Thousands:    Comma                 │
│     1:          5:         ALT-F7:    Currency:     Prefix: $             │
│     2:          6:         ALT-F8:    Date format:  MM/DD/YY              │
│     3:          7:         ALT-F9:    Time format:  HH:MM:SS              │
│     4:          8:         ALT-F10:   Negative:     Parentheses           │
│                                                                          │
│   Configuration file: C:\123R23\123.CNF                                  │
├────────────────────────────────────────────────────────────────────────┤
│                      ┌ Press any key to continue ┐                       │
└────────────────────────────────────────────────────────────────────────┘
05-Nov-91  09:17 AM                                        NUM
```

International Defaults

The Other option on the Defaults menu includes several useful items, the first of which is International. As you can see from the Default International Settings dialog box in Figure 7.32, this option governs several areas of formatting: Punctuation, Currency, Date, Time, and Negative. By altering these settings, you can format your worksheets in keeping with various standards used around the world. For example, in Britain the date for Christmas Day, 1992 is shown as 25/12/92 rather than 12/25/92. In France the period is used to separate thousands, as in 1.500 for one thousand five hundred. In Britain you would probably want the Currency format to use the £ sign instead of a $. You can make such adjustments with the Default International Settings dialog box, the effects of which can be seen in Figure 7.33.

Figure 7.32

The Default International Settings dialog box

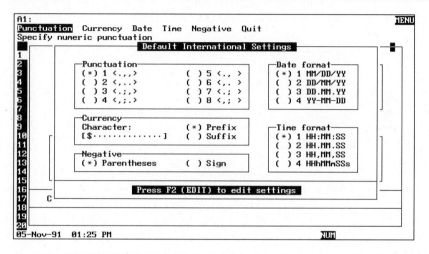

Note that when you change the International settings, all worksheets you create or retrieve will reflect these settings. If you create a worksheet with the £ as the currency symbol, and then send it to a user in the U.S. who has $ as the currency symbol, the currency format will appear with $ instead of £.

There are three types of punctuation in 1-2-3: the decimal point, the argument separator, and the thousands separator.

- The decimal point appears in several formats—such as Fixed and Currency—and is entered by the user when decimal values are needed. The default decimal point is a period, as in 1.25.

- The argument separator is entered by the user when a function uses more than one argument. For example, the function @MAX(B1,0) returns the larger of two values, the entry in B1 or 0. Both B1 and 0 are arguments and the default argument separator is a comma.

- The thousands separator is not entered by the user but appears in several formats, such as the Currency format. The default thousands separator is the comma, as in 1,500 for one thousand five hundred.

To accommodate different preferences for punctuation, 1-2-3 provides the eight options shown in Table 7.2. As you can see, option D was used in Figure 7.33. Note that the Default International Settings dialog box lists the options with numbers (1-8) and the menu uses letters (A-H).

Figure 7.33
A worksheet displayed with International options

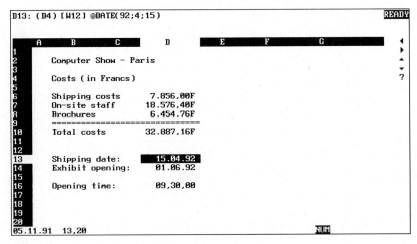

Table 7.2   Options for International Punctuation

Option Letter	Decimal Point	Argument Separator	Thousands Separator	Entry/Result in Comma Format
A	Period	Comma	Comma	1.1*@MAX(B1,0)=1,512.5
B	Comma	Period	Period	1,1*@MAX(B1.0)=1.512,5
C	Period	Semicolon	Comma	1.1*@MAX(B1;0)=1,512.5
D	Comma	Semicolon	Period	1,1*@MAX(B1;0)=1.512,5
E	Period	Comma	Space	1.1*@MAX(B1,0)=1 512.5
F	Comma	Period	Space	1,1*@MAX(B1.0)=1 512,5
G	Period	Semicolon	Space	1.1*@MAX(B1;0)=1 512.5
H	Comma	Semicolon	Space	1,1*@MAX(B1;0)=1 512,5

Under the Currency option, you enter the character you want 1-2-3 to use when you format cells with the Currency format. The default setting is the dollar sign as a prefix to the value. To change the currency symbol to a pound sign, you would select Currency, Backspace over the previous entry, and then type a pound sign. (On most keyboards you can do this by holding down Alt and then entering the ASCII code for the £ symbol, which is 156 from the numeric keypad. When you release the Alt key the symbol will appear.) When you press Enter to confirm the symbol you have typed, you will see the choices Prefix and Suffix—you can place the symbol before the value, as with the $ and the £, or after, as with the F, French franc, shown in Figure 7.33.

You can use up to 15 characters for a currency prefix or suffix. Because of this, you can use the Currency format for a custom format. For example, in Figure 7.34 the measurements of m.p.g. were entered with the International Currency command and positioned as suffixes.

Figure 7.34

An example of custom formatting

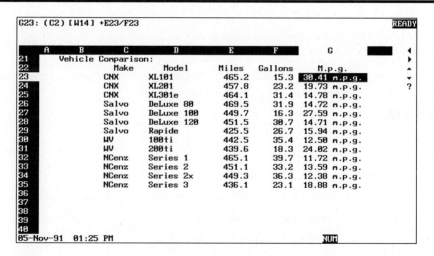

As you can see next to the cell address indicator, the cells were formatted with the Range Format Currency command. Note that a space was entered in front of m.p.g. when the suffix was set up. If you want a space between a prefix and a value, you must enter a trailing space after the text. Also note that you cannot have more than one custom format like this per worksheet.

The four options for date formatting affect the display of formats D4 and D5, the long international and the short international. The options are shown in Table 7.3. The four options for time formatting affect the display of the last two time formats 3 and 4, the long and short international (these are also known by the format identifiers D8 and D9, since the four possible time formats follow on from date formats D1 through D5). These options are also shown in Table 7.3.

Table 7.3   **Options for International Dates and Times**

Options for International Dates

Long Intn'l (D4) Format Letter	Format	Displayed As	Short Intn'l (D5) Format	Displayed As
A	MM/DD/YY	12/25/92	MM/DD	12/25
B	DD/MM/YY	25/12/92	DD/MM	25/12
C	DD.MM.YY	25.12.92	DD.MM	25.12
D	YY-MM-DD	92-12-25	MM-DD	12-25

Options for International Times

Long Intn'l (D8) Format Letter	Format	Displayed As	Short Intn'l (D9) Format	Displayed As
A	HH:MM:SS	13:25:30	HH:MM	13:25
B	HH.MM.SS	13.25.30	HH.MM	13.25
C	HH,MM,SS	13,25,30	HH.MM	13.25
D	HHhMMmSSs	13h25m30s	HHhMMm	13h25m

The negative setting affects the way that the Currency and Comma formats display negative values. Normally this setting is Parentheses, so that the Comma format shows a mathematical value of –2,000 as (2,000). However, you can change the Negative setting to Sign so that a minus sign is used instead of the parentheses, as in –2,000.

The Help Setting

The second item under the Other option on the Defaults menu is Help. There are two possibilities: Instant and Removable. This setting determines how 1-2-3 treats the help file that it uses when you press F1. The default setting is Removable, which dates from floppy-disk systems where you had to be able to remove the help file disk in case you needed to insert a data disk.

The Instant option tells 1-2-3 that the help file will always be available; you should select this setting when using 1-2-3 on hard-disk machines.

The Clock Setting

Another interesting item under the Other option on the Defaults menu is Clock, which affects how the date and time are displayed at the bottom of the 1-2-3 screen. The choices are Standard, International, None, Clock, and Filename. The first two choices determine the date and time formats used. The Standard setting uses Date format 1 and Time format 1. The International setting uses the long international format, and reflects choices you have made with the Date and Time options under the International command. You can see an example of this in Figure 7.33. The third Clock choice, None, removes the display of date and time. The fourth choice, Clock, returns the display of date and time. Finally, the Filename option substitutes the name of the current worksheet file for the date and time display. This last option is preferred by some who like to keep track of the name of the file they are working with.

The UNDO Feature

Undo is one of the most important items under the Other option on the Default menu. This option controls the UNDO feature, which allows you to reverse many 1-2-3 actions with the Undo key, Alt-F4. The best rule for preventing unnecessary and unintentional loss of data is the one you use for steady monetary accumulation: Save on a regular basis. This means saving the current worksheet at least every 15 minutes. You should also save your work before:

- Performing a file retrieve

- Turning off your PC

- Leaving your PC unattended

- Performing a major move or copy

- Executing a data sort, extract, or data fill operation

- Performing a file combine

However, even if you try to live by these rules, there is always a possibility that something will go wrong. 1-2-3's built-in UNDO feature helps out in these situations, enabling you to overcome a wide range of errors and accidents. For example, UNDO is very handy after a mistaken Range Erase or a disastrous File Combine. The following lists explain how UNDO works and when you can and cannot use it.

- UNDO must be active in order to work.

- UNDO only works when 1-2-3 is in READY mode.

- UNDO cancels the most recent operation that changed worksheet data and/or settings (1-2-3 automatically restores whatever worksheet data and settings existed the last time it was in READY mode).

- The UNDO feature can reverse the effect of an UNDO operation if you change your mind about what you just undid.

Any series of 1-2-3 commands performed after you press / to display the main menu and before 1-2-3 returns to READY mode is a single undoable operation. If you press / to select a new command but then press Esc to undo your previous operation, you will not be able to undo the previous operation. UNDO cannot undo the following operations and settings:

- Commands that create, modify, or delete files on disk, such as File Save and File Erase.

- The default directory settings commands (File Directory and Worksheet Global Default Directory).

- The Help access method (Worksheet Global Default Other Help).

- The current file's reservation status, if you use File Admin Reservation Get or Release to change it.

- Worksheet Global Default Other Undo Enable.

- Any command that attaches or detaches an add-in (Add-In Attach, Add-In Detach, Add-In Clear, or Worksheet Global Default Other Add-In Set or Cancel).

- Invoking an add-in (depending on what the add-in does).

- Movement of the cell pointer.

- Pressing Undo after using System or {SYSTEM} does not undo the effects of any operating system commands you used.

- Also, if you press Undo after using Print Printer Go, 1-2-3 undoes any changes you made to 1-2-3 print settings with the Print commands, but cannot undo any changes the command had on your printer's internal settings.

- Finally, UNDO does not work in utility programs (PrintGraph, Install, Translate, and Access).

When 1-2-3 is first installed, UNDO is active. You can tell this from the UNDO indicator on the bottom line of the screen. However, the UNDO feature takes up about 150k of memory, since in order to undo your last operation, 1-2-3 must reserve a portion of memory to keep a copy of the worksheet. If you are building a large worksheet and are running short of memory, you can turn off UNDO by issuing the Worksheet Global Default Other command and selecting Undo. Select Disable and the memory that was assigned to UNDO will be released. If you want UNDO to remain disabled in future sessions, be sure to use the Default Update command to record this change.

If you later decide to reactivate UNDO, simply follow the same commands and select Enable. You will need to do this when the worksheet is empty—at the start of a session, for example. This is because UNDO has to occupy the section of memory that is right next to the 1-2-3 program itself. Remember to use Update to record the setting for future sessions.

The Beep Command

The Beep command under the Other option on the Default menu allows you to turn off the beep that 1-2-3 makes when an error occurs. You might want to do this if you find the beep annoying; however, working without the beep can be rather confusing. Most people find that the beep provides useful feedback and come to rely on it when working with 1-2-3.

Add-Ins

The final item under the Other option on the Default menu is Add-Ins. An *add-in* is a special program written to work with 1-2-3. The Add-Ins option on the Default Other menu is used to establish default add-ins that are loaded every time 1-2-3 is loaded. There is more on add-ins later in this chapter.

Expanded Memory

Earlier you saw that the Worksheet Status command displays information about how expanded memory is used by 1-2-3. The Default Settings screen contains an item called Enhanced expanded memory on. This item is represented in the menu system by the Worksheet Global Default Other Expanded-Memory setting. As mentioned, expanded memory is RAM added to your system beyond the 640k limit normally recognized by DOS. If you have expanded memory properly installed in your computer, it will be listed in the worksheet status screen, as shown in Figure 7.35.

The EMS version item tells you what version of expanded memory you have. LIM 4.0 means version 4.0 of the Lotus/Intel/Microsoft Expanded Memory Specification. 1-2-3 gets information about the version you are using from the operating system.

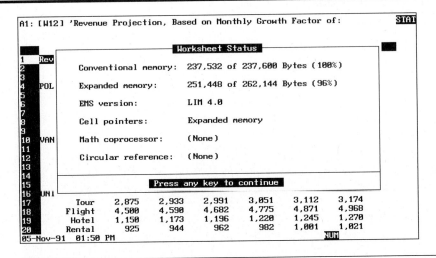

Figure 7.35
Worksheet Status
screen showing
expanded memory

The Cell pointers item indicates how you have directed 1-2-3 to utilize your expanded memory. The information in a worksheet can be divided into two parts: data, which is merely the cell contents; and cell pointers, the information about each cell and how it is formatted. You can have 1-2-3 place only data in expanded memory, while the rest of the worksheet, including the cell pointers, resides in conventional memory. Because of the way in which expanded memory works, this makes for faster operation than storing the entire worksheet, including data and cell pointers, in expanded memory.

If you issue the Worksheet Global Default Other Expanded-Memory command, you can choose between Standard and Enhanced. If you select Standard, only data will be stored in expanded memory and cell pointers will be stored in conventional memory. (This will be indicated by the words "Conventional memory" next to the Cell pointer item on the worksheet status screen.) Selecting Standard is the same as turning off the Default Settings item called Enhanced expanded memory on.

If you chose Enhanced from the Worksheet Global Default Other Expanded-Memory menu, 1-2-3 can store all spreadsheet information in expanded memory, allowing you to build much larger worksheets. (Accordingly, the Cell pointer item on the worksheet status screen will say "Expanded memory.") Choosing Enhanced is the same as selecting the Enhanced expanded memory on item in the Default Settings dialog box.

Note that you cannot use the enhanced option if you have versions of EMS earlier than LIM 4.0. Also note that if you use expanded memory to build large worksheets, they may grow too large to load on computers that have no expanded memory.

Autoexec Macros

The last option on the Default menu is Autoexec. This option will not really be significant until you work with macros in 1-2-3, a subject covered in Chapter 12. A macro is essentially a series of instructions stored in a worksheet and carried out by 1-2-3. It is sometimes helpful to run a particular macro as soon as the worksheet in which it is stored is loaded. To do this, you must assign the macro the special name \0 and set Autoexec to Yes. When Autoexec is set to Yes, macros called \0 are run automatically. When Autoexec is set to No, such macros must be run by the user.

Suppose your work with 1-2-3 involves heavy use of one particular worksheet. You can have 1-2-3 retrieve a worksheet file automatically whenever the program is loaded simply by naming the file AUTO123.WK1 and storing it in the default data directory. When 1-2-3 is being loaded, it always checks the data directory for a file called AUTO123.WK1. If such a file is found, 1-2-3 loads it. 1-2-3's auto file loading feature is also always in effect regardless of the default settings. By placing an autoexecuting macro, \0, in this file, and making sure that the Autoexec option is set to Yes, you can trigger file loading and a series of commands just by starting 1-2-3. For more about macros, see Chapter 13.

Working with Add-Ins

1-2-3's extensive range of commands provides many of the features you need for your work. However, you might find yourself wishing for added features in one or two areas. If Lotus included every feature that users have requested, the program simply would not fit on most personal computers. Instead, Lotus created *add-in applications* to augment 1-2-3's power without making the main program too large. This section shows you how to load add-ins and activate them in 1-2-3 sessions. Later in this chapter the Viewer, Wysiwyg, and Auditor add-ins are discussed.

Attaching Add-Ins

1-2-3 comes with five add-ins, and others are available from third-party software developers. You can attach add-in applications during a session to provide extra functions without removing the 1-2-3 program or the current worksheet from memory. However, because add-ins make additional demands on memory you may not be able to load all of the add-ins at once. You can pick and choose which add-ins you want to have available during a 1-2-3 session.

To manipulate add-ins, you use the Add-In command on the main 1-2-3 menu. The Add-In menu contains four commands: Attach, Detach, Invoke, and Clear. To make an add-in available, you Attach it to 1-2-3. When it is no longer needed, you Detach it. To use an attached add-in, you Invoke it. To remove all attached add-ins, you Clear them.

The following steps demonstrate how to attach the Auditor add-in, which enables you to analyze the structure of 1-2-3 worksheets. (The procedure is similar when attaching other add-ins.)

1. Activate the main menu and select Add-In, or press Alt-F10.

2. Select Attach. 1-2-3 presents a list of ADN files from the program directory, as shown in Figure 7.36.

3. Press F3 or click List if you want to see a full-screen list of add-ins. You can press Esc or click the right mouse button to edit the file path if you have stored the add-in files in a different directory.

4. Select the file called AUDITOR.ADN. You will be asked whether or not you want to assign the add-in to a key. The choices are No-Key, 7 8 9 10. Choose 7. You will be returned to the Add-In menu.

5. At this point, you could select Invoke to use the Auditor add-in. However, use Quit to leave the menu system so you can explore the other methods of invoking an add-in.

Figure 7.36

Using the Add-In Attach command

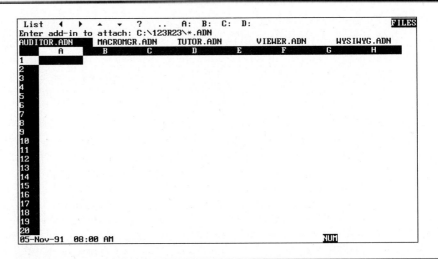

Note that you cannot see any change in 1-2-3 at this point. There are several ways of invoking an attached add-in. Some add-ins create a new menu item. For example, when you attach the Viewer add-in, a View command is added to the File menu. You can also attach an add-in to one of four keys: Alt-F7, Alt-F8, Alt-F9, or Alt-F10. For example, if you attach the Auditor add-in to Alt-F7, pressing Alt-F7 brings up the Auditor menu.

You can also use the Add-In Invoke command to invoke an add-in. This command lists the currently attached add-ins and allows you to pick one. When working with add-ins, you can use the Alt-F10 key to call up the Add-In menu without first activating the main menu. However, if you attach an add-in to Alt-F10, you can no longer use it for this purpose. In the case of the Auditor application, you will press Alt-F7, the key you assigned to it when you attached it. A menu and dialog box will appear, as shown in Figure 7.37.

Details of how to use the Auditor add-in are given later in this chapter. At this point you can select Quit or press Escape to leave the Auditor add-in.

Figure 7.37

The Auditor add-in

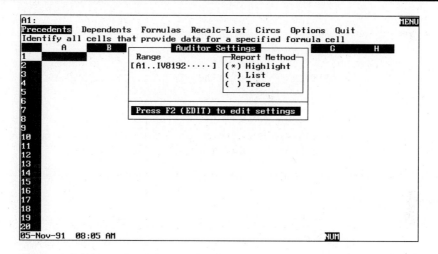

Detaching Add-ins

Once an add-in is attached, it remains attached until you exit 1-2-3. This means that you can invoke it during a session whenever you need it. If you know you are not going to use the add-in again, you should detach it from 1-2-3 so that it no longer takes up precious memory. You can do this in one of two ways.

If you only want to detach one add-in, select Detach from the Add-In menu. This command shows you a list of currently attached applications. Highlight the one you want to detach and press Enter. To detach all the attached add-ins with one command, select Clear from the Add-In menu.

Permanent Attachments

If you use a particular add-in on a regular basis, you can have it attached automatically every time you load 1-2-3. You can create an auto-attach add-in through the Invoke item in the Auto-attach add-ins section of the Default

Settings dialog box that appears when you issue the Worksheet Global Default command. Alternatively you can create an auto-attach add-in through the menu system. The Add-In option on the Default Other menu produces the menu seen at the top of Figure 7.38. Note that in this case the Viewer add-in has already been set up as an auto-attach add-in.

Figure 7.38

The Default Other Add-In menu

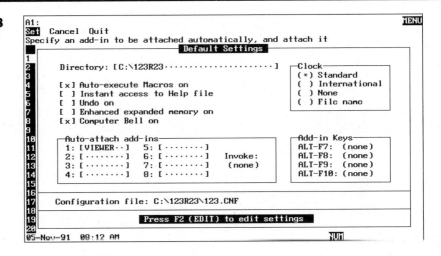

Using the menu approach, you select Set to create an auto-attach add-in or Cancel to remove one. Both commands lead to a list of numbers, from 1 through 8. Simply choose the number of the auto-attach add-in you want to create or remove. When you create an auto-attach add-in, you are asked what key to use for it. After this you must decide whether or not the add-in should be invoked whenever you start 1-2-3.

Remember that attaching an add-in merely makes it available; invoking an add-in actually puts it to work. Typically, this means that the add-in menu is displayed. In most cases, it is not appropriate to invoke an add-in automatically. Furthermore, while up to eight add-ins can be automatically attached, only one add-in can be automatically invoked.

When you finish choosing an auto-attach add-in, either through the Set command or the dialog box, 1-2-3 loads the add-in if it is not already loaded. To record your choice of auto-attach add-ins for the next session, you must select Update from the Default menu or the Default Settings dialog box. This updates the configuration file on disk. If you cancel or remove an add-in from the Default Settings dialog box, 1-2-3 will also remove the add-in from memory.

If you decide to operate the auto-attach add-in feature by editing the Default Settings dialog box, bear in mind that you can choose an add-in from a list of files. When you have activated field 1 in the Auto-attach add-ins group, you can press F3 to display a list of add-in files from which you can choose, as shown in Figure 7.39.

Figure 7.39

Listing add-in files

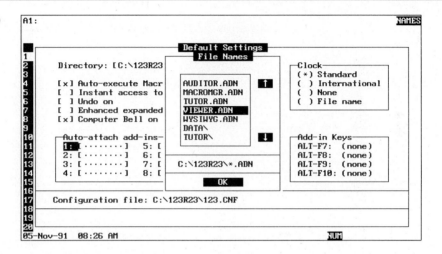

You can also use a list with the Invoke feature. If you press F3 when editing the Invoke field, you will get a list of the add-ins that you have chosen for auto-attach. You can choose one of them for Invoke, or you can choose the item called None, which appears at the top of the list.

Using the Viewer Add-In

The Lotus Magellan Viewer add-in, called Viewer for short, helps with file management. When you attach Viewer, a new option called View is offered on the File menu. For this reason, there is no need to assign an add-in key to Viewer.

Exploring Viewer

Selecting View from the File menu brings up the choices Retrieve, Link, and Browse, as shown in Figure 7.40. All three commands list files for you to examine and select. However, the Retrieve command lists files so that you can select a file to be retrieved, and is a sophisticated alternative to the regular File Retrieve command. The Link command lists files so that you can establish links between them, a 1-2-3 feature described in detail earlier in this chapter.

The Browse command, shown at work in Figure 7.41, simply lists files so that you can explore your disks and only allows you to view the files.

Figure 7.40

The File View menu

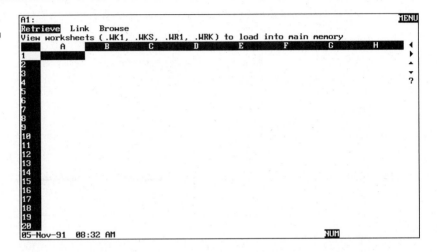

As you can see from Figure 7.41, the Viewer screen replaces the regular worksheet display and lists files on the left. As you scroll through the list of files, the contents of the highlighted file name appear in the View window on the right. (If nothing appears in the View window, Viewer cannot display that type of file.) The Browse command lists all files, using the file specification *.*. The Retrieve and Link commands list worksheet files, using a file specification of *.W??.

Being able to see an accurate display of the contents of worksheet files considerably enhances your ability to manage files. Using the File View Retrieve command, you can check the contents of a worksheet before you retrieve it. As you will see in a moment, the File View Link command enables you to check the contents of a worksheet and establish links with it, without retrieving the file.

When you have highlighted a worksheet file in the list of files, you can explore the entire contents of the file, not just its upper-left corner. Keyboard users can press the Right Arrow key to place a cell pointer in A1 of the worksheet, and can then use normal spreadsheet navigation keys to explore the file, including End and Home (do not use the Goto key, F5). Mouse users can simply click in the displayed worksheet to activate the cell pointer. A mouse palette is provided on the right side of the screen.

The task of displaying the contents of worksheets is performed by two files: VIEWER.123 and VIEWER.SYM. These viewer files convert into screen images the contents of 1-2-3 and Symphony worksheets, respectively.

Figure 7.41

Using the File View
Browse command

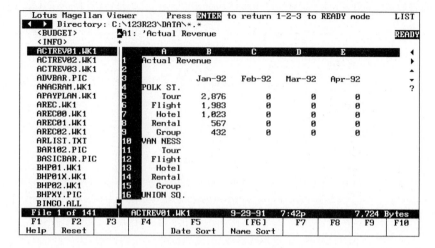

Another conversion file, VIEWER.TXT, allows you to see the contents of
text files, plus some parts of nontext files. For example, if you highlight a
dBASE file, Viewer reveals the field names and some of the records in the
file. If you highlight a 1-2-3 graph file in the PIC format, Viewer displays the
titles and legends. The text file viewer is the default, used if the file does not
match a worksheet format.

To properly view other types of files, including word processing and
graphic files, you may want to purchase the full Lotus Magellan program.
This software offers other features besides file viewing. Magellan has a fast
file search either by file name or by words or phrases within files and can
launch applications based on the file you are viewing (similar to the document launching facility on the Apple Macintosh). It also provides a variety
of utilities such as file delete, backup, file compression (to save disk space),
plus a file-integrity-checking function that can alert you to computer viruses.

Working with Viewer

As you can see from Figure 7.41, the Viewer screen efficiently conveys information about the files in your current 1-2-3 directory. The Viewer screen consists of the following parts:

- The status line at the top of the screen displays prompts for the retrieving, linking, and browsing commands. It also contains a mode indicator
  that tells you if the highlight is in the List or View window. The mode
  indicator may also temporarily display the word WAIT while it redraws
  the view screen.

- The directory path shows the name of the directory in which you are viewing files. To the left of the directory path are left and right arrows for changing the directory with your mouse.

- The List window on the left contains a list of file names in the current Viewer directory.

- The View window on the right displays the contents of the currently highlighted file in the List window. If you are using a mouse and viewing a worksheet file, Viewer displays a mouse palette to the right of the window, with scroll arrows.

- The information line beneath the List and View windows lists the total number of files in the directory and the number of the highlighted file. Below the View window is the file name, the date and time the file was last saved, and the file size in bytes.

- The function key bar at the bottom of the screen lists the function keys available in Viewer. If you are using a mouse, you can click these instead of pressing the keys.

When you first use Viewer, you will see a list of files in the default data directory, the one listed when you use the Worksheet Global Default command. You can change the directory being viewed. While in the List window, press the Left Arrow key or click the left arrow symbol to the left of the directory path. This changes the directory to the one above the current directory. As you keep pressing Left Arrow or clicking the left arrow symbol, you will eventually see a list of drive names.

To make a directory current in Viewer, highlight its name in the list and press Right Arrow or click the right arrow symbol to the left of the directory path. Repeat this step until you reach the directory you want. The name of the current Viewer directory always appears below the status line. This directory does not have to be the same as your current directory in 1-2-3. When you start Viewer for the first time, however, the directory it uses is the current directory in 1-2-3.

If you change the current directory within Viewer, Viewer remembers this directory from one Viewer session to the next. Even if you change the current directory with the File Directory command, Viewer continues to use the directory you set while in Viewer. To make the Viewer directory the same as the current directory in 1-2-3, just press F2 while using Viewer or click the box called Reset.

The List window on the left of the Viewer screen contains a list of files that is normally in alphabetical order. You can press F5 or click on the Date Sort button at the bottom of the screen to change the order of files to the date of storage. Use F6 to return to a list sorted by name. You can move around the List and View windows using the cursor-movement keys. The keys used in navigating the List window are listed in Table 7.4. The pointer-movement keys act according to which viewer is active, and are also listed in Table 7.4.

Table 7.4   **The Viewer Keys**

In both windows:*

F2	Makes the current directory in 1-2-3 the current Viewer directory.
F5	Sorts files in List window by date.
F6	Sorts files in List window by name.

In the List window:

Left Arrow	Displays a list of directories or drives.
Right Arrow	Moves the highlight to the View window if the List window contains file names. If the List window contains directory names, makes the highlighted directory current.
Up Arrow	Moves the highlight up one line.
Down Arrow	Moves the highlight down one line.
End	Moves the highlight to the last line.
Home	Moves the highlight to the first line.
PgDn	Moves the highlight down one screen.
PgUp	Moves the highlight up one screen.

In the View window:**

Left Arrow	Moves highlighting to the List window, or one column to the left in the worksheet being viewed.
Right Arrow	Moves the highlight right one column in the worksheet being viewed.

* When using View Retrieve, the Enter key, pressed in the List or View window, retrieves the currently viewed worksheet.
** When the View window is current and contains a worksheet, you can use the standard cursor-movement keys to move the cell pointer and examine the worksheet. When using View Link, pressing Enter in the View window links the highlighted cell to the current cell of the worksheet in 1-2-3. (To link a range of cells, highlight the first cell, type a period to anchor the range, extend the range using the cursor keys, and press Enter.)

File View Browsing

The File View Browse command displays all the files in the current directory in the List window. You can scroll through the list of files and view their contents in the View window. Press Esc to quit Browsing and return to the File View menu. Press Ctrl-Break to return directly to the 1-2-3 worksheet.

File View Retrieval

Because the File View Retrieve command will replace any file already in memory with the file you select for retrieval, when you issue the command 1-2-3 prompts you to save the current file if you have changed it since the last time you saved to disk. As you can see from Figure 7.42, the File View Retrieve command displays worksheet files in the current directory in the List window and prompts you to select and retrieve a file from the list.

Figure 7.42

Using File View Retrieve

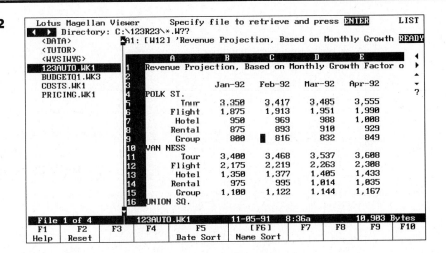

To retrieve a file with the Viewer, highlight it in the List window and press Enter. If you have moved into the View window to view the file, you can press Enter to retrieve the file while still in the View window.

File View Linking

When you link files with Viewer, you can see the contents of the *source file*, which supplies the data for the link to the current file, called the *target file*. This lets you ensure that you are selecting the correct cell as the source cell. Viewer automatically writes the correct linking formula in the target cell of the current worksheet. When you leave Viewer and return to the target cell, the cell contains the linking formula.

When you use the Viewer, you don't have to know the address of the cell to which you wanted to link, which is difficult to do if you have no diagram of the source file and are not familiar with its layout. The following steps demonstrate how Viewer assists you in creating file links.

1. First make sure that the Viewer add-in is attached. From the main menu, select Add-In followed by Attach. Select VIEWER.ADN followed by No-Key. The add-in will be attached. (If it is already attached, 1-2-3 will tell you.) Press Esc to return to READY mode.

2. In cell A1 of a fresh worksheet, enter the label **This is a link:** and then move the cell pointer to B2. This is where the link into the current worksheet will appear.

3. From the File menu, select View. Choose the Link option and scroll the list of files that is displayed until the supporting worksheet to which you want to link is highlighted. In this case, you can use the revenue projection created in the last chapter, or any other sizable worksheet.

4. Following the instruction at the top of the screen, press Right Arrow to move the highlighting into the righthand window. As you can see from Figure 7.43, the file you selected is still marked by an underline or highlight in the file list.

Figure 7.43

Using File View Link

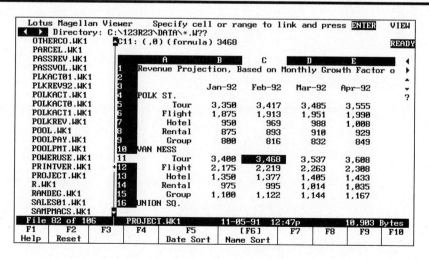

5. Move the highlighting, which now acts like a cell pointer, to the cell you want to link with. If you are using the revenue projection from the last chapter, try selecting N29. Note that the upper-left corner of the View window tells you the address of the current cell and its contents. Press Enter to confirm the link.

6. You are immediately returned to READY mode with the link formula in place. You can see the result in Figure 7.44. Note that 1-2-3 records the full path of the file you are linking to when you create the link with the View Link command.

The View Link command saves any guesswork over correct file names and cell addresses, since you can clearly view the file you are linking to.

Figure 7.44

Results of linking

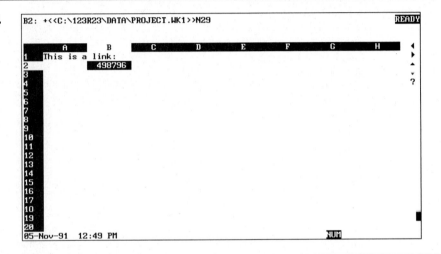

Using the Wysiwyg Add-In

The Wysiwyg add-in is probably the most important of those provided with 1-2-3 Release 2.3. You can use Wysiwyg with 1-2-3 Release 2.3 as long as you have a graphics monitor and at least 512k of RAM. When you attach Wysiwyg, you have the ability to:

- Format text and numbers in a variety of fonts, styles, and sizes

- Draw lines, boxes, and grids around spreadsheet cells for display and reporting purposes

- Combine graphics and text within the worksheet, including freehand art work and clip-art

- Customize the 1-2-3 display, including colors, frame styles, and zoom factor

The first three areas are discussed in detail in Chapter 10, but the last one, the ability to customize your display, is dealt with here since it has direct bearing on your default mode of operation.

The Wysiwyg Effect

As you can see from Figure 7.45, attaching Wysiwyg enhances the worksheet frame: A grid of lines outlines the cells, and the cell pointer is shown as an outline rather than solid shading. This change occurs when you load Wysiwyg, even before you invoke it.

Figure 7.45

The 1-2-3 screen with Wysiwyg attached

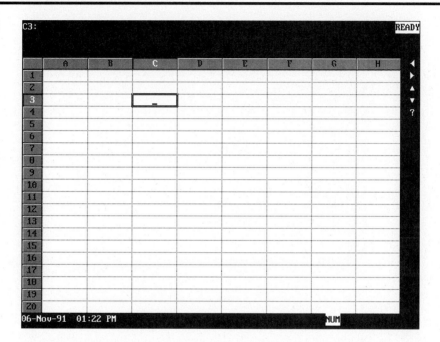

Note that Wysiwyg may have a slightly different effect on your system. (The exact appearance of 1-2-3 when running Wysiwyg depends upon the Wysiwyg Display command, which is described in a moment.) Once you have tried Wysiwyg, you may want to use it all the time, in which case you can use the Worksheet Global Default Other command to select Wysiwyg as an auto-attach add-in. Once you have experimented with the Wysiwyg Display command and its ability to customize the 1-2-3 screen, you may also want to use the Display Default command to record your preferences so that they are used every time Wysiwyg is attached.

The Wysiwyg Menu

You do not need to assign Wysiwyg to an add-in key because it has its own menu, as shown at the top of Figure 7.46. To use Wysiwyg commands, you

need to activate the Wysiwyg menu either by typing a colon (:) or by moving
the mouse pointer into the menu area.

Figure 7.46

The Wysiwyg menu

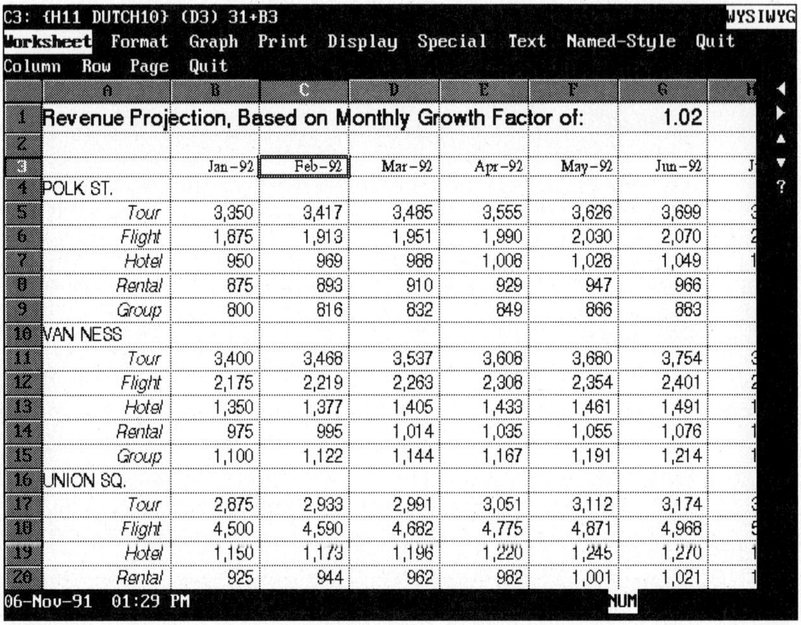

The Wysiwyg menu uses the two-line system plus dialog boxes, just like
the regular 1-2-3 menu. Of course, moving the mouse pointer into the menu
area normally activates the regular 1-2-3 menu. But with Wysiwyg attached,
this action can also activate the Wysiwyg menu: The program responds with
whichever menu you used last. You can toggle between the two menus by
pressing the right mouse button.

Since the Wysiwyg menu uses the colon as a menu key, it is normal to
write Wysiwyg commands preceded by a colon, as in :Worksheet Column.
This helps to distinguish Wysiwyg commands from regular 1-2-3 commands.

The Wysiwyg Display Commands

As you can see from the worksheet in Figure 7.46, Wysiwyg can transform
ordinary data into something more visually appealing. As described in Chapter 10, Wysiwyg can also print the results exactly as they appear on screen.
This section covers the :Display commands, which allow you to customize
and store as defaults your preference for the 1-2-3 display.

Mode

The :Display Mode command allows you to switch between several different types of display. The default setting is Graphics, which shows your
worksheet as it will appear when printed. The alternative to this is Text,
which is the way the 1-2-3 screen appears without Wysiwyg loaded (see Figure 7.44 and earlier illustrations in this chapter). The Mode command also
offers a choice between B&W and Color. The B&W option displays everything in black and white and the Color option enables you to display colors
if you have a color monitor.

Zoom

The :Display Zoom command allows you to shrink or enlarge the 1-2-3 worksheet so that you can see more or less of it at once. Normal display is referred
to as 100% zoom. Percentages less than 100% shrink the worksheet, and percentages greater than 100% enlarge it. For example, Figure 7.47 shows the
effect of 63% zoom. This allows you to see a full 12-month projection. Note
that in this screen the grid lines shown in Figure 7.46 have been removed.

When you choose the Zoom command, you have a choice of five preset
zoom percentages, plus Manual, which allows you to enter any percentage
between 25% and 400%. The preset percentages are: Tiny: 63%, Small:
87%, Normal: 100%, Large: 125%, and Huge: 150%. The Large and Huge
settings are helpful when you want to examine Wysiwyg formatting in detail.
Figure 7.48 shows an example of Zoom Large. It also shows the :Display
Color menu, which is described next.

When you select Manual, you can type in a number for the percentage.
Alternatively, you can use the Right and Left Arrow keys, or the right and
left mouse arrows, to increase (right) or decrease (left) the current value.
The display will change as you increase or decrease the zoom percentage.

Colors

The :Display Colors command is used to alter the color of the 1-2-3 screen
when Wysiwyg is attached. The screen is divided into nine areas, which
appear as the first nine items in the :Display Color menu. Most of these
items are self-explanatory. When you select an area, such as Background, a
single-line list of eight colors appears from which you can choose. The Background option alters the worksheet background color, but does not affect
areas outside the worksheet frame.

The color of labels and values in the worksheet entries is determined by
the Text setting. The Unprot choice affects the color of unprotected cells.
The color of the cell pointer is determined by the Cell-Pointer option, but
this does not affect the style of the cell pointer, which is covered by the :Dis-
play Options Cell-Pointer command. If you are using a grid of lines on the
worksheet, determined by the :Display Options Grid command, the color of
the lines is determined by the :Display Color Grid option. The column and

row frame of the worksheet is colored by the Frame option. If you want negative values to appear in a different color, use the Neg option. The Lines option controls the color of lines added to the worksheet by the Wysiwyg :Format Lines command. If you use the :Format Lines Shadow command to add a drop shadow to cells, you can alter the color of the shadow by using the :Display Color Shadow option.

Figure 7.47

Using 63% zoom

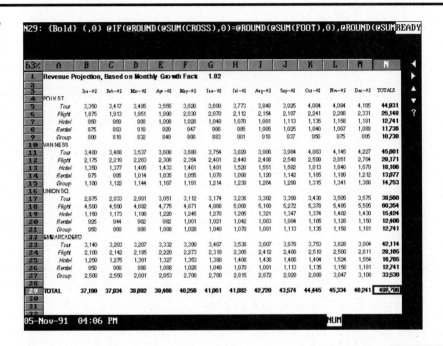

Besides Quit, the only other option on the :Display Color menu is Replace. You use this option to change the way that Wysiwyg displays colors. Each of the 8 colors available under Wysiwyg can be changed to one of the 64 colors displayed by your monitor. Wysiwyg uses the values 0 through 63 to represent the available choices. When you select a color to change, you can type in a number for the color value. Alternatively, you can use the Right and Left Arrow keys, or right and left mouse arrows, to increase (right) or decrease (left) the current value. You need to experiment with your computer to see which values look best.

Options

The :Display Options command covers six areas of screen activity. Using the available options, you can radically alter the way 1-2-3 looks. You can turn off the frame, turn on a grid, and even adjust the brightness of your display.

Figure 7.48
Using 125% zoom

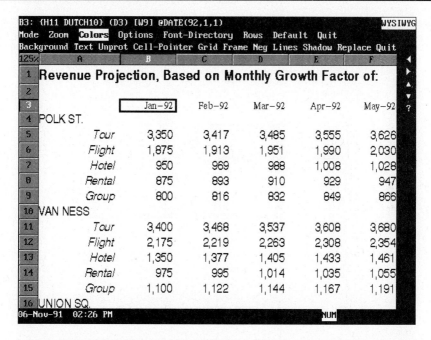

```
B3: {H11 DUTCH10} (D3) [W9] @DATE(92,1,1)                    WYSIWYG
Mode  Zoom  Colors  Options  Font-Directory  Rows  Default  Quit
Background Text Unprot Cell-Pointer Grid Frame Neg Lines Shadow Replace Quit
```

	A	B	C	D	E	F
1	Revenue Projection, Based on Monthly Growth Factor of:					
2						
3		Jan–92	Feb–92	Mar–92	Apr–92	May–92
4	POLK ST.					
5	Tour	3,350	3,417	3,485	3,555	3,626
6	Flight	1,875	1,913	1,951	1,990	2,030
7	Hotel	950	969	988	1,008	1,028
8	Rental	875	893	910	929	947
9	Group	800	816	832	849	866
10	VAN NESS					
11	Tour	3,400	3,468	3,537	3,608	3,680
12	Flight	2,175	2,219	2,263	2,308	2,354
13	Hotel	1,350	1,377	1,405	1,433	1,461
14	Rental	975	995	1,014	1,035	1,055
15	Group	1,100	1,122	1,144	1,167	1,191
16	UNION SQ.					

```
06-Nov-91  02:26 PM                                           NUM
```

Frame   There are five options for the style of frame used in Wysiwyg. The first option is 1-2-3, which produces a standard frame with row numbers, column letters, and no lines between column letters or row numbers. The Enhanced option places lines between column letters and row numbers. The Relief option, seen in Figure 7.48, adds a sculpted look to the column and row headings.

The Frame Special option allows you to customize the frame to provide information about the size of your worksheet. This can be measured in four different ways:

- The Characters option measures the worksheet according to the number of lines and characters, based on six lines per inch and ten characters per inch.

- The Inches option measures the worksheet by inches. You can see this in Figure 7.49. Note that as you zoom the worksheet the scale changes proportionately.

- The Metric option measures the worksheet by centimeters.

- The Points/Pica option measures the worksheet in points and picas.

Figure 7.49
Using the Inches
frame

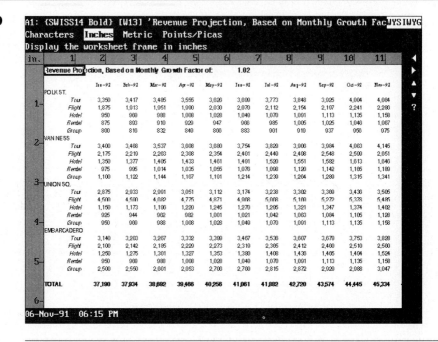

The final Frame option is None, which turns off the display of column and row headings. Although this might seem a little strange, the uncluttered look offered by None may be desirable for presentations. Figure 7.50 shows a graph pasted into the worksheet with Wysiwyg and then displayed alongside numbers. The frame has been turned off, as has the worksheet grid.

Grid   The :Display Options Grid command offers a simple choice between No and Yes. Choose No and the grid lines disappear; choose Yes and they are restored.

Page-Breaks   You can use the Wysiwyg print commands to see where in the worksheet page breaks will occur—the page breaks appear as dotted lines. With :Display Options Page-Breaks, you can select Yes to show the page breaks or No to hide them.

Cell-Pointer   The cell pointer in Wysiwyg can appear as either an outline, as shown in Figure 7.50, or as a shaded rectangle. The Cell-Pointer options are thus Solid or Outline.

Intensity   You can switch your screen between two Intensity settings: Normal or High. High increases the brightness of colors used by Wysiwyg.

Figure 7.50
A worksheet
without a frame

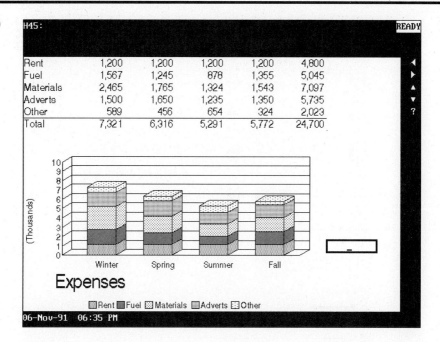

Adapter   Normally, Wysiwyg can correctly detect the type of display
adapter you are using. However, if Wysiwyg does not appear to work correctly on your screen, you may need to tell it about your particular combination of adapter and monitor. When you select Adapter, your choices are
Auto, which tells Wysiwyg to use its auto-sensing feature, or one of the following items:

1   VGA adapter with color or monochrome monitor

2   MCGA adapter with color or monochrome monitor

3   EGA adapter with color or monochrome monitor

4   EGA adapter with monochrome monitor

5   EGA adapter with low-resolution color monitor

6   Hercules monochrome graphics adapter

7   CGA adapter with color or monochrome monitor

8   ATT/Compaq/Olivetti 400 lines plasma display

9   Text mode

The last option for Adapter is Blink, which allows you to choose Yes for a blinking cursor or No to stop the cursor from blinking.

Font-Directory

When you install 1-2-3 Release 2.3, a subdirectory called WYSIWYG is created below the program directory. Font files required by Wysiwyg are copied into this area and Wysiwyg assumes that it will be able to find fonts there. If you want to use a different area of your hard disk for these font files, you use the :Display Font-Directory option to tell Wysiwyg of the new location. When you use the :Display Default Update command, your choice of directory is recorded for future sessions.

Rows

While the :Display Zoom command shrinks or enlarges the worksheet by a given percentage, the :Display Rows command simply alters the number of rows that appear on the screen. This command does not alter the number of columns that are visible and so may distort worksheet entries. The setting can be from 16 to 60. When you select Rows, you can type in a number. Alternatively, you can use the Right and Left Arrow keys, or the right and left mouse arrows, to increase (right) or decrease (left) the current value.

Default

When you are ready to record the choices you have made with the Display command, you should choose the Default option. This command offers two choices: Restore and Update. The Restore command changes the settings back to what they were when you last used the Update command. The Update command records the current choices as the new defaults, storing them in a file called WYSIWYG.CNF. This file also stores the printer currently selected by the Wysiwyg Print Config command as the default printer. See Chapter 10 for more on Print Config and the other Wysiwyg commands. The Worksheet Global Default command and the :Display command work together to give you a version of 1-2-3 that suits your needs.

Using the Auditor Add-In

With the Auditor add-in, you can analyze the logical structure of worksheets by examining the formulas they contain. For example, you can list all formulas that depend upon a particular cell, or identify all cells involved in a circular reference.

The Auditor Menus

When you attach Auditor, you should choose an add-in key for it; otherwise, it will not appear on any 1-2-3 or Wysiwyg menu. When you activate Auditor, a menu and dialog box appear, as shown in Figure 7.51.

Figure 7.51

The Auditor menu and dialog box

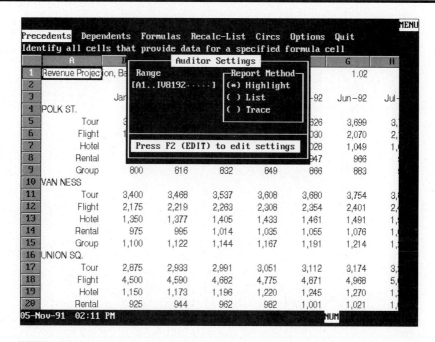

There are two main items in the Audit Setting dialog box: Range and Report Method. Range refers to the area of worksheet that you want Auditor to examine; the default setting is the entire worksheet. There are three Report Methods: Highlight, List, or Trace, which determine how Auditor responds when you ask it to locate information for you:

- Highlight identifies cells by displaying them in a bright intensity or different color.

- List lists information about identified cells in a worksheet range you specify.

- Trace displays identified cells one at a time.

As you can see from the dialog box, the Highlight method is the default choice.

There are seven items on the Auditor menu:

- Precedents identifies all cells referred to by a particular formula in the audit range.

- Dependents identifies all formulas that depend on a particular cell in the audit range.

- Formulas identifies all formulas in the audit range.

- Recalc-List identifies all formulas in the order in which 1-2-3 recalculates them.

- Circs identifies all cells involved in a circular reference.

- Options sets or resets options such as the audit range or the way in which Auditor identifies cells.

- Quit returns 1-2-3 to READY mode.

The Options menu contains options for Highlight, List, and Trace, which work just like the previously described option buttons in the dialog box. The other three Options are as follows:

- Audit-Range allows you to specify the worksheet range you want to audit.

- Reset clears any highlights from cells and resets the options to the defaults.

- Quit returns you to the main Auditor menu.

The default audit range is the entire worksheet from A1 through IV8192. There is no need to change this default unless you specifically want to exclude a particular area of the worksheet.

Finding Precedents

The Precedents command identifies all the cells and ranges that provide data to a formula. These are the cells that 1-2-3 has to refer to in order to calculate the result of the formula. For example, if cell D5 contains the formula @SUM(D2..D4)*A1, cells D2, D3, D4, and A1 are all precedents of cell D5.

How Auditor identifies precedents and other items such as Dependents and Formulas depends on whether you select Highlight, List, or Trace from the Options list. For example, Figure 7.52 displays the results of the Precedents command issued with List as the report method.

When you issue the Precedents command, you are asked to identify the source cell, meaning the cell whose precedents you are attempting to locate. In the example in Figure 7.52, the source cell was N5. If the List option is selected, you must also identify a cell or cells to contain the results. This should be an unused area of the worksheet, as the list can be quite extensive.

You can see from the list in Figure 7.52 that each cell is given, along with the value or formula in that cell. The title in P5 was entered by Auditor.

Figure 7.52
Results of
Precedents
command

```
N5: (,0) @SUM(B5..M5)                                            READY

        A         L        M        N       O      P        Q      ◄
1  Revenue Projection,                                                 ►
2                                                                      ▲
3                 Nov-92   Dec-92   TOTALS                             ▼
4  POLK ST.                                                            ?
5            Tour   4,084   4,165   44,931         Precedents of Cell N5
6            Flight 2,286   2,331   25,148         B5: 3350
7            Hotel  1,158   1,181   12,741         C5: +$G$1*B5
8            Rental 1,067   1,088   11,736         D5: +$G$1*C5
9            Group    975     995   10,730         E5: +$G$1*D5
10 VAN NESS                                        F5: +$G$1*E5
11           Tour   4,145   4,227   45,601         G5: +$G$1*F5
12           Flight 2,651   2,704   29,171         H5: +$G$1*G5
13           Hotel  1,646   1,679   18,106         I5: +$G$1*H5
14           Rental 1,189   1,212   13,077         J5: +$G$1*I5
15           Group  1,341   1,368   14,753         K5: +$G$1*J5
16 UNION SQ.                                       L5: +$G$1*K5
17           Tour   3,505   3,575   38,560         M5: +$G$1*L5
18           Flight 5,485   5,595   60,354         G1: 1.02
19           Hotel  1,402   1,430   15,424
20           Rental 1,128   1,150   12,406
05-Nov-91  02:49 PM                                            NUM
```

If you selected Highlight as the Report Method, Auditor highlights all precedents in the worksheet using a brighter color. On some monitors, this might be difficult to see. To clear the highlighting, use the Options Reset Highlight command. If you selected Options Trace as your Report Method, the first precedent cell is highlighted in the worksheet and a three-item menu appears: Forward, Backward, and Quit. Select Forward to see the next precedent, Backward to review earlier precedents, or Quit to end the command.

Finding Dependents

The Dependents command works just like the Precedents command except that it identifies all formulas in the audit range that reference a particular cell. For example, if you chose Dependents in Figure 7.52 and selected cell M5 as the source cell, N5 would be a dependent cell, as would the grand total in N29 at the bottom of the column of totals. You can use Dependents when you need to see whether a particular cell you are about to alter or erase is referenced in any formulas.

Finding Formulas

The Formulas command identifies all the formulas (including linking formulas to cells in other files) in the audit range. How Auditor identifies formulas depends on whether you selected Options Highlight, Options List, or Options Trace.

Getting a Recalc List

The Recalc-List command identifies formulas in the worksheet in the order of recalculation. Remember that the default order of recalculation is Natural. Using the Worksheet Global Recalculation command, you can alter this to Columnwise. Auditor always begins by identifying the formula that 1-2-3 calculates first and ends with the formula that 1-2-3 calculates last. Note that Auditor does not identify linking formulas when you use Recalc-List.

Circular References

The Circs command on the Auditor menu identifies all the cells in the worksheet that are involved in a circular reference. A circular reference occurs when a formula refers to itself. For example, the formula @SUM(D2..D5) would be circular if it were entered in D5. 1-2-3 would add the sum to the sum every time the spreadsheet is recalculated, adding D2+D3+D4+ the current value of D5. (Circular references only occur when the recalculation order is Natural.) A formula can refer to itself either directly or indirectly. The previous example is a direct reference. If cell B1 contains +B2, cell B2 contains +B3, and cell B3 contains +B1, the circular reference is indirect.

When 1-2-3 detects a circular reference, it displays the CIRC indicator on the status line. You can use the Worksheet Status command to check the location of a circular formula, but the Auditor Circs command can identify all of the cells involved in the circular reference. How Auditor identifies the cells in the circular reference depends on your Report Method selection.

Summary

Although 1-2-3 is relatively easy to set up and use, there are many housekeeping chores that you need to attend to as soon as you start to make extensive use of the program. File saving, organizing, and protecting are important to preserve the investment of time and effort you make in your work with 1-2-3. The file-linking feature offers you a new way of organizing complex tasks and sharing information between users. In addition, by careful attention to defaults, you can save considerable time during each session. The next two chapters take you beyond spreadsheet calculations and into 1-2-3's database management and graph-making capabilities.

8

Database Commands

THIS CHAPTER EXAMINES SORTING AND DATABASE MANAGEMENT. SORT-
ing is the ability to reorder one or more columns of information
based on one or more key columns. This capability is particularly useful for, but not limited to, the task of database management. A *database* is a collection of information arranged in a meaningful way. The processes of organizing, updating, and extracting information from databases
are known as *database management.*

Sorting Lists

Many spreadsheets, both large and small, contain lists, or information organized into columns and rows. The worksheet in Figure 8.1 contains a simple
list. 1-2-3 enables you to sort lists, placing labels in alphabetical order and
numbers in numerical order. You can also sort a list based on several different items of information. For example, you can sort the list of people in Figure 8.2 by last name, and then subsort it by first name.

Figure 8.1
Simple list

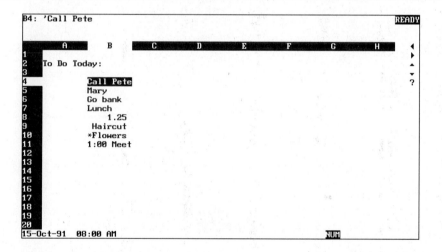

This chapter will use the lists shown in Figures 8.1 and 8.2 to illustrate the
process of sorting. If you want to follow the examples, create these lists in
separate worksheets. The only formatted entries are the dollar amounts in
column G of Figure 8.2. These were assigned the Currency format, with two
decimal places. All of the column widths are the standard nine characters.
Note that the label Haircut in column B of Figure 8.1 actually begins with a
space. Also, the 1:00 entry in B11 will need a preceding apostrophe since it
begins with a value but is in fact a label.

A Simple Sort

The list Figure 8.1 is a simple collection of things to be done. Suppose that you want to sort this list alphabetically. A good place to begin is with the cell pointer on the first piece of data to be sorted, in this case, cell B4. Now press / and select Data followed by Sort. This brings up the Sort menu and the Sort Settings dialog box, as shown in Figure 8.3.

Figure 8.2

Employee list

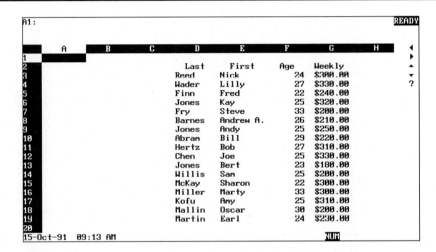

Figure 8.3

The Sort menu and Sort Settings dialog box

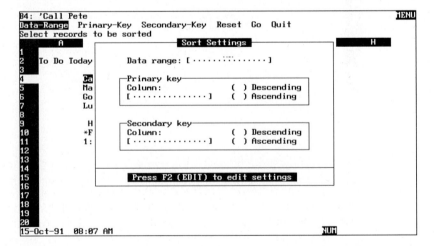

The Sort Settings dialog box will record options you choose for the Sort operation from the Sort menu. Alternatively, you can edit the settings within the box without using the menu. To perform a sort, 1-2-3 first needs to know the range that contains the data to be sorted, known as the *data range*. Since the cells to be sorted are B4 through B11, you would select Data-Range and highlight B4..B11. (Keyboard users can type a period to anchor the beginning cell of the range at B4, and then press End followed by Down Arrow; mouse users can select the range with the mouse.)

Next 1-2-3 needs to know the *sort key;* The column of information on which the sort will be based. When your list includes more than one column, you must choose the column or columns that will determine the order of items in the list. When the list is only one column wide, you select Primary-Key and point to any cell in the column that contains the list. When you press Enter, 1-2-3 requests the sort order, as shown in Figure 8.4.

Figure 8.4
Selecting the sort order

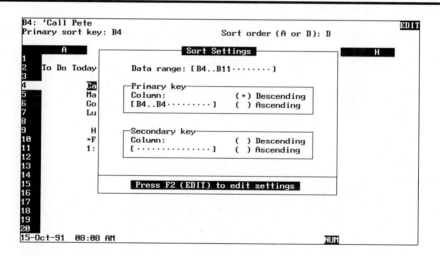

The sort order can either be descending or ascending. As you can see from Figure 8.4, 1-2-3 initially suggests Descending, as indicated by the letter D next to the "Sort order" prompt. However, you should type **A** since you want to select Ascending. The Ascending option sorts labels from A to Z and values from small to large. The Descending option sorts in the opposite order: labels from Z to A, numbers from large to small. After selecting the desired order, press Enter to confirm it. Your choice will be recorded in the Sort Settings dialog box along with the data range and the location of the primary key. If you are editing the Sort Settings dialog box, you can simply click on Ascending to select it.

With the data range, primary key, and sort order set, you can select Go to execute the sort and then return to READY mode. Figure 8.5 shows the results for this example. As you can see, the items are roughly in alphabetical order. However, note that the item Haircut appears at the top of the list because its first character is a space, and labels beginning with spaces are placed at the top of an ascending sort. (You can think of a space as the letter before A in the alphabet.) Also note that the item 1.25 is at the bottom of the list. Items that are values are placed below labels in an ascending sort. (1:00 Meet is a label, even though it starts with a number.) The item *Flowers is below Mary because it begins with an asterisk, and labels that begin with punctuation characters come after those that begin with regular letters in ascending sorts. The order of priority in sorting is discussed further under "Rules of Order."

Figure 8.5

The sorted to do list

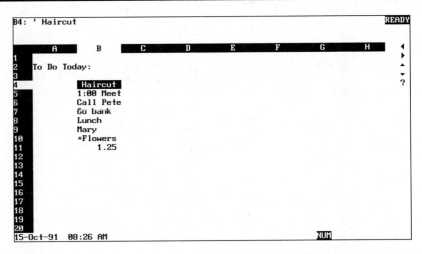

Suppose that you want to sort this list according to your priorities for the day. To do this, you can enter numbers in column A that represent a priority level from 1 to 5, with 5 the most important, as shown in Figure 8.6.

This new column of numbers will now be the basis for the sort. Activate the menu and select Data followed by Sort. Note that 1-2-3 remembers the data range. Select Data-Range from the menu or dialog box. Extend the range from B4 through to A11, and then press Enter to confirm. (It's okay to define a range from right to left.) As you will see from the Sort Settings dialog box, the range is recorded as A4..B11.

Since the previous setting for the primary key is remembered and you want to sort the list based on column A, you need to change the primary key. Select Primary-Key and choose a cell in column A. Note that the sort key coordinates are not locked when you are pointing them out. After selecting a cell in column A, note that the previously selected order, Ascending, is still in effect. In this case, however, you want to sort in descending order to place priority 5 items at the top of the list. Type **D** and press Enter to select Descending and then choose Go to complete the sort, the results of which can be seen in Figure 8.7.

Figure 8.6

Prioritizing the list

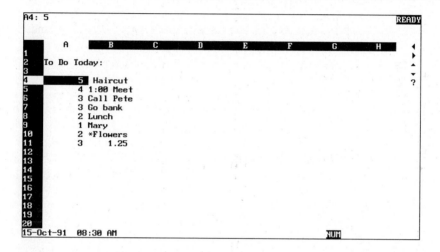

Figure 8.7

The list sorted by column A

You can undo the Sort command with the UNDO feature. Since 1-2-3 remembers the sort settings, you can quickly repeat the command. For example, if you edit some entries in the list, you can resort by selecting Data, Sort, and then Go. Suppose that you want to make Mary a higher priority. Entering 6 as her priority number and then reissuing the Sort command will place her at the top of the list.

A Two-Level Sort

Suppose that you want to sort alphabetically the list of names in Figure 8.2. Activate the menu and select Data followed by Sort. Now select Data-Range and make the setting D3..G19. You must exclude the labels above the data to be sorted; otherwise, 1-2-3 will treat them as part of the list and insert them into the data in alphabetical order.

Now select Primary-Key and choose any cell in column D, the Last column. Choose Ascending as the order. To make sure that any people with the same last name are sorted according to first name, you need to select a secondary key, which can be any cell in column E, the First column. Again choose Ascending as the order. The settings will appear as shown in Figure 8.8.

Figure 8.8

The sort settings

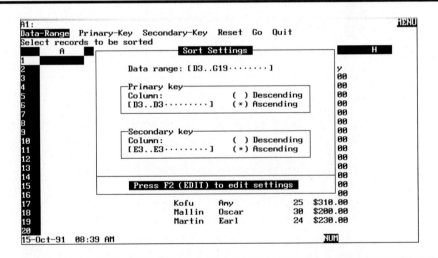

Before issuing the Go command to perform a large sort, you should check the settings. Remember that when you are highlighting a large range you can use the period key (.) to view all four corners of the range setting. Note that when performing a multicolumn sort you must include all of the columns of the list, even though only two of them can form the basis of the sort. In the example, you do *not* want to sort just columns D and E. You

want to sort columns D through G, *based on* columns D and E. If you just used D and E as the data range, 1-2-3 would disconnect the names from their associated ages and salaries. Because such mistakes are easily made, it is a good idea to save the file before performing a large sort. Also note that Sort is one of the commands that you can reverse with UNDO. The properly completed sort will look like Figure 8.9. Note that the three people with the last name Jones are subsorted according to their first names.

Figure 8.9
The completed two-level sort

```
A1:                                                                    READY

          A      │ B    │ C    │   D   │   E    │ F  │   G     │ H   │  ◄
1                                                                       ►
2                              Last     First    Age   Weekly           ▲
3                              Abram     Bill      29   $220.00          ▼
4                              Barnes    Andrew A. 26   $210.00          ?
5                              Chen      Joe       25   $330.00
6                              Finn      Fred      22   $240.00
7                              Fry       Steve     33   $200.00
8                              Hertz     Bob       27   $310.00
9                              Jones     Andy      25   $250.00
10                             Jones     Bert      23   $180.00
11                             Jones     Kay       25   $320.00
12                             Kofu      Amy       25   $310.00
13                             Mallin    Oscar     30   $200.00
14                             Martin    Earl      24   $230.00
15                             McKay     Sharon    22   $300.00
16                             Miller    Marty     33   $300.00
17                             Reed      Nick      24   $300.00
18                             Wader     Lilly     27   $330.00
19                             Willis    Sam       25   $200.00
20
15-Oct-91   09:09 AM                                            NUM
```

Rules of Order

You may wonder how 1-2-3 decides the exact order in which to place the rows of the data range when you issue the Go command. The program looks at the primary key, sorts it, and moves the rest of the cells according to their entries in the primary column. If there are matching values in the primary column, 1-2-3 looks to the secondary column as a tie breaker.

Typically, a column will consist of all labels or all values, in which case the order is fairly easy to predict. If you have picked Ascending, numbers are sorted from lowest to highest, words are sorted from A to Z, and dates are sorted from oldest to most recent. However, there are some subtleties to alphabetical order, and some rules that 1-2-3 uses to determine sort order when a key column contains a mixture of values and labels. 1-2-3 normally puts numbers before labels in a descending sort when a column contains both numbers and labels. 1-2-3 is not case sensitive when sorting label data. The sort rules are summarized in Table 8.1. Later in this chapter you will learn how to apply the Sort command to information arranged in fields and records as a database.

There is a way to alter the order in which 1-2-3 arranges records in a database. This involves using the Install program, which is described in detail in Appendix A. The Modify Current Driver Set option on the Install menu allows you to alter a setting called Collating Sequence. The collating sequence determines the order in which 1-2-3 sorts label entries that include both numbers and letters. There are three options: ASCII, Numbers first, and Numbers last. The default setting is Numbers first. The following shows the results of a sort in ascending order, using the three different collating sequences:

ASCII	Numbers first	Numbers last
33 Saw Lane	33 Saw Lane	Six rolling city
34 Crescent Ave.	34 Crescent Ave.	Six Rolons Place
69 Cucumber St.	69 Cucumber St.	Square Plaza
Six Rolons Place	Six rolling city	Three City Plaza
Six rolling city	Six Rolons Place	33 Saw Lane
Square Plaza	Square Plaza	34 Crescent Ave.
Three City Plaza	Three City Plaza	69 Cucumber St.

Table 8.1   The Sort Rules

Type of Data	Position in List
Blank cells	Appear at the top of the list, even before cells that contain only blank spaces.
Labels beginning with spaces	Come after blank cells. Are arranged according to the number of spaces preceding the first character, with more spaces preceding less. Are then arranged alphabetically from A to Z.
Labels beginning with numbers	Are placed after labels that begin with spaces, before labels that begin with letters, and are arranged numerically.
Labels beginning with letters	Are arranged alphabetically from A to Z.
Labels beginning with special characters	Characters like @ and $ come after Z. Two labels that begin with the same special character are arranged according to the second character. The special characters are listed, from lowest to highest, in the following order: ! " # $ % & ( ) * + . / : ; < = > ? @ [\ ] ^ ` { | } ~
Values	Values come after labels that begin with special characters, and are arranged from lowest to highest according to their numeric value, regardless of their format and of whether they are formulas or numeric constants.

If you want 1-2-3 to use a sort sequence other than Numbers first, you must load the Install program and make the change there, storing the new setting in your 1-2-3 configuration file. You cannot change the sort sequence within the 1-2-3 program itself.

Adding and Deleting Items

There are several techniques for adding items to a list that has already been sorted. If you simply type new items at the bottom of the list, they will not automatically be included in the data range and you will have to issue the Data Sort Data-Range command to redefine the setting to include the new items. You will also have to issue the Data Sort Go command to sort the new items into their proper place within the list.

An alternative approach is to insert the new item into the list using the Worksheet Insert Row command. For example, if you want to add an employee called Sam Waites to the list in Figure 8.9, you can place the cell pointer on row 19, issue the Worksheet Insert Row command, and press Enter to insert a fresh row. The new row is placed above old row 19, which now becomes row 20, and 1-2-3 automatically expands the data range to include the new row. You can then type the new item on the new row.

The row insert method generally allows you to put new items into the list in correct order while automatically including them in the data range. However, you cannot place items above the first or after the last item with this method without redefining the data range. In fact, it's a good idea to check the data range whenever you have made many changes or additions to your list.

The Worksheet Insert Row command is a poor choice if you have other entries in the worksheet that occupy the same rows as the list. For example, suppose you want to insert a fresh row above row 8 of Figure 8.9 for a new employee named Fred Hegel. Doing so could introduce an unwanted blank line in any other list stored on the left or right of the employee list. An alternative in a situation like this is to make room in the list by moving part of the list. In this case, you could issue the Move command with the cell pointer in D8, define D8..G19 as the source range, D9 as the destination range, and move the bottom part of the employee list down one row without affecting the rest of the worksheet. 1-2-3 will expand the data range to reflect the new coordinates, D3..H20, and the new entry on row 8 will be part of the list.

Deleting items from a list presents a similar set of problems. You can either use Worksheet Delete Row to remove a row or use the Move command to close up a list over the items to be deleted. 1-2-3 will automatically adjust the data range after a Worksheet Delete Row command unless you delete the first or last row of the range. Deleting the first or last row of a range wipes out the range coordinates (this is also true of named ranges, ranges in formulas, and ranges in menu settings). The Worksheet Delete Row command may also affect areas of the worksheet parallel to the list.

The Move command avoids this problem. Suppose that you want to remove Steve Fry from the list in Figure 8.9. If you use Move with a source range of D8..G19 and a destination range of D7, the Data-Range setting is automatically adjusted to D3..H18.

Sorting Tips

You have seen that 1-2-3 remembers the sort settings from one sort operation to another. Normally this is helpful. However, if you have sorted one section of a worksheet and then want to sort a second one, you may find the remembered settings a problem. You must change the data range so that it corresponds to the second list you want to sort. Then you must change the primary key. If the second list does not need a secondary key, you may be left with a secondary key setting left over from the first list you sorted. Attempting to sort when both keys are not within the current data range results in an error. To prevent this error, you can use the Reset command on the Data Sort menu. This clears all three range settings. Alternatively, you can edit the Sort Settings dialog box and clear the secondary range if it is not needed. Simply press Escape or the right mouse button when the key column box is active. This clears the range coordinates. You can then click OK or press Shift-Enter to continue.

Like many other range settings in 1-2-3, the data range used by the Sort command can be selected before activating the menu system. Do this by dragging with the mouse or by using the keyboard as follows:

1. Place the cell pointer in the upper-left cell of the range to be selected.

2. Press F4 to activate the range prompt on the second line of the screen.

3. Move the cell pointer to the lower-right cell of the range to be selected.

4. Press Enter and then activate the menu.

When you choose Data Sort from the menu, 1-2-3 does not immediately assume that you want to use the preselected range as the Data-Range. However, as soon as you select Data-Range from the Data Sort menu or activate the data range field in the Sort Settings dialog box, the coordinates of the preselected range are entered for you. Unfortunately, if you activate the primary key column or secondary key column in the Sort Settings dialog box, 1-2-3 will also assume that you want the same preselected range for your key setting. To avoid this problem, you can use the Primary-Key and Secondary-Key items on the Sort menu to establish the primary or secondary key settings, since the menu command does not assume that you want to use the preselected cells. Remember that if you do have to edit range settings you can point out the desired cells in the worksheet by pressing F4 to switch between the dialog box SETTINGS mode and the worksheet POINT mode.

There are a number of reasons for sorting a list, apart from a natural desire to organize your data. For example, if you want to find who in Figure 8.9 is earning the most, you would perform a descending sort by the Weekly column. This would reveal both the highest and lowest earners (the lowest earner would fall at the end of the list). The same would apply to finding the most recently hired employee. In fact, sorting is a valuable tool for discovering information about a database.

Database Concepts

A database management program enables you to enter, store, and manipulate facts or data. Much of the information you deal with on a daily basis comes from databases. Whether the information is laid out in a table of columns and rows or consists of a collection of separate forms, almost anything from medical records to an inventory list can be considered a database. The company personnel records, your customer account files, even the passenger volume figures used in several earlier chapters can all be considered databases.

Suppose you are using a spreadsheet to total the day's sales figures. These begin as a stack of numbered receipts. You might enter the receipts into a spreadsheet and sort them in numerical order to check that they are all accounted for. You may also want to know how many of which items have been sold—that is, you want to sort the list by product name. In addition, you might want to review the major sales of the day, sorting them out by amount of sale. You might want to locate a specific receipt or create a separate list of all receipts for sales of a particular item. Performing these kinds of tasks is called *database management*.

Database Basics

There are two basic elements in a database. Each category of information is called a *field*. Thus, the telephone book has three fields: name, address, phone number. Each set of information is called a *record*. For example, this entry in a phone book constitutes a record:

```
Doe, John 13 Elm Street 555-4321
```

There are two basic arrangements for tracking data. The telephone book is a *tabular database*. The information is arranged in a table of columns and rows, as outlined in Figure 8.10. The vertical columns are the fields; the horizontal rows are records. This type of database can also be called *list-oriented*; the information is simply arranged in a list. This is the type of database you can create with 1-2-3.

The same information can be arranged in a *form-oriented* database. The right portion of Figure 8.10 shows each record on a separate form, much like a card file. To see all of the records, you have to page through all of the forms. Form-oriented database software usually offers users a fill-in-the-blank approach to data entry, popular with people who must enter a lot of data. However, a tabular database gives you a broader perspective on your data, allowing you to see at least part of 20 records at once or more if you use Wysiwyg and zoom the display, as described in Chapter 7.

Figure 8.10
Diagram of two database layouts

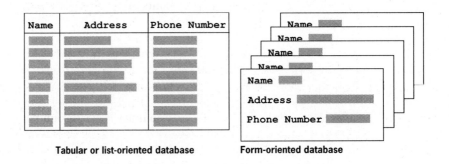

Tabular or list-oriented database   Form-oriented database

1-2-3 as a Database

A 1-2-3 database is essentially a list with column headings. Each column is a separate field and each field has a name, which is placed at the top of the column. In fact, the list in Figure 8.9 is a database.

Database Structure

A 1-2-3 database is composed of a series of consecutive columns. Each column should contain consistent types of data—either all values, all labels, or all dates. The columns should also have unique titles, located immediately above the first row of data. Each record—that is, the entire set of data related to each customer in a customer database or order in an orders database—must occupy a single row. Records should be placed one after another with no empty rows between them.

1-2-3 has two database functions: sorting and querying data. The sort capability lets you reorder data according to your specifications. As you have seen, this ability is not only used in database management. *Querying* a database means asking 1-2-3 to find or extract selected data. For example, 1-2-3 can search the database in Figure 8.2 for everyone that has the value 200 in the Weekly column or extract a list of all records where the age is greater than 29.

Database Limits

Since 1-2-3 databases are blocks of consecutive rows and columns, some limits apply to their dimensions. The maximum number of fields is 256, which is the total number of columns. The maximum number of records is the total number of rows minus one row for the field names, or 8,191. The maximum field size is 239 characters long, which is also the maximum column width minus 1 for the label prefix. As you might imagine, you are likely to run out of memory before you reach the limits of 1-2-3's database capacity.

Many different software packages offer some level of database management abilities. These programs can be divided into two groups: relational and flat-file. A *relational database* can relate the data in several different files based on common elements. Many of these programs also have a command language that can be used to compose complex sets of instructions in order to present users with complete menu-driven applications. Such programs are referred to as programmable relational databases. Examples include Ashton-Tate's dBASE series and Paradox from Borland International.

Although 1-2-3 is not a relational database, it can keep a sizable amount of related information in one worksheet. In addition, because 1-2-3 is memory-based it is relatively fast when performing database operations. Since 1-2-3's database commands resemble its spreadsheet commands, you can perform database management tasks without learning a new program. You have all the power of 1-2-3's built-in functions and graphics to analyze your data. You can even use 1-2-3's macro command to build customized menu-driven database applications.

Flat-file databases are the personal computer equivalent of card files, and are designed to make it as easy as possible to create, sort, and search records. However, such programs often lack the graphics and math capabilities found in 1-2-3. For this reason, you will probably want to use 1-2-3 for basic database applications if you are already learning it for spreadsheet work. If you later decide that you need a dedicated database management program, you can export data that you have accumulated in 1-2-3 without retyping it, since all popular database managers read WK1 files.

Database Creation

1-2-3 considers as a database any data that you enter into a worksheet in consecutive rows and named columns, and that you treat as a database (by sorting and querying). Consider the list of employees in Figure 8.11. This is a small database much like the one seen in Figure 8.9. The fields are Last, First, Age, and Weekly, plus a new field, DoH (for date of hire).

If you want to follow the examples in the next section, you can create this worksheet from the previous example by adding the dates in column H, or you can build the worksheet from scratch. All of the columns are the default width of nine characters. The entries in column G are formatted with the Currency format, using two decimal places. The entries in column H use the @DATE function so that H3, for example, is @DATE(88,11,25). Column H entries are formatted with Date format 4.

Figure 8.11

A spreadsheet database

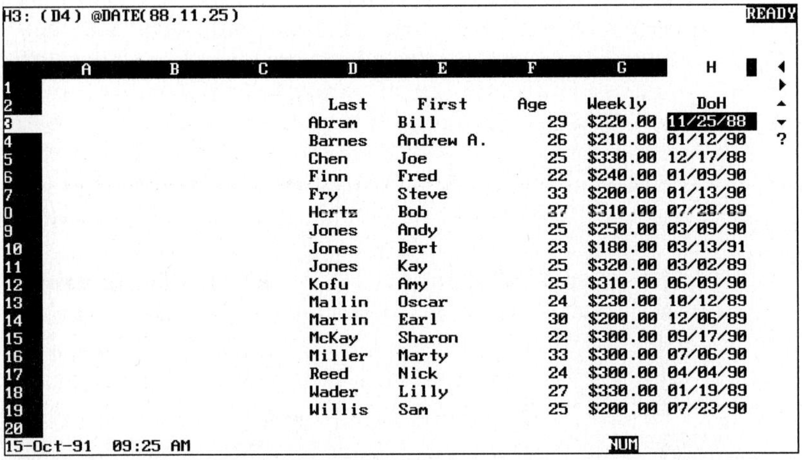

```
H3: (D4) @DATE(88,11,25)                                          READY
┌──────────────────────────────────────────────────────────────────┐
        A       B       C       D        E       F       G       H  ■  ◀
1                                                                      ▶
2                             Last    First    Age    Weekly   DoH    ▲
3                             Abram   Bill      29    $220.00 11/25/88 ▼
4                             Barnes  Andrew A. 26    $210.00 01/12/90 ?
5                             Chen    Joe       25    $330.00 12/17/88
6                             Finn    Fred      22    $240.00 01/09/90
7                             Fry     Steve     33    $200.00 01/13/90
8                             Hertz   Bob       37    $310.00 07/28/89
9                             Jones   Andy      25    $250.00 03/09/90
10                            Jones   Bert      23    $180.00 03/13/91
11                            Jones   Kay       25    $320.00 03/02/89
12                            Kofu    Amy       25    $310.00 06/09/90
13                            Mallin  Oscar     24    $230.00 10/12/89
14                            Martin  Earl      30    $200.00 12/06/89
15                            McKay   Sharon    22    $300.00 09/17/90
16                            Miller  Marty     33    $300.00 07/06/90
17                            Reed    Nick      24    $300.00 04/04/90
18                            Wader   Lilly     27    $330.00 01/19/89
19                            Willis  Sam       25    $200.00 07/23/90
20
15-Oct-91   09:25 AM                                       NUM
└──────────────────────────────────────────────────────────────────┘
```

The Contents of Your Database

Entries in a database may be labels or values. The labels can be left, right, or center aligned—their alignment will not affect the operation of the database commands. In the example in Figure 8.11, the employee names are labels. The values can be either numbers or formulas. 1-2-3's numeric dates, described in Chapter 3, are particularly important in databases since many collections of information include dates. Records will often need to be sorted or selected according to dates.

Many databases also contain nonnumeric numbers—that is, numbers that are entered as labels. A typical example would be zip codes in addresses. If you enter the zip code 01234 as a number, it will appear as 1234 in the cell because a leading 0 in a number does not register. To circumvent this problem, you must enter such figures as numbers preceded by label prefixes. You should also use this strategy for nine-digit zip codes, telephone numbers, and part numbers that contain letters as well as digits. If not, the zip code 94109-4109 entered as a number would result in 9000 because 1-2-3 will read the dash as a minus sign. Note that when you enter a telephone number with an area code, beginning the entry with a square bracket will make it a label, as in [800] 555-1212. In 1-2-3 you can sort and search for numbers even if you enter them as labels.

Columnar Arrangements

Since 1-2-3 allows only one row for each record in a database, you may need to widen the columns of fields containing lengthy information. To compensate for widening, you can narrow the columns containing short data. In Figure 8.12, column D has been widened to 12 characters to accept the correction from Hertz to Hertzfield, while column F has been reduced to six characters since it does not need to be any wider. Bear in mind that columns needn't show all the data that they contain for 1-2-3 to store long entries accurately. However, if you want all of your data to print and to be visible on the screen, you may need to expand columns.

Figure 8.12
Adjusted database
list

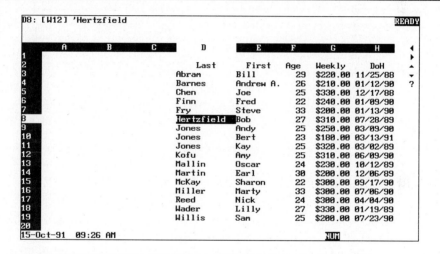

Making Enquiries

Using the Data Query command, you can quickly find specific records or groups of records. Then you can browse through and edit these records. You can even copy the selected records to a separate list. As you will see, the Data Query feature is quite different from the Search/Replace command described in Chapter 4.

Lines of Questioning

Suppose that you want to know the names of all employees earning $310 per week in the list in Figure 8.12. You can phrase this as the query "Find employees who have the value 310 in the Weekly column." The conditions you define for selecting data in 1-2-3 are called *criteria*. To find data that matches your criteria, 1-2-3 needs to know where the data is. This is the Data Query input range, which contains the entire database, including the field names. 1-2-3 also needs to know where the criteria are. This is the Data Query criteria range, which contains field names and values/formulas that specify the criteria of your search.

After you give 1-2-3 these two pieces of information, you can use the Find command to highlight matching records. If you provide a third piece of information, the output range, 1-2-3 can extract a list of items into that area of the worksheet.

Where the Data Is

To use the Data Query Find command, you first need to define the input range, or the location of the database. The database in Figure 8.12 occupies D2..H19. You may want to preselect this range or at least place the cell pointer in the upper-left cell of the database (D2) before issuing the Data command. When you select Data from the main menu and then pick Query, 1-2-3 presents the Query menu and Query Settings dialog box shown in Figure 8.13. You can use the Window key, F6, to erase and redisplay the Query Settings box, in case you want to peek at the underlying spreadsheet.

Figure 8.13

The Query menu and Query Settings box

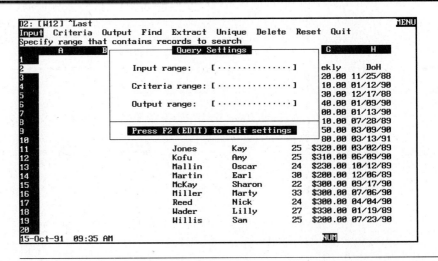

The input range for a query must encompass the entire database, including the field names. Choose Input from the menu or click in the input range field in the dialog box. If you preselected the range, it will be entered for you. If you need to point out the range, you can use the End key quite effectively. After anchoring the range at D2, press End and then Right Arrow.

Press End again, and then press Down Arrow. This will highlight the entire database from D2 to H19, as the data occupies contiguous columns and rows. Press Enter to confirm this range. The input range appears in the settings box and you are ready to tell 1-2-3 what records you want to find.

Note that if you have just used the Data Sort command to sort your database, you might think that you have already answered the question "Where is the data?" After all, the Sort menu asked you to define a range of data. However, while the procedure used in Query is similar to that used in Sort, the Data Query input range includes the field names. In addition, you do not have to include the entire database in the range to be searched; you can leave some records off the bottom of the range if you do not need 1-2-3 to consider them in its search. However, you must include field names for the columns you are searching and you should be familiar with the Query command before defining anything less than the entire database as your input range.

Which Data to Find

To tell 1-2-3 which data to look for, you establish a criteria range—a small table that consists, in its simplest form, of a field name above a piece of data. In this example, you want to find all personnel in the sample database who have 310 in the Weekly column. The criteria range or table will thus be Weekly (the field name) and 310 (the data to match). You actually enter this information into cells of your worksheet, as shown in Figure 8.14. You must select Quit to leave the Data Query menu before entering this data.

Figure 8.14

The criteria range

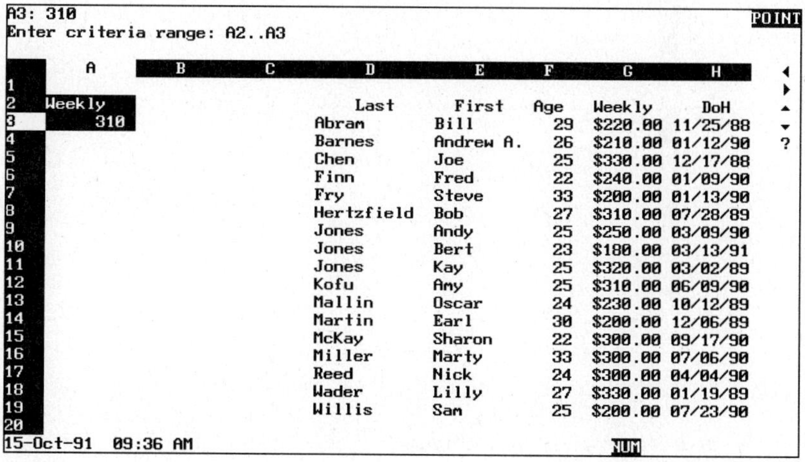

```
A3: 310                                                    POINT
Enter criteria range: A2..A3

      A        B      C       D        E      F      G        H      ◄
1                                                                     ►
2   Weekly                          Last    First  Age   Weekly  DoH  ▲
3      310                   Abram    Bill    29   $220.00 11/25/88   ▼
4                           Barnes  Andrew A. 26   $210.00 01/12/90   ?
5                           Chen     Joe      25   $330.00 12/17/88
6                           Finn     Fred     22   $240.00 01/09/90
7                           Fry      Steve    33   $200.00 01/13/90
8                           Hertzfield Bob    27   $310.00 07/28/89
9                           Jones    Andy     25   $250.00 03/09/90
10                          Jones    Bert     23   $180.00 03/13/91
11                          Jones    Kay      25   $320.00 03/02/89
12                          Kofu     Amy      25   $310.00 06/09/90
13                          Mallin   Oscar    24   $230.00 10/12/89
14                          Martin   Earl     30   $200.00 12/06/89
15                          McKay    Sharon   22   $300.00 09/17/90
16                          Miller   Marty    33   $300.00 07/06/90
17                          Reed     Nick     24   $300.00 04/04/90
18                          Wader    Lilly    27   $330.00 01/19/89
19                          Willis   Sam      25   $200.00 07/23/90
20
15-Oct-91  09:36 AM                                        NUM
```

The next step is to tell 1-2-3 the location of the criteria. Do this by selecting Criteria from the Data Query menu and then highlighting the appropriate range of cells, as shown in Figure 8.14. The most common error at this point is to include a blank line in the criteria range, which tells 1-2-3 to find all of the records in the database.

When you press Enter to confirm the criteria range, you are ready to ask 1-2-3 to find the records. Select the Find command from the Data Query menu. 1-2-3 will now try to match the data you have entered in the criteria range to each row of the appropriate column in the input range. In this example, 1-2-3 looks in the field/column called Weekly, checking for the value 310. When a match for this value is found, the entire record is highlighted, as shown in Figure 8.15.

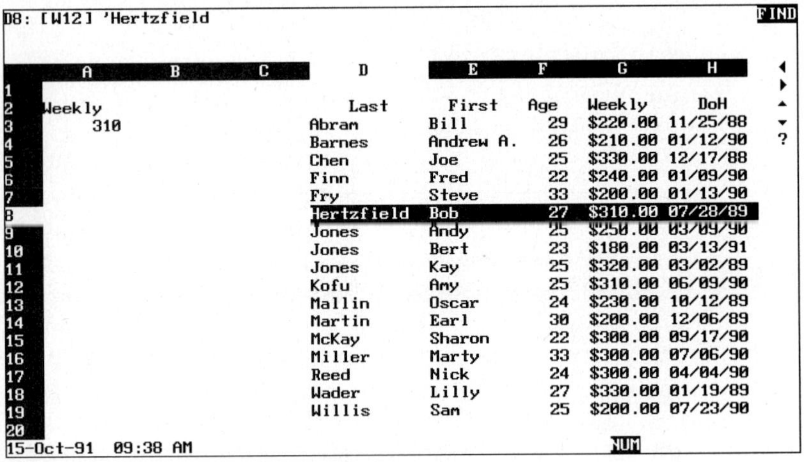

Figure 8.15

The first matching record

```
D8: [W12] 'Hertzfield                                           FIND

         A         B         C         D      E      F       G       H
1
2    Weekly                            Last   First  Age    Weekly   DoH
3         310                          Abran  Bill    29   $220.00 11/25/88
4                                       Barnes Andrew A. 26 $210.00 01/12/90
5                                       Chen   Joe     25   $330.00 12/17/88
6                                       Finn   Fred    22   $240.00 01/09/90
7                                       Fry    Steve   33   $200.00 01/13/90
8                                      Hertzfield Bob  27   $310.00 07/28/89
9                                       Jones  Andy    25   $250.00 03/09/90
10                                      Jones  Bert    23   $180.00 03/13/91
11                                      Jones  Kay     25   $320.00 03/02/89
12                                      Kofu   Amy     25   $310.00 06/09/90
13                                      Mallin Oscar   24   $230.00 10/12/89
14                                      Martin Earl    30   $200.00 12/06/89
15                                      McKay  Sharon  22   $300.00 09/17/90
16                                      Miller Marty   33   $300.00 07/06/90
17                                      Reed   Nick    24   $300.00 04/04/90
18                                      Wader  Lilly   27   $330.00 01/19/89
19                                      Willis Sam     25   $200.00 07/23/90
20
15-Oct-91  09:38 AM                                             NUM
```

Working with Find

When you successfully execute the Find command, the mode indicator says FIND. As you can see from Figure 8.15, a highlighting bar runs the full length of the first record that meets your criteria. You can then move to the next record that meets the criteria by pressing the Down Arrow key. When you get to the last matching record and press Down Arrow, 1-2-3 will beep. You can move back up one record with the Up Arrow key and continue to browse through the matching items by using the Up or Down Arrow key. (In this case, there are only two matching records.) The End key takes you to the last record in the database, while Home takes you to the first.

If you issue the Find command and 1-2-3 does not find any records within the input range that match your criteria, you will get a beep. No error message appears but you will be returned to the menu. Use the Query Settings box to verify that you have selected the right cells for the input and criteria ranges. You can repeat these commands to make sure of the range settings or adjust them if necessary. Remember that the the Query input range includes the field names, but the Sort data range doesn't. Also check that you have correctly spelled the field name in the criteria range. An easy way to ensure this is to copy the label directly from the database. You can actually capitalize the field name differently in the two ranges, but the spelling must be accurate. You must also check the data you enter under the field name in the criteria range: If it is a value, check whether such a value exists in the database; if it is text, check whether it is spelled correctly.

Notice that in the FIND mode a cursor flashes within the Find highlight bar. You can move this cursor across the bar with the Right Arrow and Left Arrow keys. The cursor moves from the center of one column to the center of the next. This is to allow you to edit entries for the highlighted record. You can press F2 and edit the cell contents. The mode indicator will then change to EDIT. After you have altered the cell contents, return them to the cell with the Enter key. Be careful when you press Enter to exit the EDIT mode, since pressing Enter in FIND mode is one way of ending the Find operation. Instead of editing a cell within the Find bar, you can replace it by placing your cursor in the appropriate column, typing the new entry, and then carefully pressing Enter. (If you press Enter for too long, 1-2-3 will act as if you had pressed it twice, and will return to the Query menu.)

You exit the FIND mode by pressing either Enter, Esc, F7, or Ctrl-Break. If you entered the FIND mode from the Query menu, Enter or Esc takes you back to the Query menu, where you can make changes to the settings. You can press Ctrl-Break or pick Quit from the Query menu to return to READY mode. If you return to READY mode with any of these methods, 1-2-3 returns the cell pointer to the cell it occupied when the Find was executed. In contrast, F7 (the Query key) ends the Find command and leaves you in READY mode with the cell pointer on the record that was highlighted when you pressed F7. The pointer will be in the cell that contained the Find bar when you pressed F7. In this way, F7 acts as a "goto" key, a quick way to move the cell pointer to a specific cell within a database.

Repeating a Query

Suppose you need to find all employees making $300 per week. Having returned to READY mode, you can change the previous entry of 310 to 300. When you are in READY mode, the Query key (F7) will repeat the last query you performed, using the same input and criteria range settings and the current entries in those cells. Thus you can browse through the entries that meet the new criteria, press Esc to return to READY mode, and then enter new criteria for yet another search. You only have to return to the Data Query menu if you change the coordinates of the input and criteria ranges.

Suppose you have to update numerous employee records within a large database. You would have a criteria table with Last and First as headings. You would type the name of the desired employee under the Last name and First name headings in the criteria table and then select Find. The next time you needed to look up an employee's record, you could simply type the name of the employee in the criteria range and press F7. The same input criteria range settings will be used, but with the new entry in the range. In this way, you can easily find a succession of employees from a long list.

Note that the Query key only institutes a query from READY mode. If you use the Query key and no records match your criteria, 1-2-3 will beep and return you to READY mode. If you press the Query key while in the FIND mode, you will be returned to READY mode and your cell pointer will be placed in the cell containing the field of the record you were browsing when you pressed the key. Also note that the Query key repeats the last type of query that you performed. There are two types of queries: Find and Extract (Extract is described in the next section.) If the last query you last performed was a Find, F7 performs a Find. If the last query you performed was an Extract, F7 performs an Extract.

The Find feature is useful for quick searches when you don't want to print a separate list—for example, to perform a quick check of a specific item in stock, an employee record, and so on. It is also useful when you want to edit the selected records. If you want to copy the selected records to another part of the worksheet or to another worksheet, you need to use the Extract command.

Listing Records with Query Extract

You may want 1-2-3 to provide you with a list of items matching your criteria instead of simply highlighting them in the database. You can do this with the Query Extract command, which copies matching records to a range of cells in the current worksheet.

What 1-2-3 Needs to Know

To use the Query Extract command, you need to provide 1-2-3 with four pieces of information:

- Where the data is located, or the input range.

- Which records to extract. This is the criteria range, containing field names and values/formulas that specify the records to select.

- Where to put the extracted records. This is the output range, or the cells in which to place the extracted data.

- What data to output, or the field names used in the output range.

If you have already used the Find command, you will have established the first two items. The last two involve the output range.

The Output Range

When extracting a list of matching records from a database, you must decide which pieces of information you want and where you want them. For example, suppose you want to create a list of all people paid $300 per week. You want the list to show last name and date of hire. To do this, you enter the field names Last and DoH in a separate area of the worksheet. In Figure 8.16, field names Last and DoH have been entered on row 6 and are being defined as the output range.

Figure 8.16
Defining the output range

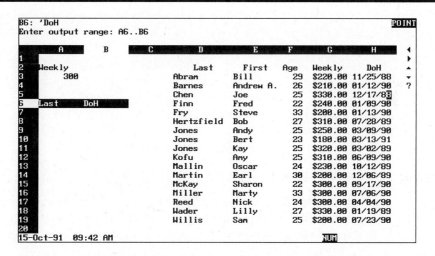

The output range can contain any number of fields in any order. You do not need to include fields that are part of the criteria in the output range, but doing so can help you verify that you selected the desired records.

The size of the output range is a matter for you to decide. You can choose between an unlimited output range or a limited one. Using just the field names as the output range creates an unlimited list area, in effect telling 1-2-3 that it can use any number of rows below the field names for the results of the Extract command. If there is nothing entered in the worksheet below the field names, this method is fine. Otherwise, you will want to limit the size of the output range to something just slightly longer than the list you expect the command to create. A useful key at this point is PgDn: Pressing PgDn once while pointing out the output range adds 20 rows.

The problem with limiting the output range is that a list requiring more space than you have allocated will be incomplete and will produce an error message. The problem with not limiting the range is that an unexpectedly long list could overlap cell entries you wanted to keep and the results of the Extract command take precedence over other cells. The most common cause of unexpectedly long extract lists is an error in the criteria. A typical error is including a blank line in the criteria range, which, as mentioned, tells 1-2-3 to select all of the records in the database.

To record the output range, place the cell pointer in the leftmost field name and select Output from the Query menu. Anchor the cell you are in and press End and Right Arrow to include all of the field names. Then press Enter if you want an unlimited output range, or use the Down Arrow and PgDn keys to include the desired number of rows in a limited output range, and then press Enter. You will see the settings recorded as shown in Figure 8.17.

Figure 8.17
Query settings in place

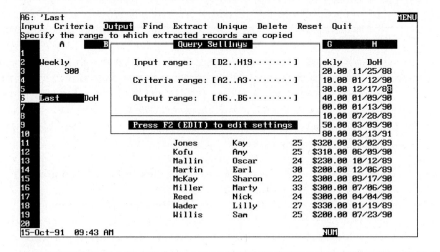

Extracting Records

With the input, criteria, and output ranges defined, you can choose Extract to place the items identified by your criteria into the output cells. The results for the example can be seen in Figure 8.18. If 1-2-3 does not find any records matching your request, it beeps and returns you to the Data Query menu. Note that the dialog box was turned off with F6 in order to see all of the worksheet.

Figure 8.18

The completed
Extract operation

```
A6: 'Last                                                          MENU
Input  Criteria  Output  Find  Extract  Unique  Delete  Reset  Quit
Copy all records that match criteria to output range
        A        B        C        D        E       F       G       H        ◄
 1                                                                           ►
 2   Weekly                        Last     First   Age  Weekly    DoH       ▲
 3       300                       Abran    Bill    29   $220.00 11/25/88    ▼
 4                                 Barnes   Andrew A. 26  $210.00 01/12/90    ?
 5                                 Chen     Joe     25   $330.00 12/17/89
 6   Last      DoH                 Finn     Fred    22   $240.00 01/09/90
 7   McKay     09/17/90            Fry      Steve   33   $200.00 01/13/90
 8   Miller    07/06/90            Hertzfield Bob   27   $310.00 07/28/89
 9   Reed      04/04/90            Jones    Andy    25   $250.00 03/09/90
10                                 Jones    Bert    23   $180.00 03/13/91
11                                 Jones    Kay     25   $320.00 03/02/89
12                                 Kofu     Amy     25   $310.00 06/09/90
13                                 Mallin   Oscar   24   $230.00 10/12/89
14                                 Martin   Earl    30   $200.00 12/06/89
15                                 McKay    Sharon  22   $300.00 09/17/90
16                                 Miller   Marty   33   $300.00 07/06/90
17                                 Reed     Nick    24   $300.00 04/04/90
18                                 Wader    Lilly   27   $330.00 01/19/89
19                                 Willis   Sam     25   $200.00 07/23/90
20
15-Oct-91   09:45 AM                                          NUM
```

When 1-2-3 extracts formulas from a database to an output range, it converts them to their numeric values. The dates in Figure 8.18 have been converted from @DATE entries to date serial numbers. However, formats for extracted values are retained (hence the dates still look like dates).

As with the Find command, you can repeat the Extract command with F7. If the last Query command you executed was Extract, F7 will perform Extract. Suppose you want a list of employees making $320 per week. You simply enter the value 320 in A3 and then press F7. The previous Extract results are erased and a new list is placed in the output range, as shown in Figure 8.19.

Note that 1-2-3 does not just write the new list over the previous one. The old list area is cleared of all entries and formats before the new entries are copied from the input range.

Once you have performed an Extract, you might want to dress up the results. For example, you might need to print the list to pass it on to someone else. If there are many entries in the list, you might want to sort them with the Data Sort command. In Figure 8.18, the extracted list in columns A and B is already in alphabetical order. This is because the entries were extracted from a database that was already sorted by name, and 1-2-3 copies extracted records row by row. You can test this by changing the criteria in A3 to 200 and pressing F7. The new list will be

```
Last            DoH
Fry             01/13/90
Martin          12/06/89
Willis          07/23/90
```

However, suppose that you want to sort this list by the DoH field. First, you would issue the Data Sort command and check the Sort Settings. Select Reset from the Sort menu if there are already settings in place for sorting a different range. Then select Data-Range and indicate A7..B9 as the range. Next choose Primary-Key and choose a cell in column B. Select D for Descending as the sort order, and select Go to complete the command. The sort will place the most recent date at the top of the list. Although this is a small example, the same principle applies to much larger examples. The data you extract from a database with the Data Query command can be sorted with the Data Sort command, just like any other list.

Figure 8.19
A revised output

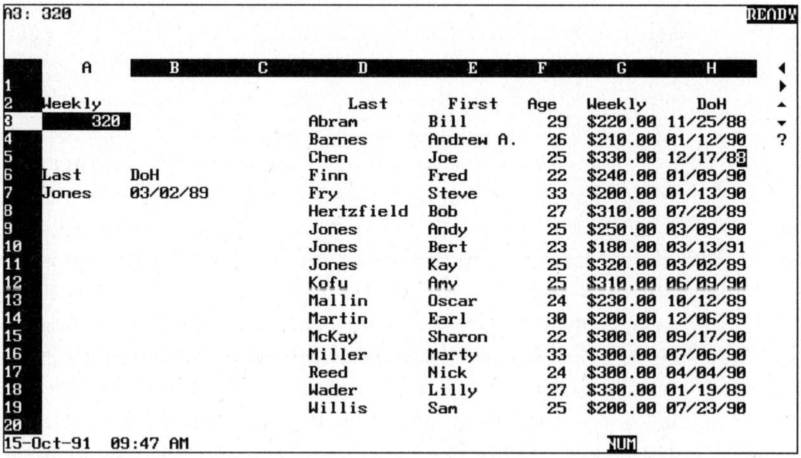

Unique Records

When the Extract command is executed, 1-2-3 copies every matching record from the input range to the output range. If some records are duplicates, 1-2-3 copies both, which is usually what you want. For example, if your criteria was last name Jones, an output list of Last and Age would list all three Jones in the sample database if you used the Extract command. However, two of the entries in the output list would be identical: Jones/25. You can prevent this by using Unique rather than Extract from the Query menu. 1-2-3 will only create one of each unique output entry record. This helps you to create reports in some types of database.

Suppose you have a database of wines for a private cellar. You have a field called Origin that lists country of origin. Another field called Type denotes the type of wine. There are other fields, such as Vintage, and one record for each bottle of wine. Suppose you want a list of all the different types of French wine. Simply enter French under the field name Origin in your criteria table. Your output range consists of the field Type. The result is a list that only shows one entry for each type, not a list showing the type for each bottle that comes from France.

Bear in mind that Unique excludes only records that have identical entries in the fields specified in the output range. Unique does not delete duplicate records from the input range. When you create large databases, it is not unusual for duplicate records to occur, particularly if more than one person is using the database. However, sorting the database will reveal duplicates which can then be deleted if desired.

Deleting Records

When you are maintaining a database, you may need to get rid of records. You can find the record and then delete it with the Worksheet Delete Row command. However, this method may remove any data that is on the same row as the deleted record, all the way across the worksheet. For example, suppose that Mr. Hertzfield leaves the company. As you can see from Figure 8.18, removing row 8 would interfere with the output range. Fortunately, the Query menu provides a special Delete command that removes records without affecting cells outside the database. The Delete command erases records that meet your criteria and then closes up the input range (performing the equivalent of a series of Range Erase and Move commands).

To use Query Delete, first set the criteria for the records you want deleted. It's a good precaution to test the criteria with the Find command before using the Delete command. If the Find command correctly locates the records you want to delete, select Delete. You will be prompted to confirm this action as it is removing data from the worksheet. Choose Cancel if you don't want to proceed; select Delete to confirm the command. Another safeguard is to make sure that the UNDO feature is enabled. This will allow you to reverse the effects of Query Delete by pressing the Undo key, Alt-F4. Note that the Query key, F7, does not activate the Delete command.

If you use the sample database and a criterion of 200 in A3, the Query Extract command produces a list of three names. If you next use the Query Delete command, confirm the Delete, and then press F6 to remove the Query Settings window, your results should resemble Figure 8.20.

Note that the extracted list of data in columns A and B is not affected by the alterations to the input range. 1-2-3 erases the cells within the input range containing the records that meet the criteria, and then closes up the range, *without* disturbing the surrounding cells. In this case, you can undo the Query Delete, so quit from the Query menu to READY mode and press Undo (Alt-F4).

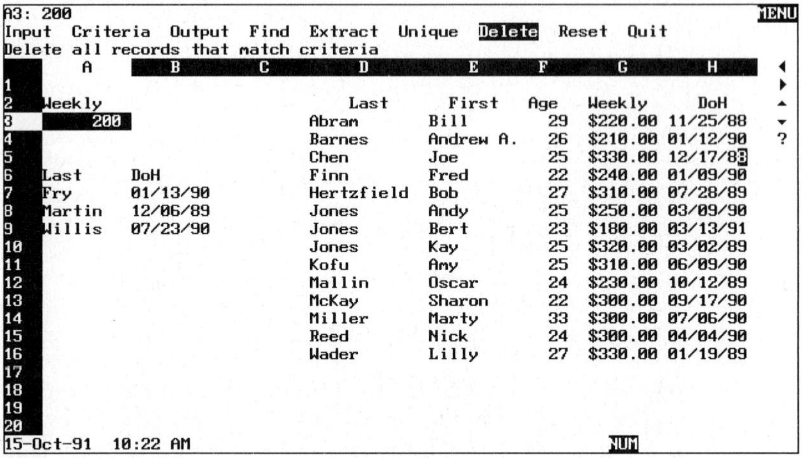

Figure 8.20

The results of
Query Delete

```
A3: 200                                                          MENU
Input  Criteria  Output  Find  Extract  Unique  Delete  Reset  Quit
Delete all records that match criteria
     A        B        C        D        E      F      G       H     ◀
                                                                     ▶
 1
 2  Weekly                           Last     First   Age  Weekly    DoH    ▼
 3       200                         Abram    Bill    29  $220.00 11/25/88   ?
 4                                   Barnes   Andrew A. 26 $210.00 01/12/90
 5                                   Chen     Joe     25  $330.00 12/17/83
 6  Last     DoH                     Finn     Fred    22  $240.00 01/09/90
 7  Fry      01/13/90                Hertzfield Bob   27  $310.00 07/28/89
 8  Martin   12/06/89                Jones    Andy    25  $250.00 03/09/90
 9  Willis   07/23/90                Jones    Bert    23  $180.00 03/13/91
10                                   Jones    Kay     25  $320.00 03/02/89
11                                   Kofu     Amy     25  $310.00 06/09/90
12                                   Mallin   Oscar   24  $230.00 10/12/89
13                                   McKay    Sharon  22  $300.00 09/17/90
14                                   Miller   Marty   33  $300.00 07/06/90
15                                   Reed     Nick    24  $300.00 04/04/90
16                                   Wader    Lilly   27  $330.00 01/19/89
17
18
19
20
15-Oct-91   10:22 AM                                        NUM
```

Adding Records

There are several techniques for adding records to a database after it has been defined as the Query input range. If you simply type new items at the bottom of the database, they will not automatically be included in the input range and you will have to issue the Data Query Input command to redefine the setting so that it includes the new items.

Alternatively, you can insert the new item into the list using the Worksheet Insert Row command. Provided you insert the row below the field names and above the last record in the database, 1-2-3 will automatically expand the input range to include the new row.

The Worksheet Insert Row command doesn't work well if you have other entries in the worksheet that occupy the same rows as the database. For example, suppose you want to insert a fresh row above row 3 of Figure 8.19 for a new employee call Bert Abelarde. Doing so would interfere with the criteria range. An alternative is to move part of the list. In this case, you could issue the Move command with the cell pointer in D3, define D3..H19 as the source range, D4 as the destination range, and the bulk of the database would be moved down one row without affecting the rest of the worksheet. 1-2-3 would expand the input range setting to reflect the new coordinates, D3..H20, and the new entry on row 3 would be part of the list.

All About Criteria

So far, only one criterion at a time has been used with the sample databases, but 1-2-3 can handle more complex criteria. For example, you can

use multiple fields for criteria and you can use formulas to specify ranges
of matching values instead of a single value.

Multiple Criteria

Suppose that you want to find out whether anyone in the sample database
earns $200 per week and is 25. To do this, you add a second field, Age, to the
criteria table, with the value 30 below it. You must expand the Criteria setting to include this new information, as shown in Figure 8.21.

Figure 8.21

Expanding the
criteria table

```
B3: 25                                                            POINT
Enter criteria range: A2..B3
          A         B      C       D          E      F      G         H       ◀
1                                                                             ▶
2   Weekly     Age                   Last     First    Age   Weekly    DoH    ▲
3       200          25              Abran    Bill     29   $220.00 11/25/88  ▼
4                                    Barnes   Andrew A. 26   $210.00 01/12/90 ?
5                                    Chen     Joe      25   $330.00 12/17/83
6   Last       DoH                   Finn     Fred     22   $240.00 01/09/90
7   Fry        01/13/90              Fry      Steve    33   $200.00 01/13/90
8   Martin     12/06/89              Hertzfield Bob    27   $310.00 07/28/89
9   Willis     07/23/90              Jones    Andy     25   $250.00 03/09/90
10                                   Jones    Bert     23   $180.00 03/13/91
11                                   Jones    Kay      25   $320.00 03/02/89
12                                   Kofu     Amy      25   $310.00 06/09/90
13                                   Mallin   Oscar    24   $230.00 10/12/89
14                                   Martin   Earl     30   $200.00 12/06/89
15                                   McKay    Sharon   22   $300.00 09/17/90
16                                   Miller   Marty    33   $300.00 07/06/90
17                                   Reed     Nick     24   $300.00 04/04/90
18                                   Wader    Lilly    27   $330.00 01/19/89
19                                   Willis   San      25   $200.00 07/23/90
20
15-Oct-91   10:24 AM                                          NUM
```

If the entries beneath the field names in a criteria table are all on the
same line, as in Figure 8.21, then the relationship between them is AND.
This means that a record must meet both criteria (the first criterion *and* the
second) to be included in the locate operation. If you executed an Extract
with the criteria range as defined in Figure 8.21, only one record would be
listed in the output range: Willis 07/23/90. If the entries under the field names
in the criteria table are on separate lines, the relationship between them is
OR. This means that 1-2-3 locates records that match any one of the criteria
(one criterion *or* the other). For example, in Figure 8.22 the value of 25 was
moved from B3 to B4. The criteria range was defined as A2..B4 so the
Extract command listed everyone who is earning $200, regardless of age,
plus everyone who is 25, regardless of earnings.

When you want to use multiple AND criteria, you can quickly create the
criteria table by copying the entire set of field names to a suitable location in
the worksheet and then defining these names and the row beneath them as
the criteria range. You can then enter the data to be matched under the

appropriate field name prior to a search, and then delete it when the search is completed. You don't have to have an entry in every column of the criteria table for it to work. You can also copy the field names a second time to create an output range that includes all fields.

Figure 8.22

Criteria relationship established as OR

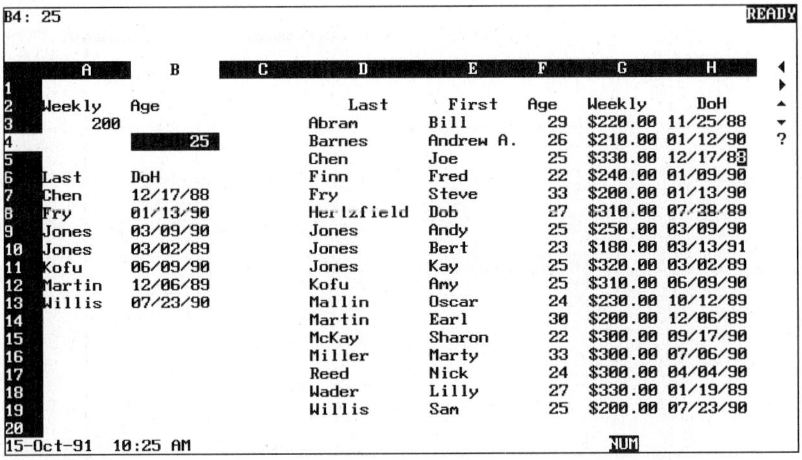

```
B4: 25                                                          READY
       A        B        C        D         E      F      G        H
1
2  Weekly   Age                   Last     First   Age  Weekly    DoH
3      200                        Abran    Bill    29   $220.00 11/25/88
4               25                Barnes   Andrew A. 26  $210.00 01/12/90
5                                 Chen     Joe     25   $330.00 12/17/88
6  Last     DoH                   Finn     Fred    22   $240.00 01/09/90
7  Chen     12/17/88              Fry      Steve   33   $200.00 01/13/90
8  Fry      01/13/90              Herlzfield Dob   27   $310.00 07/38/89
9  Jones    03/09/90              Jones    Andy    25   $250.00 03/09/90
10 Jones    03/02/89              Jones    Bert    23   $180.00 03/13/91
11 Kofu     06/09/90              Jones    Kay     25   $320.00 03/02/89
12 Martin   12/06/89              Kofu     Amy     25   $310.00 06/09/90
13 Willis   07/23/90              Mallin   Oscar   24   $230.00 10/12/89
14                                Martin   Earl    30   $200.00 12/06/89
15                                McKay    Sharon  22   $300.00 09/17/90
16                                Miller   Marty   33   $300.00 07/06/90
17                                Reed     Nick    24   $300.00 04/04/90
18                                Wader    Lilly   27   $330.00 01/19/89
19                                Willis   Sam     25   $200.00 07/23/90
20
15-Oct-91  10:25 AM                                         NUM
```

An arrangement of this sort for the sample database is shown in Figure 8.23, where A21..E22 has been defined as the criteria range and A25..E25 is the new output range. The criteria you see in Figure 8.23 will find anyone in the database who has the last name Jones or the first name Bert. Note that 1-2-3 finds all records that match all of the criteria on any one row of the criteria table. Remember to reduce the size of the criteria range if you decide to use less rows of criteria.

Formulas in Criteria

You have seen that a criteria table offers a simple but effective way of indicating the parameters of your search for data. All the criteria used so far have compared records to set values, but sometimes you will want to find records that match a range of values. You can expand the usefulness of the criteria table by using formulas and range names to create detailed search specifications and match a range of values. The formula +F3>27 in cell C22 of Figure 8.24 is a typical example of a criteria formula. It tells 1-2-3 to find all records in the database where the entry under Age is a value greater than 27. This type of formula is known as a *true/false formula*, since the only possible answers are true or false. The formula +F3>27 actually asks whether F3 is greater than 27. The answer yes or true is represented by 1, while the answer no or false is represented by 0. A true/false formula can also be called a *conditional formula* since it asks 1-2-3 to evaluate a condition—in this case, the value of F3 relative to 27.

Figure 8.23
A full set of field names for output and criteria

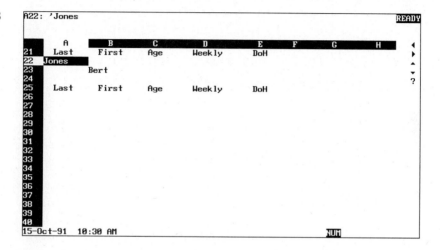

Figure 8.24
A list of all records with Age > 27

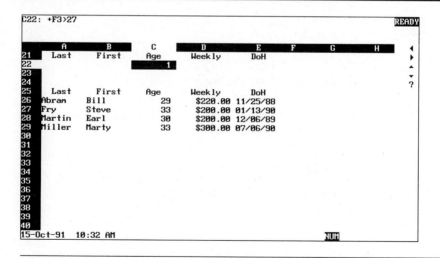

When a true/false formula is used in a criteria table, 1-2-3 evaluates all the records in the database relative to the condition when performing the Find or Extract command. Cell F3 contains the Age field for the first record in the database, which is the field being evaluated by the formula. When performing the Find or Extract, 1-2-3 checks whether the entry in F3 is greater than 27. If it is, the record on row 3 is selected. Next 1-2-3 applies the same formula relative to the next row in the database. Although you don't see this happen, the formula is changed to +F4>27 and if the answer is true the record on row 4 is selected. If the answer is false, the record is not selected. 1-2-3 proceeds through the database, evaluating each row in turn. In Figure 8.24, you can see the results of the Extract using the formula +F3>27. (If you want to try this yourself, be sure to redefine the criteria and output ranges before performing the Extract.)

Assigning Names

You can use the Range Name commands to simplify writing criteria formulas like the one in Figure 8.24. If you assign a name to the cell immediately below the field name, you can then use that name in the formula. Thus, if you named F3 as AGE, you could enter the criterion in cell C22 as +AGE>27. The Range Name Labels Down command is a quick way to assign the appropriate name to each cell in the first record of the database. If you issue this command and select D2..H2 of the sample database as the label range, you will give range names to each cell in the second row of your database, using the field names in the first row. If you now use the Range Name Create command, you will see a list of the range names you have just created. If you press the Name key (F3), you can see the cell coordinates listed next to the names when they are highlighted, as shown in Figure 8.25.

Figure 8.25

Range names listed with Name

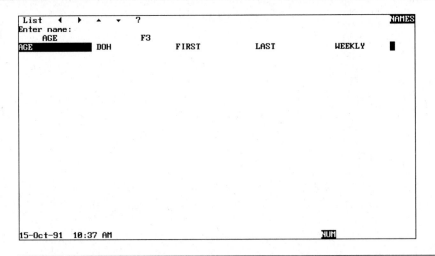

Note that the cell called AGE is F3, the cell below the label used to name it. The cell called LAST is D3, FIRST is E3, and so on. Also note that the range name AGE is immediately substituted for the cell coordinate F3 in the formula in C22.

As you can see from Figure 8.25, the range names are stored in capital letters. In fact, 1-2-3 is not case sensitive when it comes to the Query command. When you put together formulated criteria, you can refer to field names in either upper- or lowercase. Suppose you want to find all people in the sample database who are under 30 and earn more than 300. You would enter +AGE<30 in the criteria table under Age. To create this formula, you can actually type **+** and then press Name for a list of range names. Highlight AGE and press Enter to include it in the formula, and then type **<** followed by **30**. Press Enter to complete the formula. In D22, enter the formula **+WEEKLY>300**. The results of an Extract operation based on these criteria are shown in Figure 8.26.

Figure 8.26
A new Extract operation

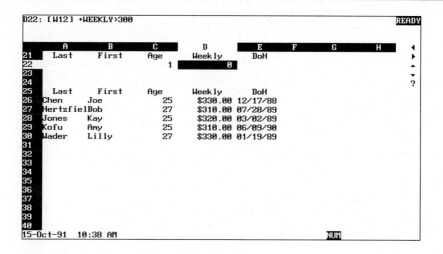

Revealing Formulated Criteria

Naming ranges makes formula criteria easier to write and easier to read when the cell is highlighted. Nevertheless, the entries in C22 and D22 of Figure 8.26 still look rather odd. It helps to format the cells with the Range Format Text command. The Text format displays formulas as formulas, not as their results. The effect can be seen in Figure 8.27, where a further criteria has been added.

The only drawback to the Text format is that the formulas are still values and are thus limited by the rules for displaying values. This means that the formula in E22 cannot flow into the next cell as it would if the entry were a label.

Figure 8.27

Using the Text
format to reveal
formulas

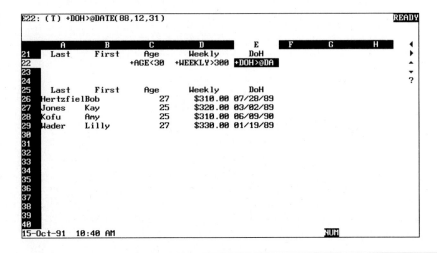

```
E22: (T) +DOH>@DATE(88,12,31)                                    READY

         A        B        C        D        E     F     G     H    ◀
21    Last     First     Age     Weekly     DoH                     ▶
22                      +AGE<30  +WEEKLY>300 +DOH>@DA               ▲
23                                                                  ▼
24                                                                  ?
25    Last     First     Age     Weekly     DoH
26  Hertzfiel Bob         27      $310.00   07/28/89
27  Jones     Kay         25      $320.00   03/02/89
28  Kofu      Amy         25      $310.00   06/09/90
29  Nader     Lilly       27      $330.00   01/19/89
30
31
32
33
34
35
36
37
38
39
40
15-Oct-91  10:40 AM                              NUM
```

The entry in E22 of Figure 8.27 shows how dates are used in criteria formulas. This particular formula,

    +DOH>@DATE(88,12,31)

selects dates in 1989 and beyond. Note that you could use the date serial number instead of @DATE, entering the formula as +DOH>32508. However, this is typically more difficult to enter and even harder to read.

More About Formulated Criteria

Formulas in the criteria table use what are called *comparison operators*. Each criteria table formula includes three elements—field, comparison operator, and value—telling 1-2-3 which field contains the value you want to match, whether you want to match an exact value or a range of values, and the value itself. In the earlier example, the request for all employees older than 27 was expressed as +AGE>27. The plus sign was used because this is a formula. AGE is the field name, while > is the comparison operator meaning greater than, and 27 is the value. The comparison operators you can use are as follows:

- The > operator means greater than. (+AGE>27 means 28, 29, and so on.)

- The < operator means less than. (+AGE<27 means 26, 25, and so on.)

- The >= operator means greater than or equal to. (+AGE>=27 means 27, 28, and so on.)

- The <= operator means less than or equal to. (+AGE<=27 means 27, 26, and so on.)

- The <> operator means not equal to. (+AGE<>27 means any value other than 27.)

- The = operator means equal to. (+AGE=27 means only 27.)

Note that you generally will not use +AGE=27 unless it is part of a larger formula, since you needn't use a formula if the criterion is a single value. Instead, you can simply use 27 as the criterion. Also note that 1-2-3 doesn't mind which field name you use above a criterion formula as long as the formula makes the appropriate field name reference. Thus you can enter +AGE>27 under the field name Last and use those two cells alone as the criteria range. This feature is useful when you work with multiple conditions.

You can create more complex formulas for selecting records by using the logical operators #AND#, #OR#, and #NOT# (AND, OR, and NOT). When you combine two conditions with #AND#, 1-2-3 will only select records for which both conditions are true. In contrast, when you combine conditions with #OR#, 1-2-3 selects records for which either condition is true. When you preface a condition with #NOT#, 1-2-3 selects records for which the condition is false.

For example, the formula

```
+WEEKLY=300#AND#AGE>27
```

selects Miller. The formula

```
+WEEKLY=240#OR#WEEKLY=210
```

selects Barnes and Finn. The formula

```
#NOT#FIRST="Marty"
```

selects everyone but Miller.

You must place the logical operator in the formula within # signs, as shown in the examples. You create multiple conditions with logical operators to make your search more specific and to avoid multiple formulas. You can use a single formula with a multiple condition under any field name. Thus, the following formula, entered under Last, will work even if the field name and the formula are the only two cells in the criteria table:

```
+WEEKLY=240#OR#WEEKLY=210
```

Matching Text

So far, you have seen how 1-2-3 relates to values in criteria. At times, however, you may want to match text in a criterion. That is, suppose something was entered as a label and you want to incorporate it into a formula. You must place the text in double quotes; for example, "Steve" will find STEVE, steve, and Steve. When you use the comparison operators with labels, 1-2-3 interprets > as meaning higher in the alphabet. This means you can use these operators with nonnumeric fields like zip codes to specify codes equal to or greater than, say, 94100, which would be written +ZIP>"94100".

To add scope to your searches for a text match, you can use wildcards. These are the question mark (?), the asterisk (*), and the tilde (~). The question mark stands for any character in that position in a string: T?M would find TAM, TIM, TOM, and so on. The asterisk means anything from this character to the end of the label: FRED* would find anything beginning with FRED, including FREDDY, FREDERICK, and so on. The tilde means not: ~FRED would find anyone but FRED.

Database Functions

Storing your databases in 1-2-3 enables you to use the program's extensive math capabilities. For example, you might want to sum a column of figures to find the total value of a field. You might also want to find the average of all values in a field. 1-2-3's database functions provide the tools for this type of math, besides enabling you to perform selective calculations. The functions use the concepts of input and criteria ranges to calculate such things as the total weekly pay of everyone hired after a certain date, or the average age of everyone earning less than a certain amount.

Regular Database Math

Before we go into database functions, you need to know how other functions and formulas are applied in the context of a database. Figure 8.28 shows a revised version of the sample database that makes greater use of 1-2-3 formulas. The three calculations on row 23 show the number of people in the database, their average age, and the total of the values in the Weekly column.

The formula in G23 is a simple aggregate, using the @SUM function. However, the range being summed includes the field names on row 3 and the line of labels on row 20. This is means that the formula will remain accurate if a row is added to the database to accommodate a new record, or if a record is deleted (remember that deleting a column or row that is used as a range coordinate will corrupt the range reference). This approach is also used for the @COUNT function in E23 and the average calculation in F23. However, since the @COUNT function does not distinguish between labels and values the actual formula in E23 is @COUNT(E3..E20)–2, to compensate for the two extra rows included in the range argument.

Figure 8.28
Database with added calculations

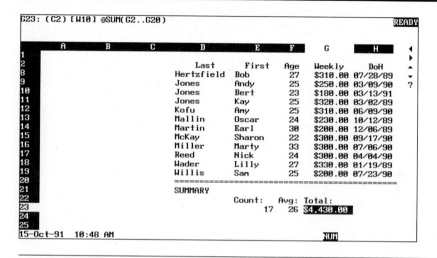

```
G23: (C2) [W10] @SUM(G2..G20)                                      READY

       A        B        C        D          E         F      G         H       ◀
 1                                                                             ▶
 2                                  Last      First    Age   Weekly    DoH      ▲
 8                                  Hertzfield Bob       27   $310.00 07/28/89  ▼
 9                                  Jones     Andy       25   $250.00 03/09/90  ?
10                                  Jones     Bert       23   $180.00 03/13/91
11                                  Jones     Kay        25   $320.00 03/02/89
12                                  Kofu      Amy        25   $310.00 06/09/90
13                                  Mallin    Oscar      24   $230.00 10/12/89
14                                  Martin    Earl       30   $200.00 12/06/89
15                                  McKay     Sharon     22   $300.00 09/17/90
16                                  Miller    Marty      33   $300.00 07/06/90
17                                  Reed      Nick       24   $300.00 04/04/90
18                                  Wader     Lilly      27   $330.00 01/19/89
19                                  Willis    San        25   $200.00 07/23/90
20                                  =======================================
21                                  SUMMARY
22
23                                           Count:   Avg:  Total:
24                                              17     26   $4,430.00
25
15-Oct-91  10:48 AM                                          NUM
```

In the calculation of the average age, note that the @AVG function is actually @SUM divided by @COUNT. Consequently, @AVG(F3..F20) will not be accurate because two of the entries in this range are labels so that you are, in effect, averaging in two zeros. Since an accurate count exists in E23, the formula used in F23 is in fact @SUM(F2..F20)/E23.

When performing math with a database, you must also consider the role of cell references. Suppose that you want to add to the sample database a field that shows raises for all employees based on an increase of 9%. If the Raise field were added in column I of the worksheet, the formula in the first record, in cell I3, would be +G3*0.9. This formula could be copied down the column to I19. Sorting the database would not affect the formula, nor would a Query Extract. The calculated field could be used in criteria and output ranges. However, when 1-2-3 copies cells from the input range to the output range during an Extract, the operation is the equivalent of a Range Value rather than a Copy—that is, formulas are converted to their resulting values.

An alternative approach is to place the rate of increase outside of the database—for example, in B3. The formula in I3 should then be +$B$3*G3. The reference to B3 is made absolute to allow accurate copying of the formula down the column, and to permit sorting of the database without corrupting the formula. You'll have problems with formulas in databases if you don't remember the need for absolute references. For example, suppose that all employees were to be given a raise based on an individual rate. If these rates were entered in B3 through B19, the formula in I3 could be +B3*G3, and this could be copied down the column so that I4 was +B4*G4 and so on. However, if the database (columns D through I) were then sorted, the formulas would be incorrect. Whatever employee ended up on row 3 after the sort would get the rate that was in B3. There are two ways to solve this problem: You can either include the rate column within the database, or make each reference to the rate column absolute. In other words, there are two rules for calculations within databases:

- Make sure that values used in formulas in the database are placed within the database whenever possible.

- When formulas in the database use values that are outside the database, make sure that references to cells outside the database are absolute.

How Database Functions Work

When you want to find the total of the values in a database field, you normally use the aggregate function @SUM. Likewise, to calculate the number of items in a field, you use the @COUNT function. However, if you want the sum or average of selected values in a column, you turn to the database functions. For example, you could sum the weekly earnings of all people in the sample database who were under 25.

The database functions are summarized in Table 8.2. The syntax of all database functions is the same. For example, the @DSUM function can be stated as:

@DSUM(*input_range*, *field*, *criteria_range*)

The *input_range* argument is the collection of data that is the subject of the calculation, which typically corresponds to the Database Query Input setting. The field names are included in this range. In the sample database in both Figures 8.22 and 8.28, the *input_range* would be D2..H19.

Table 8.2   **The Role of Database Functions**

Function Name	Action
@DSUM	Sums selected values in a range
@DAVG	Averages selected values in a range
@DCOUNT	Counts selected entries in a range
@DMAX	Finds the largest value among selected values in a range
@DMIN	Finds the smallest value among selected values in a range
@DSTD	Returns the standard deviation of selected values in a range
@DVAR	Measures the variance of selected values in a range

The *field* argument is a number representing the database field to which you want the calculation applied. The numbering begins with 0 for the first field. Thus to sum selected values in the Weekly field of the sample database, you would use the *field* argument 3 (this number is sometimes referred to as the *offset column*, since it counts how many columns the target column is offset from the first column).

The *criteria_range* argument is an area of the worksheet in which you have entered the criteria for the calculation. This need not be the same range that is the current Data Query Criteria setting. For example, to calculate the sum of the Weekly field entries for all people 25 or younger, you could enter the field name Age in B10 and the criteria +F3<=25 in B11, and then use B10..B11 as the criteria range argument.

The complete formula to calculate the total weekly earnings of everyone 25 or younger would be

```
@DSUM(D2..H19,3,B10..B11)
```

This type of calculation is much easier if you name your ranges—for example, if you call the input range DATABASE and the criteria range something like DBCRIT1. Using field names to name the cells in the first record in your database will allow you to use those field names in criteria, as in +AGE<=25. Figure 8.29 shows several of the database functions at work.

Figure 8.29
Database functions at work

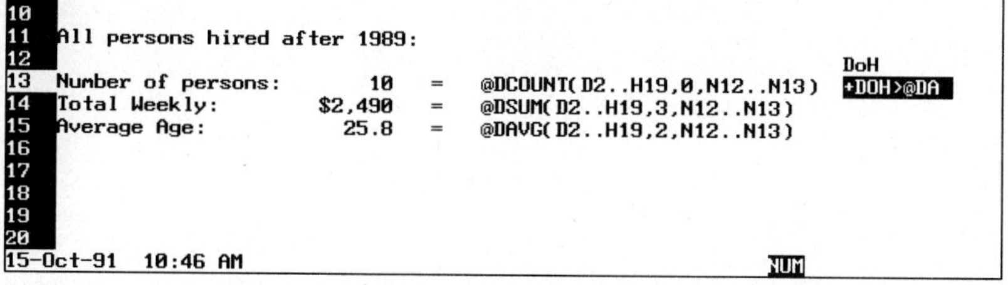

The database functions provide you with the means of calculating a variety of useful statistics about your database. In addition, you can use them

with the Data Table command to produce cross tabulations, as described in Chapter 12.

Summary

The ability to sort and search large quantities of data is a very valuable component of 1-2-3. While the database commands are sometimes less obvious then those used in straightforward spreadsheet work, they are well worth learning. In addition to the commands covered in this chapter, database users may want to explore the use of database functions in data tables, covered in Chapter 12, and the input macros described in Chapter 15. The next chapter explores 1-2-3's graph making capabilities.

9

Graphs and Charts

HERE ARE A VARIETY OF GRAPH STYLES IN 1-2-3 RELEASE 2.3 AND A whole range of options with which to dress up your graphs. This chapter explains how to design, print, and manage charts and graphs created from your spreadsheet data and how to customize them to your needs. You will also learn how to generate and save multiple graphs using a single worksheet and how to print graphs using a separate program called PrintGraph.

Graph Basics

To work effectively with graphs in 1-2-3, you need to become familiar with the terms and concepts that 1-2-3 uses in its Graph commands. Figure 9.1 shows a typical 1-2-3 graph labeled with the commonly used terms. These terms will all be described as they are introduced in the course of the chapter.

Figure 9.1
Annotated graph

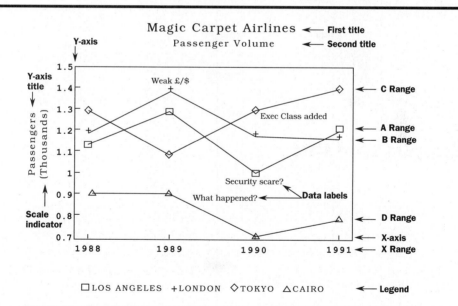

In Figure 9.2 you can see the worksheet that generated the graph in Figure 9.1. This worksheet has been annotated to show which cells supply the information displayed in the graph. This sample worksheet records the number of passengers carried by an airline to each of four cities over a four-year period. (If you want to use a similar worksheet to follow the examples in this chapter, refer to the section "Working with Ranges" in Chapter 2.)

The graphs you generate from your worksheets are dynamically linked to the data. This means that changes to the values being graphed result in changes to the graph the next time you view it. However, when you store a graph as a picture file for printing, this image is frozen and is not linked to the data. This allows you to create a graph with one set of values, save a picture of it, and then change the values and save the new picture that results. Saving graphs in picture files is covered towards the end of the chapter under "Printing Graphs."

Figure 9.2

Sample worksheet

Legend range

X-axis range
A data range
B data range
C data range
D data range

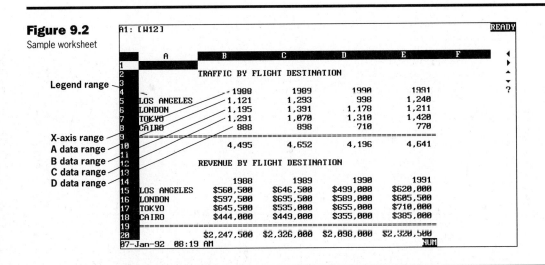

Graph Types

When graphing with 1-2-3, you first need to decide which type of graph best suits the information you want to convey. Although you can change graph types after designing a graph, the choice of type determines how you graph the data and what impression the chart will make. 1-2-3 provides six basic graph types: line (the default), bar, XY, stacked bar, pie, and high-low-close-open (HLCO). It also provides a graph type called mixed, which is a blend of bar and line graph.

Line Charts

When you want values to appear as points with lines connecting them, you need the line graph type. Each value in each data range is represented by a separate point. This method is effective for showing changes in data over time. For example, the chart in Figure 9.1 graphs the volume figures from Figure 9.2. You can use different shapes for the symbols that represent data points; you can also turn these off, leaving just the lines that connect the points. Alternatively, you can turn off the lines and just use symbols for the data.

A line chart is said to have two axes, the x-axis and the y-axis. The x-axis in Figure 9.1 is formed by the years over which the volume figures are graphed. The y-axis provides a scale from which you can measure the size of the values represented by the data points. 1-2-3 automatically creates the y-axis for you, based on the quantities being graphed; however, you can adjust the y-axis manually if you want.

Bar Charts

Two of 1-2-3's graph types, bar and stacked bar, are variations of the basic bar chart. In a regular (as opposed to stacked) bar, each piece of data in each data range is represented by a separate bar, as shown in Figure 9.3. This chart allows you to compare the relative performance for each destination in each year.

Figure 9.3

A bar chart

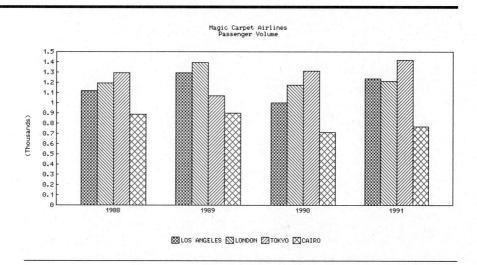

Note that the relative overall performance for each year is more difficult to gauge. Also note that the font used for the graph text in Figure 9.3 is different from that in Figure 9.1. When you print a graph with 1-2-3, you can choose from a variety of fonts. The font used in Figure 9.3 is called Roman while the font in Figure 9.1 is Block, which is the default font.

Rather than show each value as a separate bar, the stacked bar chart creates just one bar for each year, totaling the year's figures and showing the relative contribution of each destination as a portion of the whole bar. The stacked bar is thus a good way to show relative performance of cumulative values. For example, Figure 9.4 shows clearly that total volume varied from year to year. Note that the scale of the graph in Figure 9.4 differs from that in

Figure 9.3 (and Figure 9.1) because the values represented by the individual bars are larger. 1-2-3 adjusts the scale automatically.

You can also see that the graph in Figure 9.4 has a 3-D effect, one of the new features introduced to graphs in 1-2-3 Release 2.3.

Figure 9.4
A stacked bar chart

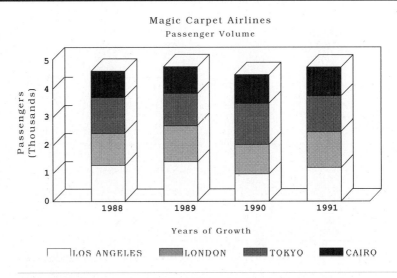

XY Charts

The XY chart is rather like a line chart but is the only 1-2-3 graph type to use values for the x-axis. The XY chart is mainly used to show the distribution of values, and is helpful when analyzing statistics and performing regression, but is not appropriate for the data graphed so far in this chapter. A sample XY chart is shown in Figure 9.5, which graphs engine performance. The graph plots the intersections between two sets of values (torque and speed) and shows their correlation.

Note that, unlike the years in Figure 9.1, the x-axis is not simply a fixed set of values used as labels. In an XY graph, you can adjust the scale of the x-axis and set the upper and lower limits manually. Also note the text in Figure 9.5 is all the same size. This is how the graph appears when displayed on screen with the Graph View command, described in a moment.

Pie Charts

A pie chart can be an effective image when you want to display the proportional breakdown of values within a single whole. A pie chart is thus a one-dimensional graph; it uses only one range of values. If you selected Pie as the graph type for the data values in Figure 9.1 or 9.3, you would see the breakdown of the first data series—that is, the Paris volume broken down by year.

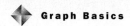

Graph Basics

345

What you would probably prefer to see is the total volume for one year broken down by destination, as shown in Figure 9.6, which graphs the volumes for 1990.

Figure 9.5

An XY graph

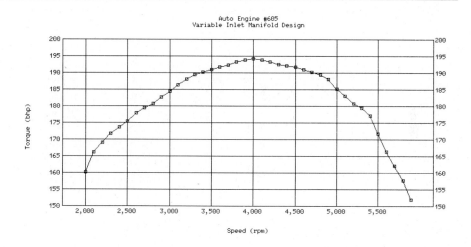

Figure 9.6

A sample pie chart

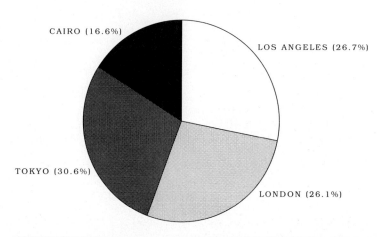

This chart was created by defining one column of values as the data range. (In this case E4..E6 was used to show the breakdown for 1990.) A pie chart can use an x-axis range, in this case A4..A6, to label the pie slices. As you can see from Figure 9.6, the percentage of the total represented by each slice is provided next to the slice names. This is one of the many elements of a pie chart that you can change, as described later in the section "Dressing Up Pie Charts."

High-Low-Close-Open Charts

If you work with stocks or commodities, you know that the terms high, low, close, and open refer to the prices set by trading during a specific time period. For example, in a day of trading a stock *opens* at a certain price and *closes* at a certain price. During the day, the highest price paid for the stock sets the *high*, while the lowest price determines the *low*. All four of these figures can be represented by a simple graphic convention. The high and low can be drawn as vertical line between the two values. The open can be drawn as a horizontal line to the left of the high-low line, and the close can be shown as a horizontal line to the right of the high-low line. You can see this arrangement in Figure 9.7, in which one stock is tracked over a two-week period.

Figure 9.7

A high-low-close-open graph

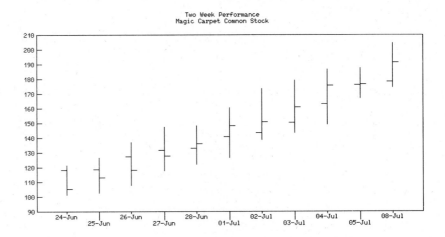

Mixed Charts

At times you may want a graph to show two different types of information. For example, you might want to graph actual sales as bars and projected sales as a line. You can do this using a mixed graph. You can have three of the data ranges appear as bars, and three more as lines. Figure 9.8 shows an example of a mixed chart.

Figure 9.8

A mixed chart

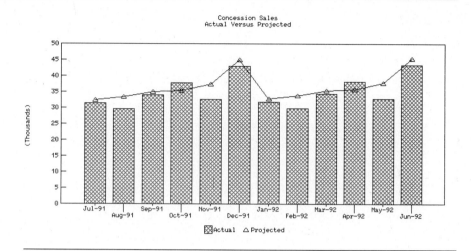

Features

One option under the Graph Type command does not represent a graph type: Feature. This option includes a number of commands for altering the appearance of several of the graph types:

- Vertical is the default setting for charts. The x-axis is drawn across the bottom of the screen and bars in bar charts appear vertical.

- Horizontal alters the orientation of graphs, drawing the x-axis up the left side of the screen and rotating bars so that they appear as in Figure 9.9.

- Stacked applies to line, bar, mixed, and XY graphs. It tells 1-2-3 to plot values in data ranges one on top of another. Applying Stacked to a bar chart creates a stacked bar chart.

- Frame allows you to turn on or off the sides of the graph frame and the display of zero lines. The graph in Figure 9.9 has two sides turned off, giving a less cluttered look. In Figure 9.10, two zero lines are displayed in an XY graph where the values are represented by symbols instead of lines.

- 3D-Effect works with bar or stacked bar charts to give an impression of depth to the chart. You can see examples of this in Figure 9.4 and Figure 9.9.

The Horizontal option enables you to create charts like the one in Figure 9.9, which emphasizes the performance of the leading item. Since the x-axis information is not numeric and does not represent a time line, it was possible to sort the order of items in the data range so that the largest value was placed first in the graph.

Figure 9.9

Using the
Horizontal and 3-D
features

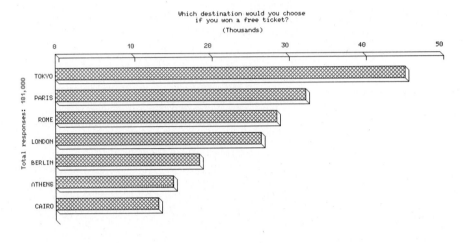

Figure 9.10

XY graph with zero
lines

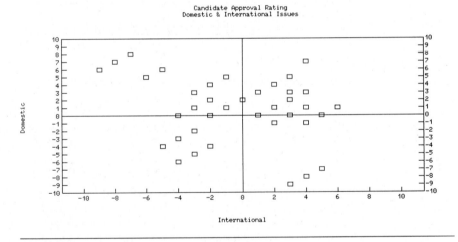

Building a Graph

This section describes how to create the stacked bar graph shown in Figure
9.4, using a worksheet like the one shown in Figure 9.2. In the process, you
will learn how the basic Graph commands work and how to attach explana-
tory text to graphs.

The Graph Menu

The first step, after loading the worksheet, is to press / and select Graph from the menu. The main Graph menu appears, along with the Graph Settings dialog box, as shown in Figure 9.11. Remember that you can press the Window key, F6, to reveal the underlying worksheet and turn off the dialog box.

Figure 9.11

The main Graph menu

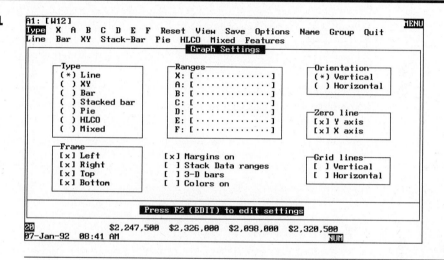

Choose Type followed by Stack-Bar. You can now set the ranges to be graphed. These include the X range and data ranges A through F. Notice that 1-2-3 refers to data range A as the first data range, data range B as the second data range, and so on. 1-2-3 allows a maximum of six data ranges.

If you are using a mouse with 1-2-3, you can issue graph commands through your choices in the Graph Settings dialog box. To choose stacked bar as the graph type, simply click in the appropriate field of the Type box. Graph options, which are described in the course of this chapter, appear as settings in one of three dialog boxes: Graph Settings, Legends & Titles, or Scale Options. You can access both the Legends & Titles and Scale Options dialog boxes via the special buttons that appear when you edit the Graph Settings dialog box. You can also use the keyboard to establish your graph settings by editing the dialog boxes.

Both keyboard and mouse users can press F4 to activate POINT mode in the worksheet when editing range settings. When editing dialog boxes, you must confirm your choices by selecting OK or pressing Shift-Enter. If you press Esc or click the right mouse button to exit the SETTINGS mode, the settings will revert to what they were before you edited them. This is particularly important when working with dialog boxes like Legends & Titles and Scale Options, which pop up over the main Graph Settings dialog box.

The X Range

The x-axis forms the baseline of most graphs. The X range is a series of consecutive cells, arranged in either a column or a row, that contain either values or labels. In many graphs, the X range values provide a time scale. However, in all but XY graphs, the X range entries simply act as labels, even if they are values. These labels help identify the values represented in the graph—labeling the points in a line graph, the bars in a bar graph, or the slices in a pie graph.

To graph the passenger volume in Figure 9.2 over a four-year period, you will select B4..E4 (the years 1988 through 1991) as the X range. All of the Graph commands allow you to select ranges either by pointing them out, by typing the coordinates, or by entering a preassigned range name. When you have entered the X range, the coordinates appear in the Graph Settings dialog box. If the range you have identified has a range name, that also will appear in the settings box.

The Data Ranges

The volume figures that you want to graph are in cells B5 through E8. Each row of values in this block constitutes a data range. The first of these is range A. When you select A from the main Graph menu, you enter the coordinates B5..E5. You can then select B to enter B6..E6, C to enter B7..E7, and D to enter B8..E8. Each of these ranges will be recorded in the Graph Settings dialog box, as shown in Figure 9.12.

The Graph View

Although the graph is not really complete at this point, you will probably want to view your progress. Select View from the main Graph menu or press the Graph key, F10. The results will look like those shown in Figure 9.13. (Don't type anything until you're done looking at the graph, since any key you press will take you back to the main Graph menu.)

As you can see, 1-2-3 does a lot of the work for you. For example, the scale of the y-axis has been set automatically, from 0 to 5. The text "Thousands" has been added to show the units used in the scale. Each data range has been shaded differently and each year's worth of data has been totaled to create a single bar, proportionately subdivided according to the relative value of each data range in that year.

The Graph View command always shows you the current graph—that is, the one whose settings are in the Graph Settings box. Later in this chapter you will learn how to make a number of different graphs from one work-sheet; however, only one graph can be current at any one time. You remove the graph from view and return to the main Graph menu by pressing any key.

Figure 9.12

The completed range settings

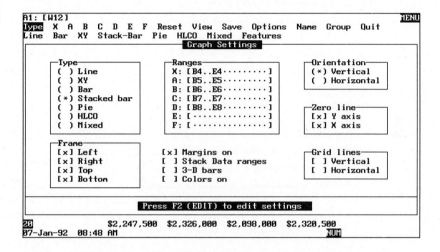

Figure 9.13

The preliminary graph seen with View

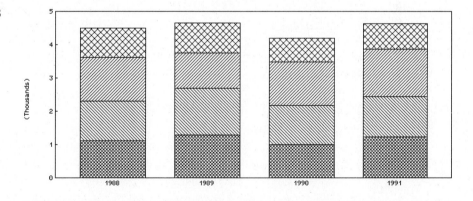

The Graph key, F10, is closely related to the Graph View command. Pressing F10 displays the current graph. The next key you press returns you to the mode you were in before pressing F10. In 1-2-3 Release 2.3, the F10 key works in MENU mode as well as in READY mode.

Notice that the graph appears in a single color on a black background, even if you are using a color monitor. This is because 1-2-3 has two modes for graph viewing: Color and B&W. B&W (short for black and white) is the default mode. You set the viewing mode option with the Graph Options command, described in a moment. (If your graph *does* appear in color, someone has already activated the Color option.)

If you don't see a graph when you press the Graph key or select View from the Graph menu, you may not have 1-2-3 installed correctly. Check the installation procedure described in Appendix A, particularly the Screen Display setting. The only systems that cannot display graphs are PCs that use the original IBM monochrome adapter.

Graph Save

Although the graph is not yet finished, you may want to make sure that you have saved the graph settings established so far. You might be tempted to choose the Save item on the Graph menu, but this is not the purpose of the Graph Save command. To save your graph settings so that they will be in place the next time you use the worksheet, use the File Save command. This saves all the settings for the current graph as well as all your worksheet data. The Graph Save command stores a snapshot of the current graph in a special file that is used by the PrintGraph program to print the graph. This graph picture file, which has the extension .PIC, is not dynamically linked to the worksheet that generates the graph. The graph settings are part of the worksheet and, like other 1-2-3 menu settings, will not be stored unless the worksheet is stored. Press any key to return to the Graph menu. Then press Esc to return to the main menu and issue the File Save command. The section "Further Graph Commands" discusses how to store more than one group of graph settings in a single worksheet file. The Graph Save command is covered under "Printing Graphs."

Graph Options

At this point, the basic structure of the graph has been established but it needs further work, particularly in the area of labeling. To label the graph and customize its appearance, you use the Graph Options command. When you issue this command, 1-2-3 displays a menu with the following options:

- The Legend option adds legends describing the A through F data ranges, such as those seen at the bottom of Figure 9.4.

- The Format option controls the display of lines and symbols in line and XY graphs.

- The Titles option adds text to label the graph and the two axes, as seen in Figure 9.4.

- The Grid option adds or removes graph grid lines such as those seen in Figure 9.5.

- The Scale option controls the appearance of the y-axis and x-axis scales. It also sets a skip factor for x-axis labels.

- The Color option turns on the use of color when displaying graphs and saving graph images for printing.

- The B&W option turns off the use of color when displaying graphs and saving graph images for printing.

- The Data-Labels option allows you to create labels within graphs, as seen in Figure 9.1.

Some of these options, such as Scale, are quite complex and will be dealt with under "Customizing Graphs." You can use the Color and B&W commands to switch between color and monochrome display mode for graphs. The B&W mode is the default. In B&W mode, 1-2-3 shades graphs with different patterns (hatching) to distinguish data ranges. When you switch to Color mode, 1-2-3 uses different colors for shading. When you add shading to a pie chart, it appears as colors in Color mode and hatching in B&W mode. Note that the choice you make appears in the Graph Settings box as Color on.

Obviously, you have to have a color monitor to see the colors, but you may need to select Color even if you have a monochrome system. This is because the choice of Color or B&W affects the printing of graphs. If you want a graph to print in color, you must issue the Graph Save command while the Color on setting is checked. If you plan to print the graph on a black-and-white printer, you must save it with the Color on option unchecked. For more on the Graph Save command, see the section "Printing Graphs."

The Legends and Titles options, dealt with in the next two sections, allow you to add descriptive text to the graph. The text can be typed or it can be supplied by worksheet cell entries. If you edit the Graph Settings dialog box, you will see a three-dot button labeled "Legends & Titles" that leads you to the dialog box shown in Figure 9.14.

Legend Text

The legend text, located below the graph, identifies the data ranges represented by each symbol, color, or hatch pattern in the graph. There are several ways of supplying the text for legends. When you select Options from the Graph menu and then select Legend, you see the following choices:

A B C D E F Range

When you select one of the letters, you are prompted to enter legend text for the corresponding data range. The entry can be either the actual text you want to use—such as LOS ANGELES or Los Angeles for data range A in this example—or a reference to a cell containing the text you want to use.

Figure 9.14

The Graph Legends & Titles dialog box

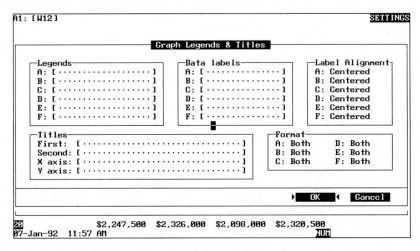

Cell references must be preceded by a backslash so that, in this example, you could enter **\A5** for data range A. After you have typed either the actual text or a cell reference, press Enter. You are returned to the Options menu and your entry is recorded in the Graph Settings box. To set the legend text for another range, you must first select Legend again.

The Range option on the Legend menu allows you to set all of the legend text at once. You do this by indicating a worksheet range that contains the required text in consecutive cells. In the bar graph you have been constructing, you could use the range A5..A8. The Legend Range command presents a typical range definition prompt, allowing you to type in the coordinates or point them out in the worksheet. However, when you press Enter to confirm the range, the cells are recorded as \A5, \A6, and so on. 1-2-3 uses the first entry in the range as the A data range legend, the second entry as the B data range legend, and so on.

Figure 9.15 shows the results of using A5..A8 as the legend range. 1-2-3 places the legend underneath the graph. A box containing the correct shading is used to key the text to the data range it describes. If the graph type is line or XY, the legend uses the appropriate symbols, as seen in Figure 9.15. You cannot add legends to pie charts. Each data range can have legend text up to 19 characters. If there is not enough room for all of the legends on one line, an extra line will be used. In some cases, Wysiwyg can actually make the legend difficult to read. If you are using Wysiwyg and your legend text overlaps, try detaching the add-in with the Add-In Detach command.

Note that the cells supplying the legend text do not have to be adjacent to the data ranges they are labeling. You could just as easily use A15..A18 for the legend text instead of A5..A8. In addition, although using cell addresses for legend text saves you typing and allows you to change the legend text by changing the contents of the referenced cell, these cell references are not dynamic. This can lead to errors if you move cells after specifying them as the legend text. If you moved the contents of cell A5 after selecting it for data range A, 1-2-3 would not update the setting for you. This is true whether you use the Legend Range command to select the cells or set the cells for each range individually.

Figure 9.15

Graph with legend and titles

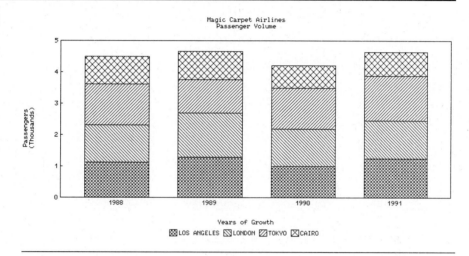

One way around this problem of nondynamic cell references is to enter a range name for the legend text. For example, you could use the Range Name command to name A5 as LEGENDA, and then enter \LEGENDA as the legend text for data range A. The contents of the range LEGENDA would be used for the legend text, even if you moved this single-cell named range to another location. However, this is a lot of trouble, particularly if you don't expect to move the cell supplying the legend text.

Text for Titles

The two lines of title text at the top of Figure 9.15 were created with the Titles command on the Graph Options menu. 1-2-3 displays four options when you select Titles: First, Second, X-Axis, and Y-Axis. These work much like the legend text options. When you select First, you can enter the text of the first line of the title, the coordinates of a cell containing the desired text preceded by a backslash, or a block name preceded by a backslash. In this example, the text "Magic Carpet Airlines" was typed.

When you press Enter to confirm a title, you are returned to the Options menu, but the Titles option remains highlighted. This allows you to reselect it quickly and choose the next title option: Second. In this case, the text "Passenger Volume" was entered, but the label in cell B2 could conceivably have been used, and would be entered as \B2. The text "Years of Growth" was entered after selecting Titles and then X-Axis. The text "Passengers" was entered for the y-axis. Note that each of the four pieces of title text can be up to 39 characters long. The resulting graph, complete with the four added titles, looks like the one you saw in Figure 9.4, except for the 3-D effect, discussed later in the "Using Graph Type Features" section.

Further Graph Commands

So far you have seen how to choose the graph settings needed to produce a simple but effective graph from worksheet data. You have seen that the graph settings are stored with the worksheet in the worksheet file. In this section, you will learn how to switch graph types and how to name graph settings so that you can generate several different graphs from the same worksheet. You will also learn how to reset graph settings to simplify the task of redefining graphs. This section also looks at the Group command, used to assign several graph ranges simultaneously.

Changing Graph Types

Suppose you have created your stacked bar graph showing four years' worth of passenger volume by destination. You have added a legend and titles to the graph. Then you decide to see what the chart looks like as a regular bar graph. To do this, simply select Type from the Graph menu and select Bar. You are returned to the Graph menu and can select View to see the results, which will look like the chart in Figure 9.3. Note that the scale on the y-axis has been altered because the bars represent smaller values than those in Figure 9.4. There is one bar for each value in the data ranges.

If you leave the Graph menu, perform more work on the spreadsheet, and then press F10, you will see the bar chart and not the stacked bar. This is because the Graph key and the Graph View command both graph the current graph settings. However, changing the Type setting for a graph does not affect any of the other graph settings. 1-2-3 is still graphing the same four data ranges, with the same legend and title text. Similarly, if you now select Type and choose Line, you will see a line chart with the same data and text. The data ranges A through D are still appropriate to this chart type, as is the X range setting.

Changing graph type does not always produce acceptable results. If you choose Pie as the type, you will get a chart like the one in Figure 9.16. This chart breaks down the A range, Los Angeles, according to year, although this is not immediately apparent from the graph itself.

You get this result because pie charts are one-dimensional. They graph only one data range, A, and use the X range as labels for the pie slices. (For more on pie charts, see "Dressing Up Pie Charts.") If you want a pie chart that breaks down one year's worth of volume according to destination, you have to alter many of the graph settings. This raises the question of how to define a second set of graph settings without losing the first. The answer is to store the first graph's settings with the Graph Name command.

Figure 9.16

A pie chart by year

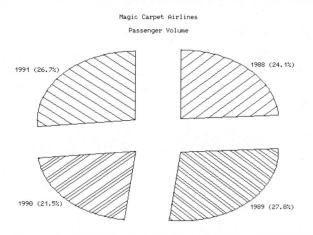

Graph Names

The Graph Name command allows you to save the current graph settings. You can then return to those settings later with a single command. If you then define another graph that you want to save, you can attach a different name to the new settings and switch between old and new settings without losing either set.

When you select Name from the Graph menu, you get a menu similar to the one provided by the Range Name command. There are five choices: Use, Create, Delete, Reset, and Table. The Use option reinstates a graph you have already named, making it the current graph. When you select Use, you are shown a list of graph names. When you choose a name from the list, the graph is displayed and its settings are placed in the Graph Settings box.

You use the Graph Name Create command to attach a name to the current graph. When you choose Create, you can type a new name or select one from the list of existing names, overwriting the settings previously stored for that name. Note that a graph name only preserves the settings used to draw the graph; it does not freeze the values that are graphed. If the data in the underlying worksheet changes, the graph will change accordingly. Also note that graph names can be up to 15 characters long, and should not include spaces and punctuation.

You use the Delete command to remove a single name from the list and the Reset command to remove all names from the list. 1-2-3 does not ask you to confirm either of these commands, so you should use them with care. However, you can reverse both commands with the Undo key. To help you manage graph names, the Table command lists all of the existing names in the worksheet in an area of your choosing.

Suppose that you want to preserve the stacked bar chart you have created, but also want to create a different graph, perhaps a pie chart, from the same worksheet. You would follow this procedure:

1. Select Graph View to make sure the settings of the current graph are correct. (If you have experimented with other graph types, you may need to change the type back to Stack-Bar.)

2. Select Graph Name and choose Create.

3. Type a name for the graph, for example STACKBAR1, and then press Enter.

4. Make any changes you want to the graph settings in order to produce the second graph.

5. View the second graph to make sure the settings are correct.

6. Choose Graph Name Create and enter a name for the second graph, for example PIE90.

7. Use the File Save command.

The last step is very important since none of your work with either the graph settings or graph names is stored until the worksheet is stored. When you have stored the worksheet, you can safely switch between the two graphs. For example, to view the graph named STACKBAR1, select Name from the Graph menu and then pick STACKBAR1 from the list that's presented, as shown in Figure 9.17.

The graph you select is displayed and its settings are placed in the Graph Settings box. In other words, the named graph is made the current graph. Any changes you make to the graph settings at this point will affect the current graph. However, you must reissue the Graph Name Create command to record these changes. For example, if you want to alter the formatting of STACKBAR1, you must first make it the current graph with Name Use, make the changes, issue the Name Create command, and select STACKBAR1 as the name under which to store the new version of the graph. If not, the next time you issue the Name Use command to make a different graph current, the latest changes to STACKBAR1 will be lost. If you are following along with the examples, go ahead and save the current settings now (if you haven't done so already). Later you can try embellishing the graph in a variety of ways.

Figure 9.17

Choosing a named graph with Name Use

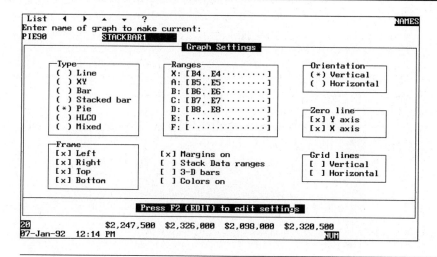

```
 List    ◄   ►   ▲   ▼   ?                                              NAMES
 Enter name of graph to make current:
 PIE90         STACKBAR1
┌─────────────────────────────── Graph Settings ───────────────────────────────┐
│   ┌─Type──────────┐   ┌─Ranges──────────────┐   ┌─Orientation──────┐          │
│   ( ) Line          X: [B4..E4·········]       (*) Vertical        │
│   ( ) XY            A: [B5..E5·········]       ( ) Horizontal       │
│   ( ) Bar           B: [B6..E6·········]                           │
│   ( ) Stacked bar   C: [B7..E7·········]                           │
│   (*) Pie           D: [B8..E8·········]       ┌─Zero line─────┐   │
│   ( ) HLCO          E: [·············]         [x] Y axis          │
│   ( ) Mixed         F: [·············]         [x] X axis          │
│   └───────────────┘ └─────────────────────┘                       │
│   ┌─Frame─────────┐                            ┌─Grid lines────┐   │
│   [x] Left          [x] Margins on             [ ] Vertical        │
│   [x] Right         [ ] Stack Data ranges      [ ] Horizontal      │
│   [x] Top           [ ] 3-D bars                                  │
│   [x] Bottom        [ ] Colors on                                 │
│                                                                   │
│              ┌─ Press F2 (EDIT) to edit settings ─┐              │
└───────────────────────────────────────────────────────────────────┘
 20         $2,247,500  $2,326,000  $2,098,000  $2,320,500
 07-Jan-92   12:14 PM                                          NUM
```

Graph Reset

If you create a stacked bar chart like the one in Figure 9.15 and then want to create a pie chart like the one in Figure 9.6, you will need to make numerous changes to the graph settings. Rather than alter each setting in turn, you can clear out some or all of the settings with the Graph Reset command. When you select this command, you are presented with the following menu:

```
Graph X A B C D E F Ranges Options Quit
```

The first option, Graph, clears all of the graph settings. Obviously, this is a command to use with caution. The single-letter options reset the respective ranges without affecting any of the other settings. The Ranges option simultaneously resets all of the range settings in the graph—that is, A through F and X. When you select Graph Reset Options, 1-2-3 clears out all of the graph settings made with the Graph Options command, including titles and legends as well as the data labels and scale settings described in the next section.

If you use the dialog boxes to establish your graph settings, the Reset command is not needed. You can remove or alter many settings simply by clicking or editing the appropriate check box. When you need to cancel a range setting, you can activate the appropriate range field and press Esc to clear the coordinates. If you need to change range coordinates, you can press F4 to switch to POINT mode in the worksheet.

Graph Group

The Graph Group command can, in one single action, set the X range and all of the data ranges for a graph. When you select Group, you are prompted to point out a range of cells to be used for a graph. For example, Figure 9.18 shows the Group command being used with the sample worksheet.

Figure 9.18

The Graph Group command

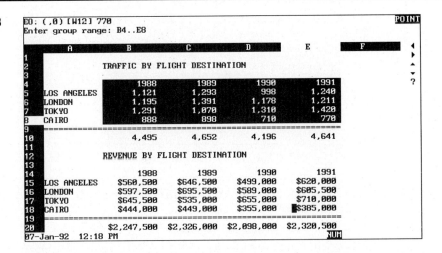

The cells containing the X range and data ranges A through D are highlighted. When you enter the group range, 1-2-3 asks you to choose between Columnwise and Rowwise. If you select Columnwise, the first column within the range is used as the X range and the remaining columns are used as data ranges. If you select Rowwise, the first row is read as the X range and the remaining rows as data ranges. Rowwise is the appropriate choice for the sample data. When you select this option, the range settings for the graph will be the same as in Figure 9.12.

This all-at-once approach to graph building is convenient, but only if the worksheet data fits a certain pattern. All of the ranges must be in contiguous parallel cells. For example, if there were blank rows between each of the destinations in the sample worksheet, the Group command would not work properly. The Group command clears any previous range settings, so you cannot use it to add ranges to an existing graph. Please note that this command resets all preexisting X ranges and data ranges. That is, if you have a

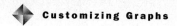

graph with four data ranges and use Group to define a graph with only three data ranges, you don't need to reset range D. However, the command leaves any preexisting titles unchanged.

Customizing Graphs

In this section, you will learn how to further improve and adjust graphs for the desired effect. The commands covered here allow you to enhance a graph's visual impact.

Grid Options

The Grid command turns on and off the use of grid lines in a graph. (1-2-3 displays no grid lines by default.) All graph types except pie charts can include grids. The Grid command offers four options:

- The Horizontal option draws grid lines across the graph from the y-axis.

- The Vertical option draws grid lines up the graph from the x-axis.

- The Both option draws both horizontal and vertical grid lines.

- The Clear option clears all grid lines.

The XY graph shown in Figure 9.5 is an example of the Both option. Figure 9.19 shows the stacked bar chart from Figure 9.15, with the addition of horizontal grid lines and several other changes that are described in a moment. If you want, try adding grid lines to your own stacked bar graph. (If you already reset the graph, use the Graph Name Use command to reinstate those graph settings.)

Scale Options

When you are unhappy with 1-2-3's scaling for the y-axis, or with the format of the numbers on the scale, use the Graph Options Scale command to adjust these aspects of the graph manually. For example, in Figure 9.3 the numbers on the y-axis are not formatted consistently. The values of 0 and 1 are shown with no decimal places, while all of the other numbers have one decimal place. In this case, you might prefer to apply a Fixed format to the axis so that all the numbers show the same number of decimal places. Figure 9.19 illustrates several modifications to the y-axis that you can make with the Graph Options Scale command. The y-axis numbers are formatted to one decimal place whereas there are no decimal places in the original version of this graph shown in Figure 9.15. The "Thousands" scale indicator that 1-2-3 added automatically has been removed. The scale is now displayed on the left and right of the graph. Finally, the high point of the scale has been increased from 5 to 6. The 3-D effect was added with the Features command described later in this chapter.

Figure 9.19

Stacked bar chart with several options in use

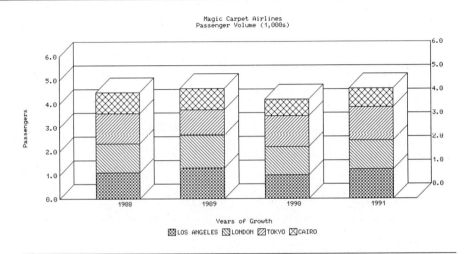

You use the Graph Options Scale command to adjust the scaling and for-matting of the x-axis in an XY graph. You also use Scale to set the number of x-axis labels displayed in XY, line, bar, and stacked bar graphs. For example, in Figure 9.5 the numbering on the x-axis progresses in increments of 1,000 while there are grid lines every 500 units. In this case, 1-2-3 was told to skip every other value in the scale.

When you select Scale from the Graph Options menu, you have the three choices Y-Scale, X-Scale, and Skip. Also, a new dialog box appears, as shown in Figure 9.20.

The Skip option will be reviewed in a moment. The Y-Scale option is used to adjust the y-axis, and the X-Scale option controls the x-axis. The X-Scale option is only valid if the graph type is XY.

Using Y-Scale

The Y-Scale command gives you considerable control over the visual impact of a graph. For example, the bar chart in Figure 9.3 gives the impression that the airline is doing very well. However, what if Magic Carpet Airlines were aiming for passenger volumes of 1,500 for all destinations by 1991? The graph in Figure 9.3 tends to suggest that the airline came close. However, if you alter the Y-Scale settings, you can create a different impression, as illus-trated in Figure 9.21.

Figure 9.20

The Graph Scale
Settings dialog box

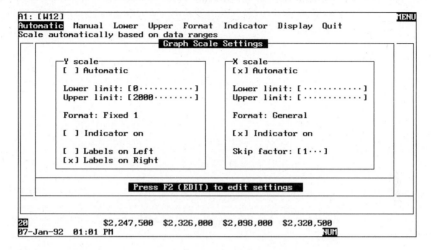

Figure 9.21

Bar chart with
adjusted y-axis

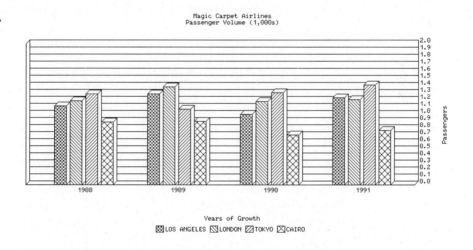

This graph has the upper limit of the y-axis extended to 2,000. It also has the horizontal grid option in place and uses a Fixed format with one decimal place for the numbers on the y-axis. The scale is displayed on the right. When you select Y-Scale from the Graph Options Scale menu, you must select one of the following options:

■ The Automatic option draws the scale automatically, with upper and lower limits based on the values in the data ranges. Automatic is the default setting.

- The Manual option draws a scale with upper and lower limits based on values supplied by the Lower and Upper settings.

- The Lower option sets the lower limit for a graph when displayed with the Manual setting.

- The Upper option sets the upper limit for a graph when displayed with the Manual setting.

- The Format option sets the display format used for numbers on the scale, based on the standard format options Fixed, Sci, Currency, and so on.

- The Indicator option displays or hides the scale indicator (such as "Thousands").

- The Display option controls the use of y-axis labels and tick marks, the choices being Left, Right, Both, or None. The Left option places the y-axis markings in the usual position, while Right places them on the right. The Both option repeats the markings on the left and right, while None removes them completely.

In addition, there is a Quit option that returns you to the Options menu. By default the Automatic setting is in effect, there are no entries for Upper and Lower, the format is General, and the indicator is displayed. The first time you select Manual, the Upper and Lower settings both change to 0 and nothing is displayed in the graph. If you want to use Manual, you must at least set the Upper limit to a number that is appropriate to the values being graphed. For example, in Figure 9.21 the setting for Upper is 2000. You can leave the Lower limit at 0 or alter it, as described in a moment.

If you select Manual, set your own Upper and Lower values, and then decide you want the original scale, simply select Automatic. This appears to wipe out your Upper and Lower settings. However, if you select Manual again, the Upper and Lower values will reappear.

The Format command presents you with a standard list of 1-2-3 formats to choose from. The most likely choices are Fixed, Currency, and Comma. The General format is the default format. Remember, 1-2-3 chooses the measuring unit for the scale and this is reflected in the indicator. If the indicator says "Thousands" and the values on the y-axis are from 0 to 1.7, for example, there is no point using the Comma format since there are no more than two digits to display. However, you need to provide at least one decimal place in the format or else the decimal portion of the scale will disappear.

You cannot alter the factor that 1-2-3 uses for the y-axis. If 1-2-3 selects Thousands, you must live with that. However, you can remove the indicator text from display by issuing the Y-Scale Indicator command and selecting No.

If you do this, make sure that the scale of the graph is either self-explanatory or adequately described in one of the Title settings. For example, in Figure 9.22 the text "1 = 1,000" was created with the Title Y-Axis command.

Figure 9.22

Graph with origin of 1,000

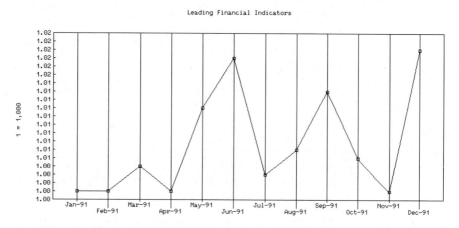

About Origins

The *origin* of a graph is the starting point of the y-axis. In some cases, you can make the graph more useful by making the Y-Scale Lower a value greater than 0. For example, if you were graphing a financial indicator with values from 1001 to 1019, you could set Lower to 1000 and Upper to 1020 so that the differences between values would be easier to observe. An example of this is shown in Figure 9.22.

On the other hand, a value of less than 0 may be necessary to graph negative values. For example, a graph of company profits may need to show a negative figure when the company makes a loss. In fact, when 1-2-3 graphs negative values it automatically makes room for them in the default scale. You can see an example of this in Figure 9.23.

When you are working with negative numbers, it is helpful to see a line that represents the value of zero. Referred to as the *zero line*, this line can be turned on or off in a graph by checking the appropriate field in the Graph Settings dialog box, or by issuing the Graph Type Features Frame Zero-Line command. You can see a y-axis zero line in Figure 9.23. If you are working with an XY graph, you can also place a zero line on the x-axis. You cannot use an x-axis zero line on other types of graphs.

When you adjust the origin, keep in mind that, on bar graphs, 1-2-3 will ignore the Lower setting if it means part of a bar will be obscured. Thus, the graph in Figure 9.22 works because the type is Line. If you changed the type to Bar, 1-2-3 would draw it with 0 as the origin, overriding your entry of 1000 in the Lower setting. In addition, when you alter the scale of the y-axis to move the graph origin, 1-2-3 does not alter the on-screen size of the graph. The graph is always expanded to fill the screen and is always the same shape with a constant ratio of y-axis to x-axis. However, you can adjust the shape of a graph when printing it, as described later under "Printing Graphs."

Figure 9.23

Graphing negative values

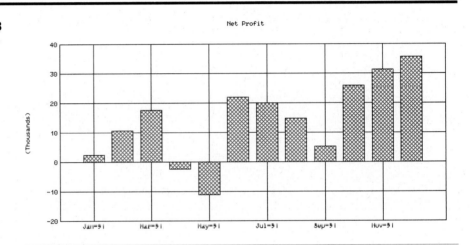

Adjusting the X-Axis

For line, bar, and stacked bar graphs, you can use the Scale Skip option to control the display of x-axis labels. You do this by setting a *skip factor.* When you select Skip, you are asked to specify a number. The default entry is 1, which causes 1-2-3 to display all x-axis labels. If you enter 2, 1-2-3 displays every other x-axis label, as in Figure 9.23. If you enter 3, you get every third label, and so on. Note that the skip factor does not affect the "stacking" of values on the x-axis that you see in Figure 9.22. 1-2-3 makes this adjustment automatically to make the x-axis easier to read. If the x-axis labels are unreadable even after 1-2-3 has stacked them, you can increase the skip factor to make the axis more readable.

If the X range contains values, they will be displayed according to the format of the cells in the worksheet—unless the graph is of the XY type, in which case you can use the X-Scale Format command to alter their appearance. The X-Scale command controls the scale of the x-axis, much as Y-Scale affects the y-axis, *if* the graph type is XY. For other graph types, 1-2-3 simply displays the cell entries in the X range as they appear in the worksheet, evenly spaced across the graph.

Using Data Labels

The Titles and Legend commands are not the only way of adding text to a graph. You can enter labels in the worksheet, associating them with the points in a line or XY chart or the bars in a bar graph. To do this, you use the Graph Options Data-Labels command. Once mastered, this command enables you to annotate graphs beyond the rigid limits of the Legend and Titles commands.

With data labels, you enter the text that you want shown on the graph in a range of worksheet cells. This range, known as a *data-label range,* should equal in size the data range to which you want the text attached. You place the text in the cell within the range that corresponds to the position of the data value you want to annotate. You can then choose the position of the text relative to the data value. For example, Figure 9.24 shows four pieces of text arranged within a graph. This was accomplished with the cells shown in Figure 9.25.

Figure 9.24

A graph with data labels

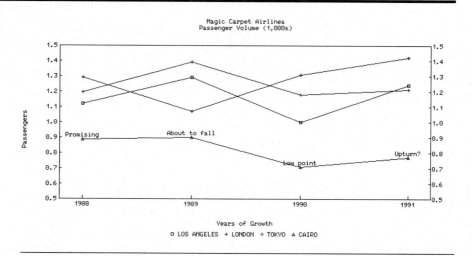

These entries were set up in an unused part of the worksheet and labeled Graph Notes. The years in G23..G26 are not used by the graph settings; they are merely entered to label the entries in H23..H26. The entries in H23..H26 are the actual labels used in the graph with the Data-Labels command.

When you select the Legends & Titles button while editing the Graph Settings dialog box, you will get the dialog box shown earlier in Figure 9.14, which contains the data label settings. Alternatively, you can select Data-Labels from the Graph Options menu. This command offers the following choices:

```
A B C D E F Group Quit
```

Figure 9.25

Setting a data-label range

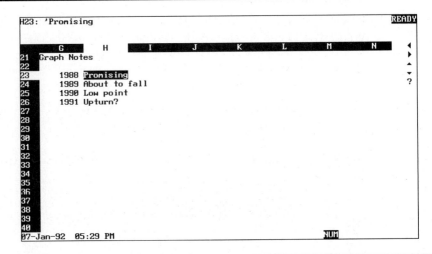

The single-letter options allow you to set individual data-label ranges for each of the graph's data ranges. The Group option allows you to set a number of data-label ranges at once. To create the graph shown in Figure 9.24, option D was selected from the Data-Labels menu and II23..II26 was indicated as the range. When you have pointed out a range, either a single or a group range, 1-2-3 asks where you want the labels positioned relative to the data values. The choices are Center, Left, Above, Right, and Below. In Figure 9.24 the Above option was used. When you make your position choice, it appears in the Data labels section of the Graph Settings box next to the range coordinates.

If you are using the Group command to set more than one data-label range at once, the position you select applies to all of the ranges. This can be a problem if you want some labels to be above and others below. To mix label positions, set each data-label range individually. In Figure 9.26 you can see the actual worksheet entries used to create Figure 9.1.

The years were entered in H2 through K2 to make the data-label range easier to work with, and the right-aligned labels A through D were entered in column G. The actual data-label range is the area highlighted in Figure 9.26, that is, H3..K6. The four labels in this range (J3, I4, J5, and J6) will be attached to the graph. They are placed according to their relative position in the range, so that "Fears of unrest?" is associated with the first data range at the third value on the x-axis, while "Weak $/£" is associated with the second data range, second value.

In Figure 9.27, you can see the graph settings used in Figure 9.1. Note that the A range label "Security scare?" is below, while the B range label "Weak $/£" is above. The label attached to the third value of the data range,

"Exec Class added," is positioned on the right of the value, and uses a trick to distance itself from the data point: A number of spaces were placed at the beginning of the label to push it even further to the right. Also note that you can use more than one label per data-label range. (If you want to try creating this graph yourself, just change your graph type from Stack-Bar to Line and then define the data-label ranges as described.)

Figure 9.26
Data-label entries

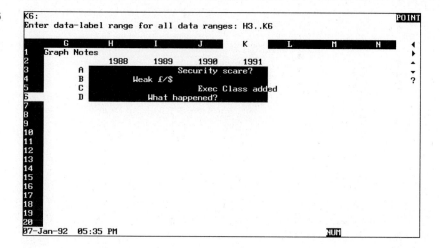

Figure 9.27
Data-label settings

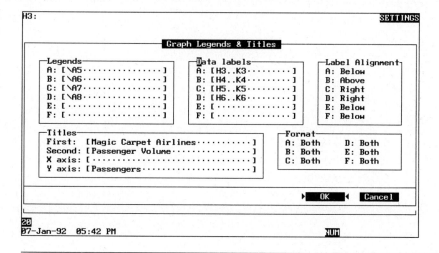

One further trick is to set up a fake data range on a graph, just to position labels. Figure 9.28 displays the worksheet that generates the XY graph in Figure 9.29. The X range for this graph is the set of numbers in column B. (These extend further down the worksheet to 5,900.) Data range A consists of the torque readings in column D. The actual X range is B4..B43 and the A range is D4..D43.

Figure 9.28

The engine power worksheet

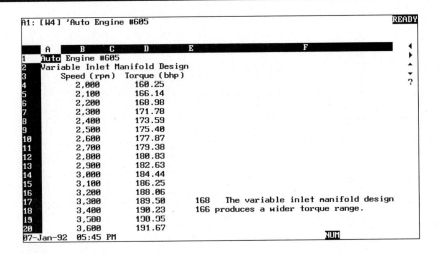

Figure 9.29

Graph with floating text

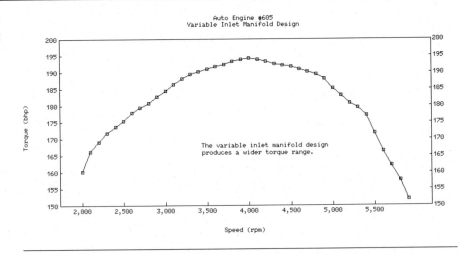

In column E you can see two values, 168 in cell E17 and 166 in cell E18. In fact, the range E4..E43 constitutes data range B. The range F4..F43, which contains two labels adjacent to the values in data range E, forms the data-label range. The result of this arrangement is that 1-2-3 only graphs two values for data range B and places the labels in column F in the spot where those two values appear on the graph. The effect is the appearance of floating text seen below the curve in Figure 9.29.

You may notice that the two values in data range B do not actually show up: There are no symbols or lines. This is achieved with the Format setting described in the next section. This use of a "phantom" data range allows you a measure of creativity when using data labels. Figure 9.30 shows the data-label settings that produce the graph in Figure 9.29.

Figure 9.30

The power curve data-label settings

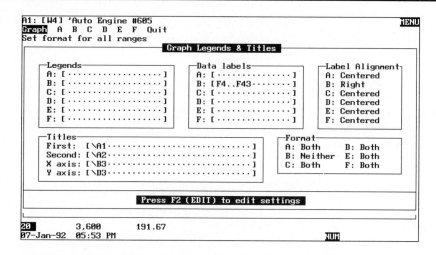

The Format of Line Charts

In a rare example of inconsistent terminology, the Graph Options Format command in 1-2-3 has nothing to do with the appearance of numbers. Instead, it controls the "format" of data points in line and XY graphs. Both of these chart types can represent data points as symbols and draw lines between the points. You can also omit either the symbols, the lines, or both. For example, in Figure 9.29 the values 168 and 166, shown as part of the B range in Figure 9.28, do not actually appear on the chart. However, you cannot alter the choice of symbols used in line and XY charts. These are always as follows:

■ A, the first data range, is represented by a square.

- B, the second data range, is represented by a cross.

- C, the third data range, is represented by a diamond.

- D, the fourth data range, is represented by a triangle.

- E, the fifth data range, is represented by an asterisk.

- F, the sixth data range, is represented by an inverted triangle.

When you select Format from the Graph Options menu you get the choices seen at the top of Figure 9.30. These allow you to set the format for all ranges (Graph) or for each range individually (A through F). Choosing one of these options brings up the following four-item menu:

- The Lines option connects the data points with lines.

- The Symbols option displays a symbol at each data point along the line.

- The Both option displays both lines and symbols (this is the default setting).

- The Neither option displays neither lines nor symbols, hiding the data points on the graph (this option is used to position data labels).

- The Area option draws shading between the lines in a line graph (not used with an XY graph). This produces a graph like the one shown in Figure 9.31.

The format settings are located on the Legends & Titles dialog box.

Figure 9.31

A line graph using the Area option

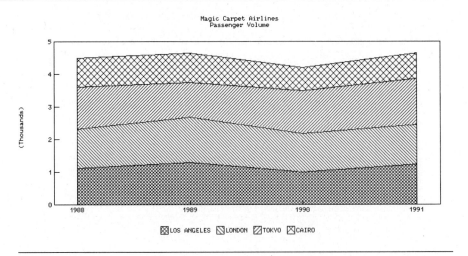

You have seen how the Neither option works, and the default setting, Both, is the one used in Figure 9.1. The Lines option is useful when drawing trend lines where each data point does not need to be emphasized. For example, Figure 9.29 might look better without each data reading marked on the power curve. Figure 9.32 displays Predicted Sales as a line drawn with the Line option. This graph also shows the Symbols option, which plots scattered data points representing Actual Sales without connecting them. Figure 9.32 is an example of an XY graph, described in more detail in the section on XY graphs.

Figure 9.32

An XY graph of
sales plotted
against advertising

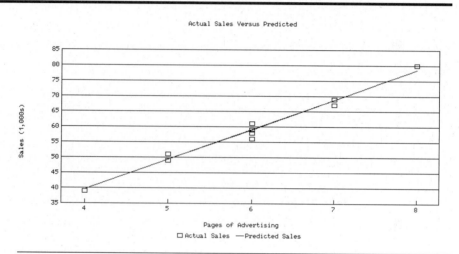

Special Graph Types

This section reviews special settings and commands for HLCO, mixed, XY, and pie charts. It also examines the Features command found on the Type menu, used to further customize graphs.

Using Graph Type Features

Besides the Graph Options menu, you can use the Features option on the Graph Type menu to alter and enhance the appearance of your graphs. Features offers the following possibilities:

- Vertical draws the x-axis across the bottom of the screen, making bars in bar charts appear vertical.

- Horizontal alters the orientation of graphs. It draws the x-axis up the left side of the screen and rotates bars.

- Stacked applies to line, bar, mixed, and XY graphs. It tells 1-2-3 to plot values in data ranges one on top of another.

- Frame allows you to turn on or off the sides of the graph frame and the display of zero lines.

- 3D-Effect works with bar or stacked bar charts to give an impression of depth to the chart.

The possibilities these options provide are best discovered by experimentation. You may well want to use 3D-Effect in most of your bar charts—it adds visual interest, as seen in Figure 9.33.

Figure 9.33

Chart using several Features options

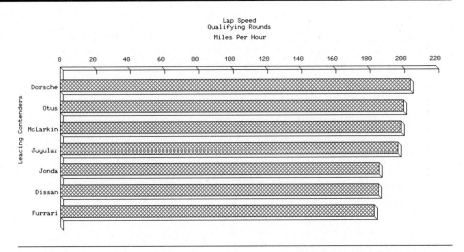

The Horizontal option is useful for adding variety to presentations and is well suited to charts that show rankings and performance, such as the racing car lap speeds shown in Figure 9.33. However, when you use Horizontal, the top of the graph is displayed on the right of the screen, so you must transpose grid and other options accordingly. For example, the grid lines in Figure 9.33 were applied by activating the Vertical option, even though they appear horizontal. Also note that the effect of ranking values from largest to smallest comes from sorting the data range.

The Frame option on the Features menu leads to a submenu with the choices All, Left, Right, Top, Bottom, None, Zero-Line, Margins, and Quit. The first six choices control how many sides of the graph are framed with a line. The default setting is All. The Left, Right, Top, and Bottom options turn off the respective sides of the graph, with None being the choice if you want no lines around the graph. In Figure 9.33, two sides of the graph are turned off. Because the graph is drawn with the Horizontal feature in effect, which rotates the graph, the Right and Top choices on the Frame menu were used. Note that if you use grid lines on a graph, you may not notice that part of the frame is turned off.

The Zero-Line option on the Frame menu controls the drawing of a line at the value of 0 on y-axis scales, and on x-axis scales in XY graphs. This is helpful if negative values are being displayed but may be removed to give a less cluttered look to the graph. The Margins option adjusts graph appearances by adding or removing the margins normally placed on the left and right of the graph. These can be seen in Figure 9.32 between the y-axis lines and the first and last data values. Margins on is the default setting in 1-2-3, but you can turn them off if appropriate.

Creating HLCO Graphs

As mentioned, HLCO (high-low-close-open) is a way of describing prices for commodities or stocks set during a specific time period. The high and low are drawn as a vertical line between the two values. The open is drawn as a horizontal line to the left of the high-low line. The close can be shown as a horizontal line to the right of the high-low line.

To create an HLCO graph like the one shown in Figure 9.34, you select HLCO as the Type and use the following range settings:

A range   High values
B range   Low values
C range   Closing prices
D range   Opening prices
X range   Time period

Note that 1-2-3 will stagger the x-axis labels if there are too many to fit on one line. When you need to graph a large number of time periods, you may not want to use an X range setting to avoid cluttering the graph. Note that in Figure 9.34 the Y-Scale Display Both command was used to label both sides of the chart and the Features Frame Top command was used to remove the line across the top of the chart frame.

Creating a Mixed Graph

You use the Mixed Graph type when you want a graph to show two different types of information. For example, if you graph actual sales as bars you might want to superimpose a line showing projected sales. You can see an example of a mixed chart in Figure 9.35. You do not have to use all of the ranges to create a mixed graph. Figure 9.35 was created by selecting the actual sales as the A range and the projected sales as the D range. The 3D-Effect option was used and the margins were turned off, allowing 1-2-3 to place the first and last bars against the graph frame.

Figure 9.34

A HLCO graph

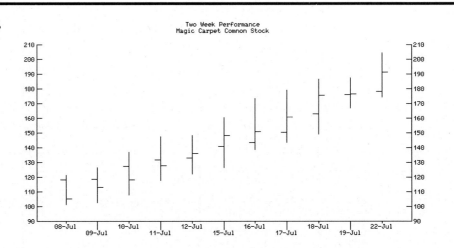

Figure 9.35

A mixed graph using 3D-Effect

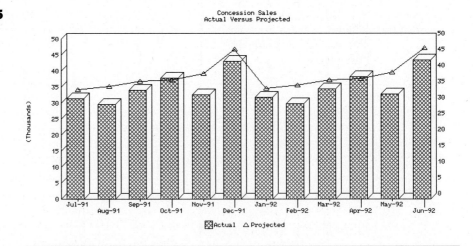

XY Graphs

The power curve shown earlier in Figure 9.29 doesn't use all of the power of the XY graph. The XY graph accepts numerical data for the X range and does not require that the data be sorted numerically. For example, consider the values listed in the worksheet in Figure 9.36. These show how many pages of advertising copy a company purchased, per month, for one year. The actual sales figures for each month are listed, along with the predicted sales.

You could use this worksheet to draw a line chart of sales by month over the year. You would set the months as the X range. The actual sales could be the A range, and predicted sales could be the B range. Suppose, however, that you wanted to graph the correlation between ad pages and sales—that is, you wanted to graph actual and predicted sales against ad pages. This would mean using the ad pages as the x-axis. In fact, this is how the XY graph in Figure 9.32 was created. The distance between each of the sales figures and the y-axis is based on value, not the order in which they appear in the X range. Thus the coordinates of the January figure of 39 for actual sales could be described as 4,39, while the February figure is plotted at 5,51.

Figure 9.36
Worksheet for sales plotted against advertising

```
A1:  'Ad Pages Versus Sales ( in 1,000s )                          READY

         A         B         C         D        E      F      G    ◄
1    Ad Pages Versus Sales ( in 1,000s )                            ►
2                                                                   ▲
3                Actual    Actual    Predicted                      ▼
4    Month:      Pages:    91 Sales: 91 Sales:                      ?
5    Jan-91         4         39         40
6    Feb-91         5         51         49
7    Mar-91         6         58         59
8    Apr-91         5         51         49
9    May-91         6         61         59
10   Jun-91         7         67         69
11   Jul-91         5         49         49
12   Aug-91         6         59         59
13   Sep-91         5         49         49
14   Oct-91         6         56         59
15   Nov-91         7         69         69
16   Dec-91         8         80         78
17
18
19
20
10-Jan-92   11:20 AM                                    NUM
```

In Figure 9.32, the actual sales are displayed with the Symbols option so that no line is drawn between them. The predicted sales are drawn with the Lines options so that no data points appear, just the lines connecting them. Note that this line is straight because the prediction of sales is based on regression analysis, a specialized area of statistics that is covered in Chapter 11. One conclusion that you can draw from Figure 9.32 is that the predicted sales closely match the actual sales, indicating that the method of prediction was very accurate.

Dressing Up Pie Charts

Pie charts differ from the other 1-2-3 graph types in that they are one-dimensional. They show a collection of values as portions of the whole.

The sample worksheet seen earlier in Figure 9.18 included volume figures for an airline flying to four destinations. Suppose that you want to show how much each destination contributed to the total volume in 1990. If you have already charted numbers from the same worksheet, you might begin by naming any existing graph and then saving the worksheet. This would allow you to safely employ the Graph Reset command to clear any previous range and option settings that might not be appropriate to a pie chart.

Then you would change the Graph Type to Pie and select D5..D8 as the A range. The resulting pie chart will look like the one in Figure 9.37, which is bland and quite uninformative. The pie slices show the percentages of the whole that each slice represents, beginning with Paris at the 12 o'clock position, but there is nothing to tell the viewer which slice is which. In addition, all of the slices are unshaded.

Figure 9.37

Basic pie chart

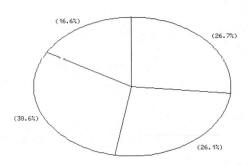

```
Magic Carpet Airlines
1990 Volume By City
```

To remedy these problems, you can add a first and second title line (x-axis and y-axis titles do not appear on a pie chart). To identify the values on the graph, set an X range that contains labels for each of the slices. In this case, you could use A5..A8 of the sample worksheet.

To distinguish the pie slices better, you can add shading to them. You do this by setting a second data range (Graph B) in which you place numbers that invoke different shading. While 0 represents no shading, 1 assigns shading 1, 2 assigns shading 2, and so on. In Figure 9.38, Los Angeles has shading 0, while London is 1, Tokyo is 2, and Cairo is 3. The worksheet entries that do this can be seen in Figure 9.39.

Note that the third entry is not simply 2, but 102. Adding 100 to the entry tells 1-2-3 to *explode* the corresponding slice, which is how the slice representing Tokyo was set apart from the others, in Figure 9.38.

Figure 9.38

Pie chart with shading and exploded slice

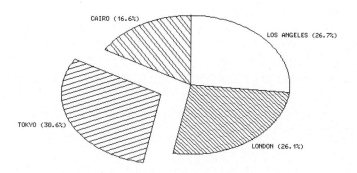

Figure 9.39

Setting a second data range for pie shading

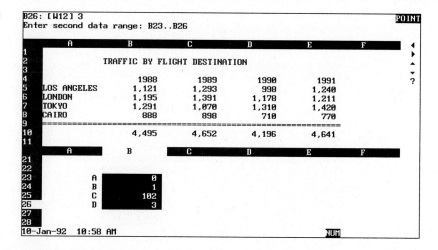

Printing Graphs

Since you need a high level of control over hardware to print a detailed graphic image, you also need complex software. In Release 2.3, Lotus does not include this software in the main 1-2-3 program so that it can run within a modest amount of RAM. Instead, graph printing capabilities are provided by two supplemental programs supplied with Release 2.3: PrintGraph and Wysiwyg. The Wysiwyg add-in is described in detail in the next chapter. PrintGraph, the older of the two programs, has changed little since the days of 1-2-3 Release 1A.

This section explains how to save your graphs in PIC files and print them with PrintGraph. You will learn how to apply fonts and colors, and how to size and position your graphs on the printed page. You will also learn how to preview your graphs with PrintGraph so that you can see what they will look like before you print them.

Graph Save

If you want to print graphs with PrintGraph, you must create a PIC file of the graph. To do this, first set up the graph exactly as you want it, and then select Save from the Graph menu. 1-2-3 shows you a list of existing PIC files in the current data directory. This file listing is just like the one for File Save but the file specification is *.pic. Next, you type a suitable name for the file or select one from the list to overwrite a previous file. When you press Enter to complete the command, the file is stored with the .PIC extension. You can then use PrintGraph to print the file. There is also other graphics software that can read files in the PIC format. (If you have been following the examples in this chapter, issue the Graph Save command now so you can experiment with Print Graph. Assign any name you like to the PIC files.)

Using PrintGraph

To print a graph with PrintGraph, first exit 1-2-3. If you have loaded 1-2-3 from the 1-2-3 Access System, you can select PrintGraph from the system menu. Otherwise, if you are at the DOS prompt in the 1-2-3 program directory, you can enter **PGRAPH** to load the program. When the program has loaded, you will see the menu shown in Figure 9.40. The area below the double line is a collection of settings that indicate how 1-2-3 will be printing your graphs.

There are six options on the main PrintGraph menu. You use the first, Image-Select, to select the PIC files you want to print. You can choose more than one file at a time, which enables you to print a batch of graphs one after another. Graphs you choose with Image-Select are then listed under the heading GRAPHS TO PRINT on the left of the screen. The Settings option allows you to adjust three areas—Image, Hardware, and Action—the current settings for which are described below the menu. Note that the settings shown in Figure 9.40 are the defaults when you first install the program.

The Go, Align, and Page options correspond to their namesakes on the 1-2-3 Print menu. The Go option tells PrintGraph to start printing. The Align option tells 1-2-3 that it is printing at the top of the page. The Page option tells 1-2-3 to advance to the next page. You use the Exit command to leave PrintGraph.

Figure 9.40
The PrintGraph
menu and initial
settings

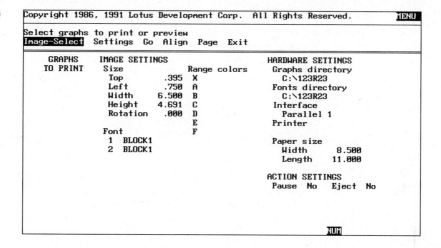

```
                                                                    MENU
Select graphs to print or preview
Image-Select  Settings  Go  Align  Page  Exit

     GRAPHS     IMAGE SETTINGS                  HARDWARE SETTINGS
     TO PRINT   Size                Range colors  Graphs directory
                  Top       .395    X               C:\123R23
                  Left      .750    A             Fonts directory
                  Width    6.500    B               C:\123R23
                  Height   4.691    C             Interface
                  Rotation  .000    D               Parallel 1
                                    E             Printer
                Font                F
                1  BLOCK1
                2  BLOCK1                         Paper size
                                                    Width      8.500
                                                    Length    11.000

                                                ACTION SETTINGS
                                                  Pause  No   Eject  No




                                                           NUM
```

The PrintGraph Settings

The first time you use PrintGraph, you may need to adjust the settings, particularly those for Hardware, before you can print anything. When you select Settings from the main PrintGraph menu, you get these options:

- The Image option defines graph settings (font, color, size).

- The Hardware option defines the printer and directories for fonts and graph files.

- The Action option controls printer actions (ejecting paper, pausing between graphs).

- The Save option saves PrintGraph settings in a special configuration file.

- The Reset option restores the PrintGraph settings from the configuration file.

- The Quit option returns you to the main PrintGraph menu.

Whenever you start PrintGraph, the program reads settings stored in a configuration file called PGRAPH.CNF. You can change these settings during a PrintGraph session. If you need to use the new settings in a future session, you must store them in the PGRAPH.CNF file by using the Settings Save command before exiting PrintGraph. This is equivalent to the Worksheet Global Default Update command in the main 1-2-3 program. If you change some settings and then decide to restore the original settings, you can use Settings Reset. In Figure 9.41 you can see the Settings menu and a typical collection of settings.

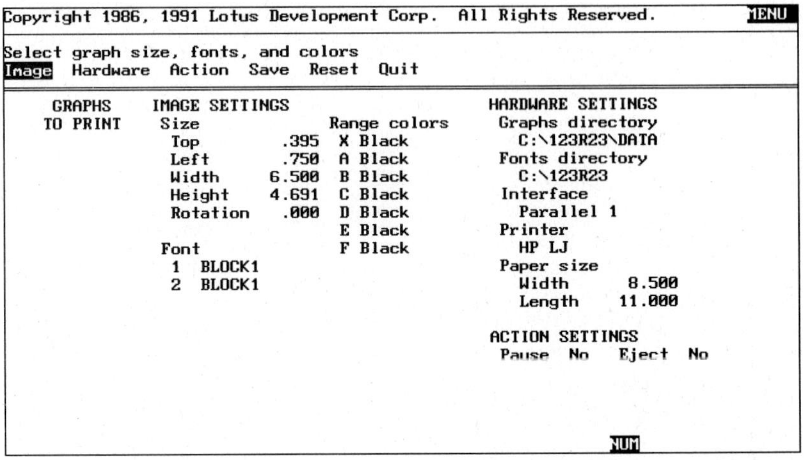

Figure 9.41

Typical PrintGraph
settings

```
Copyright 1986, 1991 Lotus Development Corp.  All Rights Reserved.        MENU

Select graph size, fonts, and colors
Image  Hardware  Action  Save  Reset  Quit

   GRAPHS     IMAGE SETTINGS                       HARDWARE SETTINGS
   TO PRINT   Size                 Range colors    Graphs directory
              Top         .395     X Black            C:\123R23\DATA
              Left        .750     A Black          Fonts directory
              Width      6.500     B Black            C:\123R23
              Height     4.691     C Black          Interface
              Rotation    .000     D Black            Parallel 1
                                   E Black          Printer
              Font                 F Black            HP LJ
              1   BLOCK1                            Paper size
              2   BLOCK1                              Width     8.500
                                                      Length   11.000

                                                    ACTION SETTINGS
                                                    Pause  No   Eject  No



                                                 NUM
```

The Hardware Setup

The Settings Hardware option defines your printer model, specifies the correct graph and font directories, and selects the printer interface and paper size. Of particular importance are the directory settings, because when 1-2-3 is first installed the directory setting for PrintGraph is the program directory, which is only correct if you are using the program directory to store PIC files.

Graphs-Directory   The Graphs-Directory setting specifies the drive and directory that contain the graph (PIC) files you want to print—for example, C:\123\DATA. When you use the Image-Select option to indicate which graphs you want to print, PrintGraph lists the graph files in the directory you specify. If you have stored PIC files in several directories, you can select the most commonly used directory, or the root directory. If you select the root directory, the Image-Select prompt will list all subdirectories and you can then choose the directory you want to print from.

Fonts-Directory   The Fonts-Directory setting specifies the directory that contains the font (FNT) files used to print PIC files. Before printing or displaying a graph, PrintGraph looks for the fonts in the fonts directory you specify here. Enter the name of the directory, including the drive, that contains the PrintGraph fonts. Typically, this is the 1-2-3 program directory and is already set correctly.

Interface   The Interface setting defines the interface used by your graphics printer, either parallel or serial. You must choose the proper interface before PrintGraph can communicate with your printer. When you select Interface, 1-2-3 offers the following options.

- 1 represents parallel (the interface used by most printers, also known as LPT1). This is the initial default setting.

- 2 stands for serial (the interface sometimes used by plotters, known as COM1).

- 3 is second parallel (a second parallel port, known as LPT2).

- 4 represents second serial (a second serial port, known as COM2).

- 5–8 represent remote devices (called DOS Device LPT1 through LPT4). These are used when printing on a network, as described in Appendix B.

If you select a serial printer (choice 2 or 4), you must also indicate the speed at which it receives data. This is known as the *baud rate* and the choices are:

```
1:110      2:150      3:300      4:600      5:1200
6:2400     7:4800     8:9600     9:19200
```

Check your printer/plotter control panel and manual to find out the correct baud setting.

Printer   The Printer setting identifies the model of printer or plotter to use. When you select this option, PrintGraph displays the names of the printers you chose when you used the Install program. Some printer models appear more than once because PrintGraph can operate them in different modes. For example, an Epson FX can print graphs in either low-density or high-density mode. High-density mode produces a more detailed image but takes longer. Low-density mode is faster but results in a less detailed image. Thus, you might want to check this setting even if you only chose one make and model of graphics printer when you installed 1-2-3.

Bear in mind that this setting displays the printers you chose with the Graphics Printer option in the Install program. Text printers will not be listed. If you need to select a graphics printer, exit PrintGraph, run Install, and use Graphic Printer to select the appropriate model. Then return to PrintGraph and select the model with the Settings Hardware Printer command. Note that PrintGraph does not work with all of the printers that you can use with Wysiwyg. Since the Graph Printer option in Install actually installs printers for both PrintGraph and Wysiwyg, you may have chosen a printer in Install that does not get listed by PrintGraph. Most notably, PrintGraph does not work with PostScript printers such as the Apple LaserWriter. To print graphs on such printers, use the Wysiwyg feature described in the next chapter.

A typical list of printers produced by the Settings Hardware Printer command appears in Figure 9.42. The current printer has a # symbol to the left of its name. To select a printer from the list, highlight its name and press the spacebar. The # symbol appears next to your selection. You can select only one printer at a time.

In Figure 9.42, the current printer is the Epson FX in high-density mode. However, the highlighting is currently on the HP 7470A plotter entry. If you pressed Enter at this point, the Epson would remain the current printer. However, if you pressed the spacebar, the # symbol would move from the Epson to the highlighted HP. If you then pressed Enter, the HP would become the current printer. Pressing Esc will return you to the Settings menu, leaving Epson as the current printer selection.

Figure 9.42

Selecting the printer

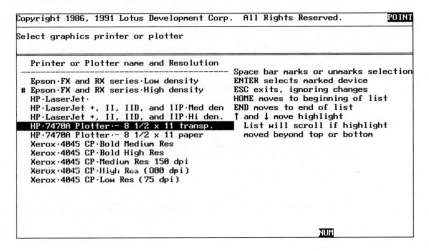

Also note that the HP 7470A appears twice in the list. This is because 1-2-3 operates it differently when printing on transparencies rather than paper. If you are using an HP laser printer with only 512k of printer memory, you will only be able to print half-page graphs in the high-density mode. (Fortunately this is the default graph size setting.)

Size-Paper The Size-Paper setting specifies the default page size for your graphs. You can set length and width. The choices are made in inches, and the initial default settings are 11 for the length and 8.5 for the width.

The Image Settings The Image Settings command controls the following three areas of graph printing:

■ The Size option controls the size of the graph on the page, including height, width, and angle of rotation.

- The Font option chooses fonts for printing the text in the graph.

- The Range-Colors option assigns colors to graph data ranges if you have a color printer or plotter.

Image Size   The Size option on the Image menu determines the size and proportion of the printed graph. There are three options: Full, Half, and Manual.

- The Full option sizes the graph so that it fills as much of an 8½-by-11-inch page as possible. The graph is rotated 90 degrees so that it appears sideways on the page—in other words, with the x-axis aligned with the direction of printing. This is sometimes referred to as *landscape mode*.

- The Half option tells PrintGraph to fill approximately half of an 8½-by-11-inch page with the graph. The x-axis is thus perpendicular to the direction of printing. This is sometimes referred to as *portrait mode*.

- The Manual option allows you to set the dimensions of the graph yourself using five different parameters, all of which are measured in inches except for the rotation:

  - Left represents the distance between the left edge of the paper and the left margin.

  - Top represents the distance between the top edge of the paper and the top margin.

  - Width represents the width of the graph, measured from the left margin.

  - Height stands for the height of the graph, measured from the top margin.

  - Rotation is the rotation of the x-axis from the horizontal, measured in degrees, so that a setting of 90 degrees results in landscape mode.

The width, height, and rotation that you choose affect the proportions of the printed graph. Figure 9.43 displays a graph printed with a large width setting but a small height setting. The effect is a flatter-looking curve than a taller graph of the same data.

Image Font   The Font option on the Image menu selects the fonts or typefaces used for text in the graph. When you view graphs in the main 1-2-3 program, a standard sans serif font is used for all of the text. However, when you print a graph, you can use any of the following fonts:

Font Name	Size of Font (in bytes)
BLOCK1	5732
BLOCK2	9273

Font Name	Size of Font (in bytes)
BOLD	8684
FORUM	9767
ITALIC1	8974
ITALIC2	11865
LOTUS	8686
ROMAN1	6843
ROMAN2	11615
SCRIPT1	8064
SCRIPT2	10367

Note that the fonts numbered 2 are simply bold versions of the fonts numbered 1. The graph in Figure 9.43 was printed with the first line of the title in Roman2 and the rest of the text in Block2.

Figure 9.43

Wide low graph

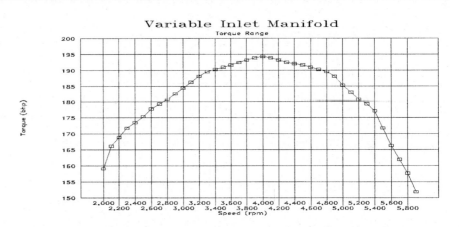

PrintGraph lets you choose two different fonts within the same graph. Font 1 is for the first line of the graph title while Font 2 is for the rest of the text in the graph. (This numbering is not connected with the numbering of the font names.) If you want the same font for all the text on the graph, select only Font 1 and then choose a font from the list that PrintGraph displays. This will appear in both the Font 1 and Font 2 slots in the settings area unless you have previously selected and saved a different font for Font 2. If you want a different typeface for Font 2, select Font 2 and make your choice. It will appear in the settings area. Note that the font is not in any way attached to the graph files you are printing. All graphs that you print will use the current font setting.

Image Range-Colors   The Range-Colors option on the Image menu assigns colors to the graph data ranges. The colors PrintGraph displays for you to choose from will depend on your printer. If you do not have a color printer, black is your only choice. First select a range (X, A through F) and then select a color to assign to that range. At this point you can choose another range or select Quit to return to the Image menu.

Selecting Images   When you choose Image-Select, PrintGraph looks for graph (PIC) files in the graph directory you specify with Settings Hardware. You can change the directory by editing the prompt, as with the File Retrieve prompt. A vertical list of files in the directory is presented, as shown in Figure 9.44.

Figure 9.44
Selecting images

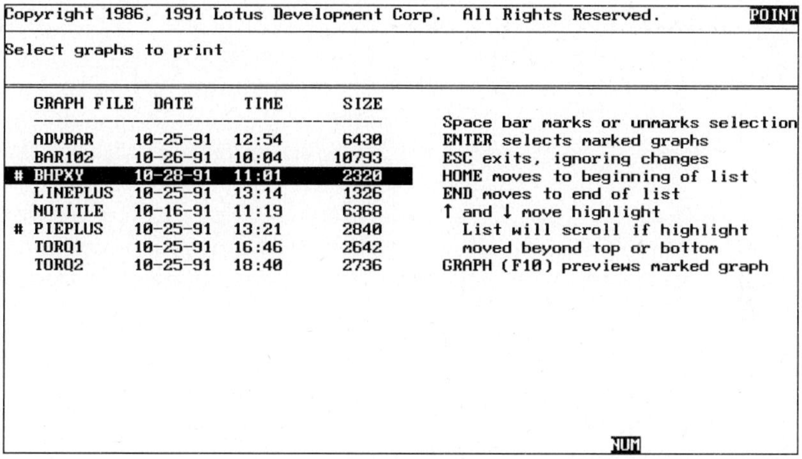

```
Copyright 1986, 1991 Lotus Development Corp.  All Rights Reserved.      POINT

Select graphs to print


   GRAPH FILE  DATE      TIME      SIZE
   --------------------------------------      Space bar marks or unmarks selection
     ADVBAR    10-25-91  12:54     6430         ENTER selects marked graphs
     BAR102    10-26-91  10:04    10793         ESC exits, ignoring changes
   # BHPXY     10-28-91  11:01     2320         HOME moves to beginning of list
     LINEPLUS  10-25-91  13:14     1326         END moves to end of list
     NOTITLE   10-16-91  11:19     6368         ↑ and ↓ move highlight
   # PIEPLUS   10-25-91  13:21     2840           List will scroll if highlight
     TORQ1     10-25-91  16:46     2642           moved beyond top or bottom
     TORQ2     10-25-91  18:40     2736         GRAPH (F10) previews marked graph







                                                               NUM
```

You can move the highlight bar through the list of graph files and press the spacebar to indicate that you want to print the highlighted graph. Print-Graph then places a # symbol next to the graph. You can choose more than one graph from the list and PrintGraph will print them all at once. To cancel selection of a graph, highlight its name and press the spacebar; the # symbol disappears. When you have finished selecting, press Enter. To print the graph or graphs you have selected, you use the Align and Go commands, which are described in the next section.

You can also use Image-Select to view graphs on the screen. Highlight the graph file name and press Graph (F10). The graph appears with the current font setting. This allows you to check that you have the right graph. Note that this view is not exactly WYSIWYG (what you see is what you get). The size and proportions of the graph will not necessarily be accurate.

Ready to Print

When you have made all of your choices for the settings and selected the images you want to print, you can choose Align from the main PrintGraph menu and then select Go. The Align command tells PrintGraph to start printing at the top of the page. If the graph stays in the printer when the printing is complete, you can use the Page command to eject the page. If you always want the graph ejected after printing, you can change the Action Eject setting to Yes. You shouldn't do this if you want to print more than one graph on a page, in which case you print the second graph without issuing the Align or Page command. If you are printing a batch of graphs, the Action Eject setting becomes quite important. You should set it to Yes if you want each graph on a separate page. Set Eject to No if you want PrintGraph to print as many graphs as possible on each page.

The actual printing process may take quite a while. First 1-2-3 loads the image and font files, then it processes them, and finally it sends the combined data to the printer. Some printers take a long time to print, particularly in high-density mode. You may want to print a sample using your printer's low-density mode before printing a large batch of graphs. The Ctrl-Break key will cancel graph printing. If you are printing with a plotter, you may be asked to insert certain pens into the machine during the printing process. Note that when you are printing on a system that requires you to load each sheet of paper by hand, you should select Yes for the Action Pause setting. You will then be prompted by PrintGraph to insert fresh paper as required.

Summary

In this chapter, you learned how to construct a variety of different graphs with 1-2-3. You saw how these graphs can be customized with a whole range of options before being saved as image files for later output with the PrintGraph program. Using the Graph Name commands, you learned how to manage many different graphs associated with the same worksheet. In the next chapter, you will read about how to use the Wysiwyg add-in to customize graphs further and print them along with worksheet cells for professional-looking spreadsheet reports. Indeed, you may find it more convenient to use Wysiwyg for all of your graph printing, rather than exiting from 1-2-3 to use PrintGraph.

CHAPTER

10

Spreadsheet Publishing with Wysiwyg

I N CHAPTER 6, YOU LEARNED HOW TO USE THE STANDARD PRINT COMMAND to produce printed reports of spreadsheet data. Chapter 9 explained how to use the Graph commands to chart spreadsheet data, which you can then print with the PrintGraph program. Chapter 7 discussed how add-in programs supply added features to 1-2-3, and how the Wysiwyg add-in can be used to customize the 1-2-3 display. This chapter describes how to use the Wysiwyg add-in to improve the appearance of your reports and graphs, both on screen and in print. This area of *spreadsheet publishing* will help you create presentation quality output from data stored in 1-2-3 work-sheets. You can see an example of this in Figure 10.1.

Wysiwyg: The Means to Get What You See

As you know by now, Wysiwyg is an acronym for "what-you-see-is-what-you-get," meaning that documents appear on the screen in a format that very closely resembles the printed output. This is a relatively recent concept in computing. The first word processing programs on the IBM PC displayed only the words in documents—not the margins, not the spacing, and certainly not the typeface that the printer was using. Because the best quality printers at that time used a fixed set of characters to print documents, and the monitors used a fixed set of characters to display them, it was possible to coordinate display and printout in simple documents, if not match them exactly. However, there were often surprises when a letter emerged from the printer, such as unwanted gaps between words, or columns that were not properly aligned.

The problem was worse when it came to printing spreadsheets. Even though the spreadsheet data is arranged in strict columns and rows, it often does not match the space available on a piece of paper. As you saw in Chapter 6, printing reports from 1-2-3 with the regular Print command requires a working knowledge of characters and lines per inch, and often involves trial and error to get the right data in the right place on the page.

Furthermore, the regular Print command makes little allowance for the increasingly sophisticated capabilities of printers, many of which can now create a variety of typefaces or fonts, in a variety of styles and sizes, as well as lines, shading, and pictures. Earlier versions of 1-2-3 provided limited support for printer features by allowing you to enter setup strings either through the Option Setup command or in cells in the worksheet. However, there was no visual feedback on screen; you had to print the spreadsheet to the setup strings' effects.

The Wysiwyg add-in changes all this, letting you use sophisticated graphic features such as fonts, shading, and drawing tools to enhance your documents. It also lets you print graphs and pictures as part of your spread-sheets. Best of all, it lets you view your documents on screen exactly as they

Figure 10.1
Report created with
Wysiwyg

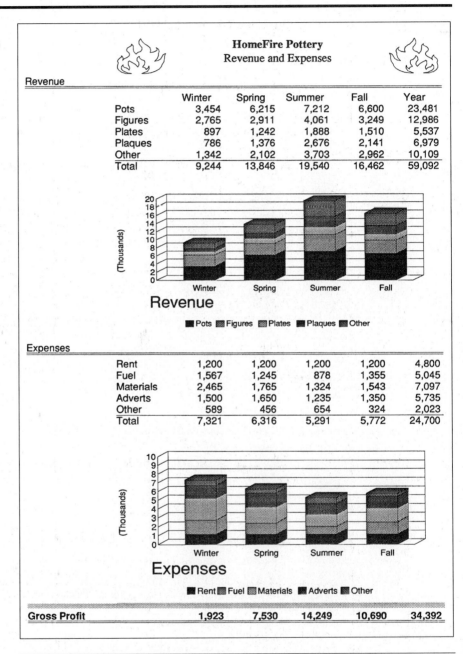

HomeFire Pottery
Revenue and Expenses

Revenue

	Winter	Spring	Summer	Fall	Year
Pots	3,454	6,215	7,212	6,600	23,481
Figures	2,765	2,911	4,061	3,249	12,986
Plates	897	1,242	1,888	1,510	5,537
Plaques	786	1,376	2,676	2,141	6,979
Other	1,342	2,102	3,703	2,962	10,109
Total	9,244	13,846	19,540	16,462	59,092

Expenses

	Winter	Spring	Summer	Fall	Year
Rent	1,200	1,200	1,200	1,200	4,800
Fuel	1,567	1,245	878	1,355	5,045
Materials	2,465	1,765	1,324	1,543	7,097
Adverts	1,500	1,650	1,235	1,350	5,735
Other	589	456	654	324	2,023
Total	7,321	6,316	5,291	5,772	24,700

| **Gross Profit** | 1,923 | 7,530 | 14,249 | 10,690 | 34,392 |

will appear when printed. As you can see in Figure 10.1, the results can be quite impressive.

How Wysiwyg Works with 1-2-3

The 1-2-3 program emerged before publishing and presentation technology. Many users have been happy to stay with the familiar 1-2-3 menu system. However, the number of new commands required for spreadsheet publishing would not fit into the regular menu system. What is more, the size of program required to execute these commands would exceed the limits of many computers running earlier versions of 1-2-3. Storing all of the extra instructions about fonts and graphics would require a major change to the WK1 file format widely used for information exchange. For this reason, Wysiwyg is a separate program, and loading it is optional. The Wysiwyg menu, shown in Figure 10.2, works just like the 1-2-3 menu (you press : instead of / to get the Wysiwyg menu), but the mode indicator is WYSIWYG.

Figure 10.2

The Wysiwyg menu

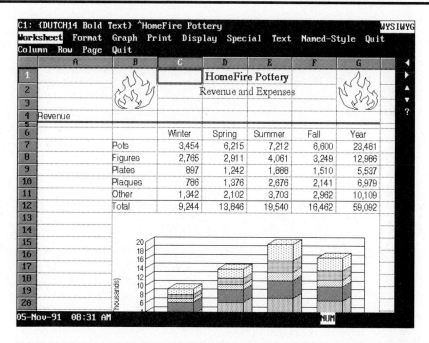

Note that the Wysiwyg menu includes several options that also appear on the main 1-2-3 menu, including Worksheet, Graph, and Print. These options work differently in Wysiwyg than they do in 1-2-3. For example, the

Wysiwyg :Print command (the colon is used to distinguish Wysiwyg commands from regular 1-2-3 commands with the same name) is used to print areas of the worksheet together with their Wysiwyg formatting. You can still perform a regular print from the same worksheet, but the :Print command is much more powerful and includes a preview feature to show you exactly how each page will look when printed.

Wysiwyg does not alter the data within the 1-2-3 files. The formatting information used by Wysiwyg to display and print enhanced worksheets is stored in a separate file with the extension .FMT. For example, if you use Wysiwyg to enhance a worksheet called SALES.WK1, a file called SALES.FMT is automatically created to store the Wysiwyg formatting information.

The following information is saved in the Wysiwyg format file:

- All Wysiwyg formats set with the Format, Graph, Named-Style, and Text commands.

- The font set for the corresponding worksheet file.

- The eight named styles for the corresponding worksheet file.

- The Wysiwyg print range (set with :Print Range Set).

- The Print Layout settings and the settings for printing the worksheet frame and grid (set with :Print Settings Frame and :Print Settings Grid).

- The colors for negative values, lines, and drop shadows (set with :Display Colors Neg, :Display Colors Lines, and :Display Colors Shadow).

- Row heights (set with :Worksheet Row).

- Page breaks (set with :Worksheet Page).

Remember to save your work whenever you make formatting changes that you want to preserve, even if you did not change the data in the worksheet. The formatting changes you make with the Wysiwyg commands do not become permanent until you save the worksheet file. If you end 1-2-3 without saving the worksheet file, any changes you made with Wysiwyg commands (as well as changes you made to the worksheet itself) will be lost.

Each cell affected by Wysiwyg formatting is given a formatting code. This code is not apparent when working without Wysiwyg, but when Wysiwyg is loaded, the code appears, as shown in Figure 10.2, where cell C1 contains the following:

```
{DUTCH14 Bold Text} ^HomeFire Pottery
```

The code is placed in curly braces. What appears after the code are the contents of cell C1, in this case the label HomeFire Pottery. The code itself contains three elements. DUTCH14 is the font, and Bold is the style. Text indicates that C1 is part of a text range, a special Wysiwyg feature that allows text to be justified within a range of cells. In this case, C1..F2 was made a text range, allowing the two lines of the title to be centered within that range. There will be more about format codes as the Wysiwyg commands are examined in greater detail.

Accessing Wysiwyg

To gain access to the Wysiwyg commands, you have to attach the WYSIWYG-.ADN file to 1-2-3, by using the Add-In Attach command described in Chapter 7. Alternatively, you can make Wysiwyg permanently available by using the Worksheet Global Default command (Other Add-In). Once the WYSIWYG-.ADN file is attached, you can activate the Wysiwyg menu by typing a colon (:) or by moving the mouse pointer into the top area of the screen. If the regular 1-2-3 menu appears, click the right menu button to display the Wysiwyg menu.

Learning the Wysiwyg Commands

The rest of this chapter is devoted to a review of the Wysiwyg commands. You will learn how they work and see what they do. Since Wysiwyg allows you to be more creative in designing your spreadsheets and reports, the emphasis is on explaining how Wysiwyg works rather than telling you how to perform a specific series of actions. Much of the power of Wysiwyg comes from creating just the right mix of elements. Once you are familiar with the commands, you will be able to combine them in ways that are effective for your type of work.

The Wysiwyg Worksheet and Format Commands

Using the :Worksheet and :Format commands, you can control much of the layout and style of your reports. The three :Worksheet commands—Column, Row, and Page—let you control row height, column width, and page breaks. The :Format commands let you format worksheet entries in different fonts, colors, and styles. They also let you add horizontal and vertical lines, outlines, and shading to the worksheet. There are eight fonts and eight colors. The available styles are bold, italics, and underlining.

:Worksheet Column

The :Worksheet Column command duplicates the regular Worksheet Column Column-Range command, allowing you to set or reset the widths of several columns at once. When you start working with Wysiwyg fonts, you will need to make minor adjustments to columns because the default Wysiwyg font is proportional, with each letter having a different width. In contrast, the regular 1-2-3 screen font is monospaced. With a monospaced font, you always know how many characters will fit in a given column width—for example, nine characters when the column width setting is 9. With a proportional font, you may get more or less than nine characters in the cell. If you want to use a monospaced font in Wysiwyg, use Courier.

In Wysiwyg mode, you can see the effect of applying a different font and adjust the column widths accordingly. Having the :Worksheet Column command saves switching back to the regular 1-2-3 menu. Because you can have many fonts in a worksheet and the character widths vary with different fonts, 1-2-3 uses a standard measure for the width of a character when setting column widths: One character equals one tenth of an inch. In other words, a 10-character-wide column will be exactly 1 inch wide, regardless of the fonts it contains.

:Worksheet Row

You use the :Worksheet Row command to adjust the height of rows. The row height is measured in points and may need to be adjusted when you are working with Wysiwyg fonts. Every worksheet has a default font, known as font 1, which determines the appearance of characters in the worksheet that are not specifically formatted with the :Format Font command. When you first install Wysiwyg, the default font is Swiss 12 point, meaning a typeface known as Swiss and a size of 12 *points*, or 12 times $1/72$ of an inch. This is the font in which the revenue figures in Figure 10.2 are displayed.

The default font determines the starting height of rows in the worksheet. If the default font is 12 points, the row height will be 14 points. A row height 2 points greater than the actual font gives about the right amount of space for the characters to be displayed and printed clearly. If you apply a font larger than the default, Wysiwyg automatically increases the height of the row to make room for the larger font. If you look carefully at the first two rows in Figure 10.2, you can see that they are slightly higher than rows 6 through 12. This is because of the 14-point fonts used for the two lines of title text.

If you format a cell with a font that is smaller than the default, Wysiwyg does not automatically reduce the row height. Wysiwyg always makes the row height appropriate to the largest font in the row, or the default font, whichever is larger. If all of the entries on a row are in a small font and you want to reduce the row height, you can use the :Worksheet Row Set-Height command, which allows you to set the height for a number of rows at once.

You set the height by using the Up Arrow or Down Arrow key, which alters the height one point at a time, or by entering the desired number of points. The row height will change on the screen. You can use the :Worksheet

Row Auto command to return control of row heights to Wysiwyg. All cells in a row with a fixed height will have a format code of H followed by the number of points, as in {H9} for a row height of 9 points.

The Row command has other uses. For example, it allows you to fine-tune the amount of vertical space between items in a worksheet. For example, the height of rows 51 and 52 in Figure 10.3 was substantially reduced to bring the numbers in row 53 closer to the graph above them. Altering the row height is effective when you have added shading to a row. You can reduce row height to create narrow bands of shading, like the one in row 52 at the bottom of Figure 10.3. Bear in mind that if you manually set the row height too low for the characters in a row, they will appear on screen and in the printout with the tops cut off.

Figure 10.3

Varying row heights

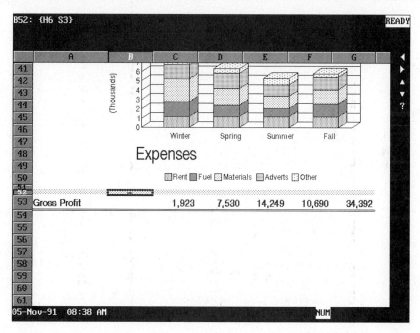

Note that in Figure 10.3 the grid has been turned off with the Display Options Grid command. This makes it easier to see some Wysiwyg features such as lines and shading.

The :Worksheet Page command allows you to add and remove both horizontal and vertical page breaks anywhere in your worksheets (Wysiwyg ignores the horizontal page breaks created by the regular Worksheet Page command). When you set a print range with Wysiwyg, a set of dashed lines appears on screen to show you where the soft page breaks will fall. You can then use :Worksheet Page to add hard page breaks.

Figure 10.4 shows the lower portion of the report in Figure 10.1. The vertical line of dashes is the automatically inserted vertical page break, the horizontal line of dashes is the horizontal page break. Cells immediately below and to the left of page break lines carry the format code {Page}.

Figure 10.4

Vertical and horizontal page breaks

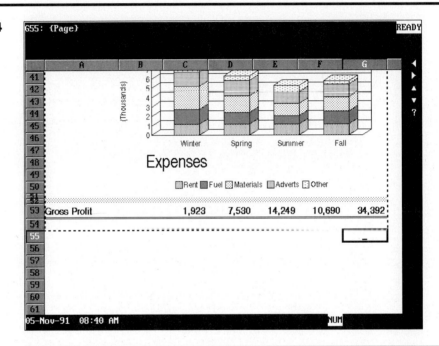

The :Worksheet Page Row command inserts a horizontal page break above the current row. The :Worksheet Page Column command inserts a vertical page break to the left of the current column. Manually inserted page breaks create a format code of {MPage} and are shown by a line with longer dashes than those used to indicate soft page breaks.

The :Worksheet Page Delete command deletes any manually inserted page breaks above and/or to the left of the cell pointer. Note that if you set a Wysiwyg print range that is smaller than one page, the page break lines will appear as a box around the print range.

:Format Font

The appearance of individual letters and numbers is determined by their font, size, and style. Wysiwyg provides you with a collection of fonts, including Swiss, Dutch, Courier, and Xsymbol in a variety of sizes from 3 to 24 points. Figure 10.5 shows examples of these fonts. Note that the Xsymbol font is used to provide arrows and other special characters instead of regular letters.

Figure 10.5

Wysiwyg fonts

Wysiwyg Fonts
Bitstream Swiss 12 point : 1-2-3 and Wysiwyg
Bitstream Swiss 14 point : 1-2-3 and Wysiwyg
Bitstream Swiss 24 point : 1-2-3 and Wysiwyg
Bitstream Dutch 6 point : 1-2-3 and Wysiwyg
Bitstream Dutch 8 point : 1-2-3 and Wysiwyg
Bitstream Dutch 10 point : 1-2-3 and Wysiwyg
Bitstream Dutch 12 point : 1-2-3 and Wysiwyg
Xsymbol 12 point : ⑥②⑦② ➡⇨➤ ↕↗↘➡⇨↙↗↑
(printed from Wysiwyg on a laser printer)

You can have up to eight different font/size combinations in one worksheet. Thus you might choose Swiss 10, 12, 14, and 24 point together with Dutch 10, 12, 14, and 24 point. You can create a variety of font sets and name them, allowing you to quickly switch from one set to another. All fonts can be printed with one or more of three styles: bold, italic, and underline.

Figure 10.5 shows the fonts provided by 1-2-3. When you apply one of these fonts to a worksheet, 1-2-3 uses its built-in screen font files to display characters on the screen. 1-2-3 also allows you to use fonts that are built into your printer, such as LaserJet cartridges or resident PostScript fonts. However, because 1-2-3 has no matching screen fonts for these printer-specific fonts, it will use the screen font that most closely resembles the selected fonts.

The :Format Font command is used to apply fonts to worksheet cells and manage the use of fonts within a worksheet. When you choose the Font command from the :Format menu, you see a list of fonts, as shown in Figure 10.6. This Wysiwyg Font Selection menu lists the names and sizes of the eight fonts currently selected for this worksheet. The first font in the list is the default font.

To assign one of the eight fonts to a cell or cells in the worksheet, you pick the number you want either by selecting it from the menu bar or by checking the entry in the list box. If you check the list box entry, a pair of OK/Cancel buttons appear and you must pick OK to confirm your choice. Having chosen a font, you are asked to indicate the range of cells to which you want it applied (unless you have preselected the range, in which case the font is automatically applied to your selection).

Figure 10.6

The Wysiwyg Font Selection menu

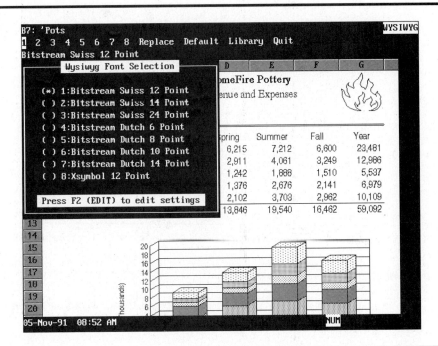

When you have assigned a font to a range of cells, the cell format code will reflect the change, as in {SWISS 14} if you applied the second font from the list in Figure 10.6. Note that there is no format code in the case of font 1, the default code, since this would require every cell in the worksheet to carry a format code. If you apply a font larger than the default, the row height increases automatically to accommodate the larger characters.

The :Format Font menu also includes three commands for managing fonts: Replace, Default, and Library. The Replace command allows you to replace fonts in the Wysiwyg Font Selection menu. For example, suppose you want to use Dutch 14 point instead of Xsymbol 12 point, which is currently font number 8. Select Replace to view a numbered list of the current fonts. Pick the number of the font you want to change, in this case 8, and Wysiwyg presents a menu of available fonts. These include the standard Wysiwyg bitstream fonts (Swiss, Dutch, Courier, and Xsymbol) plus Other, which represents printer-specific fonts that depend on the printer you have installed. In Figure 10.7, Other has been selected. The list shows printer fonts for a Hewlett-Packard LaserJet after having listed the regular bit-stream fonts.

Figure 10.7

Replacing a font

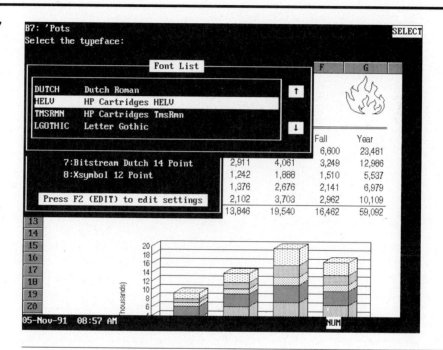

When you choose the replacement font, the Wysiwyg Font Selection menu is updated. Any cells formatted with the font you have changed will automatically reflect the new font assignment. Thus cells formatted as Xsymbol when Xsymbol was font 8 will now appear as Courier if you replaced Xsymbol with Courier as font 8. The current Wysiwyg font selection is saved with the worksheet. The Replace command does not affect the font list for other worksheets.

To make a permanent change to the font list for all worksheets, you use the Default command on the :Format Font menu. This allows you to restore the default selection to the font list, or update the defaults so that they reflect the current font list. Since you may want to have several different font lists handy, the Library commands Retrieve, Save, and Erase are provided. You can use these commands to manipulate font library files, which have the extension .AFS. To store the current font list in a library file, select Library Save and then provide a name for the file (the extension

.AFS is added automatically). To replace the current font selection with a previously saved list of fonts, use Library Restore and choose from the list of previously saved AFS files. The selection in the retrieved AFS file replaces the current font selection. However, you can still use Default Restore to retrieve the font selection you saved with Default Update.

:Format Bold and :Format Italic

You can draw attention to the cell by formatting it with boldface or italics. When you issue either the :Format Bold or :Format Italic command, you must choose Set to assign the attribute or Clear to remove it. You can either preselect cells and then issue the command, or issue the command and then indicate the cells to be affected. The format code for bold is {Bold} and the code for italic is {Italic}. You can assign both bold and italic to a cell, in which case the format code appears as {Bold Italic}. Figure 10.8 displays samples of the bold, italic, and underline formats.

Figure 10.8
The bold, italic, and underline formats

Using Bold, Italic, and Underline
Bold : **1-2-3 and Wysiwyg**
Italic : *1-2-3 and Wysiwyg*
Underline -Single : 1-2-3 and Wysiwyg
Underline - Double : 1-2-3 and Wysiwyg
Underline - Wide : 1-2-3 and Wysiwyg

(printed from Wysiwyg on a laser printer)

:Format Underline

When you select :Format Underline, you have a choice of three underlining styles: Single, Double, and Wide, as illustrated in Figure 10.8. The style you choose is applied to the cells you indicate, or to the preselected range. You cannot combine underline styles in one cell. If you have used the Single style and then apply the Double style, the single underlining is changed to double. You use the :Format Underline Clear command to remove underlining from a cell. Note that the underlining applies to spaces between words, but does not apply to the entire cell, only to characters entered in the cell.

:Format Color

The :Format Color command allows you to assign colors to cell entries and their background. If you have a color output device, reports will be printed in the colors you assign with the :Format Colors command. If you have a black-and-white printer, Wysiwyg approximates the colors with shades of gray.

The :Format Color Text command alters the color of the text and numbers in a range. When you select the command, you are presented with a list of colors from which to choose. The :Format Color Background command alters the background color for a range of the worksheet. When you select the command, you are presented with a list of colors from which to choose. You can see an example of the Background command in Figure 10.9, where most of the bottom part of an invoice was given a different color. Note the format code {/ Green} in cell A19. The / indicates that this is a background color code.

Figure 10.9
Use of color,
shading, and lines

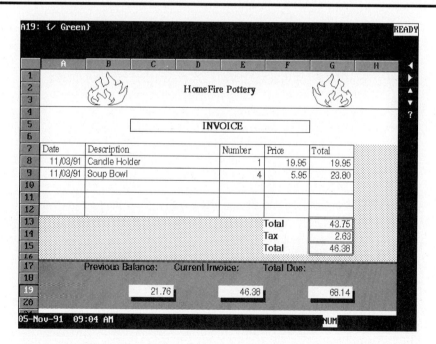

Cells for the three amounts on row 19 were colored with the normal or default color and these appear to stand out. The shading on these three cells is a result of the :Format Lines Shadow command, described in a moment.

The :Format Color Negative command allows you to have the color red automatically appear when values in a range of cells are negative. You can turn this option off by selecting :Format Colors Negative Normal, which tells Wysiwyg to use the default color for all values in the range, whether or not they are negative. For special emphasis, you can reverse the coloring for a section of the worksheet by using the :Format Color Reverse command. This switches the text and background colors within the indicated range of cells.

:Format Lines

The invoice in Figure 10.9 shows several applications of the :Format Lines command. The options on the :Format Lines menu are Outline, Left, Right, Top, Bottom, All, Double, Wide, Clear, and Shadow. The first six items apply a line of single thickness to the cells you select. The Outline command draws a line all around the selected cell or cells. For example, the box around the word INVOICE was created with the Outline command applied to the range C5..F5.

The Left and Right commands draw lines down the left and right sides of cells. These commands were used to create the columnar grid for the invoice items. The codes for these formats are {L} and {R}, respectively. The Top and Bottom commands draw lines across the top or the bottom of cells. The codes for these formats are {T} and {B}, respectively. The line between rows 3 and 4 was actually created by using the Top command on cells A4..H4, but it could also have been generated by applying the Bottom command on cells A3..H3.

The All command draws a line on each side of every cell in a range, creating a grid effect. The resulting code is {LRTB}, which stands for Left, Right, Top, and Bottom. While this command is sometimes handy, it may not always be what you need. For example, the grid in cells A7..G12 of Figure 10.9 could not be created with the All command, since that would have placed unwanted lines between columns B, C, and D. The All command was issued separately for A7..A12 and for E7..G12. When you want a large grid, you may consider using the :Print Settings Grid command, which prints the worksheet grid on every page of your report.

The lines drawn with the first six commands on the :Format Lines menu are single width. The :Format Lines Double option brings up a five-item menu containing commands for drawing double lines around sections of the worksheet: Outline, Left, Right, Bottom, and All. In Figure 10.9, the Double All command was applied to G13..G15. A similar five choices are provided for the :Format Lines Wide command, which applies a thick line to cells.

You use the :Format Lines Clear command to remove lines from cells. It brings up the options Outline, Left, Right, Bottom, and All. When you select Clear, you can choose which lines to remove. The Clear command removes single, double, and wide lines at the same time.

You use the :Format Lines Shadow command to set or clear a drop shadow for a range of cells. This command works with single cells, as in C19 in Figure 10.9, or with a group of cells. A thick line is drawn along the bottom of the selected cells and up the right side to give the shadow effect. This is not to be confused with the shading effect, which is described next.

:Format Shade

The :Format Shade command provides the four options Light, Dark, Solid, and Clear. You use the first three to shade an area of the worksheet with dark, light, or solid shading. You use the Clear command to remove shading from a row of cells. Shading was used in Figure 10.9, in column H and in rows 13 through 16.

   The light shading allows underlying cell entries to remain partially visible. If you want just a thin band of shading, apply shading to a column or row of cells and then use the :Worksheet command to reduce the width of the column or height of the row. Similarly, you can use the Shade Solid command to draw a thick dark line by varying the column or row width.

:Format Reset

When you want to remove all formatting from a range of cells, use the :Format Reset command. This command also restores the default font to the cells you select and resets the row height. To remove individual formats, such as shading and lines, use the corresponding Clear command.

The Wysiwyg Graph Commands

Though the PrintGraph program described in the last chapter does an adequate job of printing graphs, it does not allow for much customizing, or for mixing graphs and other information, as shown in Figure 10.10. However, graphs often form part of a report that contains text and numbers.

   With Wysiwyg you can use the :Graph commands to paste a named 1-2-3 graph into a worksheet range, the size of the range determining the size of the graph. Figure 10.11 includes part of the worksheet that produced the report in Figure 10.10. The current cell contains the format code {Graph EXP-SBAR}, which is the name of the graph that is pasted in that cell. The same code appears when you highlight any cell in the graph range B36..G50. When you include a pasted graph in a Wysiwyg print range, the graph is printed along with the rest of the worksheet.

   Pasting graphs into a worksheet is also the prerequisite for using Wysiwyg's :Graph Edit command to enhance your graph with text, arrows, lines, and shapes. In addition, pasting a graph into a worksheet is the key to two of Wysiwyg's most creative features: freehand graphics and clip art. To create a freehand drawing like the triangles on the left side of the report in

Figure 10.10, you paste a blank graph into an area of the worksheet and then edit it. This provides you with a blank canvas upon which to draw whatever you want. You can see a graphic being edited in Figure 10.12.

Figure 10.10
Report mixing graphs and numbers

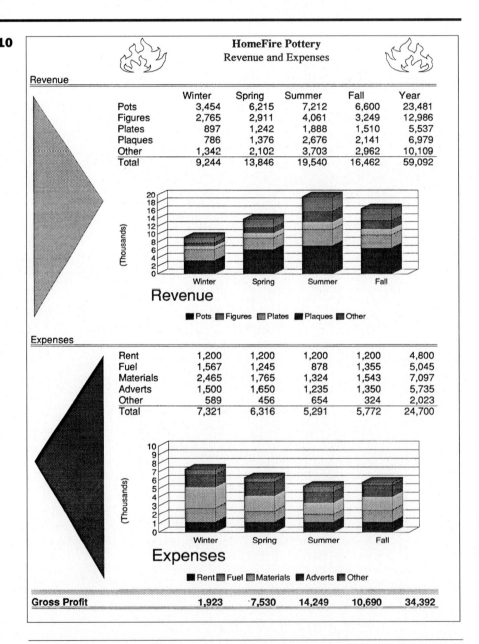

	Winter	Spring	Summer	Fall	Year
HomeFire Pottery					
Revenue and Expenses					
Revenue					
Pots	3,454	6,215	7,212	6,600	23,481
Figures	2,765	2,911	4,061	3,249	12,986
Plates	897	1,242	1,888	1,510	5,537
Plaques	786	1,376	2,676	2,141	6,979
Other	1,342	2,102	3,703	2,962	10,109
Total	9,244	13,846	19,540	16,462	59,092
Expenses					
Rent	1,200	1,200	1,200	1,200	4,800
Fuel	1,567	1,245	878	1,355	5,045
Materials	2,465	1,765	1,324	1,543	7,097
Adverts	1,500	1,650	1,235	1,350	5,735
Other	589	456	654	324	2,023
Total	7,321	6,316	5,291	5,772	24,700
Gross Profit	1,923	7,530	14,249	10,690	34,392

Figure 10.11

A graph pasted in a worksheet with Wysiwyg

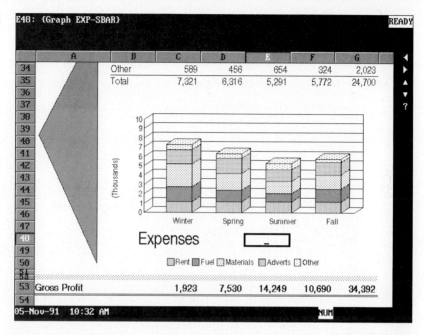

Instead of drawing your own graphics, you can use 1-2-3's collection of clip art. This clip art is stored in files with the extension .CGM, for Computer Graphics Metafile. The flames at the top of the report in Figure 10.10 come from the file FLAMES.CGM. As you can see from Figure 10.13, these were pasted into the worksheet. The size of the range into which the clip art is pasted determines its dimensions.

:Graph Add

To place a graph in a worksheet, you use :Graph Add. You can add the following types of graphs:

- Current is the graph that is now in memory for the current worksheet.

- Named is one of the graphs stored in the current worksheet with the regular Graph Name Create command.

- PIC is a graph saved on disk in a PIC file with the regular Graph Save command.

- Metafile is a drawing created with an art program and stored on disk in the CGM format.

- Blank is an area in which you can create drawings of your own.

Figure 10.12

Editing a graphic

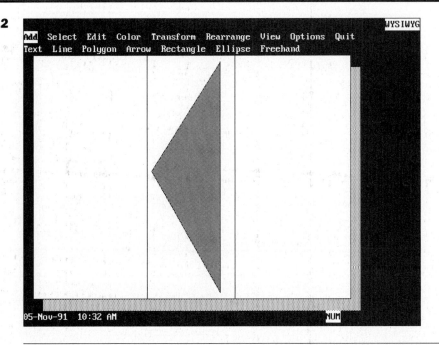

After you decide what type of graph you want to add, you indicate an area of the worksheet in which the graph will reside. Wysiwyg then draws the image to fit the range. For example, in Figure 10.13, the flame image was added to B1..B3 from the file FLAMES.CGM. In Figure 10.14, the range occupied by the stacked bar chart of revenue is B13..G26. The proportions of the graph depend upon the shape of the range you select. You can alter the range later without removing the graph by using the :Graph Settings Range command.

Graphs that you add are visible in the worksheet unless you change the :Graph Settings Display setting to No. The cells occupied by the graph contain a {Graph} format command that gives the name of the graph. If the graph is a PIC or Metafile, the code will look like this:

```
{Graph Drive:\Directory\Filename}
```

If you add the same graph twice, the graphs are numbered. For example, in Figure 10.13, the two sets of flames are the same Metafile image pasted in two different places. The first one is called

```
{Graph D:\123R23\FLAMES.CGM.1}
```

and the second is called

```
{Graph D:\123R23\FLAMES.CGM.2}
```

(Note that the second image was reversed using the :Graph Edit command.)

When you add a Blank graph, the code is {Graph <BLANK>} and the area appears at first to be whited out. You must use the :Graph Edit command, described in a moment, to draw your design within the blank area. When you have several blank graphics, they are numbered <BLANK>, <BLANK>.1, <BLANK>.2, and so on.

Figure 10.13
Pasting a CGM clip art file

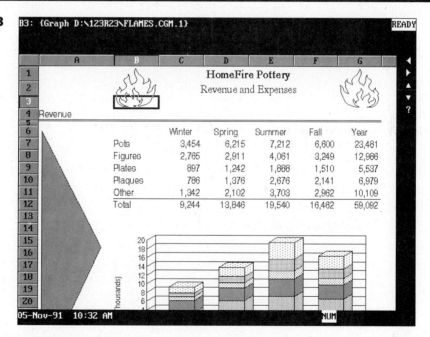

:Graph Remove

To remove a graph that has been pasted into the worksheet, you use the :Graph Remove command. Wysiwyg lists the inserted graphs and you can select the one you want to remove. Underlying data is not affected by the removal of a graph. If an inserted graph obscured cell entries, they will reappear when you remove the graph.

Figure 10.14

The range
occupied by the
revenue graph

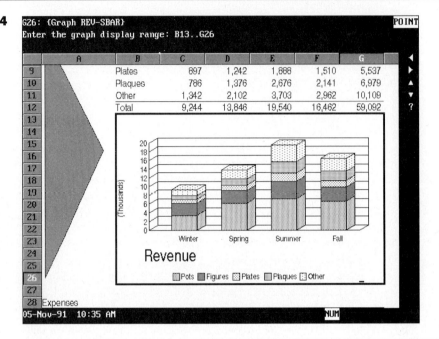

:Graph Goto

When you have many graphs inserted in your worksheet and want to move quickly to a particular one, you can use the :Graph Goto command. Simply select the graph you want to move to from the list that is provided.

:Graph Settings

The :Graph Settings command provides several options for manipulating inserted graphs. The :Graph Settings Graph option allows you to point to a graph in the worksheet and then select a different graph to be used in its place. Note that whenever you are asked to point out a graph in a Wysiwyg command, you can press F3 to list the graphs currently added to the worksheet.

The :Graph Settings Range command allows you to point at a graph and then alter its size or move it a short distance. When you have indicated the desired graph, a box is placed around its perimeter. You can then expand or contract this box with either the mouse or the cursor-movement keys. You can also move it by dragging the edges to a new location. You can use the period key (.) to change the active edge of the box, just as you do with a regular range setting. In Figure 10.14, there is a range setting box around the revenue graph. (The :Graph Move command, described in a moment, is preferable when you want to move a graph to a completely different location.)

One of the main benefits of the :Graph Settings Range command is that it enables you to alter the proportions of a graph. For example, if the range into which you add a graph is too wide, the graph will appear flattened. If it is too tall, the graph will appear elongated. The :Graph Settings Range command allows you to experiment with different proportions without removing the graph and trying again.

When you add a Named or Current chart of data to your worksheet, you may want it to be updated to reflect changes in the worksheet data, or you may want it to remain unchanged. For example, suppose you are graphing a sales projection based on a growth rate. You create a graph of the sales data based on a 10% growth rate, name it, then add it to the worksheet. Now you change the growth rate to 12%, name the graph, and paste in the new projection. You want your report to show the difference between the two graphs, but you know that a named graph is a collection of settings, not a fixed set of data. This means that if Wysiwyg automatically updates all of your graphs, both graphs will show the same rate, not the difference between 10% and 12%.

The :Graph Settings Sync command lets you tell Wysiwyg which graphs are to be updated automatically—that is, synchronized with the worksheet data. Graphs are synchronized by default. To unsynchronize a graph, select No and then pick out the graph. To resynchronize a graph, select No and then point out the graph, or press F3 and select it from the list of added graphs. Unfortunately, there is nothing in the format code for a graph to tell you whether or not it is synchronized.

The :Graph Settings Display command allows you to turn on or off the display of added graphs in the worksheet. Turning off the display can make spreadsheet operations a little quicker.

The :Graph Settings Opaque command determines how the data under an added graph is viewed. Typically, you will not want to add a graph to a range occupied by cell entries, since the graph obscures the entries. By default, added graphs are opaque. In some cases, you may want to use a graph to hide entries that are used in calculating but not reporting. However, you can change the Opaque setting to No in order to have data visible through the graph. For example, in Figure 10.15, the graph is actually placed over the last two rows of the table (the graph range extends up to row 11), moving the bars closer to the numbers they represent. Keep in mind that you can only see through areas of the graph that are not occupied by shaded or colored objects.

:Graph Move

When you want to move a graph from one location to another in a worksheet, you use :Graph Move. Select the graph to be moved and then point to the upper-left corner of the new location.

Figure 10.15

A graph displayed over figures

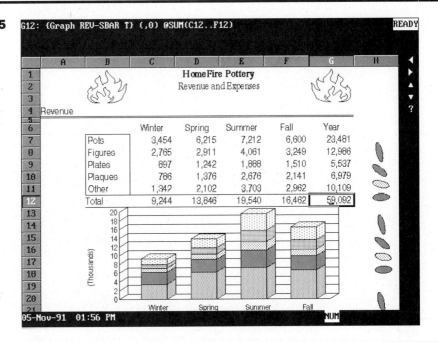

:Graph Zoom

Sometimes the graphs you add will appear quite small. The :Graph Zoom option allows you to zoom a selected graph to full-screen size to view details. When you have selected a graph and viewed it, press any key to return the graph to normal size and get back to the :Graph menu.

:Graph Compute

When you change data in the worksheet, inserted PIC and Metafile images are not affected. However, Current and Named graphs can be updated to reflect changes in the data being charged. As mentioned, the Graph Setting Sync command is used to tell Wysiwyg not to update added graphs. You can use the :Graph Compute command to override the Sync setting and update all graphs in the worksheet, regardless of their Sync setting. Be sure that you want all graphs to be updated before you issue this command.

:Graph View

When you want to add a PIC or Metafile (CGM) image to a worksheet, it is handy to be able to see the contents of the file to check if you have the right one. The :Graph View command allows you to list PIC or CGM files. Just select a file from the list to view it full screen without adding it to the worksheet.

:Graph Edit

One of Wysiwyg's most exciting commands is :Graph Edit, which allows you to add your own touches to graphs. When you issue the :Graph Edit command, you must tell Wysiwyg which graph you want to edit. (This graph must have been added to the worksheet with the :Graph Add command.) There are several ways to indicate the graph you want to edit. You can place the cell pointer in one of the cells occupied by the graph and press Enter, or double-click the left mouse button while the mouse pointer is on the graph. Alternatively, you can press F3 to produce a list of the available graphs from which you can choose. Pressing F3 a second time, or clicking on List in the special mouse palette, allows you to see a full-screen list of graphs.

When you have chosen a graph, you enter the drawing board, as shown in Figure 10.16. Here you can see the revenue graph from Figure 10.14 being edited. The word "Revenue" in a large font was added to the basic graph. The graph itself was created with the regular graph commands. It was then named and added to the worksheet with the :Graph Add Named command.

Figure 10.16
Using :Graph Edit

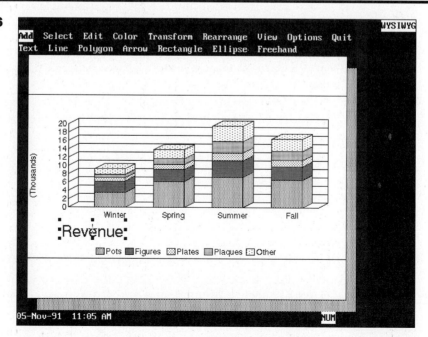

You can edit graphs with or without a mouse. In either case, a movable pointer is used. You can edit any of the graph types. When editing PIC and CGM graphs, the edits are not saved in the original PIC or CGM disk file. The first time you edit a Blank graph, the editing area is blank except for lines indicating the boundaries of the graph. The :Graph Edit commands, which constitute a complete set of drawing tools, are described in the following sections. Using these commands, you can add text, geometric shapes, and freehand designs to the graph, and then color and shade them however you want.

:Graph Edit Add

The :Graph Edit menu works just like other 1-2-3 menus. To add something to a graph, you select the Add command. This presents you with a list of seven different items, as shown on the second line of the menu in Figure 10.16. Suppose you want to add an arrow to the graph in Figure 10.16 to highlight the general trend in revenue. To begin, select the fourth item in the Add menu: Arrow.

A Wysiwyg arrow consists of a straight line connecting one or more points with an arrowhead at the end. When you select Arrow, the Add menu disappears and you are in POINT mode. A prompt on the second line of the screen asks you to indicate the first point of the arrow. Above this, you see the x and y coordinates of the pointer, which has been changed into a cross-hair, as shown in Figure 10.17. You can move the cross-hair pointer either with the mouse or with the arrow keys on the keyboard.

Every graph you edit is divided into a grid of tiny rectangles, 4,096 across (x coordinate) by 4,096 down (y coordinate). The upper-left corner of the graph is designated as 0,0 and the lower-right corner is 4,095:4,095 (the x coordinate is always given first). This grid helps you align objects and keep track of their location. (You can use the Options command to place a visible grid of squares on the graph edit area, as described later in this chapter.)

Suppose you decide that the arrow will begin above the stacked bar representing Winter revenue. Move the cross-hair there and mark the point by clicking the left mouse button or pressing Enter. The prompt at the top of the screen now says "Stretch to the next point." When you move the cross-hair, a line appears, stretching from the first point to the cross-hair. Now you can position the cross-hair where you want the second point of the arrow to be placed. This second point can be the end of the arrow, or one of several points through which the arrow passes.

To end the arrow, press Enter or double-click the left mouse button (press it twice in quick succession). To mark a second point for the arrow and move on to a third, press the spacebar or click the left mouse button. Having marked a second point, you can move the cross-hair to the third point. If you want to unlock the last point, press Esc or click the right mouse button.

Figure 10.17

The POINT mode
when editing a
graph

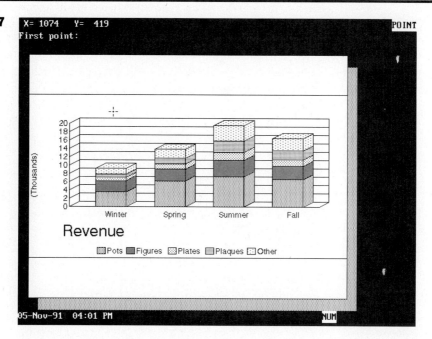

If you press Enter or double-click to complete the arrow, the arrowhead
will be drawn and the menu will reappear. Figure 10.18 displays a completed
arrow with four points, one above each bar. Note the square markers or *handles* on the arrow.

All of the items you add to a graph are called objects. In Figure 10.16,
the word "Revenue," which is a text object, has handles on it, represented by
small squares. Similarly, the arrow in Figure 10.18 has handles on it. The handles indicate that an object is selected. This means that it is the current
object and will be affected by the next command. For example, if you select
the Color Text command in Figure 10.16, the command will alter the color of
the word Revenue. Choosing Edit Width with the arrow selected will apply
the command to the arrow.

You can attach the following seven different types of objects to a graph
with :Graph Edit Add. Examples of the objects are shown in Figure 10.19.

■ Text is used to add text to graphs. You type on an edit line at the top of the
screen using the usual 1-2-3 edit keys. When you press Enter, you are
prompted to place the text on the graph. Do this by moving the cross-hair
to the correct location and pressing Enter or clicking the left mouse button. You can add text from the worksheet by using \ and the cell address.
For example, \A4 would add the word "Revenue" in Figure 10.16.

Figure 10.18

The completed arrow

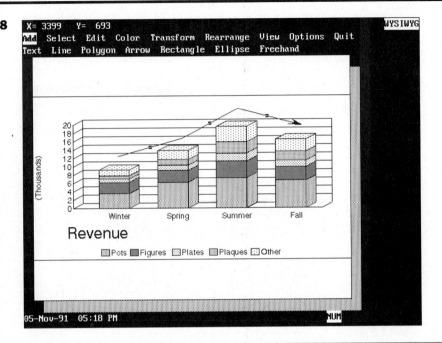

- Line is used to create a straight line between two points, or a jointed line between more than two points. The command works just like the Arrow command described previously. Once you have drawn a line, you can use :Graph Edit Edit to alter the style and width of the line, or smooth it into a curve and add arrowheads.

- Polygon is used to create a multisided enclosed shape, such as a triangle. This command works just like Arrow, except that when you press Enter or double-click the left mouse button to complete the polygon, Wysiwyg automatically connects the last point with the first. Once you have drawn a polygon, you can use :Graph Edit Edit to alter the style and width of the line, or smooth it into a curved shape. You can shade the inside of the shape with the Color command.

- Arrow is used to create arrows, as described previously. Once you have drawn an arrow, you can use :Graph Edit Edit to alter the style and width of the line, or smooth it into a curve and alter the arrowheads.

- Rectangle is used to create squares and rectangles. Make the shape by moving the cross-hair to where you want one corner of the rectangle to appear. At that point, press the spacebar to fix the corner or hold down the left mouse button and move the cross-hair to locate the opposite corner. A box appears between the two points. Press Enter or release the left mouse button to complete the object. You can shade the inside of the rectangle with the Color command.

Figure 10.19

Objects added to a graph

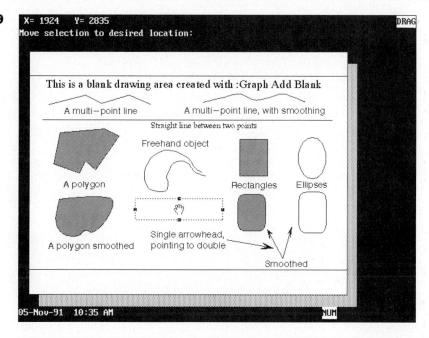

■ Ellipse is used to create circles and ellipses. You lay out the shape as a rectangular box that defines the perimeter of the ellipse. First move the cross-hair to where you want one corner of the rectangle to appear. To fix the corner, press the spacebar or hold down the left mouse button, then move the cross-hair to indicate the position of the opposite corner. Press Enter or release the left mouse button to complete the object. You can shade the inside of the object with the Color command.

■ Freehand is used to draw free-form shapes using the pointer as a pencil. Activate the pencil by holding down the left mouse button, and complete the shape by releasing the button. Alternatively, press the spacebar to lock the first point of the drawing and then move the pointer, using the space-bar to lock successive points and Esc to unlock the last point. You can enclose an area by placing the last point over the first point. You can color the inside of such shapes. Use :Graph Edit Edit to alter the style and width of the line, or smooth it into a curve.

When you complete any of the preceding objects, the :Graph Edit menu reappears and the object is selected with handles. This makes it easy to correct mistakes right after you have drawn them. For example, if the object you have just added is all wrong, you can delete it by pressing the Delete key, which erases whatever is currently selected. If you have added the right object in the wrong place, you can move it. With a mouse, simply point to the object and hold down the left mouse button while you point to the new location, dragging the object with you (keyboard users need to issue the Rearrange Move command first). When you move an object, the pointer changes into a hand, as seen in Figure 10.19 where a rectangle is being moved.

When you are drawing or moving objects with the mouse you can hold down the Shift key to restrict the mouse movement to straight lines. For example, when drawing a line, Shift will keep the line vertical, horizontal, or to the nearest 45-degree angle. When moving an object, Shift allows you to slide it as a straight line, horizontally, vertically, or at 45 degrees from its original location. Use Shift with Rectangle to draw a square and Shift with Ellipse to draw a circle.

Adding objects to a graph with :Graph Edit Add is just the beginning: You can also enhance these objects with other commands on the Edit menu. You can color the lines and insides of shapes with Color. You can rotate, flip, and slant objects with Transform. You can use Rearrange to move and copy objects as well as place them above or below other objects. You can use the Edit command to format text, alter line styles and widths, adjust arrowheads, and smooth straight lines into curves.

:Graph Edit Select

Objects that you add to a graph can be moved and rearranged. To select an object with the mouse, simply point and click. This places handles on the object to let you know it is selected. You can then drag the object to a new location. A small hand icon appears on the object as it is being moved. You can select objects without a mouse by using the Select menu. The first option on this menu, One, allows you to move the pointer on the screen with the cursor-movement keys until it is over the object you want to select. You then press Enter to select it. Other commands, such as All, None, and More/Less allow you to select and deselect additional objects. The Select Cycle option allows you to select each object in the graph in turn. You press the cursor-movement keys to cycle through the objects, and empty handles appear on each object as it is made current. You press the spacebar to select the current object, at which point the handles are filled in. This enables you to select several objects. You press Enter when your selection is complete. The objects you chose are then ready for the next command.

The Select command is handy even if you are using a mouse because selecting several different objects with the mouse can be difficult. Normally, to select a group of objects with the mouse, you point to a location above and to the left of the objects and then click and drag a selection rectangle over the various objects you want to select. However, this is difficult if the objects are placed on top of others that you do not want to select. You can either use the Select command to choose the objects, or you can use Shift-Click (point at an object and click on it while holding down the Shift key). This selects the object you are pointing at without deselecting the other objects already selected. If you have selected several objects, you can Shift-Click on one of them to deselect it without deselecting the entire group. If you need to select the original graphic but not the objects added to it, then use Select Graph.

:Graph Edit Edit

There are numerous aspects of graph objects that you can alter with the :Graph Edit Edit commands. The first of these commands is Text, which allows you to edit text you have added to a graph (not the text of the graph itself). Only issue this command after first selecting a text object. You can use the regular 1-2-3 editing keys, plus the Wysiwyg formatting sequences described later in the chapter to alter the text. You can use these to alter the font, style, or color of part of a piece of text. Press Enter when you are done editing.

The second :Graph Edit Edit command is Centering, which offers the three choices Left, Center, and Right. Only issue this command after first selecting a text object. These choices determine the alignment of a text object relative to the original center point of the text.

The Edit Font command allows you to alter the font of text you have added to a graph, offering choices from 1 through 8, which match choices in the current font selection. Use the formatting sequences described later to alter the font of a section of text.

The Edit Line-Style command offers a range of styles that can alter the look of lines used in any of the nontext objects added to a graph. The choices include Solid, Dashed, Dotted, and Hidden, which removes the line from view. This is handy when you have colored the inside of an object and don't want the edge to be visible.

The Edit Width command offers five choices for the width of lines on nontext objects, from Very Narrow to Very Wide. You can alter lines added with Line, Arrow, and Freehand with the Edit Arrowheads command. You can have arrowheads on both ends of a line (Two), on one end or the other (One), or switch an arrowhead from one end to the other (Switch). You can also remove arrows with None.

The Edit Smoothing command allows you to turn straight lines into curves. This command works with all nontext objects except lines and arrows that only have two points. The Smoothing choices are None, Tight, and Medium. Medium gives the most curve and None returns the lines to the original configuration. Smoothing used on rectangles creates rounded corners. Smoothing used on ellipses creates the same affect, as you can see in Figure 10.19.

:Graph Edit Color

You can manipulate the color of added objects with the Color commands. The first of these, Lines, allows you to color the lines used to draw all non-text objects. You get a choice of eight colors plus Hidden, which makes the line invisible. The second Color command, Inside, can be used to shade the inside of a rectangle, ellipse, or polygon, as shown in Figure 10.19. This command presents a full-screen palette of choices. You can see a black-and-white version on the palette in Figure 10.20. The current color is highlighted on the palette. (All colors are numbered; if the object has just been drawn, however, it will not have a color number assigned to it.) Move the highlight to the desired shade and press Enter to select it, or click on it with the mouse. The Home and End keys highlight the first and last colors, respectively.

You color text objects with the Text command, which offers eight colors, plus Hidden. Note that you can use the text format codes described later in this chapter to color part of a piece of added text.

Figure 10.20

The color palette

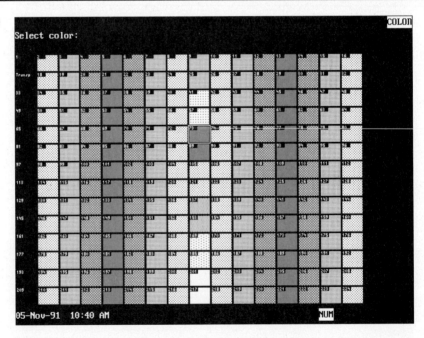

The Map command allows you to alter the color of the underlying graphic, such as the chart in Figure 10.18. The colors of the graphic are numbered 1 through 8, and when you pick a number you are presented with the color palette in which the current color is highlighted. Select the color you want and the appropriate areas of the graph will be assigned that color.

The Color Background command alters the background of the entire graphic, allowing you to choose from the full-screen palette of colors seen in Figure 10.20.

:Graph Edit Transform

Once you have added an object to the graph, you can alter it considerably by selecting it and then using the :Graph Edit Transform command. The Size command places a box around the object, which you can then adjust with the mouse or the arrow keys. These move the lower-right corner of the box. If you move the lower-right corner of the box out from the object, it will be enlarged. Move the box in on the object and it will be reduced. Hold down the Shift key while adjusting the box and the proportions of the object will be maintained as the size is increased or decreased. If you don't use Shift, you can radically alter the shape of the object by moving the free corner of the box. If you pass it across the top of the object, you "flip" the object.

The Transform Rotate command allows you to rotate the object through 360 degrees, using a rotating arm that appears when you issue the command. You can see this in Figure 10.21, where a tall rectangle is being rotated clockwise. Use the Up Arrow or Down Arrow key if you need to rotate an object with the keyboard. Press Enter when the angle of rotation is correct. The grid on the drawing area in Figure 10.21 is activated by the Options command, which is described in a moment.

To rotate an object about its own axis in exact 90-degree increments, use the Transform Quarter-Turn command. The rectangle in the upper-right corner of Figure 10.21 was drawn as a tall object, and then rotated with Quarter-Turn. Be careful if you use Q to issue the Quarter-Turn command, since the main :Graph Edit menu reappears when the command is executed; if you press Q a second time without first selecting Transform, you will choose Quit and will leave the editing screen and return to the worksheet.

The Transform X-Flip and Y-Flip commands flip objects along the x and y axis, respectively. For example, suppose you wanted to make a large X shape using a pair of slanted rectangles like the one at the bottom of Figure 10.21. You would first duplicate the object (with Rearrange Copy) and then use X-Flip to make it slant the other way. In contrast, the Horizontal and Vertical commands allow you to distort an object along either the x or y axis. For example, the slanted rectangle in Figure 10.21 was constructed by drawing a tall rectangle and then using the Horizontal command to drag the lower-right corner farther to the right. If you do not like the effect of a Transform operation, you can use the Clear item on the Transform menu to reverse the last Transform command.

Figure 10.21

Transform examples

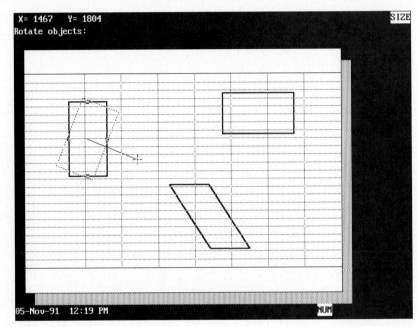

:Graph Edit Rearrange

The :Graph Edit Rearrange command allows you to delete, move, and copy objects. As you know, the Delete key deletes the currently selected objects. The Rearrange Delete command does the same thing. The Restore command puts back what the last Delete action removed. The Move command is for keyboard users to activate the hand icon that allows objects to be repositioned. The Copy command simply makes a copy of the current objects and places them in the drawing area close to the original.

Since the Delete key is easy to use by mistake, the Rearrange Lock command allows you to protect the position, shape, and other attributes of an object. You use Unlock when you need to unlock a locked object later.

Each new object in a graph is placed in front of the previous objects. The Rearrange Front command moves an object to the foreground, and the Back command puts an object behind all the others on the graph. For example, suppose you have added some text, and then a shaded box to put the text in. The box will obscure the text unless you use Front to move the text in front of the box.

:Graph Edit View

To help with detail work on graphics, the :Graph Edit View command allows you to zoom in on parts of the graph, using a variety of commands. You can also use a number of keystrokes to alter the view without using the menu. When you are at the Edit menu, the plus key (+) enlarges the graph and the minus key (–) shrinks it. The View Full command restores full-screen editing, which is the normal view.

The View In command prompts you to select a rectangle on the screen that will then be zoomed to full-screen size. Use View Full to return the screen to normal. The View Pan command allows you to change the area of the graphic being viewed when the In command has been issued. You do this with the arrow keys. You can also use the plus and minus keys at this point to zoom in closer or zoom back out. The View Up, Down, Left, and Right commands allow mouse users to adjust the area being viewed without using the cursor-movement keys.

:Graph Edit Options

The :Graph Edit Options commands can help you align objects on your graph. The Grid command places a grid on the drawing area, as seen earlier in Figure 10.21. Note that this grid matches the width pattern of underlying worksheet cells. The Options Cursor command allows you to choose between the default small cross-hair and the big cursor shown in Figure 10.22. The dotted vertical and horizontal arms of the cross-hair extend all the way to the edge of the drawing.

Figure 10.22 also shows the third Options command: Font-Magnification. This command allows you to enlarge or reduce the size of the fonts in 1-2-3 graphs you are editing. You cannot change the fonts or edit the graph text, but you can resize it. The default size is 100%. Use over 100% to increase the font size, less than 100% to shrink it. The allowed range is from 0% to 1,000%. In Figure 10.22, the setting is 130%.

:Graph Edit Tips

The best way to learn about the Wysiwyg graph editing feature is to experiment; your skill at drawing objects will improve rapidly with practice. There also are some shortcuts.

The Delete key is handy if you have just created an object you don't want to keep. By the same token, it is easy to erase the current object accidentally by inadvertently pressing Delete. The antidote to this is the Rearrange Restore command.

Though you can use the Undo feature in 1-2-3 to reverse graph editing, it only works when you return to READY mode. Pressing Alt-F4 restores the graph to the way it was before you used the :Graph Edit command—that is, it erases all editing since the last time you were in READY mode.

Figure 10.22

The big cursor

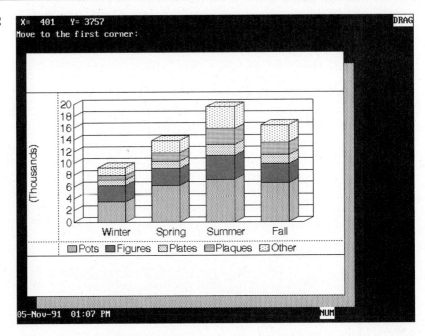

If you need several copies of an object, use the Insert key. This duplicates the current object and gives you a copy of the last object you deleted. If you need to line up objects, remember that the Shift key lets you slide objects in a straight line. To align two objects, place one exactly on top of the other and then move the top object while holding down the Shift key. If you need the inside color of an object to be transparent so that an underlying object will show through, use color 17.

When you use Quit to leave the Edit menu, the graph is automatically computed and redrawn in the worksheet. You can see typical results in Figure 10.23, where the graph shown earlier is seen in the worksheet, displayed at 125% zoom.

The Wysiwyg Print Commands

The :Print commands give you a great deal of control over page layout and printing, whether you are working with a combination of graphs and data, or simply data. The :Print commands let you print your worksheet exactly as you have formatted it on the screen. The print preview feature lets you see how your printed worksheet will look, complete with page breaks, before you print it.

Figure 10.23
Edited graph

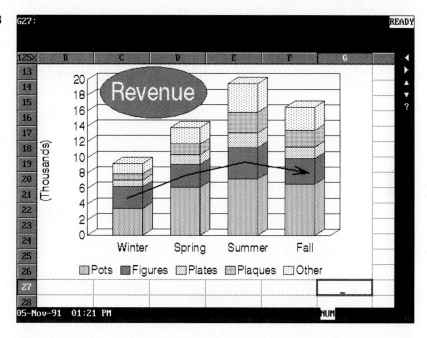

When you select :Print you see a box displaying all the current :Print settings, as shown in Figure 10.24. Use the Print Info command to remove the settings box and reveal the underlying worksheet.

:Print Go, File, and Background

The :Print Go command sends the selected print range to the printer. This command operates on the range you set with Wysiwyg, not the range set with the regular Print command. A message tells you that printing is taking place and you have to stop work until the printing is finished and the message disappears.

If you want to send your work to a file instead of to a printer, you use the :Print File command. This creates a file with the .ENC extension—that is, the file is encoded ready to print from DOS with the PRINT command. This is sometimes useful when you want to print a batch of complex files simultaneously after you have finished a Wysiwyg session. For example, if you create a file called INVOICE1.ENC in the C:\123R23\DATA directory, you can print it later by entering the following at the DOS prompt:

```
PRINT C:\123R23\DATA\INVOICE1.ENC
```

Figure 10.24

The Wysiwyg Print settings

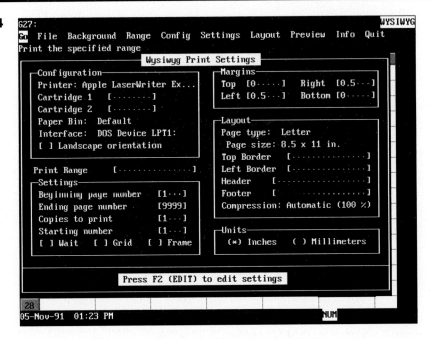

Wysiwyg also can print files while you continue working with the program. To do this, use the :Print Background command, which first creates a temporary encoded file, and then sends it to the printer. Wysiwyg may slow down while this takes place, but you can still work while the file prints.

:Print Range

You use the :Print Range command to tell Wysiwyg which cells you want printed. It works much the same as the regular Print Range command. However, remember that the Wysiwyg print range is quite separate from the regular print range.

When you select :Print Range, you have to pick Set to establish the Range or Clear to remove it. When you set a print range with Wysiwyg, a print border appears in your worksheet to show you where page breaks will occur. Because this disturbs the appearance of the worksheet if you are using it for on-screen presentation purposes, the Clear command is provided to let you erase this border from the screen.

:Print Config

You use the :Print Config command to tell Wysiwyg which printer model you are going to use and how it is attached to your system. The :Print Config command has the following options: Printer, Interface, 1st-Cart, 2nd-Cart, Orientation, and Bin. When you select Printer, Wysiwyg displays a list of the printers that you specified during installation. You will have to save your work, end your current session, and run the Install program to add further printers to the list. Note that the Printer option may list several choices for the same printer model—High Res, Medium Res, and so on—which refer to the print quality. Bear in mind that you may need extra RAM in your printer to support high-resolution printing. The higher the printing resolution, the sharper your printed graphics will appear. An option called Ext Cap, available for some models, results in even better graphics.

The Interface option tells Wysiwyg which port the printer is connected to. Eight options are provided. Normally, you will want option 1—Parallel 1. This is the connection used by most printers. However, if you are using a serial printer or plotter, you will need to select option 2 or 4. If you are using a network printer, you may need to select from options 5 through 8, which represent DOS devices, not ports.

The Cart options refer to font cartridges installed in the printer. If your printer accepts font cartridges, use these commands to tell Wysiwyg which ones are present.

The Orientation command tells Wysiwyg whether to print in landscape or portrait mode, with portrait being the default. You can see the difference between the two modes in Figure 10.25, which was drawn with the :Graph Edit command.

If your printer can feed paper from several bins, use the Bin command to tell Wysiwyg where the paper for the print job will be coming from. Note that when you select a printer model with the Printer command, Wysiwyg knows whether or not the particular model supports different Bin and Cartridge commands.

The choices you make with the Config command are saved when you save the worksheet. They remain in effect until you load a worksheet that has different printer settings. If you want to store a particular printer as the default, so that it is selected when you start a new session, issue the Display Default Update command. This will not affect your Config choices in worksheets that you have already saved.

:Print Settings

You use the :Print Settings command to tell Wysiwyg which pages of a report you want printed (Begin and End) as well as the page number to use for the first page of the report (Start-Number). For example, suppose the print range contains five pages, and you want to print the second and third pages, but number the first of these pages as number 1. You set Begin = 2, End = 3, Start-Number = 1. If you want several copies of the report, use the Copies command. If you need the printer to wait while you feed paper, use the Wait command.

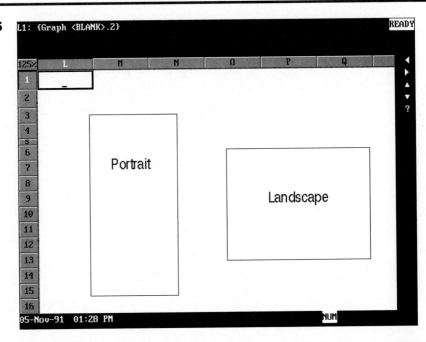

Figure 10.25
Print orientation

If you want to print the worksheet gridlines on the report, use Grid. You can use the Frame command to include column lettering and row numbering on a report; this is useful when you are documenting a worksheet for others.

The Reset command returns all print settings to their defaults but does not affect the print range setting. Note that you can edit the print settings directly rather than use the menu to choose the setting commands.

:Print Layout

The :Print Layout commands determine how the report is placed on the page, as well as the page size itself. The Page-Size command allows you to select from a range of predefined page sizes or define your own custom size. The Margins command lets you set margins on all four sides of the page. Page size and margin changes are reflected in the print borders shown in the worksheet.

The Titles command enables you to enter a header and a footer. These do not appear in the worksheet, but do show up when you print and when you use the Preview command. You use the following symbols in headers and footers to format them and to add information such as the date and page number:

#	Prints current page number
@	Prints current date
\cell address	Uses contents of a worksheet cell
|	Separates portions of the header

For example, the header

    Page #

prints as

    Page 1

The header

    Page #|Report @

prints as

    Page 1   Report 13-Nov-91

and the header

    Page #|HomeFire Pottery|@

prints as

    Page 1   HomeFire Pottery   13-Nov-91

Note that headers can be no longer than 240 characters in length.

To add styles such as boldface and underline to header and footer text, you use the text format codes, discussed later under the :Text command. As with the regular Print command, you can set print borders with Wysiwyg that are repeated on each page. Use the Layout Borders command for this.

Perhaps the most powerful Layout command is Compression, which allows you to shrink or expand the size of the print area. This command does not alter the :Print Range setting or the margin settings, but it actually scales the printed results up or down to occupy more or less space. Normally, there is no compression in effect—a setting also referred to as 100% compression. If you select Layout Compression, you can choose Manual to enter a percentage

/wR to adjust hoft of Row (handwritten)

(over 100% to expand the print area, under 100% to reduce it). Alternatively, if you use the Automatic option, Wysiwyg will try to shrink your print area so that it fits onto a single page. At maximum, Wysiwyg will shrink the print area by 700%. If this still does not reduce the print area to fit a single page, a two-page report is created. If maximum shrinkage does not reduce the print area to fit on two pages, a three-page report is created, and so on. Set Compression to None to restore full-size printing.

To save the current collection of print layout settings as the default settings for new spreadsheets, use the Layout Default Update command. Use Layout Restore to return settings to the state they were in the last time you updated the defaults.

Use the :Print Layout Library command to store the current settings in a page layout library file. This file, which automatically receives the extension .ALS, can then be retrieved for use with other worksheets. This command has three options: Retrieve, Save, and Erase. Use Retrieve to use a previously stored layout library file with the current worksheet. Use Save to create a library file for the current settings. Use Erase to remove unwanted library files from disk.

:Print Preview

The :Print Preview command shows you a reduced image of your print range so that you can see exactly what will appear on each page of your document. This lets you view the effects of commands like Compression that alter how much of what you want to print appears on each page. You can see an example of the :Print Preview feature in Figure 10.26.

The :Print Preview command displays what will be sent to your printer when you use the :Print Go command, starting with the first page. You can use the PgDn key to go to a second page, and successive pages, if there are any. Use PgUp to move back towards the first page. Pressing any key when the last page of the report is displayed will return you to the :Print menu. Remember that the :Print Info command toggles on and off the Print Settings dialog box if you need to view the underlying worksheet while using the :Print menu.

The Wysiwyg Display Commands

As you saw in Chapter 7, the :Display commands allow you to customize your screen display by selecting colors for the cell pointer, worksheet background, frame, and data. The :Display commands also let you add grid lines to the worksheet, enhance or hide the worksheet frame, and even alter the size of cells to display more or less of the worksheet. The :Display commands are also used to identify the directory containing the Wysiwyg fonts. Normally Wysiwyg assumes that the fonts will be in the WYSIWYG

program directory, but if you want to keep your fonts separate from the
rest of the Wysiwyg program files, you can tell Wysiwyg the name of the
directory with :Display Fonts-Directory.

Figure 10.26

The :Print Preview
feature

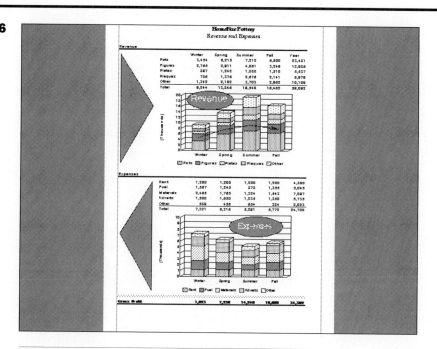

The Wysiwyg Special Commands

The :Special commands copy and move formats from one range to another.
They also import formats and graphs from other files, and export formats
and graphs from the current worksheet to files on disk.

:Special Copy and :Special Move

When you have developed a special format for a cell or group of cells, you
may want to apply it to a different range of the worksheet. You can use :Spe-
cial Copy to copy the Wysiwyg formatting from one range to another. The
:Special Move command takes the formats from one range and applies them
to another, returning the source range to the default formats.

:Special Import

The :Special Import command replaces the formats, named styles, font set,
and graphics in the current file with those from a different FMT file. (Recall
that FMT files contain all the Wysiwyg formatting codes for a spreadsheet.)

For example, suppose you have developed a file called INVOICE.WK1 and begin to format with Wysiwyg. Then you find out that a colleague has already developed an invoice format that looks great. You borrow the format file, called BILL.FMT, and use the :Special Import command to apply the formats to your own INVOICE file. The :Special Import command has four options:

- All replaces formats, fonts, named styles, and graphics in the current file with those from another FMT file on disk.

- Named-Styles replaces the named styles in the current file with named styles from a file on disk. (Named styles are covered under "Wysiwyg Named-Style.")

- Fonts replaces the current fonts set with the fonts set from a file on disk.

- Graphs copies graphs from a FMT file on disk but does not delete graphs in the current file.

Note that imported graphs will be placed on top of spreadsheet data or existing graphs if the graph range is already occupied. Graph importing is mainly for situations where the current worksheet has the same structure as the one you are importing from. Also note that Import recognizes ALL files, the format files created by the Allways add-in used with earlier versions of 1-2-3.

:Special Export

The :Special Export command allows you to use the font sets, named styles, and graphics from the current file with another worksheet. For example, if you have created a worksheet called REVENUE.WK1 and formatted it with Wysiwyg, a file called REVENUE.FMT on disk will contain the font sets, formats, named styles, and graphics you have used. Suppose you want to use similar formatting with a worksheet called EXPENSES.WK1. With REVENUE.WK1 loaded, you select :Special Export and then enter EXPENSES as the new file name. The .FMT extension will be added automatically. When you retrieve EXPENSES.WK1 and load Wysiwyg, you will see the formatting you have exported from REVENUE.FMT. When you export a format, it overrides any existing FMT file associated with the target spreadsheet. This means that you can use :Special Export to replace the formatting in an existing FMT file with that of the current worksheet. You select an existing format file from the list of files that the :Special Export command presents.

The Wysiwyg Text Commands

The :Text commands let you work with labels as if you are using a word processor. You can enter and edit data directly into a special {Text} range instead of through the input line in the control panel. You get full word wrap plus font and format control. The Text command can also align labels within a range instead of within cells, enabling you to center titles over a report.

:Text Edit

The :Text Edit command allows you to enter text as though you were using a simple word processor. When you select Edit from the :Text menu, the program prompts you for a range. When you indicate a range, the upper-left cell of the range is placed near the upper-left corner of the screen and a flashing vertical edit cursor is placed at the left edge of the cell. You can then proceed to type. For example, suppose that you wanted to add a note across the bottom of the invoice last seen in Figure 10.9. You might select cells A22..H24. You can see the note being typed in Figure 10.27.

Figure 10.27

Text being entered

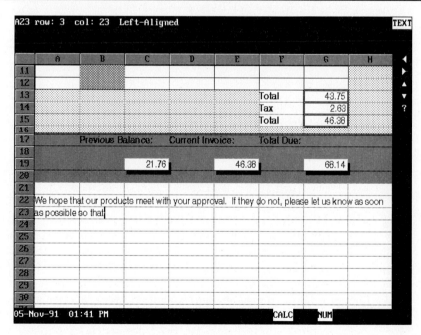

Note the row and column indicator at the top of the screen and the format Left-Aligned. Also note that the text automatically wraps around to a new line at the right edge of the range. The mode indicator in the upper-right corner of the screen tells you that you are in TEXT mode. The CALC indicator temporarily appears at the bottom of the screen to indicate that you are altering the contents of the worksheet.

You can move through the text you are typing using the text editing keys listed in Table 10.1.

Table 10.1   **Text Editing Keys**

Key	Action
Left Arrow	Moves cursor one character to the left
Right Arrow	Moves cursor one character to the right
Ctrl-Left Arrow	Moves cursor left to the beginning of previous word
Ctrl-Right Arrow	Moves cursor right to the end of next word
Home	Moves cursor to the beginning of current line
End	Moves cursor to the end of current line
Delete	Deletes the character to the right of cursor
Backspace	Deletes the character to the left of cursor
Enter	Ends current line and moves cursor to the start of new line
Esc	Ends text editing and returns to READY mode
F3	Displays menu of text formats
Insert	Switches between insert and overstrike typing modes

If you press F3 while in TEXT mode, a special text menu appears across the top of the screen, as shown in Figure 10.28. This menu allows you to turn on a variety of formatting characteristics, including boldface, italics, and underline. For example, if you decide that your next word should be bold, select Bold from the text menu. Figure 10.28 shows the last typed word in boldface. The top line of the screen displays a formatting code as a reminder. When you want to stop typing in bold, select Normal.

You can alter the format of text after you have typed it by moving the edit cursor to the point where you want a format to begin, and then selecting the format. You must move the cursor to where you want the format to end and select Normal to turn it off.

You can also format text with the format codes that are shown in Table 10.2. You must enter these codes in lowercase: You cannot use B for bold, for example. You place these codes in the text by placing the cursor right before the character you want to format and then pressing Ctrl-A followed by the appropriate code. Repeat this sequence for each code you want to use. Press Ctrl-E to stop using a particular code. Press Ctrl-N to stop using all codes and mark the end of the formatting sequence.

Figure 10.28

The text formatting menu

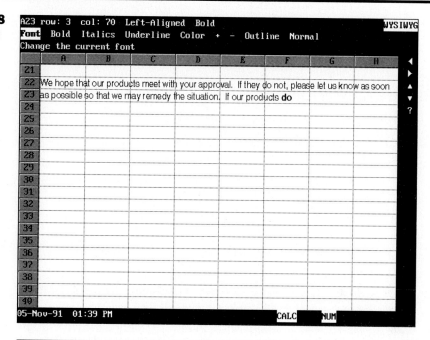

You press Esc when you have finished typing and editing your text. This returns you to READY mode. The text you have typed appears as labels in the left-hand column of the text range. In Figure 10.29, you can see the complete note on the invoice worksheet. Note that cells you have included in a text range all have the format code {Text}. You can return to editing the same range simply by issuing the :Text Edit command with the cell pointer anywhere within the range.

If you want to alter the text you have created with :Text Edit, you can either repeat the command for the same text range or edit the actual cell entries with F2. You can insert the text format codes listed in Table 10.2 into labels to format them. You can also use the same codes within headers and footers and text that you add to graphics.

:Text Align

By default, text that you enter into a text range is left-aligned. The :Text Align command allows you to center or right-align the text. The alignment

Table 10.2 **Text Formatting Codes**

Code	Result
b	Bold
d	Subscript
f	Flashing
i	Italics
o	Outline of characters
u	Superscript
x	Flip backwards
y	Flip upside down
1c	Default color
2c	Red
3c	Green
4c	Dark blue
5c	Cyan
6c	Yellow
7c	Magenta
8c	Reverse colors
1	Font 1
2	Font 2
3	Font 3
4	Font 4
5	Font 5
6	Font 6
7	Font 7
8	Font 8
1_	Single underline
2_	Double underline
3_	Wide underline
4_	Box around characters
5_	Strike through

options are Left, Right, Center, and Even. The Even option justifies all full lines of text flush with the left and right edges of the range by varying the space between words. The Center option centers each line of text between the left and right edges of the range. The Right option aligns the text with the right side of the text range.

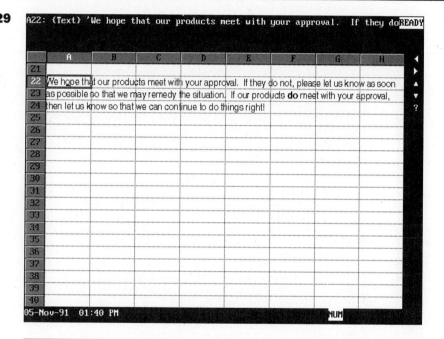

Figure 10.29
Completed text
entry

By setting a text range that is the width of a report, you can center title text over the report. In Figure 10.30, the text of the note in Figure 10.29 has been centered. Note that the ^ symbol is added to the label to accomplish centering. This symbol only affects the alignment of the text in Wysiwyg mode.

:Text Reformat

Like the Range Justify command in the regular menu system, the :Text Reformat command reads all of the labels in the range and puts them into a long paragraph, word wrapped within the confines of the range. For more on working with Range Justify, see Chapter 11.

:Text Set and :Text Clear

You use the :Text Set command to designate a cell or group of cells as a text range in preparation for using the :Text commands. This adds the {Text} code to the selected cells. Normally, a cell is automatically made a {Text} cell when you use the :Text Edit or Align command. However you may want to add this attribute to a cell before using the :Text Edit command in order to prepare it for text entry. To clear the {Text} attribute from a cell or range of cells, use the :Text Clear command.

Figure 10.30
Centered text

```
A22: {Text} ^We hope that our products meet with your approval.  If they    READY

        A        B        C        D        E        F        G        H
  21
  22   We hope that our products meet with your approval.  If they do not, please let us know as soon
  23   as possible so that we may remedy the situation.  If our products do meet with your approval,
  24              then let us know so that we can continue to do things right!
  25
  26
  27
  28
  29
  30
  31
  32
  33
  34
  35
  36
  37
  38
  39
  40
 05-Nov-91  01:38 PM                                                    NUM
```

The Wysiwyg Named-Style Command

The :Named-Style command allows you to assign names to groups of formats so you can easily and consistently format ranges with a number of formats at once. This command can save you a lot of time if you regularly prepare the same type of reports or want to maintain a consistent style in your reporting.

When you first select :Named-Style, you see a list of eight entries all called Normal and numbered from 1 to 8, and a ninth item called Define. To use the :Named-Style feature, select Define and then choose which of the eight numbered styles you want to define. For example, if you chose 2, you would be asked to point to the cell that contains the style that you want to define, and then would be asked to give style 2 a name. If the style were

Dutch 8-point italic, you might call it Fine (you are limited to six characters in the name). From now on, the :Named-Style menu will list 2:Fine and you can pick this item to assign the style it represents to any number of cells.

You can define up to eight named styles, which are stored with the current worksheet when you save it. This means you can have different named styles in different worksheets. You can copy the named styles from one worksheet to another with the Special command.

Wysiwyg Tips and Tricks

This section examines the practical aspects of working with Wysiwyg. While the Wysiwyg features are well integrated into 1-2-3, you should know about some of its limitations.

Wysiwyg and Regular Commands

While Wysiwyg does not affect data in your 1-2-3 worksheet, there are some 1-2-3 commands that affect Wysiwyg formatting. When you copy a range of data with the regular Copy command, 1-2-3 also copies all Wysiwyg formats set with the :Format, :Named-Style, and :Text commands, except lines and drop shadows added with :Format Lines. Copy does not copy named style definitions and, therefore, 1-2-3 will not update any Wysiwyg formats in the "To where?" range if you update or redefine the named style. You should use the :Special Copy command to copy named styles.

When you move a range of data with the regular Move command, 1-2-3 also moves all formats set with the :Format, :Named-Style, and :Text commands. Move also moves a graphic added to the worksheet with :Graph Add if the "Copy what?" range includes the entire graphic.

When Wysiwyg is loaded, selecting Data Parse puts Wysiwyg in text display mode. Selecting Quit from the Data Parse menu returns Wysiwyg to graphics display mode. When you use Data Sort Go, all formats set with the :Format, :Named-Style, and :Text commands, except lines and drop shadows, move with the data as 1-2-3 sorts it.

When you insert columns or rows in a worksheet with Worksheet Insert Column or Worksheet Insert Row, 1-2-3 formats the new columns or rows with the Wysiwyg formats common to the columns or rows directly on either side of them. For example, if you add a column between columns B and C, and column B is formatted as bold italics and column C is formatted as italics, the new column will be formatted as italics.

File Operations

When you read a WK1 file into memory, 1-2-3 reads the formatting information into memory from the Wysiwyg format file (FMT) by the same name, if one exists. When you save a WK1 file with File Save, 1-2-3 saves the formatting information in a Wysiwyg format file with the same name as the WK1 file but with an .FMT extension.

When you incorporate data from a worksheet file on disk into the current file with File Combine, 1-2-3 does not read the formatting information into memory from any corresponding format file. When you erase a worksheet file from disk with File Erase Worksheet, 1-2-3 will erase the corresponding Wysiwyg format file (FMT), if one exists. When you extract a range of data from an active file and save it in a worksheet file on disk with File Xtract, 1-2-3 does not create a format file for the new worksheet file.

When you create a new file in memory with File New, the file has the Wysiwyg defaults, including

- The font set

- The named styles

- The print configuration settings (except Printer and Interface)

- The :Print Layout settings

- The :Print Settings settings

The File New command does not affect :Display settings for the current Wysiwyg session (except for the colors of negative values, lines, and drop shadows).

Undoing Wysiwyg

You can use the Undo feature (Alt-F4) to reverse the effects of the most recent Wysiwyg command or series of commands. 1-2-3 treats as a single operation any series of Wysiwyg commands that you perform after you press : and before you return 1-2-3 to READY mode. When you press Undo (Alt-F4) immediately after completing the commands, 1-2-3 undoes the entire series of Wysiwyg commands. For example, if you select :Graph, complete a series of Graph commands without leaving the :Graph menu, and then return 1-2-3 to READY mode and press Undo, 1-2-3 undoes the entire series of commands.

Note that you might want to turn off the Undo feature before using Wysiwyg because it can use up a lot of memory. To turn off Undo, use Worksheet Global Default Other Undo Disable.

Wysiwyg and Macros

You can create macros to automate Wysiwyg tasks. Wysiwyg does not affect the execution of regular macros that you run while it is loaded. When you use Record (Alt-F2) to create a macro, 1-2-3 records all keystrokes, including those that perform Wysiwyg commands. This includes all mouse clicks and mouse movements. For more about macros, see Chapter 13.

Ending a Wysiwyg Session

Always use File Save before removing Wysiwyg from memory or you will lose your Wysiwyg formatting. Wysiwyg remains in memory until you use the Add-In Remove command, or until you end the 1-2-3 session.

If you are printing with Wysiwyg print commands, wait until 1-2-3 stops printing before you try to remove Wysiwyg from memory; you cannot remove Wysiwyg from memory while printing. Wysiwyg must be in memory if you want to move or copy Wysiwyg formatting along with data, or if you want to insert or delete rows or columns in a worksheet that automatically have Wysiwyg formatting assigned to them.

Summary

The Wysiwyg add-in transforms 1-2-3 from an old-fashioned character/keyboard-oriented spreadsheet into a modern graphic/mouse-based information manager. Wysiwyg accomplishes this without imposing an excessive burden on your hardware. While not every PC has enough memory to run Wysiwyg, and some older systems will operate more slowly when in graphics mode, Wysiwyg makes spreadsheet publishing available to a wide range of users. To make the most of Wysiwyg, spend some time experimenting with the commands and mixing different formats to create the effects you want. Remember that the regular print commands are always available when you want a rough-and-ready print of worksheet data, but when you have to make a good impression, switch to Wysiwyg.

11

Working with Text

ALTHOUGH SPREADSHEETS ARE PRIMARILY DESIGNED TO MANIPULATE numbers, in a number of situations you can use them to handle text. This chapter examines several 1-2-3 commands that apply to text. You'll use the Range Justify command to produce paragraphs of text from labels. You'll learn how to use the Print File command to convert spreadsheet data to text files that can be read by word processors. You'll combine the File Import and Data Parse commands to read text files from other programs. Finally, you will learn about the string functions that manipulate labels.

1-2-3 as Text Editor

Most of your worksheets will require at least a few labels, words, and phrases that describe the values in the model. Sometimes these pieces of text can be fairly lengthy. Consider the spreadsheet of projected expenses seen in Figure 11.1. The designer of this model decided to explain several of the assumptions at work in the calculations. This is a good practice, especially if the spreadsheet is going to be used or read by others.

Figure 11.1

Paragraphs of text in a worksheet

```
B14: 'Monthly growth rate (5%) reflects new sales push.              READY

        A        B       C       D       E       F       G       H     ◄
 1  Revenue Projection, Based on Monthly Growth Factor of:    1.05     ►
 2                                                                     ▲
 3           Jan-92   Feb-92  Mar-92  Apr-92  May-92  Jun-92  Jul-92   ▼
 4  POLK ST.                                                          ?
 5      Tour     3,350   3,518   3,693   3,878   4,072   4,276   4,489
 6    Flight     1,875   1,969   2,067   2,171   2,279   2,393   2,513
 7     Hotel       950     998   1,047   1,100   1,155   1,212   1,273
 8    Rental       875     919     965   1,013   1,064   1,117   1,173
 9     Group       800     840     882     926     972   1,021   1,072
10
11  TOTAL        7,850   8,243   8,655   9,087   9,542  10,019  10,520
12
13  Assumptions:
14         1 Monthly growth rate (5%) reflects new sales push.
15         2 Tour revenue will continue to be strong, reflecting
16           high disposable income in service area.
17
18
19
20
01-Nov-91   07:42 AM                                          NUM
```

To enter something like the first assumption in Figure 11.1, you simply type a long label and then press Enter. If you need to edit the text later, you can use the Edit key (F2). Remember that you can quickly pass your cursor through a long label by using the Ctrl-Right Arrow or Ctrl-Left Arrow keys, which move the cursor five spaces right or left, respectively. (The Tab and Shift-Tab keys do the same thing.)

To produce something like the second assumption, you can either enter two separate labels, in B15 and B16, or enter one long label that is then split into shorter labels to fit the available space. When you type a label longer than 80 characters, 1-2-3 scrolls the text off the screen to make room for more characters. You can see this in Figure 11.2, where the text for the second assumption is being typed.

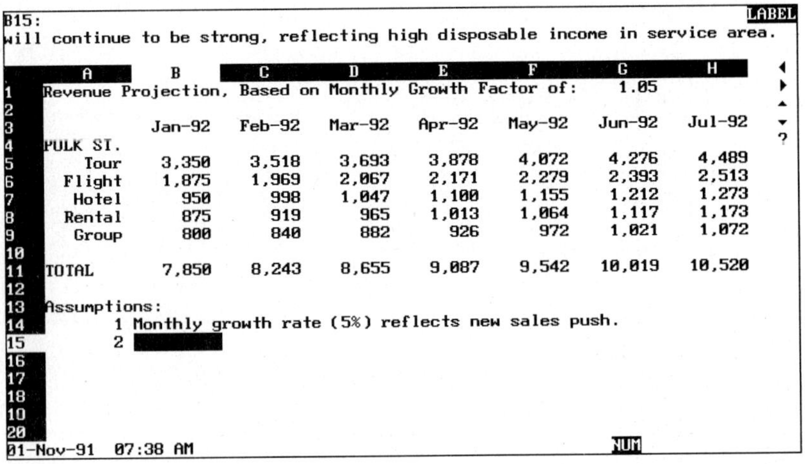

Figure 11.2

Typing a long label

```
B15:                                                                    LABEL
will continue to be strong, reflecting high disposable income in service area.
       A       B        C        D        E        F        G        H      ◀
1  Revenue Projection, Based on Monthly Growth Factor of:       1.05        ▶
2                                                                           ▲
3          Jan-92   Feb-92   Mar-92   Apr-92   May-92   Jun-92   Jul-92     ▼
4  PULK ST.                                                                 ?
5        Tour    3,350    3,518    3,693    3,878    4,072    4,276    4,489
6      Flight    1,875    1,969    2,067    2,171    2,279    2,393    2,513
7       Hotel      950      998    1,047    1,100    1,155    1,212    1,273
8      Rental      875      919      965    1,013    1,064    1,117    1,173
9       Group      800      840      882      926      972    1,021    1,072
10
11 TOTAL         7,850    8,243    8,655    9,087    9,542   10,019   10,520
12
13 Assumptions:
14           1 Monthly growth rate (5%) reflects new sales push.
15           2 ▮▮▮▮▮▮▮▮▮
16
17
18
10
20
01-Nov-91   07:38 AM                                            NUM
```

When the label is completed, it is entered and initially spreads across the columns of the worksheet. As shown in Figure 11.3, you cannot see the whole label at once, yet the entire label is stored in cell B15. Remember that 1-2-3 only allows long labels to borrow space like this when the neighboring cells are empty.

You probably want to format a long piece of text like this into a paragraph. To do this in 1-2-3, you split the long label into several shorter labels using the Range Justify command. The Range Justify command wraps the text into an area of the spreadsheet that you designate. Simply place your cell pointer on the cell containing the long label, in this case B15. Select Justify from the Range menu. When 1-2-3 requests the justify range, point out the area into which you want the long label rearranged—in this case the block of cells B15..G17, as shown in Figure 11.4.

The highlighted area should be empty except for the cell being reformatted. The range should be as wide as you would like the paragraph to be, and should extend several rows below the original cell so that there is room for the reformatted text. When you press Enter, 1-2-3 divides the long label into a series of shorter labels as wide as the highlighted range, without breaking words. The results can be seen in Figure 11.1.

Figure 11.3

A long label that borrows space

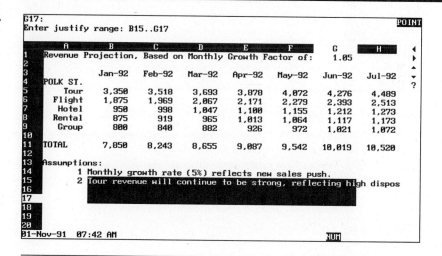

Figure 11.4

Using the Range Justify command

```
B15: 'Tour revenue will continue to be strong, reflecting high disposable i READY

        A       B        C        D        E        F        G        H      ◄
1   Revenue Projection, Based on Monthly Growth Factor of:       1.05        ►
2                                                                            ▲
3               Jan-92   Feb-92   Mar-92   Apr-92   May-92   Jun-92   Jul-92  ▼
4   POLK ST.                                                                 ?
5        Tour   3,350    3,518    3,693    3,878    4,072    4,276    4,489
6      Flight   1,875    1,969    2,067    2,171    2,279    2,393    2,513
7       Hotel     950      998    1,047    1,100    1,155    1,212    1,273
8      Rental     875      919      965    1,013    1,064    1,117    1,173
9       Group     800      840      882      926      972    1,021    1,072
10
11  TOTAL       7,850    8,243    8,655    9,087    9,542   10,019   10,520
12
13  Assumptions:
14          1 Monthly growth rate (5%) reflects new sales push.
15          2 Tour revenue will continue to be strong, reflecting high dispos
16
17
18
19
20
01-Nov-91   07:41 AM                                              NUM
```

```
G17:                                                                    POINT
Enter justify range: B15..G17

        A       B        C        D        E        F        G        H      ◄
1   Revenue Projection, Based on Monthly Growth Factor of:       1.05        ►
2                                                                            ▲
3               Jan-92   Feb-92   Mar-92   Apr-92   May-92   Jun-92   Jul-92  ▼
4   POLK ST.                                                                 ?
5        Tour   3,350    3,518    3,693    3,878    4,072    4,276    4,489
6      Flight   1,875    1,969    2,067    2,171    2,279    2,393    2,513
7       Hotel     950      998    1,047    1,100    1,155    1,212    1,273
8      Rental     875      919      965    1,013    1,064    1,117    1,173
9       Group     800      840      882      926      972    1,021    1,072
10
11  TOTAL       7,850    8,243    8,655    9,087    9,542   10,019   10,520
12
13  Assumptions:
14          1 Monthly growth rate (5%) reflects new sales push.
15          2 Tour revenue will continue to be strong, reflecting high dispos
16
17
18
19
20
01-Nov-91   07:42 AM                                              NUM
```

If you need to reformat the text into shorter labels, simply highlight the cell containing the piece of text to be edited and press F2. Be wary of making a label much shorter or longer than it was before editing: 1-2-3 does not automatically rearrange a paragraph of text after part of it has been shortened or lengthened. However, you can use the Range Justify command after editing to readjust a paragraph. For example, suppose you edit cell B15 as shown in Figure 11.5, where the first line of the second assumption is too short.

If you now use the Range Justify command and again select the range B15..G17, the first line of text will flow out to column G. The text that doesn't fit on the first row of the range is placed on the second row. 1-2-3 will actually add a space in between the words "reflects" and "high" to separate them. The results can be seen in Figure 11.6.

Figure 11.5

Edited text

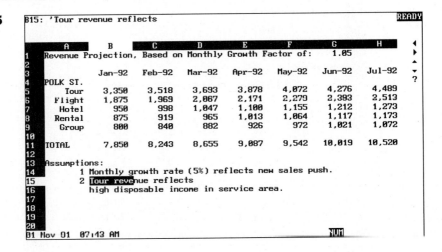

Figure 11.6

Results of rejustifying the range

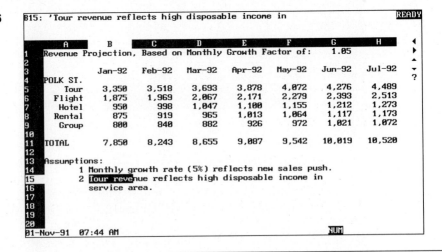

Despite its limited capabilities with text, you can use 1-2-3 to compose short documents, letters, and memos by using a series of long labels together with the Range Justify command. You can use a number of macros to simplify the successive reformatting of text, as described in Chapter 13. For more on formatting text with the Wysiwyg add-in, see Chapter 10.

Exporting with Print Files

However adept you become with 1-2-3, it won't handle your text with all of the editing and formatting features of a proper word processor. If you need to transfer information from 1-2-3 to a word processing program, you can use the Print command and choose the File option instead of Printer.

To transfer words and numbers from 1-2-3 to a word processing program, you need to create a special file that the word processor can read. As you may know, different word processing programs store their documents in different file formats, and the format determines the way that the actual letters of the document are stored on disk. Nevertheless, all popular word processing programs can read files that are stored in ASCII (American Standard Code for Information Interchange) format.

Word processing programs can read information stored in this way because they also use ASCII codes to send the letters and numbers of your documents to your printer. Indeed, this is also how 1-2-3 sends your spreadsheet data to the printer. By diverting data intended for the printer to a file on a disk, you can create a print file of spreadsheet data that consists entirely of ASCII codes. You do this by issuing the Print File command, which selects a file rather than the printer as the target of the print range. The file is normally named with the extension .PRN to distinguish it from other 1-2-3 files, and the data in it is simply a series of lines, each containing a string of letters, numbers, and spaces. Formulas are converted into their values and the values become text, including any formatting such as the dollar signs of the Currency format. ASCII files are sometimes called text files or DOS text files because they can be created with basic DOS commands.

Exporting a Print File

Suppose that you have prepared six months worth of projected revenue figures in a 1-2-3 worksheet like the one in Figure 11.7 and you want to include them in a memo that you are writing with your word processing program. Retyping the numbers from 1-2-3 into a word processing document would be a chore, and errors could arise from inaccurate typing. Instead, you decide to export the figures from 1-2-3 as an ASCII file and read them into the word processing document.

```
A1: 'Revenue Projection, Based on Monthly Growth Factor of:              READY

        A        B        C        D        E        F        G        H      ◄
1  Revenue Projection, Based on Monthly Growth Factor of:        1.06            ►
2
3              Jan-92   Feb-92   Mar-92   Apr-92   May-92   Jun-92   TOTALS      ▲
4  POLK ST.                                                                     ▼
5      Tour    3,350    3,551    3,764    3,990    4,229    4,483   23,367      ?
6    Flight    1,875    1,988    2,107    2,233    2,367    2,509   13,079
7     Hotel      950    1,007    1,067    1,131    1,199    1,271    6,627
8    Rental      875      928      983    1,042    1,105    1,171    6,103
9     Group      800      848      899      953    1,010    1,071    5,580
10
11 TOTAL       7,850    8,321    8,820    9,349    9,910   10,505   54,756
12
13 Assumptions:
14      1 Monthly growth rate (6%) reflects new sales push.
15      2 Tour revenue reflects high disposable income in
16        service area.
17
18
19
20
01-Nov-91   07:52 AM                                         NUM
```

First select Print from the main menu, and then select File. 1-2-3 immediately asks you to name the file to which you want the output sent, and displays a list of existing PRN files. You can type a fresh name or choose one of the existing names. If you select an existing name, 1-2-3 asks if you want to Cancel the command or Replace the data in the existing file with new data. To create a new PRN file in the current directory, you can simply type the file name. If you want to use the extension .PRN, leave the extension blank and 1-2-3 will supply it. Otherwise, you can enter a file name with an extension of your choice, such as .TXT or .ASC.

Once you have entered or chosen a file name, 1-2-3 opens a file on disk and prepares to receive the print data. You can now select the print range and the desired print options using the Print menu and/or the Print Settings dialog box. Then select Go from the main Print menu to write the data into the file. Only after you quit the Print menu and return to READY mode is the file closed. This allows you to select another range of cells to be printed to the same file. In fact, you can select several different ranges and send each one to the same print file by alternating the Range and Go commands.

When you're creating a print file, the print range must include all of the labels and numbers you want to export. For example, if a long label flows across several columns, you must include all of those columns for the entire label to be printed. For the revenue projection in Figure 11.7, the print range would be A3..H11 if you wanted to exclude the title and assumptions, or A1..H16 if you wanted to include them. Do not include any extra blank columns and rows in the print range; these will just add empty space to the word processing document.

To make it easier for your word processor to handle the data coming from 1-2-3, you may want to change some of the options prior to printing to disk. Use the Margin option to set the left margin to zero characters. This will prevent 1-2-3 from adding four spaces to the left of the data in the file. Similarly, selecting a top margin of zero will stop 1-2-3 from adding extra lines to the top of the print range. The right margin setting needs particular attention since the data in the file will be split into sections if you have a right margin setting narrower than the width of the print range. In general, you shouldn't use a right margin much wider than 80 if the text file is to be read by a word processor working with a standard letter page document. Otherwise, your file will contain more data per line than can comfortably fit between the document margins. In most cases, you should also use the Other Unformatted option. This will prevent 1-2-3 from adding headers, footers, and page breaks to the print file. Typically, you will add these embellishments within the word processor.

In Figure 11.8 you can see the Print Settings dialog box completed. Note that when you use the Print File command the name of the file appears in the dialog box. You can edit the file name at this point. When the file name field in the dialog box is active, you can press F3 to list file names.

Figure 11.8

The completed print settings

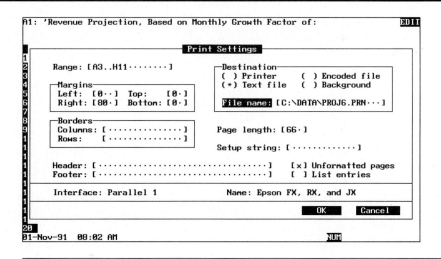

Having selected the print range and the options that you want, you can select Go from the main Print menu. Unless you want to add other cells to the print file, you should now select Quit to return to READY mode and close the print file. (If you accidentally select Go a second time before leaving the Print menu, you will end up with two copies of the same data in the file.)

Once you have created the print file, you can exit 1-2-3 and start your word processor (after first making sure you have saved any necessary changes to your worksheet). When you reach the point in your document where you want the 1-2-3 text to appear, you may want to check that your margin settings are wide enough to accommodate the incoming data before issuing the command to read in the print file. Word processors use different commands to read in ASCII text. For example, in DisplayWrite 4 the command is Get File (Ctrl-F6). In Microsoft Word, you can use Transfer Load. In WordPerfect, you use Text In/Out (Ctrl-F5). WordPerfect also allows you to read in text files from the file list presented by the List key (F5). In fact, WordPerfect 5.1 allows you to link documents to 1-2-3 worksheets and avoid the need for a print file, a feature described in the next section. Figure 11.9 shows the sample print file after it has been read directly into a WordPerfect document.

Figure 11.9

Text imported into WordPerfect

```
                              MEMORANDUM

To:        Bill Jones

From:      Fred Smith

Subj:      Six Month Projection


Bill:
       Here are the six month projection figures for the Polk St. office, based
on a monthly growth rate of 6%, as discussed last week.

            Jan-92   Feb-92   Mar-92   Apr-92   May-92   Jun-92   TOTALS
POLK ST.
     Tour    3,350    3,551    3,764    3,990    4,229    4,483   23,367
   Flight    1,875    1,988    2,107    2,233    2,367    2,509   13,079
    Hotel      950    1,007    1,067    1,131    1,199    1,271    6,627
   Rental      875      928      983    1,042    1,105    1,171    6,103
    Group      800      848      899      953    1,010    1,071    5,580

TOTAL        7,850    8,321    8,820    9,349    9,910   10,505   54,756

                                            Doc 1 Pg 1 Ln 2.95" Pos 1"
```

Once you have imported the text from 1-2-3 into your word processor, you can use traditional word processing tools like underline, boldface, and so on. Bear in mind that the columns of numbers and labels are not set up with tab stops at this point; they are simply arranged with spaces. This will make a difference in the way you edit the material in the word processing document. Most word processors can convert such text into columns, inserting tabs or other formatting codes. This might be a good step to take if you want to edit the imported data extensively.

Other Means of Sharing Data

One type of data that word processing programs treat somewhat differently are names and addresses used for *mail merging,* the customizing of a standard letter with names and other information from a list. Some word processors such as WordPerfect can read a name and address list from a spreadsheet file in a format that is ready for mail merging. Since this is a fairly specialized word processing function, you should consult your word processor's program manual or a good text on that program.

Another way that some word processors now interact with spreadsheets is through file linking. For example, in WordPerfect 5.1 the last option on the Text In/Out menu is Spreadsheet. You can use this option to read all or part of a 1-2-3 spreadsheet straight into a WordPerfect document without having to prepare the worksheet data by saving it in a text file. In fact, you can connect the worksheet to the word processing document so that changes in the worksheet cause corresponding changes in the document.

When you select Spreadsheet from the WordPerfect Text In/Out menu, you see these options:

```
1 Import   2 Create   3 Link Edit   4 Link   5 Link Options
```

The Import option reads all or part of a 1-2-3 worksheet into the current document at the current cursor location. Choosing this option brings up a four-item menu:

```
1 - Filename
2 - Range
3 - Type
4 - Perform Link
```

You must fill in the appropriate information for the first three items and then select the fourth to complete the operation.

When specifying the file name, you can use the List command to display standard WordPerfect directory lists and then select the desired worksheet file from the list. When you give WordPerfect the name of the worksheet, the file is read and the entire worksheet, from A1 through the last occupied cell, is suggested as the default range to be imported. You can select a smaller range by stating coordinates or a range name.

You then have to decide how you want WordPerfect to treat the spreadsheet data—as a table, or as a set of tabbed columns. When you have given WordPerfect the parameters for the Import command, you can select Perform Link and the spreadsheet data will be read into the document with the appropriate formatting (either a table code or a tab set code).

The Import command creates static data that does not change if the spreadsheet is updated later. In contrast, the Spreadsheet Create command establishes a special file link between your WordPerfect document and the 1-2-3 worksheet range you specify. This means that the word processing document will reflect the latest figures in the worksheet. When you select Link, you get the same four commands presented by the Import command, but the result is different. Special codes separate the imported spreadsheet data from the rest of the document, as illustrated in Figure 11.10. Note that the Text In/Out Spreadsheet Link Options command allows you to turn off the display of link codes.

Figure 11.10

A 1-2-3 worksheet linked into WordPerfect 5.1

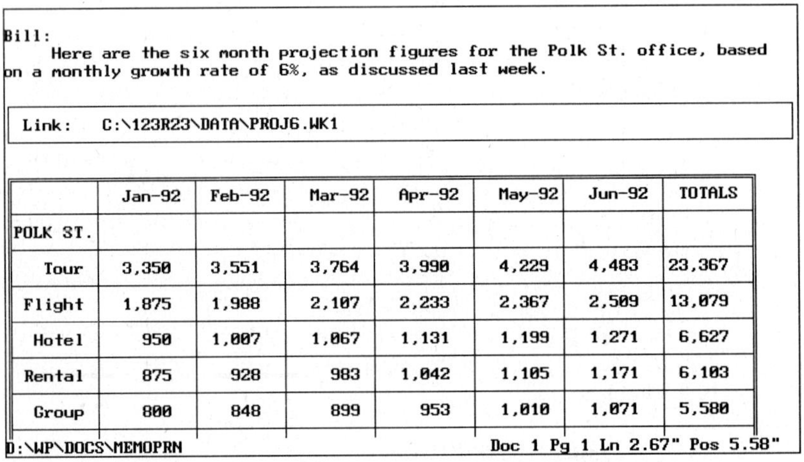

```
Bill:
    Here are the six month projection figures for the Polk St. office, based
on a monthly growth rate of 6%, as discussed last week.

  Link:    C:\123R23\DATA\PROJ6.WK1
```

	Jan-92	Feb-92	Mar-92	Apr-92	May-92	Jun-92	TOTALS
POLK ST.							
Tour	3,350	3,551	3,764	3,990	4,229	4,483	23,367
Flight	1,875	1,988	2,107	2,233	2,367	2,509	13,079
Hotel	950	1,007	1,067	1,131	1,199	1,271	6,627
Rental	875	928	983	1,042	1,105	1,171	6,103
Group	800	848	899	953	1,010	1,071	5,580

```
D:\WP\DOCS\MEMOPRN                                   Doc 1 Pg 1 Ln 2.67" Pos 5.58"
```

When you need to print the WordPerfect document, you issue the Text In/Out Spreadsheet Link Options command and select the Update All Links option. This tells WordPerfect to reread the worksheet file, making sure that the latest version is used to supply data to the document. If you set to Yes the Update on Retrieve option on the Text In/Out Spreadsheet Link Options menu, WordPerfect will update the spreadsheet link every time the document is retrieved.

Other word processors have commands similar to WordPerfect's Text In/Out Spreadsheet. For example, in Microsoft Word you can use Library Link Spreadsheet. Since 1-2-3's WK1 file format is such a well-established standard, it is supported in most file import/export commands.

Importing Text into 1-2-3

Besides creating text files that can be read by word processing programs, 1-2-3 can read text files into a spreadsheet. This feature is handy when you want to use information from a program that cannot create data files in 1-2-3 format. Suppose your company has a custom program for sales orders. The program cannot store data in 1-2-3 format; however, you would like to take a spreadsheet of recent orders with you when making sales calls. The accounting program should be able to print data to disk using the equivalent of

1-2-3's Print File command. In this example, the recent sales listing for a company has been stored in a file called RSLIST.TXT. To read this file into 1-2-3, you use the File Import command.

Before issuing the File Import command, you need to think about where in the worksheet you want to place the incoming data. The Import command works like File Combine rather than File Retrieve: It doesn't erase all of the current worksheet but simply uses as many cells of the current worksheet as it needs, beginning with the cell that is current when you issue the command. While you can use File Import to read data into an existing worksheet, it is a good idea to experiment with importing files into a blank spreadsheet first. Issuing the File Import command with the cell pointer in the wrong location can overwrite important entries. Moreover, imported data can sometimes have unexpected effects on existing entries in the spreadsheet. For example, the imported data may contain ASCII codes that 1-2-3 misinterprets as commands. Figure 11.11 shows a worksheet ready to receive the imported sales data, beginning in cell A9.

Figure 11.11
Worksheet ready
for text import

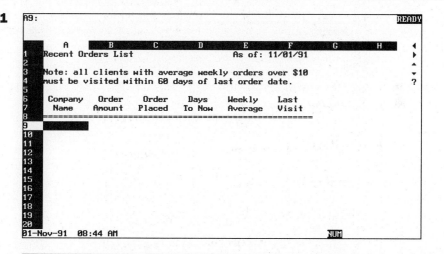

When you select Import from the File menu, you get a choice between Text and Numbers. You use the Text option when the file being imported consists purely of lines of data, with words and numbers separated by spaces. When 1-2-3 reads a simple text file like this, each line is treated as one long label. You then need to take additional steps, described shortly, to break these labels down into individual cell entries. You use the Number option to read in data from files in which the pieces of information are separated by commas, quotes, or both. Such files are sometimes referred to as BASIC data files, or comma- and quote-delimited files. Some programs that cannot export data in 1-2-3 format can create delimited files instead of or in addition to ASCII text files. Delimited files are easier for 1-2-3 to make sense of than simple text files because the delimiters help 1-2-3 break up each line of data into separate items and place each item in a separate cell.

When you have selected Text or Numbers, 1-2-3 requests the name of the file. You are presented with a list of PRN files in the current directory. To see other files in other areas, you can edit the drive and directory prompt as well as the file specification, using the techniques described in Chapter 7. When you select the file you want, 1-2-3 reads it into the worksheet at the current position of the cell pointer, as seen in Figure 11.12.

Figure 11.12
Imported text

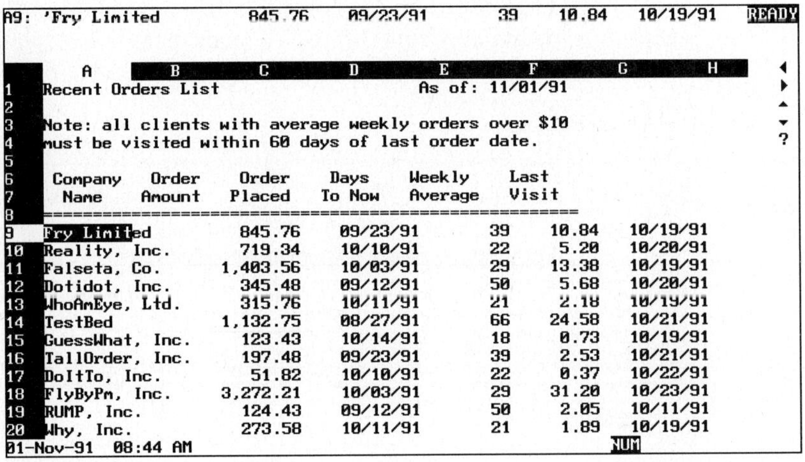

```
A9:  'Fry Limited            845.76    09/23/91       39    10.84   10/19/91  READY

      A        B        C        D        E        F        G        H      ◄
1  Recent Orders List                       As of: 11/01/91                  ►
2                                                                            ▲
3  Note: all clients with average weekly orders over $10                     ▼
4  must be visited within 60 days of last order date.                        ?
5
6  Company   Order    Order    Days    Weekly   Last
7   Name     Amount   Placed   To Now  Average  Visit
8  =====================================================================
9  Fry Limited        845.76   09/23/91    39    10.84   10/19/91
10 Reality, Inc.      719.34   10/10/91    22     5.20   10/20/91
11 Falseta, Co.     1,403.56   10/03/91    29    13.38   10/19/91
12 Dotidot, Inc.      345.48   09/12/91    50     5.68   10/20/91
13 WhoAmEye, Ltd.     315.76   10/11/91    21     2.18   10/19/91
14 TestBed          1,132.75   08/27/91    66    24.58   10/21/91
15 GuessWhat, Inc.    123.43   10/14/91    18     0.73   10/19/91
16 TallOrder, Inc.    197.48   09/23/91    39     2.53   10/21/91
17 DoItTo, Inc.        51.82   10/10/91    22     0.37   10/22/91
18 FlyByPm, Inc.    3,272.21   10/03/91    29    31.20   10/23/91
19 RUMP, Inc.         124.43   09/12/91    50     2.05   10/11/91
20 Why, Inc.          273.58   10/11/91    21     1.89   10/19/91
01-Nov-91  08:44 AM                                              NUM
```

The data in this figure was imported using the Text option. At first glance, this looks like a normal spreadsheet. However, if you look at the contents of cell A9 carefully, you will see that it is one long label. There is no data at all in columns B, C, D, and so on. There are two techniques you can use to help 1-2-3 make sense of data like this. The first technique, called *parsing,* involves breaking up the lines of data according to a set of interpretation rules. The second approach is to use the string functions described later in this chapter.

The Data Parse Command

The Data Parse command is used to divide long labels, such as those in Figure 11.12, into separate cells of information. The command passes the label through a special line of codes that filter the contents of the label into four categories: values, times, dates, and labels. To create this line, called the *format line,* you place your cell pointer on the first cell containing a label to be parsed. In Figure 11.12, this would be cell A9. You then issue the Data Parse command, which presents a small settings dialog box and a menu with the choices Format-Line, Input-Column, Output-Range, Reset, Go, and Quit. Select Format-Line. This command offers the two choices Create and Edit. At this point, you need to select Create, which both inserts a new row into the worksheet and creates a long label consisting of special characters, as shown in Figure 11.13.

Figure 11.13

Inserting the format line

```
A9: !L>>*L>>>>>*******U>>>>>****D>>>>>>>*******U>****U>>>>***D>>>>>>    MENU
Format-Line  Input-Column  Output-Range  Reset  Go  Quit
Create or edit a format line at the current cell
     A        B                    Parse Settings              G        H
1    Recent Orders L
2                         Input column: [.............]
3    Note: all clien
4    must be visited     Output range: [.............]
5
6    Company    Orde
7    Name      Anoun      Press F2 (EDIT) to edit settings
8    ===============
9    L>>*L>>>>>*******U>>>>>****D>>>>>>>*******U>****U>>>>***D>>>>>>
10   Fry Limited        845.76   09/23/91    39    10.84   10/19/91
11   Reality, Inc.      719.34   10/10/91    22     5.20   10/20/91
12   Falseta, Co.     1,403.56   10/03/91    29    13.38   10/19/91
13   Dotidot, Inc.      345.48   09/12/91    50     5.68   10/20/91
14   WhoAnEye, Ltd.     315.76   10/11/91    21     2.18   10/19/91
15   TestBed          1,132.75   08/27/91    66    24.58   10/21/91
16   GuessWhat, Inc.    123.43   10/14/91    18     0.73   10/19/91
17   TallOrder, Inc.    197.48   09/23/91    39     2.53   10/21/91
18   DoItTo, Inc.        51.82   10/10/91    22     0.37   10/22/91
19   FlyByPn, Inc.    3,272.21   10/03/91    29    31.20   10/23/91
20   RUMP, Inc.         124.43   09/12/91    50     2.05   10/11/91
01-Nov-91  08:48 AM                          CALC      NUM
```

This long label in A9, the cell that was current when the Create command was issued, begins with the ! character. Recall that ! in the leftmost column of a print range tells 1-2-3 not to print anything on that line. Following the ! character are a series of letters, asterisks, and greater-than signs. The letter L stands for label, V stands for value, D represents date, and T represents time. The letters show the points at which 1-2-3 wants to split the label into separate cells as well as the type of data 1-2-3 thinks it has found in each part. The greater-than sign (>) shows the number of characters that 1-2-3 finds in each part of the label. The asterisks represent the gaps between the parts into which 1-2-3 wants to split the long label. These will be the breaks between columns when 1-2-3 translates the lines of text into cell entries.

If you look closely at this format line, notice that the first piece of data identified by 1-2-3 is a short label that is three characters long, as indicated by L>>. This is followed by a gap and a longer label, L>>>>>>, and then the value V>>>>>. This means that 1-2-3 wants to parse the company name into two columns of data, because the space in "Fry Limited" fooled 1-2-3 into thinking there were two columns of labels although there should only be one. You correct misinterpretations like this with the Format-Line Edit command, described in a moment.

Despite this shaky beginning, 1-2-3 did well with the rest of the format line. The values and dates in the text have been correctly identified. In this example, you would simply need to change L>>*L>>>>>> to L>>>>>>>>>> for the format line to work correctly. The Format-Line Edit command on the Data Parse menu allows you to adjust the format line to reflect more accurately how the label should be divided. When you pick Format-Line and then Edit, the menu and settings box disappear so that you can make the necessary changes to the format line characters. You are automatically placed into overstrike mode, as indicated by the status line message OVR. This is because, however inappropriate the selection of characters on the parse line, there are just enough of them to describe the data. Instead of adding and deleting characters, you simply type the ones you want over the incorrect ones.

Often the parse format line created by 1-2-3 does not interpret your text entry the way you want it to. After all, determining what parts of this long label should be placed in which cells is a fairly complex task. When you have edited the line, press Enter to return to the Parse menu. (If you return to READY mode after creating a format line, you can also edit the line using the F2 key since the line is simply a label.) In Figure 11.14, you can see the edited format line and the two settings needed to complete preparations for the parse operation: input column and output range.

Figure 11.14

The edited parse line with parse settings

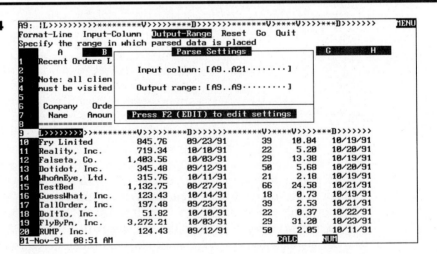

When the format line editing is completed, you must use the Input-Column and Output-Range commands. The input column is actually a single column range that begins with the parse line and extends to the last of the labels of data you want to parse, in this case A9..A21. The output range is the area of the spreadsheet you want the parsed data to occupy. You don't need to highlight the entire output range, just its upper-left corner. You can either choose an output area that is a separate part of the worksheet and so preserve the original labels, or you can output the results of the Parse over the input column of labels. Since you can reverse the Parse command with UNDO and you probably won't need the labels after they have been parsed, the second option is preferable. In this case, you can just select A9 for the Output-Range setting.

When you have specified the input column and output range, you can issue the Go command. The results are seen in Figure 11.15. Note that the values are all unformatted, with the dates appearing as serial numbers. Also note that the Parse command does not set column widths and the first column is not quite wide enough to show the company names in full.

Figure 11.15

Initial results of the Parse operation

```
A9: 'Fry Limited                                                    READY
         A         B         C        D        E         F        G         H      ◄
   5                                                                               ►
   6    Company   Order    Order    Days    Weekly    Last                         ▲
   7     Name     Amount   Placed   To Now  Average   Visit                        ▼
   8    ==========================================================================  ?
   9    Fry Limit  845.76   33504      39    10.84     33530
  10    Reality,   719.34   33521      22     5.2      33531
  11    Falseta,  1403.56   33514      29    13.38     33530
  12    Dotidot,   345.48   33493      50     5.68     33531
  13    WhoAnEye,  315.76   33522      21     2.18     33530
  14    TestBed   1132.75   33477      66    24.58     33532
  15    GuessWhat  123.43   33525      18     0.73     33530
  16    TallOrder  197.48   33504      39     2.53     33532
  17    DoItTo, I   51.82   33521      22     0.37     33533
  18    FlyByPn,  3272.21   33514      29    31.2      33534
  19    RUMP, Inc  124.43   33493      50     2.05     33522
  20    Why, Inc.  273.58   33522      21     1.89     33530
  21    Why, Inc.          273.58   10/11/91        21     1.89    10/19/91
  22
  23
  24
  01-Nov-91  08:54 AM                                              NUM
```

In this example, since the output range began in the same cell as the input column, the parse format line was overwritten. However, one of the source labels was not overwritten, which is why the entry for Why, Inc., appears to have been duplicated. You can erase the label remaining in A21. Indeed, there is usually quite a bit of tidying up to do after a Parse operation. The date serial numbers need to be formatted back to date appearance. You can apply a Comma format to columns B and E. Figure 11.16 includes a tidier version of the results; notice that the entries in column D have been converted into formulas.

Besides tidying up the Parse results, you might want to consider the purpose of putting this data in a spreadsheet. In the current scenario, the values were supplied by a sales order program that could not create files in any of the standard formats understood by 1-2-3. As a means of transferring data, the Parse command is limited. Although it creates values from labels, it does not recreate the formulas that produced those values. The entries in columns D and E will remain fixed values unless you replace them with formulas. If you do replace them with formulas, as shown in Figure 11.16, the number of days from the last order to the current date will be recalculated when the date changes.

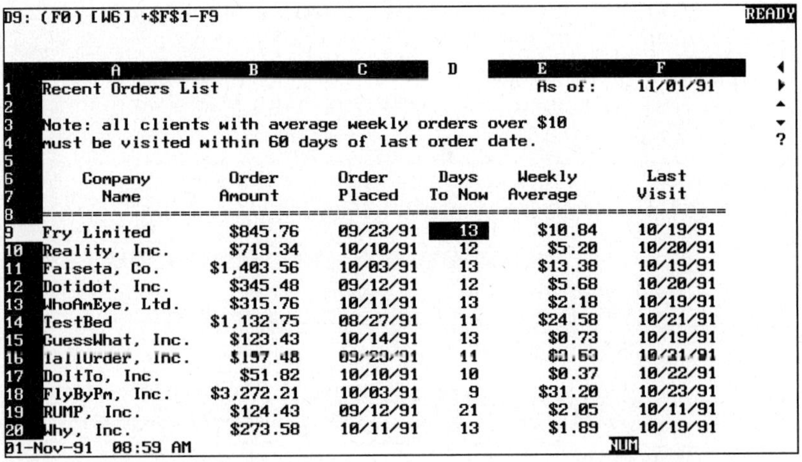

Figure 11.16

Improved Parse operation results

```
D9: (F0) [W6] +$F$1-F9                                              READY

         A              B            C        D       E            F        ◀
1    Recent Orders List                               As of:     11/01/91   ▶
2                                                                            ▲
3    Note: all clients with average weekly orders over $10                  ▼
4    must be visited within 60 days of last order date.                     ?
5
6        Company        Order        Order    Days    Weekly     Last
7         Name          Amount       Placed   To Now  Average    Visit
8    ========================================================================
9    Fry Limited        $845.76      09/23/91   13    $10.84     10/19/91
10   Reality, Inc.      $719.34      10/10/91   12    $5.20      10/20/91
11   Falseta, Co.       $1,403.56    10/03/91   13    $13.38     10/19/91
12   Dotidot, Inc.      $345.48      09/12/91   12    $5.68      10/20/91
13   WhoAmEye, Ltd.     $315.76      10/11/91   13    $2.18      10/19/91
14   TestBed            $1,132.75    08/27/91   11    $24.58     10/21/91
15   GuessWhat, Inc.    $123.43      10/14/91   13    $0.73      10/19/91
16   laiiUrder, Inc.    $157.48      09/29/91   11    $3.63      10/21/91
17   DoItTo, Inc.       $51.82       10/10/91   10    $0.37      10/22/91
18   FlyByPn, Inc.      $3,272.21    10/03/91    9    $31.20     10/23/91
19   RUMP, Inc.         $124.43      09/12/91   21    $2.05      10/11/91
20   Why, Inc.          $273.58      10/11/91   13    $1.89      10/19/91
01-Nov-91  08:59 AM                                            NUM
```

While parsing text is not a particularly common operation for most spreadsheet users, it is valuable for those who have to deal with information from programs that cannot store data in a standard worksheet format. Remember, the Translate program that comes with 1-2-3 can create WK1 files out of the following formats: DBF, DIF, Enable, SYLK, SuperCalc4, Symphony, and Visi-Calc. In general, it is better to use one of the formats than to rely on the Parse command. For more on using Translate, see Appendix B.

Text Formulas

Even though labels have no numeric value, you can use them in formulas. This expands your ability to handle a variety of tasks in your worksheets. Text formulas are particularly useful when developing macros, which are discussed in Chapters 13 and 14. You can also use them within the body of your spreadsheet. For example, you can reference a label in another cell just as you can a value, as shown in Figure 11.17. The entry +A6 in cell C3 returns

the name Mick from the table of sales. If the sales figures were updated and the list were resorted, putting a different agent in first place, the names in C3 and A6 would change.

Figure 11.17

Referencing a label

```
C3: [W13] +A6                                                        READY
         A        B         C        D          E           F         ◄
1   Sales Campaign                                                    ►
2                                                                     ▲
3   Sales leader:      Mick                                           ▼
4                                                                     ?
5      First     Last      Office      Sales    Commission   Last Sale
6   Mick      Scott     Van Ness    $941,250    $56,475    01-Nov-91
7   Jim       Weir      Embarcadero $890,670    $53,440    28-Oct-91
8   Jane      Dobbs     Polk St.    $878,590    $52,715    26-Oct-91
9   Bill      Front     Embarcadero $876,900    $52,614    25-Oct-91
10  Ron       Davis     Union Sq.   $859,600    $51,576    24-Oct-91
11  Fred      Jones     Union Sq.   $849,050    $50,943    20-Oct-91
12  Rob       Ridge     Embarcadero $804,550    $48,273    16-Oct-91
13  Mary      Grant     Polk St.    $768,545    $46,113    16-Oct-91
14  Pip       Harris    Embarcadero $760,805    $45,648    13-Oct-91
15  Joe       Smith     Union Sq.   $687,450    $41,247    12-Oct-91
16  Alan      Chan      Van Ness    $586,780    $35,207    11-Oct-91
17  Nina      Smith     Union Sq.   $500,001    $30,000    09-Oct-91
18  Tom       Clark     Van Ness    $459,870    $27,592    08-Oct-91
19  Jud       Ford      Polk St.    $458,790    $27,527    06-Oct-91
20
01-Nov-91   09:05 AM                                         NUM
```

To show the agent's full name, you might be tempted to use the formula +A6+B6. However, the result of such a formula would be 0 because 1-2-3 thinks you are trying to add two labels and labels have a value of zero. 1-2-3 can only "add" labels if you use the & sign. Thus the formula +A6&B6 has the result MickScott. Adding labels like this is referred to as *concatenation* and & is referred to as the *concatenation sign.* Unfortunately, +A68B6 concatenates the two parts of the name without any intervening spaces. You can add spaces and other text to a concatenation formula by enclosing the desired characters in quotes. Thus the formula +A6&" "&B6 produces the desired result: Mick Scott.

The formula +A6&" "&B6 concatenates three pieces of information: a cell reference (A6), text placed in quotes (in this case a space), and another cell reference (B6). The beginning plus sign lets 1-2-3 know this is a formula. Note that 1-2-3 will not accept the & sign as the first character in a formula, but you can use & within a formula, between cell references, and between strings of text. Consider this formula:

```
+A6&" "&B6&" from the "&C6&" office."
```

which produces this result:

```
Mike Scott from the Van Ness office.
```

Note that in order to create the space before the office name, you need to include it in the quotes that precede the cell reference.

You will encounter a slight problem when you want to include values in a text formula. For example, suppose you want to create the following:

```
Mick Scott with sales of $941,250
```

You might think that you could use this formula:

```
+A6&" "&B6&" with sales of "&D6
```

However, this results in ERR, because the & sign must be followed by a reference to a cell that contains a label, or a formula that results in a label. To create a label result from a cell containing a value, you use the @STRING function. This function converts a value to a label, using the following syntax:

```
@STRING(x,n)
```

The *x* argument can be the address of the cell you want converted into a value, or a formula resulting in a value. The *n* argument determines how many decimal places of *x* are shown in the resulting label. Thus @STRING(10/3,2) results in a label that reads 3.33. In the example, the formula

```
+A6&" "&B6&" with sales of $"&@STRING(D6,0)
```

produces this result:

```
Mick Scott with sales of $941250
```

Note that the @STRING function does not permit any control of formatting besides the decimal places. Thus the dollar sign has to be added as text and the thousands separator is omitted, despite the fact that the values are displayed in the table with currency format.

Despite these limitations, when you use text formulas rather than simply typing statements, the cell references in the formula are dynamic: When the top salesperson changes, the text is updated. This technique allows you to create invoices, letters, and other documents that have the appearance of static text but are in fact dynamically related to the contents of the spreadsheet. Figure 11.18 contains a memorandum composed of a mixture of ordinary labels and text formulas.

There are text formulas in rows 5, 11, 13, 14, and 17 of Figure 11.18. These combine values from the table in Figure 11.16 with strings to produce text that looks as though it were simply typed into a wide column. Figure 11.19 shows the formulas in this memo exposed by application of the Text format. Notice the use of @STRING to convert values to labels. Also note the use of leading spaces in H5 to indent the name of the person to whom the memo is addressed.

Figure 11.18
Memorandum using
string formulas

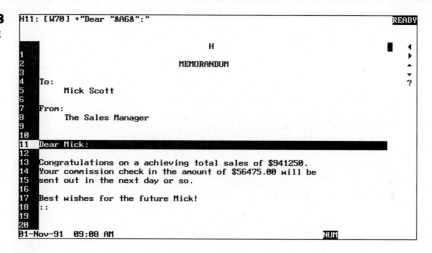

Figure 11.19
Text formulas
exposed

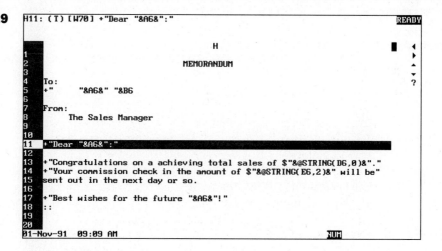

String Functions

The @STRING function is one of a number of 1-2-3 functions that are specifically designed for manipulating text. Known collectively as the string functions, they are valuable when writing string formulas and when dealing with data imported in the form of text. String functions are also used with some advanced macro commands, as described in Chapter 14.

The @EXACT Function

You can use the @EXACT function to compare character strings (text either enclosed in quotes or stored in a cell as a label). It has the syntax:

@EXACT(*string1*,*string2*)

where *string1* is a character string value and *string2* is a second string value. The @EXACT function compares the values of *string1* and *string2*. If the values are exactly identical, including capitalization, it returns a value of 1. If there are any differences, it returns 0. @EXACT ignores label prefixes. If you compare character string constants (as opposed to label cells), you must enclose the text within quotes. You can only compare character strings with @EXACT. If you attempt to compare one or more numbers or empty cells, the result is ERR.

Figure 11.20 includes an example of @EXACT. Commission checks cannot be authorized until the salesperson's report has been received. The formula in F24 returns the text Okay if the entry in column D is Yes. If the entry is No, or even YES or yes, the formula returns Pending Report.

Figure 11.20
Using @EXACT

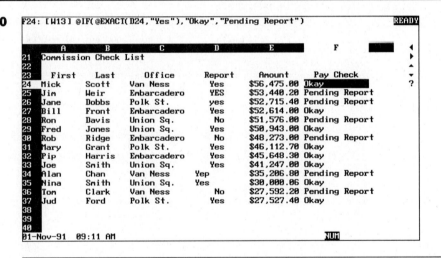

To compare strings without regard to capitalization, you can use the @IF function without @EXACT. The @IF function is not case sensitive. For example, the following formula will return Okay if D24 contains Yes, regardless of the capitalization:

@IF(D24="Yes","Okay","Pending Report")

The @FIND Function

The @FIND function locates characters within a string. For example, suppose you want to determine where the letter "t" is located within Lotus. The function returns the position of a character—that is, how many characters it is removed from the left of the label. The @FIND function uses the following syntax:

```
@FIND(search-string,string,start-number)
```

The *search-string* argument is the character or string value that you are looking for. The *string* argument represents the string you are searching within. The *start-number* argument is a numeric value of 0 or greater, representing the character position at which you want to begin searching. If you enter the label Lotus in A1, the formula

```
@FIND("t",A1,0)
```

returns 2. The @FIND function returns the character position at which the first occurrence of *search-string* was found. The number 0 represents the first character in the string, 1 represents the second character, and so on. Both the *search-string* and *string* arguments can either be a piece of text enclosed in quotes or a cell reference to a label.

Suppose that the entry in A1 were Lotus Development. The formula

```
@FIND("t",A1,3)
```

would return 16, since the letter "t" at the end of the label is 16 characters beyond the first character and the *start-number* argument tells 1-2-3 to begin the search three characters into the string, beyond the first occurrence of "t." You get an error if the value of *start-number* is more than the number of characters in *string* minus 1. You also get an error if @FIND fails to find any occurrences of *search-string*.

The @LEFT, @RIGHT, and @MID Functions

@LEFT, @RIGHT, and @MID are used to find strings of characters within labels based on the position of those characters. The syntax of @RIGHT and @MID is similar to @LEFT, which has the syntax

```
@LEFT(string,n)
```

where *string* is a string value and *n* is a numeric value of 0 or greater. The @LEFT function thus returns the leftmost characters of *string*, returning the number of characters specified by the *n* argument. For example, the following formula returns Lotus if A1 contains Lotus Development:

```
@LEFT(A1,5)
```

The @LEFT function is handy for separating names into first and last. Suppose that A1 contains Fred Smith. The formula @LEFT(A1,4) returns Fred. But if A1 is changed to Stephen Smith, the formula will return Step. To make the formula more useful, you can employ @FIND to specify how far to the left the reading of the characters must go. The following formula will work nicely:

```
@LEFT(A1,@FIND(" ",A1,0))
```

Here @FIND returns a number that is the position of the space, and this is used as the second argument in the @LEFT function.

While @LEFT reads characters beginning at the left of a label, @MID reads characters from the middle of a label, starting at the character position you specify. Thus @MID uses one more argument than @LEFT. Its syntax is as follows:

```
@MID(string,start-number,n)
```

where *string* is the label to be read, *start-number* is the character at which to start reading, and *n* is the number of characters to be read. For example, if A1 contains Lotus Development, the following formula returns Dev:

```
@MID(A1,6,3)
```

As with @LEFT and other string functions, spaces and punctuation count as characters with @MID, but label prefix characters are ignored.

The @RIGHT function reads characters from the right end of a label. Thus @RIGHT(A1,5) returns Smith if A1 contains Fred Smith or Stephen Smith. However, to cope with last names of varying lengths you need to work out the second argument so that @RIGHT begins reading after the space between the names. For example, the formula

```
@RIGHT(A1,@LENGTH(A1)-@FIND(" ",A1,0)-1)
```

uses the @LENGTH function, described next, to find out how many characters there are in the original label. The position of the space, and one more character, are subtracted from this length to give the @RIGHT function the correct second argument.

There is another way of working out the @RIGHT calculation. If the @LEFT formula that produced the first name is in B1, you could enter the following in C1:

```
@RIGHT(A1,@LENGTH(A1)-@LENGTH(B1)-1)
```

This formula creates the second @RIGHT argument by taking the length of the first name away from the length of the original label.

The @TRIM and @LENGTH Functions

The @LENGTH function simply measures the length of a label, using the following syntax:

    @LENGTH(String)

Thus @LENGTH(A1) returns 5 if A1 contains Lotus. As you saw with @RIGHT, the @LENGTH function is very useful when combined with @RIGHT and @LEFT to extract specific text from a long label.

Occasionally, you will develop a string formula that creates a label with one or more extra spaces at the beginning or end. The @TRIM function removes any extra spaces from a label, using the syntax:

    @TRIM(string)

@TRIM removes trailing spaces after the last nonspace character, spaces preceding the first nonspace character, and duplicate spaces between words. Normal spaces in strings are not affected. If *string* is empty or contains a numeric value, the @TRIM function returns ERR. This function is particularly useful when you are dealing with data from other programs that may pad some text entries to equal lengths by using trailing spaces.

The @REPLACE Function

You use the @REPLACE function to substitute one string of characters for another within a label. Its syntax is

    @REPLACE(original-string,start-number,n,new-string)

where *original-string* is the label to be worked on, *start-number* is the character position within that label where you want the replacement to begin (with the first character in *original-string* counting as 0, the second as 1, and so on), *n* is the number of characters to replace, and *new-string* is the set of characters to be used for the replacement. For example, if A1 contains Super Deleaded, the following formula will convert it to Super Unleaded:

    @REPLACE(A1,6,2,"Un")

The @REPLACE function works well with @FIND to locate the right place to make the replacement. You can also use @REPLACE to append one string to another, by specifying a *start-number* argument one greater than the number of characters in *original-string*. To delete part or all of a string, specify "" as *new-string*. Remember that you can also use the Range Search/Replace command instead of @FIND and @REPLACE to perform search and replace operations.

The @LOWER, @UPPER, and @PROPER Functions

The three functions @LOWER, @UPPER, and @PROPER change the case of a string. @LOWER, which has the syntax

```
@LOWER(string)
```

turns a string into all lowercase characters. @UPPER, which has the syntax

```
@UPPER(string)
```

returns all uppercase characters. The @PROPER function, which has the syntax

```
@PROPER(string)
```

converts the first letter of every word in the string to uppercase, and the rest of the characters to lowercase. For example, if A1 contains Lotus development, @LOWER(A1) returns lotus development, @UPPER(A1) returns LOTUS DEVELOPMENT, and @PROPER(A1) returns Lotus Development.

For the @PROPER function, a word is defined as an unbroken string of alphabetic characters; any blank spaces, punctuation symbols, or numbers mark the end of a word. In all three functions, numbers and symbols within the string are unaffected by the function. If the string is blank or is a numeric or date value, the result is ERR.

The @STRING Function

As you saw, @STRING is used to convert numbers to labels. It has the syntax

```
@STRING(x,n)
```

where x is the numeric value to be converted and n is a numeric value between 0 and 15 representing the number of decimal places to the right of the decimal point. Thus @STRING(A1,0) converts 20.01 to the label 20, rounding it to the decimal precision indicated by the n argument of 0. You can then use the label in a string formula.

Dates are a particularly difficult set of values to work with in string formulas. For example, in Figure 11.19 you saw how the labels and values from Figure 11.17 could be made into sentences. Suppose that you want to create a string formula that refers to the date in F6 of Figure 11.17, such as "Today is Nov 1, 1991." To begin with, you might consider this formula:

```
+"Today is "&@STRING(@DAY(F6),0)&"/"&
@STRING(@MONTH(F6),0)&"/"&@STRING(@YEAR(F6),0)&"."
```

By combining the @STRING function with the date part functions described in Chapter 4, this formula produces "Today is 1/11/91." Although this is not exactly what you wanted, it is a simple formula that

comes fairly close. Unfortunately, there is no function to translate a formatted date into text. To include the name of the month in your result, you would have to create this formula:

```
+"Today is "&@CHOOSE(@MONTH((F6)-1,"Jan","Feb","Mar","Apr",
"May","Jun","Jul","Aug","Sep","Oct","Nov","Dec")&" "&
@STRING(@DAY(F6),0)&","&&@STRING(@YEAR(F6)+1900,0)&"."
```

This formula uses the @CHOOSE function to return the correct three-letter abbreviation for the month.

The @VALUE Functions

@VALUE converts a label into a numeric value. Its syntax is

```
@VALUE(string)
```

where *string* is a label that appears to be a number. For example, suppose you have this label in B5:

```
The price is $1,375.95
```

You want to use the value of 1375.95 to perform a calculation. To do this you could use

```
@VALUE(@RIGHT(B5,8))
```

The @VALUE function ignores commas in thousands, but you must exclude the dollar sign using the @RIGHT function.

The @VALUE function has two companion functions, @DATEVALUE and @TIMEVALUE. These convert character strings into dates and times, respectively. For example, if B5 contains the label "Today is 1/1/90," the following formula will return 32874, the date serial number for 1/1/90:

```
@DATEVALUE(@RIGHT(B5,6))
```

If B5 contains "The time is 10:30 AM," the following formula will return 0.4375, the decimal time value of 10:30 a.m.:

```
@TIMEVALUE(@RIGHT(B5,8))
```

Both @DATEVALUE and @TIMEVALUE require that the character string being acted upon contain a date or time in a standard 1-2-3 format; otherwise, the function cannot read the value correctly and will return ERR. Acceptable date and time formats are listed in Table 11.1.

Date or time labels that follow one of the preceding formats can be converted to a value by @DATEVALUE or @TIMEVALUE. Other formats can be recognized if they are currently selected by the Worksheet Global Default Other International command.

Table 11.1   **Acceptable Date and Time Formats**

Dates	Times
25-Dec-91	11:30:45 PM
25-Dec	11:30 PM
Dec-90	23:30:45
12/25/91	23:30
12/25	

Another useful application of @DATEVALUE is to enter dates in a more convenient order than that required by @DATE. If you need to enter 12/25/92, you can use @DATEVALUE("12/25/92") instead of @DATE(92/12/25).

The @REPEAT Function

Use the @REPEAT function to repeat a string of characters a specified number of times using the syntax

```
@REPEAT(string,n)
```

where *string* is a string value and *n* is a numeric value greater than or equal to 0. The @REPEAT function returns as many copies of *string* as you specify with *n* and produces a label. While it resembles the repeating label prefix (\) used to produce dashed lines in a cell, @REPEAT lets you specify exactly how many times you want the string to be repeated. Also, the \ label prefix adjusts the number of repeated characters to fill the column, even when the width is changed. In contrast, the @REPEAT function displays a fixed number of characters that only changes if you alter the *n* argument.

When you specify a text string with @REPEAT, it must be surrounded by double quotes. Thus, the formula

```
@REPEAT("Stop",3)
```

results in this label:

```
StopStopStop
```

The number argument in the @REPEAT statement can be a formula or a cell reference. @REPEAT is handy when you want to create the effect seen in the first few rows of Figure 11.21.

Figure 11.21

Using @REPEAT

```
A61: [W6] +"Principal"&@REPEAT(".",35)                          READY

    A          B           C           D           E          F        G      ◀
61  Principal.............................   12,500.00                       ▶
62  Loan term in years....................         4                        ▲
63  Number of payments per year...........        12                        ▼
64  Annual interest rate (%A.P.R).........     12.50%                        ?
65  Payment per period....................    332.25
66  Total of payments.....................  15,948.00
67  Total interest paid...................   3,448.00
68
69  PMT   Paid in      Paid in     Cumulative  Remaining
70   #    Interest     Prinicipal  Interest    Balance
71    1     140.73       191.52       140.73   12,308.48
72    2     137.80       194.45       278.53   12,114.03
73    3     134.87       197.38       413.40   11,916.65
74    4     131.94       200.31       545.34   11,716.34
75    5     129.01       203.24       674.35   11,513.10
76    6     126.07       206.18       800.42   11,306.92
77    7     123.14       209.11       923.56   11,097.81
78    8     120.21       212.04     1,043.77   10,885.77
79    9     117.28       214.97     1,161.05   10,670.80
80   10     114.35       217.90     1,275.40   10,452.90
01-Nov-91  09:19 AM                                       NUM
```

The @REPEAT function creates the ellipses (...) between the labels on the left and the corresponding values on the right. It's fine if the number used for the *n* argument is greater than the number of repetitions required, since the value in column E cuts short the resulting label. The value of 35 can be used in each of the cells A61 through A67.

The @CHAR Function

Earlier in this chapter, you learned that many programs can share information using ASCII characters. There are 256 ASCII characters, numbered 0 through 255. Many of them are symbols not found on the keyboard, such as ASCII graphics characters. The @CHAR function can display some of these codes in 1-2-3, using the syntax

    @CHAR(x)

The *x* argument is a numeric value between 1 and 255 and the function returns the character that 1-2-3 associates with this value. Thus @CHAR(163) returns the £ sign. Unfortunately, 1-2-3 does not use the standard method of code numbering. The £ is normally ASCII 156, and you can create this code within a 1-2-3 label by typing 156 on the numeric keypad while holding down the Alt key. 1-2-3 diverges from the normal ASCII numbering because it offers an alternative method of creating many foreign characters, using the Lotus International Character Set (LICS). This is described in Appendix C.

Figure 11.22 shows the @CHAR function used to display the character corresponding to a range of code values. If you print a worksheet like this as a reference, you can determine which of the codes your printer can reproduce. Note that 1-2-3 returns a blank for code values 1 through 32. (A code value of 0 results in ERR.)

Figure 11.22
An ASCII chart produced with @CHAR

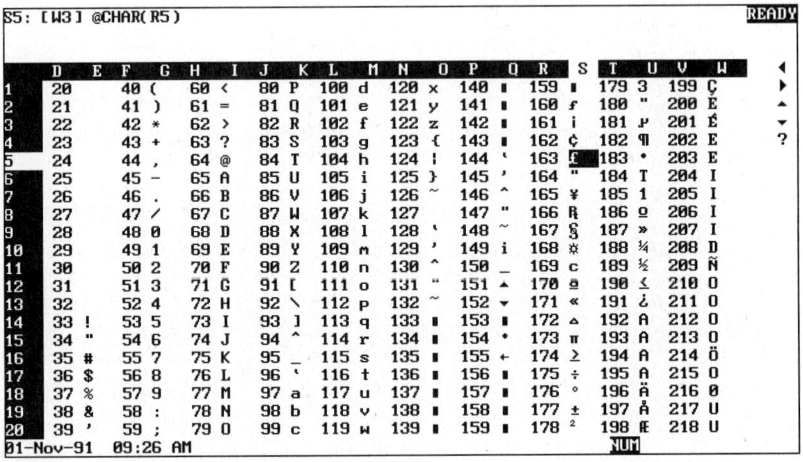

```
S5: [W3] @CHAR(R5)                                                      READY
       D    E    F    G    H    I    J    K    L    M    N    O    P    Q    R   S    T    U    V   W     ◄
 1    20      40 (      60 <      80 P     100 d     120 x     140 ∎     159 ∎    179 3    199 Ç     ►
 2    21      41 )      61 =      81 Q     101 e     121 y     141 ∎     160 ƒ    180 "    200 E     ▲
 3    22      42 *      62 >      82 R     102 f     122 z     142 ∎     161 í    181 ⊦    201 É     ▼
 4    23      43 +      63 ?      83 S     103 g     123 {     143 ∎     162 ¢    182 ¶    202 E     ?
 5    24      44 ,      64 @      84 T     104 h     124 ¦     144 '     163 £    183 •    203 E
 6    25      45 -      65 A      85 U     105 i     125 }     145 '     164 "    184 T    204 I
 7    26      46 .      66 B      86 V     106 j     126 ~     146 ^     165 ¥    185 1    205 I
 8    27      47 /      67 C      87 W     107 k     127       147 "     166 ℞    186 º    206 I
 9    28      48 0      68 D      88 X     108 l     128 `     148 ~     167 §    187 »    207 I
10    29      49 1      69 E      89 Y     109 m     129 '     149 i     168 ✕    188 ¼    208 D
11    30      50 2      70 F      90 Z     110 n     130 ^     150 _     169 c    189 ½    209 Ñ
12    31      51 3      71 G      91 [     111 o     131 "     151 ▲     170 ₒ    190 ≤    210 O
13    32      52 4      72 H      92 \     112 p     132 ~     152 ▼     171 «    191 ¿    211 O
14    33 !    53 5      73 I      93 ]     113 q     133 ∎     153 ∎     172 ⌐    192 A    212 O
15    34 "    54 6      74 J      94 ^     114 r     134 ∎     154 •     173 π    193 A    213 O
16    35 #    55 7      75 K      95 _     115 s     135 ∎     155 ←     174 ∑    194 A    214 Ö
17    36 $    56 8      76 L      96 `     116 t     136 ∎     156 ∎     175 ÷    195 A    215 O
18    37 %    57 9      77 M      97 a     117 u     137 ∎     157 ∎     176 °    196 Ä    216 0
19    38 &    58 :      78 N      98 b     118 v     138 ∎     158 ∎     177 ±    197 Å    217 U
20    39 '    59 ;      79 0      99 c     119 w     139 ∎     159 ∎     178 ²    198 Æ    218 U
01-Nov-91  09:26 AM                                                      NUM
```

The @CODE Function

The reverse of @CHAR, the @CODE function tells you the ASCII code of a special character. It uses the syntax

    @CODE(string)

where *string* is a string value, the first letter of which is evaluated by @CODE to return the ASCII code.

You can use @CODE to get an exact evaluation of user input, since each letter of the alphabet has one ASCII code for uppercase and another for lowercase. Thus you could use the condition @CODE(B5)=89 to determine whether or not the entry in B5 is Y, which has the code 89. If you simply use B5="Y," 1-2-3 will evaluate this as true whether B5 contains Y or y. Bear in mind that @CODE returns the code for the first character in a label after the label prefix, so if B5 contains Yellow, @CODE(B5) will still return 89.

More Text Formulas

The possibilities for text manipulation with 1-2-3 are extensive. Using the string functions and text in formulas, you can handle many tasks beyond the traditional number crunching for which spreadsheets were originally designed. As a final example, consider the 1-2-3 business name generator seen in Figure 11.23.

Figure 11.23
Business name
generator

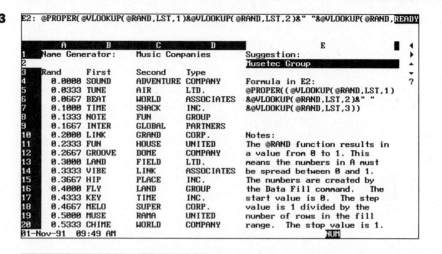

The plausible-looking company name seen in E2 was produced by a formula, the first part of which is shown at the top of the screen. The @VLOOKUP function is used to look up a random number in the table of name fragments from A1..A21. The table consists of a column of numbers roughly spaced across the possible value of @RAND, from 0 to 1. Columns B and C are typical of names used in the travel business. Column D contains several company types, repeated down the list. The & sign is used to connect the three @VLOOKUP statements, and the comma and space separate the name from the type. In cell E2, @PROPER produces a variation on normal capitalization. By repeatedly pressing F2 to edit any cell in the worksheet and then pressing Enter, you can cause 1-2-3 to recalculate and so reselect the random numbers, thus producing new name combinations. The complete formulas are as follows:

```
E2: @VLOOKUP (@RAND,TABLE,1)&VLOOKUP(@RAND,TABLE,2)
" "&@VLOOKUP(@RAND,TABLE,3)

E5: @PROPER(@VLOOKUP(@RAND,TABLE,1)&@VLOOKUP(@RAND,
TABLE,2)&" "&@VLOOKUP(@RAND,TABLE,3))

E8: @PROPER(@VLOOKUP(@RAND,TABLE,1))&@PROPER(@VLOOKUP
(@RAND,TABLE 2,))&" "&@PROPER(@VLOOKUP(@RAND,TABLE,3))
```

If you make the lookup table references absolute in the formula, you can copy the formula to many cells in a column to produce a list of possible names. By filling the table with phrases that fit the kind of business for which you are trying to create a name, you can produce some very interesting results.

Summary

In this chapter, you learned of 1-2-3's ability to juggle words and labels in a variety of ways. You can arrange words into paragraphs of text to describe and document a set of figures. Using the Wysiwyg add-in, you can dress up words with special formatting to match the output of some word processors. You can import words and figures into 1-2-3 and parse them into cell entries, or export them to form parts of documents prepared by other programs. Using string formulas, you can extract data from text entries and even create new words. In the next chapter, you will read about another advanced aspect of 1-2-3: the ability to perform statistical calculations and create cross-tabulations of worksheet data.

12

Statistics and Data Tables

Regression

Frequency Distribution

*Data Tables and
What-If Analysis*

Matrix Arithmetic

THIS CHAPTER REVIEWS THE 1-2-3 DATA COMMANDS THAT HAVE NOT YET been covered: Table, Distribution, Matrix, and Regression. Several of these commands relate to statistical analysis. The Distribution command performs frequency distributions. The Matrix command allows you to perform matrix arithmetic. The Regression command compares sets of variables and produces several statistical measurements of the extent to which they are related. This chapter also demonstrates how to use the Data Table command to create "what-if" tables of formula results and, together with the database functions, perform cross tabulations of database statistics.

Regression

When you have a collection of related facts, you may want to measure the relationship between them. For example, you may want to evaluate the relationship between goods sold and the amount of money spent advertising them, or the connection between earnings and level of education. One method of analyzing the connection between such facts is called *linear regression,* and 1-2-3 provides the Regression option on the Data menu for doing this. (Since regression analysis is fairly complex, a complete discussion of the subject is beyond the scope of this text.)

A Regression Example

Suppose you have put together the marketing data you see in the worksheet in Figure 12.1. Column B shows the number of full-page newspaper advertisements placed by the company in 1991, listed by month. The numbers in column C represent sales, in thousands, for those same months. You may want to know how closely these two sets of numbers relate. If you could measure the relationship mathematically, you might be able to use that measurement to predict future sales based on different levels of future advertising.

Regression is a measurement of the relationship between two or more factors, which are referred to as *variables.* In our example, the amount of advertising is one variable and sales is another. Because standard business philosophy presumes that the level of sales a company achieves is related to the amount of advertising it does, sales can be considered the *dependent variable,* because its value presumably depends on advertising. Advertising, in turn, can be thought of as the *independent variable.* Regression measures the effect of one or more independent variables on a dependent variable.

Setting Up Regression

When you select Regression from the Data menu, you get a menu and settings dialog box, as shown in Figure 12.2, where the appropriate settings have already been recorded. The first two items on the Regression menu refer to the variable factors in the regression calculation. The X-Range option is the independent variable; in this case it is the Actual Pages, stored in cells B5..B16. The Actual Sales in cells C5..C16 are the dependent variables, the Y-Range option. The purpose of the regression is to gauge the effect of the X range on the Y range. The X and Y ranges must contain an equal number of data points. Since there can be more than one independent variable, the X range may be several columns wide, but it must contain the same number of rows as the Y range.

Figure 12.1

Marketing data

```
A1: 'Ad Pages Versus Sales ( in 1,000s )                              READY
┌─────────────────────────────────────────────────────────────────────┐
│      A         B          C        D      E      F      G        ◄    │
│1   Ad Pages Versus Sales ( in 1,000s )                           ►    │
│2                                                                 ▲    │
│3             Actual     Actual                                   ▼    │
│4   Month:    Pages:     91 Sales:                                ?    │
│5    Jan-91      4         39                                          │
│6    Feb-91      5         51                                          │
│7    Mar-91      6         58                                          │
│8    Apr-91      5         51                                          │
│9    May-91      6         61                                          │
│10   Jun-91      7         67                                          │
│11   Jul-91      5         49                                          │
│12   Aug-91      6         59                                          │
│13   Sep-91      5         49                                          │
│14   Oot-91      6         56                                          │
│15   Nov-91      7         69                                          │
│16   Dec-91      8         80                                          │
│17                                                                     │
│18                                                                     │
│19                                                                     │
│20                                                                     │
│05-Jan-92  09:53 AM                                   NUM              │
└─────────────────────────────────────────────────────────────────────┘
```

After setting the X and Y ranges, you must set the output range. In this example, cell H1 has been chosen. The results of the regression calculation will occupy several columns and nine rows, but you only need to define the upper-left corner of the cells of the output range. There is one other Regression setting: Intercept. As you can see from Figure 12.2, the default setting is Compute; the alternative setting, Zero, will be discussed in a moment. When you have completed the four settings, select Go to complete the regression calculation. The results can be seen in Figure 12.3.

Note that H1 was the Output-Range setting but there is no entry in H1 itself. 1-2-3 uses nine rows and as many columns as it takes to lay out the results legibly, based on the column widths in the output area. With a default column width of nine, the results occupy four columns.

Figure 12.2
Data Regression
menu and
Regression
Settings box

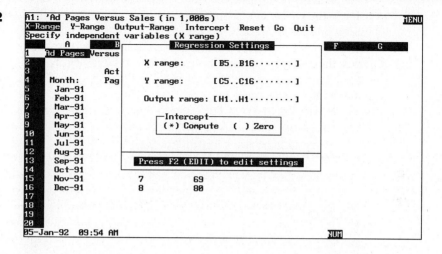

Figure 12.3
Results of
regression analysis

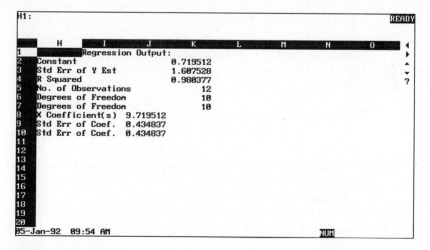

Using Regression Results

The results of a regression calculation are various measurements of the relationship between the variables, and a column of labels describing these numbers. The heading Regression Output appears more centered if you output to wider columns than the default width of nine. (Note that outputting to columns any narrower than nine will make the data difficult to read.)

Interpreting the different parts of these results involves numerous concepts from statistics. The No. of Observations should match the number of data points that were observed for the variables—in this case 12, one for each month. Degrees of Freedom represents the number of observations minus one for each variable being observed—in this case 10. The value R Squared, sometimes referred to as the coefficient of determination, measures the extent to which the variables are related, with 1 being the optimal value. In the example, where the sales are closely related to the pages, the value of R Squared is nearly 1.

The Std Err of Y Est is the estimated standard error of the Y values. This value helps measure the certainty with which the independent variables can be used to predict the dependent variables. In general, the larger this measurement the less reliable the relationship between independent and dependent variables. This standard error, like R Squared, is useful when you are deciding between different independent variables as predictors of the dependent variables.

The Std Err of Coef. gives an error measurement of the coefficients. The larger this value relative to the X Coefficient, the less certain the relationship between the variables. This measurement will tend to be smaller the more observations are included in the calculation.

Perhaps the most useful numbers in the regression output are the Constant and the X Coefficient. The Constant can be described as the y-axis intercept of the regression line that describes the relationship between Pages and Sales. You can force the Constant to be zero by changing the Regression Intercept setting from Compute to Zero. You would only do this if, when the independent variable is equal to zero, the dependent variable must also be zero—for example, when relating the hours a store is open each day to the amount of goods sold, which would have to be zero if the hours open equalled zero. The X Coefficient tells how much the dependent variable, the Sales, will change for a single unit increase in the independent variable, Pages. As you can see in Figure 12.3, this value is close to 10, and most of the Sales figures are in fact about ten times the Pages.

If you have used the Compute setting for the Regression Intercept, the Constant can be used with the X Coefficient to predict the value of sales based on different numbers of pages. In Figure 12.4, a calculation added in column D represents this formula:

```
Constant + X Coefficient * independent variable
```

In this case, cell D5 is $K$2+$J$8*B5. This formula was copied down the column to produce the "predicted" results seen, which are fairly close to the real results.

The value of this calculation comes when the pages are changed to the figures shown in column B in Figure 12.5, where the sales for 1992 are predicted. Note that the prediction seen here is only a statistical inference—not a guaranteed basis for a business decision but a suggestion that more advertisements

will produce more sales. Note that column C is ready to accept actual sales, which can then be compared with predictions for a further assessment of the correlation between advertising and sales. In general, statistical predictions will be more reliable the more they are tested against actual data.

Figure 12.4

Calculating with regression results

```
D5: (F0) [W12] +$K$2+$J$8*B5                                    READY

        A         B            C           D        E      F      G    ◄
1  Ad Pages Versus Sales (in 1,000s)                                   ►
2                                                                      ▲
3                 Actual       Actual      Predicted                   ▼
4  Month:         Pages:       91 Sales:   91 Sales:                   ?
5     Jan-91         4            39           40
6     Feb-91         5            51           49
7     Mar-91         6            58           59
8     Apr-91         5            51           49
9     May-91         6            61           59
10    Jun-91         7            67           69
11    Jul-91         5            49           49
12    Aug-91         6            59           59
13    Sep-91         5            49           49
14    Oct-91         6            56           59
15    Nov-91         7            69           69
16    Dec-91         8            80           78
17
18
19
20
05-Jan-92   09:55 AM                                           NUM
```

Figure 12.5

Predictions with regression

```
D5: (F0) [W12] +$K$2+$J$8*B5                                    READY

        A         B            C           D        E      F      G    ◄
1  Ad Pages Versus Sales (in 1,000s)                                   ►
2                                                                      ▲
3                 Planned      Actual      Predicted                   ▼
4  Month:         Pages:       92 Sales:   92 Sales:                   ?
5     Jan-92         6                         59
6     Feb-92         6                         59
7     Mar-92         6                         59
8     Apr-92         7                         69
9     May-92         7                         69
10    Jun-92         7                         69
11    Jul-92         8                         78
12    Aug-92         8                         78
13    Sep-92         8                         78
14    Oct-92         9                         88
15    Nov-92         9                         88
16    Dec-92         9                         88
17
18
19
20
05-Jan-92   09:56 AM                                           NUM
```

Multiple Variables

You can include more than one independent variable in the regression calculation. Suppose that the company is also using radio advertising. You can add the number of radio spots per month to the model and include them in the regression calculation. In Figure 12.6, you can see the radio spots in column C. The X-Range setting is now B5..C16, and the Y-Range setting is D5..D16. The results can be seen on the right of Figure 12.6.

Figure 12.6

Using two independent variables

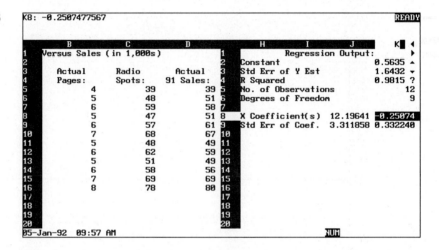

Note that the last two lines of the results now show two figures each. These represent the first and second independent variables. The measure of R Squared is 0.981545, showing a healthy relationship between the two independent variables and the dependent one. Also note that the figures shown in the regression results in Figures 12.5 and 12.6 are displayed in the General format. As you can see from cell K8 in Figure 12.6, the full result is actually a very long number.

Graphing Regression

In Chapter 9, you saw how to construct graphs, including XY graphs. There is a close relationship between the display of data in an XY graph and the calculations done in regression analysis. The marketing figures shown in Figure 12.5 give the monthly advertising page count next to the sales for the month and the projected sales based on the regression analysis on the right. If the pages are graphed as the x-axis in an XY graph, and the actual and predicted sales are graphed as the first and second data ranges, you can see the relationship between them. The resulting graph is shown in Figure 12.7.

The actual sales are shown as small squares. The predicted sales, calculated from the regression figures, are displayed as a line rather than as symbols. As you can see, the data points produced by the regression calculation create a straight line that fits the actual relationship between sales and pages as closely as possible. If you learned that five-and-a-half pages of advertising were planned for a particular month, you could read the probable sales from the y-axis (55,000).

Figure 12.7
Regression graph

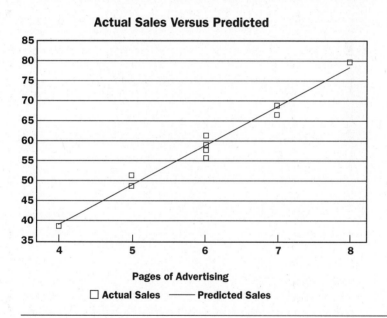

Actual Sales Versus Predicted

Pages of Advertising

□ Actual Sales   ——— Predicted Sales

Frequency Distribution

When dealing with large quantities of information, you often need to analyze the distribution of the data. For example, suppose you conducted a survey of the European travel habits of several hundred companies and recorded the results in a worksheet like the one in Figure 12.8. One of the survey questions was number of employees. You might want to know how many respondents had small work forces and how many had large. You could browse through the worksheet and find that the respondents ranged from 5 to over 500 employees. But this response would be rather vague. If you categorized the companies based on number of employees and counted how many fell into each category, you would get a better grasp of the survey respondents. This type of analysis is called a *frequency distribution,* which you can perform in 1-2-3 by using the Distribution command on the Data menu.

Figure 12.8

Survey results

```
A21: [W15] 'Company Name                                              READY

         A              B          C        D        E         F        G        ◄
21  Company Name   Employees  Code #   Code    Class     Europe    Flights   ►
22  Fry Limited          22         2 B      Business  y              4      ▲
23  Reality, Inc.       420         3 C      Business  y             40      ▼
24  Falseta, Co.        167         2 B      Coach     n              0      ?
25  Dotidot, Inc.       282         1 A      First     n             12
26  WhoAmEye, Ltd.      335         2 B      Business  y            102
27  TestBed             100         3 C      Coach     y              3
28  GuessWhat, Inc.      70         3 C      Coach     y              2
29  TallOrder, Inc.     117         5 E      First     n              5
30  DoItTo, Inc.        537         1 A      Business  y            121
31  FlyByPn, Inc.       215         1 A      Business  y             26
32  RUMP, Inc.           71         4 D      Business  n              0
33  Why, Inc.            40         3 C      Coach     y             10
34  Unouni, Inc.        111         4 D      Business  n              0
35  Amernew Assoc.       44         1 A      First     n              0
36  Bytehard, Co.       914         3 C      Coach     y            212
37  Tungvia, Inc.        76         3 C      Coach     y              6
38  Byteteam, Ltd.       41         2 B      Business  y             10
39  Zy-Comp, Inc.        84         4 D      First     n              0
40  FLEX, Ltd.          106         5 E      Coach     y             13
05-Jan-92  10:04 AM                                          NUM
```

Performing a Distribution

To perform a frequency distribution with 1-2-3, you need to supply both the range of values that are to be categorized and the column of numbers representing the range over which the values are to be distributed, also called the categories. The cells containing the category numbers are called the *bin range,* as though each number in the values range were tossed into the appropriate bin for counting. The result of the Distribution command is a list of the totals of that count placed in the column to the right of the bin numbers.

Before issuing the Data Distribution command, you must enter a series of numbers for the bin range. Be sure that the cells used for the bin range have empty cells immediately to their right. The first number in the bin range will represent all values from 0 to the number, so that 50 would represent from 0 to 50. In this example, you could use 50 through 500, in intervals of 50, as shown in Figure 12.9. You can easily enter this series of numbers with the Range Fill command.

When you select Distribution, you are first prompted for the values range—in this example, cells B22..B124. As soon as you enter this value, you are prompted for the bin range, in this case J5..J14. When you enter the bin range, 1-2-3 immediately fills in the numbers seen in K5..K15 of Figure 12.10. From this result, you can see that 23 of the companies responding to the survey had from 0 to 50 employees. There were 12 companies with 51 to 100 employees, and so on. These results provide a valuable picture of the survey data.

Figure 12.9
A bin range

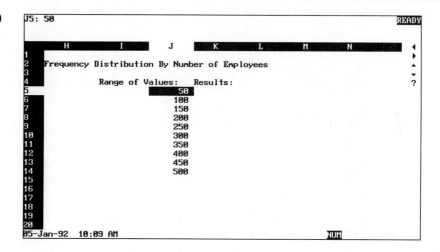

Figure 12.10
The results of the Data Distribution command

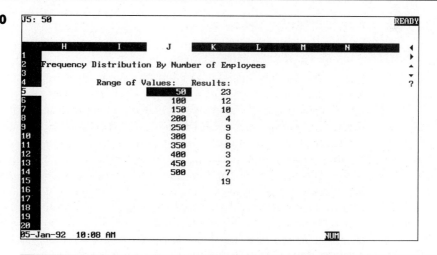

Note the last number in the results, 19. This is placed one cell below the last bin number, indicating that there are 19 companies with over 500 employees. 1-2-3 always places a result in this position, even if it is 0, to show that the Distribution command has evaluated all possible values.

Improving the Distribution Results

Since the bin numbers alone are somewhat difficult to interpret, you can add a second column, as in the worksheet in Figure 12.11. The labels in column I show the range of numbers implied by the Distribution command. Note how the labels are constructed with a string formula.

Figure 12.11

Improved
distribution results

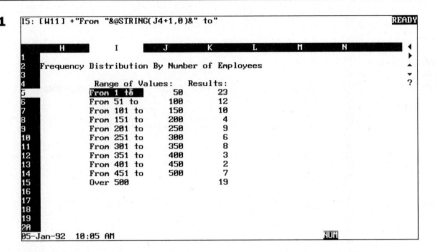

Data Tables and What-If Analysis

Quite often you establish a set of spreadsheet formulas and then change the numbers upon which the formulas are based just to see "what if." For example, you might set up a worksheet to calculate sales for the next 12 months based on a starting volume of 2,000 units increasing at 5% per month. By changing the starting figure, you can see *what* would happen *if* sales began at 2,500 instead of 2,000. By changing the growth rate, you can see *what* would happen *if* sales grew by 6% instead of 5%. Rather than trying out growth rates one at a time, you might want to create a table of total sales achieved by a whole set of rates. Such a table is sometimes referred to as a *one-way data table,* the list of results obtained from varying one factor in a calculation. You could also create a *two-way data table* by varying both the beginning sales and the rate of growth. You can automate this kind of what-if analysis by using the Data Table command.

A One-Way Data Table

Suppose you are thinking of buying a swimming pool. The spreadsheet shown in Figure 12.12 includes some of the calculations involved. The total price of the pool is calculated and the down payment subtracted to show an amount you would like to finance. The figures in D1, D2, and D3 show the principal, interest, and term of the loan, respectively. The formula in D5 is

```
@ROUND(@PMT(D1,D2/12,D3),2)
```

Figure 12.12

Preparing for a
data table

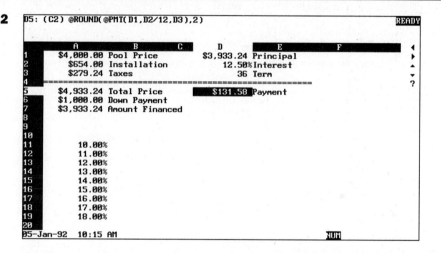

You may want to know how much the loan payments will be at different rates of interest. For example, there is a list of rates that begins at 10% in cell A11 and runs to 18%. This list was created with the Data Fill command, filling cells A11 through A19 with values starting at .1 and incremented by .01 to stop at .18. The Percent format was then applied to the cells. What you want to calculate, in B11 through B19, is the payment amount corresponding to each of these interest rates. To do this, you build a data table. The first step is to create the column of variables, in this case the rates of interest that have already been entered. The next step is to head the column of results with the formula that you want to recalculate for each of the variable values, in this case the loan payment calculation in D5. Instead of moving this formula to B10, you simply reference it, using the entry +D5 in B10. The result should be 285.05. Now you are ready to select Table from the Data menu. There are just three options: 1, 2, and Reset. You can vary one value in a set of formulas by selecting 1. You can vary two items by choosing 2. The Reset option simply clears any previous settings.

Option 1 replaces one input cell with cells from the input column, and this is what you need to calculate the loan payment for each rate of interest. When you pick 1, you are prompted for the range of cells to use as the data table. In this case, the range is cells A10 through B19. The table is all of the numbers to be fed into the formula, plus the formula at the top of the results column. When you have entered the data table range, the program prompts for "input cell 1," meaning into which cell do you want to read the values from the left column of the data table. In this case, it is the interest cell, D2.

When you have entered the input cell, the results are tabulated. 1-2-3 feeds each of the values from A10 through A19 into cell D2, recalculates the formula in B10, and places the results in the table, creating the output seen in B11 through B19 in Figure 12.13. Note that the results in the table are neatly formatted because the Worksheet Global Format has been set to Currency, with two decimal places.

Figure 12.13
One-way data table results

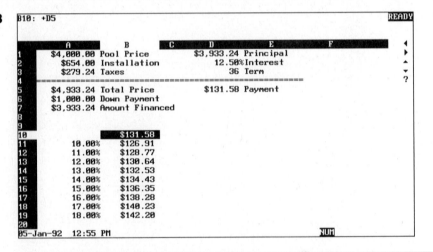

The entry in cell B10 could be formatted with the Hidden format to remove it from view and make the table less confusing to read. Note that the Data Table output consists of numbers, not formulas, and so is not dynamic. Changing the term of the loan on the spreadsheet will not cause any change in the cells of the data table unless you repeat the Data Table command to take into account changes in the model. You can quickly repeat the last Data Table command by pressing the Table key (F8). As you can see, the Data Table command is a quick way to perform a repetitive series of calculations and list the results.

Although a one-way table only varies one value in a formula, it can calculate more than one formula and show the results. For example, in Figure 12.14

you can see that the formula +D5*D3 for total payments was added in C10. This will create a second results column. The table range was then expanded to A10..C19 and the input cell D2 was used to create the results shown.

Figure 12.14

One-way table with two formulas

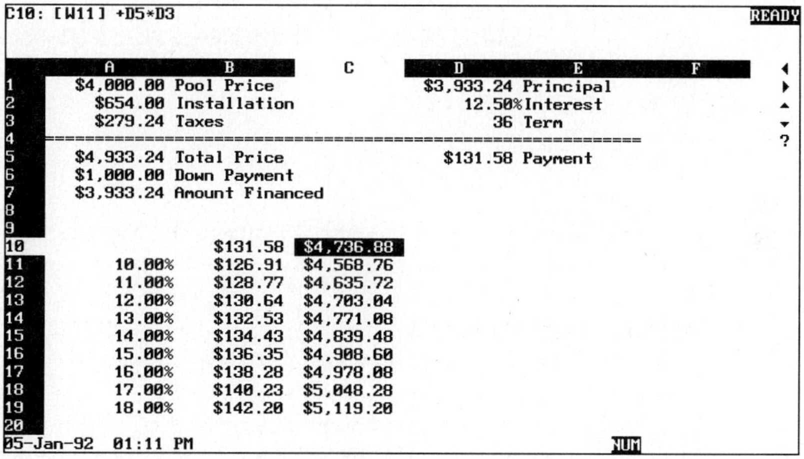

```
C10: [W11] +D5*D3                                                              READY

         A            B             C          D           E        F       ◀
1     $4,000.00  Pool Price               $3,933.24 Principal             ▶
2       $654.00  Installation             12.50% Interest                 ▲
3       $279.24  Taxes                       36  Term                     ▼
4     ==================================================================  ?
5     $4,933.24  Total Price              $131.58 Payment
6     $1,000.00  Down Payment
7     $3,933.24  Amount Financed
8
9
10                    $131.58  $4,736.88
11        10.00%      $126.91  $4,568.76
12        11.00%      $128.77  $4,635.72
13        12.00%      $130.64  $4,703.04
14        13.00%      $132.53  $4,771.08
15        14.00%      $134.43  $4,839.48
16        15.00%      $136.35  $4,908.60
17        16.00%      $138.28  $4,978.08
18        17.00%      $140.23  $5,048.28
19        18.00%      $142.20  $5,119.20
20
05-Jan-92  01:11 PM                                              NUM
```

A Two-Way Data Table

The next step is a two-way table, seen in Figure 12.15. This table shows the payments on the loan based on a variety of interest rates and four different payment terms for a pool priced at $4,000. Thus the table varies both the interest in D2 and the term in D3. The operation is performed by setting up first the interest rates down the side and then the terms across the top. The formula into which you want to input the variable values is referenced in the cell above the input column and to the left of the input row, in this case cell A10.

Next you select the Table command from the Data menu and choose 2. The data table is defined as the range formed by the column of variables and the row of variables, A10 through E19 in this case. You are then prompted for input cell 1, which is the interest in D2. This is the cell into which the variable values in the column of the table will be fed. Finally, you are prompted for input cell 2, the cell into which the variables on the top row of the table will be fed, in this case the term in cell D3.

1-2-3 then creates the results seen in Figure 12.15. You can use this table to decide what terms are best suited to your budget. You could easily produce a different table with price instead of term as a variable, to see how large a pool you could afford to finance. You can use the Reset command to clear the current settings for data table and input cells. Remember that the data table is not dynamic and will not update when you change other factors in the model from which it is derived. You must reissue the Table command or press the Table key (F8) to update the results.

Figure 12.15

A two-way data table

```
A10: (H) [W13] +D5                                                    READY
          A              B           C           D           E        F      ◄
      $4,000.00 Pool Price                   $3,933.24 Principal             ►
1                                                                            ▲
2       $654.00 Installation                   12.50% Interest               ▼
3       $279.24 Taxes                              36 Term                    ?
4     ======================================================================
5     $4,933.24 Total Price                    $131.58 Payment
6     $1,000.00 Down Payment
7     $3,933.24 Amount Financed
8
9
10                          12          24          36          48
11        10.00%      $345.79     $181.50     $126.91      $99.76
12        11.00%      $347.63     $183.32     $128.77     $101.66
13        12.00%      $349.46     $185.15     $130.64     $103.58
14        13.00%      $351.31     $186.99     $132.53     $105.52
15        14.00%      $353.15     $188.85     $134.43     $107.48
16        15.00%      $355.01     $190.71     $136.35     $109.47
17        16.00%      $356.87     $192.58     $138.28     $111.47
18        17.00%      $358.73     $194.47     $140.23     $113.49
19        18.00%      $360.60     $196.36     $142.20     $115.54
20
05-Jan-92   01:13 PM                                           NUM
```

Databases and Data Tables

One particularly powerful use of the Data Table command is performing cross tabulations of database information. For example, given the database shown in Figure 12.16, you may want to know the total weekly pay broken down by department, which has been calculated in the lower half of the screen.

To build a table like this, you combine the database functions with the Data Table command. First you create a list of the categories by which you want the results broken down—in this case, the four departments, entered in alphabetical order in E23..E26. These labels will be the input for the Data Table 1 command. Above the column that will contain the results, you enter the formula that you want to calculate. In this case, the formula, located in F22, reads

    @DSUM(INPUT,3,DBCRIT)

The range called INPUT is the database, cells B2..G19. The number 3 is the offset column—that is, the column in the database to which you want the @DSUM applied, in this case the column of weekly pay. The range DBCRIT is the criteria range that will be used to determine the results, in this case B21..B22. Note that B21 contains the heading Dept. This means that 1-2-3 will feed each of the values from the data table (E23..E26) into B22, one after another. As each department name is plugged into the criteria table, the @DSUM function is recalculated, producing the sum of the Weekly field for all records in which the Dept field matches the current criteria. The results are entered into the data table. Note that the result in F22, the table's formula cell, reflects the total weekly amounts for all employees since there is currently no entry in B22. Recall that an empty row in a criteria table tells 1-2-3 to select all records in a database. The label in E22 is merely cosmetic, describing the items below it. There is no need for this label, and no need for it to match the heading used in the database and criteria range.

Figure 12.16
One-way database data table

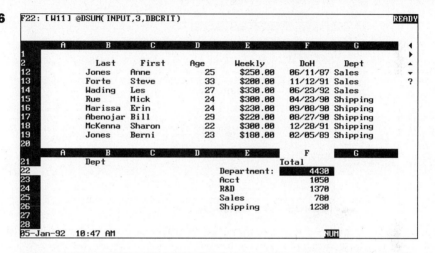

When you issue the Data Table 1 command, the range E22..F26 is selected as the table range. Cell B22 is selected as input cell 1. The results, which appear as shown in Figure 12.16, can then be formatted as you like.

You can also expand this type of operation to include a second variable. Figure 12.17 includes a two-way tabulation that uses the added column/field Gender.

The formula in E22 is the one that will be calculated in the table. This formula uses the range A22..B23 (named DB2CRIT) for the criteria. This criteria table selects records based on the values in two fields: Dept and Gender. The table range is E22..G26. Input cell 1 is A23 (underneath the Dept heading in the criteria table) while input cell 2 is B23 (underneath Gender in the criteria table). The resulting table shows a breakdown of pay by department and by gender.

Figure 12.17
Two-way database
data table

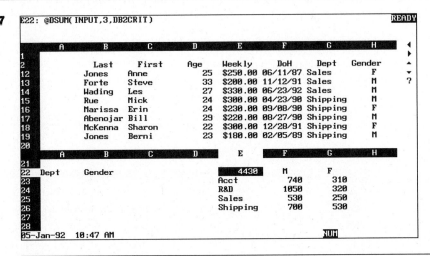

```
E22: @DSUM( INPUT,3,DB2CRIT )                                    READY
┌──────────────────────────────────────────────────────────────────┐
│    A      B       C        D      E        F        G       H   ◄  │
│ 1                                                               ►  │
│ 2        Last    First    Age   Weekly    DoH      Dept    Gender▲ │
│ 12       Jones   Anne      25   $250.00 06/11/87 Sales     F    ▼  │
│ 13       Forte   Steve     33   $200.00 11/12/91 Sales     M    ?  │
│ 14       Wading  Les       27   $330.00 06/23/92 Sales     M       │
│ 15       Rue     Mick      24   $300.00 04/23/90 Shipping  M       │
│ 16       Marissa Erin      24   $230.00 09/08/90 Shipping  F       │
│ 17       Abenojar Bill     29   $220.00 08/27/90 Shipping  M       │
│ 18       McKenna Sharon    22   $300.00 12/28/91 Shipping  F       │
│ 19       Jones   Berni     23   $180.00 02/05/89 Shipping  M       │
│ 20                                                                 │
│    A      B       C        D      E        F        G       H      │
│ 21                                                                 │
│ 22 Dept  Gender                                                    │
│ 23                                4430     M        F              │
│ 24                              Acct      740      310             │
│ 25                              R&D      1050      320             │
│ 26                              Sales     530      250             │
│ 27                              Shipping  700      530             │
│ 28                                                                 │
│ 05-Jan-92  10:47 AM                                      NUM       │
└──────────────────────────────────────────────────────────────────┘
```

Matrix Arithmetic

1-2-3 provides the Matrix commands to allow you to compute the inverse of a matrix. The Matrix command on the Data menu provides two options: Invert and Multiply, as shown in Figure 12.18. If you know what the inverse of a matrix is and need to perform matrix arithmetic in your work, the following description of the Matrix commands will probably be sufficient to get you started applying 1-2-3 to the task. If you are not familiar with inverting matrices, the following example will give you an idea of how they are used to solve practical problems.

About Matrix Arithmetic

Matrix arithmetic is employed in linear programming, a technique used when determining the optimal allocation of limited resources. While a discussion of linear programming concepts is clearly beyond the scope of this book, you can get an idea of how the Matrix commands work and how linear programming is applied with 1-2-3 from a relatively simple example.

Imagine that a shipping company needs to determine the optimal mix of cargo on a ship, choosing between sheep and goats. The data from which this mix must be calculated is the amount of fuel it takes to ship each sheep and each goat, plus the amount of loading time involved for each animal. This data is laid out in the worksheet in Figure 12.18.

At this point, the numbers shown are pure data, not formulas. The profit per sheep and goat is also listed in the worksheet. The calculation that must be performed to determine the optimal mix of sheep and goats involves the following equations:

```
2,750 Liters * Sheep + 9,250 Liters * Goats = 80,000 Liters
3 Hours * Sheep + 2 Hours * Goats = 40 Hours
```

The answer to these equations will be the number of each animal you should load to optimize allocation of the given resources. Once you have entered the data in the worksheet, you can have 1-2-3 calculate an inverse of the matrix of numbers in B4..C5 and place the results in cell E4.

Figure 12.18

A matrix math worksheet

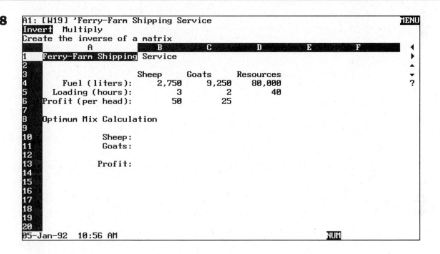

Matrix Inversion

When you select Invert from the Data Matrix menu, you are prompted for the range of cells to be inverted. In this example, the range is B4..C5. You can point out or type in the cell coordinates, just as you do at other 1-2-3 range prompts. The matrix to be inverted must be square—that is, it must have the same number of columns as rows. When you have entered the range coordinates, you are prompted for an output range; you need only point out the upper-left corner of the output range, in this case, E4. If you prefer to specify the entire range, bear in mind that the output range will be the same size as the source range. When the range is entered, the inverse matrix is produced, as shown in Figure 12.19. Note that your exact results may vary slightly from those shown due to subtle differences between computer hardware. Also note that the default column width in Figure 12.19 is ten characters, which affects the display of decimal places in the results.

Figure 12.19

Matrix Invert results

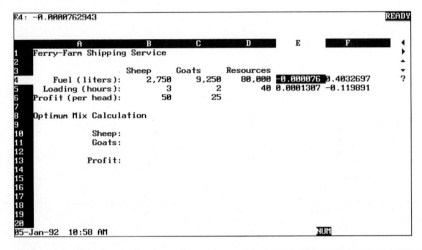

Matrix Multiplication

Having calculated the inverse matrix of the numbers, you can use the Matrix Multiply command to multiply the original resources of 80,000 liters and 40 hours by the inverse matrix. The resources, which were the constants in the previous equations, themselves constitute a matrix. The Matrix Multiply command allows you to multiply two matrices together. In this case, the results will be the number of sheep and goats that make the most efficient use of your limited resources. When you select Multiply from the Matrix menu, you are prompted to enter the first range to multiply, which will be the output of the inverse matrix, cells E4..F5. When these coordinates are entered, you are prompted to specify the second range, which will be the resources in D4..D5. After entering the second Matrix coordinates, you are prompted for an output range. In this example, you can use cell B10. When you enter the output range, the results of the calculation are produced, as shown in Figure 12.20.

The results indicate that a mix of approximately 10.03 sheep and 5.67 goats is the most efficient use of the resources available. Since you cannot load 5.67 animals, you might want to display this result without any decimal places. However, simply applying a range format with 0 decimal places will cause problems if you use the result in another calculation. This is because a format rounds numbers for display purposes only. You should use the @ROUND function if you want to eliminate the decimal places. In Figure 12.20, you can see one further calculation added to the worksheet. This shows the amount of profit made by the mix determined in B10 and B11, using the profit figures from row 6. The formula

```
+B6*B10+C6*B11
```

is used to multiply profit per unit by optimal number of units. You might modify the formula as follows, in order to use whole units of sheep and goats:

```
+B6*@ROUND(B10,0)+C6*@ROUND(B11,0)
```

Statisticians and mathematicians using 1-2-3 should note that there are limits to the numerical capabilities of personal computers in general and 1-2-3 in particular. 1-2-3 can calculate any formula whose value is between 10^{-308} and 10^{308}, but values less than 10^{-99} or greater than 10^{99} cannot be displayed in the worksheet, regardless of the format or column width you use. In such cases, 1-2-3 displays asterisks in the cell and these do not disappear even when the format is changed or the column widened. Formulas that have a value beyond the limits of 1-2-3 result in ERR.

Figure 12.20
Matrix Multiply results

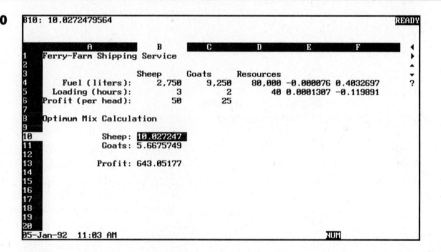

Summary

This chapter explored some of 1-2-3's more esoteric commands and functions. You may never need to use the features described in this chapter, but knowing that they are available may give you new ideas about the kind of work that 1-2-3 can perform. Statisticians and mathematicians will find the Regression, Distribution, and Matrix commands particularly useful. The Data Table command has a whole range of applications, from simple tables of results to extensive cross tabulations.

13

Introducing Macros

AS YOU APPLY 1-2-3 TO MORE AND MORE TASKS, YOU WILL WANT TO take advantage of its powerful macros feature. Macros can eliminate repetitive typing, automate the execution of frequently used commands, and even create customized menus. This chapter explains how to create basic macros and discusses the rules of macro design and organization. You will learn how to record macros with the Learn feature and how to store macros in a macro library using the Macro Library Manager add-in.

About Macros

Although you may be intimidated by macros since they tend to be associated with power users, macros are really no more difficult to use than other spreadsheet features such as functions. You don't have to be proficient in everything covered by the preceding chapters to use macros. You should be familiar with the use of range names, described in Chapter 4, but the main requirement for using macros is that you already be using 1-2-3 for a task that you want to simplify or speed up.

Macros in 1-2-3

When you find yourself repeating the same keystrokes over and over, you need a macro. Macros were first developed for word processing programs as a way to record and play back frequently used phrases; they stored multiple keystrokes under a single key or name. Other programs adopted this feature, including 1-2-3. The manual for the very first version of 1-2-3 referred to the macro feature as "the typing alternative." The manual provided little documentation of the feature, and it is rumored that Lotus almost left the feature out because they doubted whether many people would use it. However, users were quick to grasp the possibilities offered by the primitive macro feature offered in the first version of the program, and each new version has improved the power and versatility of 1-2-3 macros.

The macros you create in 1-2-3 enable you to record and play back any series of keystrokes, including those used to enter labels, numbers, and formulas, or to select menu choices. For example, suppose you have a customer order worksheet like the one in Figure 13.1, which requires you to enter the date for each order. You can create a macro that enters the @NOW function into a cell to read the current date from your system clock. The macro could then convert the function into the resulting date serial number, and could even format the date serial number with the desired date format.

A 1-2-3 *macro* can be defined as a set of keystrokes or instructions stored as labels in a named range. Numbers and letters are stored as numbers and letters; commands are stored as special symbols or words within brackets. Macros can be composed by the user or they can be recorded by 1-2-3.

Figure 13.1

A sample worksheet

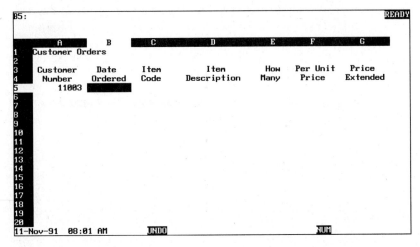

A Sample Macro

As an example, entering @NOW in a cell involves typing **@NOW** and then pressing Enter. To turn this operation into a macro, you must enter @NOW as a label rather than a value, and add a command that tells 1-2-3 to press Enter. The macro would look like this:

```
'@NOW~
```

Entering an apostrophe as the first character directs 1-2-3 to read the entry as a label and not a value. 1-2-3 understands the tilde symbol (~) to mean Enter.

Labels that are being used for macros are referred to as *macro code*. In Figure 13.2 you can see macro code entered in an empty section of the sample worksheet. Typically, you will want to keep macros separate from the data entry area of the worksheet. (The question of where to store macros will be dealt with in more detail under "Macro Organization.")

The next step in creating a macro is to assign a range name to the cell containing the macro code. You can either use a standard range name, such as ENTER_DATE, of up to 15 characters in length, or a special *hotkey* range name. A hotkey range name consists of the backslash followed by a single letter, such as \A, \B, \C, and so on. In this case, use the hotkey name \D to remind you that this macro enters the date.

Before using a macro, you should make sure that the cell pointer is in an appropriate location—in this case a cell into which you want to enter the date. If you have used a hotkey name such as \D, hold down the Alt key and press the letter used in the range name to execute the macro. For example, if the macro cell is named \D, you press Alt-D. This tells 1-2-3 to find the range

called \D and execute the instructions it contains. Figure 13.3 demonstrates the effect of running the macro shown in Figure 13.2. The @NOW function was entered in the current cell.

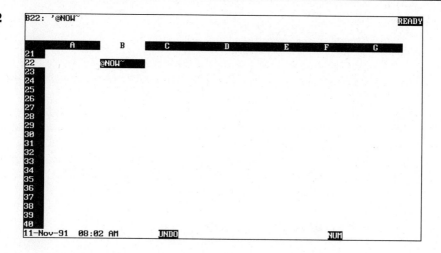

Figure 13.2
A sample macro

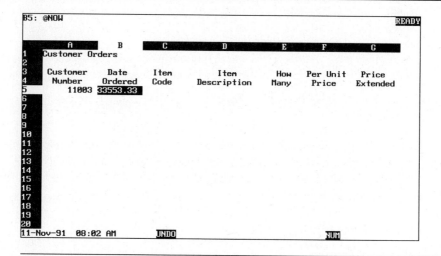

Figure 13.3
Results of running sample macro

If you don't use a hotkey name for the macro, you execute the macro by pressing Alt-F3, the Run key, and then selecting the macro from the list provided. The list includes regular range names as well as those belonging to macros, and works just like the range name list produced by Name (F3). If you press F3 after pressing Alt-F3, you get a full-screen list of range names. When you highlight or type the macro name and press Enter, the macro code in that cell is executed. The pros and cons of different macro naming systems will be discussed later under "Macro Name Strategies." Macros that are not hotkey macros will be referred to as *run* macros.

Expanding Macros

Macros can consist of much longer instructions than the simple example in Figure 13.2. For example, you probably want to improve the sample macro to format the result of the @NOW function so that it appears as a date rather than a date serial number. First you must consider the exact keystrokes involved in formatting a single cell. Normally, you select the cell with the cell pointer, press /, select Range, and then select Format. Then you choose the exact format you want and press Enter to confirm that the current cell is the range you want to format. If you want to use the MM/DD/YY format, known as D4, the keystrokes would be as follows:

/	Bring up the main menu
R	Select the Range command
F	Select the Format command
D	Select the Date formats
4	Select date format 4
~	Press Enter to confirm the current cell as the range to be formatted

In other words, what you want your macro to do can be written as /RFD4~. To add this code to the existing macro, you might edit cell B25 and type in the additional characters. The result would be

```
@NOW~/RFD4~
```

Since B25 is already called \D, pressing Alt-D would now carry out the entire instruction, entering @NOW in the current cell and formatting the cell to D4. However, adding the /RFD4~ code to the existing code in B25 is not necessarily the best way to proceed.

One Line at a Time

When a macro carries out several different operations, it is often a good idea to enter each operation into a separate cell. This makes it easier to edit the different steps if you need to alter the way the macro works or if the macro does not work correctly. For this reason, you might want to enter /RFD4~ into a cell of its own. However, there is a slight problem with entering /RFD4~ as a macro: The first character (/) normally brings up the menu.

Consequently, you must begin the entry by typing an apostrophe, just as you did when entering @NOW~. (Actually, you can also use one of the other label prefix characters—^ and "—but it's simpler to make consistent use of left-aligned labels for macro code.)

At this stage, you need to decide which cell to store your macro in. When a macro contains many instructions, the instructions are placed on successive rows of the same column. You execute a macro that consists of more than one line of instructions by indicating the first cell in the macro. 1-2-3 reads the instructions in that cell, the instructions in the next cell down, and so on, until a blank cell is encountered.

In the sample macro, the date formatting instruction can be placed below the @NOW entry, so that the \D macro looks like this:

```
@NOW~
/RFD4~
```

(From now on it is assumed that if a leading apostrophe is required it will be included when the macro code is entered.) When you press \D, the @NOW function is entered into the current cell and formatted to D4. You can see the results, and the expanded version of the macro, in Figure 13.4.

Figure 13.4

The expanded macro

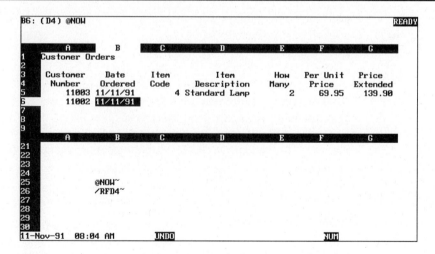

The Macro Making Process

The expanded sample macro is now fairly useful, and you have seen how easy it is to create and expand macro code. It is time to summarize the steps involved in macro making.

1. Design the code. Consider the actions that you want the macro to perform and go through a test run, noting each keystroke required. This is one situation where a pencil and paper can be helpful. Write out the macro and check that it is accurate. It's a common mistake to omit one or more tildes (~) since you are so accustomed to pressing the Enter key.

2. Enter the code as one or more labels. Break macro code into manageable pieces and write them in a column of consecutive entries. Each separate operation can be a separate label, and you should avoid labels longer than 20 characters, which will be difficult to edit if the macro does not work properly. When a piece of macro code begins with a value or a value indicator (such as + or @), or with the / character, include a leading apostrophe. If the macro code begins with text, an extra apostrophe is not required. For example, this macro would enter the word "Customer":

```
Customer~
```

3. Name the code. Macro names are usually single cell range names. Even if the macro is spread over several cells, the name only needs to be applied to the first cell. In each worksheet, you can have 26 hotkey macros, named \A through \Z. In addition to the hotkey macros, you can have any number of *run macros* with longer range names, such as ENTER_DATE or DATENTER. You execute hotkey macros by pressing Alt plus the assigned letter, and you execute run macros by first pressing the Run key (Alt-F3) and then selecting the name from the list provided.

4. Store the code. Like any other label you enter into a worksheet, macro code is not stored on disk until the worksheet is stored. Since it's easy to become engrossed in writing macros, make an extra effort to save the worksheet file on a regular basis so the latest version of the code is safely stored. This becomes particularly important as you develop more complex macros, since errors in macro code can wipe out all or part of the current worksheet.

Macro Key Codes

You could further refine the macro in Figure 13.4 so that it converts the @NOW function into a fixed date. Recall that a cell containing @NOW is updated to reflect the current date, whereas you will undoubtedly want the date on which an order is placed to remain fixed. To convert the @NOW function to a fixed date serial number, you would press the Edit key (F2), the Calc key (F9), and then Enter. But how do you type this instruction as macro code? You need to use the set of key codes provided by 1-2-3. You already know that the tilde (~) is the code for Enter. The rest of the key codes are listed in Table 13.1.

As you can see, the Edit key is entered in macros as {EDIT} and the Calc key is {CALC}. The system of codes is fairly consistent so that you can often guess what the code for a particular key will be. 1-2-3 does not have key codes for the following keys: Caps Lock, Compose (Alt-Fl), Learn (Alt-F5), Num Lock, Print Screen, Run (Alt-F3), Scroll Lock, Shift, Step (Alt-F2), and Undo (Alt-F4). You cannot use these keystrokes in macros because they would not make sense or because you can achieve the same effect in some other way. For example, writing a macro that performed an UNDO would be redundant. Using Run (Alt-F3) in a macro to run another macro is actually the same as using the {BRANCH} macro command, described later in this chapter.

Note that curly braces are included in all the key codes in the table. Do not substitute parentheses or square brackets for the curly braces. Entries beginning with a curly brace are automatically read as labels so you don't have to start them with an apostrophe. If you need a macro to type a curly brace, you must enclose it in curly braces. For example, the macro

```
Super Star {{}Model 100{}} Deluxe~
```

enters the label

```
Super Star {Model 100} Deluxe
```

into the current cell.

Returning to the \D macro, the expanded version that enters @NOW, formats the result, and then converts it to a fixed date will look like this:

```
@NOW~
/RFD4~
{EDIT}{CALC}~
```

Figure 13.5 shows this macro; it produces the results shown in cell B7.

Note that in the lower half of the figure some additions have been made to the area containing the \D macro. Labeling your macros makes it much easier to keep track of what they do and how they work. The entry in each of the cells from A23 to D23 is \=. The entry in A25 is actually '\D with a leading apostrophe because entering \D on its own would fill the cell with the letter D.

Macro Strategy and Macro Management

Your initial enthusiasm for macros may lead you to create many of them quite quickly. This is fine, *if* you take the time to organize your work. This section discusses techniques for naming and arranging macros, and includes tips for improving macro code and further examples of macros applied to common tasks.

Table 13.1   **Macro Key Codes**

Keys	Macro Code
Down Arrow	{DOWN} or {D}
Up Arrow	{UP} or {U}
Left Arrow	{LEFT} or {L}
Right Arrow	{RIGHT} or {R}
Abs (F4)	{ABS}
App1 (Alt-F7)	{APP1}
App2 (Alt-F8)	{APP2}
App3 (Alt-F9)	{APP3}
App4 (Alt-F10)	{APP4}
Backspace	{BACKSPACE} or {BS}
Calc (F9)	{CALC}
Ctrl-Left Arrow or Shift-Tab	{BIGLEFT}
Ctrl-Right Arrow or Tab	{BIGRIGHT}
Del	{DELETE} or {DEL}
Edit (F2)	{EDIT}
End	{END}
Esc	{ESCAPE} or {ESC}
Goto (F5)	{GOTO}
Graph (F10)	{GRAPH}
Help (F1)	{HELP}
Home	{HOME}
Ins	{INSERT} or {INS}
Menu	{MENU}
Name (F3)	{NAME}
PgUp	{PGUP}
PgDn	{PGDN}
Query (F7)	{QUERY}
Table (F8)	{TABLE}
Window (F6)	{WINDOW}
~ (tilde)	{~}
{ (open brace)	{{}
} (close brace)	{}}

Figure 13.5

The expanded
macro and results

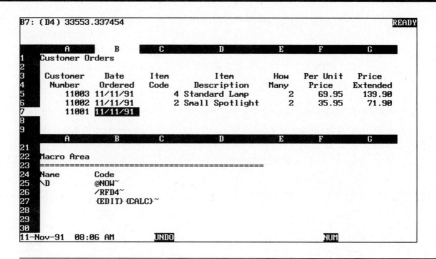

Macro Name Strategies

When you press the Run key, Alt-F3, 1-2-3 displays a list including all range
names for the current worksheet, not just macro names. For example, if you
have ranges called DATA_ENTRY and LIST in the worksheet, and then create a macro called \D, the Run key will provide this list:

```
DATA_ENTRY    LIST       \D
```

If you then create a macro called FORMAT, the list will look like this:

```
DATA_ENTRY    FORMAT    LIST       \D
```

By using a consistent pattern of names, you can segregate macro names from
regular range names. For example, if you begin all macros with the backslash
they will appear, in alphabetical order, after names beginning with letters,
like this:

```
DATA_ENTRY    LIST       \D          \FORMAT
```

If you're using many run macros and want the macro names to appear at the
beginning of the list, you can begin the macro names with the # character, as
in #SAVE, so that the list looks like this:

```
#FORMAT    #SAVE DATA_ENTRY    LIST       \D
```

Note that your hotkey macro names have to use the \ character and thus will
always appear toward the end of the list.

There is also a trick that you can use for assigning names to macro cells. In Figure 13.5, you saw that entries were added to the area containing the macro in order to label it. Entering the name of the macro in the cell to the left of the first cell of macro code is particularly handy since it allows you to name the macro with the Range Name Labels command. To see how this works, consider the macros in Figure 13.6.

Figure 13.6

Additional macros

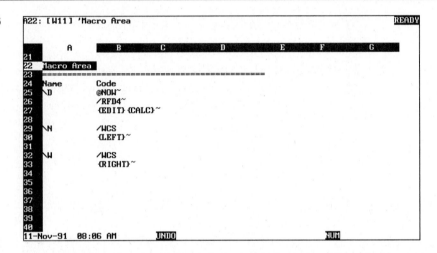

Starting in cell B29 is a macro named \N that narrows the current column by one character, while the macro that starts in B32, called \W, widens the current column by one character. Suppose you enter the code for the \D macro plus these other two all at once. Then you need to assign the names \D, \N, and \W to cells B25, B29, and B32, respectively. You enter the labels '\D, '\N, and '\W in A25, A29, and A32 to identify the macros in column B. Then you issue the Range Name Labels command and choose Right. By selecting A25..A32 as the label range, you attach any labels within that range to the cells immediately to their right, thus naming B25 with the label in A25, and so on. Empty cells in the label range are ignored. This technique allows you to assign range names *en masse* and is very handy when working with macros.

Macro Code Strategy

1-2-3 is not case sensitive when reading instructions in macro code. For example, you can use /rfd4 or /RFD4, and {edit}{calc} or {EDIT}{CALC}. However, 1-2-3 is faithful to the case you use in your macro code when entering text. For example, the following macro enters a label in the current cell and then moves the cell pointer one cell down the column:

```
Small Spotlight{DOWN}
```

"Small Spotlight" will be typed in exactly the same mixture of upper- and lowercase that you used when entering the macro, but {DOWN} could be entered as {down} or {Down} or even the shortcut {d}.

There are some shortcuts you can use when writing macro code, and these were listed in Table 13.1. Some keys have short names, such as {DEL} for {DELETE} and {ESC} for {ESCAPE}. The single-letter versions of the arrow keys are handy when you want to minimize your code. As you have seen, you can use {R} instead of {RIGHT}, although users who are not well versed in macros might find a simple {R} somewhat cryptic. Another useful way of reducing the length of macro code is to use a repetition argument. For example, instead of using this

```
{RIGHT}{RIGHT}{RIGHT}{RIGHT}
```

you can use

```
{RIGHT 4}
```

The repetition argument follows the key name and is separated from it by a space. You can employ a repetition argument whenever a macro needs two or more consecutive uses of the following keys: {BACKSPACE}, {BIGLEFT}, {BIGRIGHT}, {DELETE}, {DOWN}, {ESCAPE}, {LEFT}, {NAME}, {PGDN}, {PGUP}, {RIGHT}, {UP}.

If you combine repetition arguments with abbreviated names, you can substantially reduce the amount of code required. For example, you can turn this

```
{RIGHT}{RIGHT}{RIGHT}{DOWN}{DOWN}{PGDN}{PGDN}
```

into this

```
{R 3}{D 2}{PGDN 2}
```

There is one instance where you might want to avoid abbreviation: using the key code {MENU} in your macros, rather than the slash symbol (/), can make them easier to read.

While you can minimize the space taken up by repeated keys, it's better to avoid use of repeated keys whenever possible. This is particularly true of cursor-movement keys. Translating extensive cursor movement into macro code is prone to error. Furthermore, positioning the cell pointer with relative commands such as {UP 3}{RIGHT 2} means that later changes to the worksheet or macro could render the instructions inaccurate. A more sophisticated alternative is to use range names. For example, if a macro needs to position the cell pointer on data in cell B5, name B5 and then use {GOTO} to get there. For example, if you name B5 as TARGET, the code

```
{GOTO}TARGET~
```

will move the cell pointer to TARGET, *regardless* of where the cell pointer is before the GOTO command and *regardless* of whether the data in B5 has been moved to another cell.

When building macros, you should choose menu items with the first-letter method. This makes for more accurate code, and makes it much easier to decipher the macro. For example, the following code is very hard to read:

```
/R~{R 7}~{R 3}~~
```

However, the effect is the same as /RFD4~. You can see that using macros to select menu items by the highlight-and-enter method makes them unnecessarily complex and obscure.

When a macro needs to select a default option, such as the two decimal places that are the default setting for the Currency format, type the choice and then press Enter. A macro to format the current cell in Currency format with two decimal places should read /RFC2~~ rather than /RFC~~. The extra keystroke is well worth the trouble when you are trying to read the macro later.

Macro Organization

Macros are such fantastic tools that you'll probably begin to accumulate many of them once you know how to develop them. The placement of macros within a worksheet becomes an important factor to consider when organizing your macros.

The first rule to observe is that at least one blank cell must separate macros. In Figure 13.6, several macros were included in the same area of the worksheet as the \D macro. Because each macro is separated from the others by a blank cell, 1-2-3 can tell where one macro leaves off and the next begins. When the user presses Alt-N, for example, 1-2-3 executes the code in B29, followed by that in B30. After that the macro stops because B31 is empty. However, if the \W macro started in cell B31, 1-2-3 would execute that macro as well.

You also need to think carefully about where you place macros within your spreadsheet. The macros in Figure 13.6 are below the main work area. This location is fine unless the user decides to delete column A or B of the worksheet or insert a new column between current columns A and B. The macros might be damaged or their arrangement disrupted by major changes to the work area above them.

Suppose you moved the macros to the right of the main work area. This location is even more risky, since the user may decide to delete a row from the list in the main work area. Since both macros and work area are unlikely to be in view at the same time, it's all too easy to delete a row from the work area and accidentally delete a row of macro code. Since macros run until they encounter a blank row, even deleting a blank row or inserting a fresh row can cause problems for macros stored to the right of the work area. One way to avoid inadvertently deleting rows is to move the cursor to the right when using the Worksheet Delete Row or Worksheet Insert Row command. (You can press Ctrl-Right Arrow or the Tab key to move to the right of your work area to check for macros before deleting or inserting rows.)

Some users like to place their macros above the main work area and to the left of the spreadsheet—that is, around the home position. Here they are relatively safe from row deletion and easy to find. Perhaps the safest location is below and to the right of the main work area. Macros are fairly easy to move with the Move command since range names remain firmly attached to cells during Move operations. In Figure 13.7 the macros from Figure 13.6 have been moved to the right of the main work area. A new macro has been added and the Range Name Labels Right command is being executed to name the macro.

Figure 13.7
Macros that have
been moved and
annotated

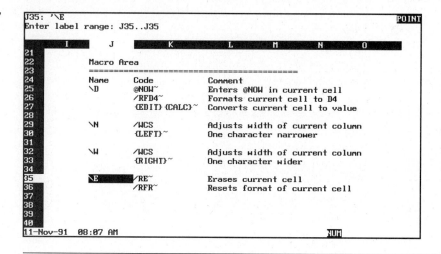

Comments have also been added to the right of the macro code in Figure 13.7. This is an important aspect of macro management, since it's quite easy to forget what a particular piece of macro code is intended to do. Adding notes to each line of macro code both states their purpose and helps you write more accurate macros.

Note that the column containing the macro code, now column K, has been widened. This prevents the macro code from appearing truncated because the cells immediately to the right are now occupied by comments. If column K were only nine characters wide, the code {EDIT}{CALC}~ in K27 would appear in the worksheet as {EDIT}{CA, although the actual contents of K27 and the performance of the macro would not be affected.

Also note that the \E macro in Figure 13.7 is very handy because it makes up for the absence of a "cell delete" command in 1-2-3. The \E macro removes the contents of the current cell and resets its format.

Macro Name Tables

Even simple macros add to the number of named ranges in a worksheet. As you tackle more complex tasks with macros, you will start making extensive use of range names. To keep track of the names and locations of all named ranges in a worksheet, you use the Range Name Table command. This produces a two-column list of the range names and their corresponding coordinates, as seen in Figure 13.8.

Figure 13.8
A range name table

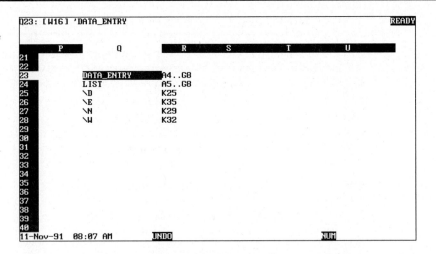

In this case, the Range Name Table command was issued with the cell selector in Q23. The table occupies columns Q and R plus as many rows as are needed to list all the current range names. You should always leave enough room for the resulting table when you issue this command; otherwise, the table will overwrite the contents of existing cells. Note that the table is not dynamic: It is not linked to the Range Name command and will not be updated automatically when new names are created or old names deleted. You must reissue the

Table command to get an updated table. However, the Table command does remember the previous table location, and if you use the same location, it will erase the old table before creating a new one.

Macro Applications

So far you have seen macros that enter data and offer shortcuts to executing a series of commands. Macros can also be very effective in changing settings. For example, when you set up a print operation in a worksheet you might have to change half a dozen settings in the Print Settings box. If you want to print a second report from the same worksheet, you might have to change the same settings again because a worksheet cannot store two sets of print settings. The solution is to create two macros, each of which will institute the appropriate settings for one report. You can employ a similar approach to store several different settings for the Data Sort settings and Data Query commands. (You can also use macros for graph settings, although the Graph Name command allows you to store and recall several different graph settings.)

When creating macros of this kind, you first need to name the ranges of the worksheet you are going to be using. For example, suppose you have a worksheet in which you want to print from two different ranges. First, name both ranges using names such as PRANGE1 and PRANGE2, or perhaps something more descriptive, like ORDERS and PRICES. If you are using a macro to sort data, name the data range. If you are querying data, name the criteria range. This allows your macro to refer to the range by name rather than by coordinates. Next include a Reset or Cancel command in the macro. Clearing previous settings prior to establishing new settings ensures that there are no inappropriate held-over settings.

Consider the following macro code, which prints a range called ORDERS after first clearing previous settings:

/ppca	Clear all print settings
rorders~	Set print range
op60~	Set page length of 60
ml5~mt3~mb4~	Set left, top, and bottom margins
s\027E~	Enter setup string
qag	Quit options, align and go

Note that there is not an entry for every single print setting. The code only needs to address those that are to be varied from the default reinstated by the Clear command.

1-2-3 can do a lot of the work involved in creating a lengthy macro of this type. By using the macro recording feature, described in the next section, you can quickly create many macros simply by recording the actions you want the macro to perform.

Recording Macros

1-2-3 offers two methods for creating macro code: writing and recording. The macros introduced so far have all been created by writing. That is, they have been designed by thinking through the action to be performed and then manually entered as the appropriate labels. The recording method is a very convenient alternative, once you understand the basic principles of macro operation. This section demonstrates how to record macros using the Learn key (Alt-F5), and how to manage the learn range. You will also find out how to modify and improve recorded macros.

The Learn Commands

Using an area of the worksheet called a *learn range*, 1-2-3 can record your actions, such as entering data and issuing commands, in the form of macro code. In a sense, 1-2-3 "learns" what you have done in order to repeat it. You can then use this recorded macro code to create macros that are employed either "as is" or as the foundation for more sophisticated macros. To start recording macro code, press the Learn key, Alt-F5. However, before you can use the Learn key you must define a learn range, a blank area of the worksheet in which the recorded code can be stored.

If you press Alt-F5 before defining a learn range, you get a beep, the mode indicator flashes ERROR, and the message "Learn range has not been defined" is displayed at the bottom of the screen. The message doesn't explain how to define a learn range, but if you press the Help key (F1) at this point, 1-2-3 advises you to select Learn from the Worksheet menu.

The Worksheet Learn command offers three possibilities: Range, Cancel, and Erase. You select the Range option and use the standard 1-2-3 range setting procedure to tell 1-2-3 which cells can be used for the recording. The Cancel command makes 1-2-3 forget the Worksheet Learn Range setting. Selecting Cancel deletes the learn range setting with no confirmation prompt and returns you to READY mode. The Erase command performs a Range Erase on all of the cells in the learn range. This command includes a standard No/Yes confirmation to complete or abort the command and return you to READY mode. If you select Erase when no learn range is defined, the command is aborted and you receive an error message.

The learn range is a single-column range extending down enough rows to receive all of the instructions that you want to record in a single recording. You cannot simply indicate a single cell for the learn range and have 1-2-3 assume that the cells below it are free to be used. In other words, until you are familiar with how 1-2-3 records your actions in LEARN mode you have to estimate an appropriate size for the learn range. You should err on the side of generosity because the learn process is aborted when the learn range is full. A simple rule of thumb is to calculate the number of keys you plan to type during the recording and include one row for each key. Pressing PgDn expands the learn range 20 rows. Make sure that there are no occupied cells within the learn range since the recording will overwrite them. If you do select a learn range that is too small, 1-2-3 displays the message "learn range is full" during recording. To recover from this error, press Esc to get back to READY mode. Then erase the learn range and expand it before trying the recording again.

A Learning Example

To see how the Learn commands work, consider the worksheet in Figure 13.9, a record of customer orders like the one seen earlier but with several more entries. The user of this worksheet wants the customer number centered in the column. At this point, the customer numbers have been entered as values and there is no 1-2-3 command for centering values in a column. However, if you convert the numbers to labels you can use the center label prefix (^) to center the numbers in the column.

Figure 13.9
Sample worksheet

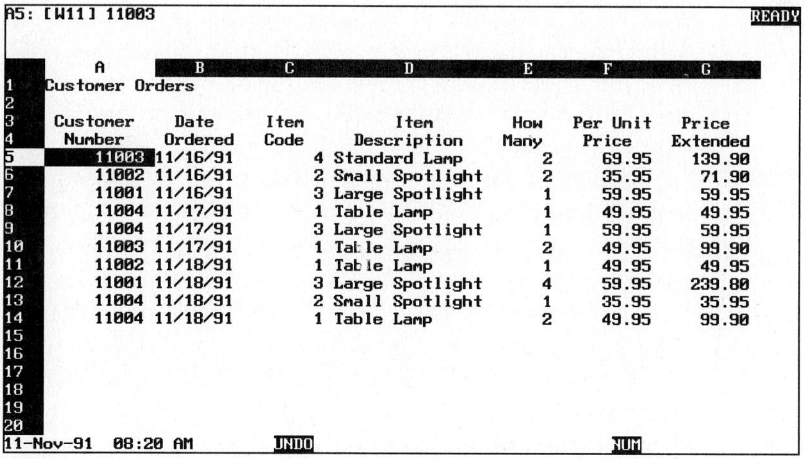

	A	B	C	D	E	F	G
	Customer Orders						
3	Customer	Date	Item	Item	How	Per Unit	Price
4	Number	Ordered	Code	Description	Many	Price	Extended
5	11003	11/16/91	4	Standard Lamp	2	69.95	139.90
6	11002	11/16/91	2	Small Spotlight	2	35.95	71.90
7	11001	11/16/91	3	Large Spotlight	1	59.95	59.95
8	11004	11/17/91	1	Table Lamp	1	49.95	49.95
9	11004	11/17/91	3	Large Spotlight	1	59.95	59.95
10	11003	11/17/91	1	Table Lamp	2	49.95	99.90
11	11002	11/18/91	1	Table Lamp	1	49.95	49.95
12	11001	11/18/91	3	Large Spotlight	4	59.95	239.80
13	11004	11/18/91	2	Small Spotlight	1	35.95	35.95
14	11004	11/18/91	1	Table Lamp	2	49.95	99.90

A5: [W11] 11003   READY

11-Nov-91 08:20 AM   UNDO   NUM

Altering the customer numbers in this way would not affect the user's ability to sort the list based on column A, and the numbers are not used in any calculations. Rather than reenter the numbers as labels, you need a macro that will center and convert to a label a number that has already been entered as a value. Suppose that it's your job to create such a macro. You decide to make the macro by performing the operation in LEARN mode, recording the keystrokes required.

First you need to define the learn range with the Worksheet Learn Range command. Suppose that this example already includes a collection of macros in column K, as in Figure 13.7. A logical place to begin the learn range is K38. To give the learn operation plenty of room you can anchor the start of the range at K38 and then press PgDn to extend the range to K38..K58. When the range is confirmed, you are returned to READY mode. Now place the cell pointer in A5, the first cell that needs to be altered, and press Learn (Alt-F5) to turn on the learn feature. The message LEARN appears at the bottom of the screen to indicate that you are in LEARN mode. Now perform the actions that you want to record: Press Edit to edit the cell contents; press Home to move the edit cursor to the beginning of the number; type the center label prefix (^); press Down Arrow to enter the edited contents and move to the next cell.

Having performed the actions required to convert a value into a centered label, you want to turn off LEARN mode. To do this, simply press Learn (Alt-F5). The LEARN message disappears and you can now move to the learn range to examine the results. In the first cell of the learn range (cell K38), you will find this label:

```
{EDIT}{HOME}^{D}
```

Note that 1-2-3 uses the abbreviated form of the code for Down Arrow. Before you can use this macro, you must name it and label it. You can add the name in J38 and a description in L38, as shown in Figure 13.10. Then you can place the cell pointer on the macro name and issue the Range Name Labels Right command. This will attach the name to the macro, in this case \C.

Sometimes during a macro recording 1-2-3 will turn on the CALC message next to the LEARN message. If this message remains on after you complete the recording, part of the recording has not yet been entered into the learn range. You should enter the rest of the code and the message will disappear when you continue working. If the message does not disappear, you can press the Calc key (F9). This will ensure that the entire code for the actions you have performed is correctly recorded in the worksheet.

Improving Your Learning

At this point, you can use the recorded macro. In this example you would place the cell pointer on a cell to be converted and press Alt-C. To convert a whole column of entries, simply keep pressing Alt-C. Since the macro finishes with the Down Arrow, the cell pointer is left in position to convert the next cell down the current column. However, after you have recorded and named a macro you need to manage the learn range. If you don't adjust the current learn range setting, pressing the Learn key (Alt-F5) again tells 1-2-3 to keep recording in the same learn range, continuing in the cell immediately below the previous recording. The learn feature does this to allow you to construct a macro from several separate actions: First you record an action, then you turn off recording, perform an unrecorded action, and resume recording. The recorded actions form one continuous macro.

Figure 13.10

The macro recorded and annotated

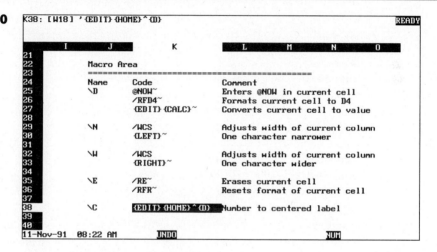

If you want to prevent Learn from adding new code to old, you can either issue the Worksheet Learn Cancel command to clear the current learn range setting, or use the Worksheet Learn Range command to alter the learn range setting. It's best to alter the learn range if you plan to do more macro recording to create additional macros. In this case, you could revise the range from K38..K58 to K40..K60, ready to record another macro under the last one.

In the example in Figure 13.10, the macro code that 1-2-3 recorded in LEARN mode was fairly compact. When recording macros, 1-2-3 uses the abbreviated key names and tries to split the code into manageable pieces. However, a long series of commands can create lengthy code such as

```
/ppcarorders~op60~ml5~mt3~mb4~\027E~qag
```

(This is the code for the printing macro introduced under "Macro Applications.") Code like this is best annotated and split into more manageable parcels.

Another problem is errors during recording. For example, suppose you are recording a print macro that includes the range name ORDERS and you

make a mistake as you type the name, typing **ores**. Then you press Backspace twice to correct it and continue. The recorded code looks like this:

```
/ppcarores{BS}{BS}ders~
```

While this code works, it would look better and work faster if you removed
the error.

Note that repetition arguments are not used in macro recording so some
codes will be repeated. If you need repeated codes, you can edit the
recorded code to change such items as {D}{D}{D}{D} to {D 4}. However,
remember to minimize the use of cursor-movement keys in macro recordings
and use range names whenever possible. They can turn this

```
/ppcar.{D}{D}{D}{END}{RIGHT}{END}{DOWN}~
```

into this:

```
/ppcarorders~
```

When you do use range names, enter them as names rather than selections
from the NAME list. Otherwise, you will get

```
/ppcar{NAME}{R}{R}~
```

which does not give you much clue as to which range is being chosen and
may not work if you add further range names to the list. Also remember to
select menu items by the first-letter method if you want to get intelligible
recordings rather than something like this:

```
/{R}{R}{R}{R}{R}~~{R}{R}{R}{R}~~{L}{L}
{L}{L}~orders~
```

The preceding code is the highlight-and-enter version of

```
/ppcarorders~
```

1-2-3 will sometimes split code awkwardly between cells. For example, in
the following code (part of a recorded print macro) 1-2-3 split the page
length setting of 60 between two cells:

```
ohBrite Lites||@~ml5~mr80~p6
0~s\015~qag
```

The first line of the macro selects Options Header and then enters the
header text Brite Lites||@ (this prints the company name Brite Lites on the
left of the header with the current date on the right). Then the macro sets the
left margin (ml5~) and the right margin (mr80~). The complete code to set
the page length is p60~ but this is split. The macro would be easier to interpret if the lines were split and annotated, as in the following.

```
ohBrite Lites||@~        Enters header
ml5~mr80~p60~            Sets margins
s\015~qag                Enters setup string then aligns &
                         prints
```

Applied Learning

One application of the Learn feature requires a slightly different sequence of commands. When you are building a worksheet, you might need a series of temporary macros. For example, you might need to enter the same set of labels in several places within the worksheet. If you establish a learn range before you enter the labels for the first time, you can record the labels. You can then name the first cell of the recording and play back the recorded macro to enter the labels in other locations. When you use it in this fashion, the learn feature provides an alternative to the Copy command.

Suppose you no longer need to repeat the labels but have to enter a series of dates in several different locations. You can use the Worksheet Learn Erase command to clear the learn range and record the date entry steps in the same range. You can then use the macro name previously used to enter the label entries to enter the date entries. If you wanted to repeat another entry in several cells, you could repeat this process, using the same learn range and macro name again.

With recorded macros it's critical to read the recording before you use it. This will help to prevent unexpected results. A common error is to include extra steps in the recording, such as cell pointer movements. Consider the sample recording, which converted the numeric value in the current cell into a centered label. The operative phrase here is current cell. Before using the macro the user is expected to position the cell pointer in an appropriate location. To record this macro properly, you must place the cell pointer in position before turning on the LEARN mode. If you turn on LEARN too soon, your recording is liable to contain positioning keys that will prevent the macro from working correctly.

Macro Control

1-2-3 contains numerous features for controlling macro execution. To get the most out of macros, you need to know how to stop them, how to interrupt them, how to make them repeat, and how to keep track of the cell pointer during macro execution. This section covers all of these aspects of macro control.

Stopping Macros

If you execute a macro and get unexpected results, you may want to stop the macro immediately. You do this with Ctrl-Break (or Ctrl-Scroll Lock on some keyboards). When you press Ctrl-Break during macro execution, 1-2-3 beeps and flashs ERROR in the mode indicator. To remove the error message and return to READY mode, just press Esc.

Macros and Undo

You can undo the effect of most macros by pressing Undo after stopping the macro. This is true even if the macro has performed several different operations. In most cases, Undo reverses all of them, restoring the worksheet to the state it was in before the macro executed. This is because Undo reverses what happened since the last time 1-2-3 was in READY mode, and you are in a special mode known as CMD while a macro is executing.

You can also use Undo to cancel a macro recording. If you record a macro and immediately decide that it is wrong, you can press Undo to wipe out the recording, and start over. This is particularly helpful when you first start using the record feature.

The {QUIT} Command

Although you learned earlier that macros stop automatically when they get to a blank cell, this is not strictly true. In the next chapter, you will work with macros that use subroutines to call other macros. You use a special macro code, entered as {QUIT}, as the last command of the macro that you want to terminate. Placing a {QUIT} command at the end of a macro called by a subroutine ends both the subroutine macro and the one that called it. You should get into the habit of using {QUIT} to mark the end of your macros. Among other things, it helps you to distinguish where one macro ends and another begins.

Cell Pointer Control

In each of the macro examples so far in this chapter, considerable emphasis was placed on the term "current cell." Cell pointer positioning is crucial to successful macro execution. As a simple example, consider a macro designed to erase the current cell. Obviously, you must be sure to position the cell pointer correctly before executing the macro. With more involved macros, the question of positioning becomes even more important. A macro designed to be executed with the cell pointer in A1 could do serious damage if it was run with the cell pointer in B5.

You may want to include commands in the macro that position the cell pointer correctly before the rest of the code is executed. Whether you are developing utility macros, such as those in Figure 13.7, or more complex macros like those described earlier under "Macro Applications," you must carefully consider the effect of cell pointer location on a macro.

Looping Macros

In some cases, you may be using a macro repeatedly. For example, the \C macro recorded earlier in the chapter centers a number in a column and moves the cell pointer down one row to the next cell, using the following code:

```
\C        {EDIT}{HOME}^{D}
```

If you are using this macro to center a very long column of numbers, you could get tired of pressing Alt-C, even though the macro substitutes one keystroke for four. Fortunately, 1-2-3 allows you to loop a macro so that it repeats itself.

The simplest way to loop a macro is to use the {BRANCH} command. Like the {QUIT} command introduced earlier, {BRANCH} is one of the special macro commands that make up the 1-2-3 macro command language. Unlike {QUIT}, however, {BRANCH} requires an argument, namely, the cell to which you want the macro to branch. Like the repetition arguments used with cursor key codes, you place macro command arguments within curly braces, separated from the command by a space. Thus you could use {BRANCH TOP} to tell a macro to carry on reading instructions in the cell named TOP. The command {BRANCH \C} would tell a macro to continue at the cell named \C.

To make the number-centering macro repeat itself, you would simply add the {BRANCH} command to it:

```
\C      {EDIT}{HOME}^{D}
        {BRANCH \C}
```

This is a simple looping macro that will work its way down a column, editing each cell in turn. When the user presses Alt-C, 1-2-3 starts to execute the macro code in the cell called \C. You might want to imagine an invisible cursor, which we will call the macro cell pointer, passing through the code. In all of the macros discussed prior to this one, the macro pointer moves straight down the column of instructions, stopping when it reaches a blank cell. In contrast, in this macro, the {BRANCH} command is used to reroute the macro pointer before it reaches an empty cell. Having passed through the instructions in the cell called \C, the macro pointer moves on to those in the next cell down the column—that is, {BRANCH \C}. This tells the macro pointer to continue with the instructions in the cell called \C, and so on, in an endless loop. In fact, you have to press Ctrl-Break to stop the macro.

Note that the flow of the macro pointer is quite separate from the movement of the cell pointer, which, in this case, is moved down one row by each loop of the macro. Also note that this is a rather rough and ready way to loop a macro, since you must press Ctrl-Break to halt the loop. However, such loops can be useful when you are creating utility macros to tidy up your work. Consider the next macro, which tells 1-2-3 to add an @ROUND function to the contents of the current cell:

```
\R        {EDIT}{HOME}@ROUND(
          {END},2){DOWN}
```

If the current cell initially contained B5*1.01, it would be replaced by @ROUND(B5*1.01) when the user pressed Alt-R.

Suppose you have a whole column of calculations that need to be rounded in this way. You could get tired of pressing Alt-R, so you add the code {BRANCH \R} to the macro. Now you can place the cell pointer in the first cell to be affected, press Alt-R, and wait until the last entry in the column has been updated, at which point you press Ctrl-Break to stop the loop. You might get a few error messages if the macro reaches a label entry or blank cell before you press Ctrl-Break, but overall, looping the macro saves a lot of keystrokes and makes life a little easier.

Fortunately, there are several ways to create a looping macro that stops itself. In the case of the \R macro, you want the macro to stop when it reaches a cell that is not a value. You need a test that tells the macro whether or not the current cell contains a value. You use the {IF} macro command to put a test into a macro. Like the @IF function, this macro command works by evaluating a true/false condition and acting upon the result. The condition is provided as the command argument. The action to be performed if the condition is true is described immediately after the {IF} command, on the same line. The code to be executed if the condition is false is placed in the cell immediately below the {IF} command; thus the syntax for the command is

```
{IF condition}do-if-true
do-if-false
```

Suppose that you want a macro called \K to loop until the value in A1 is greater than 100. You could set up the {IF} statement like this:

```
{IF A1>100}{QUIT}
{BRANCH \K}
```

Alternatively, you could reverse the condition and rearrange the elements like the following to achieve the same effect.

```
{IF A1<=100}{BRANCH \K}
{QUIT}
```

You want the \R macro to quit when the current cell contains something other than a value. The 1-2-3 @CELLPOINTER function can tell you what type of information a cell contains. This function, described in detail in the next chapter, returns useful information about the current cell. The formula @CELLPOINTER("type") returns v if the current cell contains a value, b if it is a blank cell, or l if the cell contains a label. By combining the @CELLPOINTER function with the {IF} command, you can create a macro that edits a column of values and stops when it reaches a label entry or a blank cell:

```
\R       {EDIT}{HOME}@ROUND(
         {END},2){DOWN}
         {IF @CELLPOINTER("type")="v"}{BRANCH \R}
         {QUIT}
```

Note that the result of @CELLPOINTER is a label and so must be placed in quotes in the condition statement. There's more on the {IF} command in the next chapter.

You can use a similar technique to make the \C Centering macro repeat until it encounters a blank cell. The code would look like this:

```
\C       {EDIT}{HOME}^{D}
         {IF @CELLPOINTER ("type")="b"}{BRANCH\C}
```

User Input Macros

At times you want to control the action of a macro with user input rather than a spreadsheet condition. In other words, you want the macro to stop and wait for the user to answer a question or select an option before continuing execution. The simplest way to get user input in a macro is the {?} command, which has no arguments. You place this command at any point in a macro where user input is required. When a macro encounters a {?} command, program control is handed to the user, who can type a label or number, make a menu selection, or specify a cell or range using either the pointing or typing method.

Suppose that you want a macro that formats a single cell with the Fixed format. The simplest code would be /RFF~~. This macro accepts the default decimal place setting of 2. If you want the macro to select one decimal place, you can use /RFF1~~. However, if you want the user to choose the number of decimal places, you use /RFF{?}~~, substituting the {?} command for the decimal place setting. When the macro is executed, it pauses at the "Enter number of decimal places" prompt. When the user types a number and presses Enter, or simply presses Enter to accept the default setting of 2, the macro resumes control and assigns the format to the current cell.

You can also use the {?} command whenever you want the user to supply a range setting. For example, consider the simple print macro /PPR{?}~AG, which pauses at the print range prompt. When the user selects a range and presses Enter to confirm it, the macro issues the Align and Go commands. The {?} command gives the user plenty of opportunity to respond. In this example, the range can be changed, rejected, or reselected until the user presses Enter. Of course, the user could also press Ctrl-Break to halt the macro at this point.

Note that in this macro and the previous one, the {?} command is followed by a tilde (~) to enter or confirm the user input. The first few times you use {?} in your macros you might be tempted to leave out this ~ since the user will be also be pressing Enter. If you find that your {?} macros tend to stall when you execute them, check that you have not omitted the required ~ that follows the {?} command.

The {?} command is not a particularly sophisticated method of obtaining user input, and other methods will be suggested in the next chapter. However, {?} does give you a way of controlling macros and expanding the range of actions that a single macro can perform. For example, the following macro will round the current cell to a number of decimal places entered by the user:

```
\R        {EDIT}{HOME}@ROUND(

          {END},{?}~){DOWN}
```

Unfortunately, if you want to combine the {?} command with the {IF} loop, you have to redo the whole macro since the following code would ask for user input during each loop:

```
\R        {EDIT}{HOME}@ROUND(
          {END},{?}~){DOWN}
          {IF @CELLPOINTER("type")="v"}{BRANCH \R}
          {QUIT}
```

In the next chapter, you will learn how to obtain user input and store it for use in a repeating macro.

Automatic Macros

One very convenient feature of 1-2-3 macros is that you can have the program activate a macro as soon as the file in which it is stored is retrieved. To do this, you name the macro \0, the special autoexec macro name. A macro

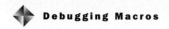

named \0 executes as soon as you retrieve the worksheet in which it is stored. For example, you might use the following code as an autoexec macro:

```
/FR{NAME}
```

This macro uses the File Retrieve command and the F3 key to present a full-screen list of files from which you can choose. If you enter this \0 macro in a worksheet called 123AUTO.WK1 and store it in the default data directory, 1-2-3 will automatically load the file and run the macro as soon as you load the 1-2-3 program. After loading 1-2-3, you'll immediately see a list of files from which to choose.

At times you may want to deactivate the autoexec macro feature. Since this feature is often used to start a series of macros for helping novices perform data entry in a worksheet, you might want to deactivate the feature while an experienced operator is using these worksheets. You deactivate the autoexec macro feature with the Worksheet Global Default Autoexec setting. Select No to deactivate the feature, and Yes to reactivate it (the default setting is Yes for active). Then select the Worksheet Global Default Update command to lock in this setting for the next time 1-2-3 is loaded.

Debugging Macros

Since 1-2-3 macros execute quickly, it may be hard to tell what goes wrong when a macro misbehaves, and it may be difficult to stop the macro before it is completed. For this reason, 1-2-3 provides a STEP mode of macro execution. This mode lets you watch your macro run one step at a time, which is very useful for debugging your macro code. As an example, consider the worksheet in Figure 13.11. This worksheet is a monthly revenue projection. The revenue is listed in columns by month. The columns are being summed on row 10 using a sum formula like the one in B10.

Two macros are visible on the worksheet. The first one, \C, is used to copy the contents of a cell across the model to the last column. The second macro, \S, is designed to sum a column. \S first types the @SUM function and the opening parenthesis. Then it moves the cell pointer to the top of the column, anchors the range to be summed at that point with a period, and includes all the cells down to the bottom of the column. Finally, it adds a closing parenthesis and enters the formula in the cell with a tilde.

The idea behind the \S macro is that the user will place the cell pointer in C10 and press Alt-S to activate the macro and sum the column. As you can see from Figure 13.12, however, the results are not as expected. Cell C10 contains the formula @SUM(C9..C8192), which is not only incorrect but a circular formula because it sums a range that includes the formula cell. (You'll notice the message "CIRC" at the bottom of the screen.) The step feature should help you locate the problem.

Figure 13.11

Sample macros

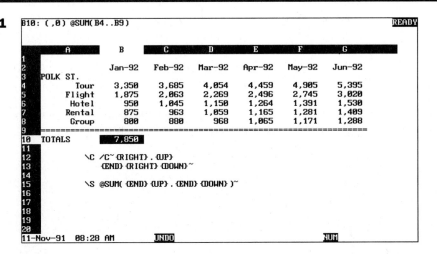

Figure 13.12

Erroneous results
from \S macro

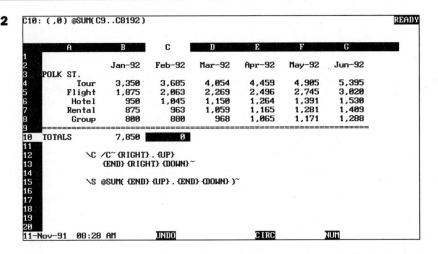

To activate STEP mode, press the Step key, Alt-F2. The message "STEP" appears at the bottom of the screen. From now until you reissue the Alt-F2 command, any macro you run will be executed in STEP mode. Before running the macro you want to debug, however, you should make sure that the conditions are correct. In Figure 13.12, the incorrect formula needs to be deleted from cell C10 before the macro is rerun. If you then press Alt-S to start the \S macro that needs to be debugged, 1-2-3 displays the macro code at the bottom of the screen and places the cursor on the first instruction. To execute the macro, you press the spacebar repeatedly. Each press causes one character to be typed or one macro code to be executed. In Figure 13.13, several instructions in the \S macro have been executed.

Figure 13.13
Running a macro in
STEP mode

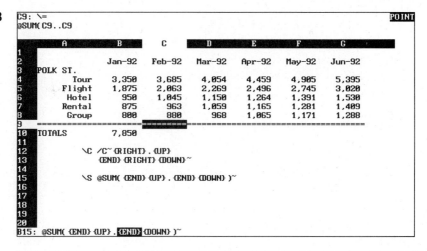

In Figure 13.13, the problem with this macro is about to become apparent. The {END}{UP} combination took the cell selector only to cell C9, where the period anchored the start of the range. The intention of the macro was to anchor the range at the top of the column of numbers. At this point, the {END}{DOWN} combination is about to take the cell selector to the bottom of the worksheet. You can abort the macro now by pressing Ctrl-Break. This returns you to READY mode but does not reverse the effect of Alt-F2, and macros will continue to be executed in STEP mode until you press Alt-F2 again. The correct code for \S is

```
@SUM({UP}{END}{UP}.{END}{DOWN}~
```

Macro Sharing and Macro Libraries

Macros stored in a regular worksheet are specific to that worksheet. They are saved in the worksheet file and are not immediately available when you retrieve a different worksheet. However, you will want to use some macros, like the \E macro shown in Figure 13.7, in all of your worksheets. You can transfer macros from one worksheet to another by using the Xtract and Combine commands on the File menu. You can also store macros in a special file called a macro library and then use them in various worksheets if you use the Macro Library Manager add-in.

Macro Transfers

You can transfer macros from one worksheet to another by first using the File Xtract command to store the code into a separate worksheet, and then reading that worksheet into the destination worksheet. For example, suppose you want to transfer the macros in Figure 13.7 to another worksheet. You would issue the File Xtract Values command and enter a suitable file name such as MACTRNS1. Then you would indicate J25..L36 as the extract range. The macro code, together with names and comments, is then written to the file MACTRNS1.WK1.

Next you load the file into which you want to transfer the macros. Then place the cell pointer in the upper-left cell of the area into which you want to read the macros. For example, in Figure 13.14 the correct cell would be P37, below the existing macro and separated from it by a blank row.

Figure 13.14

Preparing to read in macro file

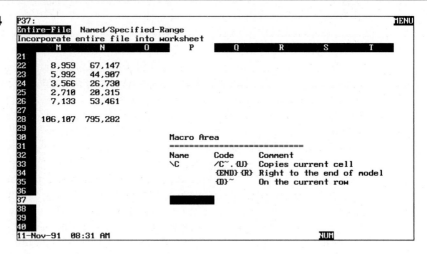

You can see that the File Combine Copy command has been issued and the user is about to choose the Entire-File option. When this is chosen, the correct file name must be specified. When the file name MACTRNS1 is entered, the macros are read in, as shown in Figure 13.15. Note that the Range Name Labels Right command is now being issued to name the new macros.

You must name the newly arrived macros because the File Combine command forgets all named ranges attached to the incoming cells. That is, to make a macro active in the worksheet to which you just copied it you must use the Range Names command. If you consistently use the three-column layout, you can use the Labels Right method to assign names quickly.

Figure 13.15

Macros combined
into a different
worksheet

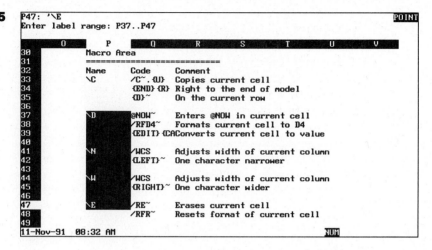

```
P47: '\E                                                        POINT
Enter label range: P37..P47
            O        P        Q        R        S        T        U        V
30                 Macro Area
31                 ============================
32                 Name     Code      Comment
33                 \C       /C~.{U}   Copies current cell
34                          {END}{R}  Right to the end of model
35                          {D}~      On the current row
36
37                 \D       @NOW~     Enters @NOW in current cell
38                          /RFD4~    Formats current cell to D4
39                          {EDIT}{CAConverts current cell to value
40
41                 \N       /WCS      Adjusts width of current column
42                          {LEFT}~   One character narrower
43
44                 \W       /WCS      Adjusts width of current column
45                          {RIGHT}~  One character wider
46
47                 \E       /RE~      Erases current cell
48                          /RFR~     Resets format of current cell
49
11-Nov-91  08:32 AM                                            NUM
```

You can also transfer macros from one worksheet to another by choosing the Named/Specified-Range option when using the File Combine command. If you know exactly where in the source worksheet the macros are located, you can read them directly from the source worksheet, without having to create an intermediate file with File Xtract. To make this easier, you can adopt a policy of always naming the macro area of your worksheets. For example, if you had used the name MACROS for the range J25..L36 in Figure 13.7 you could transfer the macros to another worksheet simply by issuing the File Combine Copy Named/Specified-Range command in the destination worksheet, entering MACROS as the range, and then specifying the source worksheet. Likewise, if the range P33..R48 in Figure 13.15 were called MACROS, you could read it into another worksheet using the same procedure.

Macro Libraries

One application of this Combine procedure is to collect macros from several worksheets into a single worksheet that contains nothing but macros. Such a file is called a *macro library* and can be copied onto a floppy disk and lent to colleagues. A common macro library worksheet shared among co-workers can help eliminate duplication of effort. However, to share macros successfully you must adhere to some basic standards of layout such as the three-column method advocated here.

In earlier versions of 1-2-3, a macro library was simply a worksheet used to collect macros. Users then copied the macros into their worksheets as needed. Using the Macro Library Manager add-in provided with 1-2-3 Release 2.3, you can create special macro library files whose macros can be used in any other worksheet at any time. The Macro Library Manager is attached to 1-2-3 just like the Wysiwyg add-in described in Chapter 10.

Normally, whenever you press Alt-F3 or Alt and a letter key to execute a macro, 1-2-3 looks for the name of the macro in the current worksheet. If the hotkey macro you have invoked is not there, you get a beep. A run macro that is not in the current worksheet will not appear in the Run list. When you invoke a macro with the Macro Library Manager add-in attached, 1-2-3 still looks in the current worksheet. However, if it does not find the macro there, it checks whether a macro library file is open. If so, the macro from the library is made available: Hotkey macros are immediately executed and macros from the library are listed when Run is pressed. Remember that 1-2-3 only looks to the macro library file if the current worksheet does not contain the macro you have asked to execute.

There are several advantages to placing macros into a macro library. First, you no longer have to copy all of your favorite macros from worksheet to worksheet. You simply place them in a library, making them accessible from any worksheet. This saves space in your worksheets. In addition, macros are likely to be safer when stored separately, in a library file, where accidental row or column deletion or insertion cannot occur.

Macro library files have the extension .MLB. They are created by a special move operation that takes entries from a regular worksheet and stores them in an .MLB file. A library file can contain up to 16,376 cells, equal to a range that is eight columns wide by 2,047 rows long. Although information in a macro library file is stored in a column and row format, you cannot retrieve a library file. To examine or edit the contents of a library file, you move the contents into a regular worksheet. You can then move the edited contents back into the library file. The commands for carrying out these operations are found on the menu presented when you invoke the Macro Library Manager. However, before you can do this, you must attach the Macro Library Manager add-in.

Setting Up the Macro Library Manager

The Macro Library Manager is in a file called MACROMGR.ADN on the Install disk that came in your 1-2-3 package. Before you can start working with the Macro Library Manager add-in, you must attach this file to 1-2-3. If you have a hard-disk system, you will have copied the contents of the Install disk to the 1-2-3 program directory on your hard disk during installation. If you have a dual-floppy system, you will have created a backup copy of the Install disk during installation and you should insert the backup Install disk in one of your computer's floppy-disk drives before you attempt to attach the Macro Library Manager.

To attach the Macro Library Manager, select Add-In from the main 1-2-3 menu and then choose Attach. 1-2-3 displays a list of files with the extension .ADN in the directory from which you started 1-2-3. If MACROMGR.ADN is not included in the list, you need to specify the drive and/or directory that contains this file (press Esc to clear the currently displayed file names, edit the drive and/or directory name, and then press Enter).

When you select MACROMGR.ADN as the add-in to attach you are prompted for the key you want to use to invoke Macro Library Manager. The options 7 through 10 assign Macro Library Manager to one of the function keys Alt-F7 through Alt-F10. Alternatively, you can choose not to assign the add-in to any key (the No-Key option). If you select No-Key, you will be able to invoke Macro Library Manager using the Invoke option on the Add-In menu. (Since Alt-F10 is initially set to display the Add-In menu, pressing this key gives you the same menu that appears when you select Add-In from the main menu. However, because you can always access the Add-In commands through the 1-2-3 menu, you can also assign Alt-F10 to any add-in.) After making your choice you are returned to the Add-In menu. Select Quit to return 1-2-3 to READY mode. Macro Library Manager is now attached, loaded in memory.

To use the add-in you must invoke it by pressing the key you assigned it to—for example APP1, Alt-F7. Alternatively, you can choose Add-In from the main 1-2-3 menu (or press Alt-F10 if you haven't already assigned this key to—a specific add-in), select Invoke, and choose MACROMGR from the list of currently attached add-ins. As soon as you invoke Macro Library Manager, the Macro Library Manager menu appears.

To set Macro Library Manager as an add-in that is automatically attached/invoked whenever you start 1-2-3, use Worksheet Global Default Other Add-In. For more information about automatic attaching and invoking of macros see Chapter 7.

The Macro Library Manager Menu

There are five commands plus a Quit option on the menu that appears when you invoke the Macro Library Manager. The commands are Load, Save, Edit, Remove, and Name-List. The Load command reads a macro library file into memory and makes the macros in it available to you. You can load up to ten library files at once.

The Save command moves cells from the current worksheet and pastes them into a library file, at the first available position. You are given an opportunity to name the library file and to assign a password to it if you wish. Note that all of the current worksheet cells that you save to the library file are removed from the current worksheet, as are their range names. The range names go with the cell contents into the library file. As soon as you save cells into a library file, that file is also loaded into memory and the macros in it are available for use.

The Edit command reads the contents of a library file into the current worksheet. This is how you can check and alter the code in a library file. The range names attached to macro code in the library are also read into the current worksheet. Since the library file may contain a range name that has also been used in the current worksheet, 1-2-3 gives you a choice between Ignore and Overwrite after you have issued the Edit command and chosen the file you want to edit. The Ignore option tells 1-2-3 not to bring in range names from the library file that conflict with existing names in the current worksheet. The Overwrite option tells 1-2-3 that it is okay to replace existing range name definitions with duplicate names from the library file.

The Remove command on the Macro Library Manager menu clears a library file from memory. This command does not affect the contents of the library file. The Name-List command simply lists the range names used in a particular library file to help you manage the file contents.

A Macro Library Example

Suppose that you have a collection of macros in a worksheet like the one in Figure 13.7. You want to place these macros in a library file. First you load the worksheet containing the macros. The process of saving macros into a library file actually removes the cells from the worksheet, so you should issue the File Save command if you have made any changes to the worksheet. This will ensure that you have a current version of the worksheet on disk in case something goes wrong during the transfer of macros to the library. After making sure that the Macro Library Manager is attached, invoke it with the keystroke you selected during the attach process. From the Macro Library Manager menu, choose Save. You get a standard 1-2-3 file naming list, like the one that appears when you use File Save. The list uses the file specification *.MLB to list any existing library files. Enter a suitable name for your library file and press Enter. If a library file of that name already exists, you will be asked whether or not you want to overwrite it.

After confirming the library file name, you are prompted for the library range, the cells that you want to move. This depends upon how much information you want the macro library to contain. You could store all of the names and comments into the library file in full three-column format—in the example in Figure 13.7 this could be J25 through L36. If you want to economize on space and memory, you can store just the code and the names, J25..K36. To minimize space and memory, you could select just K25..K36 as the library range.

When you confirm the library range, you are asked if you want to specify a password for the library file. Select No to leave the file unprotected or Yes to enter a password. The password can be up to 80 characters long. Passwords do not prevent libraries from being loaded, they simply prevent them from being edited by people who do not have the password. (They also prevent users from viewing the macro code in STEP mode.) When you save a library file with a password, you can only edit the library if you enter the exact password. (As with File Save passwords, you must match the combination of uppercase or lowercase letters in the password.)

After you select no password or enter a password, 1-2-3 completes the operation and moves the contents of the cells in the library range into a library file on disk with the name you chose. The same library file is also loaded into memory so that its macros are immediately available for use. You must now decide what to do with the worksheet from which you saved the macros. If you simply use the Worksheet Erase or File Retrieve command to erase the current worksheet, you will leave the version on disk that still has the macros in it. This is not a problem, but it does mean you are not getting the space-saving benefit of having the macros in a library file. To do this, you can clear out any remaining macro labeling and save the revised and "slenderized" worksheet.

Suppose that you want to add the macros from Figure 13.13 to the macro library (*after* correcting the error in the \S macro). You might think that you could retrieve the worksheet containing the additional macros and repeat the Save process described in the previous paragraphs. Unfortunately, this is not the case. The Save command always writes an entirely fresh library file; there is no incremental saving. What you must do is read the contents of the library file into a worksheet (using the Edit command from the Macro Library Manager menu), place the additional macros in the area to be saved, and then save the code back into the library file.

In this example, you would load the worksheet shown in 13.13, and then issue the Edit command with the cell pointer in A17. Choose the Overwrite option to give the macro library range names precedence over those in the current worksheet. Accept A17 as the range for the macro library and the contents of the library will be read in. You can now use the Save command to move all of the macros back to the library file. If you use the Edit option to bring the library into the current worksheet and then add further macros, you should check the range name of all the macros before saving them back to the library.

Managing Macro Libraries

You must attach Macro Library Manager before you attempt to save data into a library or load a library file into memory. If you detach the Macro Library Manager during a work session, the macro libraries you have saved or loaded disappear from memory but the files on disk are not affected. Each macro library is limited to 16,376 cells. The Macro Library Manager add-in places a library in memory when you select either the Load or the Save command from the Macro Library Manager menu. As mentioned, you can have up to ten libraries in memory simultaneously. When you specify the range you want to save into a library, the Macro Library Manager allocates a cell in conventional memory for each cell in the range, even if it is empty. To save memory, try to make your macro code as compact as possible and specify Save ranges with as few empty cells as possible. Saving a large amount of code into a library may reduce the memory available for creating a worksheet. As a rule, only load the libraries you need and remove them when you no longer need them.

A macro library is stored in an area of memory separate from the worksheet. There are different rules for accessing the information a library contains. A library has no cell coordinates, so macros stored in a library cannot use cell coordinates to access code or data within the library.

For example, the following macro would work if it were stored in a worksheet with the first line of code in cell B20:

```
\R      {EDIT}{HOME}@ROUND(
        {END},{?}~){DOWN}
        {IF @CELLPOINTER("type")="v"}{BRANCH B20}
        {QUIT}
```

The cell coordinate can be used in the {BRANCH} command to tell 1-2-3 where to branch to. However, if this macro were saved into a library file, it would look to B20 of the current worksheet for the branch code, not to the beginning of the macro. This is why it is vital to use range names instead of cell coordinates within macros.

The Worksheet Erase and File Retrieve commands do not erase macro libraries from memory, so you can erase all data from a worksheet or retrieve a new worksheet without affecting the libraries. Basically, you use the same techniques to run a macro stored in a library that you do with a macro in a worksheet. Remember that you must specify the name of the macro, not the name of the library. If you press Run (Alt-F3) and then press Name (F3) to display a full-screen menu of range names, 1-2-3 first lists all the range names in the worksheet in alphabetical order, as show in Figure 13.16. After the range names from the current worksheet, 1-2-3 lists the range names in each macro library that is currently loaded, also in alphabetical order. If you highlight a library range name, it is displayed at the top of the list followed by the name of its library. (If you highlight a range name that is in the current worksheet, its range coordinates are displayed at the top of the menu.)

There are a few more rules to keep in mind when creating and using libraries. You cannot have two or more libraries in memory with the same name. When you try to save a library using an existing library name, a prompt asks whether you want to overwrite the library. When you edit a library, you copy its contents, including range names, into the worksheet. To avoid conflicts with existing range names, try to use unique names for each range you save into the library. The Macro Library Manager will not let you save a range into a library if the range includes a link formula, one that references another file. When you try to save such a range, Macro Library Manager displays an error message. As you develop more complex macros, the Macro Library Manager becomes even more important, as discussed in the next chapter.

Figure 13.16

Full-screen range name list including library names

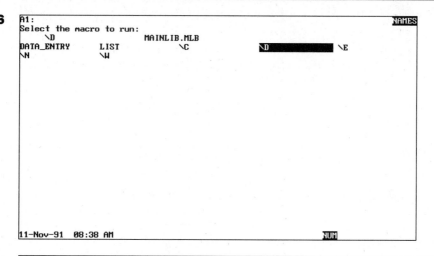

Summary

In this chapter, you learned how to write, record, and debug macros. You also learned how to organize macros professionally and how to store them in a macro library so that you can use them with any spreadsheet. You have begun to explore the 1-2-3 macro command language. In the next chapter, you will learn more about the macro commands and how you can use them to create sophisticated macros. You will see how macro menus are created and how you can combine the special functions with macros to develop advanced spreadsheets.

Advanced Macros
and Functions

THIS CHAPTER EXPLORES THE MORE ADVANCED ASPECTS OF CREATING 1-2-3 macros. You will read about the powerful macro command language that allows you to create menu-driven applications with 1-2-3. You will also learn to create macros that prompt for user input. In addition, this chapter describes a number of built-in functions that are primarily used in macros and advanced spreadsheets.

Working with Macro Commands

Simple macros merely replicate a fixed set of instructions that you might otherwise enter from the keyboard. Such macros can be extraordinarily useful and can save a great deal of typing time. At some point, however, you will want to increase the usefulness of your macros by enabling them to respond to user input—you can do this with special 1-2-3 commands. These commands can also access 1-2-3 features and functions not available from the keyboard, allowing you to create macro-driven spreadsheets that are easy for less experienced users to operate. This section shows how macro commands are applied and presents techniques that will help you design macros for others to use. It includes many examples of macro commands in action.

The Role of Macro Commands

Macro commands enable you to create macros that evaluate conditions and choose between different courses of action based on parameters you specify. For this reason, the macro commands are a lot like programming statements. This does *not*, however, mean that macro commands are just for programmers. Ordinary users are quite capable of taking advantage of macro commands, either to simplify their own work or to prepare 1-2-3 applications for others to use.

This chapter emphasizes creating macros that can be used by other, less-experienced operators. You can employ such macros to reduce lengthy and sometimes complex tasks to a few simple commands, thus making the power of 1-2-3 available to a wider range of people.

The {BRANCH} Command

In the last chapter, you learned that the macro command {BRANCH} can be very helpful when you need a macro to repeat a series of operations. As an example, you edited a column of values to include the @ROUND function. The following macro edits the current cell, moves down one cell and repeats the action, moves down again, and so on.

```
\R        {EDIT}{HOME}@ROUND({END},2){DOWN}
          {BRANCH \R}
```

The main action performed by this macro is the editing operation in the first line. The {BRANCH} statement on the second line merely tells 1-2-3 to go to the cell called \R and carry on reading the instructions from there.

Like the built-in functions, many macro commands require arguments, which you include within curly braces, separated from the name of the command by a space. When multiple arguments are required, you connect them with commas, just as in functions. The {BRANCH} command has the syntax

```
{BRANCH location}
```

where *location* is a cell address or range name. In the previous example, the argument is the range name \R. When using macro commands that require a location argument, you should generally supply a range name rather than a cell address, particularly if you are planning on running the macro from a macro library.

The {BRANCH} command is not only used for looping macros. Later in this chapter you will use {BRANCH} in several situations where macro code is split into segments that need to be linked together.

The {IF} Command and the @CELL Function

Once you execute the \R macro, it will loop continuously until you stop it with Ctrl-Break. This method of halting macro execution is crude, however, and is unsuitable for macros designed for inexperienced operators. A better approach is to check the contents of the current cell during each loop in order to determine whether to continue. To do this, you can use the @CELL and @CELLPOINTER functions in combination with the {IF} command to make the macro choose between two courses of action depending upon the contents of a particular cell. The syntax of the @CELL function is

```
@CELL(code,location)
```

where *code* is one of the codes listed in Table 14.1, and *location* is a cell address. If the *location* argument is a range name, the location is taken to be the upper-left cell of the range. For example, the formula @CELL("type",A1) returns b if A1 is blank. The same statement returns v if A1 contains a value, and l if it contains a label.

The @CELLPOINTER function returns similar information about the cell currently occupied by the cell pointer. Its syntax is

```
@CELLPOINTER(code)
```

Table 14.1   Codes Used with @CELL

Code	Response
address	The absolute address of a cell
row	The row number of the cell (from 1 to 8192)
col	The column number of the cell (from 1 to 256) corresponding to columns A through IV
contents	The actual contents of the cell
type	The type of data in the cell:
	b if the cell is blank
	v if the cell contains a number or any formula
	l if the cell contains a label
prefix	The label-prefix character of the cell:
	' if the label is left-aligned
	^ if the label is centered
	" if the label is right-aligned
	l if the label contains a print setup string or format line for parsing
	\ if the label is repeating
protect	The protected status of the cell:
	0 if the cell is not protected
	1 if the cell is protected
width	The width of the column containing the cell (between 1 and 240)
format	The current display format of the cell:
	Fn is Fixed (n=0 through 15)
	En is Exponential (n=0 through 15)
	Cn is Currency (n=0 through 15)
	+ is +/− (bar graph format)
	G is General

Table 14.1   **(continued)**

Code	Response
	P*n* is percent (*n*=0 through 15)
	D1-D5 represent Date
	1=DD-MM-YY
	2=DD-MMM
	3=MMMY
	4=MM/DD/YY
	5=MM/DD
	D6-D9 represent Time
	6=HH:MM:SS AM/PM
	7=HH:MM AM/PM
	8=HH:MM:SS (24 hour)
	9=HH:MM (24 hour)

---

where *code* is one of the codes listed in Table 14.1. Note that both the @CELL and @CELLPOINTER functions require that the *code* argument is entered in quotes. The information returned by the @CELL and @CELL-POINTER functions covers address, row, column, contents, type, prefix, protection status, width, and format.

Bear in mind that the result returned by @CELL may be a label. In this case, you may need to refer to the result as a string in quotes, as the " b" in this formula, which returns VACANT if A1 is blank:

```
@IF(@CELL("type",A1)="b","VACANT","OCCUPIED")
```

The {IF} macro command works like the @IF function in that it chooses between two possibilities. For example, you may want a macro to repeat if a certain condition exists, but quit if it does not. The syntax of the {IF} command is as follows

```
{IF condition}action1
action2
```

The *condition* argument is a conditional formula, such as A1>100, @CELL("type",A1)="b", or @CELLPOINTER("type")="v".

As with other macro commands, the {IF} command needs careful construction if it is to be effective. You need to consider the condition that {IF} evaluates relative to the situations in which the macro will be used. For example, you could control the looping \R macro like this:

```
\R        {EDIT}{HOME}@ROUND(
          {END},2){DOWN}
          {IF @CELLPOINTER("type")="b"}{QUIT}
          {BRANCH \R}
```

In this case, *action1* terminates the macro while *action2* is the branch that causes the macro to repeat. This means that the macro will quit if the current cell is blank. This would allow the macro to proceed down the column of values until there were no more left to be rounded. However, consider what would happen if the column ended in these three cells:

```
C30:          B30*1.7
C31:          =============
C32:      @SUM(C3..C31)
```

In this case, the \R macro would cause an error when it got to C31. The macro would try to enter @ROUND(\=,2) in C31, which produces an error. But because the cell is not blank, the macro cannot quit. In fact, it keeps editing C31, compounding the problem. You could change the third line of the macro to

```
{IF @CELLPOINTER("type")="l"}{QUIT}
```

to stop the macro when it hits a label entry. However, this does not stop the macro if the column has no label at the bottom. This is probably the best solution:

```
   \R     {EDIT}{HOME}@ROUND(
{END},2){DOWN}
{IF @CELLPOINTER("type")="v"}{BRANCH \R}
{QUIT}
```

This macro repeats whenever the current cell is a value entry. If the current cell is not a value entry, the macro stops. This version is safe to use if the column ends in either a blank cell or a label. You can see that the macro commands offer both power and versatility in macro design, but require you to exercise some care in their application.

Controlling Loops, Input, and Errors

The preceding \R macro only works for columns of numbers, and only rounds to two decimal places. To improve the macro and give it more flexibility, you can allow the number of decimal places to be altered. The last chapter demonstrated how to use the {?} command to pause a macro for user input. However, {?} does not provide the user with a prompt and cannot store the response. What the improved \R macro needs is a command that asks for input and places it in a designated cell. This section explores macro commands that can be used to solicit user input, methods for dealing with errors made by the user during macro execution, and the {FOR} command, which provides precise control of macro repetition.

Obtaining User Input

The {GETLABEL} command prompts the user for an entry and stores the result as a label. Its syntax is

`{GETLABEL prompt_message,location}`

The *prompt_message* argument is a word or several words. The *location* is the cell into which the label is placed when the user presses Enter. For example, the macro command

`{GETLABEL Type first name and press Enter ,FIRST}`

will produce the following prompt on the second line of the screen when the macro runs:

`Type first name and press Enter _`

When the user presses Enter, what she or he has typed is placed in the cell called FIRST. Note that the space between the message text " Enter" and the comma used as the argument separator creates the space between the text and the cursor when the command is executed. The *prompt_message* must be enclosed in double quotation marks if it uses one of these characters:

`; : .`

For example, if you want to use a colon at the end of the message text, the command statement would look like this:

`{GETLABEL "Type first name and press Enter: ",FIRST}`

Note that the space is within the quotes and there is no space between the quotes, the argument separator, and the location argument.

In the case of the \R macro, you might want to use the following {GET-LABEL} statement to elicit user input:

```
{GETLABEL "Enter number of decimal places: ",NUM}
```

The command is shown at work in Figure 14.1. Note that the response will be placed in NUM (cell B18) *as a label*. This is appropriate in this particular example because the number forms part of the macro code, and all macro code consists of text or formulas that evaluate to text.

Figure 14.1

Using {GETLABEL}

```
E4: (,2) [W9] (B4*0.125)*($E$1-C4)/365                                    EDIT
Enter number of decimal places:

           A             B          C          D          E       F
1  Accounts Receivable List                 Today is:  11/01/91
2
3     Company        Owing        Due       Contacted Interest
4  VIA Assoc.       1,115.12    10/20/91    10/29/91     4.58
5  U.S. Hay, Inc.     450.32    09/29/91    10/17/91     5.09
6  Westtung Assoc.    271.46    10/16/91    10/27/91     1.49
7  Unolink, Ltd.      281.35    10/09/91    10/25/91     2.22
8  Advwest Assoc.     244.60    09/20/91    10/27/91     3.52
9  TEAM, SA.           93.43    09/16/91    10/28/91     1.47
10 VERITas, Inc.      319.06    09/22/91    10/29/91     4.37
11 Diskky, Ltd.       280.63    09/23/91    10/17/91     3.75
12
13    Macros Area ============================================================
14 \R              {GETLABEL "Enter number of decimal places: ",NUM}
15 MAIN            {EDIT}{HOME}@ROUND(
16                 {END},
17 NUM
18                 ){DOWN}
19                 {IF @CELLPOINTER("type")="v"}{BRANCH MAIN}
20                 {QUIT}
01-Nov-91  06:10 PM                             CMD              NUM
```

When the user types a number and presses Enter, the number is placed in NUM and the macro reads the instructions below the {GETLABEL} statement. Note that the macro was rearranged to fit the contents of the NUM cell into the code. Also the *location* argument in the {BRANCH} statement has been altered to MAIN so that the {GETLABEL} statement is skipped during the looping process. The use of range name labels in the column to the left of the code makes it easy to label the required cells in one pass of the Range Labels Right command.

Formulas in Macro Code

Another technique for increasing a macro's flexibility is to create macro code out of string formulas. The formulas can be dependent upon entries in the spreadsheet and thus return different code for different conditions. Suppose that you want to make the \R macro work with either columns or rows of values. The macro might begin with the following statement:

```
{GETLABEL "Round a column or row (Enter C or R): ",MODE}
```

The result of this code is the letter C or R in the cell called MODE (cell B23). You can then use the entry in MODE as the basis for code in the macro that either repeats the rounding process down a column or right along a row. The completed macro can be seen in Figure 14.2.

Figure 14.2

Including user input in a formula

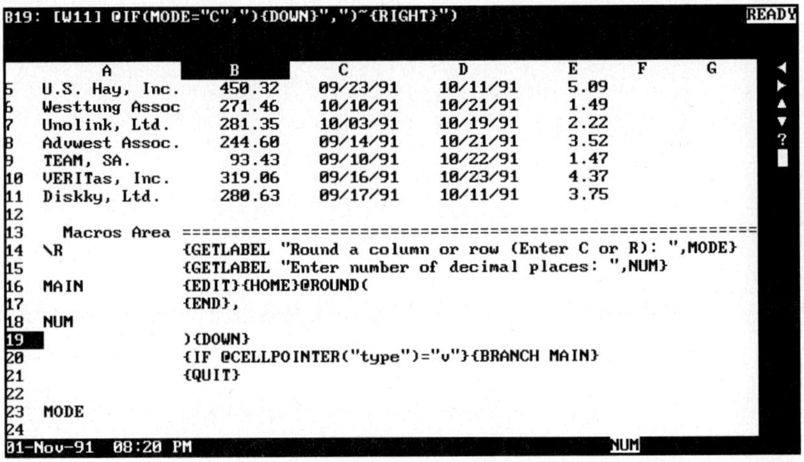

```
B19: [W11] @IF(MODE="C",")DOWN}",")~{RIGHT}")                          READY

              A              B           C           D           E       F       G
5     U.S. Hay, Inc.      450.32     09/23/91    10/11/91    5.09
6     Westtung Assoc      271.46     10/10/91    10/21/91    1.49
7     Unolink, Ltd.       281.35     10/03/91    10/19/91    2.22
8     Advwest Assoc.      244.60     09/14/91    10/21/91    3.52
9     TEAM, SA.            93.43     09/10/91    10/22/91    1.47
10    VERITas, Inc.       319.06     09/16/91    10/23/91    4.37
11    Diskky, Ltd.        280.63     09/17/91    10/11/91    3.75
12
13      Macros Area  ==============================================================
14    \R              {GETLABEL "Round a column or row (Enter C or R): ",MODE}
15                    {GETLABEL "Enter number of decimal places: ",NUM}
16    MAIN            {EDIT}{HOME}@ROUND(
17                    {END},
18    NUM
19                    ){DOWN}
20                    {IF @CELLPOINTER("type")="v"}{BRANCH MAIN}
21                    {QUIT}
22
23    MODE
24
01-Nov-91  08:20 PM                                                     NUM
```

As you can see, the entry in cell B19 is an @IF formula, the result of which is either){DOWN} or)~{RIGHT}. Note the tilde in the second response, required because Right Arrow does not enter edited cell contents.

Error Trapping

Macros that you design for your own use can be a little rough around the edges; if something goes wrong, you will be there to fix it. When designing macros for others, in contrast, you have to consider everything that might go wrong. For example, what if the user executes \R and enters something besides C or R? As the macro stands in Figure 14.2, a response other than C puts the macro into row mode. Making allowances for user error, sometimes referred to as *error-trapping,* is an important part of macro design.

In the case of trapping an erroneous response to the first {GETLABEL} in the example, you could use the code shown in Figure 14.3. This version of the \R macro also prevents the user from rounding with a decimal number greater than 4.

Figure 14.3
Macro with error trapping

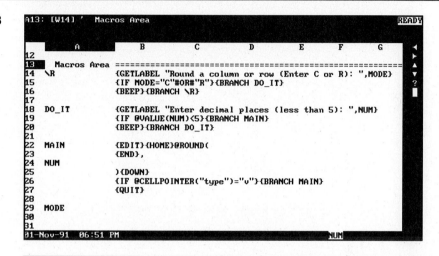

After the user replies to the first {GETLABEL} statement, the response is evaluated by the {IF} statement in cell B15. If the response is a C or an R, the macro resumes at DO_IT. Otherwise, your computer beeps and redisplays the {GETLABEL} prompt by repeating the first line of the macro. The {BEEP} command, described under "Input and Feedback," is useful for alerting the user to problems. The same procedure is used in the section of the macro now called DO_IT. If the user enters an unacceptable response to the request for the number of decimal places, the question is repeated after a beep.

The preceding code traps errors in user input. There are two other types of errors in 1-2-3 macros. There are so-called *fatal errors* caused by such basic problems as a disk drive not being ready when a File Save is being attempted. These errors return you to READY mode. You can trap these serious errors using the {ONERROR} command, which has the following syntax:

```
{ONERROR branch,message}
```

Both arguments are locations, preferably named ranges. The *branch* location is the macro code that you want 1-2-3 to branch to when a serious error occurs. The *message* location is an optional argument, a place into which

1-2-3 will write the error message. This allows you to use the message in your macro code.

The other type of error is a *syntax error:* an error in the macro code itself. Syntax errors produce an error box, usually with a message about the nature of the error. For example, if you use {BEER} instead of {BEEP}, you get the message "unrecognized key/range name" together with the address of the cell where the error occurred. Press Esc to clear the message and you will be in READY mode.

There is one other command that you may want to use when controlling user actions during macros. Normally, pressing Ctrl-Break during a macro will stop the macro. You can prevent this by using the {BREAKOFF} command early in the macro. You can restore the normal use of Ctrl-Break with the {BREAKON} command. This command is useful when you want to confine the user to macro menu choices, as described in the next section.

Extensive Input

When designing macros to make life easier for novices, you may want to prompt the user for pieces of data that the worksheet requires. An example of this is seen in Figure 14.4, a worksheet designed to calculate financing for the purchase of a swimming pool. Four pieces of information vary from one purchase to another: the price, the down payment, the term, and the interest rate. A macro has been designed to request each piece of information in turn, beginning with the price.

Figure 14.4

The pool finance worksheet

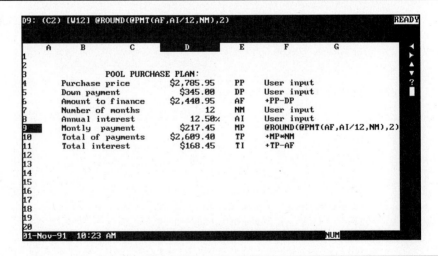

Note that the two-letter codes in column E simply document and name the elements of the calculations. The formulas in column F explain how the calculation is performed. You can hide these documentation entries from view by formatting E4..F11 with the Range Format Hidden command. In Figure 14.5, you can see some of the macro code. The first line of the macro places the price of the pool into the cell named PP (cell D9), using the {GETNUMBER} command. The {GETNUMBER} command works exactly like the {GETLABEL} command except that the response must be a numeric value—if the user enters a label, the result is an error. (A technique for trapping such errors is discussed later in this chapter under "The @IS Functions.")

Figure 14.5

Macro code for pool finance worksheet

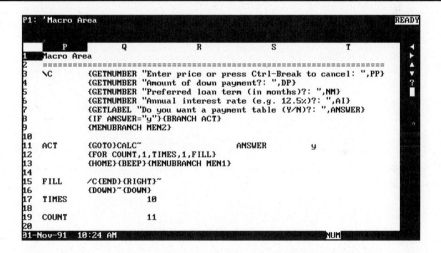

When a user types a number and presses the Enter key, the number is placed into the designated cell. The responses to the price, down payment, and term questions are placed in the appropriate cells of the loan calculation. The fifth line of the macro is a {GETLABEL} command that asks the user if she or he wants to generate a payment table. The user's response is placed in a cell named ANSWER. The next line of the macro, seen on row 8 of the worksheet, evaluates the contents of the cell ANSWER, using the {IF} command. If the cell named ANSWER contains the label y, the macro branches to a macro cell called ACT. The {ACT} macro creates the payment table. If the condition is false, meaning that ANSWER contains something other than y, the macro continues with the next line, a {MENUBRANCH} command described later in the chapter under "Macro Menus."

Using the {FOR} Command

The macro called ACT, seen in Figure 14.5, creates a payment table in the worksheet. The first three lines of the table are stored in the worksheet, as shown in Figure 14.6. The ACT macro simply expands the table in accordance with the number of payments that the finance plan requires.

Figure 14.6

The first part of the payment table

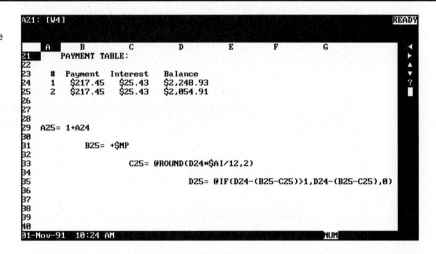

```
A21: [W4]                                                       READY
      A      B         C          D        E      F      G       ◄
21        PAYMENT TABLE:                                          ►
22                                                                ▲
23     #   Payment  Interest  Balance                             ▼
24     1   $217.45   $25.43   $2,248.93                           ?
25     2   $217.45   $25.43   $2,054.91                           ■
26
27
28
29   A25= 1+A24
30
31          B25= +$MP
32
33               C25= @ROUND(D24*$AI/12,2)
34
35                    D25= @IF(D24-(B25-C25)>1,D24-(B25-C25),0)
36
37
38
39
40
01-Nov-91  10:24 AM                                        NUM
```

The ACT macro uses the {FOR} command to control repetition of a macro called FILL. You can see from Figure 14.5 that FILL copies a line of the payment table once. The payment table is completed by repeating the copy operation so that there is one line for each payment. The {FOR} command controls repetition of a task by means of five arguments:

{FOR *counter,start,stop,step,subroutine*}

- *Counter* is the location of a cell that records the number of times the task has been repeated—in this case a cell named COUNT.

- *Start* is the starting number to be placed in the counter location—in this case 1.

- *Stop* represents the total number of times the task is to be repeated—in this case the cell called TIMES. Located lower down in column Q, this cell contains a formula that subtracts two from the number of periods in the term of the loan. This formula allows for the two lines already entered in the worksheet, as shown in Figure 14.6.

- *Step* stands for the amount to increment the counter after each iteration—in this case, 1.

- *Subroutine* is the task to be repeated—in this case, FILL. (A subroutine is a macro called from another macro.)

The results of the completed {FOR} operation in the case of a loan with 12 monthly payments can be seen in Figure 14.7. Note that the macro does not display the table at this point, but goes on to a menu of options, using the {MENUBRANCH} command described in a moment in the section "Macro Menus."

Figure 14.7

The results of the {FOR} operation

```
A21: [W4]                                                              READY

        A    B          C          D         E      F      G         ◄
       21        PAYMENT TABLE:                                        ►
       22                                                              ▲
       23    #    Payment    Interest   Balance                        ▼
       24    1    $217.45    $25.43     $2,248.93                      ?
       25    2    $217.45    $23.43     $2,054.91                      ■
       26    3    $217.45    $21.41     $1,858.87
       27    4    $217.45    $19.36     $1,660.78
       28    5    $217.45    $17.30     $1,460.63
       29    6    $217.45    $15.21     $1,258.39
       30    7    $217.45    $13.11     $1,054.05
       31    8    $217.45    $10.98       $847.58
       32    9    $217.45     $8.83       $638.96
       33   10    $217.45     $6.66       $428.17
       34   11    $217.45     $4.46       $215.18
       35   12    $217.45     $2.24         $0.00
       36
       37
       38
       39
       40
       01-Nov-91  10:24 AM                                     NUM
```

Input and Feedback

When you are designing applications to be used by others, you must consider many factors that do not arise when you are creating macros for your own use. For example, the {IF} command is not case sensitive. You can demand an exact response by using @EXACT, as in:

```
{If @EXACT(ANSWER,"Y")}{Branch PRE}
```

Here the user would have to type Y to proceed; entering y would not be acceptable. You might require correct capitalization from a user when proper names are being entered, or when some form of code is being used. An alternative to requiring correct capitalization from the user is to employ @UPPER or @PROPER to apply capitals to the input after it has been placed in the worksheet.

Figure 14.5 showed that the {BEEP} command is used in the ACT macro. This causes your computer to beep when the payment table is completed. Tasks that keep the user waiting can benefit from a {BEEP} to announce their completion. Later in this chapter, under "An Extended Example," you will find more examples of how to handle user input and provide feedback to the user.

Macro Menus

The macro code shown in Figure 14.5 features two instances of the {MENU-BRANCH} command. When the ACT macro has completed the {FOR} routine, the macro branches to a menu called MEN1. If the user does not ask for a payment table, she or he is presented with MEN2. One of the most popular uses of the macro commands is to create customized menus within a spreadsheet to simplify its operation. You can place macro menus in macro libraries to make them available in any worksheet or leave them in the current worksheet so that they are worksheet specific. This section describes the structure and application of macro menus. It also discusses the use of *subroutines,* sections of code that are called from within a macro. Subroutines are useful when designing menu macros since they make economical use of macro code and allow you to control macro flow entirely through the menu macros.

Writing Macro Menus

At the top of Figure 14.8 is the MEN1 menu that is displayed by the last line of the ACT macro code. This menu offers the user a choice between printing the loan table, changing the figures in the loan calculation, or saving the worksheet.

Macro-generated menus follow the same format as regular 1-2-3 menus: A row of options is followed by a row containing a description of the currently highlighted option. You can use both the highlight-and-enter and the first letter methods of selection to choose items. To let you know that you are still in the middle of a macro rather than a Lotus system menu, 1-2-3 automatically displays a CMD message at the bottom of the screen.

When the user selects an item from the menu in Figure 14.8, a macro is activated to carry out the menu item. You can easily create such a menu to operate macros in your worksheets. However, remember that this menu is part of this worksheet, not a part of the overall 1-2-3 menu system. You can place menus in a macro library if you want to be able to access them from any spreadsheet.

Figure 14.9 contains the instructions that make up the macro menu in Figure 14.8. Each menu item is in a separate but contiguous column, listing the parts of the menu on consecutive rows. At least three rows are required for each menu item. The first row is the name of the item as it is to appear on the menu—in this case Print, Change, Save, and Quit. Each menu item should begin with a different first letter if you want to be able to use the first letter method of selection.

Figure 14.8

A macro menu

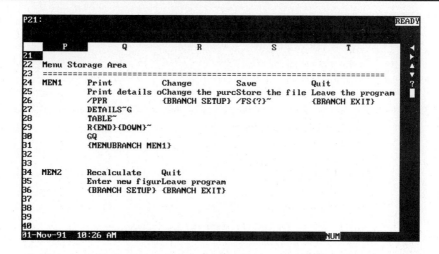

```
A1: [W4]                                                              MENU
Print  Change  Save  Quit
Print details of the purchase together with a loan table
       A       B         C          D         E      F          G
1
2
3                    POOL PURCHASE PLAN:
4         Purchase price        $2,785.95   PP    User input
5         Down payment            $345.00   DP    User input
6         Amount to finance     $2,440.95   AF    +PP-DP
7         Number of months            12    NM    User input
8         Annual interest          12.50%   AI    User input
9         Montly  payment         $217.45   MP    @ROUND(@PMT(AF,AI/12,NM),2)
10        Total of payments     $2,609.40   TP    +MP*NM
11        Total interest          $168.45   TI    +TP-AF
12
13
14
15
16
17
18
19
20
01-Nov-91  10:26 AM                              CMD              NUM
```

Figure 14.9

Menu macro code

```
P21:                                                                 READY
       P              Q            R             S            T      ◄
21                                                                   ►
22   Menu Storage Area                                               ▲
23   ================================================================ ▼
24   MEN1    Print          Change        Save         Quit          ?
25           Print details oChange the purcStore the file Leave the program ■
26           /PPR           {BRANCH SETUP} /FS{?}~       {BRANCH EXIT}
27           DETAILS~G
28           TABLE~
29           R{END}{DOWN}~
30           GQ
31           {MENUBRANCH MEN1}
32
33
34   MEN2    Recalculate    Quit
35           Enter new figurLeave program
36           {BRANCH SETUP} {BRANCH EXIT}
37
38
39
40
01-Nov-91  10:26 AM                                              NUM
```

The second line of the menu item is the explanation of the item that appears when the item is highlighted. For example, the second line of the Print item is

```
Print details of the purchase together with a loan table
```

Although menu item names can be up to 55 characters long, the explanation line can contain up to 72 characters. (Normally you would make the menu name brief and the explanation longer.)

Below the item names and explanation text are the macro commands that are executed when the item is chosen. This can be extensive macro code, as in the Print item in Figure 14.9, or a simple {BRANCH} statement that leads to further code stored elsewhere in the worksheet. Both the Change and Quit items in the example use the latter approach. The SETUP and EXIT code to which these items branch will be discussed in a moment.

Figure 14.9 shows that the placement of macros in adjacent columns as required by the menu macro command syntax can make it difficult to see all of the code on a given line, particularly if you do not want to widen the columns because they contain other data. However, this is not a problem for the execution of the macro since 1-2-3 does not care if the entire command is visible in the macro menu storage area.

The {MENUBRANCH} command that activates the menu has the syntax

```
{MENUBRANCH location}
```

where *location* is the upper-left cell of the menu. Typically, this is given a range name. In the example, cell Q24 is called MEN1.

Macro Menu Management

The macro menu called MEN1 in Figure 14.9 gives the user a chance to print details of the purchase plan, change those details, save the worksheet, or quit the program. The second menu, called MEN2, also lets the user alter figures and leave the program. This menu is called up when the user chooses not to create a loan table. Since the actions performed by this menu item are essentially the same as actions performed by the MEN1 menu, the code has been shared. There are two routines involved:

■ SETUP clears any existing loan table and the entries in several key cells.

■ EXIT takes the user out of 1-2-3 after confirming that this is what the user wants.

These routines are called from the two menus by {BRANCH} statements and are shown in Figure 14.10.

The EXIT subroutine uses the {BEEP}, {GETLABEL}, and {IF} commands to make sure that the user wants to exit. The user's response to the {GETLABEL} command is stored in a cell called REPLY, the contents of which are evaluated by the {IF} statement. The SETUP routine erases the cells ANSWER and COUNT using the {BLANK} command, which has the syntax

```
{BLANK location}
```

where *location* is the name or coordinate of a cell or range of cells that you want to erase. The {BLANK} command is an alternative to /RE (Range Erase).

Figure 14.10
Additional subroutines

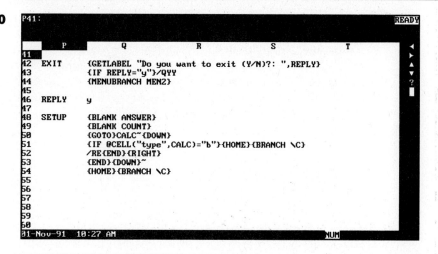

```
P41:                                                          READY

        P           Q              R            S          T
41
42  EXIT      {GETLABEL "Do you want to exit (Y/N)?: ",REPLY}
43            {IF REPLY="y"}/QYY
44            {MENUBRANCH MEN2}
45
46  REPLY     y
47
48  SETUP     {BLANK ANSWER}
49            {BLANK COUNT}
50            {GOTO}CALC~{DOWN}
51            {IF @CELL("type",CALC)="b"}{HOME}{BRANCH \C}
52            /RE{END}{RIGHT}
53            {END}{DOWN}~
54            {HOME}{BRANCH \C}
55
56
57
58
59
60
01-Nov-91  10:27 AM                              NUM
```

The cell called CALC is in fact A25, the cell right above the rows of the payment table entered by the ACT macro (see Figure 14.7). After checking that there is something in the cell below CALC, the SETUP routine erases the macro-generated part of the payment table with Range Erase, using the End and arrow keys to point out the range. This is a slightly risky procedure to use in a macro, so it must be carefully tested. However, it does have the advantage of erasing payment table entries below payment 2, no matter how large the table is.

After erasing the payment table, SETUP moves the cell pointer to the home cell to adjust the screen display, and then begins the \C macro again, prompting for new data. The \C macro also begins again if the SETUP routine detects that there is no table (@CELLPOINTER finds the cell below CALC to be blank).

Menus and Subroutines

Macro menu items can either list macro code directly within the menu area, or use the {BRANCH} command to direct macro flow from the menu item to a separate section of code. Macro code can be split into sections, called subroutines, that can then be used by more than one macro. Subroutines are an effective way to execute macro menu items. A macro that uses a subroutine is said to *call* the subroutine. In its simplest form, a subroutine is a macro name in curly braces, as in {PRINT}, entered on a line by itself. This calls a section of macro code named PRINT. When 1-2-3 encounters this statement in a macro, it looks for the macro called PRINT and executes it.

Unlike a branch, after which flow continues in the new direction, a subroutine that has been completed returns macro control automatically to the place from which it was called. The subroutine macro command is normally referred to as {subroutine} in lowercase to indicate that the argument is a variable.

In the following macro menu example, the selection of List runs the SORT_DATA macro and then the PRINT_DATA macro. The SORT_DATA macro does not contain any statements directing macro flow. After the {SORT_DATA} call in the macro, 1-2-3 automatically returns to the next line, which is a further subroutine: {PRINT_DATA}.

```
Enter  List
Enter Data      Sort and print list
{BRANCH}ENTER        {SORT DATA}
                     {PRINT DATA}
```

One main appeal of the {subroutine} command is that it enables you to assemble macros from reusable parts. Thus, the macro SORT_DATA might be a sorting operation that is used in several other macros. Instead of typing the same code each time sorting is required, you can simply reference the SORT_DATA macro as a subroutine. You might also create a simple subroutine to store the following standard steps used when printing:

```
{CALC}  Recalculate spreadsheet
/PPA    Align printer
CA      Clear all printer settings
```

Placing this code in a stand-alone macro called PRE_PRINT would permit you to execute these commands from any print macro in the spreadsheet with the simple statement {PRE_PRINT}.

Menucall and Menu Control

When the user selects any one of the items in a macro menu, control of the macro passes to the code beneath the menu item name and explanation. When the code used by the menu item is complete, macro control does not automatically return to the macro menu. Suppose that you have the following menu item called Print:

```
Print
Prints the range called list
/PPRlist~AG
```

When the Go command has been issued, the macro ends. If you want another menu to appear, you can refer the macro back to the menu with a {MENUBRANCH} command. For example, the EXIT routine shown in Figure 14.10 returns users to MEN2 if they decide not to exit the program.

An alternative approach is to use the {MENUCALL} command, which operates a menu as though it were a subroutine. When the selected menu item is completed, control automatically passes back to the macro that called the menu. The exception would be a menu option that used the {QUIT} command, which ends both the current subroutine and the macro that called it. When using {MENUCALL}, the {QUIT} option is an important way of allowing the user to leave the menu system. Conversely, if you want to confine the user to the menu system, the {QUIT} option can be left out. Figure 14.11 diagrams the difference between macro flow under {MENU-BRANCH} and {MENUCALL}.

Figure 14.11
Diagram of
{MENUCALL} and
{MENUBRANCH}

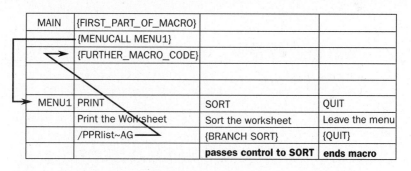

MAIN	{FIRST_PART_OF_MACRO}		
	{MENUCALL MENU1}		
	{FURTHER_MACRO_CODE}		
MENU1	PRINT	SORT	QUIT
	Print the Worksheet	Sort the worksheet	Leave the menu
	/PPRlist~AG	{BRANCH SORT}	{QUIT}
		passes control to SORT	**ends macro**

MAIN	{FIRST_PART_OF_MACRO}		
	{MENUBRANCH MEN1}		
	{FURTHER_MACRO_CODE}		
MENU1	PRINT	SORT	QUIT
	Print the Worksheet	Sort the worksheet	Leave the menu
	/PPRlist~AG	{BRANCH SORT}	{QUIT}
		passes control to SORT	**ends macro**
	ends macro		

Menu Escapes

When using macro menus, keep in mind that the user might well press Esc. This key is used in regular 1-2-3 menus to clear the menu or return to the previous level. If you do not want the user to be able to leave your macro menu by pressing Esc, you can include a {BRANCH} command that displays the menu below the {MENUCALL} or {MENUBRANCH} command. The following macro, called \M, will display MEN1. If the user presses Esc when the menu is displayed, the menu is simply redisplayed.

```
\M        {MENUBRANCH MEN1}
          {BRANCH \M}
```

You can turn off the other key that gets you out of a menu, Ctrl-Break, for the duration of a macro with the {BREAKOFF} command mentioned earlier. Be careful when using this command, however, since you do want the user to be able to stop such events as a print job gone awry.

Advanced Functions

There are several advanced functions that can be very useful in more complex macros. Sometimes called the miscellaneous functions, these allow you to perform such operations as data-entry checks and macro control.

The @@ Function

You have seen that the @CELL and @CELLPOINTER functions respond with information about cells. Another function that tells you about cells is @@, which returns the contents of a cell that is referenced as a label in another cell. Thus @@(A1) returns the answer 10 if A1 contains a reference to a cell that contains the number 10. The argument for the function can either be a cell reference (such as A2) or the name of a range, the upper-left cell of which contains 10. The @@ function can be useful when you need to reference values scattered throughout a worksheet. For example, suppose you have annual revenue calculations for three areas of revenue: sales, service, and other. Each total is in a different part of the worksheet, in a cell named for the type of revenue. Thus the sales total is in a cell called SALES and the service total is in a cell called SERVICE. You could create a lookup feature in which the user enters the name of the revenue category in one cell, while an @@ function returns the value from that category in another. You can see an example in Figure 14.12.

The @COLS and @ROWS Functions

When you need to know how many columns or rows there are in a range of cells, you use the @COLS and @ROWS functions. Thus, @COLS(DATA) returns 7 if DATA is the name given to cells A1..G20. The response to @ROWS(DATA) would be 20.

Figure 14.12
Using the @@
Function

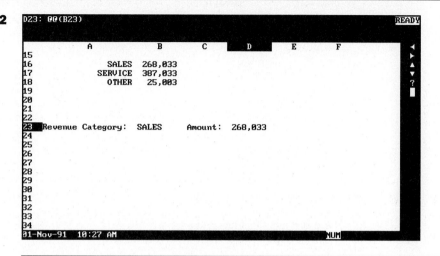

The @N and @S Functions

The @N and @S functions return useful information about a cell. They have the syntax

@N(*range*)

and

@S(*range*)

where *range* is the name or address of a cell. (If range is a multicell range, the function refers to the upper-left cell of the range.) The @N function returns the numeric value of the range, so that @N(DATA) returns the value 5 if the upper-left cell of DATA contains a 5 or a formula that results in a 5. If the upper-left cell of DATA contains a label, the result will be 0. This allows you to use @N in a test for cell contents.

The companion to @N is @S, which returns the string value of the cell it references. Thus, @S(DATA) returns Name if the upper-left cell of the range DATA contains the label Name or a string formula that results in Name. If the same cell contains a numeric value, such as 5, @S will return the empty label " ", which appears as an empty cell.

True and False Tests

In some spreadsheet designs, you may need to test whether a statement or condition is true or false. 1-2-3 represents a true statement as 1 and a false statement as 0. Thus, A1>99 results in 1 if A1 contains any number larger than 99, or 0 if A1 contains a number less than 99 or a label (labels have a 0 value). The more likely place to find true/false tests is in an @IF statement such as @IF(A1>99,1,0). Since this statement is somewhat difficult to read, you can use

```
@IF(A1>99,@TRUE,@FALSE).
```

The @TRUE and @FALSE functions return the responses 1 and 0, respectively, and require no argument. @FALSE is used with the @IS functions discussed in the next section.

The @IS Functions

There are several 1-2-3 functions that begin with IS: @ISAFF, @ISAAP, @ISERR, @ISNA, @ISNUMBER, and @ISSTRING. These are all true/false functions that give you the means to check certain conditions in a worksheet or current 1-2-3 session. The @ISERR and @ISNA functions tell you whether a formula or cell entry results in either the ERR or NA response, respectively. These functions take the form

```
@ISERR(value)
```

and

```
@ISNA(value)
```

where *value* is a cell reference or a formula. The @ISERR function returns the response 1, meaning true, if *value* results in ERR, as is the case with @ISERR(1/0) or @ISERR(A1/A2), where A2 contains the value 0.

A typical application of the @ISERR function is seen in Figure 14.13. In this figure, cell D7 contains a formula (shown next to the cell address indicator) that avoids the problem of dividing one column of numbers by another when some of the cells in the columns might be empty or contain zeros. Thus, the division of sales by the number of staff would result in an ERR message in cell D7 if the formula were simply C7/B7. The added @IF function uses @ISERR to turn the ERR result into the string of text "Not Available."

Figure 14.14 illustrates another application of the @ISERR function. Here it is used in a data entry macro that completes the simple order form in the upper half of the screen. The command {GETNUMBER} places ERR in the destination cell if the user enters a label instead of the requested number. The macro code at B23 causes 1-2-3 to beep and repeat the {GETNUMBER} command if the user accidentally enters a label.

The @ISNA function is similar to @ISERR, but it is used less frequently. The value NA is less common than ERR, since few formulas give this result unless you design them that way. The functions @ISNUMBER(*value*) and

@ISSTRING(*value*) are used to test whether the referenced value is a number or a string. Figure 14.15 shows an example of these functions at work; a set of cells in column B is being used to receive data about a piece of lost baggage.

Figure 14.13
Using @ISERR

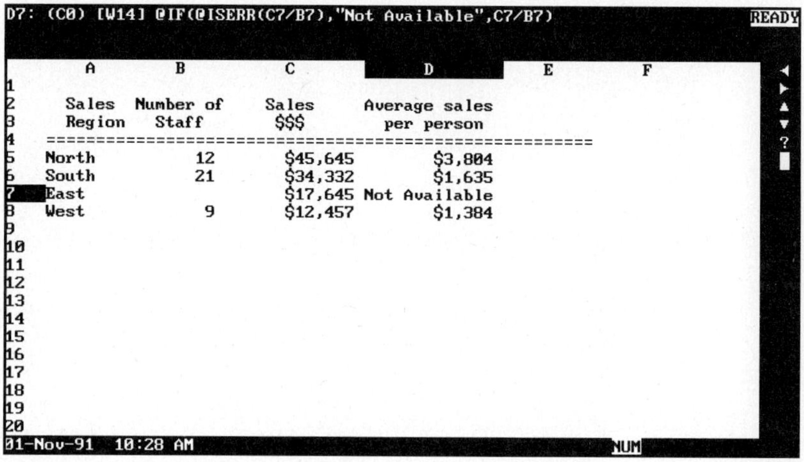

```
D7: (C0) [W14] @IF(@ISERR(C7/B7),"Not Available",C7/B7)          READY
          A          B          C          D          E          F        ◄
1                                                                         ►
2       Sales    Number of    Sales    Average sales                     ▲
3       Region    Staff       $$$       per person                       ▼
4    =========================================================           ?
5       North       12       $45,645       $3,804                        ■
6       South       21       $34,332       $1,635
7       East                 $17,645   Not Available
8       West        9        $12,457       $1,384
9
10
11
12
13
14
15
16
17
18
19
20
01-Nov-91  10:28 AM                                              NUM
```

Figure 14.14
Using @ISERR in a
macro

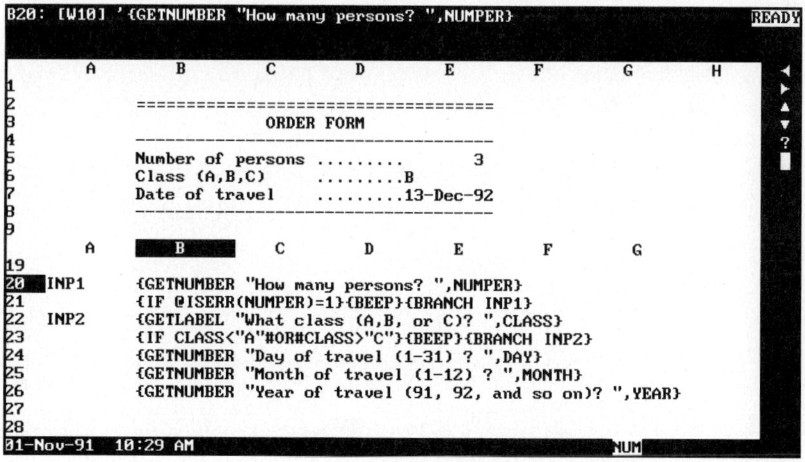

```
B20: [W10] '{GETNUMBER "How many persons? ",NUMPER}               READY
          A       B       C       D       E       F       G       H     ◄
1                                                                        ►
2              ===================================                       ▲
3                      ORDER FORM                                        ▼
4              ---------------------------------                         ?
5              Number of persons ........        3                       ■
6              Class (A,B,C)        .........B
7              Date of travel       .........13-Dec-92
8
9              ---------------------------------
          A       B       C       D       E       F       G
19
20   INP1   {GETNUMBER "How many persons? ",NUMPER}
21          {IF @ISERR(NUMPER)=1}{BEEP}{BRANCH INP1}
22   INP2   {GETLABEL "What class (A,B, or C)? ",CLASS}
23          {IF CLASS<"A"#OR#CLASS>"C"}{BEEP}{BRANCH INP2}
24          {GETNUMBER "Day of travel (1-31) ? ",DAY}
25          {GETNUMBER "Month of travel (1-12) ? ",MONTH}
26          {GETNUMBER "Year of travel (91, 92, and so on)? ",YEAR}
27
28
01-Nov-91  10:29 AM                                              NUM
```

The first piece of data, Passenger Name, has been entered in B3 and column C states "Okay." This method of data entry and prompting uses formulas next to the data entry cells to flag entries as they are made. Here are the

Figure 14.15

Using @ISNUMBER
and @ISSTRING

```
C3: [W14] @IF(@ISSTRING(B3)=0,"Enter label","Okay")              READY

              A           B              C          D        E          F       ◄
1    Lost Baggage Report              Today:    11/01/91  Time:    10:29 AM     ►
2    ================================================================           ▲
3    Passenger Name: Jones, S.  Okay                                            ▼
4         Date Lost:            Enter number                                    ?
5         Time Lost:            Enter number
6        Flying From:           Enter label                                     ■
7          Flying To:           Enter label
8          Meal Type:           Enter label
9
10
11
12
13
14
15
16
17
18
19
20
01-Nov-91  10:29 AM                                            NUM
```

formulas used in column C:

```
@IF(@ISSTRING(B3)=0,"Enter label","Okay"))
@IF(@ISNUMBER(B4)=0,"Enter number","Okay"))
@IF(@ISNUMBER(B5)=0,"Enter number","Okay"))
@IF(@ISSTRING(B6)=0,"Enter label","Okay"))
@IF(@ISSTRING(B7)=0,"Enter label","Okay"))
```

Cell C3 evaluates to "Okay" because @ISSTRING(B3) results in 1. In cell
B4 there is a blank label, a simple apostrophe. This causes the message
"Enter a number" to be displayed as the result of the formula in C4 because
@ISNUMBER produces 0 when it is applied to a cell containing a label. Of
course, the user just sees a note that the information for Date Lost must be a
number rather than a label. An alternative syntax for the preceding formulas
would be as follows:

```
@IF(@ISSTRING(B3)=@FALSE, "Enter label","Okay")
```

The use of @FALSE instead of 0 makes the formula easier for someone else
to understand.

Note that the blank entry form should start with no entries in cell B3 or
in cells B6 through B8. There should be blank labels in B4 and B5 to create
the "Enter" prompts. These formulas could be incorporated into a macro
that clears the data entry area with the {BLANK} command.

An Extended Example

This section explores a set of macros and formulas designed to facilitate the printing of mailing labels. In the process, you will learn how to break down a relatively complex task into manageable steps and how to develop a complete set of macro code.

Some Useful Commands

The mailing label macro described in a moment employs several powerful commands that you have not yet used. The {LET} command is used in several situations to transfer values from one location in a worksheet to another. The {LET} command assigns a value to a location in the spreadsheet using the format:

```
{LET location,value}
```

This saves a macro from having to move the cell selector to a location to enter data. The *location* argument is the address or block name of the cell in which you want to store the value or label. Specifying *location* as a multicell range means the upper-left cell in the block will be used. The *value* argument is the data you want assigned to the location. 1-2-3 will try to assign the value as a numeric value, but will assign it as a string if it cannot. Thus the command

```
{LET A1,101}
```

places the number 101 in cell A1. Of course, you can use cell references for the value argument.

The {RECALC} command recalculates the formulas within a specified block, proceeding by rows within the block. The format for the {RECALC} command is as follows:

```
{RECALC location,condition,iteration}
```

The range to be recalculated is specified as *location*. The *condition* is an optional argument specifying a condition that must be evaluated as True before the block is no longer recalculated. The optional *iteration* argument tells 1-2-3 how many times to repeat the calculation. While the *condition* argument evaluates to False, 1-2-3 continues to recalculate the worksheet. When used in conjunction with the *iteration* argument, the *condition* argument stops recalculation short of the maximum number of iterations if it returns True.

The point of this command, and the companion command {RECALCCOL}, is to make sure that a particular set of formulas return current values. While {CALC} recalculates the entire worksheet, {RECALC} and {RECALCCOL} evaluate just a portion, which takes less time. You use {RECALC} when the area you are recalculating is below and to the left of the cells referenced by the formulas in this area. Use {RECALCCOL} when the area you are recalculating is above and to the right of the cells referenced by the formulas in this area. You use these commands prior to printing a report to ensure that the reported data is correct but to avoid lengthy delays in updating the entire spreadsheet. (Note that if the formula to be calculated is both above and to the left of cells with new values, you must use the {CALC} command.)

Printing Mailing Labels in 1-2-3

Quite often an organization will accumulate many names and addresses in a 1-2-3 worksheet. While there are other programs that can import WK1 files and then print labels, there is no reason why you cannot print the labels directly from 1-2-3. Figure 14.16 shows part of a sample mailing list. The entries are contacts at client companies. The fields are Number, First, Last, Company, Address, City, State, and Zip.

Figure 14.16

The client database

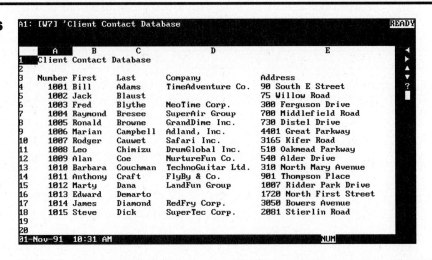

There are several ways to print mailing labels from this list. The basic task is to get from the horizontal arrangement of information in the database to the vertical arrangement used in a mailing label; that is, to get from this:

Bill Adams TimeAdventure Co. 90 SE St. Santa Rosa, CA 95404

to this:

```
Bill Adams
TimeAdventure Co.
90 SE St.
Santa Rosa, CA 95404
```

You could try to arrange all of the records into label form and then send them to the printer at once. Alternatively, you could set up a single range of cells as the print range and print the same range repeatedly, each time placing a different record's data in the range. The example that follows takes basically this approach. However, instead of using a single label form as the print range, the example uses three label forms side by side, so that you can print up to three labels on the page. This allows for most types of computer labels. The overall task can be split into four basic operations:

1. Arrange horizontal field data in a vertical label format.

2. Determine print parameters based on label size.

3. Position label data in print range.

4. Send the labels to the printer.

You can accomplish step 1 by pulling the first few records from the database into a separate part of the worksheet. Step 2 must solicit and then store three pieces of information supplied by the user:

- The number of labels. How many columns of labels will be printed across each page of labels (typically this is one across, two across, or three across).

- The number of lines. How many blank lines should be placed between each label or row of labels.

- The width of labels. How wide each label is, stated as a number of characters.

Step 3 involves arranging the label data according to the preceding print parameters and altering the print settings. If the labels are two across, the print range will need to be set accordingly. You must set the number of line feeds between each row of labels, and adjust the width of the columns containing label data to match the user's choice of lines between labels and label width.

Step 4 involves sending to the printer the data in the print area (consisting of one, two, or three labels), and then changing the records in the print area. You accomplish this by using a {FOR} statement, which repeats the basic printing process, and by using a set of formulas that change the data in the label assembly area after each iteration of the print task. These formulas form the basis of the solution to the mailing-label problem.

A Wealth of Formulas

When you want to pull a piece of data from a table of cells of known dimensions, you can use the @INDEX function. Recall that this function takes the three arguments *range*, *column*, and *row*. The *range* is the table of cells—in this example, the client database, which has been named CLIENT_DB. The *column* argument is a number representing the column containing the target data (with 0 being the first column in the range). The *row* argument is a number representing the row containing the target data (with 0 representing the first row in the range). Thus the following formula would return Bill from the sample worksheet:

```
@INDEX(CLIENT_DB,1,1)
```

A series of formulas like this could extract each of the entries required to create a label. If you made the row argument dependent upon a value that is increased by one after each label is printed, the formulas could reflect each record in turn. If you use the {FOR} command to control the repetition of the print operation, the cell named as the counter argument in the {FOR} statement will increase every cycle. This cell, called ROWS in this example, can be used in the @INDEX statement like this:

```
@INDEX($CLIENT_DB,1,$ROWS+1)
```

Note that the range names are preceded by $ signs to make them absolute. This is simply to ensure that the range reference will remain accurate if the formula is copied. The +1 is required because the value in ROWS begins at 0 and the first record is on index row number 1. This formula returns the last name entry to be inserted into the first label form

```
@INDEX($CLIENT_DB,2,$ROWS+1)
```

while this formula returns the first name to be placed in the second label form:

```
@INDEX($CLIENT_DB,1,$ROWS+2)
```

In Figure 14.17 you can see these formulas at work in what is called the Label Assembly Area. There are three formulas under each field name, creating a set of entries that can be used to build the first three labels. Figure 14.17 also shows some of the values that will be used in the macro, such as the number of lines per label, and the beginning of the label-printing macro code. The macro actually consists of the three subroutines ASK, SETUP, and DO_LABEL.

Note that three records must be assembled at once because the macro can print up to three labels across the page at once. The macro will print the first three records, then a {FOR} statement will add to the ROWS range, which will change the records reflected in the Label Assembly Area. The

increment used in the {FOR} argument will be 1, 2, or 3, depending upon the number of labels across. If the user wants two-across labels, the counter, ROWS, will be incremented by 2 for each cycle of the {DO_LABEL} routine, causing the Label Assembly Area to supply the next two records in the database. You can see the macro code in its entirety in Figure 14.18. It will be described in detail in a moment.

Figure 14.17
Label Assembly
Area

```
M4: [W14] @INDEX($CLIENT_DB,1,$ROWS+1)                              READY

         M           N          O         P        Q      R      S      ◄
1   Label Assembly Area ===========================================     ►
2                                                                       ▲
3   First       Last       Company      Address    City    State Zip    ▼
4   Bill        Adams      TimeAdventure C90 South E Santa Rosa,CA 95404 ?
5   Jack        Blaust                  0 75 Willow RMenlo Park,CA 94025
6   Fred        Blythe     NeoTime Corp. 300 FergusoMountain ViCA 94043
7
8   Code Area ==============================================================
9
10  Range Names   Values/Code
11         ROWS            0 The counter in the {FOR} statement in {DO_LABEL}
12  DEFAULT_LINES          2
13        SPACE            3
14        LINES            2
15  DEFAULT_WIDTH         40
16        WIDTH           40
17
18          \L {ASK}      Label printing macro starts here
19             {SETUP}
20             {DO_LABEL}
01-Nov-91  10:32 AM                                              NUM
```

The Label Assembly Area shown in Figure 14.17 only serves to pull the required data from the database. The actual assembly of records into label-shaped print ranges is done by another set of formulas. These employ the @S function to ensure that the data used are strings. You can see the first of the formulas in this label area in Figure 14.19. Note that if the referenced cells do not contain strings, the formulas return a blank.

The range names FIRST and LAST in the formula in V4 refer to cells M4 and N4, shown in Figure 14.17. These are the cells containing data from the first record and they were assigned names from the labels in row 3 using the Range Name Labels Down command. The formula highlighted in Figure 14.19 simply combines the first and last name entries with a space between them. It is assumed that there will be a first and last name entry for each record.

The formulas in V5 through V7 are more complex, since there may not be a company name for each client. Thus the formula needs to supply the company name if there is one; otherwise, it should supply the address, as in the second label. The formula in V5 is thus

```
@IF(@ISSTRING(COMPANY),@COMPANY,@S(ADDRESS))
```

Figure 14.18

Remaining macro
code

```
Code Area=========================================================================

Range Names      Values/Code
          ROWS            0 The counter in the {FOR} statement in {DO_LABEL}
 DEFAULT_LINES            2
         SPACE            3
         LINES            2
 DEFAULT_WIDTH           40
         WIDTH           40

            \L {ASK}          Label printing macro starts here
               {SETUP}
               {DO_LABEL}
               Q
               {let ROWS,0}{calc}{home}

           ASK {getlabel "How many labels across ? Enter 1, 2, or 3: ",ACROSS}
               {LABEL_CHK}
               {let LINES,DEFAULT_LINES}
               {getnumber "How many lines between labels (default is 2): ",LINES}
               {LINE_CHK}
               {getnumber "How wide is each column of labels (default is 40): ", WIDTH}
               {WIDTH_CHK}


     LABEL_CHK {if ACROSS="1"#or#ACROSS="2"#or#ACROSS="3"}{return}
               {beep 4}
               {getlabel "Number out of range, default is 1 ",ACROSS}
               {let ACROSS,"1"}

      LINE_CHK {if lines<>0}{return}
               {let LINES,DEFAULT_LINES}

     WIDTH_CHK {if WIDTH<>0}{WIDTH_SET}{return}
               {let WIDTH,DEFAULT_WIDTH}
     WIDTH_SET {goto}1LABEL~/wcs
               40
               ~{right}/wcs
               40
               ~{right}/wcs
               40
               ~
                              LINEFEED L
         SETUP /ppcar
        ACROSS 2
               LABEL~omr240~ouq

      DO-LABEL {for ROWS,0,@rows(CLIENT_DB)-2,@value(ACROSS),PRINT}

         PRINT {recalc FORMULAS}
               {recalc FORMULAS}g
               {for SPACE,1,LINES,1,LINEFEED}
```

That is, if there is a string in the cell called COMPANY, the result will be the contents of COMPANY; otherwise, the contents of ADDRESS will be returned. In V6 the formula must supply City, State, and Zip, properly punctuated, or the address, again dependent upon the presence of a label in the COMPANY cell:

```
@IF(@ISSTRING(COMPANY),@S(ADDRESS),@S(CITY)&",
"&@S(STATE)&"  "&@S(ZIP))
```

Figure 14.19

Further label formulas

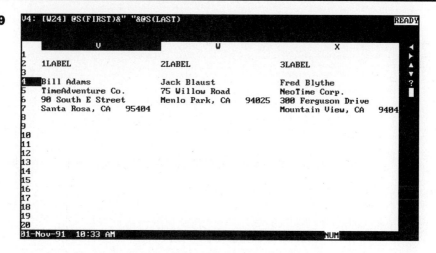

```
V4: [W24] @S(FIRST)&" "&@S(LAST)                                    READY

            V              W                    X                    ◀
1                                                                    ▶
2   1LABEL            2LABEL               3LABEL                     ▲
3                                                                    ▼
4   Bill Adams        Jack Blaust          Fred Blythe               ?
5   TimeAdventure Co. 75 Willow Road       NeoTime Corp.             ■
6   90 South E Street Menlo Park, CA  94025 300 Ferguson Drive
7   Santa Rosa, CA   95404                 Mountain View, CA   9404
8
9
10
11
12
13
14
15
16
17
18
19
20
01-Nov-91  10:33 AM                                          NUM
```

Finally, in V7 the formula must return a blank, represented by a pair of quotes (""), if there was no company name:

```
@IF(@ISSTRING(COMPANY),@S(CITY)&@S(STATE)&@S(ZIP),"")
```

In the next column, a similar set of formulas refer to the contents of row 5 of the Label Assembly Area. These cells do not have range names and are simply referred to by their cell coordinates, as in:

```
W4:@S(M5..M5)&"  "&@S(N5..N5)
W5:@IF(@ISSTRING(O5),@S(O5..O5),@S(P5..P5))
W6:@IF(@ISSTRING(O5),@S(P5..P5),@S(Q5..Q5)&@S(R5..R5)&@S
(S5..S5))
W7:@IF(@ISSTRING(O5),@S(Q5..Q5)&@S(R5..R5)&@S(S5..S5),"")
```

Note that the first label used range names because these were easily assigned to the appropriate cells with the Range Label Down command. Also note that range names make formulas much easier to read. A full table of range names used in the model is shown in Figure 14.20. A range name table becomes a vital ingredient when documenting and debugging complex macros. Note that the table in Figure 14.20 has been arranged to fit the screen.

Figure 14.20

A range name table

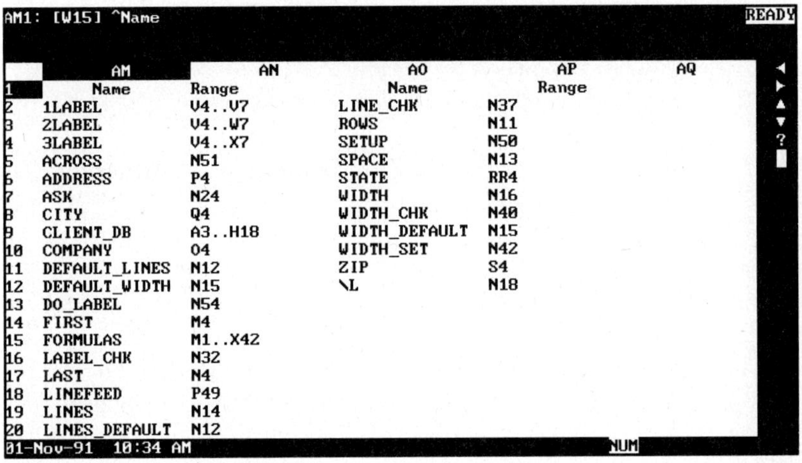

```
AM1: [W15] ^Name                                                    READY

          AM              AN              AO            AP          AQ      ◀
1     Name        Range       Name          Range                          ▶
2  1LABEL       V4..V7      LINE_CHK      N37                               ▲
3  2LABEL       V4..W7      ROWS          N11                               ▼
4  3LABEL       V4..X7      SETUP         N50                               ?
5  ACROSS       N51         SPACE         N13                               ■
6  ADDRESS      P4          STATE         RR4
7  ASK          N24         WIDTH         N16
8  CITY         Q4          WIDTH_CHK     N40
9  CLIENT_DB    A3..H18     WIDTH_DEFAULT N15
10 COMPANY      O4          WIDTH_SET     N42
11 DEFAULT_LINES N12        ZIP           S4
12 DEFAULT_WIDTH N15        \L            N18
13 DO_LABEL     N54
14 FIRST        M4
15 FORMULAS     M1..X42
16 LABEL_CHK    N32
17 LAST         N4
18 LINEFEED     P49
19 LINES        N14
20 LINES_DEFAULT N12
01-Nov-91  10:34 AM                                        NUM
```

In column X, the column coordinates of the references are the same but references are to row 6 instead of 5. While the labels are printing, the print range will be extended from column V to include column W if the user wants two-across labels. Column X will be included if the user wants three-across labels. The following three range names are set up to help with this.

```
1LABEL is cells V4..V7
2LABEL is cells V4..W7
3LABEL is cells V4..X7
```

The width of columns V, W, and X will be adjusted to match the user selection of label width.

Checking User Input

As you can see from Figure 14.18, the label printing macro actually consists of three subroutine commands—{ASK}, {SETUP}, and {DO_LABEL}—plus a few extra commands. The data for the labels is assembled using formulas so the first subroutine, ASK, can request from the user the parameters required to perform the label printing: how many across, how many lines between, and how wide. The responses are stored in the three cells ACROSS, LINES, and WIDTH. However, to avoid errors, each response is checked. Also, provision is made for a default setting for LINES and

WIDTH. The subroutines LABEL_CHK, LINE_CHK, and WIDTH_CHK take care of this.

The LABEL_CHK macro simply makes sure that the user enters 1, 2, or 3. The {RETURN} command returns control of the macro to the ASK macro that called the LABEL_CHK routine. The LINE_CHK routine checks that the user has supplied a value using the condition LINES<>0. If the user did not supply a value, the LET command is used to place the value from DEFAULT_LINES in the cell called LINES. The WIDTH_CHK routine uses a similar approach, but triggers the WIDTH_SET macro before returning macro control to the \L macro. The WIDTH_SET macro uses formulas to supply the value for the width setting. After the {GOTO} command has moved the cell pointer to the range called 1LABEL (V4..V7), the Worksheet Column Set-Width command is issued. The value of 40, seen in the macro in Figure 14.18, is supplied by this formula:

```
@STRING($WIDTH,0)
```

This formula takes the value entered as a number by the user and stored in WIDTH and converts it to a label so that it can be used as part of the macro code. The macro then applies the same value to the next two columns (W and X).

Setting Up and Printing

When the subroutines within the ASK subroutine are completed, the SETUP subroutine kicks in. This simply clears the print settings and sets the print range according to the number of labels across that the user requested. A very basic but effective technique is used for this. If the user wants two-across labels, user input is 2. This value is placed in the ACROSS cell, which precedes a cell that begins with the characters LABEL. As 1-2-3 reads the SETUP macro instructions, the print range is set to 2LABEL. Note that the right margin is set to 240 by the SETUP macro to prevent it from conflicting with the width requirement of the labels.

After SETUP is completed, control is passed to the DO_LABEL macro. This macro consists of a single {FOR} command that repeats the PRINT macro:

```
{FOR ROWS,0,@ROWS(CLIENT_DB)-2,@VALUE(ACROSS),PRINT}
```

The counter used by the {FOR} command is the cell called ROWS; the value in ROWS starts out at 0, as determined by the second argument in the statement. The stop value is one less than the number of records in the database, determined by the formula

```
@ROWS(CLIENT_DB)-2
```

Note that the first set of records is already in the print area and the total number of records in a database is the total number of rows, less one for the heading. (There are already records in the print area because the formulas in the print area refer to formulas in the Label Assembly Area. These latter formulas pull data from three rows of the database based on an evaluation of the expressions of Rows+1, Rows+2, and Rows+3, and ROWS itself has a starting value of 0.) The step by which the {FOR} command increments the counter is @VALUE(ACROSS), the number of labels across. Thus, if there are 15 records and the user enters 2 for the ACROSS value, the {FOR} command will play out as shown in Table 14.2. The @VALUE function must be used to convert the label in ACROSS to a value.

Table 14.2   **Progress of {FOR} Command in DO_LABEL Macro**

Counter	Start	Stop	Step	Subroutine
0	0	14	2	Recalc print area, based on Rows=0, then print
2	0	14	2	Recalc print area, based on Rows=2, then print
4	0	14	2	Recalc print area, based on Rows=4, then print
6	0	14	2	Recalc print area, based on Rows=6, then print
8	0	14	2	Recalc print area, based on Rows=8, then print
10	0	14	2	Recalc print area, based on Rows=10, then print
12	0	14	2	Recalc print area, based on Rows=12, then print
14	0	14	2	Recalc print area, based on Rows=14, then print
16	0	14	2	Return control to \L macro

*Note that Counter = ROWS.

The PRINT macro not only sends the print range to be printed, but recalculates the formulas that pull the records from the database into the Label Assembly Area. Remember that 1-2-3 suspends formula recalculation during macro execution. This means that a command needs to be inserted to prompt recalculation. Instead of recalculating the entire worksheet, you can name a range of cells and recalculate them with the {RECALC} command. The range called FORMULAS in this example covers the entire label assembly and the top of the macro code area (M1..X17). In fact, as you can see from Figure 14.18, the command is issued twice, just to make sure that the labels are updated before the printing begins.

The PRINT macro also has its own {FOR} command, which supplies the necessary lines between the labels, based upon the user input in LINES. The subroutine called LINEFEED consists simply of the letter L, which, when pressed at the Print menu, sends a line feed to the printer.

The Final Steps

When the {FOR} command in {DO_LABEL} completes, macro control reverts to the \L macro, which issues the command Q to Quit the Print menu. The ROWS cell is then returned to 0 with the {LET} command. Although the {FOR} command in DO_LABEL will set ROWS to 0 using the start argument the next time the macro is run, this {LET} command is at the close of the macro because the formulas in the Label Assembly Area depend upon ROWS and will not be updated correctly until the next time the macro runs. The Label Assembly Area may be blank at the end of the DO_LABEL subroutine, because the value of ROWS is greater than the number of records in the database, as explained in Table 14.2. The {LET} command ensures that the labels displayed at the end of the macro are the first records in the database.

Finally, the macro recalculates the entire worksheet and moves the cell pointer to A1 with the {HOME} command. This presents the user with a familiar sight and a fully calculated worksheet in READY mode. Of course, the \L macro could easily be incorporated into a menu of macros.

One other wrinkle in this example pertains to the formulas used in the Label Assembly Area. Now that you know how the macro works, you should realize that when the number of records is not exactly divisible by the number of labels across, there will be one or possibly two "blank" labels in the label print area. In addition, the row argument in the @INDEX formulas will exceed the number of rows in the range being indexed. The following formula gives an ERR response if ROW+1 is greater than the number of rows in CLIENT_DB:

```
@INDEX($CLIENT_DB,1,$ROWS+1)
```

This would result in ERR being printed in the "blank" labels. To get around this problem, you can modify the formula by adding an @IF formula based on the @ISERR function. The correct formula would return a blank entry, represented by double quotes (""), if the @INDEX function returned an error. The amended formula in M4 would be:

```
@IF(@ISERR(@INDEX($CLIENT_DB,1,       if an error exists
$ROWS+1),"",@INDEX($CLIENT_DB,1,      return nothing
$ROWS+1))                             else @INDEX result
```

The formulas in M4 through S6 should be amended in this way to prevent any spare labels from printing errors.

Full-Screen Effects

In several situations you may want to present the user with a clear picture of what is required or with a wide variety of options. You can use the following techniques to present a screen that is easy to read and hard to miss.

An Opening Number

Applications that will be used by novices should have "friendly" opening screens that make the operator comfortable with the program. You can do this by careful use of the \0 macro and screen positioning. You can accentuate a regular 1-2-3 macro menu to make an effective opening. In Figure 14.21, note that the user is shown the first menu and told how to use it. This was achieved using the {GOTO} command, first moving the cell pointer to the upper-left corner of the screen, and then to the highlighted label. The menu was then called.

Figure 14.21

Opening screen
and menu

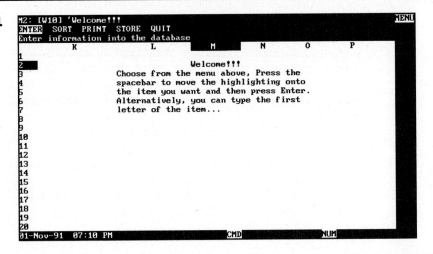

While You Wait

Most users hate to wait, so it is prudent to let them know when they have initiated a procedure that takes time, as shown in Figure 14.22. The macro that performs the printing simply moves the cell selector to this screen before issuing the Go command. You should display similar screens when the user saves the file. You might want to add an extra warning if the application is written for floppy disk users, reminding them *not* to remove the disk until the save process is complete.

Figure 14.22
Waiting screen

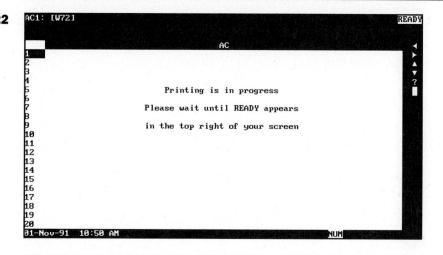

```
AC1: [W72]                                                              READY

                                       AC                               ◄
1                                                                       ►
2                                                                       ▲
3                                                                       ▼
4                                                                       ?
5              Printing is in progress                                  ■
6
7              Please wait until READY appears
8
9              in the top right of your screen
10
11
12
13
14
15
16
17
18
19
20
01-Nov-91   10:50 AM                                            NUM
```

Full-Screen Menus

You can overcome the limits of the horizontal top-of-screen 1-2-3 menu with macro techniques. Figure 14.23 displays a large menu that offers the user 14 options. Each number on the menu represents a different macro, which the user can select by typing the number of the desired option. A menu like this is effective as a first screen, activated by the \0 macro.

Figure 14.24 shows the code that processes selections from this menu. After the cell selector is positioned by a pair of {GOTO} statements, the user is prompted by a {GETNUMBER} statement to "Enter the number of your choice:". The response is placed in the cell called TEST. The series of {IF} statements branch to the chosen macros—ENTER, REVIEW, and so on. You can employ this approach in a number of different situations where the choices do not fit into a normal 1-2-3 menu.

There will be slight pause when selecting a choice with this system because 1-2-3 has to evaluate each {IF} statement. An alternative approach that provides faster response and far less code is to present the user with options that are actual subroutine names that can be highlighted using a screen like that seen in Figure 14.25. The user's menu selection is then processed with the following code:

```
MENU {GOTO}A1~{D5}~{?}{EDIT}~
     {DISPATCH WHERE}
```

The {DISPATCH} command is used to direct macro flow to the cell called WHERE. This cell contains the formula @CELLPOINTER("contents"), which reads the contents of the cell currently occupied by the cell pointer.

Figure 14.23
Menu item macro
code

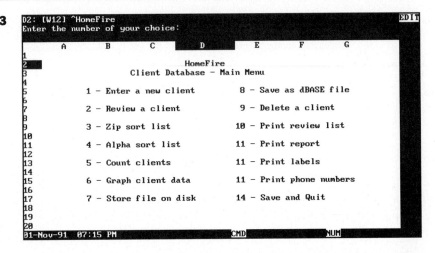

Figure 14.24
Full-screen menu

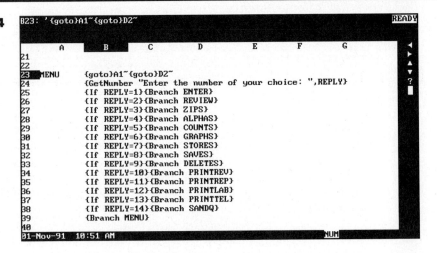

Note the {?} that provides the pause for the user to move the cell selector and press Enter. This command is followed by the code {EDIT}~, which causes 1-2-3 to update the @CELLPOINTER function in the WHERE cell. If you omit this code, WHERE may retain the cell selector's previous location and the macro will branch improperly.

Figure 14.25
Menu of subroutines

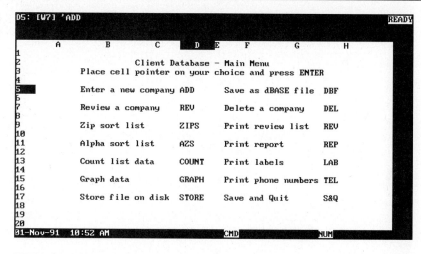

```
D5: [W7] 'ADD                                                          READY

       A         B         C       D  E      F          G        H
 1
 2                              Client Database - Main Menu
 3                    Place cell pointer on your choice and press ENTER
 4
 5              Enter a new company ADD        Save as dBASE file  DBF
 6
 7              Review a company    REV        Delete a company    DEL
 8
 9              Zip sort list       ZIPS       Print review list   REV
10
11              Alpha sort list     AZS        Print report        REP
12
13              Count list data     COUNT      Print labels        LAB
14
15              Graph data          GRAPH      Print phone numbers TEL
16
17              Store file on disk  STORE      Save and Quit       S&Q
18
19
20
01-Nov-91  10:52 AM                            CMD              NUM
```

The macro names on the menu can sometimes be normal names, but in
a large model where many names are used you may be forced to use abbre-
viations. However, this shouldn't present a problem since you can provide
descriptions on the menu.

Summary

This chapter outlined the extent to which macros can automate tasks both
for your own convenience and for the benefit of less-experienced users. By
careful use of user input commands and error-checking, you can ensure
trouble-free macro execution. In the process, you learned how many of the
most useful macro commands work. The syntax of the remaining macro
commands is provided in Appendix C.

This book has now described every aspect of 1-2-3, from simple sums,
through dynamic graphics, to macro-based automation and applications
development. However, no book can show you everything that a program as
powerful as 1-2-3 can do. With millions of users around the world, 1-2-3 is
constantly being applied to new and exciting tasks, tasks that will make people more productive, and thus that little bit closer to achieving their goals. I
hope that this book has helped you to use 1-2-3 more effectively, and made
working with it just a little bit more enjoyable.

APPENDIX A

Installing 1-2-3 Release 2.3

This appendix describes how to install 1-2-3 release 2.3 on your computer. Besides covering the basic installation procedure, it addresses several special situations, including upgrading from previous versions of 1-2-3, installing less than the full complement of 1-2-3 programs, and making changes to hardware after the initial installation.

The Basic Installation

This section outlines the basic procedures for installing 1-2-3 Release 2.3. If you are loading 1-2-3 Release 2.3 on a system that does not already have a version of 1-2-3 installed, you can follow these instructions exactly. If you are installing Release 2.3 on a system that already includes a version of 1-2-3, you should also refer to the later section of this appendix on upgrading to 1-2-3 Release 2.3. If you have limited disk space available for 1-2-3, see the section "Special Installations." If you are going to use 1-2-3 Release 2.3 on a network, also see Appendix B, "Working with Other Programs."

First Steps

1-2-3 is distributed on a number of floppy disks. Many of the files on these master disks (also called *original* or *distribution* disks) are compressed to save space. For this reason, you cannot simply copy the files from the master disks to your hard disk to install 1-2-3. In fact, the installation procedure involves running a program called Install that is located on floppy disk 1.

The Install program "uncompresses" the files from the master disks onto your hard disk and also asks you to supply several pieces of information that you should have handy before you begin. First, Install asks for your name and the name of your organization. Next, Install asks which of several companion programs you want to install on your system, presenting a screen of choices like the one shown in Figure A.1. Unless you have limited space available on your hard disk, you should install all of the items. (This requires about 6 megabytes of disk space.)

Install also wants to know the type of display adapter you have. Your adapter should be compatible with one of the following choices:

- Video Graphics Array (VGA)

- Enhanced Graphics Adapter (EGA)

- Multi-Color Graphics Adapter (MCGA)

- Color Graphics Adapter (CGA)

- Monochrome Graphics Adapter (plain IBM monochrome adapter)

- Hercules (plus compatible monochrome graphics cards)

- Toshiba

- AT&T

- GRiD

- IBM 3270

Figure A.1

Selecting
companion
programs

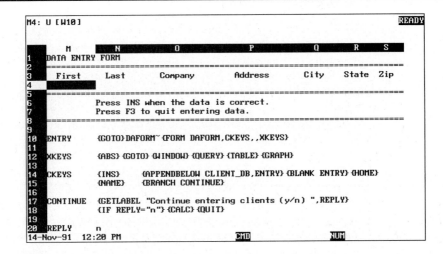

```
M4: U [W10]                                                              READY

        M         N          O             P           Q       R     S
1 DATA ENTRY FORM
2 ===============================================================================
3    First    Last     Company        Address      City    State  Zip
4
5 ===============================================================================
6          Press INS when the data is correct.
7          Press F3 to quit entering data.
8 ===============================================================================
9
10 ENTRY     {GOTO}DAFORM~{FORM DAFORM,CKEYS,,XKEYS}
11
12 XKEYS     {ABS}{GOTO}{WINDOW}{QUERY}{TABLE}{GRAPH}
13
14 CKEYS     {INS}        {APPENDBELOW CLIENT_DB,ENTRY}{BLANK ENTRY}{HOME}
15           {NAME}       {BRANCH CONTINUE}
16
17 CONTINUE  {GETLABEL "Continue entering clients (y/n) ",REPLY}
18           {IF REPLY="n"}{CALC}{QUIT}
19
20 REPLY     n
14-Nov-91  12:20 PM                          CMD              NUM
```

Do not worry if the choices do not include the exact display configuration
you are using; you can adjust the selection after the initial installation is completed. If you select a VGA or EGA adapter, you are also asked to specify
the number of characters from left to right; 80×25 (80 characters across by 25
lines) is the standard.

You are also asked to select printers. 1-2-3 divides printers into two categories: text and graphics. You use text printers to print plain spreadsheet reports,
and graphics printers to print charts and spreadsheet reports that have been
enhanced with the Wysiwyg add-in. You can install several printers of each
type. To select a printer, just choose the printer manufacturer from the list.
Then select the appropriate model. Bear in mind that you can always add additional printers after the initial installation has been completed.

Running Install
Once you know which companion programs you want to install and your
monitor and printer types, you are ready to begin installation. Place disk 1
into your floppy-disk drive and log on to that drive—that is, make that drive

the default drive, the drive that DOS assumes in any commands you issue. The drive letter of the default drive appears in the DOS prompt; for example, the prompt C> indicates that drive C is the default drive. On most hard-disk computers, drive C is the hard disk and the default drive. To log on to floppy-disk drive A, enter **A:** at the DOS prompt. Provided that there is a disk in drive A, the DOS prompt will change to A:\>, or something similar. (You can install 1-2-3 from drive B if necessary.)

After logging on to the floppy drive containing disk 1, you type **INSTALL** and press Enter to load the Install program. Throughout the installation process, you will be prompted for information or asked to perform particular actions. Follow the on-screen instructions and press F1 if you need help.

The first prompt is for your name and that of your organization. This is recorded on the original program disk as well as the computer onto which the program is installed to help prevent unauthorized duplication of your copy of 1-2-3. If you are installing 1-2-3 at work, you might want to check with your employer on how to enter the name information.

Next comes the menu of companion programs seen earlier on Figure A.1. The programs with a check mark beside them will be installed. If you want to deselect an item, use the arrow keys to move the highlighting to the item and press the spacebar to remove the check mark. You can install companion programs at a later date by again running the Install program from disk 1.

After making your choices from this menu, you are asked to name the drive and directory to be used for the 1-2-3 program files. By default, Install assumes C:\123R23—that is, a directory called 123R23 on drive C—but you can enter a different drive or directory if you want. The Install program creates the directory for you if it does not already exist. Install also creates subdirectories of this program directory for the Wysiwyg files and the Tutor files.

Do not enter 123 as the name of the program directory if you already have a copy of 1-2-3 installed in a directory called 123. See the section "Upgrading to 1-2-3 Release 2.3" for details on how to deal with earlier versions of 1-2-3.

When you have supplied the drive and directory information, Install starts transferring files to the hard disk. You will be prompted to change disks in the floppy drive until all the disks have been copied. A message "File transfer successful" will appear when the task is completed.

You must now select the display and printing equipment to use with 1-2-3. After you have made these choices, they are saved in a file on disk called a *driver set*. When you are asked whether you want to name this driver set, select No to create a driver set called 123.SET. Later you can create other SET files to allow 1-2-3 to work with a different set of equipment, as explained under "Driver Sets and Configuration Files." If you have elected to install Wysiwyg, next you are asked to select a font set. Your choices are Basic, Medium, and Extended, with Medium and Extended including several larger fonts.

This concludes the initial installation of 1-2-3. You should now be able to start the program from your hard disk. First you need to move to the disk and directory in which the 1-2-3 program files were installed. If you installed 1-2-3 in C:\123R23, log on to drive C by entering **C:** at the DOS prompt. Then move to directory 123R23 by entering **CD \123R23**. You can now load the 1-2-3 Access menu by entering **LOTUS** at the DOS prompt to bring up a menu that includes 1-2-3, PrintGraph, Translate, and Install. Simply type **1** to begin 1-2-3. You can bypass the Access menu and go straight to 1-2-3 by entering **123** instead of **LOTUS** at the DOS prompt.

Note that 1-2-3 uses several other directories in addition to the program directory. These will have been created as subdirectories of the program directory. Besides these directories, you may want to create one or more data directories to keep your 1-2-3 data files separate from program files. See the next section for more on working with directories. If you have problems starting 1-2-3, read through the next section and also refer to the section "Advanced Installation."

Fine Tuning

Once you have completed the basic installation, you can adjust the way 1-2-3 operates and how it fits into your computer system. You may want to change the DOS CONFIG.SYS file to improve performance and alter AUTOEXEC.BAT to improve access to 1-2-3. You can even create a batch file menu system to give you easy access to 1-2-3 and other programs on your hard disk.

Files and Buffers

To use 1-2-3 efficiently, you may need to fine-tune your system via the DOS CONFIG.SYS file. When your computer starts up, it looks to the floppy disk in drive A for the disk operating system (DOS). If DOS is found on the disk in drive A, it is loaded into RAM. If the system does not find DOS on the disk in drive A, it looks to the hard disk, typically drive C. If DOS is found on drive C, it is loaded into memory. The disk from which your system loads DOS is called the *boot disk*.

When loaded into memory, DOS looks for the configuration file, CON-FIG.SYS—a file on the boot disk that contains information about how your system is configured. This file is not essential, since DOS assumes certain default conditions if it does not find a CONFIG.SYS file. However, you will want to establish some settings with CONFIG.SYS when running 1-2-3.

The two CONFIG.SYS settings that affect 1-2-3 involve two aspects of the way DOS manages information in RAM: buffers and files. The number of *buffers* (temporary holding areas into which DOS can put information your programs use) is normally five. The number of open files that DOS can keep track of is normally eight. By increasing these settings with a

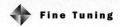

CONFIG.SYS file, you can improve the speed with which DOS manipu-
lates information in your system. Settings of 20 for buffers and 20 for files
are often used on systems running 1-2-3. You establish these settings by
placing the following instructions in the CONFIG.SYS file:

```
BUFFERS = 20
FILES = 20
```

The instructions can be upper- or lowercase letters, but must be on separate lines.

The CONFIG.SYS file may need additional information about your
hardware. For example, there may be additional commands for dealing with
various devices such as external hard disks.

You can check whether your system has a CONFIG.SYS file by typing
DIR *.SYS at the DOS prompt while in the root directory of your hard disk
or on the floppy disk with which you start your system. If you find a CON-
FIG.SYS file, you can examine its contents by entering **TYPE
CONFIG.SYS**. If you plan to change the CONFIG.SYS file or create a new
one, you should copy the original file to another file, such as CONFIG.OLD.
You do this at the DOS prompt with the command

```
COPY CONFIG.SYS CONFIG.OLD.
```

You can create a new CONFIG.SYS file with the DOS COPY command.
Type

```
COPY CON CONFIG.SYS
```

at the DOS prompt and press Enter. The cursor will move to a blank line.
Type the first instruction—for example, **FILES = 20**—and then press Enter
for another line. After the last instruction, press F6 and press Enter again.
You will see the message "1 File(s) copied," meaning that the file has been
written to the disk. (Pressing F6 produces the Ctrl-Z code, which DOS reads
as "end-of-file.") This CONFIG.SYS file is a pure ASCII file, which you can
create with SideKick's Notepad, WordStar in the nondocument mode, and
many other word processors—such as WordPerfect—that have commands
for saving text in ASCII.

Paths and Directories

Normally, the Install program places the 1-2-3 program files in a subdirectory
called 123R23. A hard-disk directory system for a computer running 1-2-3 and
WordPerfect might look like the one shown in Figure A.2. Note that the Install
program creates the following directories: 123R23, 123R23\WYSIWYG, and
123R23\TUTOR. If you want a separate directory for your 1-2-3 data files, you
must create it using the directory commands described in a moment.

Figure A.2

A hard-disk
directory system

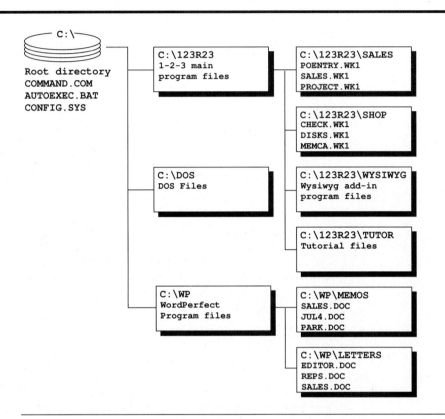

For DOS to find either a program file or a data file, you must specify a path for it to follow. For example, the path to the worksheet file called PRO-JECT.WK1 in the sales subdirectory of 123R23 is \123R23\SALES\. The backslash character is used to separate directory names and distinguish them from file names. To identify files accurately on a hard disk, you must include the path to the file as part of the file name. Thus, the full name of the PRO-JECT.WK1 file is

```
C:\123R23\SALES\PROJECT.WK1.
```

The top of the directory tree is referred to as the *root directory*, indicated by a single backslash, as in C:\.

To create a new directory, you enter the command **MD** (for Make Direc-tory) followed by the name of the directory, as in

```
MD \WORK
```

This command creates a subdirectory of the root directory called WORK. To create a subdirectory of the 123R23 directory called DATA, you would enter

```
MD \123R23\DATA
```

For more about directories and how to make and remove them, see Chapter 7.

You can always start 1-2-3 by moving to the 1-2-3 program directory before you issue the load command. However, if you enter the command **LOTUS** or **123** while you are in a directory other than the 1-2-3 program directory, DOS will not be able to carry out your command, *unless* you have already told it the path to the 1-2-3 program files. You do this by entering a PATH command at the DOS prompt. For example, you might enter a command like the following to tell DOS where to look for program files that are not in the current directory:

```
PATH=C:\;C:\DOS;C:\123R23
```

This command tells DOS to look in the root directory, the DOS directory, and the 123R23 directory on drive C any time you issue a command. You can display your computer's current PATH setting at any time simply by entering **PATH** at the DOS prompt.

Using Batch Files

Unfortunately, DOS forgets the PATH commands when you turn off the system. To solve this problem, you use a *batch file*, a collection of instructions to DOS that are delivered in a group or batch. A batch file has the extension .BAT. For example, the file P.BAT might contain the following lines:

```
ECHO OFF
PROMPT $P$G
DIR/W
```

You activate a batch file by typing the part of the file name preceding the period. Typing **P** and pressing Enter tells DOS to change the prompt and then list the files in the current directory. The ECHO OFF command tells DOS to display the results on the screen, but not the batch file's instructions.

A file called 1.BAT might contain the instructions needed to load 1-2-3:

```
CD\ 123R23
123
```

Every system can have a batch file called AUTOEXEC.BAT, which DOS looks for in the root directory when the system starts up. Because DOS executes the commands in AUTOEXEC.BAT automatically, this file is the perfect place to store commands such as PROMPT and PATH that set up the working environment the way you like it. AUTOEXEC.BAT can also be a means of loading a program every time you turn on or reboot your computer.

For example, suppose you want to go straight to 1-2-3 every time you start your computer. The following AUTOEXEC.BAT file on the hard disk would accomplish this:

```
ECHO OFF
PROMPT $P$G
PATH=C:\;C:\DOS;C:\123R23
123
```

To create this batch file, you copy the instructions from the keyboard directly into a file by typing

```
COPY CON AUTOEXEC.BAT
```

at the DOS prompt. Pressing Enter gives you the first line for an instruction. Type the instruction (for example, PROMPT PG) and press Enter for another line. After the last instruction, press F6 and press Enter again. The file will be written to the disk. This file is a pure ASCII file. Note that the last line of this batch file can include items that cause 1-2-3 to load specific worksheets or configurations, as described shortly.

Batch File Menus

If you are comfortable creating batch files, you can use them to move between 1-2-3 and other programs stored on the hard disk. This involves creating a series of batch files and a message file. Note that such an arrangement is not essential for running 1-2-3 on your computer. A *message file* is simply an ASCII file that contains text you want DOS to display. If you use the command TYPE together with the name of an ASCII file, DOS displays the text from the file on the screen. You can use this feature to create a simple menu. For example, you could create a list of programs in a file called MENU.MSG. By preceding the command TYPE MENU.MSG with the CLS command, which clears the screen, you can achieve a display such as this:

```
                      Main Menu
============================================
1      Run 1-2-3
2      Run WordPerfect
3      Run Backup
       Type the number of your choice and press ENTER
```

To display this message when you return to DOS from another program, write a batch file called Z.BAT, which changes the directory back to the root, clears the screen, and types the message, as in these four lines:

```
ECHO OFF
CD \
```

```
CLS
TYPE MENU.MSG
```

If you write a batch file called 1.BAT that starts 1-2-3, you can load 1-2-3 simply by typing **1** and pressing Enter. If the 1.BAT file that starts 1-2-3 runs the Z.BAT file after 1-2-3, you have created a loop from the menu to 1-2-3 and back to the menu. Here is what 1.BAT would look like:

```
ECHO OFF
CD \123R23
123
Z
```

(The last line, Z, directs DOS to run the batch program Z.BAT.) You could set up other batch files such as 2.BAT and 3.BAT to load other programs such as WordPerfect (2.BAT) and Backup (3.BAT).

You may want to place these batch files in a subdirectory rather than in the root directory. You can create a subdirectory called C:\BAT to store the menu files. Make sure that the PATH command in your AUTO-EXEC.BAT includes C:\BAT to let DOS know where to look for a batch file if it does not find it in the current directory. Also, the TYPE command in the Z.BAT file should include the full path to the message file, as in TYPE C:\BAT\MENU.MSG. This is because the PATH statement applies to program files, not data files. With the location of your batch files entered in the PATH command in your AUTOEXEC.BAT file, you will always be able to return to the menu and the root directory from anywhere on the disk simply by typing **Z** and then pressing Enter at the DOS prompt. You can easily adapt this system to your own needs by substituting the commands for other software programs and expanding the list.

1-2-3 Menu Options   You can issue a command to load 1-2-3 with an accompanying worksheet name, preceded by a special code (-W), so that the worksheet is retrieved from disk as soon as the program is loaded. For example, entering this command at the DOS prompt in the 1-2-3 directory

```
123 -WSALES
```

loads 1-2-3, and then loads the worksheet SALES.WK1, *if* there is a worksheet called SALES in the default directory (the one set by the Worksheet Global Default Directory command). You can use this ability to nominate a startup worksheet in batch files to load 1-2-3 in several different ways. You can set up a menu like the following to offer a choice between different 1-2-3 startup files.

```
                 1-2-3 Options
=======================================
1      Run 1-2-3 for Pricing
2      Run 1-2-3 for Budget Analysis
3      Run 1-2-3 with no file
```

The file 1.BAT used to activate this menu contains the instruction

```
123 -WPRICING
```

so that 1-2-3 loads the pricing worksheet as soon as the program loads. The 2.BAT file contains

```
123 -WBUDGET
```

and so on. You could use a variation of these instructions to load 1-2-3 for different users. Bear in mind that the file you call needs to be available to 1-2-3. To help ensure this, you can use a more specific request like:

```
123 -WC:\DATA\SALES
```

You can set up this menu system in your 1-2-3 directory. To use this system, the batch file called from the main menu to load 1-2-3 contains the following lines:

```
ECHO OFF
CD \123R23
CLS
TYPE 123.MEN
```

The file 123.MEN is the 1-2-3 Options menu shown above. Since DOS runs batch files in the current directory before those found in directories listed in the PATH setting, you can have two sets of files called 1.BAT, 2.BAT, and so on. The first set, stored in the root directory or a special subdirectory, operates the main menu. The second set, stored in the 123R23 directory, operates the 1-2-3 Options menu.

As well as nominating a startup worksheet for 1-2-3, you can invoke a specific driver set and configuration file. For more on this feature, see the next section.

You can also use a technique called *parameter passing* when constructing batch files to run 1-2-3. You add a special code to the batch file command that can be replaced by a value that you provide when you run the batch file. This is similar to the technique used by 1-2-3. When you enter **123** followed by **-W** and a file name to load 1-2-3, you are passing a parameter, in this case, the file name.

Batch file parameters are signified by a percentage sign and a number, as in %1 for the first parameter. If you create a batch file called 3.BAT that looks like this

```
ECHO OFF
CLS
123 -W%1
Z
```

you can load 1-2-3 with a worksheet by entering

```
3 filename
```

The characters %1 stand for parameter 1. The file name you supply becomes the first parameter. Parameters are handy because they do not have to be used. You could enter 3 on its own just to load 1-2-3, or enter 3 followed by a space and a file name to load 1-2-3 plus a specific file.

Driver Sets and Configuration Files

1-2-3 uses several files to record your preferences for how the program should operate. When you use the Worksheet Global Default Update command to record your preferences for items like Printer and Undo, these are recorded in a file called 123.CNF stored in the program directory. You can actually create a variety of CNF files to suit different needs and specify which one to use when you load the program. To do this, you exit 1-2-3 and copy the 123.CNF file to a new file, for example, FRED.CNF, using this command:

```
COPY 123.CNF FRED.CNF
```

Now reload 1-2-3 specifying FRED.CNF. To do this, precede the CNF file name with the code -C, for example

```
123 -CFRED
```

At first, the program will run as before, but when you use the Worksheet Global Default command you will see FRED.CNF as the configuration file on the settings sheet. After making the desired changes to the defaults, select Update, and the new settings will be recorded in FRED.CNF. By cloning a CNF and then changing it, you can create personalized configurations that you can invoke when 1-2-3 is loaded.

Other information used by 1-2-3 is recorded in files known as *driver sets,* which have the extension .SET. This is information about your hardware, recorded by the Install program. The default SET file, 123.SET, is created by the Install program when you first install 1-2-3. When you use the command 123 or LOTUS to load 1-2-3, the information in 123.SET is read automatically, as long as a file of that name is stored in the program directory.

If you use Install after the initial installation (perhaps to change a printer), the change is recorded in a SET file. You can use the default file name, 123.SET, or choose a different name. Occasionally, you might want to load 1-2-3 with a different graphics display than the one you normally use. You can store the normal graphics display in 123.SET and store an alternative choice in a different file, perhaps HIRES.SET. To invoke this driver set when loading 1-2-3, you would enter

```
123 HIRES
```

to tell 1-2-3 to use HIRES.SET instead of 123.SET. To load 1-2-3 with a special driver set and a custom configuration file called FRED.CNF, you would enter

```
123 HIRES -CFRED
```

To load a custom version of 1-2-3 and a startup worksheet called SALES-.WK1, you would enter

```
123 HIRES -CFRED -SALES
```

See the section "Advanced Installation" for more on creating a SET file.

Upgrading to 1-2-3 Release 2.3

If you already have an earlier version of 1-2-3 on your hard disk, you should remove it before installing 1-2-3 Release 2.3. This applies to Releases 1A, 2, 2.01, and 2.2. Since 1-2-3 Release 2.3 can read files created in these versions, you will have no problem using your existing data files with Release 2.3. Note that although Release 3, Release 3.1, and 1-2-3/G are chronologically earlier than Release 2.3, they are different, more powerful, programs. If your system is already equipped with one of these programs, you should not install 1-2-3 Release 2.3. For more details on sharing files between different Lotus products, see Appendix B.

To remove an existing version of 1-2-3, you should first check that there are no data files in the program directory. If there are, copy them to a different directory. First enter

```
MD \123WORK
```

to create a suitable subdirectory for these files. Then use the following command to copy all worksheet files from a program directory called 123 to the new directory called 123WORK:

```
COPY \123\*.WK? \123WORK
```

(If 1-2-3 is stored in a directory other than 123, substitute the appropriate directory name.) Note that in addition to worksheet files with the extensions .WK1 and .WKS, you might have data files with the extensions .PIC, .PRN,

.ALL, and .MLB. If so, repeat the COPY command, substituting the different file extensions for .WK?.

When all data files have been safely copied from the 123 program directory, you can issue the following command to remove all remaining program files from the directory:

```
DEL \123\*.*
```

Now check that all the files have been deleted by entering **DIR \123**. If there is still one file left, called 123.COM, with a file size of 2,000 bytes, you will need to use a procedure called *copy protection removal*. This clears out the special file used by Lotus to prevent unauthorized copying of some versions of 1-2-3. If you were using 1-2-3 Release 2, you can use the COPYOFF or COPYHARD/U command on the original System disk to remove copy protection. If you were using Release 2.01, use the Advanced Options from the Install program on the original Install disk to get rid of copy protection.

If you cannot find the original disks for your old version of 1-2-3, use the ZAP command on disk 1 of the Release 2.3 disks to remove copy protection. Insert disk 1 in drive A and enter **A:ZAP**. If you were using Release 2.01 enter **A:ZAP 2.01**.

With all of the old program files removed from your hard disk, you can use the 1-2-3 Release 2.3 Install disk to carry out a normal installation as described previously. You can use the old program directory or create a new one for the new version. If you do not use the old directory, remove it by entering **RM \123**. Note that you cannot remove a directory if it has subdirectories or contains any files. Also note that you may need to adjust the PATH statement in your AUTOEXEC.BAT if you install 1-2-3 Release 2.3 in a directory other than the one you were using for the previous version. For example, if you had 1-2-3 Release 2 installed in \123 and now have 1-2-3 Release 2.3 installed in \123R23, you may have to change PATH=\123 to PATH=\123R23.

Special Installations

Although 1-2-3 Release 2.3 is an extremely powerful package, the core of the program requires relatively little disk space. If you want to run 1-2-3 in a limited mode, perhaps from the 720k floppy disk in a laptop computer, you will need the following files:

File	Size in Bytes	File	Size in Bytes
123.CMP	169,455	123.EXE	18,448
123.CNF	429	123.LLD	16,419
123.DLD	6,640	123.RI	43,668
123.DYN	14,133	123.SET	56,788

These files take up less than 320k (note that the SET file varies in size according to the type of printer and monitor you have). With these files, you can load 1-2-3 and use all of the regular menu commands. However, you will not have the Access menu, PrintGraph, Install, Help, or Wysiwyg. If you want access to PrintGraph from your floppy disk, you can copy to your floppy the files PGRAPH.EXE, PGRAPH.HLP, PGRAPH.CNF, and all of the FNT files (BLOCK1.FNT, and so on). These take up 170k. To use the 1-2-3 Access menu, you need LOTUS.EXE and LOTUS.RI. Although the main 1-2-3 Help file (123.HLP) is over 600k, you can place it on the same disk as the preceding files if you are using a high-capacity floppy disk.

The problem with setting up 1-2-3 Release 2.3 for use on a floppy disk is that the Install program assumes you are using a hard-disk machine. It's easiest to install 1-2-3 on a hard-disk computer and then copy the files you need from the hard disk to the floppy. Before doing this, you should create a SET file that corresponds to the hardware on the machine that will be running 1-2-3 from floppy disks. See the next section for tips on creating a SET file.

Advanced Installation

Unfortunately, the basic installation procedure for 1-2-3 may not successfully install 1-2-3 on your system. The problems associated with installing 1-2-3 for a floppy-disk system were addressed in the previous section. The following sections describe how to deal with other problems relating to installation, and how to inform 1-2-3 about changes to the equipment you are using.

Returning to Install

In several situations, you may want to run the Install program after the initial installation of 1-2-3. A copy of Install was placed on your hard disk when the initial installation was performed. You can use this copy of Install to make changes to the initial installation. However, if you want to add programs that you declined to install in the initial installation, you need to use the original Install disk. Place the disk in drive A, log on to drive A, and enter **INSTALL** at the DOS prompt. This version of Install can uncompress the program files from the original floppy disks onto your hard disk.

If you want to change equipment such as a printer or the type of display, you can run Install from your hard disk. You can select Install from the 1-2-3 Access menu or enter **INSTALL** at the DOS prompt while you are in the 1-2-3 program directory. When you load Install, you must press Enter to bypass the introductory screen. You then come to the main menu shown in Figure A.3.

As you can see, the highlighted option is described in the box on the right. You use the Select Your Equipment option when you are installing 1-2-3 for the first time or if the file containing your driver set, 123.SET, has been damaged. This file is read by 1-2-3 whenever the program is loaded and contains your hardware choices. You employ the Change Selected Equipment option to tell 1-2-3 about changes after the initial installation. Specify Wysiwyg Options allows you to generate font information for the Wysiwyg program that matches your hardware choices. Typically, this is carried out automatically when you alter your hardware with the previous option. You also use Specify Wysiwyg Options to install additional bitstream fonts besides those that come with 1-2-3.

Figure A.3
The main Install menu

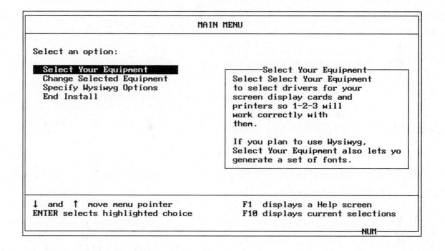

```
                              MAIN MENU


   Select an option:

     Select Your Equipment          ┌─────Select Your Equipment─────┐
     Change Selected Equipment      │Select Select Your Equipment   │
     Specify Wysiwyg Options        │to select drivers for your     │
     End Install                    │screen display cards and       │
                                    │printers so 1-2-3 will         │
                                    │work correctly with            │
                                    │them.                          │
                                    │                               │
                                    │If you plan to use Wysiwyg,    │
                                    │Select Your Equipment also lets yo
                                    │generate a set of fonts.       │
                                    └───────────────────────────────┘

   ↓ and ↑ move menu pointer         F1  displays a Help screen
   ENTER selects highlighted choice  F10 displays current selections

                                                              NUM
```

Changing Equipment

When you select Change Selected Equipment, you see the menu shown in Figure A.4. Normally, you will choose Modify the Current Driver Set, which allows you to make changes to the driver set that was used when Install was loaded. Unless you specifically requested a custom driver set, the default set called 123.SET was used. Unless you want to develop multiple driver sets, you will simply modify 123.SET and save your changes to this file. The easiest way to create additional driver sets is to use the Save the Current Driver Set command and provide a new file name. This file will then contain whatever settings were current when the command was issued.

To make current a driver set other than 123.SET, you invoke the SET file when you start Install or when you start the 1-2-3 Access menu, as in

```
INSTALL CUSTOM
```

or

```
LOTUS CUSTOM
```

both of which make the driver set stored in CUSTOM.SET the current driver set. You can also use the Make Another Driver Set Current option on the menu in Figure A.4 to choose a different driver set to be modified. Note that you cannot create a fresh driver set this way. To create a new driver set, you must use the COPY command at the DOS prompt to copy an existing SET file and give it a new name, or you must use the option called Save the Current Driver Set and provide a new name.

Figure A.4

The Change Selected Equipment menu

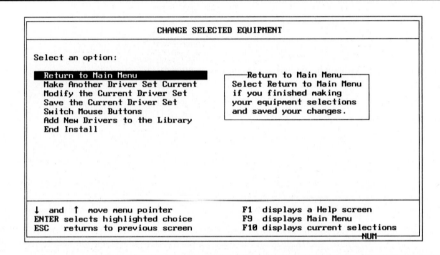

To see what the current selections are, you can press F10 to produce a display like the one shown in Figure A.5. Note that if you press F10 before you make any changes to the driver set, you will see what the current driver set contains. If you make any changes to the driver set, pressing F10 displays what settings will be saved when you choose Save the Current Driver Set. Note that Figure A.5 also displays the name of the driver set that is current—in this case CGA.SET.

When you choose Modify the Current Driver Set, you see a list of the items that you can change, as shown in Figure A.6. When highlighted, each item is explained in the box on the right. The four items after Return to Previous Menu are fairly self-explanatory hardware choices, each of which presents a list of options. You highlight the option you want and press Enter. When your choice is completed you are returned to the menu in A.4.

The Keyboard, Printer Interface, and subsequent options shown in Figure A.7 are only used in special situations—for example, if you are working with a custom keyboard or printer port. The exception to this is Collating Sequence, which determines how the Data Sort command operates for entries that contain both numbers and letters. The Help screen shown in Figure A.7 makes it clear what is offered by the three options ASCII, Numbers First, and Numbers Last.

Figure A.5

Current driver set selections

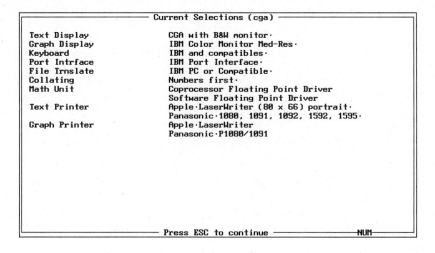

```
┌─────────────────── Current Selections (cga) ───────────────────┐
│                                                                 │
│   Text Display        CGA with B&W monitor.                     │
│   Graph Display       IBM Color Monitor Med-Res.                │
│   Keyboard            IBM and compatibles.                      │
│   Port Intrface       IBM Port Interface.                       │
│   File Trnslate       IBM PC or Compatible.                     │
│   Collating           Numbers first.                            │
│   Math Unit           Coprocessor Floating Point Driver         │
│                       Software Floating Point Driver            │
│   Text Printer        Apple·LaserWriter (80 x 66) portrait.     │
│                       Panasonic·1080, 1091, 1092, 1592, 1595.   │
│   Graph Printer       Apple·LaserWriter                         │
│                       Panasonic·P1080/1091                      │
│                                                                 │
│                                                                 │
│                                                                 │
│                                                                 │
│                                                                 │
│                                                                 │
│                                                                 │
│                                                                 │
│ ──────────────── Press ESC to continue ──────────────── NUM     │
└─────────────────────────────────────────────────────────────────┘
```

Figure A.6

The Modify Current Driver Set menu

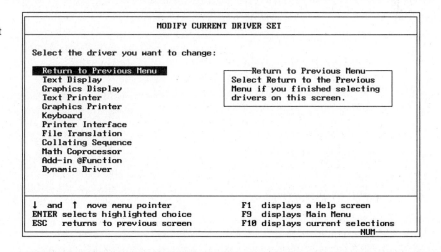

```
┌─────────────────────────────────────────────────────────────────┐
│                    MODIFY CURRENT DRIVER SET                      │
│                                                                   │
│   Select the driver you want to change:                           │
│                                                                   │
│   ▓Return to Previous Menu▓       ┌─Return to Previous Menu─┐      │
│    Text Display                   │ Select Return to the Previous │
│    Graphics Display               │ Menu if you finished selecting│
│    Text Printer                   │ drivers on this screen.       │
│    Graphics Printer               └──────────────────────────┘    │
│    Keyboard                                                       │
│    Printer Interface                                              │
│    File Translation                                               │
│    Collating Sequence                                             │
│    Math Coprocessor                                               │
│    Add-in @Function                                               │
│    Dynamic Driver                                                 │
│                                                                   │
│   ↓ and ↑ move menu pointer        F1  displays a Help screen     │
│   ENTER selects highlighted choice F9  displays Main Menu         │
│   ESC   returns to previous screen F10 displays current selections│
│                                                              NUM  │
└─────────────────────────────────────────────────────────────────┘
```

After making your choice, you can return to the previous menu, Change Selected Equipment. This menu includes two items that you may need to use before saving the modified driver set and exiting the Install program. The Switch Mouse Buttons option in the Change Selected Equipment menu allows you to make your mouse left-handed instead of right-handed. You use the Add New Drivers to the Library option when you purchase new equipment that comes with its own 1-2-3 drivers.

Figure A.7

Choices for
Collating Sequence

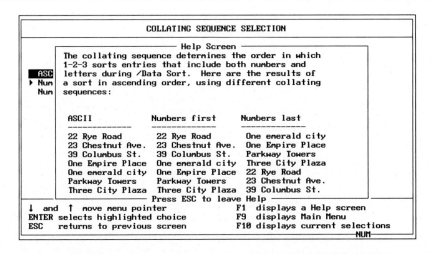

When you are ready to store your changes, press F10 to check the current selections, and then select Save the Current Driver Set. You will be prompted with the name of the driver set file that is current, but you can change the name to store the new settings in a new file. The extension .SET is automatically added to the file name you provide. If you enter the file extension yourself, Install gives you an error message.

If the changes you have made require additional font information to be created for use by Wysiwyg, you get the chance to choose from Basic, Medium, or Extended font sets. The Extended set takes the most time to generate but gives you the widest choice of fonts. The Basic set is quick but limits the number of font sizes you can use in Wysiwyg. To avoid generating font information, you can press F9 to get to the main menu and select End Install. If you later decide you need the font information, you can choose Specify Wysiwyg Options from the main menu.

APPENDIX B

Working with Other Programs

This appendix discusses how to share information between 1-2-3 Release 2.3 and other programs. These include products from Lotus as well as "foreign" programs such as dBASE. There are also tips on using 1-2-3 Release 2.3 on a network.

Importing and Exporting

Although 1-2-3 Release 2.3 is a powerful spreadsheet, database manager, and graphing program, it is not the only program that is used for these tasks. At times you may want to export data from 1-2-3 Release 2.3, making it available to other programs, or import data prepared by a program other than 1-2-3 Release 2.3.

The WK1 Format

When you save a worksheet in 1-2-3 Release 2.3, it is stored in a file with the .WK1 extension. This file consists of the actual values, formulas, and labels that you have entered in the worksheet, plus any print and graph settings you have created. The arrangement of this information in the file is known as the *file format*. Over the years, the WK1 format has become something of a standard among computer programs. Quattro Pro, Excel, and Paradox can read and write information using the WK1 format. Popular Macintosh programs like FileMaker Pro and Excel can also import and export data in the WK1 format. Some programs, such as WordPerfect, cannot create WK1 files but can import data stored in WK1 format.

For this reason, you will often be able to make information from your 1-2-3 worksheets available to other users with little or no special effort. However, there are some limitations involved in using the WK1 format. When sharing data between two different programs, the principle of lowest common denominator tends to apply. For example, many entries in a 1-2-3 worksheet may in fact be formulas. If the program that is reading your WK1 file cannot read formulas as formulas, it may translate those formulas to values.

In addition, the WK1 format has been in existence since Release 2.0 of 1-2-3, but new features have been added to 1-2-3 since then. For example, 1-2-3 Release 2.3 allows you to create link references between worksheets. These are stored in the WK1 format, but unless the program reading the WK1 file can reproduce a worksheet link, the link will be lost. Before sharing files with another program via the WK1 format, you should check the program's documentation for information about any 1-2-3 features that may be lost in translation.

Sharing Data with Other Lotus Products

You may want to share data with users of other Lotus products, such as Symphony, or a different version of 1-2-3. Table B.1 lists the Lotus products and the file extensions they normally use.

Table A.1 **Lotus Products and Their Default File Formats**

1-2-3 Release 1A	WKS
1-2-3 Release 2.0	WK1
1-2-3 Release 2.2	WK1
1-2-3 Release 3.0	WK3
1-2-3 Release 3.1	WK3
1-2-3/G	WG1
Symphony Release 1	WRK
Symphony Release 1.1	WR1
Symphony Release 2.0	WR1
Symphony Release 2.2	WR1

Although not all Lotus products use WK1 as their default format, all versions of Symphony and all versions of 1-2-3 after Release 1A allow you to save worksheets as WK1 files. This means that the files can be read by Release 2.3. You can also share files you create in Release 2.3 with products like 1-2-3 Release 3.0, 1-2-3/G, and Symphony because they can read the WK1 format.

Importing Release 3.0 and 1-2-3/G Files   1-2-3 Release 2.3 can only read worksheets created in Release 3.0 or 1-2-3/G if those worksheets have been saved in WK1 format. There are also some practical limitations involved with this form of sharing. If you use 1-2-3 Release 2.3 to read a WK1 file created in 1-2-3 Release 3.0 or 1-2-3/G, labels are truncated after 240 characters (this number includes the label prefix). Functions that do not exist in Release 2.3 appear in the worksheet as add-in functions, and are displayed as @?. If the original formula had arguments, a list of arguments follows the question mark. Cells containing these functions evaluate to NA since 1-2-3 Release 2.3 cannot evaluate them or convert them to their original values.

Formulas imported to 1-2-3 Release 2.3 from Release 3.0 or 1-2-3/G may contain more than 240 characters. However, if you edit such formulas, they are automatically truncated after 240 characters. 1-2-3 Release 2.3 can handle link references to other worksheets, but not references to other worksheets within formulas. If you read in a Release 3 or 1-2-3/G worksheet that contains formulas that reference other files, they will appear like this:

```
'@@("<<filename>>range").
```

While Release 3.0 and 1-2-3/G can accept formulas that contain undefined range names, Release 2.3 cannot. Undefined range names in imported worksheets appear in Release 2.3 as ERR. For example, the formula @SUM(SALES) becomes @SUM(ERR) in Release 2.3 if the range name SALES is not defined.

When using 1-2-3 Release 3.0 to save a WK3 file as a WK1 file, you need to consider how your data is organized, since Release 3.0 can create several worksheets within one file. If the WK3 file has data in only one worksheet, you can safely use File Save to store the file in WK1 format. If the WK3 file stores more than one worksheet in the file, you should use the Translate utility, described in a moment, to convert the file to WK1 format. The Translate utility creates a separate WK1 file for each worksheet in the WK3 file.

Macros written in Release 3.0 are generally compatible with Release 2.3. However, macros that include functions, keywords, or commands that are unique to Release 3.0 obviously cannot run properly in Release 2.3. Macros from Release 3.0 that use cell addresses that include the worksheet letter will not work. Macros that use @CHAR and @CODE with the Lotus Multibyte Character Set (LMBCS) characters or values will create Lotus International Character Set (LICS) characters or values in Release 2.3. Also note that Release 2.3 has a different number of items on some menus, and so macros that select menu items by using arrow commands will not be accurate. (You should always use letters to pick menu items, not the highlight-and-enter method.)

Exporting Data to 1-2-3 Release 3.0 and 1-2-3/G   You can use 1-2-3/G files in Release 2.3 by saving a WG1 file as a WK1 file. However, since 1-2-3/G contains features not available in any other release of 1-2-3, these features, together with associated data, may be lost when you save a WG1 worksheet as a .WK1 file. If a 1-2-3/G file does not include features unique to 1-2-3/G, you can save it in the Release 2.3 format by naming the file with the .WK1 extension when you use the File Save command. If the 1-2-3/G file contains data in more than one worksheet in the file, you must copy the data to a single worksheet in another file before you can save it as a WK1 file.

If you use 1-2-3 Release 3.0 to retrieve a WK1 file created by Release 2.3, you can save the file using its original WK1 format or convert it to a Release

3.0 file by saving it with the .WK3 extension. Macros written in Release 2.3 are generally compatible with Release 3.0. However, macros that include commands unique to Release 2.3 will not run properly in Release 3.0 (this includes some Graph options and some Wysiwyg commands). Macros that select menu options using arrow keys instead of letters may not work properly.

In 1-2-3/G you can retrieve and work with files created in Release 2.3. After working with the file, you can either save it in WK1 format or convert it to a 1-2-3/G file by saving it with the .WG1 extension. In 1-2-3/G, you can run macros created in Release 2.3, but if the macro contains commands that are not exactly the same in 1-2-3/G you should translate the commands into their 1-2-3/G equivalents before running the macro. You can do this by using the Utility Macros Translate command in 1-2-3/G.

Trading Files with Symphony   Release 2.3 lets you retrieve a WRK and WR1 file created in Symphony. However, when you retrieve the WRK or WR1 file, features unique to Symphony (such as multiple windows or database forms) are lost. 1-2-3 Release 2.3 cannot run macros created in Symphony. If you are using Symphony Release 2.0, you can retrieve and work with a file created in 1-2-3 Release 2.3. You can then save the file in its original WK1 format or convert it to a Symphony file by saving it with the .WR1 extension. Note that if you use 1-2-3 Release 2.3 with expanded memory, you can create a worksheet that is too large for Symphony to retrieve. If you plan on sharing worksheets with Symphony, restrict yourself to conventional memory in 1-2-3 Release 2.3.

The Translate Utility
1-2-3 Release 2.3 comes with a special program called Translate that can convert data files between different formats. You can run this program from the DOS prompt by entering **TRANS**. You can also run Translate from the 1-2-3 Access menu. When you load Translate, you see a screen like the one shown in Figure B.1, which lists all of the formats you can translate from.

When you pick a format from the FROM list, you are presented with a TO list that indicates which formats you can translate to. The TO list varies according to the format you choose in the FROM list. If you select 1-2-3 2 through 2.3 as the FROM format, you get the TO list shown in Figure B.2, which displays the formats into which you can convert your 1-2-3 Release 2.3 files.

When you have chosen your FROM and TO formats, you are usually presented with a set of informational notes. For example, suppose you want to translate from 1-2-3 Release 2.3 to dBASE III, converting your WK1 data to a DBF file. The Translate notes tell you that the entire file or range in your WK1 worksheet must be a database. The first row of the file or range must consist of field names that are label cells beginning with a letter. The second row must be the first data record, and each cell in this row must contain data or be formatted (avoiding the Scientific format, since there is no equivalent format in dBASE). The columns must be wide enough to display the data they contain in order to prevent the data from being truncated in the DBF file.

Figure A.1

The Translate FROM list

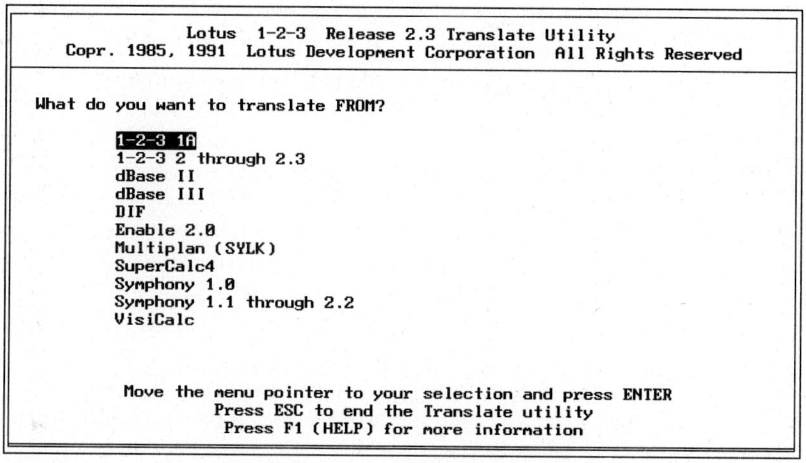

```
                    Lotus   1-2-3   Release 2.3  Translate Utility
          Copr. 1985, 1991  Lotus Development Corporation  All Rights Reserved

   What do you want to translate FROM?

         1-2-3 1A
         1-2-3 2 through 2.3
         dBase II
         dBase III
         DIF
         Enable 2.0
         Multiplan (SYLK)
         SuperCalc4
         Symphony 1.0
         Symphony 1.1 through 2.2
         VisiCalc


             Move the menu pointer to your selection and press ENTER
                     Press ESC to end the Translate utility
                     Press F1 (HELP) for more information
```

Figure A.2

The Translate TO list

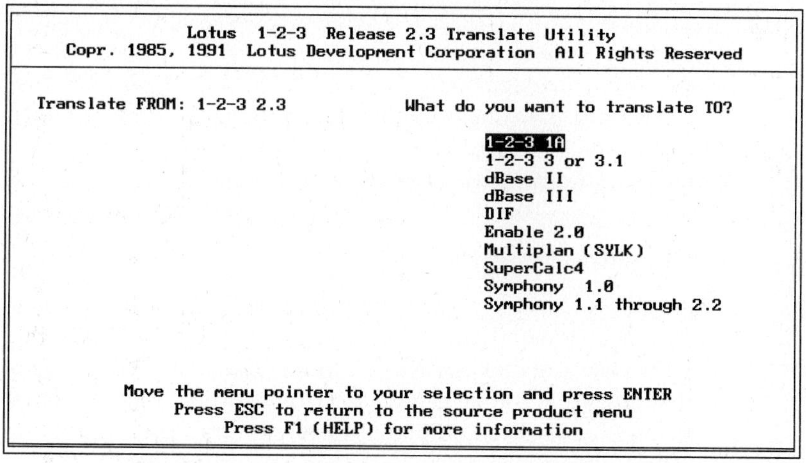

```
                    Lotus   1-2-3   Release 2.3  Translate Utility
          Copr. 1985, 1991  Lotus Development Corporation  All Rights Reserved

   Translate FROM: 1-2-3 2.3            What do you want to translate TO?

                                        1-2-3 1A
                                        1-2-3 3 or 3.1
                                        dBase II
                                        dBase III
                                        DIF
                                        Enable 2.0
                                        Multiplan (SYLK)
                                        SuperCalc4
                                        Symphony  1.0
                                        Symphony 1.1 through 2.2


             Move the menu pointer to your selection and press ENTER
                   Press ESC to return to the source product menu
                     Press F1 (HELP) for more information
```

There may be several information screens before you come to the file selection screen, which is shown in Figure B.3. You press Enter to see each screen of notes in turn or press Escape to go directly to the next step: choosing the source file you want to translate from the list provided. You can only select one file at a time from the list.

Figure A.3

The source file list

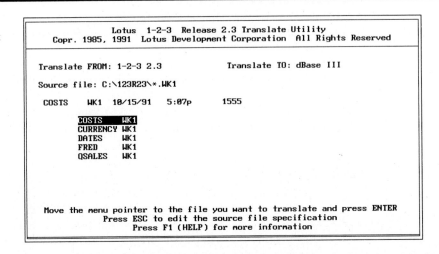

```
┌─────────────────────────────────────────────────────────────┐
│             Lotus  1-2-3  Release 2.3 Translate Utility      │
│       Copr. 1985, 1991  Lotus Development Corporation  All Rights Reserved │
│                                                             │
│   Translate FROM: 1-2-3 2.3           Translate TO: dBase III │
│                                                             │
│   Source file: C:\123R23\*.WK1                              │
│                                                             │
│   COSTS    WK1  10/15/91    5:07p       1555                │
│                                                             │
│           ┌COSTS    WK1┐                                    │
│            CURRENCY WK1                                      │
│            DATES    WK1                                      │
│            FRED     WK1                                      │
│            QSALES   WK1                                      │
│                                                             │
│                                                             │
│      Move the menu pointer to the file you want to translate and press ENTER │
│             Press ESC to edit the source file specification │
│                 Press F1 (HELP) for more information        │
└─────────────────────────────────────────────────────────────┘
```

In some translations, such as the one from 1-2-3 Release 2.3 to dBASE III, after you have selected the file you must choose between translating the entire file or just a range of cells within the file. The range can be stated as coordinates, such as A4..K89, or as a range name, provided you have assigned the name correctly in the WK1 file. After you have indicated what should be translated, the actual process is initiated. Since this can take time, a progress meter is provided on screen. When the process is completed, you may see a message box indicating any problems encountered during the translation. You might need to make changes to the source file and repeat the translation to remove the error. Note that Translate will warn you before overwriting an existing file of the same name.

Networking with 1-2-3

As personal computers proliferate, there is an increasing need to share information between them without recourse to printouts or floppy disks. It is now quite easy and inexpensive to connect PCs in a LAN, or local area network, that allows files to be shared electronically. A LAN also allows several users to share expensive equipment such as laser printers, modems, and high-capacity hard-disk drives with tape backup facilities.

LAN Organization

A LAN is a combination of hardware and software. The hardware is typically a set of cables; the software is a set of programs that control the flow of information through the cables. Some LANs require that you install an adapter board in your PC, and others use one of the ports you already have.

When you are connected to a LAN, you can access data files and program files on another PC. Other users may also be able to access your files. Since such an arrangement involves considerable cooperation and consensus, someone is usually appointed LAN manager.

The LAN manager is responsible for installing software on the LAN and issuing instructions to users. There is a special network edition of 1-2-3 Release 2.3 that contains full details of network installation. This version of the program can be shared by multiple users who all load the same program files. You should not install the single-user version for this type of network use.

File Reservations

If you are using 1-2-3 on a network where data files are shared, you should be aware of the File Admin Reservation commands. Each file has a *reservation* on it that prevents more than one person from saving changes in the same file at the same time. Only the user who has the file reservation can save changes to the file, even though several users may load the file at the same time.

The File Admin Reservation commands, Get and Release, let users on a network control the reservation. When you retrieve a worksheet that nobody else is using, you have the reservation. If you do not need to save changes to the file and think that other users might need to alter the file contents, you can use the Release command to make the reservation available to others. If you retrieve a file for which someone else already has the reservation, you will see the message RO in the status line. This stands for read-only, indicating that you can work with the file but cannot store it under its original name. RO appears only when someone else has the reservation.

If you are working on a file and do not have the reservation, you can use the Get command to request the reservation. You will be given the reservation if it is currently available and if the file has not been changed since you retrieved it. The RO indicator will disappear and you will be able to save changes in the file under its original name.

If you do not want other people to access your files, be sure to save them in an area that other users cannot access, such as in a private directory or on your local hard disk.

A P P E N D I X   C

A Directory of Macro Commands

Chapter 14 explained how to use macro commands to create macro-driven spreadsheet applications. However, that chapter did not cover every macro command. This appendix reviews all of the macro commands, detailing their syntax and arguments and, in some cases, illustrating how they are applied.

Macro Command Syntax

1-2-3's macro commands can be categorized in several ways. Some do not have arguments, while some do. Both types include a key word in braces. (Braces are recognized as label indicators by 1-2-3.) The format of the nonargument commands is simply a key word enclosed in braces, as in {RETURN}. Subroutine calls have a similar structure, except that the characters inside the braces represent a macro name instead of a key word.

The format of the commands that use arguments consists of the key word followed by a blank space and a list of one or more arguments separated by commas. As with function arguments, no spaces are allowed between or within arguments. The entire statement, complete with arguments, is enclosed in curly braces.

Screen and Response Commands

You can employ macro screen and response commands to control the updating of the display screen and the 1-2-3 control panel. The macro commands in this group also allow you to customize the mode indicator and to give audible feedback to the user.

The {BEEP} Command

The {BEEP} command produces a sound from your computer's speaker, somewhat like the one 1-2-3 makes when you press an invalid key (such as Backspace in READY mode). The syntax for the {BEEP} command is

```
{BEEP number}
```

where *number* is an optional argument that you can use to affect the pitch of the sound. The *number* argument can have any value from 1 to 4; when no number is specified, 1, the lowest pitch, is the default value.

You can use the beep to alert the operator to an error, indicate that you expect input, periodically show that a macro is still functioning during a lengthy set of instructions, or signify the conclusion of a step. Try using several beeps of a different pitch to really catch the user's attention, and to distinguish between actions. (Try tones 1,1,2,2,3,3,2—this produces "Twinkle Twinkle Little Star" on some systems.)

The {BORDERSOFF} and {BORDERSON} Commands

The {BORDERSOFF} command, which takes no argument, turns off the border around the worksheet, as well as the column lettering and row numbering. This is helpful when you want the user to have as few distractions as possible—for example, when entering data. 1-2-3 automatically restores the frame when the macro is completed. You can use the {BORDERSON} command to restore the frame during macro execution. These two commands are identical to the {FRAMEOFF} and {FRAMEON} commands.

The {FRAMEOFF} and {FRAMEON} Commands

The {FRAMEOFF} command, which takes no argument, turns off the frame around the worksheet, as well as the column lettering and row numbering. Again, this is helpful when you want the user to have as few distractions as possible—for example, when entering data. 1-2-3 automatically restores the frame when the macro is completed. You can use the {FRAMEON} command to restore the frame during macro execution. These two commands are identical to the {BORDERSOFF} and {BORDERSON} commands.

The {GRAPHOFF} and {GRAPHON} Commands

You can use the {GRAPHON} command to display graphs. You can use the function key equivalent, {GRAPH}, in a macro to display the current graph, but it pauses the macro while the graph is displayed. The {GRAPHON} command allows the macro to continue and keeps the graph displayed until one of the following is encountered:

- A {GRAPHOFF} command

- Another {GRAPHON} command

- An {INDICATE} command

- A {?} command

- Any other command that displays a prompt, including {GETLABEL}, {GETNUMBER}, {MENUCALL}, {MENUBRANCH}, /XL, /XM, and /XN

All of the above cancel the {GRAPHON} command and restore the worksheet.

The {GRAPHON} command produces a full-screen display of the current graph. The {GRAPHON} command with the optional name argument produces a full-screen display of the named graph using the current graph settings, as in:

```
{GRAPHON PIE-CHART}
```

With the nodisplay argument, you can use the {GRAPHON} command to make a named graph current without actually displaying it, as in

```
{GRAPHON PIE-CHART,nodisplay}
```

One handy use of {GRAPHON} is to create a slide show, as in the following example, which shows three graphs at 3-second intervals:

```
{GRAPHON BUDGET}
{WAIT @NOW+@TIME(0,0,3)}
{GRAPHON REVENUE}
{WAIT @NOW+@TIME(0,0,3)}
{GRAPHON EXPENSES}
{WAIT @NOW+@TIME(0,0,3)}
{GRAPHOFF}
```

The {INDICATE} Command

The {INDICATE} command allows you to customize the mode indicator in the lower-right corner of the screen—the indicator that normally says READY. The syntax for the {INDICATE} command is

```
{INDICATE string}
```

where *string* is any character string. Actually, the mode indicator can only be five characters long, so {INDICATE} will use only the first five characters of the string. You can blank out the indicator by using an empty string, as in {INDICATE ""}.

The indicator you establish with {INDICATE} remains in effect until you use the command again, either to establish a new setting or to return it to the default, READY. In fact, the {INDICATE} setting continues beyond the completion of a macro. Setting the indicator to PAUSE in a macro causes the word PAUSE to remain on the screen even if you return to READY mode. Use {INDICATE}, without any argument, to restore 1-2-3's normal indicator display at the conclusion of the macro.

The {INDICATE} command is useful if you have a series of menu selections for the operator to use. It can supply a string reflecting the menu selection and provide positive feedback as to the user's selection. For example, you can insert the command {INDICATE "SORT"} near the beginning of a macro that performs a sort operation. The user can then see that sort has been selected.

The {PANELOFF} and {PANELON} Commands

The {PANELOFF} and {PANELON} commands control the redrawing of the control panel, the upper and lower areas of the screen that normally show you the progress of an action or command. The syntax for the {PANEL-OFF} command is simply

    {PANELOFF}

The {PANELON} command restores the default setting, instructing 1-2-3 to update the control panel with each instruction executed. Its syntax is

    {PANELON}

These commands have no arguments.

You can use {PANELOFF} and {PANELON} to temporarily obscure the details of a macro's execution. After a macro reads the {PANELOFF} command, the entries on the input line are not visible as they are typed by the macro. When the macro reads {PANELON}, the normal display is restored. These commands were intended to control the annoying screen jitters that occurred when 1-2-3 executed macro instructions, particularly those involving menu choices. This is less of a problem now since the menu equivalents bypass menu selection. The {PANELOFF} and {PANELON} commands are still useful if you do not want the operator to see the macro code. Even if a user invokes DEBUG to slow down the operation of the macro, the control panel will not be updated while {PANELOFF} is in effect.

The {WINDOWSOFF} and {WINDOWSON} Commands
The {WINDOWSOFF} command freezes the entire screen, except for the control panel. Its syntax is

    {WINDOWSOFF}

The {WINDOWSON} instruction returns the normal mode of screen updating. Its syntax is

    {WINDOWSON}

Neither command uses an argument. Like the panel commands, the windows commands reduce the flicker that occurs on the screen with some macro instructions. They can also speed execution of long macros, since 1-2-3 does not have to redraw the screen every time the macro moves the cursor or changes data. You can use {PANELOFF} and {WINDOWSOFF} together with {INDICATE "WAIT"} to display the WAIT message and simply suspend further screen changes until a macro is complete. Of course, you should use {WINDOWSON} near the end of a macro to have the screen updated with the current results.

Interactive Macro Commands

When you want the user to have input during a macro's execution, you turn to the interactive macro commands. These commands can streamline data entry and add flexibility to macro designs.

The {?} Command

The {?} command, one of the most convenient and powerful of the macro commands, allows the operator to enter information from the keyboard. This command has no arguments and has the simple syntax

```
{?}
```

You place this command at any point in a macro where you need to obtain information from the operator. After a macro encounters a {?} command, program control is handed to the user, who can type a label or number, make a menu selection, or highlight an area of the spreadsheet. As soon as the user presses Enter, the macro resumes control. For this reason, the {?} is followed by an Enter (~) to actually enter or confirm the user's input.

One disadvantage of {?} is that the user can access the menu system and destructive options as long as he or she does not press Enter. For this reason, some people consider {?} better suited to personal macros rather than applications designed for inexperienced users. If you want to prompt the user for specific types of input, {GETNUMBER} and {GETLABEL} are more useful.

The {GET} Command

The {GET} command is designed to accept the entry of a single character from the keyboard. The syntax for the {GET} command is

```
{GET location}
```

where *location* is the storage location for the single character entered from the keyboard. Thus you could use {GET ANSWER} to place the response letter Y or N into the cell named ANSWER. The response to GET can be any key, letter, number, or function key. This command is yet another option to consider when you need to incorporate keyboard input in a macro. For example, you could use the following to prompt for a single-letter piece of information:

```
Type Y/N
{GET ANSWER}
{ESC}
```

The text "Type Y/N" will appear on the input line. The next character typed will be placed in ANSWER. The {ESC} command will then clear the input line.

The {GETLABEL} Command

You use the {GETLABEL} command to handle the entry of a label from the keyboard in response to a prompt message. It has the following syntax

```
{GETLABEL prompt-message,location}
```

The *prompt-message* argument is a word or words. The *location* is the cell into which the label is placed when the user presses Enter. For example, you might use

```
{GETLABEL Type product name and press Enter ,PROD}
```

to produce the following prompt on the second line of the screen when the macro runs:

```
Type product name and press Enter
```

When the user presses Enter, what he or she has typed is placed in the cell called PROD. Note that the space between the message text "Enter" and the comma used as the argument separator creates the space between the text and the cursor when the command is executed. The *prompt-message* must be enclosed in double quotation marks if it uses one of these characters:

```
;    :    .
```

For example, if you want to use a colon at the end of the message text, the command statement would look like this:

```
{GETLABEL "Type product name and press Enter: ",PROD}
```

Note that the space is within the quotes and there is no space between the quotes, the argument separator, and the *location* argument. In addition, note that the response to {GETLABEL} is placed in the location cell as a *label*. The {GETNUMBER} command handles input that must be stored as numbers.

The {GETNUMBER} Command

The {GETNUMBER} command is similar to {GETLABEL} and is used to elicit numeric information from the user in response to a prompt message. The syntax for {GETNUMBER} is

```
{GETNUMBER prompt-message, location}
```

The rules for the *prompt-message* argument are the same as for {GET-LABEL}.

The elements of the prompt text string can be stored in a separate cell and referenced if you use a string formula to construct the macro. When used with a whole series of data cells, the formula can even determine whether to use the {GETLABEL} or {GETNUMBER} command. Thus the formula

```
+"{GET"&@IF(@CELL("type",D3)="v","NUMBER","LABEL")
```

returns the characters {GETNUMBER} if cell D3 contains a value, and {GETLABEL} if it contains a label. You can combine that with a formula that produces the prompt message from a label in cell C3:

```
+"{GET"&@IF(@CELL("type",D3)="v","NUMBER","LABEL)"&"
"&C3&"? ,D3}"
```

This formula will give you the {GETLABEL} prompt "Last Name?" if cell C3 contains the label Last Name and D3 contains a label. The formula gives you a {GETNUMBER} prompt "Age?" if C3 contains the label Age and D3 contains a value. This is very convenient when you have a series of labels for a column of mixed number and label data and want data entry macro prompts for each one.

If the user enters a label in response to a {GETNUMBER} prompt, the response in the location cell is ERR. This makes for a convenient method of trapping entry errors. If you follow a {GETNUMBER} command with an {IF} command that tests the value of the @ISERR function, you can direct the flow of the macro to an instruction in another cell if the user does not enter a number, as in

```
{GETNUMBER Age? ,ANSWER}
{IF @ISERR(ANSWER)}{BEEP}{BRANCH MESSAGE}
```

where the macro flow goes to MESSAGE when the contents of ANSWER are @ERR. Of course, MESSAGE could be a loop back to the {GETNUM-BER} command, but it could also be an error message display routine.

The {LOOK} Command
The syntax for the {LOOK} command is

```
{LOOK location}
```

The {LOOK} command is similar to {GET}, except with {LOOK} the operator can type the entry before the macro execution reaches the {LOOK} command and the macro will still find it. This is because {LOOK} checks the keyboard buffer for data and records the buffer's first character as a label in the location specified in the command. If the keyboard buffer is blank when the {LOOK} command is executed, an empty string is entered in the location cell. Whereas the {GET} instruction suspends a macro's execution while waiting for a response, {LOOK} does not. This makes {LOOK} suitable for use in a loop where you want to give the user some time to respond before the application is aborted.

For example, in the following macro, called Reply, the user has 10 seconds to press a key. If a key is pressed, the macro branches to the code labeled Act2. If the user does not press a key within 10 seconds, the macro branches to the code called Act1. The branch to the code called Check makes the macro keep checking the keystroke buffer for the time period defined by Start+@TIME(0,0,10). This macro code uses two named ranges to hold the data required. The cell called Start holds the result of @NOW and the cell called Key holds the next keystroke.

```
Reply  {LET Start,@NOW}

Check  {LOOK Key}{IF Key=""}{IF @NOW>Start+@TIME(0,0,10){BRANCH Act2}

       {IF Key<>""}{BRANCH Act1}

       {BRANCH Check}
```

The {MENUBRANCH} Command

As you saw in Chapter 14, the {MENUBRANCH} command diverts macro flow to a set of cells into which you have placed the elements of a custom menu. The syntax for the {MENUBRANCH} command is

```
{MENUBRANCH location}
```

where *location* is the cell in the upper-left corner of the area used for menu storage.

Information for the customized menu must be organized according to certain rules. The top row of the menu area must contain the words used for the menu items, entered one per cell, in contiguous columns. Each of these words should begin with a different character, just as in 1-2-3's menus, if you want to be able to select a menu option by pressing the first letter of an item. (If you use menu items with the same first letters, 1-2-3 will pick the first one with that letter, starting from the left.) Menu selection words can be up to 55 characters long, but the longer the word, the wider the menu, and thus the more obtrusive it will be. You can have up to eight items in a menu and their total length, including delimiting spaces, cannot exceed the screen width.

The second row of the menu area contains the expanded description for each menu choice—this description will display at the top of the screen when you highlight the menu selection. These explanations are likely to exceed the width of the column into which they are entered, particularly as they will occupy contiguous columns—this may be unsightly, but it will not affect macro performance.

The third row of the menu area contains the actual macro instructions for each menu choice. These instructions begin in the cell immediately under the description. They can extend down the column or branch to a subroutine. The

subroutine approach makes for cleaner design, since macro instructions in contiguous columns can be hard to read, edit, and annotate.

The column to the right of the last menu option must be left blank to tell 1-2-3 that there are no more options.

The {MENUCALL} Command

The {MENUCALL} command works like {MENUBRANCH}. However, a macro using {MENUBRANCH} ends when the code for the selected option completes, whereas a {MENUCALL} returns control to the statement following it in the main code for the macro, and execution resumes at that location. This locks the user into the menu system, returning to a menu when the action chosen from the menu is complete. The syntax for the {MENUCALL} command is

```
{MENUCALL location}
```

where *location* is a cell address or block name that represents the upper-left cell in the area for menu storage. The rules for the menu building are the same as those for {MENUBRANCH}.

The {WAIT} Command

The {WAIT} command is the hold-up command—it enables you to stop the execution of a macro until a stated time. Its syntax is

```
{WAIT time serial number}
```

where *time serial number* is a decimal value that represents the serial time number for the time of day you want execution to resume. Suppose you want a user to read a lengthy instruction on the screen. You need to pause the macro long enough for this information to be read, say 45 seconds. You can accomplish this with the following instruction:

```
{WAIT @NOW+@TIME(0,0,45)}
```

The wait value is computed by adding a time value to the value returned by @NOW, resulting in a measured delay. The instruction adds the 45 seconds to the current time and waits until that time is reached before continuing execution. The mode indicator will say WAIT while 1-2-3 is waiting.

Program Flow Macros

Normally a macro is read line by line, proceeding down a column from the cell that bears the macro name. However, you can use the program flow macro commands to redirect flow in many different ways, branching to other locations or calling subroutines.

The {BRANCH} Command

The {BRANCH} command transfers the flow of a macro to a new location. Its syntax is

```
{BRANCH location}
```

where *location* is a cell address or block name that contains the next instruction to be executed. The {BRANCH} command is often combined with the {IF} command to change the flow of execution based on a test condition. The classic example of this combination is the loop controller, seen here in a macro called CENTER that turns a column of values into a centered label:

```
{EDIT}{HOME}^~{DOWN}
{IF @CELLPOINTER("type")="b"}{QUIT}
{BRANCH CENTER}
```

After the edit is performed, the macro moves the cell selector down one cell. The {IF} command checks the cell currently occupied by the cell selector and returns the cell's "type." If the type is b for blank (as opposed to v for value or l for label), the macro will quit. If the cell is not blank, the macro will branch back to its beginning, the macro called CENTER.

Remember that {BRANCH} controls macro flow, not cell selector positioning. Do not confuse {BRANCH}, which redirects the macro's execution flow but does not move the cell selector, with {GOTO}, which repositions the cell selector without affecting the macro's flow.

The {DEFINE} Command

When you use a subroutine in a macro, you can provide arguments for the subroutine. You then need to provide the subroutine with locations for the arguments—cells in which they can be stored. You do this with the {DEFINE} command, which has the syntax

```
{DEFINE location}
```

where *location* is a cell coordinate or a range name. (The upper-left cell will be used if the location argument is a multicell range.)

Suppose you want to call a subroutine named ROUND that rounds the number in the current cell and then moves down to the next cell. The code for ROUND might look like this:

```
{EDIT}{HOME}@ROUND({END},2){DOWN}
```

if the rounding is to two decimal places. The line of macro code that calls this subroutine in this case is simply

```
{ROUND}
```

However, suppose you decide to supply the number of decimal places for the rounding operation when you call the ROUND routine. You could use this code to supply a value of 2 for the decimal place:

```
{ROUND 2}
```

For a subroutine to use arguments passed to it like this, it *must* begin with a {DEFINE} statement that names the arguments. The modified ROUND macro would then be arranged as follows, where PLACES is a named cell into which the {DEFINE} statement places the subroutine argument:

```
ROUND {DEFINE PLACES}
      {EDIT}{HOME}@ROUND({END},
PLACES
      ){DOWN}
```

You can also use multiple subroutine arguments. Simply place a space between the command and the first argument, and separate further arguments by commas. For example, the subroutine cell to pass the three arguments required for a loan payment calculation might look like this:

```
{PAYMENT 2500,0.01,36)
```

The first line of the PAYMENT subroutine could then be

```
{DEFINE PRINCIPAL,INTEREST,TERM}
```

which places the three values in cells called PRINCIPAL, INTEREST, and TERM. Calls to subroutines and {DEFINE} statements can include up to 31 arguments, separated by commas.

The {DEFINE} command stores arguments as labels. If you need to store a subroutine argument as a value, add the :value argument, which can be abbreviated as :v, like this:

```
{DEFINE 2500:v,0.01:v,36:v)
```

Note that each use of the :v argument counts towards the maximum of 31 arguments allowed by {DEFINE}. You can use a further argument of :string or :s to force an argument to be stored as a label, even if it appears to be a number.

The {DISPATCH} Command

The {DISPATCH} command is used to direct macro flow to another cell, specified within the command's location argument. Its syntax is

```
{DISPATCH location}
```

so that the command

```
{DISPATCH Action}
```

directs macro flow to the range name or cell address specified in the cell called Action. This can be varied according to conditions in the worksheet. For example, the following code directs macro flow to a cell called Good if the value of Profit is greater than 0:

```
{IF Profit>0}{LET Fork,"Good"}
{IF Profit=0}{LET Fork,"Even"}
{IF Profit<0}{LET Fork,"Poor"}
{DISPATCH Fork}
```

The value of Profit determines the range name entered in the cell called Fork, which is then used as the argument for {DISPATCH}.

The {FOR} Command
You use the {FOR} command to control repetition of a task by means of the following arguments:

```
{FOR counter,start,stop,step,subroutine}
```

The subroutine task is repeated a number of times, based on the five arguments, which are defined as follows:

- *Counter* is the location of a cell that records the number of times the task has been repeated.

- *Start* is the starting number to be placed in the counter location.

- *Stop* is the total number of times the task is to be repeated.

- *Step* is the amount to increment the counter after each iteration.

- *Subroutine* is the task to be repeated.

For example, the following macro code provides for six repetitions of the subroutine called INPUT:

```
{FOR COUNT,1,6,1,INPUT}
```

Note that the cell named COUNT is used to keep track of the progress of the {FOR} operation. Chapter 14 gives a full example of the {FOR} command. The {FOR} command can be interrupted by the {FORBREAK} command.

The {FORBREAK} Command
Use the {FORBREAK} command, which takes no argument, to interrupt a {FOR} operation. Typically, you will place the {FORBREAK} command in

the subroutine. For example, the following {FOR} statement runs the INPUT routine six times and then branches to the SORT routine:

```
{FOR COUNT,1,10,1,INPUT}
{BRANCH SORT}
```

The following INPUT routine has the user type a label, which is entered in the current cell.

```
{GETLABEL "Enter product name: ",@CELLPOINTER("address")}
{IF @CELLPOINTER(contents)=""}{FORBREAK}
{DOWN}
```

After the label is entered, the cell pointer is moved down one row and the operation is repeated, up to six times. But the repetition ends if the user presses Enter without typing a label. The {FORBREAK} command returns macro control to the line after the {FOR} command, in this case the branch to SORT.

The {IF} Command

Like the @IF function, the {IF} macro command chooses between two possibilities. The syntax of the {IF} command is

```
{IF condition}action1
action2
```

The *condition* argument is a conditional formula, such as A1>100, @CELL("type",A1)="b", or @CELLPOINTER("type")="v". You can use this command to repeat an operation if a certain condition exists, but quit if it does not. For example, you could control a looping macro called \C that centers labels like this:

```
{EDIT}{HOME}^
{IF @CELLPOINTER("type")="b"}{QUIT}
{BRANCH \C}
```

In this case, *action1* terminates the macro while *action2* is the branch that causes the macro to repeat. The @CELLPOINTER function causes the macro to quit if the current cell is blank. This allows the macro to proceed down the column of labels until there are no more labels left to center.

The {ONERROR} Command

You can trap serious errors during macro execution using the {ONERROR} command. Serious errors return you to READY mode—they are not simple

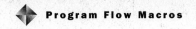

macro syntax errors that result in the macro error box. The {ONERROR} command has the following syntax:

```
{ONERROR branch,message}
```

Both arguments are locations, preferably named ranges. The *branch* location is the macro code that you want 1-2-3 to branch to when a serious error occurs. The *message* location is an optional argument, a place into which 1-2-3 will write the error message. This allows you to use the message in your macro code.

The {QUIT} Command

The {QUIT} command is used to terminate a macro. This command has no argument: You simply place {QUIT} where you want to stop the macro execution. Although it can be said that macros automatically stop when they get to a blank cell, this is not strictly true. If a macro has been called by {*subroutine*} or {MENUCALL}, 1-2-3 returns to the calling point when it gets to a blank line. Placing a {QUIT} command at the end of a macro called by a subroutine ends both the subroutine macro and the one that called it. Assigning the {QUIT} command to the Quit option in a {MENUCALL} menu provides the user with a way out of the menu. {QUIT} is also useful at the end of an {IF} command. When the {IF} condition evaluates as True, the macro, including all subroutines, terminates.

The {RESTART} Command

The {RESTART} command cancels the return sequence of a set of nested subroutines so that macro control is not automatically passed back to the calling macro when the subroutine ends. Because {RESTART} cancels all pointers to higher-level routines, macro execution will terminate at the end of the subroutine unless the instructions following {RESTART} transfer macro control elsewhere. The {RESTART} command has no arguments.

The {RETURN} Command

The {RETURN} command is used to return from a subroutine to the calling routine, and has no arguments. Used in conjunction with {MENUCALL} and {*subroutine*} this command has the same effect on macro flow as a blank cell. When 1-2-3 reads {RETURN} in a called subroutine, it leaves the current subroutine, returns to the calling macro or subroutine, and performs the instructions beneath the one that called the subroutine.

The {*subroutine*} Command

The {*subroutine*} command calls a specific macro subroutine. Its syntax is

```
{subroutine argument1,argument2,argumentN}
```

where *subroutine* is a macro name, and the arguments (and there can be many of them) are values or strings to be passed to the subroutine. These arguments must have corresponding entries in a {DEFINE} statement at the beginning of the subroutine you are calling.

The {*subroutine*} is a great way to reuse common sections of macro code in a spreadsheet and to spread out macro sections for clarity. Remember that unless the macro called by the {*subroutine*} ends in {QUIT}, program flow returns to the line below the {*subroutine*} command.

The {BREAKOFF} and {BREAKON} Commands

The {BREAKOFF} command is used to disable the Ctrl-Break key function, thereby preventing the interruption of a macro. Its syntax is

```
{BREAKOFF}
```

with no arguments. The {BREAKON} command reinstates the Ctrl-Break key's function so that you can again press Ctrl-Break to interrupt a macro. Its syntax is

```
{BREAKON}
```

with no arguments.

Normally, Ctrl-Break can be used to stop a macro. When you press Ctrl-Break, the mode indicator will change to ERROR. You can then press Escape to return to READY mode. However, when you want to ensure the integrity of an automated application by maintaining control throughout the operator's use of the worksheet, you will want to disable the Ctrl-Break feature by placing {BREAKOFF} in your macro. Be sure you have tested the macro before doing this; the only way to stop a macro that contains an infinite loop and {BREAKOFF} is by turning off or rebooting the machine.

You can disable the Ctrl-Break function during part of a macro and then restore its operation for a later section, such as printing or data entry. In any case, the Ctrl-Break function is automatically restored at the end of a macro.

Data Entry Commands

There are several macro commands that automate aspects of data entry. These include the {FORM}, {APPENDBELOW}, and {APPENDRIGHT} commands. While fairly complex to use, these commands offer an alternative to designing your own methods of adding records to databases and restricting user input. This section also describes the Range Input command, which can be effective within data entry macros.

The Range Input Command

If someone who is not well versed in spreadsheets is entering data for you, you can construct an input form to assist them. You can do this with the {FORM} command, described in a moment, or the Input command on the Range menu. When using Range Input, the first step is to protect the entire spreadsheet by issuing the Worksheet Global Protection command. This prevents any data from being altered. Now you can use the Range Unprot command to unprotect those cells where the data will be entered or edited. When you are ready to have someone enter data, you issue the Range Input command and highlight a range of the worksheet that includes the unprotected cells. When you press Enter, this area becomes the data input range. User access is now limited to any unprotected cells in the range.

Although the mode indicator will say READY, the cursor-movement keys will not take you outside of the defined range of cells and will only move to unprotected cells within the range. You can type data and press Enter or edit data with F2 and reenter it. The program menu is not available, so typing a / begins a new label instead of activating the menu.

It is very easy to override the Range Input command. You simply press Esc or Enter while the INPUT message is displayed. In fact, the command is most effective when used in macros that further control the user's access to keys.

The {FORM} Command

The {FORM} command is complex but is also extremely useful when you are designing applications for others to use. It temporarily suspends macro execution to allow data entry and editing in unprotected cells within a specified input location. Its syntax is

```
{FORM input-location,[call-table],[include-list],[exclude-list]}
```

Input-location is a range of any size that contains unprotected cells. This is the range where you enter data. The input location cannot include hidden columns and must include at least one unprotected cell. When the {FORM} command is executed, the cell pointer is placed in the upper-left unprotected cell in the *input-location* range. The macro is suspended and 1-2-3 waits for you to press a key. The mode indicator will say READY.

Call-table is an optional two-column range that assigns tasks to certain keys. Each cell in the first column contains one or more key names. Each adjacent cell in the second column contains a set of macro instructions to be performed when you press the corresponding key listed in the first column. For example, this call-table defines roles for Ins and Name (the F3 key):

```
{INS}   {APPENDBELOW CLIENT_DB,ENTRY}{BLANK ENTRY}{HOME}
{NAME}  {BRANCH CONTINUE}
```

Note that this call table is a four-cell range and all four cells must be included in the coordinates provided as the *call-table* argument.

Include-list is an optional range listing allowable keystrokes. You can specify any character key and any key name. Each cell in the range can contain one or more of the character keys as well as the key names listed at the end of this appendix. This list allows you to severely restrict what the user can type.

Exclude-list is another optional range, in this case listing unacceptable keystrokes. Each cell in the range can contain one or more keystrokes. 1-2-3 beeps when you press an excluded key.

In executing the {FORM} command, 1-2-3 uses only one list argument. If you specify an include list, do not specify an exclude list, and if you specify an exclude list, leave out the include list. If you specify both an include list and an exclude list, 1-2-3 uses the include list. To use an optional argument without using the ones that precede it, insert an extra comma (or default argument separator) as a placeholder. For example, to use a call table and an exclude list without an include list, use the following syntax:

```
{FORM input-location,call-table,,exclude-list}
```

Note that the *call-table*, *include-list*, and *exclude-list* arguments are case-sensitive. If the include list contains an uppercase *C*, but not a lowercase *c*, you can only enter uppercase *C*'s during the {FORM} command. Lowercase *c*'s are ignored. There should be no punctuation between the names of the keys listed in the call table, the include list, and the exclude list.

The {FORM} command is similar to the Range Input command, but the three optional arguments (*call-table*, *include-list*, and *exclude-list*) give you more control over user entries than you get with Range Input. When you issue the {FORM} command, 1-2-3 processes keystrokes exactly as it does during Range Input and you are actually placed in READY mode. To cancel the {FORM} command in READY mode, press Enter or Escape. 1-2-3 continues the macro at the instruction following the {FORM) command, and leaves the cell pointer where it was when you pressed Enter or Escape. If you use an include list, you must include tilde (~) and {ESC} in the list or you cannot use these keys to end the {FORM} command.

Consider the example shown in Figure C.1. The top half of the screen shows a data entry form used to enter clients in a database. Cells M1 through S8 have been named DAFORM. The only unprotected cells in this range are M4 through S4. The ENTRY macro that uses the {FORM} command begins with a {GOTO} command that positions the entry form on screen. Typically, the entry form will be located some distance from the macro code and the database, so a positioning action like this is appropriate. Then the {FORM} command is issued. The *input-location* is defined as DAFORM, M1..S8. The cell pointer is moved to M1, the upper-left unprotected cell in the range, and the mode indicator says READY, as shown in Figure C.1.

Note that the CMD indicator is still on, reminding you that a macro is still in effect. You can see that the *call-table* argument in this example is CKEYS, the four-cell range N14..O15. This tells 1-2-3 what to do when the user presses either Ins or F3 (the Name key). Note that you *cannot* use the Range Name Labels Right command to name the call table, as it is not a single-cell range.

When the {FORM} command has been issued and the user presses a key, 1-2-3 looks to {FORM} for a *call table* argument. 1-2-3 then checks the first column of the call table. If the keystroke is listed, 1-2-3 executes the macro code in the second column. This is done as a subroutine so that when the code is completed, control returns to the {FORM} command. 1-2-3 then waits for another key. If you specified {ESC} or ~ in a call table subroutine, 1-2-3 suspends the {FORM} command and allows the user to select 1-2-3 keys and menus. If a keystroke that is not listed in *call table* is used, and the {FORM} command has an *include-list* argument, 1-2-3 checks the list. If the keystroke is in the include list, 1-2-3 performs the keystroke; otherwise, 1-2-3 simply beeps and ignores the keystroke.

Figure A.1

A data entry form

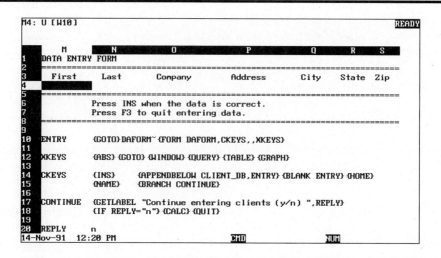

If the user presses a key that is not listed in *call table* and the {FORM} command has an exclude list, 1-2-3 checks the exclude list. If the keystroke is in the exclude list, 1-2-3 beeps and ignores the keystroke. If the keystroke is not in the exclude list, 1-2-3 performs the keystroke. This may simply mean that the character typed appears in the input line.

Putting {ESC} or ~ in a call table subroutine means that the user can move the cell pointer out of the unprotected cells of the input area and use all 1-2-3 keys and menus for the rest of the subroutine. When the call table subroutine ends, 1-2-3 moves the cell pointer to wherever it was when the call table subroutine started (unless the cell pointer is within the unprotected part of the input range when the subroutine ends, in which case 1-2-3 leaves the cell pointer where it is). 1-2-3 then reinstates use of keys as defined by the {FORM} command.

To end a macro from within a call table subroutine, use {RESTART} or {QUIT} in the subroutine. To end a {FORM} command from within a call table subroutine and continue the macro, use {FORMBREAK} to leave the {FORM} command and continue the macro at the instruction immediately following the {FORM} command.

In the example in Figure C.1, pressing Ins during the {FORM} command causes 1-2-3 to append the data in ENTRY to the database called CLIENT_DB, erase ENTRY, place the cell pointer in M4, and then return to the {FORM} command. (This block of code and the {APPENDBELOW} command in general are explained in the next section.) Pressing F3 during the {FORM} command tells 1-2-3 to branch to a subroutine called CONTINUE, which uses a {GETLABEL} command to ask whether the user wants to continue data entry. If the user enters n at the {GETLABEL} prompt, the {QUIT} command ends the {FORM} command (after issuing the {CALC} command to make sure the worksheet is up to date). Typing any other character at the {GETLABEL} prompt causes 1-2-3 to return to the {FORM} command since CONTINUE is called as a subroutine rather than a branch.

Note that the exclude list in Figure C.1 is called XKEYS and contains several key names, including {ABS} and {GOTO}. If you press any of these keys during the {FORM} command, 1-2-3 ignores the keystroke. Also note that if you use {FORM} from a macro library, the *input-location* argument must be a worksheet range. However, you can specify a *call-table*, *include-list*, and *exclude-list* argument from a macro library or the worksheet. You can also nest forms—that is, place one form within another form. You do this by making a {FORM} call from a key defined in the first {FORM} command. 1-2-3 allows nesting of up to eight forms.

The {FORMBREAK} Command
The {FORMBREAK} command ends a {FORM} command. Use {FORMBREAK} to leave the current form. The macro will continue at the command following the {FORM} command. Also use {FORMBREAK} to end a nested {FORM} command and return to the previous form. Only use {FORMBREAK} within a call table subroutine or a subroutine to which you transfer control from a call table subroutine with {BRANCH} or {DISPATCH}. If you use {FORMBREAK} without first using a {FORM} command, 1-2-3 ends the macro and displays an error.

The {APPENDBELOW} and {APPENDRIGHT} Commands

The {APPENDBELOW} and {APPENDRIGHT} commands are designed to automate the process of copying data into a named range, expanding the range to include the new information. The syntax for {APPENDBELOW} is

```
{APPENDBELOW target,source}
```

where *source* is a range of cells, the contents of which are copied to the rows immediately below the *target* range, which is then expanded to include the new data. The syntax for {APPENDRIGHT} is

```
{APPENDRIGHT target,source}
```

where *source* is a range of cells, the contents of which are copied to the columns immediately to the right of the *target* range, which is then expanded to include the new data.

If any of the cells in the source range are formulas, they are converted to values in the target range. Both commands will fail if their completion would overwrite data in the worksheet, or if the cells below or to the right of the target range are protected.

Figure C.1 shows a typical use of the {APPENDBELOW} command in the context of a data entry form. The {APPENDBELOW} command is attached to the {INS} or Insert key. When the user presses Insert, the following code is executed

```
{APPENDBELOW CLIENT_DB,ENTRY}{BLANK ENTRY}{HOME}
```

The contents of the range called ENTRY (M4..S4) are copied to the row below the range called CLIENT_DB and 1-2-3 automatically expands CLIENT_DB to include the new row. The macro continues by blanking the ENTRY range so it can be used for the new record, and moving the cell pointer to the first cell by using the Home key. (Because the {FORM} command is still in effect, {HOME} moves the cell pointer to the upper-left corner of the unprotected section of the spreadsheet rather than to cell A1.)

The /X Macro Commands

In earlier versions of 1-2-3, typing-alternative macros were supplemented by special macro commands that all began with /X. These commands, an early macro command language, provided limited logic and program flow control for macro execution. Still functional in 1-2-3 Release 2.3, each one now has a macro language equivalent. Refer to that equivalent for a full explanation of the /X commands. Unlike the macro language commands, the /X commands are preceded by a slash (/) and are not enclosed in braces. There is no space between the command and its arguments.

The /XC Command

The /XC or "call" command corresponds to the {subroutine} command. Its syntax is

```
/XClocation~
```

where *location* is the address or block name of a cell containing the subroutine that you are calling. After /XC executes the routine or when it encounters the /XR or {RETURN} statement at the end of the routine, control returns to the macro line following the /XC instruction.

The /XG Command

The /XG command is the {BRANCH} command, directing the flow of a macro by branching to a new location containing the commands that will be entered next. Its syntax is

```
/XGlocation~
```

where *location* is the address containing the commands that you want executed next.

The /XI Command

The /XI command is the equivalent of the {IF} command. Its syntax is

```
/XIcondition~true
```

where *condition* is a comparison of two values in cells or a formula. If the *condition* evaluates as True, the macro will execute the instructions on the same macro line as the /XI statement. If the condition is False, the next instructions executed will be on the macro line that follows the condition. The argument *true* is any valid macro instruction.

The /XL Command

The /XL command, equivalent to {GETLABEL}, causes 1-2-3 to wait for the operator to input a character string from the keyboard. Then 1-2-3 stores the entry in a specified location. Its syntax is

```
/XLprompt~location~
```

where *prompt* is a message of up to 39 characters that prompts the user for label input, and *location* is where the user's input will be stored.

The /XM Command

The /XM command is the equivalent of {MENUBRANCH}, directing the macro flow to a set of cells that form a custom menu. The rules for the custom menu are the same as for the {MENUBRANCH} command.

The /XN Command

/XN is the equivalent of {GETNUMBER}. Its syntax is

```
/XNprompt~location~
```

prompting the user for numeric input and entering it in the cell specified as *location*. If the user enters a label instead of a number, the location cell will return @ERR.

The /XQ Command

Used to terminate a macro, the /XQ command is the same as {QUIT} and is normally used at the end of a macro to ensure that it terminates correctly.

The /XR Command

The equivalent of the {RETURN} command, the /XR command returns the flow of a macro to the point at which it was called as a subroutine. There are no arguments to this command.

The Cell Commands

1-2-3 groups the following macro commands as "cell" commands because they let you manipulate values and strings stored in spreadsheet cells. You can use these commands to blank out a section of the spreadsheet or to store a value or a string in a cell. This group also includes commands that you can use to recalculate the worksheet in row or column order.

The {BLANK} Command

A macro command alternative to the Range Erase menu option, {BLANK} erases a block of cells on the worksheet using the format

```
{BLANK location}
```

where *location* is the address of a block of cells or a block name. Generally used to clean out a data entry area for new data, {BLANK} is effective when a macro has to reuse an area of the worksheet. Use a block name as the argument for better control, and remember that {BLANK} does not reset cell formatting information, it just removes the contents.

The {CONTENTS} Command

The {CONTENTS} command copies the contents of one cell into another, converting it to a label of specified format and width in the process. Its syntax is

```
{CONTENTS destination,source,width,format}
```

The *destination* argument is the location where you wish the resulting label to be stored, stated as a cell address or a block name. The *source* argument is the cell address or block name of the value entry you want copied into *destination* as a label. The *width* and *format* arguments are optional. Thus the command

```
{CONTENTS A1,B1}
```

takes the number 2001 from the fixed-format (zero decimal places) cell A1 and copies it into B1 as the left-aligned label 2001.

The *width* argument is only required if you want to control width or specify *format*. The *width* argument determines the width of the resulting label, so omitting it lets 1-2-3 use the width of the source location. If you use a *width* argument wider than the original width, 1-2-3 will pad the label with leading blank spaces. If the *width* argument is narrower than the original number of characters, you will get a label full of asterisks. *Format* is an optional argument that provides control over the appearance of the value copied into the destination. Thus the command

```
{CONTENTS A1,B1,12,34}
```

copies the same 2001 into B1 as $2,001.00 with three leading spaces. This is because 12 is the specified cell width and 34 is the code for Currency format with two decimal places.

The codes used for the different formats in the {CONTENTS} command are found in Table C.1.

The {LET} Command

The {LET} command assigns a value to a location in the spreadsheet using the syntax

```
{LET location,value:type}
```

This saves a macro from having to move the cell selector to a location to enter data. The *location* argument is the address or block name of the cell in which you want to store the value or label. (Specifying *location* as a multicell block means the upper-left cell in the block will be used.) The *value* is the data you want assigned to the location. If *value* consists of numeric digits, 1-2-3 will enter it as a numeric value. If *value* contains a valid numeric formula, 1-2-3 will enter its results. Otherwise, 1-2-3 will treat *value* as a string. You can use the optional *type* argument to control how the value is handled. The *type* argument must be either the word "value," the word "string," or a reference to a label containing one of those words. Thus the command

```
{LET A1,101}
```

places the number 101 in cell A1. The command

```
{LET A1,101:string}
```

places the left-aligned label 101 in cell A1.

Table A.1   **Format Arguments Used with {CONTENTS}**

Format Number	Format
0 through 15	Fixed, 0 through 15 decimal places
16 through 31	Scientific, 0 through 15 decimal places
32 through 47	Currency, 0 through 15 decimal places
48 through 63	Percent, 0 through 15 decimal places
64 through 79	Comma, 0 through 15 decimal places
112	Bar graph (+/−)
113	General
114	D1 (dd-mmm-yy)
115	D2 (dd-mmm)
116	D3 (mmm-yy)
117	Text
118	Hidden
119	D6 (hh:mm:ss AM/PM)
120	D7 (hh:mm AM/PM)
121	D4 (long international date)
122	D5 (short international date)
123	D8 (long international time)
124	D9 (short international time)
127	Global format (as set by Worksheet Global Format)

The {PUT} Command

Unlike {LET}, which accepts only a cell address, {PUT} allows you to place a value in a location by selecting a row and column offset within a block. Its syntax is

```
{PUT location,column,row,value:type}
```

where *location* is the block of cells, identified by cell addresses or a block name, into which you want to place the data. The *column* argument is the column number of the cell within the block you want to use for the data. (As in other 1-2-3 commands such as @VLOOKUP, the first column in the block is column 0.) The *row* argument works the same way, the first row being 0. Thus the command

```
{PUT A1..C5,0,0,20:string}
```

places the label 20 in cell B2. The command

```
{PUT A1..C5,1,1,Help}
```

places the label Help in cell B1.

The {RECALC} Command

The {RECALC} command recalculates the formulas within a specified block, proceeding rowwise within the block. Its syntax is

```
{RECALC location,condition,iteration}
```

The block to be recalculated is specified as *location*. The *condition* is an optional argument specifying a condition that must be evaluated as True before the block is no longer recalculated. As long as the condition evaluates to False, 1-2-3 continues to recalculate the worksheet. (When used in conjunction with *iteration*, which specifies a maximum number of iterations, the *condition* stops recalculation short of the maximum number of iterations if it returns True.)

The point of the {RECALC} command, and the companion command {RECALCCOL}, is to avoid unnecessary delays in processing data. When a worksheet gets large, it is normal to make recalculation manual as opposed to automatic. New entries do not cause dependent data in the rest of the spreadsheet to be updated. Instead, you do this by returning to automatic calculation, pressing the F9 (Calc) key, or using the {CALC} command. While this recalculates the entire worksheet, the {RECALC} and {RECALCCOL} commands evaluate just a portion of it, which naturally takes far less time. You use {RECALC} when the area you are recalculating is below and to the left of the cells referenced by the formulas in the area. Use {RECALCCOL} when the area you are recalculating is above and to the right of the cells referenced by the formulas in this area. Use these commands prior to printing a report to ensure that the reported data is correct while avoiding the lengthy delays produced by updating the entire spreadsheet. (Note that if the formula to be calculated is both above and to the left of cells with new values, you must use the Calc key or {CALC} command.)

The {RECALCCOL} Command

The {RECALCCOL} command recalculates the formulas within the specified block, just like {RECALC}, except that it proceeds column by column. Its syntax is

```
{RECALCCOL location,condition,iteration}
```

using the same argument definitions as {RECALC}.

The File I/O Macro Commands

The file I/O macro commands permit you to manipulate data in a disk file, somewhat like the sequential file-handling capabilities you get in many programming languages. In your macros, these commands allow you to read and write data in ASCII files. This is a fairly advanced activity, which has the potential to corrupt valuable data files if not handled correctly, so use the file control commands with care and test them on expendable data files.

Using I/O Commands

The I/O commands work with ASCII or text files. These are files like the ones created by the 1-2-3 Print File command. Such files are sometimes used for exchanging information between programs that cannot read more sophisticated file formats.

A typical application of these commands is when you want to write information, one line at a time, to a text file. The following macro code writes the contents of cell A21 to a file called INFO.DAT:

```
{OPEN "INFO.DAT",M}
{FILESIZE SIZE}
{SETPOS SIZE}
{WRITELN A21}
{CLOSE}
```

The macro opens the file to be modified, reads the size of the file in bytes into a cell called SIZE, and then positions the byte pointer at the end of the file. (The *byte pointer* is like an invisible cursor within the disk file you open.) When a file is first opened, the byte pointer is located at the first character of the file. Any reading from or writing to the file occurs at the location of the byte pointer. You can position the byte pointer with {SETPOS}. Each of the file manipulation commands is described in the following sections. (Note that an alternative to the first three lines of the above macro would be to use the {OPEN} command with the A argument, which places the byte pointer at the end of the file.)

The {CLOSE} Command

The {CLOSE} command closes a file that was opened with the {OPEN} macro command. It takes no arguments. {CLOSE} is one of several commands that enable macros to read from files on disk and write information to disk files.

The {FILESIZE} Command

The {FILESIZE} command has the syntax

```
{FILESIZE location}
```

It records the size of an open file, stated as a number of bytes, in the cell specified as *location*, which can be a cell or range name.

The {GETPOS} Command

The {GETPOS} command has the syntax

```
{GETPOS location}
```

It records (in the cell specified by the *location* argument) the byte pointer's current position. The position is read as an offset number; the first character of a file is 0, the second is 1, and so on.

The {OPEN} Command

The {OPEN} command has the syntax

```
{OPEN filename,access mode}
```

It opens a file named as *filename* for reading, writing, or both. The *access mode* argument is one of these four characters:

W   Opens a new disk file to which you can write information. This is potentially dangerous, since there is nothing to stop you from overwriting an existing file. Be sure that the *filename* argument does not refer to a file that you want to preserve.

M   Opens an existing file so that you can modify it. This allows you to use the read and write commands. It, too, is dangerous; what you write to a file will overwrite existing data if the byte pointer is not positioned at the end of the file.

R   Opens a file so that you can read information from it. This is the safest form of file access, since it prevents writing to the file.

A   Opens a file and automatically positions the byte pointer at the end of the file. Does not allow changes to existing material in the file— only allows addition of new data.

The {READ} Command

The {READ} command has the syntax

```
{READ byte count,location}
```

The {READ} command copies the number of characters, specified by the *byte count* argument, from the file to the cell specified by the *location* argument. The command starts reading at the current position of the byte pointer.

The {READLN} Command

The {READLN} command has the syntax

```
{READLN location}
```

This command copies a line of data from the file to the cell specified by the *location* argument. The command starts reading at the current position of the byte pointer and stops at the end of the current line.

The {SETPOS} Command

The {SETPOS} command has the syntax

```
{SETPOS file position}
```

This command sets a new position for the byte pointer in the currently open file. If you read the file size and use this as the *file position* argument, you will locate the end of the file and be able to add data to it. Bear in mind that the first position is 0, the second is 1, and so on.

The {WRITE} Command

The {WRITE} command has the syntax

```
{WRITE string}
```

It copies characters into an open file at the byte pointer's current location. The *string* argument can be a single cell or a named single-cell range. The command does not add a line feed at the end of what is written.

The {WRITELN} Command

The {WRITELN} command has the syntax

```
{WRITELN string}
```

It copies characters into an open file. The *string* argument can be a single cell or a named single-cell range. The command adds a line feed sequence at the end of the string of characters as it writes the string to the file. Thus, you can use a series of {WRITELN} statements to add successive lines of data to a file.

Utility Commands

There are a few commands that make it easier for the macro writer to handle the chores of documentation and design. These allow you to insert comments and blank lines in your macros.

The {;} Command

When you want to place a comment in a macro, you use the {;} command. Entering

```
{;This line is a comment}
```

in a macro allows the comment to appear in the spreadsheet without affecting the way the macro runs. The macro skips this line during execution. This is useful for documenting macros, particularly where space considerations prevent the use of comments to the right of the code cells.

The {} Command

To skip a cell completely during macro execution, you can use {}, which lets a macro come as close as possible to containing a blank cell without stopping. This is sometimes useful when you want to have two macros arranged so that comparable commands are in adjacent cells but one macro is not as complex as the other, as in this example:

```
Enter                List
Enter Data           Sort and print list
{ENTER}              {SORT DATA}
{}                   {PRINT DATA}
{QUIT}               {QUIT}
```

The {SYSTEM} Command

The {SYSTEM} command lets you issue a DOS command during a macro. It temporarily suspends the 1-2-3 work session, performs the specified DOS command, and then automatically returns control to the macro. The syntax for the {SYSTEM} command is

```
{SYSTEM} "command"
```

where *command* is any DOS command, including a batch command, up to 128 characters in length. The command name must be enclosed in quotes.

For example, the command

```
{SYSTEM CHKDSK}
```

carries out the CHKDSK command at the DOS prompt. However, since you are returned to the worksheet immediately after running CHKDSK you may want to devise a means of capturing CHKDSK's results. For example, if you

want to read the results of the CHKDSK command into the current worksheet you can use

```
{SYSTEM CHKDSK >disk.prn}
```

This will place the results of the CHKDSK command into an ASCII text file called DISK.PRN. You can then read this into the current worksheet with the File Import Text command.

If you are using DOS 3.0 or higher, you can include a path in *command* if you enclose the entire thing in quotes. For example, to call a batch program called PRNFILE.BAT, located in a directory called BATCH on drive C, you would use the command

```
{SYSTEM "C:\BATCH\PRNFILE"}
```

Note that you should not use the {SYSTEM} command to run software that affects memory allocation, such as terminate-and-stay-resident programs. Also note that {SYSTEM} does not accept arguments that contain a colon, such as CHKDSK A: >disk.prn. You can place commands requiring colons into batch files, described in Appendix A, to get around this problem, and then use SYSTEM to run the batch file.

Key Equivalent Commands

The following macro commands represent keystrokes that you want typed during macro execution. Note that in addition to the {MENU} code, you can use / (slash) or < (less than) to activate the menu.

{DOWN} or {D}	Down Arrow
{UP} or {U}	Up Arrow
{LEFT} or {L}	Left Arrow
{RIGHT} or {R}	Right Arrow
{ABS}	Abs (F4)
{APP1}	App1 (Alt-F7)
{APP2}	App2 (Alt-F8)
{APP3}	App3 (Alt-F9)
{APP4}	App4 (Alt-F10)
{BACKSPACE} or {BS}	Backspace
{BIGLEFT}	Ctrl-Left Arrow or Shift-Tab
{BIGRIGHT}	Ctrl-Right Arrow or Tab
{CALC}	Calc (F9)

{DELETE} or {DEL}	Delete
{EDIT}	Edit (F2)
{END}	End
{ESCAPE} or {ESC}	Escape
{GOTO}	Goto (F5)
{GRAPH}	Graph (F10)
{HELP}	Help (F1)
{HOME}	Home
{INSERT} or {INS}	Insert
{MENU}	Menu
{NAME}	Name (F3)
{PGUP}	PgUp
{PGDN}	PgDn
{QUERY}	Query (F7)
{TABLE}	Table (F8)
{WINDOW}	Window (F6)
{~}	~ (tilde)
{{}	{ (open brace)
{}}	} (close brace)

INDEX